T0134130

Configuring Internal Controls for Software as a Service

Configuring Internal Controls for Software as a Service

as a Service
Between Fragility and Forgiveness

Chong Ee

CRC Press
Taylor & Francis Group
Boca Raton London New York

CRC Press is an imprint of the
Taylor & Francis Group, an **informa** business

The opinions expressed in this book are the author's own and do not necessarily represent the views of past, current, or future employers.

CRC Press
Taylor & Francis Group
6000 Broken Sound Parkway NW, Suite 300
Boca Raton, FL 33487-2742

© 2019 by Taylor & Francis Group, LLC
CRC Press is an imprint of Taylor & Francis Group, an Informa business

No claim to original U.S. Government works

Printed on acid-free paper

International Standard Book Number-13: 978-1-4822-5978-0 (Hardback)

Visit the Taylor & Francis Web site at
http://www.taylorandfrancis.com

and the CRC Press Web site at
http://www.crcpress.com

For my mother.

For my mother

Contents

Contents

Author

Dedicated, driven, passionate, and someone you can approach with any idea from left-field to make it a reality are some of the words clients have for Chong Ee. A former Big Four consultant and auditor, Chong brings over 19 years of industry experience in financial systems, cloud computing, and regulatory compliance from working with startups to large companies. More recently, he assisted with public company readiness efforts at Trulia, Twilio, and Okta in San Francisco. Chong is a director of financial business systems and teaches a graduate class on accounting information systems in his spare time. A graduate from Carnegie Mellon University, Chong holds active NetSuite consultant and administrator certifications from NetSuite-Oracle as well as audit and governance certifications from the Information Systems Audit and Control Association (ISACA). In 2010, he received the Michael Cangemi Best Article/Book award from ISACA.

Prologue: An Introduction

> A picture held us captive. And we
> could not get outside it, for it lay in
> our language, and our language
> seemed to repeat it to us
> inexorably.[1]
>
> **Ludwig Wittgenstein**

The title of this book, as you can imagine, has undergone several iterations:

1. Head in the Clouds: Software as a Service and Internal Controls
2. Automated Humans, Manual Machines
3. Configured Accounts in Software as a Service

Each time I reached out to my publisher, I could only see him chuckling to himself upon receiving yet another change request. During this time, I've changed employers twice, and thrown in a personal relationship and residence to boot, although these, thankfully, have only had to happen once. I've also begun teaching a weekly evening *Accounting Information Systems* class at a local university, thus beginning a dialogue with students that has, to a considerable degree, cast and recast my work in a different light, work that I've nevertheless grown accustomed to day in and day out. An internal control begins with an account; yet accounts can mean different things to different people. For accountants, a chart of accounts comes to mind. Sales professionals, on the other hand, are more inclined to think of customer accounts. For auditors, accounts are synonymous with accountability: who is responsible for what and when. There is also the act of giving an account of something or someone, to attempt at a characterization, however brief, to give color and, ideally, context. When we say "on account of," we are in fact attributing a cause and telling a story.

In many ways, the recent rise of as-a-service, and therein Software as a Service (SaaS), taps into our fundamental notions of what it means to formulate, augment, and give an account, as well as our propensity for accounts and stories. Is what we see before us itself accountable to the account we have ascribed? To the extent that SaaS makes it easier for nontechnical enterprise users to configure it to meet specific needs, the configurability of accounts, or of configured accounts, starts to enter the picture. We all can and often do become storytellers. Finally, whose account are we talking about? The vendor, customer, or employee? Even within the same SaaS consuming client enterprise, various accounts – accounting, operations, sales, procurement, legal, and human resources, to name a few – often compete and jostle, intersecting with as well as diverging from one another. It is an altogether raucous sight, a hullabaloo in the orchard.

To inquire into the nature of internal controls for SaaS, we would have to draw upon what would at first appear to be irrelevant and irreverent – the stars, the moon, and everything else in between. We can tell from the iterative book titles that we are apt to have our heads stuck in the clouds, or the sand, depending on your perspective. In fact, if we were to take the vendor's value propositions at face value then no maintenance would have been required for SaaS purchased off-the-shelf, as it were. Instead of having business processes automated, we can argue that what enterprise users are expecting is having their responses automated, so that what has been effectively rendered out-of-sight is therefore out-of-mind.

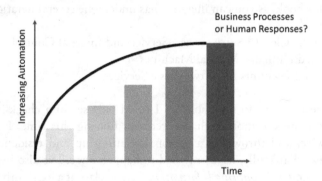

Alas, like all else, SaaS itself is not immune to insults to integrity. Like accounts, fragility can mean one of several things. When it comes to SaaS, most folks think of availability, though it is probably the least interesting kind. Another type of fragility can be attributed to an inability to be configurable to end user needs, so that rather than configure SaaS to meet these needs, the reverse happens when the users are configured to meet the demands of the SaaS at hand. An example here is a prescribed though often taken-for-granted sequence of events. Consider the following:

1. Sales order, fulfillment, invoice, credit and/or payment
2. Sales order, payment, fulfillment, invoice, credit
3. Fulfillment, sales order, invoice, credit and/or payment

I divided students in my class into groups of three where they had to determine which of the previous options held true in real life and, where applicable, illustrate with an example. The first sequence of events most resembles the textbook answer. One group had the example of a visit to a local café to purchase a cup of coffee. Yet students in other groups voiced an all too common scenario where we would first place, and pay for, our order at the counter before waiting in line for the barista to prepare our beverage. In this manner, the example was more applicable to the second sequence of events. A counter-response given was that this would depend on the choice of beverage ordered and type of café. A regular coffee drip would have been easily fulfilled at the counter prior to payment. Likewise, there are cafés where we can stand in line to order directly from the barista and receive our drink before heading to the cashier for payment. For the second sequence of events, one group gave the example of a prepaid SIM card that allowed the subscriber to draw down the minutes purchased and be invoiced for overages. Other groups pointed out that for material orders, the magnitude would have resulted in some form of initial down payment before the order was worked on with subsequent invoices issued when specific milestones were met.

The third sequence of events was the most contentious dividing the class into those who believed it to hold true and those who believed it to be false. For those in the former group, an example given was the fulfillment of medical prescriptions. We typically get a call from the pharmacy when our prescription is filled before we head over to the local pharmacy for pickup and payment. Groups that disagreed with this example argued that the prescriptions were "ordered" by our physician so in this sense, the order still preceded the fulfillment. Others saw the prescription almost like a multi-year sales order that would be fulfilled and invoiced quarterly. Groups that believed the third sequence of events to be false pointed out that there should have been some level of oversight or review before fulfillment was made and likely evidenced in an order of some kind. This raises the question of what constitutes orders: can something taken down over the phone constitute an order or does one need to sign a formal contract? Likewise, in all examples given, payment can be made via credit card and often in the absence of any issued invoice. So just as questions are surfaced on what constitutes an order, the same question can apply to invoices and other transaction types identified in all three sequences of events.

Because the events presented are deliberately kept vague and high level, some groups exercised creative freedom in re-interpreting the underlying embodied logic. For the second sequence of events, some gave an example of an entity procuring raw materials to manufacture goods to in turn sell to customers. Another group, for the third sequence of events, interpreted fulfillment not so much as a good or service but of desire, so that conceivably one we could whet our visual appetite in perusing items before placing an order. The question remains: can the third sequence of events hold true? Although it appears to belie a lack of control, it can very well reflect a more real-life portrayal of what happens in the handling of last minute orders that change by the minute, and only get documented after the fact as an order even though fulfillment has already occurred.

Often, in an audit, we work backwards from a payment to an invoice to a fulfillment to an order, and even if we can successfully thread through these artifacts in the SaaS, it is by no means a guarantee this sequence in reverse is followed in the moment-to-moment unfolding from start to finish. In fact, there is nothing to prevent someone from recording an invoice without evidencing delivery or an authorized trigger in the form of a sales order. The question becomes: with the SaaS at hand, which account applies, and, perhaps more importantly, is it accountable to other scenarios such as those that do not even make it to the printed page? The answer to the latter gives us a glimpse into just how fragile an account is. How fragile it is in turn tells us how forgiving it can be when real-life affairs are not immediately accountable to the configured account. As is often the case, there is more than meets the eye: what appears generic and out-of-the-box may yet be highly configurable. Conversely, what comes armed with complex feature gadgetry out of the gate may end up limiting the degrees of freedom available to a user in configuring the system's account to align with reality.

When we transcend beyond any one given SaaS and peer into an enterprise's *internal* cloud architecture comprised of *external* plug and play SaaS, fragility takes on new meaning: we may be more concerned about finding the weakest link and putting in place alerts where appropriate so that what appears to be fragile – a notification received on a failed sync between integrated SaaS – may really be a useful fuse in surfacing and thus defusing a bigger problem at hand. In addition to insults to sequential or architectural integrity, there are likely potential insults to transactional integrity as well:

1. What if we make a mistake in recording a transaction, updating a configuration or granting access?
2. What if we don't make a mistake but fail to perform any or all the earlier in a complete manner? In other words, not all requisite data may be recorded, configurations may be omitted and left on default settings, or access permissions may not be granted in their entirety even for a single role?
3. What if any, or all, of the earlier were performed with no valid or just cause?

To the uninitiated, it would appear unwise, risky even, to only get to the definition of SaaS and cloud computing in the third chapter, and yet at a different level, the form chosen feels strangely accountable to its content. Having taught post-graduate classes that needed to be compliant with the mandated college syllabus, I long for a different format: like Alice stumbling upon and down a rabbit hole in *Through the Looking Glass*, the shared narratives, while appearing tentative and meandering at the outset, nonetheless yield deeper finds that can be mined for real-life application once we retreat from the safe, controlled, and yet no more real world to which we are accustomed.

It is the latter that I have in mind when formulating exercises at the close of each chapter that serve as their own reward or exorcism. Rather than sketch out a sequential account first focusing on the Order-to-Cash business cycle and next on Procure-to-Pay, or a chronological one that begins with mainframes and ends with cloud computing, or yet a categorical one differentiating business, developer, vendor, and auditor needs, I've chosen to intersperse these throughout in circles and cycles, recalling the words of Rainer Maria Rilke: "I live my life in widening rings."[2] A day in the life of working with SaaS is far too complicated an affair – often punctuated by unexpected swings from major to minor – to be bound by contrived boundaries. I can only hope that you will have as much fun reading and re-reading this book as I've had writing and re-writing it.

Endnotes

[1] Wittgenstein, L. (1965). *Philosophical Investigations*. New York: Macmillan Company.
[2] Rilke, R. M., Barrows, A., and Macy, J. (2005). *Rilke's Book of Hours: Love Poems to God*. New York: Riverhead Books.

Chapter 1

Singularized Plurality

Me. Always the water

changed, but the river stood

still.[1]

Richard Powers

August 2007: The water in the Gulf of Mexico would have felt like bathwater so that by the time the sun sets, it would have been even warmer than the surrounding air. Out here in the open, miles away from the Florida coast where sand, soft and white as powder, stretches out as far as the eye can see, the sea ebbs and flows to a standstill, itself a mirror of the clear, cloudless expanse above. Deep below, schools of red groupers congregate around strategically angled baitfish. Barely 6 days into its expedition, Miss Katie, a commercial fishing boat encountered, unexpected, if not unwelcome, guests.[2] As part of a routine offshore patrol, officers from the Florida Fish and Wildlife Conservation Commission came on board and set out to count the number of fish that fell under the 20-inch minimal legal length stipulated by federal conservation regulations.[3] They would soon discover 72 fish in its catch that were under minimal legal length; these were in turn separated and placed in distinct wooden crates.[4] Yet 4 days after Miss Katie docked in Cortez, Florida, the fish from these crates appeared to have curiously grown in length.[5] Upon further investigation, a crew member admitted to having been directed by the boat captain to toss the undersized fish overboard and replace them with bigger size counterparts.[6] Nearly 3 years later, the captain would be prosecuted under a provision of the Sarbanes–Oxley Act (SOX) that imposes a maximum sentence of 20 years.[7]

Barely 5 years before Miss Katie's run-in with the authorities, the U.S. Congress enacted SOX in the wake of massive accounting fraud uncovered at Enron, the giant energy company. The provision used against Miss Katie's captain seeks to prevent a recurrence of systematic destruction of incriminating evidence such as the actions of Enron's external auditor, Arthur Anderson. Yet, boundaries drawn over what is right versus what is wrong can remain ever shifting just like the crated undersized fish that ultimately eluded the grasp of the hungry officer's hands. By the time criminal charges were lodged against Miss Katie, the minimal legal length allowed for a red grouper caught in the Gulf of Mexico was lowered from 20 to 18 inches.[8] As it turned out, none of the catch aboard Miss Katie fell below this new limit.[9] A red grouper by any other length would taste just as sweet. When cooked right, it is like a cloud: soft, white, and thick, flaking ever so tenderly.

Geography itself would prove to be a precarious construct. Had one of the officers not been deputized as a federal agent by the National Marine Fisheries Service, he would not have had the authority or wherewithal to enforce federal, in addition to state, fishing laws. After all, by the time the officers boarded Miss Katie, she was far enough from the Florida coast to be deemed in exclusively federal waters. Finally, there is the curious matter of wildlife conservation. Despite the tampering of evidence to be used in a court of law, what if the undersized fish cast overboard managed to survive? Which is preferable: the restoration of life or that of auditable albeit perishable evidence? More importantly, what does SOX have to do with fishing, or the accounting of undersized fish? What does all this have to do with internal controls for software as a service (SaaS)?

In an attempt to answer the questions, it helps to turn to a different type of fish: salmon. August also happens to be the warmest weather on a salmon farm in western Norway.[10] In place of fishing boats casting baitfish in open waters, we see a rooftop home for about 600,000 salmon, a floating warehouse that workers carefully tend.[11] In place of undersized fish in wooden crates, we find a similar cohort of categorically marked undersized fish languishing in a tank with limited fresh water.[12] Feed comprises about 60% of the cost of producing fish.[13] Thus, supply is controlled by a computer program called *Fishtalk*, where it is streamed through galvanized ceiling pipes and sprayed onto the surface of water in delineated pens.[14] In debating the charge issued against the boat captain for violating the SOX provision, an argument put forth in his defense was that fish are not tangible objects: we can't in effect make an entry in fish.[15] Salmon dead or alive, on the other hand, undergo a rigorous series of sorting and categorization at the Norwegian fish farm. Dead fish are first identified and consigned to a tank of formic acid, removed from the live ones to reduce the rate of infection.[16] The live fish are vaccinated and fed; those deemed undersized, though perhaps no more than undernourished, are squirreled away into the "dead" tank containing barely a meter of water with no lighting nor, perhaps more importantly, oxygen supply.

The handling of the undersized salmon bears remarkable parallels with the manner we behave towards our own species in the annals of human history. In the 1890s, Grant Avenue in San Francisco's Chinatown was known as Dupont Avenue, home to sex slaves brought from China.[17] In a mere span of years, these young women would become mentally and physically anguished, left to perish with no more than a "cup of water, another of boiled rice, and a little metal lamp" in a locked room.[18] Back on the Norwegian farm, 11 centimeters is the minimal length for a healthy salmon. This translates to 4.331 inches to be exact. The red groupers under 20 inches that were cast overboard at least had a fighting chance to survive when reintroduced into their element. The same can't be said for the undersized salmon. Through an almost prescient sleight of hand, they are consigned to an inevitable fate. In the larger scheme of things however, all salmon, whether large or small, are bound for the same fate, whether left to die in a dimly lit and barely oxygenated tank or carefully adorned on a dinner plate. Something fishy is going on. Despite their obvious difference, the red groupers caught at sea share the same precariousness of fate, and of categorization, as their salmon counterparts in a fish farm. Just as the minimal legal length shifted for the red grouper, eluding easy grasp each time, the shifting of salmon into live and healthy fish – the latter more a function of size than of actual performance – is a slippery endeavor whether it involves grabbing hold of the dead fish to put it in a separate tank or vaccinating the live ones in batches.[19]

Regardless of the comparison of wild-caught red groupers with farm-raised salmon, the question remains: what does all this have to do with SaaS and internal controls? I am not suggesting that using SaaS is like catching red groupers in the Gulf of Mexico or farming salmon in western Norway; yet the very basis upon which easy distinctions are drawn between right versus wrong, legal versus illegal, healthy versus unhealthy, rests on an unvarying fundamental: that the very criteria for conservation or health remains unwavering, unchanging, or, in other words, the same. In the case of the undersized red groupers, we saw the lowering of the minimal legal length from 20 to 18 inches in the mere passage of 32 months, from the time the patrol officers boarded the commercial fishing boat to the time charges were pressed against the boat captain. In the case of the farm-raised salmon, field notes from workers reveal the slippery nature of separating the dead fish from live ones, or healthy fish from undernourished ones, of working with the cold, wet texture of the subjects at hand, of confirming with a precise manner those needing to be dropped into the grooves of a conveyer belt en route to a vaccination machine.[20] Even the computer program *Fishtalk* requires human judgment to determine the right level of feed.[21] As with all manual endeavors, mistakes happen, vaccines run out, salmon dropped the wrong way make the machine beep.[22]

Compare that scenario with recording a customer sale in a SaaS. What constitutes a sale? Did delivery occur? Was a contract executed with the customer? For an invoice to be recorded, we would assume that delivery has already occurred, and a contract executed. This transaction is like the healthy salmon that have made the rounds through vaccination and feeding to grow to be beyond 11 centimeters. But like the work in the fish farm, slips can occur with the recording of the customer sale – a contract gets modified, delivery occurred but of the wrong items, or the shipment gets sent to a wrong address – just as easily as the slippery salmon can elude eager and hungry farm hands. And like the minimal legal length for keeping wild-caught red groupers from the Gulf of Mexico, parameters change with the passage of time. When we update the tax codes assigned to an item for sale, this update can introduce a conundrum of sorts when a credit memo applied to a prior invoice computes a different sales tax liability because different tax codes are applied from the time the invoice is recorded to the time a credit memo is created.

Thus, like the computer program *Fishtalk* in use at fish farms that advocates "we make your fish talk,"[23] would the SaaS in use ideally make the customer sale speak? This talk can take the form of alerts such as delivery not made or contract not executed, not unlike the beeping and flashing light the machine displays when a salmon is dropped in an incorrect manner into the grooves of the conveyor belt.[24] Alerts can also call attention to changes in what we are more likely to take for granted to stay the same, whether that relates to the tax code assigned to the same item over time, or changes to the contractual clause tied to the customer sale recorded in the SaaS. All of which presents a possibility for a false entry, in fish or otherwise. The SOX provision that the boat captain was charged with violating applies to anyone who "alters, destroys, mutilates, conceals, covers up, falsifies, or makes a false entry in any record, document, or tangible object."[25] In the case of Miss Katie, the question remains: "how does one make a false entry in fish?"[26] Yet as the salmon farm in western Norway illustrates, not only can we make a false entry in vaccinations or fish feed, we can also make a false entry in healthy fish: who is to say that fish under 11 centimeters are not unhealthy but are merely consuming feed at a far less accelerated pace to be deemed healthy enough to end up in anxious bellies?

The changing legal minimal length for retaining wild-caught fish underscores the importance of dates and times. Granted that we can't step into the same river twice,[27] how do we establish point-in-time rigor? By the time charges were pressed against the boat captain, all the catch would have been complying with the prevailing standard at that time, yet the argument put forth is that if we had to go back in time the length of the catch would not have complied. When we turn our attention to SaaS, transactions are likewise subject to period lock or closure controls. After all, we would not want to go back in time and modify the numbers that have already been reported to the public markets. This action notwithstanding, the customer sale or invoice may need to be updated even if the period is locked. To assist with timeliness of invoice payment, the customer's purchase order (PO) number, otherwise its internal authorization identifier for purchase, may need to be included on the invoice so that it shows up in a payment reminder or dunning notification of overdue payment. Locking all fields on the invoice for update while supporting tightened month-end closing procedures would not make sense from an operational perspective when it comes to billing and collections.

In this manner, the invoice resembles our Gulf of Mexico red groupers or Norwegian salmon, slippery and fast moving. Assuming a user can overwrite locked or closed periods, what happens when the user accidentally changes an amount or quantity field? Or what if the user accidentally updates an item that has had a prior tax code assigned so that the new tax code and corresponding sales tax liability gets computed? Or what if the SaaS defaults the invoice from the prior to the current open period effectively pulling into the future revenue recorded from a prior month? Where is the control, we may ask, in period closure or reliable financials? Here is another variation: consider an integration scenario between an upstream and downstream SaaS. What happens if an upstream transaction has synced over downstream but is consequently voided upstream when it is deemed to be a duplicate transaction? The slippery salmon that make it to the healthy fish tank despite their petite size come to mind. Do we go ahead and delete the synced over transaction downstream? Is it appropriate to simply delete it and does the SaaS at hand retain appropriate audit trails? Deletion of duplicate records here is no different than casting undersized red groupers overboard. What happens if the period is already locked in the downstream SaaS thus preventing users from deleting the transaction or transactions in question? If the user was to re-open a locked period, the user runs the risk of syncing-in other transactions into the wrong period. Like the fast-flowing water of the Gulf of Mexico, whatever point-in-time rigor established begins to sound less rigorous by the minute.

Let us dive deeper. What if the item that is updated on an invoice is associated with a revenue recognition schedule that recognizes revenue ratably over a specific period? What if the revenue recognition period remains unchanged or becomes decoupled from the invoice period which is in turn decoupled from the invoice date? Here, we have a change upon a change, much like the change in the minimal conservation length of the Gulf of Mexico catch even as it finds itself swimming against the tide of change in federal conservation laws. How can internal controls make the invoice talk? Much like how the computer software *Fishtalk* would alert farm workers if the salmon need food, when envisioning internal controls for the SaaS, we ask how these controls would provide timely alerts of changes, however inadvertent, to key attributes, and perhaps more importantly, whether these changes matter to the way revenue has been recorded. Just as the machine at the salmon farm would beep or provide a flashing light,[28] alerts can come in a myriad of forms from exception reports manually executed comparing data from varied sources to automated email alerts on any one single identified change. Here is another example of a change with likely impact: when the name for an item for sale is updated, does the SaaS reflect this change prospectively for all new sales performed for this item, or retrospectively as well, so that when we look back at all past sales, it would appear as if the new name were already in use? In the latter scenario, what controls would we need to employ to make sure that in the event the past invoices needed to be resent, or a credit needs to be applied, that the former item name is used in place of the new one? Although point-in-time rigor is applied in the charges pressed against the boat captain or in reported financials, the underlying SaaS itself may not be capable of the same point-in-time rigor in the changes made to master item data, so that much like how the undersized catch can be easily exchanged for their larger sized cousins, a newly renamed item would appear to have already existed.

Dates and times, or point-in-time rigor, also matter when we look at the data that needs to be migrated when deploying a new SaaS. How do we handle historical transactions that may have been recorded in an older, on-premise solution? Do we mirror these one-to-one in their respective accounting periods by opening a prior period in the new SaaS, inputting them and closing the period along with the requisite tasks such as running consolidated currency revaluations but this time taking care to use the same rate as the one used in the on-premise software? This process would have been like sorting wild-caught red groupers from the Gulf of Mexico into different time periods and assessing them for compliance with minimal length at different times periods. Surely this is a lot of work and, depending on the value of having these historical transactions in the new SaaS, may not be cost justifiable. At the other extreme is to simply make a journal entry to reflect period or month-end balances and start anew by only recording new transactions going forward in the new SaaS while still referring to its on-premise predecessor when performing an inquiry into past records. Yet, even this approach is not without tradeoffs. What happens if the customer invoices housed in the on-premise software remain unpaid and dunning or collections need to be performed as part of receivables aging? And rewinding a step further, what if the on-premise SaaS houses sales orders that are expected to generate future invoices? If we do consider bringing these into the new SaaS, are we concerned with inputting them in each of their prior accounting periods? This decision depends in part on the nature of the goods we are selling, whether inventory or non-inventory. But even after inputting them into the new SaaS, there is also the matter of having to make a manual journal entry reclass to reverse the general ledger impact; after all, we would not want to record the same sale twice, first in the on-premise software and then in the new SaaS, just as we would not want to step into the same river twice. How do we manage cutoff?

When do we make the switch; in other words, if the new SaaS is integrated with another upstream software, how do we resolve potential duplicates during go-live that may be synced in an automated manner and yet already be reflected as processed in the on-premise software? The likelihood of encountering double counting is not as remote as you would think; during a recent visit to my favorite dim sum restaurant, I noticed that the restaurant management introduced a new way of taking orders by having customers make menu selections at the start in addition to taking orders from circulating carts. Each time an item was delivered whether selected beforehand from the menu or in the moment from carts that showed up from time to time, wait staff continued to check off items on a slip of paper at each table, as they had in the past. Upon receiving our bill, I realized that the cashier unintentionally double-counted by adding the menu selections to the list of manually checked off items at the table. As this dim sum example illustrates, double-counting is even more likely during an organizational transition involving a new software, process, or team so that the old gets commingled with the new. In the case of Miss Katie, cutoff was established at the point the catch was brought on board. In other words, it did not matter that by the time charges were pressed and the case was brought to court, the length of the wild-caught red groupers in question complied with the minimal length for retention at that time.

It can be hard to arrive at specific dates, or points in time, when refreshing a sandbox environment with a current production copy for the purposes of testing. What happens when despite the production refresh, the sandbox environment nevertheless doesn't contain all the data points? As an example, for some SaaS, sandbox environments do not support system audit trails behind historical transactions recorded in production and refreshed into the sandbox instances – to peer into the history of who-did-what-when, we would have to look up the same transaction in the production environment. At first glance, this seems to be fine and dandy: why would anyone look to the sandbox environment for audit trail history? Yet, if we circle back to our prior example of data preparation for go-live, what if we were only interested in migrating transactions that have been approved in their respective prior periods so that they may be migrated into the same accounting periods in the new SaaS? When performing test validations in sandbox, we would need to be able to peer into transaction audit history to find out just when these transactions were approved. In the absence of audit history, other attributes that more closely approximate approval date may be transaction and creation dates. After all, by the time these have been refreshed into a sandbox environment, most, if not all, of them would have arrived at their final approved state. In the Norwegian salmon farm example, this would have been like asking *when* each of the salmon that has made its way to the final dead tank is assessed for being undersized and slotting them into the respective period accordingly.

Notwithstanding the winds of regulatory change, the length of the red groupers once caught and brought on board Miss Katie remains the same. Whether they ended up being swapped out for larger-sized counterparts is another story. Only the minimal length mandating their release keeps changing, so that what was out of compliance is presently in compliance. Thus, it is not so much the size of the red groupers that matters as it is in relation to the direction of the regulatory wind at bay. In *Alice's Adventures in Wonderland*, when Alice first arrives, she is too big to make it through the little door into the beautiful garden yet after she drinks from the mysterious bottle, she becomes too small to reach the key.[29] When she eats the special cake, she becomes way too big only to be reduced back to size by the White Rabbit's fan.[30] While in the rabbit's house, another bottle of mystery cordial makes her so big that she gets stuck in the room only to find relief by eating the cake that is transformed from pebbles thrown in the window.[31] The moment Alice thinks she can gain control of her size by nibbling on pieces of mushroom as taught by the Caterpillar, she begins growing yet again in the courtroom, until everyone around her becomes a pack of cards.[32] Sound familiar in the world of regulatory compliance? Just when we think we have gotten a handle on what auditors expect, their requests change yet again when they show up the following year. We can argue that rather than focusing on Alice's changing figure, like the changing public perception of the idealized female silhouette through time, it is in fact everyone else around her that keeps changing in relation to her so that it is really Alice who has stayed the same, like the undersized red groupers aboard Miss Katie. As Donna Haraway puts it, "categories are not frozen."[33] What is let in, and what is left out continues to be debated, assessed, and re-assessed. Thus, categorization can itself prove to be a slippery proposition; errors can arise with tossing out undersized salmon or miscounting undersized red groupers or recognizing premature revenue; in this manner, the categories we in turn use for categories are themselves susceptible to slippage. We have seen this in the varying minimal legal length for wild-caught red groupers but also in the varying tax code assigned to the same item earmarked for sale on an invoice.

What is an invoice anyway? One way of answering this question may be to ask about its function. When we enter invoice in the Google search bar, we see its definition as "a list of goods sent or services provided, with a statement of the sum due for these."[34] Another way to answer the question is to list the attributes that are typically associated with an invoice: a customer, its bill to and ship to address, the payment terms, the goods that are provided, the unit and extended quantity and amounts, a memo field to document the aforementioned customer PO number to ease timeliness of processing (such as 3-way match) on the customer end to ideally culminate in timely payment. Yet a third way of describing an invoice is to draw upon its relations. As alluded to previously, an invoice would enter the picture only after goods or services have been rendered; from a SaaS perspective, this may translate into seeing a 'Bill' or 'Invoice' button only on item or service fulfillment, not on the sales order or even quote. To the extent that the invoice unit price needs to reflect the sales order negotiated price, then a prerequisite for the invoice may be for an upstream approved sales order. To the extent that a sales order is associated with multiple future invoices expected when specific milestones are met or good delivered, then the invoice needs to have been generated at the right time by a billing schedule rather than manually created. To the extent that the customer would like to see the executed contract or statement of work upon invoice receipt to review and verify against both individual line as well as aggregate amounts, then an invoice generated and sent to the customer would need to have either an accompanying link to or copy of the executed contract. To the extent that the customer needs to know how to submit payment, then the customer email containing the invoice and contract attachments also needs to describe the preferred means of payment as well as the company's bank account information. In this manner, the invoice is characterized by the presence of a fulfillment, order, contract, and email verbiage on payment information. Described in this way, the invoice mirrors the Melanesian "multiply-authored" identity identified in Marilyn Strathern's study of the Highland New Guinea society in 1998.[35] Rather than seen as something that is standalone or intrinsic, our identity arises from the ongoing relations that we have with others.[36] We can use the same approach to characterize farm-raised salmon, focusing on what is done unto the fish – vaccination, manhandling, feeding – rather than simply on any inherent quality that distinguishes it from wild-caught salmon.

This relational perspective underlies exceptions identified in an audit of internal controls to support SOX. There are three types of deficiencies that can be identified:

1. Control deficiency
2. Significant deficiency
3. Material weakness

A control deficiency can refer to an internal weakness in a public company's processes and procedures in preventing or detecting misstatements in a timely manner. An aggregation of control weaknesses, or a control deficiency alone, can contribute to a significant deficiency that has more than a remote likelihood and more than inconsequential financial impact. Unlike a control deficiency, a significant deficiency is reportable to a company's audit committee. Typically comprised of members selected from the company's board of directors, an audit committee is charged with the oversight of financial reporting and disclosure. SOX itself contains other provisions on the role of the audit committee including having at least one member deemed "audit committee financial expert" independent of management, selecting and overseeing the work of independent auditors, as well as managing the process and procedures for handling complaints on the company's accounting practices. In continuing with the same pattern in characterizing a significant deficiency, a material weakness can arise from either an aggregation of significant deficiencies or a single significant deficiency that has material impact to the books and needs to be publicly reported. Whether a significant deficiency or material weakness can arise in turn depends on multiple variables that are not always immediately apparent as opposed to clear, precise lines of demarcation leading to unequivocal cause and effect. Where aggregation of deficiencies is concerned, it would be like saying that so long as the number of undersized wild-caught red groupers doesn't exceed a number deemed significant or material, the weakness uncovered would remain a control deficiency that doesn't have to be reported to higher authorities. Even the presence of material weakness is itself at best a nebulous indicator of potential fraud; invariably an uncovered misstatement leads to efforts to revisit past internal control validations to explain for the material weakness, a case of the tail wagging the dog. That easy answers are in short supply when it comes out as a simple and straightforward causality attribution reveals not so much the absence of causality but the "multiply-authored" causes at hand. As Meyer put it, "The world is seen as a single interrelated field or continuum in which everything that interacts with – is the 'cause' of – everything else; there are no separable causes and effects."[37]

A relational view of an otherwise individually drawn construct is applicable now more so than ever in the age of open application programming interfaces (APIs) and cloud computing compared to an previous time of monolithic customer-hosted on-premise software. Looking back, we can argue that the age-old relational data-base, that contains primary and foreign keys, the latter a reminder of the presence of others, is a herald of this change of perspective. In place of a traditional customer invoice that is sent out monthly, picture a self-service e-commerce checkout cart. The customer self-serves by selecting the items for purchase and enters credit card information that is in turn integrated with an external payment processing gateway. To relay the requisite sale information, such as customer name, bill to address, item sold, quantity and amount to the company's financial SaaS to make up an invoice, a third-party integration platform as a service (iPaaS) may be employed. This same facility may also relay payment information from the payment gateway back to the financial SaaS to be auto-matched with the invoices created. The composite product: the invoice and its accompanying attributes are more of a function of piecing together upstream and downstream artifacts, rather than any inherent, self-generated qualities. In other instances, the iPaaS may also transform the transmitted data, replacing null values or updating text to numeric formats for downstream SaaS consumption. Thus, just like the Melanesian people before, the invoice is "multiply-authored." Viewing the invoice in this way changes the way we think about designing internal controls for SaaS.

First, with relational aspects coming to the forefront, this can mean that at any given time, if relations change, the identity of the invoice changes and along with this, a necessary change in the way internal controls are configured. If our internal financial system of record is capable of e-commerce capability and this is activated, then, instead of checking to see that all transactions processed on a third-party checkout cart are synced over in a complete manner, a more appropriate validation may be to ensure that only items authorized for sale are exposed on the external facing customer site. Haraway herself states, "You can make categories interrupt each other. You can turn up the volume on some categories, and down on others."[38]

Notwithstanding the emphasis of this book on transactions processed in SaaS with financial impact, accounting is not the universal language it purports to be for business management. In fact, there are grumblings from business functions that the age-old enterprise resource planning (ERP) engine associated with legacy and on-premise software often foregrounds accounting and financial reporting at the expense of other more pressing operational needs. Within accounting alone, as our PO inclusion on the customer invoice illustrates, there can be conflicting demands, whether it is keeping the invoice locked down in a closed period or granting users the ability to add attributes to accelerate customer payment and improve cash flow.

In the same manner, a large part of internal controls for SaaS involves counteracting one best-in-breed and integrated solution with another. In other words, it matters more that we compare the item master data between the external facing site and the internal financial SaaS to make sure that they are aligned rather than focus a great deal on controls in either system in sheer exclusivity of the other. The more "multiply-authored" a transaction is, the more noise or false positives we would have to sieve through in exception handling. Suppose we receive an email that a transaction has failed to be synced over because of expired login credentials of the account used. Yet upon closer inspection, we realize this situation has more to do with sandbox rather than production login credentials and that the exception message should have been more specific on which environments are impacted, a sync between test or sandbox instances, or where it truly matters, among production environments.

Second, when it comes to configuring internal controls for SaaS, we run the risk of designing them to validate categories of categories. What comes to mind are Marilyn Strathern's remark as quoted by Donna Haraway: "It matters which categories you use to think other categories with."[39] Strathern herself refers to Michael Power whose study of the audit explosion in Britain led him to observe that "what is audited is whether there is a system which embodies standards and the standards of performance themselves are shaped by the need to be auditable."[40] In other words, audit for audit's sake, or more pointedly, internal controls for internal controls' sake. In the salmon farm, a control designed in this manner would validate whether the software is distributing the feed at preconfigured intervals instead of whether the fish are consuming the pellets or whether the pellets themselves are crowding out the water. Instead, farm workers intervene to provide the necessary human oversight albeit manual whether that is scooping out the feed to see how the fish would respond as it hits the water or reducing the feed altogether when observing a reduction in fish appetites in warmer waters in specific pens.[41] This careful tending to, and at times withholding of, is possibly the closest thing next to getting the fish to talk. In place of making the fish talk, the control of insuring feed dispensation at agreed intervals as designed only serves to make the control talk.

In the invoice context, think of a control that comprises a billing schedule that generates a future invoice from the sales order at agreed intervals. Much like the software controlling fish feed at expected intervals, the billing schedule doesn't validate whether goods or services have been rendered. Thus, if the control were simply bent on having a billing schedule applied on the sales order, it doesn't quite go quite far enough to ensure that services or goods have been rendered to support the revenue recorded. Power calls this "a formal 'loop' by which the system observes itself."[42] Put another way, the system of internal controls either audits or validates itself, rather than the transaction at hand. This has led some in the industry to see an audit of internal controls as a ritualistic affair rather than as any real means of addressing deep-rooted fissures underpinning symptomatic concerns. Ironically, the system of internal controls that is supposed to make us accountable to fish or to the invoice, ends up validating, in the final analysis, whether we are accountable to itself. We can also ask: would the amount generated on the future invoice change if the sales order was itself updated? Just as the level of fish feed administered by *Fishtalk* did not quite change in response to the overheated water that reduced the fish appetite, to what extent does the SaaS at hand either assist or doesn't assist in modifying the billing schedule to mirror the sales order update?

Third, when applying a relational lens on accountability, there is an acknowledgment that accountability is more than an *interior* ability to answer to, or comply with, *exterior* standards or regulations. Instead, relations with others can change the way we understand, define, or articulate accountability. In our previous examples, we see integrations between a customer-facing online storefront and an internal-facing financial SaaS to sync over customer and invoice information, as well as to sync over credit card payments between the internal financial SaaS and the payment processing gateway. Here, accountability is "multiply-authored" whether it is ensuring Payment Card Industry (PCI) compliance during cart checkout and payment processing or completeness of transactions recorded so that all credit card sales recorded in the financial SaaS are ultimately matched with payments from the payment processing gateway. If any one of the relations changes, so too does the understanding, definition, and performance of actions to support accountability. If the financial SaaS is extended with web storefront functionality instead of relying on a third-party cart checkout provider, we ask about the storage of the credit card token in the financial SaaS and whether it is PCI compliant.

Relations do not just refer to like-on-like, whether software on software or user on user. As the charges pressed against the boat captain of Miss Katie illustrate, had the inspectors boarded the boat for the routine patrol a couple of years later, its entire catch would have been compliant with the minimal legal length of 18 inches. Variable Interest Entity (VIE) rules came into existence to force companies to place their off-balance debt on their balance sheet after Enron was found to be using Special Purpose Entities (SPE), owned by Enron's treasurer, to carry large sums of debt loaned to Enron.[43] Since Enron did not directly own any share of the SPEs, the corporation did not record the debt on its balance sheet, effectively making it appear as though Enron was debt free and profitable when it was actually the opposite. Alibaba, a Chinese e-commerce company heavily regulated in China with limits on how much of the company can be owned by foreign investors, established its VIE in the Cayman Islands outside the jurisdiction of the Chinese government to receive the profits from the Chinese company and its assets.[44] By carrying the assets of companies that it doesn't own into the balance sheet, Alibaba was able to leverage the VIE rules to its benefit to gain access to U.S. trading markets and raise $25 billion in an initial public offering.[45]

But more than the slip and slide tectonics of regulatory change, the way we exist in situ, that is, in the context of existing and changing relations matters. In our example on the third-party cart checkout and payment gateway, if only non-sensitive credit card information such as payment gateway, transaction identifier, and amount is synced from the payment gateway to the internal-facing financial SaaS, the controls can be less stringent. Even with iPaaS in place to facilitate the syncs, a key manual control to consider is the reconciliation of transactions across SaaS such as payments synced to the financial system with those reported in the gateway, as well as customers synced over for creation in the financial SaaS with those set up at the third-party e-commerce site. In this context, less reliance is placed on the importance of having service organization controls (SOC) reports from each individual vendor than on having a set of controls that can effectively orchestrate the relations among the various players to account for exception handling procedures, such as when a customer's credit card fails to be processed, or when a customer cancels an initial order placed and requests a refund.

Even if SOC reports were readily proffered by vendor software providers, we almost always note an important section on compensating controls that emphasizes the obligations and responsibilities of the client organization, such as controls on access administration and requisite reviews. Client personnel are almost confounded when dealing with inaccuracies in complex software computations, such as over tax or sales commission. When following up with their third-party providers, they are confronted with the response: our software only computes what has been communicated or else designated; insofar as there are other unknown scenarios not documented, we are not responsible for the errors made; and oh, by the way, you signed off on the user acceptance testing performed on your end prior to go-live.

As we start prefacing the relational over the individual, we start to see how designing for internal controls for SaaS, much like the red groupers congregating around baitfish beneath Miss Katie in the Gulf of Mexico, is like what Garfinkel terms congregational work.[46] Take a queue for example. According to Garfinkel, members of the queue are not mere bystanders; should a newcomer enter the picture and step out of line, they actively instruct a newcomer to be accountable to the sequence or order observed with "the line starts here" or "no it starts there."[47] When asking about internal control accountability and the like, we should also ask: accountable to what. There is the obvious answer of being answerable to externally mandated requirements or a societal code of ethics of sorts. Public companies in the United States need to comply with U.S. Securities and Exchange Commission (SEC) guidelines on fair and complete financial reporting and disclosures.

There is also an answer that is more aligned with the spirit of who watches the watchers. With SOX, for example, auditors are answerable to the Public Company Accounting Oversight Board (PCAOB) that provides independent inspection of audit work in the wake of Arthur Anderson's destruction of audit evidence on Enron. In response to PCOAB Alerts 11 or 12, what the auditor focuses on when auditing clients can in turn change from one year to the next to align with shifting winds. More attention may be centered on gaining comfort with system-generated reports, otherwise information provided by entity (IPE), to reduce the level of substantive manual testing. Client personnel may have to evidence

1. The process it takes to generate reports
2. The criteria used
3. The last time changes were made
4. Folks who have access to make configurational changes

Power's argument is that the system of internal controls ends up being accountable to itself, accountability for accountability sake. In the context of the queue, we can argue that the newcomer is automatically answerable to others already standing in queue. And as we have seen, depending on how SaaS is integrated, different players are answerable to different requirements, whether that is PCI compliance, transaction completeness and accuracy, or pure operational competency.

There is yet a different kind of accountability. In attempting to replicate Galileo's incline plane demonstration of the real motion of falling bodies, Garfinkel focuses on losing what he termed the phenomenon.[48] Rather than reconstruct Galileo's experiment in its entirety blow by blow, he places emphasis on the little ways his version may differ from Galileo's and how each variation in turn lends itself to losing the phenomenon.[49] To be able to time the rolls, for example, requires us to release the balls smoothly: otherwise, the desired outcome mirroring Galileo's experiment is lost.[50] For the results to be reproducible each time, rather than simply observing how things naturally unfold, what is required is a strict adherence to the *constraints* in which Galileo's experiment is *accountable*.

Like Power's critique of audit as merely a means to validate itself, Garfinkel questions the scientific mode of inquiry as a series of steps undertaken to work backwards from a conclusion already formed in the beginning. In so doing, he distinguishes a theorized account from a naturalized one, with the former running a risk of losing the phenomenon each time the experiment is not held accountable to the enforced constraints.[51] An internal control that ensures service or good fulfillment behind every invoice may simply be a thinly veiled attempt at concealing the amount of behind the scenes work that goes on to validate that a delivery is made *after* rather than *before* an invoice is generated. Rather than act as an automated control that prevents unauthorized billing in the first place, it functions more like a detective control that assembles or lines up the necessary artifacts after the fact. No wonder then that in some circles the increase in internal control rhetoric is simply that – a self-reinforcing prophecy on the need for a system of internal controls rather than pointing to any real improvement in actual process.

In the same manner, we can say that the captain of Miss Katie is accountable to the constraints of the matter at hand: the minimal legal length mandating a near automated release of its live catch back to the sea. Likewise, the salmon from the farm that ends up on our dinner plate is accountable to the constraining 11 centimeters that separated the healthy fish from the rest. Rather than serve as a naturalized account of wildlife conservation or farm-raised fish, these theorized accounts are answerable to carefully outlined constraints and often mistaken as empirical and real. Rather than tend to the fish in the farm, we tend to the controls that idealize the software's ability to make fish talk, software that is itself reliant on the presence of manual human oversight, busy hands at work through slip and slide. Seen in this light, when we preface the relational over the individual, we are really showing a preference for the real over the rhetoric.

Popular parlance has it that internal controls are accountable to appliance standards and regulations. It is an odd juxtaposition in a way that what has been designed to operate internally is really intended to comply with what is external. Yet, just as what is internal is achieved among multi-varied functional stakeholders, what is external is bought through coalition building among varied interests. We need look no further than the Financial Accounting Standard Board (FASB) proposal in December 2015 to recast materiality from an accounting to a legal perspective for deciding what information should be included in financial statement footnotes.

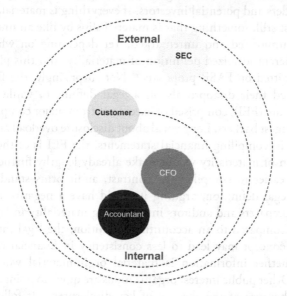

As early as August 1999, the SEC issued the Staff Accounting Bulletin No. 99 (SAB 99), reminding commission staff that "exclusive reliance on certain quantitative benchmarks to assess materiality in preparing financial statements and performing audits of those financial statements is inappropriate; misstatements are not immaterial simply because they fall beneath a numerical threshold."[52] In September 2015, the FASB released a pair of proposals on materiality, the first reframing materiality as a legal concept (rather than an accounting one), and the second applying this very same concept to assessing the appropriateness of footnote disclosures in financial statements, so that in effect, an immaterial disclosure would not be considered an error. The argument that FASB put forth is that it is trying to help organizations eliminate unnecessary disclosures in financial statements to reduce disclosure overload. According to the FASB, the concept of materiality in their conceptual framework is inconsistent with the concept of materiality established by the U.S. Supreme Court. These proposals lay bare the gulf that lies between an accounting and a legal definition of materiality. As law firm Cahill Gordon & Reindel explained, where on the one hand, the FASB Conceptual Framework states that information is deemed material "if omitting it or misstating it could influence decisions that users make on the basis of the financial information of a specific reporting entity," information is deemed material in the courts on the other hand "if there is a substantial likelihood that the omitted or misstated item would have been viewed by a reasonable resource provider as having significantly altered the total mix of information."[53]

Another argument given by the FASB is that the proposals are intended to help organizations improve the effectiveness of their disclosures by eliminating immaterial information and focusing on providing material and important facts for the stakeholders and potential investors. If everything is material, then nothing really is, or worst still, something that is material slips by like an undersized farm-raised salmon, unnoticed and unremarked. Yet depending on whom we speak to, we get a different idealized definition of materiality, and this plays out in the comments submitted on FASB proposals.[54] Not surprisingly, the Big Four audit firms have voiced their disapprovals on a legal definition, while the Financial Executives Institute (FEI), comprised of executives from major companies, emerges as one of its strongest backers. Long vocal about disclosure overload and the burdens companies face in compiling financial statements, the FEI is of the opinion that a legal definition of materiality would make already lengthy financial statements less costly and easier to compile.[55] In contrast, audit firms stand their ground in opposing a legal definition, arguing it would have a negative impact on the ability of both preparers and auditors in discussing materiality in any meaningful kind of way.[56] Compared to an accounting definition, the legal interpretation of the materiality concept may lead to less consistency in financial reporting since determining whether information is material or immaterial would be a close judgment call. Other public interest organizations are quick to point out that Enron arose precisely because of the absence of key disclosures.[57] It follows that more information would be better for investors and this proposal would achieve quite the opposite by reducing the amount of disclosed information made available.[58]

What does it mean to reframe accountability differently in the context of SaaS? Like our previous examples on the health of farm-raised fish being accountable to 12 centimeters or the conservation of wild-caught fish being accountable to 20 inches or under in length, we can very well argue that internal controls are accountable to the parameters configured within the SaaS. Take an automated control that checks for completeness of data entered on a vendor invoice. If incomplete data is submitted, the SaaS gives an error warning and prevents the transaction from being saved. This insures that specific data attributes that are key to financial reporting, such as cost center, are present for us to report on operating expenses on the income statement in categories (sales and marketing, research and development as well as general and administrative) aligned with generally accepted accounting principles (GAAP). Viewed another way, the control is accountable to the fields that have been configured as mandatory, no more, no less. If location or other fields are available for use, these continue to appear in vendor invoices in a less than consistent manner simply because no mandatory check is provided for complete data capture.

We can take this discussion a step further by looking at field level security in the context of possible updates to already submitted and saved vendor invoices. If the SaaS at hand doesn't provide field-level security to restrict users from updating specific key attributes that have financial reporting impact, then already saved and submitted invoices are at risk for inadvertent changes. There are various ways things can go awry. For example, a vendor invoice may be submitted with a wrong cost center at the outset likely because the user entering the transaction doesn't know which one to code to. In effect, more knowledgeable and thus authorized users need access to be able to update this field. Without field level security, these users and others would have access to update the cost center even for vendor invoices that have been coded correctly in the first place. In place of field level security, a compensating control can be designed for executing queries periodically on updates to vendor invoices to surface those that impact sensitive fields and email alerts can be sent to users based on results of these queries.

Another way incorrect cost centers can get assigned to operating expenses can be attributed to the way employees are first set up in an upstream human capital management (HCM) SaaS and whether they have been classified in the right cost centers to start with. Even so, what happens when they transfer to other cost centers in the same organization? Would a downstream SaaS, such as an expense management SaaS, be able to handle the cost center change and yet still be able to percolate the changes farther downstream to an accounting SaaS? Put differently, in addition to syncing transactions, are employees or cost centers also synced? What if the cost center change arises not from an internal employee transfer among existing cost centers but from an addition of a new cost center or inactivation of an existing one? What controls, manual or automated, exist to mitigate the risks of having expenses classified in correct GAAP categories on published financials despite cost center changes? From a configuration perspective, can a workflow be easily spun up to default all vendor invoices manually entered for a specific vendor to be automatically defaulted with a specific cost center to mitigate the risk of user entry errors?

The question is as much about association as it is about degrees of freedom. Insofar as internal controls are accountable to software parameters, then to the extent that these are configurable, this extends the range of possibilities for designing internal controls. It follows then that range of internal controls that can be employed is directly correlated with the degree of configurability of parameters set up in the SaaS. The less configurable a SaaS is, the more it becomes accountable to its constraints, and the more likely internal controls devised are beholden to theorized accounts. So, if the prescribed sequence of sales order–fulfillment–invoice were in effect, then the internal controls devised assumes a theorized flow. Even if a fulfillment may precede an order creation, the internal control assumes otherwise, a surefire guarantee that busy hands would once again be at work behind the scenes to put together an orderly sequence. Conversely, the more configurable a SaaS is, the less it can be held accountable to its constraints. Another way of asking this is: How can controls remain accountable to constraints if the constraints themselves are amenable to change? In effect, is it more appropriate to say that controls are accountable to configurations, or what has been configured? On the other hand, when we are accountable to configurability – the ability to configure parameters or constraints – we become accountable to the invisible hand that sets the floor for wild-caught red groupers to be immediately released or for farm-raised fish to be worthy enough to land on your plates. In effect, we can argue that this is what an audit is intended to do, that is, set the floor or lowest common denominator for compliance with external regulations.

Not all SaaS are built the same. There is in effect some level of jostling where specific vendors appropriate the SaaS verbiage when describing their software to give prospective customers the illusion that what they are buying or getting is SaaS when it is really a solution cloaked in SaaS clothing. How SaaS-y a product is itself a topic that will be covered later. It suffices to say that how we view and historically worked with or on internal controls takes on new meaning in the context of SaaS. To pretend otherwise or to continue in the same manner as before with on-premise software would be to miss out on an opportunity to refresh the toolkit that we have grown accustomed to, or gain buy in from present-day users of SaaS on the relevance of internal controls. After all, there is a sense that SaaS is easy, seamless, and economical, so why bother at all with internal controls when the whole point is to outsource what we do not have time for or quite frankly do not care very much for?

What happens when the lines drawn in the sand get redrawn? For if we were to peer beneath the surface and look at the role of configurability, audit is elevated to a meta layer not so much to itself as it is to change, in this case to configurational change. With the ability for users to configure the SaaS to their needs, a system of internal controls that emphasizes change is ironically a stronger foundation than one focused on evidencing static snapshots arrested in time. Rather than obsess with performative aspects such as who performed what when, we hone in on the degrees of freedom or variation that a configured control affords. The question becomes who has access to update what configurations when. The problem is that not all SaaS is built the same, so not all configuration updates have accompanying audit trails that are available for querying and notification. That is like having the boat captain plead ignorance at the time the catch was inspected because he did not know whether the minimal legal length of catch changed or stayed the same. On the fish farm, imagine if someone were to change the amount of feed, so that the fish either grew too quickly or too slowly. The length of health that ends up being sold and on our plates changes as a result. In this case, consumers would notice the change albeit after the fact.

It follows that in using a SaaS, the immediate or extended users, whether employees, management, customers, or vendors, can be relied upon as a last resort to notice a change at least in the output to ask whether parameters have been changed upstream even if this is not ideal as reports may have already been filed in a prior period. A change in the SaaS configuration can itself introduce a wrinkle in time that appears to transcend time. Consider a multi-year sales order that is expected to be billed multiple times depending on whether the annual subscription is up for renewal or when milestones are fulfilled. When it is first created, line level tax is not configured so that the sales tax incurred is solely based on the shipping jurisdiction and ends up distributed across all lines. What happens when line level tax is enabled in the future so that all sales orders created no longer inherit the same tax amount across all lines but vary depending on the type of product selected at the line level? New sales orders created after this configuration change would reflect the right sales tax amounts at any given line but the same sales order that is created prior to the change would continue to have future invoices that do not show tax specific lines. Thus, a change to the configuration for tax line computation resulted in a time rift of sorts where two realities, both line specific as well as order specific tax computations, coexist at the same time.

The window was open for dual realities when charges were pressed against the boat captain. Outside the court room, the minimal legal length fell to 18 inches for fish caught in the wild even if simultaneously inside the courtroom the boat captain was put on the stand for fish exceeding 18 inches. Compliance or an audit of differences can come into play when the object of dispute remains, oddly enough, indisputable. The boat captain is charged with violating the minimal catch requirement because all concerned assume that there is only one minimal legal length: it can't be both 18 and 20 inches. Otherwise, the difference in opinion starts to lose currency. Perhaps it is this loss of stability that the audit firms fear. What makes a piece of information material enough for a public company to disclose? Auditors are more accustomed to an accounting metric such as 5% of net income than a subjective judgement call facilitated by the legal team that accounts for a myriad of factors specific to the nature of the business at hand. A line drawn in the sand is better than nothing, but sometimes it leads to a tunnel vision. After all, as observed in insider threat studies conducted by Carnegie Mellon University's Software Engineering Institute (SEI), misappropriation of company assets or funds often happens in little drips, well below the materiality threshold established even as over time they aggregate to a level of significance that lends itself to easier detection or discovery.[59]

The concern expressed by audit firms over the FASB proposal of a legal definition of materiality stems from a discomfort in having to deal with dual realities – how the same article of information can be both material as well as immaterial. After all, the premise behind an audit of differences (the process to arrive at whether company personnel are compliant with a given standard or regulation) rests on the assumption that there is a rudimentary agreement on what to disagree about, and that this relates specifically to an altogether agreeable construct. When controls are accountable to parameters that themselves are amenable to change, accountability is grounded in quicksand. Like the ebb and flow of the waves, configurations can and do change. Yet, like the sea, the management of configuration changes stays the same. A careful distinction must be made that the design effectiveness of an internal control lies not so much in any one parameter or configuration change but in the overall management of all changes.

Not all configuration changes are forgiving. In other words, when configured the first time, the change can't be overwritten. The setup of subsidiaries in a company is one such irreversible change. Once parent and child subsidiaries are created and transactions booked with general ledger impact, we can no longer unwind them. It is for this reason that in some SaaS implementations, we find an intermediary rollup subsidiary that may be regional such as Asia Pacific at the mid-level even if the volume of transactions in its child subsidiaries such as Singapore doesn't justify the creation of a second tier. This placeholder of sorts allows the enterprise to expand or contract without necessarily having to update the entire corporate structure altogether. Otherwise, any change to subsidiaries – such as the creation of a new one to take advantage of tax implications associated with the sale of specific goods and services in specific jurisdictions – necessitates significant rework, resulting in likely a "re-implementation" of the SaaS. In the latter scenario, we become concerned with more than the management of configuration changes, that is, the change management processes that govern software implementation. Another example of an irreversible change is the account type chosen for a newly created account. When transactions have been coded to this account, the account type can no longer be changed even as a rationale may emerge for future updates if only to assist with the ease of developing and maintaining key financial reports.

Despite our emphasis on the management of configuration changes, reversible or otherwise, software vendors, on-premise or SaaS, are likely to discourage any given enterprise customer from overly customizing the application at hand. To counteract against this possibility, horror stories abound of clients that customize apps to the point that they become unsustainable, unsupportable, or else un-upgradable. Whether they are exaggerated or otherwise is itself a subject of contention. For some providers, customization has become a dirty word, with emphasis placed on configuration and not so much customization. The whole point with going with a third-party solution, they argue, is that a generalized need is met, so why expend unnecessary resources on tailoring shared services such as human resources, accounting, and reporting when they can be far better utilized towards the development of new competencies or products that an organization is selling. Furthermore, they argue, from an audit perspective, the more we customize, the more there is a need for configuration change management, and thus the more there is to audit.

Yet, other SaaS vendors freely interchange configurations with customizations. Salesforce, for example, at its annual DreamForce conference in San Francisco devotes an entire day to the Salesforce administrators covering topics such as declarative programming that explores how through simple point-and-click, nontechnical personnel can put in place fields and workflows that are tailored to their organization's needs using available Force.com resources. The administrator is viewed as a heroic figure capable of understanding SaaS speak and, more importantly, the divide between the broad array of vanilla functionality on display and the specific organizational needs simmering within. Organizations continue to grapple with the differences between configuration and customization. The students in my *Accounting Information Systems* class experience this firsthand when attempting develop specific reports, workflows, transaction templates, and fields. Is this a configuration or customization? Is it a one-time or one-off change? How many one-off changes does it take for them to be taken more seriously as recurring requests, no longer exceptional one-offs?

The narratives we weave, the stories we develop and tell ourselves amount to this: a change is not just a change. It can be a configuration, reversible or otherwise, or it can be a customization that somehow changes the way a software is supposed to behave. Depending on which side we are on, we can be viewed as aberrant customers who over-customize to the point of rendering a third-party vendor product un-maintainable, or client-centric administrators who are able to avail ourselves of the out-of-the-box configuration furnished. The vendor narrative that forewarns of impending doom from flagrant customization as opposed to authorized configuration illustrates the effort invested in presenting a singular reality even if it masks the plurality of interweaving accounts. Think management of configuration changes as a gateway to understanding a multitude of changes. Likewise, a red grouper caught in the Gulf of Mexico is not a just a red grouper. It can be below the minimal legal length mandating an immediate release or it can be deemed legal to retain. Farm-raised salmon is not just salmon. It can be salmon that is vaccinated, fed, and grown to a healthy size, perceived to be unhealthy because of their length, or quite simply dead.

Materiality is not just materiality: it can be framed in a legal perspective in line with the FASB guidance or it can continue to be inscribed in an accounting umbrella of quantitative and qualitative analyses. Compliance is not just compli-ance: it can be *out* of compliance as in the case of Enron's use of SPEs to avoid reporting assets on the books, or *in* compliance in the case of Alibaba availing itself of VIE rules that come into effect post-Enron to go public.[60] Enron itself was able to exploit an previous 3% rule, a product of an ongoing task force on emerging accounting issues formed by the FASB in 1990.[61] The rule stated that if a SPE had at least 3% of its total capital from an outside source, then the business enterprise did not have to consolidate the SPE with its own affairs.[62] Using SPEs owned by its treasurer, Andrew Fastow, to borrow significant sums, Enron ended up keeping $30 billion of debt off the balance sheet.[63]

In the wake of the Enron debacle, accounting standard setters closed this loop-hole by creating new VIE accounting rules that require financial consolidation when a company is controlled through means other than stock ownership. Chinese compa-nies have been able to use these VIE rules to their advantage, bringing new meaning to complying with the letter rather than the spirit of the law. By consolidating the assets of Chinese subsidiaries with their U.S. virtual counterparts, firms like Alibaba are able to qualify for an initial public offering in the United States with little capital-ization.[64] As Charles Niemeier, chief accountant for SEC's enforcement division puts it, "One can violate SEC laws and still comply with GAAP."[65] Or take Judge Elena Kagan's remarks in the U.S. Supreme Court hearing over charges pressed against the boat captain: "A person who hides a murder victim's body is no less culpable than one who burns the victim's diary. ... A fisherman ... who dumps undersized fish to avoid a fine is no less blameworthy than one who shreds his vessel's catch log for the same reason."[66] What is ludicrous is not so much the one-time application of SOX to wild-life conservation, or accounting records to red groupers, but the everyday application of SOX to mundane operational processes so that what is monitored to be in or out of compliance is taken for granted, all-pervasive, and omnipresent, unquestioned over time like the waters the red groupers swim in or the oxygen piped into Norwegian fish tanks. Do controls for our SaaS make our customer sales or vendor purchases talk, or do they serve to refract the prevailing regulatory demands of the day? Do they reflect a-day-in-the-life or are they mere theorized accounts?

What is in and out of compliance is thus an ongoing active process of navigation and negotiation. Steve Woolgar and Javier Lezaun reviewed a British tabloid article that screams: *Another Day Another Potty Penalty.*[67] In the United Kingdom, an unmarried mother of four was fined by her local council for putting out her trash in her own bin bags rather than the authorized ones issued by the council.[68] In highlighting the sheer injustice and incredulity of the matter, the article singled out the "barmy council bosses" from the hapless mother "with kids to feed."[69] Had there not been a lull of collections during the festive season, she would not have accumulated extra trash in the first place.[70] Although the matter at hand may be different – garbage disposal versus wildlife conservation, farm-raised fish, or financial records – the fundamentals nevertheless remain the same. There is a wrong bin bag, just as there is a wrong-sized catch, wrong-sized farm-raised fish, wrong sales tax computation at the header instead of the line level on a sales invoice, or wrong definition of materiality.

For this dualistic portrayal of right versus wrong to work, there can only be one version of reality even if at any given moment there are different bin bags in question, all the same black color. The tabloid article, as Woolgar and Lezaun pointed out, characterized the conflict between the governing council and the local citizen as if it were over the same object when both parties each referred to different bin bags.[71] Take 404. It is the error message you receive when attempting to locate a web page whose uniform resource locator (URL) is no longer found and may have been updated. All it takes is a mere character typo in the URL to result in a 404. That this 404 error has nothing to do with Section 404 of the SOX or the much-mythologized room 404 believed to house the web's first servers at the European Organization for Nuclear Research in Switzerland speaks to the wondrous serendipity we encounter every so often in our everyday.[72]

In asking what controls are accountable to, we begin by describing accountability to a regulation or standard whether it relates to fish conservation, fish consumption, or SOX compliance before acknowledging the composite of multifaceted cast at work. We next explore the accountability of controls to the constraints at hand; with SaaS this becomes an accountability to configured parameters. While we review various types of configuration changes veering from excessive customization on the one end to inheritance of default configurations out-of-the-box on the other, as well as reversible versus irreversible changes, we merely glimpsed the multi-composite nature of configuration change characterized by configuration management in a singular way of encompassing a seeming universe of changes. In truth, even for one single configuration change, a multiple cast is at hand: consider the lack of segregation of duties in a smaller enterprise where an accountant has access to both configure the way the transactions are processed as well as process the transactions themselves. In effect, the accountant can swap out the council-issued bin bag for her or his own, or undersized catch for a larger one. This scene is vastly different from an enterprise where roles and permissions are locked down and changes to configurations are put through a change management process. Seeing the plurality behind a singularized veil, it is no wonder that internal controls devised for configuration management can vary from one organization to another. Other factors like humans, transactional volumes, and the nature of the business can come into play. The very simple matter of configuration management for one enterprise may mean compensating manual controls in reviewing for and handling exceptions insofar as access to configuration changes can't be too tightly restricted. For yet a different company where the transactions to be processed are not as sensitive, sales quotes, as opposed to invoices, for example, compensating checks can even be redistributed to the end customer. The maturity of the company implementing the SaaS also plays a role. Configuration changes can't be locked down too soon in part because it too is trying to figure out which ones work best in actuality rather than in theory. Thus, when all is said and done, internal controls around configuration changes are accountable to an entire assortment of characters.

What happens when auditors come upon the scene, armed with loads of control narratives, walkthroughs, risk and control matrices, and test plans? What doesn't fit inadvertently gets tossed aside. A control employed in comparing account balances between the general ledger in an accounting SaaS with account reconciliations in Excel spreadsheets in a data storage SaaS may not be articulated simply because it is not a question on the boilerplate checklist to begin with, so why even attempt to fit a square peg into a round hole? The challenge lies in not stopping to tell stories, abandoning all artifacts altogether, but in cultivating a healthy skepticism of the accounts we rely on or stories we tell ourselves. Sometimes this may mean that we choose to deliberately go against the story to uncover fundamental assumptions that could well do with a change of scene. If an enterprise were to employ a single sign-on cloud platform that allows timely provisioning and deprovisioning of access to all in scope cloud applications, then do we still need to review access in each in-scope application against a current employee list every month? The latter is a commonplace control that an auditor is quick to brandish from her toolbox but to what extent are we not using the meta-control aspects of the cloud to pit cloud against cloud? Controls once devised take on a life of their own. Rarely are they revisited or retired; such is the nature of the audit and compliance work, an unstinting recycle of the same old same-old validated quarter after quarter, year after year. This consistent narrative is thus consistent with Michael Power's portrayal of the self-reinforcing loop that audit finds itself in.

In the final analysis, controls can be said to be accountable to a singular reality even if it remains largely a fragile artifact. In the case of SaaS, we have seen how a mere failure in the ability to configure mandatory field capture for cost centers and other attributes can lead to a less than consistent documentation of transaction records. From this perspective, controls can be seen to be directly accountable to the parameters configured. Yet, we can argue that to the extent that controls are utilized to mitigate risk, they are more applicable to mitigating risk arising from known unknowns than unknown unknowns. There is a deeper subtext. The undersized fish tossed out and replaced with a larger sized catch before Miss Katie docked has something in common with the council-issued bin bags the single mother in the United Kingdom replaced with her own. In both cases, we can argue they comply with the spirit of the law rather than the letter. If the fish in the undersized catch were still alive when returned to the sea, and the trash was still disposed of in bags rather than left unattended as it were, we can argue that neither wildlife conservation nor garbage disposal were placed at any significant risk. Conversely, to what extent is an insistence on internal controls itself a hindrance to complying with the spirit of the law? Or in our SaaS example, how are we not mitigating more egregious risks by focusing only on known unknowns, so that what has no precedence cannot be parameterized, cannot be configured, and therefore cannot be controlled for. Enron is one such example, so it can be considered ironic that the very means that has been amassed in its wake would likely fail to preclude it from occurring in the first place. There is also the matter of a "multiply-authored" cast. The fragility of a singular representation belies multiple actors that come onto the scene. In the case of Miss Katie, had the offshore patrol officer not been certified in federal waters, had the inspection occurred a couple of years later when the legal minimal length fell to 18 inches, or had Miss Katie sailed out on a different day perhaps when the patrol was not on duty, charges would not have been pressed. Contrary to the insinuation in the British tabloid headline, *Another Day, Another Potty Offender*, had it been a different day when garbage collection ran like clockwork in non-festive season, had the mother not had four kids to amass garbage, or had the garbage collectors mistaken the black sacks for council issued bin bags, there would have been no fine nor faux pas to broadcast.

The same can be said for newly public companies having to assert to the operating effectiveness of internal controls under SOX 404 (a) containing the management assertion and SOX 404 (b) containing the independent auditor validation. The Dodd-Frank Act of 2010 and the JOBS Act of 2012, which, among other provisions, grants newly public emerging growth companies as many as 5 years to phase in auditor attestations of internal controls as part of 404 if they remain small non-accelerated filers. The tipping point for becoming a large accelerated filer is when the newly public company has a market capitalization of more than $700 million measured as of the last business day of its most recently completed second fiscal quarter. A large accelerated filer would no longer be exempted from having to evidence operating effectiveness of internal controls. In a reverse logic of sorts, this is reminiscent of how, at different points in time, whether the length of wild-caught red groupers from the Gulf of Mexico exceeds 18 or 20 inches automatically exempts it from having to be tossed out back into the ocean. Just as GAAP is "as much a product of political action as it is of careful logic or empirical findings,"[73] the JOBS Act itself is comprised of recommendations from a task force formed in 2011 to specifically address the decline in initial public offerings (IPOs) since the late 1990s technology boom. Since coming into effect in April 2012, the number of IPOs nonetheless dropped to a new low in 2016 since the 2008–2009 financial crisis after peaking in 2014. It reflects other market variables at work, one of which surely relates to the vibrancy of the private equity financing as seen with Uber and Airbnb.[74] In 2015, in a narrowly divided U.S. Supreme Court, the decision was made to throw out the conviction against Miss Katie's captain. As Justice Ginsburg put it, "Fish one may fry but may one falsify, or make a false entry in the sea dwelling creatures?"[75]

Just as the media is apt to oversimplify the nature of internal control or compliance efforts undertaken by public companies over financial reporting, portraying at times a singularized plurality – us versus them, good versus evil – instead of acknowledging the role regulations or regulatory bodies themselves play in the pendulum shift in emphasis over time. In the context of SaaS, we become aware of a plurality of paths to take, rather than a singular one, towards a less fragile, more forgiving environment. Take an example where, because of required financial disclosures mandated by a regulatory standard and in this case *ASU 2016–2008, Principal versus Agent Considerations (Reporting Revenue Gross versus Net)*, sales transactions recorded in a specific SaaS need to be classified into principal versus agent sales. Whereas the latter involves a sale to a third-party distributor or reseller of the good and service, the former relates to a direct sale with no intermediary. The following outlines at least 6 different configuration approaches in the SaaS:

1. Create a custom field on the sales transaction. Have users manually enter "Principal" versus "Agent" values based on a review of each sales transaction.
2. Create a custom field on the sales transaction with a built-in formula that looks up to see if a separate end customer is populated; if so, "Agent" is assigned; otherwise, "Principal" is defaulted.
3. Create a custom field as well as a custom workflow, such that every time a sales transaction is created or updated, an automated process is triggered to verify if the sales transaction is principal versus agent and assigns the appropriate value to the custom field.
4. Create a custom field as well as a custom script, such that every time a sales transaction is created or updated, the script is triggered to verify if the sales transaction is principal versus agent and assigns the appropriate value to the custom field.
5. In place of a custom field, create a custom record that can hold multiple custom fields, including the new custom field for direct versus indirect sales. Associate the custom record with sales transactions and undertake one of the options (1 through 4) in selecting the means to populate the values into the record.
6. In place of a custom field, create a custom accounting segment that can be applied to a myriad of transaction types including sales transactions. Associate the custom accounting segment with sales transactions and undertake one of the options (1 through 4) in selecting the means to populate the values into the segment.

When walking through the myriad of approaches with my *Accounting Information Systems* class, the first reaction was sheer surprise at the amount of work that nevertheless needs to be undertaken with an off-the-shelf accounting SaaS solution. When attempting Option 3 in class, the resulting workflow did not work as intended for all but one student. In other words, when creating a new invoice for a specific customer to record a direct sale, the Customer Category field did not populate as Principal. Deeper investigation after class surfaced a missing step in the workflow: I would have needed to set the trigger to before record submit, so that the user upon creating an invoice would see the Principal value default automatically in the Customer Category field even before saving or submitting the invoice. As it turns out, the earlier options all mask the specific steps or design decisions needed to make each one work. With the workflow approach in Option 3, for example, users need to be able to specify not only the workflow trigger, whether it is before or after record submission as well as field edit, but also choose the right custom field (in this case Customer Category) to be set based on the condition on whether specific attributes such as End Customer and other fields are completed on the sales transaction.

Because we were not able to make the workflow work during class, we reverted to Option 1, and manually inputted the 'Principal' value directly in a direct sale. After saving the invoice and noticing the credit to the revenue account, we proceeded to pull up the standard out-of-the-box income statement report. Yet, when attempting to slice the revenue numbers by the Customer Category field, we could not find an existing report dimension or filter; existing ones pertain to cost center, subsidiary, and location. This lack necessitated a revisiting of the approach and in effect an adoption of Option 6. It turns out that accounting segments are not just necessary in configuring general ledger impact but also in slicing across companywide data in any pervasive way when it comes to reporting. Yet, just like Option 3 with the workflow previously, Option 6 when unpacked exposes a series of steps not least of which is a need to enable custom segment as part of the overall SaaS configuration to begin with, as well as a need to expose the custom segment only for sales rather than purchase transactions. When we start to be more precise in configuration work, we could be dealing with at least 20 alternatives after unpacking the level of work behind the 6 options identified. The six paths presented are themselves misleading, for contained within Option 5 and 6 are alternate paths to take depending on which of the Options 1 through 3 are reused and recombined. Thus, even without imploding the underlying detail behind each option, we are already looking at 12 instead of 6 paths.

Faced with the daunting level of work and re-work, a student asked, why would it matter to classify revenue into principal versus agent sales? To answer this question, it helps to understand that the primary driver behind revenue recognition in Accounting Standards Codification (ASC) 606 *Revenue from Contracts with Customers*. Issued jointly by the FASB and the International Accounting Standards Board (IASB). The question is whether a provider has satisfied its performance obligation when transferring the promised good or service. The emphasis is on transfer of control rather than on risk and reward to achieve convergence with international reporting standards set by IASB. Issued in May 2014 and enforced for public companies for reporting periods after December 15, 2017, ASC 606 outlines five key steps to recognize revenue:

1. Identify the contract with a customer
2. Identify the performance obligations in the contract
3. Determine the transaction price
4. Allocate the transaction price
5. Recognize revenue when or as the entity satisfies a performance obligation[76]

Wesley Bricker, deputy chief accountant of the SEC, said in a May 2016 speech, "The new revenue standard has the potential to change not only the top line, but also the bottom line," alluding to how revenue may be recognized upfront as opposed to over the length of the contract.[77] Ironically, for SaaS providers, because software is "continuously updated" over time, it can still be recognized over the length of the contract.[78] Other areas such as sales compensation may be deferred, thus resulting in increased profitability in the short term by moving expenses from the income statement to the balance sheet.

Much like the varying minimal length set for wildlife conservation, companies complying with ASC 606 can choose from a couple of options, either restating revenue from prior years or opting for a modified compliance route, applying new guidance on transactions going forward rather than going back in time. How does this impact year over year metrics that are scrutinized in public markets? If Workday, the first software vendor to comply with ASC 606, is any indication, the consequences are less than predictable. Its stock price plunged in February 2017 when it stopped giving a guidance on bookings, or billings in future periods even as it adopted 606, culminating, in the words of Morgan Stanley analysts, "in lack of clarity on the near-term growth trajectory."[79] As a *Seeking Alpha* article suggests, year-on-year comparison of deferred revenue, long used as an indicator of a company's growth, is no longer reported, casting its future growth in question.[80] This is perhaps why recasting materiality to a legal perspective can be so contentious. When what we are accustomed to is taken away, whether that be official bin bags or year-on-year indicators, how do we proceed? The stock market's reaction to Workday bears a remarkable resemblance to the way the Council reacted to the wrong bin bags used by the mother of four. Here too, note that the confluence of factors behind the "potty offender," accumulation of trash from less than frequent pickup and a family of four kids, also comes into play for Workday: market conditions, compliance with ASC 606, and changes in reporting.

In circling back to our configuration example on direct versus indirect sales, a principal sale would recognize revenue in the gross amount to which it is entitled to receive, whereas an agent sale would record revenue net of any fee or commission that the third party is entitled to in arranging for the sale to the end customer. Had agent revenue been reported as gross, it would have been overstated. The option that we settled on, Option 6, is but one of the multiple paths to take, thus even though the ASC 606 regulatory standard is singularly prescriptive in its approach, the plurality of means to comply is anything but. From an audit perspective, what option is pursued is not without additional resource implications and corresponding cost benefit tradeoffs. Option 1, while not incurring additional configuration changes to the SaaS, and thus the need to audit for changes, nevertheless requires manual reviews and entries for every singular sales invoice recorded. Option 3, while automating the default of principal versus agent values in sales transactions without additional manual entry and possibility of manual errors or omissions, nonetheless requires additional configuration work undertaken to develop and test the workflow. Possible gaps that emerge during testing may be manual bulk uploads of invoices that bypass workflow triggering altogether and thus circumventing the default of customer category values. Even so, Option 3 doesn't quite yet address the reporting gap, the need to be able to slice revenue by customer category without so much as modifying the standard income statement report and hence the need to turn to Option 6.

We have not even touched upon the difference among Options 2, 3, and 4: all three choices attempt to get the Customer Category field populated by default rather than through manual input, yet each differs in the amount of work needed to implement and to maintain, to have and to hold. A formula in a custom field, Option 2, is perhaps the easiest to deploy from the perspective of a non-technical end user, with the ability to devise a workflow through point-and-click with Option 3 falling in the middle and scripting in Option 4 on the other end of the technical expertise continuum. Even if more technical resources were available to pursue Option 4, we must still ask whether it is the most feasible approach from a maintenance perspective. In real life, the same entity that is associated with a principal sale may also resell or distribute goods and services to other entities; thus, the same customer can be associated with both principal and agent sales; what does this do to our assumptions and control design? For a consolidated invoice to the same entity to show a breakout of direct versus indirect sales, defaulted values for the Customer Category field may need to be further unpacked from Principal versus Reseller to include an additional Principal and Reseller value. Thus, much like our previous example where our configuration choices are imploded from 6 to 20, can non-technical users make this change, or do they require technical intervention?

The functionality of SaaS can also come into play. In the case of the SaaS in use by the students, whether the Customer Category field is a header or line level attribute makes a difference: workflows can only manipulate fields residing in the header level while scripts can manipulate line level fields. Why would line level fields matter, we may ask, if the entire invoice is only associated with one customer? Insofar as journal entries need to be made downstream to allocate the revenue ratably over say a subscription period, it would help to code specific journal lines to a principal versus agent customer category if only to have the corresponding general ledger impact made transparent on the resulting income statement. Taken apart, analyzed, and recombined, the ultimate combination we undertake is tested time and again in so many ways. Option 5, which we have not yet discussed bakes in this latitude or buffer for resilience, by opting for additional significant work in the creation of a custom record to house more than one custom field, even if the initial ask is for one, namely the Customer Category field. The choice we make not only has to make sense at the current time but also needs to be able to withstand the test of time. Insofar as change is needed, as in the case of having multiple customer categories identified at the line level not just on a journal but on a consolidated invoice, which option lends itself to less rework or update and not just by technical resources? An ability to scale and adapt enters the fold.

Thus far, we have merely scratched the surface when talking about change. The changes we covered focused on changes over custom configurations, but as we dive deeper, there are nuances over line level versus header level attribute or field changes. ASC 606 looks at whether each line of the sales transaction has fulfilled its performance obligation to determine if revenue can be recognized. This emphasis at the line level recalls our previous example of line versus header level sales tax computation on an order. Would the accounting SaaS at hand be able to handle this change? To be sure, this is a change upon change. Put simply, the ability to track changes to individual lines on any given sales order. What if the SaaS only displays audit trails for changes to the order at the header level only and not at the line level? What compensating manual controls need to be in place to be able to track changes to performance obligations to individual lines? The needle or unit of analysis therefore needs to be more precise, even as it is a little wave in a sea of configurational, SaaS, or regulatory changes.

Within the confines of SaaS, internal controls do not work in isolation. Configuration management depends on access management, which in turn depends on timely management reviews that depend on communicated processes and procedures or articulated job descriptions. What appears to be accountability to a singular construct like SOX is really accountability to a multitudinous cast, so that even the singular management of configuration changes for any one SaaS can take on different shades of meanings depending on the nature of the transaction, cast of internal and external actors, and artifacts at hand, not to mention the maturity of the organization. Each part, as it were, reveals a story. We find stories within stories. Is there a conversation among different parts? Or is a cacophony more likely? Ideally, when we continue to perform the necessary configuration work, and the controls over this configuration work, we can get to a point where the multiple voices can each retain their very own clarity and distinctness even as they interweave to arrive at an equal music. Perhaps there is no better way to illustrate the "multiply-authored" nature behind deceptively simplistic black and white accounts of what is in and out of compliance than to point out that, as I write this today, it was 150 years ago[81] that Major General Gordon Granger and his troops rode into Galveston, Texas, to deliver President Abraham Lincoln's Emancipation Proclamation. To be sure, this message arrived 2 months after the end of the Civil War, and 2½ years after Lincoln issued the order. In a state reeling from an economically bankrupt Confederate banking system against the larger backdrop of a war-ravaged nation, it was more than sheer coincidence that the news only arrived well after the crops had been planted and harvested.

Exercise 1.1

1. Who are the stakeholders of SaaS? List down as many as you can.
2. For each stakeholder, identify whether these are internal or external to the consuming SaaS organization.
3. For each stakeholder, identify which category they belong to: users or non-users.

Discussion

When asked these questions, students in my *Accounting Information Systems* class came up with a myriad of stakeholders from usual suspects, such as SaaS internal users in different departments and SaaS vendors to less than usual suspects such as public investors and regulators. Looking back, because my class had a lab component in which students logged into an accounting SaaS, I focused on immediate users of SaaS, such as accountants and slowly branched outwards to customers, vendors, or implementation partners. Yet to what extent do other stakeholders – regulatory, compliance, audit, analyst, and those who are not immediate users – nevertheless shape, and continue to shape, its worldview, design, and configuration in unforeseen ways? To what extent do these unseen stakeholders pull at the strings of more immediate or apparent users?

Exercise 1.2

1. Think of a SaaS in use in your organization. What are the records captured?
2. To what extent does the SaaS make the records talk or sing? In other words, do we know how the records got there, or when and why they are even relevant or in scope?
3. Conversely, to what extent does the SaaS render the records silent or invisible in specific areas?

Discussion

Students in my *Accounting Information Systems* class are more inclined to talk about what gets captured, specifically who did what, when, than to bring up the notion of why it gets captured in the first place; fewer still can point out what doesn't get captured. The question at hand is not so much the completeness of capture, but the politics of forgetting. Like the unseen SaaS stakeholders, what processes are deemed out of scope, and thus remain undocumented and thus unseen, even as they make up the underground SaaS machinery behind every transaction or entry?

Exercise 1.3

1. Can we live in dual realities, where an organization can be both in and out of compliance? If so, can you think of an example?
2. To what extent can an organization negotiate its compliance stance?
3. When an organization updates the configurations in the SaaS at hand, to what extent does it encourage multiple realities so that transactions recorded before the change continue to behave one way, while those recorded after the change behave altogether differently?

Discussion

Just as how SPEs or VIEs are compliant at different intervals of history, this exercise forces the point: how the same action can be both compliant and non-compliant at different points in time. To what extent does a myopic focus on complying with an expressed *exterior* requirement take away our *interior* ability to achieve operating effectiveness? Conversely, to what extent does having an expanded emphasis, that extends beyond compliance and to operations, end up addressing compliance as a by-product? Ironically, but not focusing squarely on compliance, an entity is able to put in place processes and procedures that are just as, if not more, operationally sound and robust enough to handle varied real-life permutations.

Endnotes

1. Powers, R. (2006). *The Echo Maker*. New York: Farrar, Straus and Giroux.
2. Supreme Court of the United States. (February 25, 2015). Yates V. United States. https://www.supremecourt.gov/opinions/14pdf/13-7451_m64o.pdf
3. Ibid.
4. Ibid.
5. Ibid.
6. Ibid.
7. Ibid.
8. Ibid.
9. Ibid.
10. Law, J. and Lien, M. (2012). Slippery: Field notes in empirical ontology. *Social Studies of Science*, 43(3), 363–378.
11. Ibid.
12. Ibid.
13. Ibid.
14. Ibid.
15. Supreme Court of the United States. Yates V. United States.
16. Law, J. and Lien, M. Slippery: Field notes in empirical ontology.
17. Kamiya, G. (January 6, 2018). Chinese sex salves' origin in Gold Rush. *San Francisco Chronicle*.
18. Ibid.
19. Law, J. and Lien, M. Slippery: Field notes in empirical ontology.
20. Ibid.
21. Ibid.

22 Ibid.

23 Ibid.

24 Ibid.

25 18 U.S. Code § 1519—Destruction, alteration, or falsification of records in Federal investigations and bankruptcy.

26 Supreme Court of the United States. Yates V. United States.

27 Plato. (1921). *Plato in Twelve Volumes*, Vol. 12 translated by Harold N. Fowler. Cambridge, MA: Harvard University Press; London, William Heinemann.

28 Law, J. and Lien, M. Slippery: Field notes in empirical ontology.

29 Carroll, L., Haughton, H., and Carroll, L. (2009). *Alice's Adventures in Wonderland*; and, *Through the Looking-glass and What Alice Found There*. New York: Penguin Classics.

30 Ibid.

31 Ibid.

32 Ibid.

33 Haraway, D.J. (2003). *The Haraway Reader*. New York: Routledge.

34 Oxford University Press. Invoice. *Oxford Living Dictionaries*. https://en.oxford dictionaries.com/definition/invoice

35 Strathern, M. (1988). The Gender of the Gift: Problems with Women and Problems with Society in Melanesia. Berkeley, CA: University of California Press.

36 Ibid.

37 Meyer, L.B. (1967). *Music, the Arts, and Ideas*. Chicago, IL: University of Chicago Press.

38 Haraway, D. J. *The Haraway Reader*.

39 Ibid.

40 Power, M. (1994). *The Audit Explosion*. London, UK: Demos.

41 Law, J. and Lien, M. Slippery: Field notes in empirical ontology.

42 Power, M. *The Audit Explosion*.

43 Gillis, P. (October 28, 2014). Son of Enron? *Foreign Affairs*. https://www.foreignaffairs. com/articles/china/2014-10-28/son-enron

44 Ibid.

45 Ibid.

46 Garfinkel, H. (2002). *Ethnomethodology's Program: Working Out Durkheim's Aphorism*. Lanham, MD: Rowman & Littlefield.

47 Ibid.

48 Ibid.

49 Ibid.

50 Ibid.

51 Ibid.

52 Securities and Exchange Commission. (August 12, 1999). 17 CFR Part 211 [Release No. SAB 99] Staff Accounting Bulletin No. 99. https://www.sec.gov/interps/account/ sab99.htm

53 Cahill Gordon and Reindel LLP. (December 26, 2007). SEC publishes final rules for financial disclosures of U.S.-Registered Foreign Companies. https://www.cahill.com/ publications/firm-memoranda/0000062/_res/id=File1/122607_SEC%20Publishes %20Final%20Rules%20for%20Finanical%20Disclosures%20of%20U%20S%20-Registered%20Foreign%20Companies.pdf

[54] Thomson Reuters Tax & Accounting. (December 30, 2015). Comment letters on materiality proposal expose sharp divide between investors, companies. *Thomson Reuters Tax & Accounting News.* https://tax.thomsonreuters.com/media-resources/news-media-resources/checkpoint-news/daily-newsstand/comment-letters-on-materiality-proposal-expose-sharp-divide-between-investors-companies/

[55] Ibid.

[56] Ibid.

[57] Ibid.

[58] Ibid.

[59] Silowash, G., Cappelli, D., Moore, A., Trzeciak, R., Shimeall, T. J., and Flynn, L. (December 2012). *Common Sense Guide to Mitigating Insider Threats* (4th ed.). Carnegie Mellon University Software Engineering Institute. Technical Report. CMU/SEI-2012-TR-012. https://www.sei.cmu.edu/reports/12tr012.pdf

[60] Gillis, P. Son of Enron?

[61] Norris, F. (January 13, 2003). Accounting rules changed to bar tactics used by Enron. *The New York Times.* http://www.nytimes.com/2003/01/16/business/accounting-rules-changed-to-bar-tactics-used-by-enron.html

[62] Ibid.

[63] Ibid.

[64] Gillis, P. (October 28, 2014). Son of Enron?

[65] Liesman, S. (February 12, 2002). SEC accounting Cop's warning: Playing by the rules may not head off fraud issues. *Wall Street Journal.* https://www.wsj.com/articles/SB1013464544838814280

[66] Liptak, A. (February 25, 2015). In overturning conviction, Supreme Court says fish are not always tangible. *The New York Times.* Retrieved from https://www.nytimes.com/2015/02/26/us/justices-overturn-a-fishermans-conviction-for-tossing-undersize-catch.html?_r=1

[67] Woolgar, S. and Lezaun, J. (June 10, 2013). The wrong bin bag: A turn to ontology in science and technology studies? *Social Studies of Science,* 43(3), 321–340.

[68] Ibid.

[69] Ibid.

[70] Ibid.

[71] Ibid.

[72] Wiener, A. (December 4, 2017). Page not found: A brief history of the 404 Error. *Wired.* https://www.wired.com/story/page-not-found-a-brief-history-of-the-404-error/

[73] Kieso, D. E. (2002). *Intermediate Accounting.* Toronto, ON: John Wiley & Sons.

[74] Bullock, N., Wigglesworth, R., and Jopson, B. (April 4, 2017). Sluggish US IPO activity needs more than a new Jobs Act. *Financial Times.* https://www.ft.com/content/adcbb10a-0f55-11e7-b030-768954394623

[75] Calamur, K. (February 25, 2015). Supreme Court sides with fisherman in case of the missing fish. *National Public Radio.* https://www.npr.org/sections/thetwo-way/2015/02/25/389005176/supreme-court-sides-with-fisherman-in-case-of-the-missing-fish

[76] AICPA Financial Reporting Center. (September 2016). Financial reporting brief: Roadmap to understanding the new revenue recognition standards. https://www.aicpa.org/InterestAreas/FRC/AccountingFinancialReporting/RevenueRecognition/DownloadableDocuments/FRC_Brief_Revenue_Recognition.pdf

[77] Krause, R. (August 5, 2016). Why everyone from AT&T to Disney and Microsoft is bracing for revenue rule. *Investor's Business Daily.* https://www.investors.com/news/technology/fasb-606-revenue-accounting-hits-software-telecom/

[78] Ibid.

[79] Krause, R. (February 28, 2017). Workday ends billings guidance in accounting shift, stock falls. *Investor's Business Daily.* https://www.investors.com/news/technology/workday-ends-billings-guidance-in-accounting-shift-stock-falls/

[80] Seeking Alpha. (June 6, 2017). Workday: The stock price appears to be working harder than the company. https://seekingalpha.com/article/4079330-workday-stock-price-appears-working-harder-company

[81] June 19, 1865.

Chapter 2

Present Absence

> Forgetting belongs to all action, just as not only
> light but also darkness belongs in the life of all
> organic things.[1]

Friedrich Nietzsche

It is funny how an account works. I remember performing a review of internal controls at an external service organization with the intent of putting together what was then a Standard on Auditing Standards (SAS) 70 report on internal controls. As a junior associate, I spoke with almost everyone, tracked down every lead, and left no stone unturned. When it came time to put together the report, the external service organization provided me with a template of what the report should look like. Turns out that the template would omit what was relevant and thus particular to the client even from a risk perspective, simply because the findings didn't conform to the template at hand. I remember ending the engagement and remarking to myself what a shame it was that all that information waiting for mining had not made its way into the final report. For those of you who have seen a SAS 70 report, or its present-day incarnation, a SOC (System and Organization Controls) report, you can probably attest to how one report remarkably resembles another. Sure, if the service organization is selling payroll instead of procurement software, the description changes, but when it comes down to the identification, and in the case of Type II reports, the validation of internal controls, these pretty much mirror the usual information technology (IT) general control suspects in access, change, and operations management. The report places little if any emphasis on automated controls within the vendor application, let alone unique features that can be effective in mitigating transaction risk on completeness, accuracy, or validity when configured in an appropriate manner.

Fast forward 10 years later, I was in a different role, this time in implementing a third party financial Software as a Service (SaaS) for internal employees. When reviewing requirements on processing a purchase requisition, we started, once again, with the usual suspects – vendor, amount, item or service for purchase, purchase approver, and possibly additional reviews from finance – but it soon became clear that other data attributes not deemed as important from an accounting perspective matter a great deal more to end users. Project codes come to mind: rather than having every purchase requisition tied to a specific vendor, management would like to be able to approve spending for an entire project, say a marketing outreach program with multiple associated vendors from assisting with publicity campaigns to tradeshow setup. Project artifacts beyond accounting also come into focus:

1. The vendor management team would review the vendor response to a request for information (RFI) or request for proposal (RFP), for example.
2. Security would review the security documentation, such as the vendor's information security policies, system, and network architecture, as well as any associated and penetration tests.
3. The legal team would review terms and other conditions stipulated in a contract or a statement of work.

All of this would take place before the purchase approver and the finance or accounting team would review the financials – initial one-time and recurring costs as well as payment terms.

Free form text fields like description or memo are especially useful in communicating to the approver in a concise manner just what the purchase requisition is about. Other implementation specifics such as ability of the vendor to engage or commit to implementation resources help clarify what is to come as well as accelerate the review and approval of the requisition itself if only to establish adequate runway or lead-time for deployment and go-live. With these considerations and more notwithstanding, when we circle back to the output of the deployed procurement SaaS, we ended up with what we could have easily mistaken for a sale rather than purchase order (PO) with vendor name interchangeable for customer name and purchase item for sale item. When it came down to documenting details surrounding the purchase, this process prioritized only fields perceived to have direct accounting impact in the Day 1 go-live. Other more operational attributes, such as project codes or links to other project artifacts, fell by the wayside. The process prioritized even more apparent financial-related data, such as department budget information that an approver would review against when assessing the proposed spend, as a Day 2 enhancement owing to the additional work needed in integrating with a different financial budgeting application. The vendor we worked with used our requirements to gain farther inroads to augmenting its purchase requisitioning capability as well as extending its customer base. As is the nature of a fast-paced project, as soon as we deployed the procurement software, we moved on to the next challenge at hand, never truly mining the opportunities that would have made the software more impactful for users actively engaged in sourcing purchases.

Fast forward 5 years later, when researching online to put together a syllabus for a graduate level accounting information systems class, I came upon a university advocating accounting as a universal language for business. In and of itself, it is not a particularly noteworthy proposition. Yet, accounting, pertinent as it may be to the world of financial reporting, has in more rubber-meets-the-road circles led to painfully learned woes of how rigid account segments and surrounding controls can be in the operational context of the day-to-day. Despite being a purported universal language, it is known more for what it keeps out than what it keeps in and, thus for many, leaves much to be desired in terms of what it truly accounts for.

To help peel back the layers that make up an account – because contrary to what Sherlock Holmes would have said, it is not elementary my dear Watson – let's turn to medical records. Unlike financial or personal records, the impact of errors in medical records could well mean a matter of between life and death or as a controller once remarked to me with a wink in her eye: "We're trying to close the books here; [sic] not in the business of saving lives." As recently as June 2017, despite billions spent in the last 2 decades, not to mention gargantuan amounts of time and resource to get to an almost 100% use or planned use of an electronic medical record system, more than half of 15,000 physicians admit to spending less time with their patients as a result of more time spent on medical records. The *San Francisco Chronicle* states rather emphatically, "We've replaced the medical chart with a patchwork of systems."[2]

To understand the challenges behind medical records, an account, or any account for that matter, it may help to dial the clock back a little farther to 1967 when Harold Garfinkel and his team began by asking what criteria, if any, were used to admit patients for treatment at the Outpatient Psychiatric Clinic at UCLA Medical Center.[3] In combing through medical records filed in clinic folders (themselves products of self-reporting procedures), it soon became apparent just what little information was available for the researchers to get at for answers.[4] For example, when soliciting the motivation or rationale for undergoing therapy, no information was available 32% of the time. Likewise, to get at psychological mindedness, no information was available 40.2% of the time.[5] In their place, researchers found an overwhelming abundance of data – 90% and upwards – on intake information such as name of therapist assigned and name of first therapist, on patient demographics such as sex and age, on first contact information such as clinic individuals involved, as well as on intake and on test documentation such as interview disposition and outcome of psychological tests.[6]

It dawned on the researchers that the extent and degree of information amassed led to the creation of a contractual rather than an actuarial record. Instead of explaining the how and why that contribute to treatment admission, the question that lies at the very heart of the research inquiries, the data points amassed defense artifacts to facilitate any future investigations of what the practitioner had done to whom in the event of a legal inquiry.[7] In other words, from a contractual perspective, these data make pretty good medical records in terms of accuracy and completeness. Even if from a research perspective, little content was available to explain the how or why of what took place – hence, the apt title of Garfinkel's work, "good" organizational reasons for "bad" clinical records.

Seen from this perspective, the journey that I underwent as a junior associate in documenting a service provider's SAS 70 report makes sense, or at least organizational sense. It isn't so much the specifics of the software delivered or the personnel involved. It is the evidencing of a best practice set of management controls around access, change, and operations that emphasizes, for new client prospects, the service provider's (auditable) credibility and reinforces, for current clients, their ascribed obligations and responsibilities. So while the service provider continues to be accountable for code maintenance and change management, clients need to be accountable for access management, reviews, and approvals as well as data quality around completeness, validity, and accuracy.

Even in the domain access management, we don't split hairs by differentiating between vendor developer and superuser access versus client personnel and end user access. In the event access is compromised, the service provider would ask questions that point back to client practices or lack thereof. Is an access management process in place to review and approve changes in access? Are users granted access based on a need-to-know or least privileged basis commensurate with their role and responsibilities? How clients choose to grant access is in fact what the software provider has no control over. The SAS 70 or SOC report thus serves as a contractual record that spells out mutual rights and obligations in the event something goes awry, such as when there is a breach in access.

As I write this, the development of a new version of the SSAE (Statement on Standards for Attestation Engagements), specifically SSAE 18 – the SSAE had replaced SAS 70 earlier – is underway to replace SSAE 16. As a reflection of the times, the intent of SSAE 18 is to address controls of controls, those outsourced by service organizations themselves to other providers so that a SaaS provider, for example, may yet rely on an Infrastructure as a Service (IaaS) provider or third-party data center. SSAE 18 requires identification of all subservice organizations to the primary cloud provider, in particular, "subservice organizational controls" it "relies on to provide the primary services to its customers."[8]

A key differentiating factor between SSAE 18 and SSAE 16 is the recognition that the monitoring of these subservice organizations needs to be ongoing and not merely a one-time exercise performed such as during initial vendor selection. Even here, the procurement SaaS we reviewed earlier is lacking in its ability to encompass or embrace multiple accounts from vendor management, security, and legal teams.

Which of the following better describes the purpose of having a record?

1. *Authentic testimony of the actions, processes, and procedures which brought them into being ... means of carrying out activities and not as ends in themselves ... capable of revealing the truth about these activities.*[9]	2. *Archives are created and received in the conduct of personal or organizational activity, and ... carry, in consequence, a particular weight as primary evidence of suppositions made, or conclusions drawn, about that activity.*[10]

Heather McNeil's article on archival theory and practice contains both descriptions. The description on the left, from a textbook is in turn quoted by McNeil from a list of archival terminology from the School of Library, Archival, and Information Studies at the University of British Columbia. Yet, as we have seen, reality mirrors more the description on the right, with less than complete clinical records reflecting more "suppositions" or "conclusions"[11] that support a contractual reading than any inherent "truth about these activities."[12] Garfinkel goes on to suggest that what is accounted for "much less than revealing an order of interaction, presuppose an understanding of that order for a correct reading" – meaning it doesn't so much reveal the actual as it does the expected nature of the relations "in accord with expectations of sanctionable performances."[13]

Nowhere is this more evident than in the fieldwork conducted by Pentland and Van Maanen in audit and police documentation.[14] Audit working papers, despite the working descriptive, are anything but a work in progress. As pointed out by Pentland, they function more like cemented artifacts that organizations can summon whenever there is a challenge to the audit work or when the threat of litigation looms at hand.[15] In the case of Enron, Arthur Anderson's poor handling, or, perhaps more pointedly, blatant destruction of audit evidence led to its eventual dissolution. It also led to the Sarbanes–Oxley Act of 2002 (SOX) provision that the court charged Miss Katie's boat captain, discussed in Chapter 1, in violation of. "Produced to document a performance of a given organizational task," audit working papers, for example, favor the use of "judgmental" over "statistical" selection to emphasize the sampling performed in lieu of validation of an entire population. Care is also taken to refer to "fairly" over "correctly" stated financials.[16]

Having served two stints at two different big four audit firms, I can attest to Pentlands findings. Rather than proclaim a clean bill of health, audit findings are quick to asset that they noted no exceptions in sampled selections. Audit working papers themselves go through internal validation. What do you mean when you write that records were inspected? How many samples were pulled from a population of how many? What does it mean to say that review was evidenced? By whom and what is the reviewer's organizational title? Often, in response to internal reviewer questions and coaching notes, I have had to return to the scene of the crime if only to augment necessary details to firm up a bulletproof or airtight case on file. In the wake of Enron, the oversight of auditors and audit of audit work by the Public Company Accounting Oversight Board (PCAOB) provides increased scrutiny on the quality of audits performed.

At first glance, police documentation appears vastly different from audit documentation. Yet, Van Mannen's examination reveals underlying similarities. Like my personal account of having to revisit working papers from a prior client engagement or strain a service organization's internal control procedures through the sieve of generic reporting templates, police officers undertake significant retrospective work to increase the likelihood for the intervention to be judged valid and legitimate so as not to pose a risk to the reputation and standing of the governing organization.[17] Thus, in place of "stand up drunk," a "public intoxication" charge is filed.[18] After all, much like the charges pressed against Miss Katie's captain, court proceedings take place well after the actual incident. All the more important perhaps that resulting police intervention is deemed necessary on account of a "suspicious behavior" or "furtive glance" as opposed to an "unexpected appearance of a black face in a white neighborhood."[19] Like Garfinkel before them, Pentland and Van Mannen, when reviewing the documented account, arrive at a contractual over actuarial reading, such that "what is recorded is never simply 'what happened.'"[20] In fact, "checkers and administrators ... whose job is to discover flaws in the files" toil behind the scenes so that "what is constructed from the procedures is a version of the incident such that the reputation and stature of the organization ... are not harmed."[21]

Let's return to Garfinkel's attempts at replicating Galileo's incline plane demonstration of falling bodies where he focused on what could go wrong, natural rather than classic accountability.[22] The latter begins with a predetermined conclusion ahead of time and comprises a series of steps that work backwards retrospectively. The destination stays the same because it actively constructs its own phenomenon.[23] The former runs the risk of "losing the phenomenon" as stakeholders figure out what needs to be done to reach a conclusion from a prospective perspective.[24] Like a police officer prospectively completing initial paperwork and then having to revisit it retrospectively to prevent it from being viewed in a negative light, a theorized account in this respect doesn't run the risk of "losing the phenomenon" in the same manner a natural account would. What does all this have to do with configuring SaaS and internal controls? Well, if our account of what happened isn't so much a naturalized blow-by-blow rendition of what can go wrong but rather an idealized affair, more in accordance with what is sanctioned or deemed appropriate, then the SaaS parameters configured don't so much automate the process to reduce manual work as it mitigates the risk of noncompliance, focused, as it were, on the demonstration of control design and operating effectiveness to internal and external auditors alike.

Take a simple access control of precluding personnel from deleting journal entries. From an audit perspective, this is a good control to have. What better way to bring about a complete lockdown to preclude the account balance from changing at the eleventh hour prior to locking or closing the period? Yet, upon closer inspection, we realize that errors are part and parcel of everyday occurrences for an accountant, such as for these types of journal entries:

1. Manually created
2. Associated with reversals to be automatically generated the following month (think reversal of expense accruals)
3. Bulk generated via manual import
4. Automatically scheduled as part revenue recognition that redistributes deferred revenue to revenue over a rateable period
5. Automatically scheduled as part of expense amortization that redistributes prepaid expenses from a clearing all-purpose account to respective individual accounts specific to an expense such as software

With carte blanche revoke of access to delete all journal entries – whether pending approval or already approved – we presume that either someone made mistakes or someone or some group of individuals with access to delete entries are meticulously going back retrospectively to assist others in deleting entries incorrectly created and still in pending approval status or wrongful approval status. Had this been a more naturalized account, the organization would have initiated a dialogue to explore the possibilities of configuring the SaaS to be better able at anticipating and handling the range of real-life scenarios. As it is, is serves up a monologue rather than a dialogue. In recalling Chapter 1, in place of a conversation among different and distinct parts, such as between accounting and operations, here even within the auspices of accounting, the process doesn't entertain other possibilities. In place of cacophony, we have deafening silence. Rather than explore likely checkpoints from a prospective perspective as we are going through the process, the process places an emphasis on dotting the t's and i's after the fact.

When revisiting this with management, their first response is why even allow anyone to delete journals to begin with? And yet, why not? If this relates to journals that are pending approval and thus don't yet have general ledger impact, why not allow users to delete them? For one thing, this process reduces the list of entries pending approval and precludes anyone from accidentally approving an inadvertent submission. It also fosters a SaaS that is far more forgiving in letting users unwind their actions. An emphasis only on transactions with financial impact doesn't quite mitigate the risk of dealing with journals erroneously submitted for approval and fails to acknowledge how these ultimately impact the entries that an organization approves to register an accounting or financial impact.

The 3-way match control between PO, receipt, and vendor invoice is a classic internal control that masks more naturalized accounts. When receiving an invoice without an apparent upstream authorization for spending evidenced in an approved purchase requisition or PO, there is nothing to stop us from retrospectively creating the purchase requisition or order well after we receive the invoice but before we actually enter it in the SaaS. So then, when we look into the system audit trails, we can still evidence the creation of a requisition or PO before the entry of a receipt and invoice to arrive at the 3-way coup de grâce. From an audit perspective, when it comes to the judgmental sampling of invoices to review against receipts and POs, we would have noted no exceptions. Yet, we are hardly convinced that this process fulfils the spirit of the control, especially since the intent of purchase requisition approvals is to have the anticipated spend reviewed against the department budget *before* rather than *after* the organization makes and receives the purchases, leaving the enterprise in the unfortunate position of being liable to pay and in accordance with agreed vendor terms even if caught off guard.

Unlike Garfinkel's medical record that at best serve as *good enough* collateral in investigations of any inappropriate behavior, the purchase artifacts here while serving as *good enough* audit artifacts, are not quite *good enough* legal records to fall back on when disputing the purchase, especially if it is a significant amount. So much for mitigating risk of uncontrolled organizational spending. When we start to look beyond the classic account of the 3-way match and look for traces of a natural rendering of the actual sequence of affairs:

1. The absence of upfront notification of future spending ahead of time
2. A possible incorrect routing of vendor invoices so that they continue to be sent to the wrong emails and get stuck in the queue even before making their way into the accounting SaaS for timely recording
3. The absence of any identifying PO number on the invoice, so that even if routed correctly and entered in the SaaS in a timely manner, either we can't apply it to an existing PO or may well apply it to the wrong PO

It is as if we put on a fresh pair of eyes. Underneath what appears to be mundane control work recycled year after year lies endless possibilities to re-imagine if only to revise and re-engage. Just because a vendor's payment terms have been correctly set up doesn't mean that we have paid their invoices on a timely basis if we continue to route them to the wrong internal recipient or that we have accounted for them correctly if there simply isn't enough information on the invoices to begin with.

In effect, how we account for a specific look and feel of a transaction depends a great deal on how its attributes align with our worldview of what it should look like. The account we arrive at is as much a function of how we conceptualize it in our mind's eye as it is about characterizing the objective characteristics that lend it color and depth. If, for example, we only care about capturing transactions that have an accounting impact in a SaaS, effectively donning the accountant's perspective, we may pay more attention to the accounts assigned to the items set up for purchase in the procurement SaaS. Here, a Russian doll phenomenon of sorts is at work when we are logging purchase requisitions in a SaaS for obtaining approval to purchase a subscription to yet a different SaaS.

Depending on the timing of the purchase and nature of use, we can account it as a prepaid subscription or else expense it immediately. What items an end user selects in a purchase requisition would thus matter from an accounting perspective even if it makes little difference to the end user creating the requisition and the assigned purchase approver, so long as the spend is valid and within budget. In fact, a popular incident management SaaS tool such as JIRA, may be more user friendly than the procurement SaaS in routing the purchase requisition to the right parties for approval. The end user could attach vendor terms and conditions to route to the legal team for review. If the end user deems the data processed by the SaaS, whether at rest or in transit, as sensitive, the end user could route the same ticket to the security team. Here, the JIRA incident management SaaS has been repurposed to fold in legal and security perspectives that matter just as much as the accounting perspective in a software subscription.

In truth, we may use other applications to complete those reviews: use of a penetration testing tool in a security review and use of the Microsoft Word application or a Google doc to make redline edits to vendor terms and conditions. Yet, when we speak of internal controls when it comes to purchase requisition – and here again in thinking back to my Big Four audit experience, control checklists or practice aides come to mind – we almost always only think of the Enterprise Resource Planning (ERP) or procurement software at hand. In truth, organizations create the purchase requisition even as they spin off a separate JIRA ticket on parallel tracks, never the twain shall meet.

Let us take a closer look at the purchase requisition in the procurement SaaS. If, like Garfinkel's inquiry into the admission criteria for patients, we were to ask about the selection process for new software vendors, what are we likely to find? Garfinkel found no ready answers in a contractual (as opposed to actuarial) reading and thus documentation of clinical records, and here we too are hard pressed to uncover the internal validation processes that an organization undergoes just by examining the attributes of the purchase requisition. We may find the vendor payment terms describing the length of time expected to pay the vendor after software delivery. We may also find other pieces of information that would help us pay the vendor, such as its billing address for one. Additional documentation needed to begin setting up the new vendor is a W-9 to record the tax identification number to dovetail into year-end tax reporting. Notice all these threads bear the accounting insignia, as well as perhaps an audit stamp of approval. Vendor payment terms is an input to a review of accounts payable aging and has implications for how the organization manages cash. For a sidebar foray into an extreme manipulation of vendor payment terms to reflect greater cash at hand, check out the controversies surrounding Groupon's extension of the time taken to pay its vendors (payment terms) that resulted in an improved view of its operating cash flow while spiking its current liabilities.[25]

Back to accounting and audit, the purchase requisition also serves as a good artifact for evidencing the 2-way match with vendor invoice – what is ordered is in fact what has been billed. When evidencing for appropriate vendor payments, we can also check to see that what the organization has paid to the vendor is also what the parties agreed upon whether in the invoice or requisition. All this sounds great but what of our initial inquiry: what is the vendor selection process? To unpack this question, let's ask the following sub-questions:

1. Is there a request for information or proposal? What requirements did the organization communicate?
2. Which vendors has the organization contacted to submit a response to the RFI or RFP?
3. What are the benefits and costs associated with each competing product presented?
4. Are there customer reference calls to verify actual customer experiences?
5. Is there an eventual ranking of competing products? Which resources perform the selection?
6. Is a cross-functional committee of vested stakeholders involved?
7. If the organization has chosen a product, is an implementation timeline scoped out, and if so, what possible additional configurations or enhancements does the organization need to fulfill communicated requirements?

Whoa, all this sounds too operational, we might protest. Surely, we would not expect one third-party procurement SaaS to do all this and more. It would defeat the purpose of a best-in-breed solution. As already alluded to, other SaaS may come into play, not the least of which is JIRA for facilitating internal cross-functional reviews or use of a contract management SaaS such as DocuSign or EchoSign for executing the contract. Yet, it is precisely because the purchase requisition is silent on all these fronts – that it merely suffices as a contractual record for evidencing the organization's obligation to pay an external vendor as well as to properly account for its liability on the balance sheet – that the organization fails to use it as an actuarial reading of what truly happens even if there are procurement, security, and legal controls at work. In fact, by only showing the "good" aspects – even here good mostly pertains to accounting or audit components – the contractual purchase requisition arguably conceals as much as it purports to reveal.

Who is to say that the ultimate vendor or software product selected may not be the most appropriate either because a more formalized selection process was not in place or selected stakeholders who should have been part of the selection committee were conveniently if not conspicuously left out of the picture? In other words, what if the selected product fails to deliver on its committed promises? In going back to the purchase requisition in the procurement SaaS, we would be hard pressed to find out just what these requirements are, let alone perform any level of root cause analysis as to just what has gone awry. We can argue that we are expecting too much: the intent if a procurement SaaS, after all, is for a specific audience, just as the intent of an accompanying JIRA or DocuSign subscription is itself for other audiences.

But insofar as we continue to invest credence in the overall "spirit" of the control, rather than the letter, and organizations place emphasis on risk mitigation rather than on a check-the-box exercise, then vendor selection and the artifacts documented and retained can and do matter a great deal when it comes to internal controls.

First, in the case of a software implementation gone awry, we can peel back the assumptions or concessions made in an attempt not just to resolve what went wrong in the immediate term but also to put in place measures to prevent it from recurring in the future. This is in effect what the Information Technology Infrastructure Library (ITIL) seeks to impress upon the IT staff – the infinitesimal difference between incident and problem management. In the absence of any necessary artifacts to facilitate any kind of retrospective worth its salt, the organization is stuck in a perpetual firefighting loop solving incidents rather than problems that underpin incidents. Here, refer to studies by the Carnegie Mellon University's Software Engineering Institute (SEI) in reviewing an organization's capability maturity model (CMM). Firefighting itself has spillover impact on unplanned work which in turn affects the timely completion of planned work (a new SaaS deployment comes to mind).

The Institute of Internal Auditors (IIA) pointed this out in a Global Technology Audit Guide (GTAG) put forth in 2005.[26] In fact, one of the co-authors of the GTAG, Gene Kim, is a co-founder of the Information Technology Process Institute (ITPI). When benchmarking IT organizations from 2003 through 2006, ITPI came to the conclusion that a key subset of foundational IT controls could explain for much of the difference between high and low performing IT organizations.[27] Examples of key IT controls include reviewing for unauthorized changes, specifying clear outcomes, managing configurations, and monitoring the rate at which the organization deployed changes to production without failures or need for rollback.[28] What is revolutionary is the correlation of organizational performance with internal controls – more than contractual artifacts to evidence compliance, and ultimately meaningful in an everyday IT operational context – a foreign concept indeed!

Second, even if we were to put aside the possibility of a software deployment gone wrong, when circling back to our initial inquiry – what is the admission criteria for vendors, as opposed to patients – we are not left with any leads to follow up on for what would otherwise appear as a complete and valid purchase requisition record with all the t's and i's checked ends up revealing all too little when it comes to the actual work that went on behind the scenes to secure the vendor product. What stands before us is a semblance of big data – details on top vendor spend, types of spend, month over month variance, and so on – yet behind these jazzy statistics, how much organizational knowledge or know-how we can mine in successfully acquiring and leveraging internal use of a third-party SaaS product?

What our earlier reference to Groupon also illustrates is that even if the product met client expectations, conceivably even with a complete, valid, and accurate purchase requisition in the procurement SaaS validated and cross validated against a downstream invoice and payment, an enterprise can still run the risk of inappropriately stretching the time it takes to pay vendors in a bid to appear favorable from an operating cash flow stance. The checked t's and i's function more like smoke and mirrors, a red herring that alludes that the enterprise has conducted appropriate reviews. Instead of fussing over who has access to set up vendors, create requisitions, invoices, and payments and whether or not the enterprise has enforced segregation of duties, we can argue that we should devote time and resource to surfacing what the process has eliminated from plain sight – vendors, information about vendors, selection process, information about the selection process, reviewers and so on – relegated to the background even as our attention remains transfixed at the circus gymnastics of requisition, invoice, and payment approvals on display. If it is not a transactional type variety, then it is one of control frameworks: many an internal control or audit conference I have attended has at least one session looking at consolidating internal control frameworks used whether from ITIL or COBIT which stands for Control Objectives for Information and Related Technologies created by the Information Systems Audit and Control Association (ISACA).

What comes to mind is a conversation I had with an internal auditor on whether we would need in-house backup jobs for a SaaS in use to address a control identified in one of the governing frameworks. Even though the answer here was no, we were relying on the SaaS provider, and this, in fact, is the reason why we went for a cloud solution to begin with. In fact, we are still addressing it as part of an internal control simply because it belongs to a framework we are using which speaks to the widening divide between official and natural accounts. It is almost as if we were looking far too hard, up close and personal, at the creases and folds to notice the forest for the trees.

If a foundational pervasive control is to have a core set of vendor management practices for vendors both large and small, we would hardly expect the same level of rigor in reviews for a small vendor whose product, for example, is simply to track project statuses with little personally identifiable or company proprietary information. In many ways, such pervasive practices occur irrespective of whether software is present, on-premise or in the cloud. But other possibilities can begin to enter the picture other than an accountant's mere account of what goes on. With the ease of configurability that is all too likely associated with the cloud, we need to recognize the need for all too often, less authorized though no less compelling procurement, legal, and security perspectives in authorizing a purchase requisition, when configuring the procurement SaaS at hand.

This brings us to the third reason for peeling back an official account to reveal its naturalized interior. Even if the software deployment didn't go wrong and the enterprise selected the correct vendor, we can, in effect, tap into the out-of-the-box configurational SaaS capability to support or bolster a financial transaction as it unfolds. A simple checkbox whether marked or unmarked can indicate whether a review – legal or security, where applicable – has taken place prior to purchase requisition approval. This indication comes with the understanding that money is but one of the multiple variables that come into play when making a sourcing or strategic partnership decision. Other attributes that may trigger necessary intervention insofar as a SaaS purchase is concerned may comprise of an impact analysis on other upstream or downstream applications that process the same transaction whether from an Order-to-Cash or a Procure-to-Pay perspective. To this end, the placement of a dropdown field for the user to select other applications impacted from the SaaS purchase may be useful.

We may also need to consider other work not so much in the first phase as is in the later ensuing phases to include having to sync transactions across SaaS and necessary integration. How enterprises define and set up units of analysis, in turn, in one SaaS may differ from another, so that if the enterprise deployed the new SaaS, we would likely need a set of fields to bridge it with those in existing applications. We would need to bring over the unique customer identifier auto-generated by the SaaS, because SaaS ties the identifier to transactions and even transaction lines. With the Accounting Standards Codification (ASC) 606, a change to any given line in the sales order changes the entire mix or composition in terms of revenue allocation, so that if transactions from the new SaaS are imported albeit manually into another at least in the first phase, then insofar as changes to sales orders occur, we not only need a unique order but also order line identification numbers if only to be able to relate changes made back to the precise line in the originating order.

Thus, when we start to layer in other less than "official" although no less compelling accounts, and herein official means audit, the way we start to view a purchase requisition starts to change as well. More than a zero-sum equation evidencing the ubiquitous debit and credit entries behind every accounting entry, we view the purchase requisition more holistically so that an otherwise straightforward purchase when fully fleshed out in the clear light of day may uncover unplanned consequences. If the new SaaS that the enterprise plans to purchase requires specific location fields set up in a downstream accounting SaaS, and these in turn impact the way the enterprise calculates sales tax, then we need to factor in necessary work not only for prepping the new SaaS for testing and go-live but also for updating the configuration of surrounding SaaS or on-premise software in context.

Although accounting may not be the universal language that it claims to be at least among the enterprise business community, our examination of accounting particularities, on the one hand, reveals a susceptibility to not seeing the full picture, and, on the other hand, raises questions on how one-sided or biased we may have been even while claiming that we were focused on being fair and unbiased. ASC 606, after all, is a means for the U.S. Financial Accounting Standards Board (FASB) to converge with International Financial Reporting Standards (IFRS) promulgated by the International Accounting Standards Board (IASB), thus alluding to differences that nonetheless exist behind the seemingly uniform banner of universality. In the context of SaaS, the specifics looked at only arguably fall within the scope of an accounting lens or any review of transactions with financial or general ledger impact. Although such a lens is especially useful in quickly identifying impact and only auditing transactions and supporting systems with financial impact to mitigate direct risks to reported financials, it only favors the accounting perspective over other and quite frankly more immediate and rubber-meets-the-road challenges such as actual SaaS deployment and impact to any transactions that may be in flight.

We also have examined journals and requisitions in flight for approval. Consider this time an upgrade to a more advanced platform of an expense management SaaS. Questions that can arise are: what would happen to expenses reports that the enterprise has approved and that are waiting for payment processing? What about those pending approval? Or how about those in pending review or draft status? To be sure, these are change management controls that an enterprise would not likely account for in a purchase requisition, but whether the enterprise considers these questions upfront during product assessment may mean a difference as to whether the eventual upgrade is seamless or borders on catastrophic dimensions.

Whether the enterprise receives satisfactory answers to these questions or at least receives a fair level of attention to them also makes a dent on whether they purchase the upgraded SaaS, and when. A deployment during a quarter end close would seem foolhardy with no buffer to handle possible exceptions or kinks that may arise. As an example, during the upgrade, the enterprise may need to recreate expense reports that are in flight for approval as the new "advanced" platform no longer supports approval routing for these "older" unapproved expense reports. If we want to be particular, we can argue that we are not being specific enough, insofar as taking in a multiplicity of accounts. By not being specific enough, we configure the SaaS to be fragile even as it is compliant with a circumscribed set of parameters deemed in scope for audit.

There is a prospective view and there is a retrospective view. The latter shapes the former, so that when we give an account, we are in fact sharing the sequence of steps to take. With an audit account, we account for only the steps that we deem within an audit or accounting purview, no more, no less. We are ill-prepared to react when something does go wrong or veers away from the documented script. A control on a 2- or 3-way match is simply that. Although there is mention of a review of exceptions that arise, it does not quite enumerate the exceptions that are likely to occur or steps to take to resolve them. In recording episodes of office conversations taking place in an accounting office processing cash disbursements in a large corporation, Lucy Suchman described a particular scenario when an accounts payable (A/P) clerk received an overdue invoice in the mail.[29] In accordance with the normative or prescribed sequencing of processing vendor payments, the clerk began by looking for evidence of a related upstream PO authorizing spend for the item, as well as for an item receipt evidencing that enterprise had indeed received the items invoice.[30] Yet, after searching through the files, the clerk, and by then having roped in the assistance of her accounting supervisor, realizes that there was no source PO.[31] A receiving document was found, but only a subset of the received items reflected payments for invoices already on file.[32] A subsequent investigation of the sequencing of control numbers on checks issued for payment to the vendor revealed a missing invoice page for items which the enterprise received and paid for, as well as the need to nevertheless pay for a smaller subset of items that the enterprise received but had not paid for.[33] All this contributed to the legitimacy of the received overdue invoice, despite the absence of clear and unambiguous audit trails showing prior spending authorization. For Suchman, the resolution of the overdue invoices was the outcome of "some prescribed sequence of steps" even if the organization constituted this sequence of PO–receipt–invoice events *after* the fact when the accounting staff contacted the vendor to send over the missing invoice page with items for which the enterprise made payment.[34]

What implications does this have for software design? Office technology designed on the assumption that real work follows the classic or idealized PO–receipt–invoice flow, while succeeding in standardizing the capture and thus reporting of operating expenses, nonetheless relegates much of the ad-hoc back-and-forth exchange witnessed in our example to that which remains outside of the system. It continues unabated behind the scenes as the work it would take to prepare the data in a format deemed acceptable for entry. In a sense, we have not gone very far from the

1. Admission criteria for patients to
2. Admission criteria for vendors to
3. Admission criteria for data

Suchman advocated for an alternative option where the system would acknowledge and incorporate the uncertainties surrounding the real work performed rather than act as a black box that only accepts as input a set of consistent parameters, the very output of real work "done in advance of its entry."[35]

Consider the following: because the SaaS at hand assumes an idealized sequence of affairs, we don't have an ability to input invoices for which no POs or receipts exist. From an internal control perspective, this process is a classic 3-way match, an automated or application control. Yet, the received invoice upon further investigation does relate to a received good that, although the enterprise didn't create a PO, the enterprise still needs to pay. To comply with the 3-way match, the enterprise retroactively creates a PO and a goods receipt for the invoice for capture and payment processing. The idealized PO–receipt–invoice flow thus constitutes a product of, rather than a driver to, getting the vendor paid. Suchman's point is that the daily consistency of accounting records predicates a system's design. Its design is not so much conceived with an activity in mind as it is on the intended outcome of the activity. Contrast this with what the auditors espouse, that is the very presence and operation of a 3-way match that achieves the completeness of accounting record, not the other way around. The 3-way match checks for record validity, so when an accounting clerk looks for an associated PO and item receipt, the clerk verifies if the overdue invoice received from the vendor is indeed legitimate to pay. That an official account of this same control would preclude entry of an invoice into the SaaS because there is no record of an order or an item received to begin with sounds logical enough in theory, but it can also lead to an unintended consequence of slowing down the entry of received invoices insofar as they trigger a search for the all too elusive PO or goods receipt. It also assumes that other upstream Procure-to-Pay controls are in place such as having the PO routed for approval *before* the enterprise establishes a contractual obligation with the vendor and a process to evidence the item received. In hindsight, had the organization had these controls in place, we could argue that the organization would not have received an overdue invoice in the first place, especially since proactive efforts underway would have identified missing invoices when comparing the items received with existing POs.

Strictly speaking, the receipt date, rather than the invoice date, drives the recording of the associated expense. This is one key difference between accrual and cost-based accounting. The former, practiced by public companies, recognizes an expense the moment they receive a service even if no cash has left the organization's bank account. The latter, practiced by most individuals in their day-to-day accounting, recognizes an expense only when they pay it. Precisely because the SaaS doesn't accept invoices without upstream support – recall that the consuming organization is liable to pay even if approval for the spending is not obtained beforehand – or other artifacts that allude to the receipt of services in the absence of received invoices (an email acknowledgement comes to mind), organizations need to expend more time and resources in manually identifying and recording accruals. What if the SaaS can be configurable to accept the entry of invoices without related POs or service acknowledgments in the form of email? In effect, there would be a holding area, a work in progress of sorts for artifacts hovering between the bounds of legitimacy and illegitimacy. As part of month end close procedures, the accounting staff could clear this work-in-progress queue, rather than start from scratch either retaining invoices without associated POs elsewhere on desks or combing through email mailboxes to evidence service receipts.

A system-imbued PO–receipt–invoice sequence thus deflects rather than incorporates the uncertainty that abounds in everyday work. The controls over completeness, accuracy, and validity – whether the description, quantity, and amount of the invoice match the item received and order placed – when "hardcoded" into the design of the SaaS in the processing of transactions mid-stream, hinders rather than aids in the complete and timely capture of expenses. From an accounting perspective, it is easy to see why these "controls" continue to be promulgated. Completeness, accuracy, and validity directly map to financial statement assertions over whether transactions recorded have taken place – those that the organization should have recorded, they have recorded and at the appropriate amounts. But having a work-in-progress area to record ghost or specter invoices doesn't dilute these assertions. If nothing else, it shores up the ability of the software to account for contingencies that arise in the daily accounting rather than assume an idealized state.

We can even go so far as to describe an almost iterative quality to the recording of invoices. Like the iterative development phases of software – as it cycles through requirement gathering, coding, testing, and release – the search for missing POs or item receipts iteratively surfaces more detail each time to augment the accounting record. Ironically, the missing upstream support artifacts are symptoms of deeper flaws, such as the absence of a companywide procurement policy above a specific threshold or clear guidance on how and where the company maintains receipt records. Like the progressive inclusion of late changes to requirements during software development to clarify and determine just what the client needs even as it takes on a new nuance each time, the progressive augmentation or revision to an already recorded record provides continual assurance of its relevancy and accuracy. Because the organization embraces change or mutability, the resulting system of internal controls is more mobile, or universally applicable, across local contingent settings in different contexts. This iterative process of revisiting, revising, and tightening aligns the design of internal controls with what happens as opposed to what should happen.

In contrast, because the SaaS at hand presumes that the date of receipt as well as that of the PO must precede that of invoice receipt, it follows that it can't allow association of an earlier dated invoice with these later dated records. Rather than entertain the uncertainty to allow for the transparency handling of shortcomings associated with missing POs and goods receipts, it conceals the complexity involved in securing the consistency of accounting records by requiring that organizations enter POs and item receipts before invoices, reaffirming Suchman's point that the real work is "done in advance of its entry."[36] In the process, the SaaS whittles away the messiness down a clean interface and admits data if and only if it agrees to defined parameters, under the guise of internal controls, to support easily accountable, comparable, and thus transferable views. Organizations can't use work-in-progress invoices without an explicit reference back to POs or good receipts at the outset, let alone reuse them – a "code block" where the organization can't revisit, revise, or else unwind relationships among entities once inscribed in a stone tablet of sorts.

Perhaps more insidious but no less important is the way that the process has imposed certainty on the actual currency of affairs, so that in all audited transactions, a PO does precede an item receipt as it would an invoice even when uncertainty is the rule rather than the exception. In this manner, the articulation work performed to put together the idealized or classic sequence of events is itself pivotal in shaping the documented account of what went on. Today, it is amazing just how much reliance an organization still places on having a requisite PO number to enter and record a vendor invoice into a SaaS – Suchman's study was performed more than 25 years ago in 1992 – giving credence to the adage, the more things change, the more they stay the same. From a customer billing perspective, this very same PO number would help ease and thus accelerate customer payment. From this perspective, we can argue that the better an enterprise is at processing vendor purchases, the better it is able to flip the script in including the customer's internal PO number on the invoices it remits.

Even if the organization can trace the received invoice back to an originating PO and receipt and can directly enter it in the SaaS, there is still the possibility of corrective actions taken to fix erroneous entries. In the case of miscategorized expenses on a vendor invoice inherited from incorrectly selected items on the purchase requisition, such as software coded to an expense account rather than to a fixed asset, an accountant may make the necessary corrections downstream on the invoice rather than on the upstream PO. This brings up an interesting question: if the PO has additional associated invoices expected in the future, this manual correction to the purchase item type would have to happen each time the organization receives a new invoice. Because it is manual, there is a possibility that the company may omit this correction for some invoices. But because the PO results from an already approved purchase requisition, what options does the SaaS offer in terms of forgiveness? In other words, can users swap out the item selected for the right one to facilitate a recording of the desired accounting impact without necessarily retriggering the entire chain of approvals all over again? Even then, if we were to perform a deep dive of root cause, we can argue that simply having an accountant correct the PO doesn't quite go far enough in engaging user awareness of which item categories to code purchases to when creating new requisitions on an everyday basis to begin with. Despite the claim that accounting is a universal language for business, when creating a requisition, it is not uncommon for users to know what purchase item or service to select: that is, where do we code the purchase to? We can record software in many ways:

1. Code to a fixed asset account and depreciated accordingly
2. Code to a prepaid account on the balance sheet so that the company can amortize and recognize expenses as expenses on the income statement monthly
3. Expense the full amount outright on the income statement

When faced with roadblocks in revising the item selected in upstream transactions, an accountant may simply create a manual journal entry that reclasses the invoices to the right fixed asset account, so that the company amortizes expenses over the length of the life of the asset rather than all at once. This shortcut isn't without tradeoffs. Issues can arise later when we attempt to trace the depreciation expense recorded on the income statement all the way upstream to the originating vendor invoice and purchase requisition. Because of the intervening journal recorded to reclass the accounting impact, we can't quite jump from the depreciation expense to the originating vendor invoice to verify if the company has already paid the invoice. When all is said and done, the intervening journal, that is itself attributed to the limitations posed by the SaaS, broke the link between an upstream vendor invoice and a downstream depreciation journal. Viewed prospectively, the process breaks the purchase requisition–PO–receipt–invoice–journal sequence. Rather than simply hide prospective history, the process erases it altogether.

In July 1976, an 18-year-old auto mechanic died when the multipiece truck wheel he mounted and inflated using a safety cage exploded.[37] More than 3 years later, the Institute of Highway Safety issued a press release detailing actions taken to remedy the danger posed by the multipiece wheel in the workplace because of its explosive potential.[38] In M.D. Baccus' research, there is much that goes into inflating a multipiece rim or wheel.[39] Depending on type of tire – typically inflated to a 90–120 psi range – blow-outs can happen because of a combination of a sudden loss of pressure a with continued load exertion on the tire and wheel assembly.[40] The Occupational Safety and Health Administration (OSHA) eventual recommendation was for the mechanic to use a safety cage at all times and at no time use a hammer to hit the tire or rim during the inflation process.[41] Over the course of 2 days, Baccus observed the work performed at

1. Three truck tire facilities
2. Two manufacturer's service shops
3. One truck fleet garage

He identified two local practices not covered in OSHA documentation.[42] The mandatory safety cage assumes that wheel inflation would happen in an enclosed space when in reality a majority of the work was performed out in the field where one of three substitute tools used for containment, a U-shaped tool, had earned the street credence of "suicide' bar."[43] As Baccus pointed out, OSHA standards didn't mention these alternative tools nor were they surfaced in any of the comments submitted to the proposed guidance.[44] The second situated practice was rooted in a need to keep checking that the lock ring is securely seated leaving no possibility or room for any separation during initial airing.[45] A safety cage from this perspective could actually exacerbate matters by obstructing the ring from direct line of vision.[46] An "old hand" trick was to tap periodically at the ring assembly typically with a hammer or a tool with a head shaped like a hammer, the very thing that OSHA advised against.[47] Here, Baccus introduced the concept of embodied logic within logic – the idea that the very object at hand, in this case the seating of the lock ring, "invites" tapping if only to insure no separation when the mechanic inflates the tire.[48]

In taking a page from the lack of clarity on patient admission criteria from our earlier review of purchase requisitions, we more than alluded to a similar lack of clarity on vendor admission criteria. In continuing with this train of thought, how likely is it that we need to submit a purchase requisition ahead of time even without knowing which vendor or product the company will select? What use is a purchase requisition as an artifact to secure approval for spend ahead of time if the company can create it only after they cement the vendor and product information? Because with the procurement SaaS requires that the company associate a vendor with every requisition, it slows down the very process that was the intent of the design to facilitate.

Even here, note that for every requisition, there can only be a one-to-one relationship with a vendor so that even though an implementation or product launch is likely to involve multiple vendors. Recall our earlier e-commerce example from Chapter 1 enabled through a multi-SaaS combo of front-end online shopping carts, backend payment card processing gateway, and integration syncs with existing downstream accounting SaaS. A purchase approver would have to approve multiple requisitions each associated with a different vendor even if they all belong to the same project budget.

From an accounting perspective, having one and only one vendor recorded in a requisition can make sense since the process copies the same information over to a PO and onto a subsequent receipt and invoice. How would we perform a review of accounts payable aging if an invoice contains multiple vendor payment terms? The fact remains that we would receive an invoice from each vendor and would have to pay each one individually even if there were multiple ones involved in a project implementation.

Just as the lock ring invited tapping when inflating the multipiece wheel despite the OSHA recommendation, the purchase requisition – because of the way it is accounted for and in this case to one vendor each time but then again only upon finalization of the chosen vendor – invites us to create a requisition too little too late only after the company has chosen a vendor and ironed out the details, even if this is precisely the intent of the design to avoid – employees engaging a vendor without having the spending reviewed against budget, or security of the purchased product validated against internal requirements. Thus, instead of having the purchase requisition created and approved prior to engagement with the vendor, the reverse happens in reality. The company ends up creating the purchase requisition after it has already executed the contract and rendered the service or item putting the organization at a liability of having to pay the vendor, the very thing for which the company erects internal controls to prevent from happening. The very way the purchase requisition is set up and accounted for, an insistence on actual "hard" numbers, despite being a "soft" estimate of actual spend to begin with, "invites" users to only think about creating *after* rather than *before* the company procures a service or software.

Even if the company has already chosen a vendor for entry in a new purchase requisition, associated details like billing address, specific items for purchase, quantity and so on, can and often does change. This means that the contents of a purchase cart in use in a procurement SaaS used to manage spending are by no means static and the company can expect them to change as they embellish it with more detail over time. After all, we can argue that the point of having a vendor selection process is for the client and the provider to come to an agreement on pricing and quantity. As part of vendor negotiations, the provider may apply discounts and here too it may differ by item type. Some areas to consider:

1. For a recurring annual subscription, the company may place emphasis on the incremental cost per user license. Does it make sense, for example, to up the number of anticipated users in any given year, or add these as we go along, pro-rating the incremental cost to co-term with the annual subscription agreement?

2. Because it is SaaS, there is the matter of a possible peanut butter spread to account for the ongoing customer support as a percentage of the overall software subscribed.
3. Also, as part of the negotiation, the provider may add more products to the proposed bundle to entice a cost-conscious enterprise customer who may be reticent to engage – who likes changes after all? – or other competitive, not to mention more compelling options, lure them.

When all is said and done, the contents of the purchase requisition cart would have looked quite different. How then do we account for it upstream prospectively as opposed to retrospectively with the luxury of hindsight? It is commonplace for users when asked to comply with company procurement policy to question the accuracy of amounts recorded. Yet, is this not a chicken or egg thing? Which comes first?

1. Settled numbers recorded in a requisition or numbers still in flux and actively negotiated
2. A vendor already selected, set up, and ready for consumption in a purchase requisition or competing vendors jostling for a competitive edge in an RFP response

From this perspective, it is no wonder that users often mistake all too easily the difference between a purchase requisition and an invoice, attaching an invoice to a purchase requisition to route for approval, and then questioning why they had to intervene all over again to approve the invoice for vendor payment. Does it have to be this way? We could after all conceive of a blanket PO so long as actual spending is under the approved amount. Wouldn't that be swell? Also, couldn't individual vendor purchase requisitions be created and associated in some way to this approved blanket PO? These considerations in turn present a myriad of possibilities for configuring the procurement process, and ultimately the purchase requisition in the SaaS. Does the SaaS at hand let us create a custom record that bridges operational, strategic, and compliance demands, so that the company can review and approve organizational spending upfront using a system of records in a manner that lets us easily slice by project, vendor, and account dimensions?

But all too often, the accounting or audit paradigm, much like the OSHA-issued safety standards in response to workplace related accidents, is in full force. Just as there is a chasm between theorized and naturalized accounts – mechanics perform the inflation of multipiece truck wheels mostly in the field with no access to the safety cage deemed mandatory by OSHA – we can argue that most of the requisitions companies have to create and route for approval don't have the requisite data attributes cemented upstream. In place of the safety cage, other tools like the "suicide bar" are used.[49] In place of the purchase requisition as a transaction record for facilitating procurement, legal, and security reviews, other "tools" like JIRA enter the picture.

Embodied logics come in when the artifact in question draws us in, encouraging a specific course of action over others. At a local public library, for example, a user mistakenly uses a library card scanner for scanning checked out books, much to the chagrin of librarians who face the inconvenience of having to perform additional work when checking returned items. In place of the library card scanner, the user should have used the docking station; however, the small print of the recommended use instruction was illegible except to the most discerning eye. We can see the same pattern in purchase requisitions raised on behalf of someone else – in this case, an administrative assistant likely on behalf of another department. Like the small print associated with the library scanner, unless paying attention, the administrator would simply submit the purchase requisition without changing the department on the requisition to the department belonging to the requestor for whom she is acting on behalf of. It is the same for selecting a prepaid item instead of an immediately expensed one. Embodied logics don't quite figure into official accounts whether they comprise of safety standards, incident management, or recording of SaaS transactions. As Baccus is quick to point out, OSHA targets its response at managing accidents rather than preventing them from arising in the first place.[50] In incident and problem management, we can ask a similar question: are they mostly concerned with the management of incidents and problems rather than delving into any real specifics of how to resolve an incident or problem? Seen from this angle, the ubiquitous purchase requisition is really an artifact for managing purchases, rather than a means of how to make effective purchases. In returning to my stints as a Big Four auditor at client engagements, internal control design and test of operating effectiveness are more akin to the management of internal controls – the rinse and repeat walkthrough, sampled validation, remediation, remediation testing, and report – than the actual ways and means of mitigating risks to financial statements. Is it any wonder that Michael Power described auditing as a "formal loop" by which the system observes itself?[51]

Let us return to the universal nature of accounting as business language. In following the multi-threaded elements of the examples presented thus far, we can argue that what appears as rather specific to a unique set of circumstances – admission criteria for patients, vendors, or multipiece rims – nonetheless all share specific universalities. The interventional management of clinical records, procurement, policing, waste, multipiece wheels, and internal controls all presuppose, or impose, a lens that reveals more about the way regulating officials or in-house employees entrusted with such responsibilities think or theorize about the way things work and less about the way they truly work. When these accounts are in turn used to inform the way that we configure a SaaS to optimize existing manual processes, the outcome is self-serving, addressing the specific requirements identified in a governing management framework rather than underlying root causes.

Audit engagements emphasizing operating effectiveness attempt to automate internal controls using the documented official accounts as a trigger or script rather than begin by questioning their veracity. So, in the case of implementing a procurement management SaaS, a recommendation may center on configuring approval workflows for the purchase requisition to send out periodic reminders of requests pending review and to enable super users to switch approvers when the primary personnel are out of office. All this speeds up, or else streamlines the process of approving purchase requisitions even as it fails to address any underlying foundational cracks. Constraints on having precise details on vendors, purchase carts, amounts, or other attributes cemented or agreed upon prior to requisition submission directly conflict with the need to have the dialogue initiated earlier rather than later, part of prospective steps to take to approve a purchase rather than a retrospective introspection performed in hindsight.

In a specific SaaS I worked on, the company couldn't even save draft purchase requisitions without submitting them as finalized, further reducing the likelihood of proactive engagement *before* rather than *after* the company has made the purchasing decisions. Subsequent downstream busywork – whether that means re-categorizing purchases in requisitions into appropriate accounts, departments or cost centers, or making manual journal entries after the fact to insure appropriate accounting – remains just that, busywork, too little too late, an audit loop unto itself. Like the firefighting loop evidenced in IT incident management described by the Carnegie Mellon University SEI,[52] the accounting busywork that transpires behind the scenes – sifting, coding, redistributing, and reporting – remains decoupled from the end users' submission and approval of purchase requisitions. It is a self-fulfilling prophecy: as the enterprise grows to the hum of increased purchasing volumes, the more accounting does, and the more it would have to do, much like IT's firefighting efforts. Requests that come in may center on automating the purchase requisition workflow further: this time to route changes to purchased orders, themselves products of approved purchase requisitions. This is yet another symptom of the disconnect evidenced between theorized and system-configured accounts when it comes to the cost benefit analysis, vendor selection, and negotiation, as well as accompanying security and legal reviews. Baccus describes how "an investigator's concept of a phenomenon is primarily informed by investigatory practices and rules rather than from the phenomenon itself."[53] Purchase requisitions created after the company has received invoices, or frequent changes to POs are but varied symptoms of a much deeper and arguably more universalized flaw in the way we think and talk about transactions yet act altogether differently in real life.

Rather than tap into specific local practices, theorized accounts continue to operate at a level that supports officiated and thus sanctioned perspectives while arguably omitting or even "erasing" local and thus actual goings-on.[54] Retrospectives can do just that, communicating merely a silver of what just happened – that which aligns with our conceptual paradigms – or worse still, not much of anything else. Negative space is still space regardless with the devil continuing to reside in the finer details. Ironically, a real retrospective would have delved much deeper into what truly happens, and rather be ensnared by detail. We should be able to see how varied specificities are by turns merely symptomatic and like fingers collectively pointing at the moon really speak to root universals. Like the credit card token that is system generated and used as a unique transaction identifier in a payment processing gateway as well as secured means of pointing back to the credit card in use without compromising sensitive credit card detail, the symptoms we discussed thus far function like tokens, or as Baccus calls them, signs.[55] To be apt at uncovering underlying root causes is not unlike tea leaf reading in that it relates to a reading of signs, whether this relates to a recurrence of IT incidences, late requisition submissions, or frequent changes to PO. We may interpret the spike in liabilities in Groupon's liabilities as a sign, or a shorthand index, or token that signifies longer than usual vendor payment terms.

If we go yet one level higher, both are signs that make us question whether there is an appropriate manipulation of the operating cash flow. With all our emphasis on internal controls over financial reporting, and in spite of the presence of multiple special interest groups, regulated bodies, including the SEC, FASB, and PCAOB, as well as public companies that fall under their oversight, it can be easy to forget that financial reports are no more predictable than the reading of tea leaves for public investors in making investment decisions. Alas, for Groupon, liabilities are not the only area under scrutiny. In its initial public offering, Groupon debuted a new accounting metric, adjusted consolidated segment operating income (CSOI), a measure of "operating profitability before marketing costs incurred for long-term growth."[56] In the first quarter of 2011, Groupon generated $81.6 million in adjusted CSOI; yet, had they included marketing costs, they would have incurred a loss of $98 million for the same period.[57] Recall the previous discussion of principal versus agent revenue in Chapter 1. There, if agent revenue didn't factor in any associated fees or commissions owed to third parties responsible for arranging the sale of the good or service, the company would have overstated revenue reported as gross. Likewise, the use of CSOI presents an interesting conundrum. In this manner, the health of the financial indicators comes under suspicion even as the recorded numbers and risk factors disclosed remind us of the inevitable winds of change.

When we inquire into the very heart or abyss of SaaS internal controls, we may yet realize that the criteria for what makes up or doesn't quite make up the financial numbers, much like our oft-mentioned admission criteria for patients or vendors, gets taken for granted or swept under the rug. Earlier, we talked about how public companies trading in U.S. markets need to perform accrual accounting, so that even if a company received no vendor invoice for a fulfilled requisition, the company would have to make entries evidencing the organization's liability to pay even if the cash hasn't exchanged hands. When it comes to the recording of revenue, a matching principle applies so that even if a company hasn't received cash in hand, they record income at the point of sales and fulfillment. Strangely enough, it is in this regard that most accounting or financial SaaS is strangely quiet on. Preferring to concern themselves with debiting or crediting the correct accounts – a vendor invoice, for example, would debit expenses and credit accounts payable – thus frees the user from having to worry about the correct general ledger impact when booking a new transaction; the SaaS can be surprisingly indifferent to the way we make an entry, betraying a susceptibility to inadvertent mistakes.

Take accruals, typically manual journal entries that auto-reverse the following month. The input for accruals can come from running a report on or query of unbilled received POs in the SaaS. To address validity and completeness, accounting may perform month-over-month variance reviews with key purchasing personnel in respective departments. A search for unbilled received POs in turn depends a great deal on timely creation of purchase requisitions ideally prospectively rather than retrospectively almost as an afterthought. In effect, it is entirely conceivable that without these manual interventions, we can easily forget to account for an organization's liability in a correct manner in the current reporting period even if SaaS approval workflows were to hum along uninterrupted and therefore unexamined. Insofar as the contents of the POs are related to services, these POs don't have an accounting impact. If not for the manual accrual entries, the company would record financial impact only upon receipt of vendor invoices since in this case the company has received no actual goods. Yet, to make an accrual entry with accounting or general ledger impact, we would have to, ironically enough, circle back to unbilled received POs with no accounting or general ledger impact. The audit emphasis on transactions, with financial impact notwithstanding, is an emphasis on unbilled received POs with no accounting impact that helps accountants in turn present a more complete picture of the organization's short- and long-term liability on the balance sheet.

Does the SaaS let you	Enter	Update	Report
1. *Work in progress* invoices with no upstream requisitions	✖	✖	✖
2. Purchase requisitions with incomplete information	✖	✖	✖
3. Vendors with incomplete information	✖	✖	✖

We started with how an accounting or audit lens can shape how a transaction, such as a vendor invoice or purchase requisition looks, smells, or moves. This initial imprint drives what attributes the company captures and in turn what processes the company configures. With all our emphasis on admission criteria and missing or changing attributes, we haven't yet explored a second-order attribute, or deeper present absence.

1. Do medical records or the use of electronic medical records (EMR) make us better doctors?
2. Does the procurement SaaS make us more astute or cost-conscious buyers?
3. Does the procurement SaaS make us better at reporting spending?

From an Order-to-Cash perspective, we can ask the same question: does the billing SaaS make us better at accounting for revenue? To what extent does an inspection of sales transactions in a billing or accounting SaaS illuminate the criteria for revenue recording? In teaching the *Accounting Information Systems* class, I shared the following scenario from Ronald Clark, a professor in the School of Accountancy at Auburn University.[58] Picture walking into a dealership on the last day of the year and finding the car of your dreams.[59] You complete the paperwork for the sale and keep the car in the dealership lot overnight to complete servicing.[60] Because you choose to obtain financing through a local bank rather than through the dealership's financing bank, you won't be able to release the check to the dealership until January 2 when the bank reopens.[61] When Dr. Clark described this case to nearly 700 Certified Public Accountants (CPAs) he taught, most elected to have the transaction recorded as a December 31 sale.[62] According to SAB 101, Revenue Recognition in Financial Statements, released in 1999 and revised in 2003, the SEC described four criteria for recording revenue:

1. Persuasive evidence of an arrangement exists
2. The price is fixed or determinable
3. Collectability is reasonably assured
4. Delivery has occurred[63]

Students agreed that the first and second criteria were met as both buyer and seller executed the sales contract with an agreed upon price. When it comes to collectability, some students raised the possibility that the bank may reject financing when it reopens on January 2. When it comes to evidencing delivery, others asked what were to happen if the car were damaged or stolen while parked in the dealership lot overnight. Thus, when it comes to recording the purchase in time for year-end books as revenue, it all boils down to a series of interpretations.

Clearly, the accounting treatment for the car purchase is not unambiguous for all CPAs. Like Garfinkel before who explored the varied ways of "losing the phenomenon" when reconstructing Galileo's experiment, Clark proceeded to ask a series of what-ifs. Suppose the sales manager and bookkeeper got together and came to a decision to record the sale as revenue in time for December 31 as it was deemed immaterial in its overall financial impact to the income statement.[64] Come the following year, because of the precedence set in the prior year, the sales manager manages to convince the bookkeeper to record a few more of these cut-off transactions as current period revenue so that sales professionals can earn their commission on time.[65] The year after, the combined amount of these borderline sales becomes significant enough to trigger a review for fraud.[66]

While SAB 101, like its predecessor released in 1981, SFAS 48, *Revenue Recognition When Right of Return Exists*, clarifies that a buyer's obligation to the seller wouldn't change in the event of the theft, physical destruction, or damage of the product, Clark points out that some auto dealers and states for that matter do provide for a right of return in sales contracts.[67] Recall from Chapter 1 the competing accounting versus legal definitions of materiality. Thus, in a small but tangible way, the right of return in our dealership example illustrates the difference between accounting and legal interpretations. Clark next asks: what happens when the buyer, afforded the right of return, returns the car on January 3 and it is damaged while waiting for inspection in the lot overnight?[68] Who assumes the liability for the damages in the event the return paperwork hasn't yet been processed? The dealership? The buyer or more likely the auto insurance company?

We can argue that it is precisely because different CPAs can come to different conclusions that we should make the criteria for revenue recognition more, not less, explicit in a SaaS, and especially for an accounting one at that. Yet, like peering into medical records, we may be hard pressed when looking to a SaaS to gain additional insights beyond who recorded what and when. If we brought the impinging considerations that we discussed previously into consideration and we performed an analytical review, we are more likely to find this information buried in a Word memo by the management shared with auditors to justify the approach used for recognizing revenue and recording the impact in the SaaS.

Like before, where in Garfinkel's examination of good organizational reasons for bad clinical records, the admission criteria for patients remains curiously out of sight. A closer look at approved requisitions or sales not only reveals little about the admission criteria employed for vendors or customers, it also doesn't quite explicate the criteria for either taking in or else carving out numbers that make up a company's financials published to Wall Street. The same configured account deemed necessary for capturing or reporting accurate or reliable financials, and in turn applied towards automation, doesn't quite go to any lengths to assure data completeness or validity. Like the surfacing of who did what to whom and when in the clinical records examined by Garfinkel, we can obtain easy answers on the routing of what purchase requisitions to whom and when in the procurement SaaS and likewise and on routing what sales invoices to whom and when in a billing SaaS.

Whether all this busywork truly makes a difference in an enterprise's recorded liability or deferred revenue is a different story. As we have seen, the software itself doesn't preclude the possibility of garbage in garbage out, that is, preventing a user from recording a fictitious or even a live transaction in an inappropriate manner. Even among CPAs, there is already a need to surface and review what we take for granted, so you can only imagine the plethora of perspectives to account for in a wider circle of constituents to include not only sales and marketing and other departments inside an organization but also customers and vendors outside. We wonder perhaps if in an alternative universe we made the admission criteria for an account, or any account for that matter, more explicit, we would have embarked on a different conversation altogether, recognizing almost fortuitously the need to turn our assumptions from inside out as well as from outside in.

For if the overarching goal is to bridge an enterprise's need to procure third-party services with an ability to record liabilities in a complete and timely manner, then the emphasis of internal controls needs to transcend the pure mechanics of who does what to whom and when to get at the untapped domain of why. If we were to take off the blinders imposed by a specific account, we would have recognized that for specific company expenses, it may not even make intuitive sense to rely on purchase requisitions as a means of reviewing and thus controlling spending. If the nature of the spending at hand relates to laptops for every new hire, then the finance team can in effect estimate the projected spending for the year from the anticipated growth in headcount without necessarily having to require the internal IT team to create a requisition each time for a block of new hires on behalf of a specific department.

This also raises the question of the nature of purchase requisitions themselves. Are they needed for recurring spending such as the continued rent payment of office facilities or are they really a means to manage unanticipated and thus unplanned expenses that arise? In the latter scenario, it is more likely that cemented data on vendors or purchases are not available at the outset. Thus, like the regular tapping at the lock ring to ensure continual contact with the multipiece tire rim, we can configure the SaaS at hand to allow users to enter less than complete records at the outset with opportunities, not to mention gentle reminders, to intervene later to augment missing information. Just as it is ironic that the safety cage, an artifact that OSHA deems mandatory when airing a multipiece wheel, is also most likely to obstruct from plain sight the air introduced between the ring and the wheel, so our very insistence on what an account should look, feel, or taste like hampers us. All it took was 2 days of observation at five facilities to lead Baccus to uncover why tradesmen continued to perform tapping with a hammer and to observe that out in the field the safety cage was likely not available and how the "suicide bar" used in its place could be anything but suicidal.

When an organization creates purchase requisitions after receiving invoices, and accounting for accruals is based on a search on unbilled and received requisitions, we see a compounding effect, where not only is the organization unable to proactively identify spending ahead of time, but it is also ill equipped to identify spending in a complete manner after the fact. Not only are requisitions late in creation, but also the organization can't create enough in a timely manner for the accruals to be complete for the month end close. The logic embodied in this specific set of circumstances makes it easy for the procurement SaaS configured to misreport on, rather than reflect in truth, the extent to which the enterprise is liable to external vendors even as it continues to receive a clean bill of health from its auditors, even if caveated with "no exceptions noted" rather than a carte blanche seal of approval.

The way we conceive of and employ a purchase requisition doesn't lend itself to any timely detection of any under-captured accruals, simply because the internal controls don't so much reveal what can happen and in fact go wrong as they reinforce the way we already preconceive or think. So as part of SOX compliance activities in process walkthrough and testing, internal and external auditors alike check for evidence of purchase requisition approval, matching against received vendor invoices, and timely payment to vendors based on agreed terms. The fact that under-reported accruals – services received for which the organization didn't create purchase requisitions simply because they hadn't yet received invoices to trigger the need for purchase requisitions in the first place – can remain undetected arises from the fact that no indicators have yet been formulated either within or around the use of the SaaS to alert users to their real-world presence. The very absence of these accruals when configuring controls for the SaaS speaks volumes.

Likewise, as we turn our attention from Procure-to-Pay to Order-to-Cash, because the company may not articulate criteria for revenue recognition in the SaaS, they may code all customer invoices to deferred revenue. The company then downloads them into a separate Excel spreadsheet where they amortize revenue perhaps rateably over the respective service period and booked as a monthly revenue entry back in the financial SaaS, essentially reclassing it from deferred revenue to revenue. Recall our earlier example of how an intervening journal entry that reclasses the accounting impact of a vendor invoice from expense to fixed asset can break any link between the resulting depreciation with its originating invoice and PO. In the same manner, a manual revenue journal entry that a company uploads based on an Excel amortization of revenue breaks the link between the resulting revenue journal and any originating sales invoices.

As we proceed from the present absences that lead us to question whether the SaaS at hand truly helps us get better at our jobs, we come upon present absences hinted at:

1. Manual updates of customer invoice attributes downstream because the company didn't sync them over the integration Platform as a Service (iPaaS)
2. Manual plug-in of values in bank reconciliations because SaaS query is not able to report on remaining unpaid balance but full amount of open vendor invoices
3. Omission of receipts required for expense reports submitted by delegates because the SaaS doesn't let delegates submit receipts on behalf of primary users

To the unsuspecting user, the manually entered values and curtailed policies reveal nothing awry, yet much like the inability of the procurement SaaS in identifying and monitoring unstructured purchase data, the examples listed are classic accounts of the tail wagging the dog. Because of SaaS limitations, perceived or otherwise, not only do we not get better at what we do, the nature of our work also changes in a way that justifies rather than addresses underlying present absences.

There is yet a different kind of present absence that can be just as insidious. In a SOX meeting on change management, imagine someone voicing the presence of unauthorized production changes. Impossible, the auditor responds, all changes submitted have been approved by appropriate parties. The counter-response? We are talking not so much about changes that have been submitted for approval as about those that have *not* been submitted for approval. At first glance, this seems to be a straightforward proposition, yet when we dive deeper, a can of worms emerges. Most SaaS have an audit trail for transactional and master data changes, such as invoices and customers. But when we start to peer further into configuration changes, such as over pervasive application features like enabling vendor-specific objective evidence (VSOE) – the discussion in the next chapter – we may fall short in evidencing just the when of the change and the by whom.

Other changes include updates to roles and permissions. When a process grants users excessive access to billing schedules which can impact the way revenue gets recognized, does this inadvertent change to access fall under change control, and if so, is there a system audit trail report that can be run to compare updates against all access requests submitted and approved to ensure deployment of approved changes only? What is to stop an IT administrator from inadvertently making a change to a user's access without an authorized request?

As we dig deeper into the availability of system audit trails, we may yet realize that the same audit trails for header field level changes to customer terms and address may not necessarily exist for line level changes to revenue recognition start and end dates, even if any change here has direct implications for revenue recognition. Do we have to run periodic revenue recognition reports to compensate for the possibility of an inadvertent revenue schedule change however unlikely?

In an audit on changes, the question centers on whether we can work backwards from a list of changes evidenced in the system to authorizing artifacts like approved change requests. This is because when we proceed chronologically from authorized requests to actual system changes, the outcome almost always guarantees no exceptions. Another question to ask is: are only configuration changes that impact the way transactions in scope? How about changes to key reports? Insofar as internal controls under SOX focus on the accuracy of financial reporting, how do we track changes to key reports and have we assessed them for impact and approved? In other words, are changes to key reports first made in a sandbox environment and validated prior to production deployment? After all, in our earlier example, we use a report run periodically to compensate for the lack of audit trails on changes to line level attributes that impact revenue schedules. As we dig even deeper, we may find a Pandora's box of change upon change. In other words, to what extent does the design of accounts, departments, locations, and subsidiaries impact the way we have configured key reports and the ensuing likelihood of frequent change? Here, we are referring to a second-order present absence of sorts, foundational tenets that impact the design and operating effectiveness of internal controls that hover on the surface.

The fact that SaaS allows nontechnical users to make configuration changes more easily through point-and-click using workflow, rather than merely to rely on technical personnel to script, presents new possibilities for rethinking and thus controlling for the entire spectrum of program changes. Changes, for example, to the approval workflow for a sales invoice may inadvertently result in excluding those uploaded in bulk, such as through a CSV import from necessary oversight and review. Who catches these exceptions and, perhaps more to the point, are system audit trails available to both track and report on such changes to workflow?

Couple the ease of configuring changes, whether to access or program, with an all-too-easy tendency to rely on third-party SOC reports for presence of internal controls and you get a perfect storm brewing quietly in the backdrop. When we read SOC reports, we are struck by the lack of mention of key controls over transaction processing such as invoice approvals or key reports. After all, service organizations typically deem these to be user-end controls that SaaS clients should have in place. Put another way, how each individual client enterprise uses the SaaS up to them; yet, these are the very controls that can directly impact the accuracy, completeness, and validity of publicly released financials.

External rules and regulations are a kind of absent presence. In Chapter 1, we saw how the minimal length of wild-caught red groupers kept changing so that by the time the court brought charges against Miss Katie, the length of the catch would have been legal. We get a sense of the pervasive impact of macro industry changes when reading the transcript of an interview with Cynthia Cooper. A former vice-president of internal audit, Cooper helped uncover nearly 3.8 billion dollars of accounting fraud at MCI WorldCom and, together with other financial debacles such as Enron, paved the way for the passage of SOX. In the interview, she describes how we can attribute cyclical crises experienced in the financial markets to deregulation, citing the repeal of the Glass–Steagall Act as an example.[69] Passed in the 1930s following the stock market crash of 1929 and ensuing banking crisis, the act disallowed commercial and investment banking within the same company. Its repeal led to a build-up of conflicts of interest culminating in banking failures in the late 1990s.[70]

To recognize these second-order present absences, we would first need to acknowledge the "multiply-authored" reality that makes up a system record. To transcend what is immediately apparent to get at what lies beneath shimmering and waiting. Not unlike red groupers congregated around angled baits, we would have to undertake a journey that breaks boundaries, itself a border crossing of sorts. Earlier, we reviewed how the process resigns artifacts – work-in-progress invoices, vendors under selection, as well as products in flux – to the wretched outer fringes, denied admission into SaaS. Recall from Clark's fictitious auto-dealer example, how, with each passing year, the sales manager convinces the bookkeeper to include more of the same transactions conducted on the last day of the year as revenue in the current fiscal year so that sales professionals can earn their commission on time.[71] It bears remarkable parallels with Cooper's telling of MCI WorldCom, where each passing quarter, the chief financial officer persuaded two mid-level managers to present an alternate version of the published financials.[72]

Originally coined by Lucy Suchman to describe the ubiquitous and thus taken for granted "bookkeeper's record ledger, the record of accounts paid and those still outstanding," "technologies of accountability" that we can just as easily apply to

SaaS "aimed at the inscription and documentation of actions to which parties are accountable."[73] What happens when a billing lens is applied on health or medical records rather than an emphasis on quality of patient-doctor interactions? A 2013 productivity analysis of electronic medical records in a community hospital found that emergency department physicians spend significantly more time entering data into electronic medical records than on any other activity, including direct patient care.[74]

As it turns out, the company bolted electronic health or medical records onto billing systems rather than design them at the outset to improve a physician's clinical workflow. It is no wonder that many physicians report that they felt like data-pushing clerks. A more recent American Medical Association Study published in 2016 followed 57 doctors and found that for every hour spent with patients, the doctors devoted 2 hours to working with health records.[75] Firsthand accounts recount the sheer number of clicks needed to record a singular patient encounter. In fact, during a busy 10-hour shift, the 2013 productivity study reported that there were close to 4,000 mouse clicks.[76] With EMR, filling prescriptions takes on new challenges when we aren't able to easily recall an auto-filled prescription or need to enter custom prescriptions not immediately recognized by the system.[77]

The same challenges exist with identifying the right Current Procedural Terminology (CPT) codes to apply to medical procedures. Used in conjunction with ICD-9-CM or ICD-10-CM numerical diagnostic coding during the electronic medical billing process, it can be tricky to find the right CPT even for the same procedure. Take balloon-occluded retrograde transvenous obliteration (BRTO), an endovascular technique used as a therapeutic adjunct or alternative to transjugular intrahepatic shunts (TIPS) in the management of gastric varices. If performed through a catheter, 37204/75894 could apply.[78] However, when varices ablation is through a direct venous access, the 36475-36479 or 37765-37785 series may apply.[79] In an interesting twist where billing and compliance threads converge, when the federal government introduced financial incentives for meaningful use (MU) of EMR, vendors focused on functionality that check-the-box for complying with MU at the expense of enhancing current software usability.

Despite purported technology advances, physicians spend more, rather than less time, on record maintenance, to the point of requiring separate scribes to key in data. In some emergency departments, the number of data entry personnel well exceeds those involved in direct patient care. To read the EMR as an actuarial account with the intent of helping physicians make better decisions based on shared data across hospitals and across time in a patient's individual history mirrors, in some ways, Garfinkel's attempt to elicit the admission criteria from patient clinical records in 1967. When we speak of using SaaS to record our transactions, it is interesting to see how little we have changed our worldview of records since the early 1900s. Much like archive theorist Sir Hilary Jenkinson, we tend to see records, like archives, "as capable of bearing 'authentic testimony of the actions, processes, and procedures which brought them to being'…created as 'a means of carrying activities and not as ends in themselves, and therefore inherently capable of revealing truth of these activities.'"[80] What we don't document is out of sight. What is out of sight is out of mind. Even what we document is susceptible to a present absence. "Records are not neutral, factual, technical documents alone … designed - implicitly or explicitly – to produce some kind of effect on an audience" that as Van Maanen and Pentland remind us, "itself actively uses records to interpret events."[81]

The iterative nature of financial fraud, whether it is year over year in Clark's auto dealership example, or quarter after quarter in the case of MCI WorldCom, suggests the story of Pinocchio.[82] Created by Geppetto, a woodcarver, Pinocchio is a marionette that comes to life when Geppetto wishes upon seeing a shooting star.[83] Yet, his ability to talk and move with no strings attached isn't granted with no strings attached. As stipulated by the Blue Fairy, Pinocchio needs to remain truthful, brave, and unselfish.[84] For every time he tells a lie, Pinocchio's nose would grow, and he would appear less human despite Geppetto's best wishes.[85] The lie upon lie, like the year over year or quarter after quarter manipulation of financials, become an all too heavy burden. Instead of going to school, Pinocchio would eventually be roped into joining a puppet show.[86] Like the protagonist in Italian writer Carlo Collodi's tale, we become more puppet-like in our response in using SaaS when we preface surface approvals over underlying complex reviews, or standard input criteria over messy real-life unstructured if not incomplete data, compelled by invisible social strings, as it were. A whale swallows Geppetto while he is searching for Pinocchio.[87] It is only when Pinocchio dives into the ocean to join Geppetto in the whale's belly that he begins to earn his badge to be human.[88] The whale's belly, buoyed by the wildlife in the ocean, isn't unlike the abyss that makes up a heart, or as Laozi put it:

> Cut holes and windows for a room;
> It is the holes which make it useful.[89]

In Chapter 1, for all our posturing, we merely resided on the surface even as we experienced a spillover effect in the courts. This chapter invites us to dive in and break the water's surface. Being swallowed by a gargantuan abyss of a whale's belly if only to regain or recover our humanity isn't unlike putting aside the feature gadgetry that comes with SaaS – configurable parameters, attributes, records, and workflows – if only to begin asking questions about what is not immediately in plain sight and whether it matters more than what is at hand. As we have seen in varied permutations, when we recognize a systematic inability to capture transactions when their real-life attributes are less than compliant with pre-programmed and idealized SaaS worldviews and investigate for signs of life that reside at the margins, we begin to gain a unique perspective and appreciation of a "usefulness from what is not there."[90]

Exercise 2.1

1. Identify a risk you face in your enterprise. This can be any risk, whether strategic, tactical, or operational.
2. For the risk identified, come up with a list of ways to mitigate this risk.
3. What does an internal control resemble? How would it look, smell, move, or feel?
4. Revisit the risk and risk mitigation strategies identified. In what ways do they map or not map to our notions of internal controls?

Discussion

When I ask students in my *Accounting Information Systems* class what an internal control is, I am met with blank stares. Sure, there is the textbook or SEC version of management internal controls. But as we go about the course of our work, to what extent do we consciously or unconsciously employ internal controls? When asked how they would deliver quality in their day jobs, students are more effusive in sharing varied examples to ensure accuracy, validity, and completeness. Even here, examples pertain more to accuracy (what) than validity (why).

Even in this simple control identification exercise, we can see how internal controls strain reality through a specific sieve or lens. When using documentation to characterize actual goings-on, it would seem almost inevitable that we continue to ignore life that resides in the margins. Like a bumbling anthropologist, the process leads the auditor to only seeing and reporting back what he or she needs to enter in prepopulated blanks on the fieldwork questionnaire.

Exercise 2.2

When asked to audit SaaS, an auditor inevitably focuses on software with financial impact. As an example, we may consider Salesforce which tracks customer quotations out of scope if sufficient mitigating detective controls are present downstream for sales orders synced over to a financial reporting SaaS such as NetSuite.

1. To what extent does a focus on systems with only accounting or financial impact preclude an identification of risks that may end up having a financial impact?
2. To what extent does a focus on transactions with financial or general ledger impact in a financial SaaS preclude an identification of risks that may end up having financial impact?

Discussion

As discussed in this chapter, an organization may kick off a review for prospective vendors by submitting a JIRA ticket to legal and security teams. JIRA, a ticket tracking system not unlike Zendesk or ServiceNow, may not be in scope for audit even if evidence on JIRA tickets indicates approvals. Other more conventional applications such as Word or Google docs used for redlining edits arguably play a more pivotal role in securing favorable terms and conditions than a cursory review and approval of purchase requisitions in a procurement SaaS.

As for focusing merely on transactions with financial impact in a financial in-scope SaaS, assess this stance against in-flight journals, requisitions, and expense reports pending approval. Purchase requisitions hosting services for purchase are likely not to have general ledger or accounting impact, yet companies use them to accrue for monthly spending when they don't receive invoices for rendered services.

Likewise, standing master data by itself has no immediate general ledger or accounting impact. Yet, the ability to both create vendors and process disbursements can introduce the possibility of fraudulent payments to fictitious vendors. Even with an authorized and newly created vendor, an incorrect update to the negotiated payment terms would inadvertently skew accounts payable aging of outstanding unpaid bills.

Exercise 2.3

Select a transaction of your choice in your current financial system of record. This can be a SaaS or on-premise software.

1. What attributes or fields does it have?
2. Are there any missing attributes or fields you can think of?
3. Does the transaction tell a complete story? In other words, does it provide any clues as to how it got there? Put differently, what was the criteria of admission?
4. To what extent does the current financial system in use fail to document other transactions that are relevant to the nature of your business but not generic enough for easy coding or categorization in the off-the-shelf third-party solution?

Discussion

Even when looking at transactions recorded in a system deemed to have financial impact and thus in scope for SOX, key attributes can still be missing. The value-add of a configurable SaaS is that it enables nontechnical users to create custom fields through point-and-click functionality. This added value is not as straightforward if a company needs to sync-in data for these custom fields from a different upstream system. When we take a step back and examine the admission criteria of a recorded transaction, the holes in the big picture, however, can be glaring. We may be uncertain as to why a transaction is recorded at all, and worst still, a possibility may exist where it is recorded without an authorized input or just cause. In other words, a sale recorded without the customer contract being ever executed (for more on this, jump ahead to the Peritus example discussed in Chapter 4). Conversely, we may not capture a transaction at all when we have to sync it in from an upstream SaaS or on-premise software and it remains stuck in an exceptions queue for processing because we have not yet created the necessary customer, vendor, or employee or it has been inactivated. Finally, wouldn't it be nice if you were able to create custom records to document transactions specific to your company's business? Recipes in a food catering business anyone?

Endnotes

1. Nietzsche, F. W., Breazeale, D., and Hollingdale, R. J. (1997). *Untimely Meditations.* Cambridge, UK: Cambridge University Press.

2. Fracassa, D. (June 12, 2017). Why doctors hate electronic records—And what could change that. *San Francisco Chronicle.* Retrieved from http://www.sfchronicle.com/business/article/Why-doctors-hate-electronic-records-and-what-11206986.php

3. Garfinkel, H. (1967). *Studies in Ethnomethodology.* Englewood Cliffs, NJ: Prentice Hall.

4. Ibid.

5. Ibid.

6. Ibid.

7. Ibid.

8. Statement on Standards for Attestation Engagements 18. (April 2016). American Institute of Certified Public Accountants (AICPA). https://www.aicpa.org/Research/Standards/AuditAttest/DownloadableDocuments/SSAE_No_18.pdf

9. School of Library, Archival and Information Studies, University of British Columbia, *Select List of Archival Terminology* (Unpublished glossary, n.d.), p. 11.

10. McNeil, H. (Spring 1994). Archival theory and practice: Between two paradigms. *Archivaria, The Journal of the Association of Canadian Archivists,* 37, 6–20.

11. Ibid.

12. School of Library, *Select List of Archival Terminology.*

13. Garfinkel, H. *Studies in Ethnomethodology.*

14. Van Maanen, J. and Pentland, B. T. (1994). Cops and auditors: The rhetoric of records. In S. B. Sitkin and R. J. Bies (Eds.), *The Legalistic Organization.* Beverly Hills, CA: Sage, pp. 53–90.

15. Ibid.

16. Ibid.

17. Ibid.

18. Ibid.

19. Ibid.

20. Ibid.

21. Ibid.

22. Garfinkel, H. (2002). *Ethnomethodology's Program: Working Out Durkheim's Aphorism.* Lanham, MD: Rowman & Littlefield.

23. Ibid.

24. Ibid.

25. Coenen, T. L. (April 1, 2012). Groupon's latest accounting problem. Morrisville, NC: Sequence. http://www.sequenceinc.com/fraudfiles/2012/04/groupons-latest-accounting-problem/

26. Taylor, J. R., Allen, J. H., Hyatt, G. L., and Kim, G. H. (2005). Change and patch management controls: Critical for organizational success. *Global Technology Audit Guide.* Lake Mary, FL: The Institute of Internal Auditors.

27. Phelps, D., Kim, G., and Milne, K. (October 2006). Prioritizing IT controls for effective, measurable security. Software Engineering Institute. Pittsburgh, PA: Carnegie Mellon University. https://resources.sei.cmu.edu/asset_files/WhitePaper/2013_019_001_297211.pdf

28. Ibid.

29 Suchman, L. A. (1983). Office procedure as practical action: Models of work and system design. *ACM Transactions on Information Systems*, 1(4), 320–328.
30 Ibid.
31 Ibid.
32 Ibid.
33 Ibid.
34 Ibid.
35 Ibid.
36 Ibid.
37 Baccus, M. D. (1986). Multipiece truck wheel accidents and their regulations. In H. Garfinkel (Ed.), *Ethnomethodological Studies of Work*. London, UK: Routledge, pp. 20–59.
38 Ibid.
39 Ibid.
40 Ibid.
41 Ibid.
42 Ibid.
43 Ibid.
44 Ibid.
45 Ibid.
46 Ibid.
47 Ibid.
48 Ibid.
49 Ibid.
50 Ibid.
51 Power, M. (1994). *The Audit Explosion*. Demos.
52 Novak, W. and Levine, L. (September 2010). Success in acquisition: Using archetypes to beat the odds. Carnegie Mellon University. Software Engineering Institute (SEI). http://repository.cmu.edu/cgi/viewcontent.cgi?article=1262&context=sei
53 Baccus, M. D. Multipiece truck wheel accidents and their regulations.
54 Ibid.
55 Ibid.
56 De La Merced, M. J. (July 2, 2011). The Groupon I.P.O.: What is adjusted CSOI? *The New York Times*. https://dealbook.nytimes.com/2011/06/02/the-groupon-i-p-o-what-is-adjusted-csoi/
57 Ibid.
58 Clark, R. L. (October 2006). Revenue-recognition decisions: A slippery slope? *The CPA Journal*. http://archives.cpajournal.com/2006/1006/perspectives/p6.htm
59 Ibid.
60 Ibid.
61 Ibid.
62 Ibid.
63 Securities Exchange Commission. (December 3, 1999). SEC staff accounting bulletin: No. 101–Revenue recognition in financial statements. Staff Accounting Bulletin No. 101. https://www.sec.gov/interps/account/sab101.htm#FOOTNOTE_6
64 Clark, R. L. Revenue-recognition decisions: A slippery slope?
65 Ibid.
66 Ibid.

67 Ibid.

68 Ibid.

69 Carozza, D. (March/April 2008). Extraordinary circumstances. *Fraud Magazine.* http://www.fraud-magazine.com/article.aspx?id=210

70 Ibid.

71 Clark, R. L. Revenue-recognition decisions: A slippery slope?

72 Mieszala, K. (April 5, 2017). Cynthia cooper—Extraordinary circumstances: The journey of a corporate whistleblower. YouTube. https://www.youtube.com/watch?v=6bh7bI19N3Q

73 Suchman, L. (1993). Do Categories have politics? The language/action perspective reconsidered. *Third European Conference on Computer Supported Cooperative Work ECSCW93.* Milan, Italy: Kluwer Academic Publishers.

74 Hill, R. G. Jr, Sears, L. M., and Melanson, S. W. (November 2013). 4000 clicks: A productivity analysis of electronic medical records in a community hospital ED. *American Journal of Emergency Medicine,* 31(11), 1591–1594.

75 Lee, B. (September 7, 2016). Doctors wasting over two-thirds of their time doing paperwork. *Forbes.* https://www.forbes.com/sites/brucelee/2016/09/07doctors-wasting-over- two-thirds-of-their-time-doing-paperwork/#1fc039995d7b

76 Hill, R. G. Jr, Sears, L. M., and Melanson, S. W. 4000 clicks: A productivity analysis of electronic medical records in a community hospital ED.

77 Lee, B. Doctors wasting over two-thirds of their time doing paperwork.

78 True Blue. (July 17, 2009). Brto. AAPC medical billing and coding forum. https://www.aapc.com/memberarea/forums/20411-brto.html

79 Ibid.

80 Jenkinson, H., Sir. (1984). Reflections of an srchivist. Maygene E Daniels and Timothy Walch (Eds.), *A Modern Archives Reader: Basic Readings on Archival Theory and Practice* (Washington, DC, p. 15), quoted in MacNeil, H. Archival Theory and Practice: Between Two Paradigms. *Archivaria 37* (Spring 1994): 8–9.

81 Van Maanen, J. and Pentland, B. T. Cops and auditors: The rhetoric of records.

82 Collodi, C., Murray, M. A., Leone, M., Pyle, H., and Leone, S. (1965). *The Adventures of Pinocchio.* New York: Grosset & Dunlap.

83 Ibid.

84 Ibid.

85 Ibid.

86 Ibid.

87 Ibid.

88 Ibid.

89 Laozi and Mitchell, S. (1988). *Tao Te Ching: A New English Version.* New York: Harper & Row.

90 Ibid.

Chapter 3

Universal Particulars

But then, a layer beneath the particulars,

the *universals* are hidden.[1]

Alain de Botton

Looking back at what would appear to be a lifetime of moves, I remember moving to San Francisco and living in a fifty-unit apartment complex. All things considered, I was lucky to have the rental studio all to myself. Laundry was in a shared space in the basement, and the premise was virtually overrun by kids of all ages with families of five or more crammed like sardines into a single unit. I think back to the configuration of my own living space, "splurging" at IKEA, picking up matching drapes, and a foldable table and chairs, and when friends came over, with one broad sweep of the hand, showcase the entire living quarters. Memory is itself a rose-tinted lens. Other times, I would hear an occasional knock on the door and open to find no one there. In the evenings, there was running up and down the shared hallway and the smell of cooking wafting through. At least once a month, we would scurry to the streets in various states of disarray in the wee hours of the morning when a tenant would inadvertently set off the fire alarm. Years later, I would find myself in a two-bedroom, one-floor flat in a 3-unit building. With a larger living space, my hitherto modest furniture went beyond the folding table and chairs. I added a couch, a display unit, and some bookcases. The bigger kitchen in the condo also provided ample opportunities for a real meal rather than instant noodles. And yet, there are times where I would curse at the folks from the unit above, running around it would seem on laminated floors. For no apparent reason, loud music would start playing at odd hours and just when I thought my patience had run out, stop unexpectedly as if out of spite. As above, so below. There were also times when I would get complaints from the neighbor below each time I would run the in-unit laundry, vacuum the floors on weekends, or move furniture to recon-figure the living space. And yet, as I sit writing this now, who would have thought that I would be quietly sequestered and tucked away in a hilltop duplex, save an unexpected intrusion of birds upon a sliver of a back porch and the occasional tap-tap of the boughs against green-lined roof tops.

Recalling my moves feels like sitting faced in the opposite direction of a com-muter train. At no time does this feel more disorientating than when the train slows to a standstill right across from the train traversing the opposite direction. When the other resumes, it is easy to think that it is your train that is moving, an inevitable return to a beginning of sorts. For a fleeting moment, you feel like you are going with the flow. Are you coming or going? Approaching or leaving? Think of Janus, the Roman god typified by twin faces, one looking forward at the future, the other back at the past. In some way, my personal journey mirrors the path taken by software used by enterprise customers and developed by external vendors. Our love affair with tapping into a common computing infrastructure began as early as 1961. John McCarthy, one of the founders of artificial intelligence, had this to say at Massachusetts Institute of Technology (MIT)'s Centennial celebration:

> *If computers of the kind I have advocated become the computers of the future, then computing may someday be organized as a public utility just as the telephone system is a public utility ... The computer utility could become the basis of a new and important industry.*[2]

In what would become a foretelling of the future, he adds:

> *Computing may someday be organized as a public utility just as the telephone system is a public utility ... Each subscriber needs to pay only for the capacity he actually uses, but he has access to all programming languages characteristic of a very large system ... Certain subscribers might offer service to other subscribers ... The computer utility could become the basis of a new and important industry.*[3]

Software as a Service (SaaS) customers, like public utility customers, can also experience downtime, just as in each of my residences: I have experienced an unexpected power or internet outage or have had no access to running water or gas due to scheduled maintenances. We need look no further than the public registration statements, or S-1s, filed by SaaS startups, where buried in the risk factors may be a brief nod to a reliance on a third-party infrastructure as a service (IaaS). Coupa, a procurement SaaS that went public in 2016 described in their S-1 how they architected their software to use Amazon Web Services' (AWS) data storage and other services and that any disruption to AWS may affect their operations, and by extension their business.[4] As it turns out, Coupa customers could not use Coupa when AWS went down in February 2017; Coupa publishes metrics on system uptime online.[5] Amazon later attributed the outage to an employee who took down more servers than intended when debugging a billing system.[6] When a significant amount of capacity was removed from subsystems, each one underwent a full restart and became incapable of handling simultaneous service requests.[7]

When Workday, a SaaS that offers human capital management (HCM) among other services, came out with a blog update communicating an intent to release zero downtime updates beginning in 2016,[8] we can be forgiven for not remembering a time in 2009 when Workday would experience a 35-hour outage.[9] In an interesting turn of events, the redundant backup to a system – a network attached storage (NAS) that stored operating system files for production servers – took itself offline when it detected a corrupted node with a backup RAID array.[10] In talking to a reporter, the Workday communications director spoke of going "old school" during the outage by reaching out to customers to describe just what happened and the action taken as part of resolution.[11] For one customer, the outage took down the ability to enter HR transactions while trying to deploy Workday in a different subsidiary.[12] This downtime notwithstanding, they were able to make changes to their project tasks and go live as planned.[13] The consensus that was communicated? Outages are a fact of life in the SaaS world: what matters are the remedial actions taken to resolve an issue at hand. In some respects, this seems highly reasonable. SaaS priced on an annual subscription basis or pay-as-you-go model, based on the number of transactions processed in any given month, is much more economical than traditional and therefore costlier on-premise or custom developed software, where resources are deployed to specifically address an enterprise's individual needs. Contrast this with the SaaS model where enhancements to the product are likely based on extent of applicability to other customers so that any identified specific need is assessed for whether it can be productized to sell to other client enterprises. Universal specifics come to mind. Generic customization is how one vendor describes it. Another emphasizes configurability over customization. The former lets customers use what is available out-of-the-box to tailor their use of the software, whereas the latter involves heavy scripting to change the way the product behaves altogether. SaaS vendors, much like their earlier on-premise counterparts, are quick to warn of the dangers of over-customization that renders the software unsupportable and unable to support future upgrades pushed out to all customers.

The story is not altogether rosy. Depending on the nature of a company's business and the type of data we are dealing with, the level of indifference to outages or downtimes can vary. Put simply, are we in the business of saving lives? Even if availability were not an issue, upgrades themselves when performed by the vendor's developers and disseminated to all customers nonetheless carry a certain level of risk, not just on the maturity of new functionality introduced but also in how it may impact existing functionality and the rather particular ways an organization uses it as well as any customized fields, records, and workflows already in place. Here, I recall a trick question I had for students in my *Accounting Information Systems* class: what version of SaaS are you on? The answer? The same version as everyone else. In a career spanning the development, testing, deployment, maintenance, and audit of varied software applications, I have seen a spectrum of outcomes with scheduled upgrades from the run-of-the-mill kind completed with minimal fuss in the dead of the night to systemwide outages lasting days. Between these two extremes, there are varied permutations of what could and has gone wrong. Inadvertent changes to standard reports may necessitate an immediate patch release to varied tranches of customers at a time depending on which tenant they belong to. More forward-looking customers have been able to negotiate to be on the second or third wave of upgrades if only to have the first wave of customers experience and surface any early adopter challenges. For being a SaaS customer is not unlike residing in a 50-unit building. Even for "customization" or configuration using out-of-the-box customization or configuration capability, governance limits may apply to preclude one customer from interrupting the operations of another sharing the same tenant.

The tenancy concept itself merits a deeper review. Our predilection for off-the-shelf packaged solutions hasn't changed over time, only the manner they have been delivered and consumed. As far back as the 1960s, IBM and other mainframe providers offered time-sharing computing power and database storage to banks and other large organizations at worldwide data centers. Companies shifted accounting and inventory management from paper records to mainframe computers. In the 1970s, greater processing mainframe ability combined with minicomputers gave rise to Material Resource Planning (MRP) that provided bill of material (BOM), inventory, and production schedule management. The 1970s saw the inception of SAP, Lawson Software, Oracle, and JD Edwards. During the 1980s, client server computing emerged even as MRP evolved to MRP II integrating materials planning with finance. In the 1990s, on the heels of Gartner Group's coinage of Enterprise Resource Planning (ERP) to describe enterprise software applications, SAP introduced its client server (R/3) architecture. In 2000, the ubiquitous web browser was born and became a means for enterprises to access enterprise software and data hosted in data centers. As the decade drew to a close, a web-based architecture emerged; unlike the client-server architecture where a single tenant consumes its own database, a multi-tenant SaaS architecture can support various clients on the same database through virtualization, which basically lets multiple applications and operating systems run on the same server. By 2009, a customer relationship management (CRM) SaaS provider, Salesforce, crossed the $1 billion revenue mark.[14] Historically, software vendors have had to contend with offering a universal solution on the one hand and meeting customer specific requirements on the other. To some extent, this burden has been alleviated by third parties such as Value-Added Resellers (VARs) that bridge the needs of smaller and medium sized enterprises. The multi-tenant cloud architecture disrupts this age-old contestation between the universal and the specific, enabling customers to define, for example, custom fields to meet their business needs despite sharing the same database.

Chong, Carraro, and WolterOne from Microsoft describe a flavor of a multi-tenant architecture.[15] Custom fields are defined in a metadata table that associates each tenant with its own set of custom fields.[16] When a customer saves a record containing the custom field, a unique Record ID is recorded in the primary table that forms the underlying base schema.[17] The Record ID is in turn used to refer to an extension table where the inputted value is mapped to the ID associated with the custom field.[18] When the customer later queries this same record with the custom field, the application looks up its value in the extension table and ensures that it is reflected in the correct data type based on the custom field defined in the metadata table.[19]

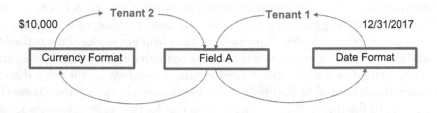

As you can see from this example, tenants 1 and 2 may assess the same custom field yet it is reflected to the date format for tenant 1 and currency format for tenant 2. In the context of the 50-unit building I lived in, this would be like giving each tenant the ability to configure the space they live in. Imagine the walls taking on the color of white or black or whichever color we fancy. Upon receiving a request, the building consults its color palette against the preference of any given tenant and only reflects the wall color they desire.

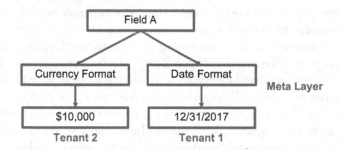

The metadata table holds the key to tenant-specific configurations. Suppose an intruder accesses the primary database table – the raw data would not make sense until the metadata table pieces it together when the application fires up in memory. Memory can retain frequently accessed data while the disk can hold the audit logs written to it that are less frequently accessed.[20] Stan Swete, Chief Technology Officer (CTO) of Workday, spoke of getting "smarter and smarter about how we use memory and what we keep in memory."[21] No wonder then the Force.com platform behind Salesforce employs massive metadata caches to maintain recently used metadata in memory to improve application response times. Metadata can also ease configurational updates without breaking the underlying architecture.[22] Rather than changing the underlying database schema, changing an application feature for Workday can be as simple as updating the metadata that defines relationships between objects.[23]

Governance limits may be placed on the number of custom fields or records that can be spun up at any given client instance. As an organization grows and continues to make rapid gains both in number of users and volume of transactions, a SaaS provider may propose a different kind of upgrade to transition it from a multi-tenant to a single tenant environment, where they can perform further tailoring, not unlike graduating from a 50-unit rental building to a 3-unit condo and to a more private duplex. Separately, we can't help but wonder how malleable or scalable the SaaS architecture is if complete configurability to some extent can't be fully realized in a multi-tenant environment. Downtime is still not a distant concern; this is not unlike having an entire neighborhood evacuate their homes in the event of a fire threat. What is surprising is that for enterprise customers accustomed to on-premise software presided by a Chinese wall, the idea of a disruption is entirely unfathomable, let alone tolerated. What they fail to realize is the cost benefit equation that accompanies SaaS use: by agreeing to be SaaS customers, they are in effect agreeing to be somewhat *indifferent* to the level availability and, in some respects, the degree of specificity they receive. At one time, Amazon EC2, an IaaS, charged customers 8.5 cents per hour for consuming a small Linux-based on-demand instance.[24] This is not to say that advances have been made in cloud computing such that outages, while no longer an artifact of the past, are not responded to swiftly to render minimal disruption to a company's ongoing operations. Netflix touts its homegrown monitoring tool, Chaos Monkey, that actively shuts down its AWS instances proactively to continually assess its current state of fail-over and fall-back procedures when something does go awry.[25] Contrary to what we might think, some even argue that service uptimes and recovery on the part of SaaS providers may very well exceed those belonging to an insular IT department of an enterprise for which IT operations is simply not a core competency. When exploring the real-life example of experiencing a power outage with students in my *Accounting Information Systems* class, we talked about how we are more likely to get a response when the entire neighborhood contacts the utility provider rather than merely one or two individuals. Group dynamics foster visibility, a subtle internal control of sorts. Finally, from an architectural perspective, by abstracting specific customer needs and having these addressed by a common metadata layer, the SaaS itself manages to remain somewhat *indifferent* and thus fragile to the particularities and idiosyncrasies that accompany each client instance.

In truth, McCarthy's concept of utility computing clarifies as much as it obfuscates, applying more to some SaaS than others. Storage or email are hardly means to gain a competitive advantage over other companies, and, in this respect, mirror a more ubiquitous commodity like electricity or water, although even in the world of data storage, a vendor may tout its product as more secure and enterprise ready than another's. In his book *The Big Switch*, Nicholas Carr argued that the adoption of vanilla boilerplate cloud utility solutions would lead to a corrosion of competitive advantage.[26] Much like electricity or water, the SaaS provided in the same industry vertical would result in a same look and feel regardless of provider, in effect a "McDonaldization" of software.[27] After all, when an enterprise customer agrees to use a SaaS from a third-party provider, it is giving up control to distinguish itself from its peers in the way it consumes a service, whether that be customer relationship management or payroll. How a client enterprise views a SaaS offering, whether as best practices or homogeneity out-of-the-box, is more reflective of where it is in its maturity lifecycle since inception. For a young startup or even a medium-sized company, a shared service is simply that – mundane back-office everyday necessities that do not warrant core expertise or competencies and therefore a prime target for engaging with a SaaS provider. The likelihood of an enterprise engaging with a SaaS provider to record or process specific transactions depends in part on its level of indifference to the value it expects.

Yet, when framed against the possibility of configurability and tailoring of out-of-the-box functionality, SaaS applications can and do tout a value proposition vastly different from plain old water or electricity. Close more sales deals using our SaaS tools, an ad compels. In continuing the theme from Chapter 2, when we review SaaS products as part of vendor selection, do we assess how SaaS-y it truly is? Is it accessible via any web browser? Do all clients get the same version? Are upgrades pushed out to all clients at around the same time? Can the pricing change based on the number of user licenses consumed or transactions processed? The differentiating factor maybe resides not so much on what is on immediate display out-of-the-box as it is on how the product would be used, and the array of options presented for tailoring such use. A common misconception is that the offered functionality would be just good enough for the masses with little need or possibility for tailoring to specific enterprise needs. It is useful to consider the factors that make a SaaS SaaS-y. All too often, web applications that do not look, smell, or behave remotely like SaaS under the hood nevertheless get marketed with modern-day SaaS verbiage, a wolf in sheep's clothing. A quick litmus test is to ask if the software needs a separate operating environment such as Citrix. More than ease of access, availability and low entry costs, a SaaS can get an enterprise started on a journey of configurability. The Force.com platform belonging to Salesforce allows for specific administrator configurations or "hacks" through point-and-click,[28] engaging in what the company refers to as declarative over programmatic customization.[29] From this perspective, SaaS is not only characterized by an ease of adoption, it can also differ from prior legacy or on-premise solutions by the ease of "customization" by nontechnical users. Thus, it is precisely because SaaS is seen and treated like a utility – recall the rising level of indifference in user responses from the *Introduction* – that consuming enterprises can fail to avail themselves of the configuration capability at hand.

We can also characterize SaaS by its degree of integration with other SaaS products. At this point, it helps to revisit SaaS as one of the three service models characterized by cloud computing. Defined by National Institute of Standards and Technology (NIST) in 2011 as a "model for enabling ubiquitous, convenient, on-demand network access to a shared pool of configurable computing resources (e.g., networks, servers, storage, applications, and services) that can be rapidly provisioned and released with minimal management effort or service provider interaction," cloud computing comprises of[30]

- Software as a Service (SaaS) where consumers access applications run on a provider's cloud infrastructure through a thin client interface such as a web browser
- Platform as a Service (PaaS) where consumers deploy applications using programming languages, libraries, services, and tools supported by the provider
- Infrastructure as a Service (IaaS) where consumers deploy applications and operating systems using processing, storage, networks, and other fundamental computing resources provisioned by the provider[31]

The cloud gives enterprises the ability to delegate parts of the stack that they do not want to manage to third parties. As we move up the cloud stack, each layer provides a greater level of abstraction. On one end of the spectrum, SaaS conceals the entire stack from the enterprise client; while users access and likely configure the applications they use, they do not develop, deploy, or maintain the applications and their underlying infrastructure. On the other end of the spectrum, IaaS automates the management and provisioning of virtual machines, network, and storage. As we move one level up, components needed for applications to run, installed runtimes such as Java and auxiliary services such as load balancers and databases, are freed from PaaS clients whose developers remain focused on business functionality and deploying applications.

Students in my *Accounting Information Systems* class had the most difficulty distinguishing PaaS from SaaS and IaaS. Coupa in its S-1 referred to its solution as a platform, even though its procurement software is categorized more as a SaaS than a PaaS. Today, these divisions are blurring. At its 2013 Dreamforce event in San Francisco, Salesforce called its Salesforce1 release a platform, no longer branding itself as merely SaaS.[32] Replacing the "Chatter" app, Salesforce1 offers greater support for customizations within Salesforce.com, as well as linkages with other apps.[33] It expands the number of application programming interfaces (APIs) to integrate Salesforce-hosted data with other products.[34] Scott Holden, vice president of platform marketing at Salesforce, said at an interview, "Now we can do more linking into the Salesforce data model, using API calls instead of building everything on Force.com."[35] Dropbox, Evernote, and LinkedIn are among the independent software vendors (ISVs) building apps on Salesforce1, and selling them on Salesforce's AppExchange marketplace.[36] Just as SaaS companies make their way down the stack, building out platforms to support a broader ecosystem, and thus a more complete value proposition, IaaS providers are likewise attempting to scale the stack, providing PaaS-like offerings to gain a competitive advantage.

Open APIs thus enable a mash-up of sorts by allowing data across two or more applications to "speak" to or otherwise integrate seamlessly with one another, so that an enterprise can and often does end up selecting multiple best in breed SaaS that integrate or play well together so that the same purchase or sale is interwoven through a myriad of SaaS products all the time oblivious to the naked eye. APIs bring to mind Metcalfe's law often illustrated using the fax machine. The premise is that a fax machine by itself is not of much use but its value increases with more fax machines added to its network. Used to characterize the value of the telecommunications network, Metcalfe's law would be challenged by Odlyzko and Tilly in 2005 for overestimating the value of each new added connection so that "the value of a network of size n grows like $n \log(n)$" as opposed to n^2 as proposed by Metcalfe's law.[37] When we circle back to the rise of APIs, the need for API management has not gone unnoticed in integration platform as a service (iPaaS) vendors. As pointed out by Pezzin and Lheureu in a Gartner 2011 research note, for many user organizations, their first taste of PaaS would be via iPaaS because of the need to integrate varied applications, as opposed to new application development.[38] iPaaS products such as Boomi and Celigo let an enterprise client play the role of an internal orchestrator, piecing together in a coherent manner what would have been otherwise disparate services from multiple providers. When you think about it, AWS EC2 comprises a set of cloud APIs that allow consumers to control the hosting of machine images on Amazon servers. APIs evolve from the Service Oriented Architecture (SOA) framework that espouses the reuse of existing business applications in the 1990s using adapters to transcend the multitude of ways they can differ.

Ever wonder how Amazon went from being an online bookseller to a dominant IaaS player? An accidental posting from Google employee and ex-Amazon engineer Steve Yegge in 2011 revealed how Jeff Bezos, as early as 2002, compelled employees to adopt a SOA approach for all internal communications among teams to be made "externalizable" to external developers via service interfaces.[39] In 2003, Pinkham and Black presented a paper describing a vision for Amazon's retail computing infrastructure that would be completely standardized and automated, relying extensively on web services for services such as storage, in effect alluding to internal work already underway.[40] In the 6 years that Yegge stayed with Amazon, he would witness its transformation from online retail to the gold standard for IaaS cloud computing. By 2014, the Gartner Group called AWS "the overwhelming market share leader, with more than 5 times the cloud IaaS compute capacity in use than the aggregate total of the other 14 providers in this Magic Quadrant."[41] In effect, by turning its internal services from inside out, Amazon paved the way for a set of tools that lets other enterprises turn their organizations from outside in by transitioning from their own infrastructure to AWS as well as collaborating with others to gain new sources of revenue. Two years after Walgreens opened its photo printing via APIs and a Software Development Kit (SDK) to partnering mobile apps, digital photo prints grew from 1% to 40% of its photo developing business.[42] Ironically enough, by making its own product indifferent to different, often unanticipated modes of consumption, an enterprise becomes less indifferent to its customer's needs, and quite simply more client-centric. This is what a SaaS aspires to be, and in effect what Amazon has done so well with AWS.

All this sifting, tweaking, inter-mixing, and rework recall the package paradox experienced in the 1990s with the dominance of monolithic enterprise resource planning (ERP) solutions. When adopted, some level of customization or tailoring is almost always required, yet how much ends up executed or left on the cutting room floor is a continual dance between what can be accomplished with standard functionality and just what is needed to meet specific needs, although this too is not without accompanying enhancement and maintenance costs. Yet as pointed out by Pollock in *Software and Organizations: The Biography of the Enterprise Solution or How SAP Conquered the World*, the choice that an enterprise makes between having to work with bricks on the one hand – hard-to-change ERP packages – and clay on the other – smaller independent suppliers – is often supplemented by a plethora of options where different industry players offer configuration technology that lets the enterprise pick and choose features as if from a restaurant menu.[43] From this perspective, the configurability offered by some SaaS over others isn't a novel concept. Nor is the delegation or outsourcing of an internal service to an external provider as we have seen with mainframes and the concept of utility computing. This could be what Larry Ellison, Oracle's CEO, had in mind when he uttered these (in)famous words at the 2008 OracleWorld:

> *The interesting thing about cloud computing is that we've redefined cloud computing to include everything that we already do. I can't think of anything that isn't cloud computing with all of these announcements. The computer industry is the only industry that is more fashion-driven than women's fashion. Maybe I'm an idiot, but I have no idea what anyone is talking about. What is it? It's complete gibberish. It's insane. When is this idiocy going to stop?*[44]

In the 1990s, Application Service Providers (ASPs) hosted and managed client-server business applications that require installation of software on users' personal computers. These applications are typically developed by software vendors separate from the ASPs. Customers typically pay for license usage upfront to be able to use it indefinitely. An annual maintenance fee, a percent of the original license fee, is incurred to cover bug fix, enhancements and version upgrades. Ellison's remarks notwithstanding, SaaS are less cost prohibitive than ASP when compared to this perpetual license model for hosted client-server applications. Where an annual subscription fee can be charged based on the number of user licenses consumed, other SaaS offers a monthly fee based on transactions processed. In this way, a capital expense incurred pre-SaaS would have been an operating expense post-SaaS.

Compared to ASP-hosted applications, SaaS providers are more likely to develop and maintain their own software. As we have seen, in place of separate instances, SaaS rely on a multi-tenant architecture capable of partitioning data to serve multiple customers, many of whom are smaller and medium sized enterprises. This multi-tenant architecture is worth exploring in greater depth when reviewing service organizations to a request for information or proposal for SaaS. Vendor responses specifically can sound suspicious when they contain verbiage encouraging clients to "upgrade" from multi-tenant to single tenant environments to build custom fields, records, and workflows. Fact or customer reference checking is also in order when a SaaS vendor claims to have multiple release versions for multiple customers, is on an aggressive weekly release schedule that casts a shadow over the product stability, or else is in the throes of migrating their application architecture to a multi-tenant one.

Today, the boundaries are not just blurring between SaaS, PaaS, and IaaS, but also between traditional ERP giants and SaaS. Eight years after Ellison's remarks at OracleWorld, Oracle acquired NetSuite, "the very first cloud company."[45] In 1998, years before SaaS gained common currency in tech circles, NetSuite began with financial backing from Ellison's venture capital entity, Tako Ventures, and, for a brief time, was licensed under the banner of The Oracle Small Business Suite.[46] NetSuite would go public in December 2007 and secure a 149% increase in revenue in the 5-year period from 2009 to 2014.[47] NetSuite founders, at annual SuiteWorld conferences, would contrast their rapid growth rate against declining fortunes of their on-premise predecessors of which Oracle is one. In retrospect, Ellison's words would seem to ring true: they foreshadowed what would become inevitable – that a long-standing ERP giant, even as it has, much like its peers in recent years, embraced a cloud presence, would not be displaced by a cloud upstart. An altogether different perspective may be that Oracle mirrors an Ouroboros of sorts, that in fact its acquisition of NetSuite isn't unlike a snake eating its own tail, an alchemical, self-sustaining act that is nothing short of transformational. Through NetSuite, Oracle is in effect able to access a different market, small- and medium-sized enterprises that could not afford the hefty price tag of larger scale ERP software but nonetheless needed a solution that can be easily implemented to process, record, and report on enterprise-wide transactions consistently though, as we have seen from Chapter 2, not in the same sequence each time. If NetSuite had been a tail, it would have been a longer one, although, when compared with the entire expanse of a lifetime, can seem relatively brief. After all, despite SaaS's rapid growth rates, traditional software still takes the bulk of the enterprise software market. *Apps That Run The World*, a publication that sizes the market for applications, reports that in 2016, SAP took the lion's share of the human capital management (HCM) market at 10% with 1.4 billion of product revenue, followed by ADP and Oracle at 6% apiece.[48] In comparison, Workday, a "pure" cloud or SaaS company, came in fourth at 5%.[49] The question remains: the more things change, the more they stay the same? When we observe how Workday's CEO was the former CEO of the ERP giant PeopleSoft, or how Salesforce's CEO held various positions at Oracle, we may be tempted to circle back to Ellison's suggestion and ask if SaaS is the emperor's new clothes.

Let's switch gears. In a Latourian sense, SaaS, or any software for that matter, can be described as an immutable mobile. Latour tells the story of a French explorer La Perouse journeying to the Pacific, presumably modern-day Southeast Asia, for Louis XVI and coming upon an island called Sakhalin.[50] This would have taken place in the late eighteenth century. He asks the local natives, the Chinese, if the bit of land they are on is an island or a peninsula.[51] In response, the oldest drops to the sand and draws a map.[52] Upon seeing the tide is about to wash out the map, his son retraces it in the European's logbook.[53] For Latour, therein lies a key difference between the Chinese and the Europeans; while both understand the value of maps, the former appears indifferent to notion of preservation whereas the latter seeks a permanent representation of the real thing.[54] I can't help but detect Eurocentrism in Latour's depiction of the Chinese. After all, the Chinese language is one of the oldest writing system still in use today, dating back to 1250–1192 BC.[55] Not to mention, if their objective were not so much to preserve the European log as it were to preserve their localness from foreign prying eyes, the medium chosen for drawing a map is sand precisely because it can be washed away. For Latour, the log is an immutable mobile. It has the properties "of being *mobile* but also *immutable, presentable, readable,* and *combinable* with one another."[56] Sounds like a SaaS? Though configurable via a metadata layer, SaaS maintains its structural integrity and thus identity, while at the same time easily integrating with another SaaS. More than just clever invective, universal mobiles comprise various threads. To be transportable and yet remain distinguishable and intact, this very artifact would have to be indifferent somehow. This is in fact what an ERP package would have challenges with as seen in Pollock's study of an ERP implementation at a British university (affectionately) named the Big Civic.[57] Far more than a simple plug and play, significant efforts had to be undertaken to adapt local practices to the specific demands of a supposedly universal solution. The same question can be asked of an internal control. Is it an immutable mobile? Recall *Exercise 2-1* from Chapter 2 where I describe attempts to elicit feedback from students in my *Accounting Information Systems* class on what an internal control would look like rather than relying on textbook definitions.

More than an artifact that we bring back from our travels – the software's sojourns to multiple client sites – is what Latour calls "optical consistency," the sheer volume of documentation or artifacts that anchors and supports a specific way we think of and articulate the real thing.[58] After all, the all-seeing eye, the panopticon, as described by Michel Foucault of the ever-present comprises of "files, accounting books, time-tables and drill" that matter to an institution.[59] Designed by the English philosopher and social theorist Jeremy Bentham in the late eighteenth century and used to inform the design of nineteenth century prisons, the panopticon allows a single watchman to observe (-opticon) all (pan-) inmates of an institution without letting any of them know whether they are being watched. In *Discipline and Punish* in 1975, Foucault observes how Bentham's panopticon has not only shaped prison design but also management hierarchical structures.[60] As Latour put it, the mind becomes "domesticated." He taps into Fabian's account of visualization in anthropology where explorers actively map out foreign lands, yet locals or what Fabian referred to as "savages," had no maps of their own.[61] Explorers appear to come equipped with written calendars that locals do not seem to possess, and along with it the ability to record a chronological event sequence. For Latour, "asymmetry is created because we created a space and time in which we place other cultures, but they do not do the same."[62] Because of this "violence committed," Fabian's argument, is "we will not understand savages anymore."[63]

Putting aside the likelihood that the locals themselves would possess tools, just not the ones that the Europeans can immediately identify with, there is a certain level of indifference, even insouciance to presume that the tools Europeans have at their disposal for understanding the locals would even apply or make sense in their context. Conversely, we can argue that they would have to work hard to prevent themselves from projecting their very own assumptions and biases onto the other. Yet for Latour, other than a continual reliance on immutable mobiles, there is no other way of presenting something from far afield. In his words, "Fabian would have to give up 'knowing' or give up making hard facts."[64] If we were to cast the university personnel as locals to be measured, assessed, and benchmarked by the travelling immutable mobile of an ERP package, we see examples of such asymmetry. At Big Civic, prior to systematized purchase requisitions introduced by the ERP package, Pollock describes how non-authorized staff would make orders over the phone and complete the necessary paperwork later.[65] With the implementation of the ERP however, Big Civic's suppliers were informed that all requisitions need to be communicated via authorized paperwork and bearing a unique order number generated by the ERP.[66] To work around time-sensitive situations such as getting a travel ticket at the last minute, university personnel without access to the ERP would generate a copy of the purchase requisition form in Word and assign it a pseudo number.[67] The busywork of cleanup and rationalization makes it appear as if the purchase requisition process inscribed by the ERP was complied with even as it takes place well after the fact. In some ways, it feels like moving forward in a train while all the time facing the opposite direction. Likewise, the use of maps to draw up foreign lands for which natives had no maps of their own is mirrored in the SaaS's insistence on a sequence of events. Recall the sales order–fulfillment–invoice sequence presented in the *Introduction* or the purchase requisition–receipt–invoice sequence from Chapter 2. From this perspective, internal controls are immutable mobiles, in use in various organizations, and yet, depending on local context, take on particular combinations or permutations.

With all the emphasis on immutable mobiles, and the way user behaviors can be inscribed by a system's script, it can be easy to underestimate the role played by the contextual organizational environment. In a university context, Pollock draws on four organizational archetypes outlined by McNay:

1. Collegium (loose policy as well as loose control of implementation)
2. Bureaucracy (loose policy but tight control of implementation)
3. Corporation (tight policy as well as tight control of implementation)
4. Enterprise (tight policy but loose control of implementation)[68]

McNay's work is drawn from management theorist Charles Handy. Thus far, we have used the words enterprise, company, corporation, and organization rather interchangeably so it is interesting to see here how a more precise delineation can help us discern differences in policy or control of implementation. To some extent, most organizations possess all four archetypes, although the resulting mix or composition may differ depending on the industry they are in and the nature of the business. How collegial, bureaucratic, corporate, or enterprising depends on a larger set of factors not least of which are tone at the top and leadership personalities. Even as I write this, Travis Kalanick, whom many see as synonymous with the Uber brand, resigned from his position as CEO following mounting investor pressure over recent scandals from a U.S. Department of Justice federal investigation of a competitor as well as claims of an internal culture of sexism and bullying.[69] Like Airbnb, Uber belongs to the Web 3.0 slew of startups that are more known for breaking rather than playing by the rules. Going beyond Web 1.0 where the internet was a one-way source of information and Web 2.0 that fosters a two-way dialogue for users to post and share information, Uber and Airbnb fundamentally changed the way we order and provide for rides and accommodations. In many ways, there are heightened risks in taking the road less travelled and often in less hospitable terrain. Uber and Airbnb are like immutable mobiles that travel from site to site, even as they encounter public opposition from some more than others – Paris taxi drivers who burn Uber-affiliated vehicles come to mind.[70]

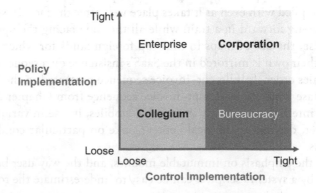

But back to Big Civic, there is much we can glean from an ERP implementation in one specific site and in so doing obtain a glimpse into the interdynamics between immutable mobiles (software) with users as well as immutable mobiles with institutions (Big Civic). Big Civic possesses all four archetypes where a complex structure of committees, each of a heterogeneous composition, governs the university.[71] Having grown accustomed to the level of flexibility that comes with either a loose policy definition or a loose control of implementation or both, university personnel often don't have a formalized, consistent policy to follow resulting in varied practices in various departments.[72] When a decision needs to be made on which path to take in configuring process routing and workflows, the committees could not make up their minds fast enough, so they delegated the decision to the immediate project implementation team that in turn relied on out-of-the-box workflows, of which requisition to invoice to payment is one such example.[73] As Pollock put it, "Big Civic changed its processes to match the system rather than the other way around."[74] Pollock describes an example where, prior to the ERP implementation, individual departments were able to determine postgraduate course fees on a case-by-case basis to respond more nimbly to changing market conditions and student financial needs. Post-ERP implementation, the university had to create a change approval working group to approve changes to course fees, all of which they then had to translate into preset categories, codes, and fees within the ERP. Recall from Chapter 2 the politics of coding. When something can't be easily coded, it presents a formidable roadblock of sorts.

Yet, faced with system indifference, organizations may resort to manual workarounds not unlike those described earlier in the handling of last minute purchase requisitions. In this manner, the ERP package as immutable mobile is said to have shaped the governing panopticon of university administration and, in the process, evolved its organizational archetypal mix from collegial to corporate. This brings us to the crux of Pollock's analysis: the ways and means in which an ERP is re-tooled or reshaped can end up reshaping its users. In many respects, this is the same pattern we have seen in the bolting of billing systems onto electronic medical records (EMR) in the physician work described in Chapter 2, with its insistence on preset billing codes and prescription levels. In a SaaS deployment, it isn't uncommon to encounter user resistance or subterfuge. Much like university personnel creating a facsimile of the actual purchase requisition to make it appear as if it were system generated in order to process a last-minute request and yet comply with the university procurement policy post-ERP implementation, users accessing a billing SaaS, when responding to specific customer inquiries that challenge standard out-of-the-box SaaS functionality, may create manual copies of customer invoices in Word documents to surface greater detail in line-level credit or sales tax computed. The creation of purchase requisitions after the fact also dovetails into paperwork performed by university personnel after rather than before communications with suppliers. In the context of McNay's four organizational archetypes, what end of the spectrum the SaaS consuming enterprise falls into — the degree of tightness (heaviness) or looseness (lightness) from policy and control implementation – paints varied shades of grey in the way the SaaS is deployed and maintained, from whether default configurations are inherited with little change to defaulted settings to whether custom workflows are devised to automate otherwise manual controls specific to internal needs. As an organization grows in volume and scale, it may choose to re-architect its internal architecture to better handle fail-over. From an IaaS perspective, this may mean looking beyond AWS and considering Microsoft Azure.

Much like the map drawn in the sand by the Chinese island local, the shifting boundaries among SaaS, PaaS, and IaaS, as well as between traditional ERP on-premise and the cloud software, are drawn or redrawn each time. There are specific considerations to be accounted for, such as assessing the veracity of vendor claims on just how SaaS-y an application truly is. We also saw how the use of metadata tables can help bridge the universal with the specific, so that a specific universality is seen to underpin what appear to be specific particularities. Yet like a set of Russian nesting dolls, the myth of the universal solution speaks to the masking of efforts undertaken in local contexts. Whether through adaptation of existing practices to fit the system's newfound paradigm or through behind-the-scenes work-arounds, the next unveiling reveals yet another and another, particularities that lie waiting for the unsuspecting. What remains unseen and thus undocumented continues to be hidden behind an official façade of an immutable mobile and not integrated into the overall panopticon. Unnoticed, it is like a ticking time bomb waiting to implode if left unchecked over time. Take Rap Genius, a website that provides insights into rap song lyrics and relies on Heroku, a PaaS vendor to run its service on customized on-demand Amazon EC2 instances, otherwise known as dynos.[75] Despite the large number of dynos leased by the website, in 2013, Rap Genius reported unusually long average response times.[76] Upon further investigation, Rap Genius engineer James Somers discovered that, in place of claims of "intelligent scaling" used to route web requests to the next available machine, the distribution was actually random so that numerous requests could end up stuck in a queue even as idle dynos lay waiting.[77] Barely a day after his widely read blog finding was posted, Heroku's general manager Oren Teich admitted that Heroku quietly changed the way it distributed tasks across the Amazon EC2 machines without alerting developers and that "over the past 3 years," Heroku users had already been experiencing "a degradation in performance."[78]

If it is an inevitable artifact that represents the real thing, how then do we improve upon the veracity of the account provided by an immutable mobile? Considerable efforts need to be expended to work against the pull of the tides, so to speak, that run counter to any prevailing dominant narrative or, as Latour would say, go out of the way if only to make it back.[79] For an immutable mobile also alludes to the ways and means we erect a science, itself a series of cascading inscriptions where any potential disagreeing point of view is cornered by yet another new text, diagram, or publication.[80] That a cascading inscription is inherently fragile betrays a pressing need for continual staging. The system of internal controls established in an organization is a series of cascading inscriptions. Woven and interwoven over time, it presents a formidable obstacle to handling ongoing people, technology, or strategy change. There is a science, or method, to the development of controls. As an example, the mix of varying control frequencies allow room for exceptions so that a monthly control when validated and "failed" still leaves enough room for remediation to be performed and remediation testing by year end to evidence operating effectiveness. For this reason, monthly controls are intermixed with quarterly and annual controls. Control frequency is also driven by the nature of the activity at hand so that if an organization pays out commissions to sales agents on a weekly basis, then a detective control to review computed commissions against any change in commission plans and associated rates is also weekly in nature. In this system or "science" of internal controls, fragility can be said to be observed through the mix of preventive versus detective controls, automated or manual; the more preventive controls are, the less fragile the system of internal controls can be said to be. Detective controls, in the other hand, add to the forgiveness aspect, compensating for any gaps or shortfalls not mitigated upstream. In this manner, the entire setup of controls resembles a series of cascading inscriptions.

It can be argued that I am doing the same here, interweaving in and out what at first appears to be disparate threads across time and culture. Just as Rap Genius' Somers had to evidence idle dynos to break the myth of intelligent routing,[81] we are compelled to see past the beguiling nature of immutable mobiles: each "contains that which no longer needs to be considered, those things whose contents have become a matter of indifference."[82] In this respect, they are black boxes concealing the mutability behind the numbers, diagrams, or printed text. A case in point is the 2008 U.S. financial crisis that was precipitated by subprime and other risky mortgages on the books of government-sponsored enterprises (GSEs) Fannie Mae and Freddie Mac.[83] As far back as 1992, Congress adopted a program requiring the GSEs to allocate 30% of loans acquired in any given year to home buyers at or below median income.[84] From 1993 through 2008, the Department of Housing and Urban Development raised the target percent to 56%.[85] To meet this target, GSEs went from accepting prime mortgages, where buyers were putting down 10% to 20% down payment, to subprime mortgages.[86] These loans were in turn packaged into complex financial structures and billed as sound investment products to less than suspecting institutional buyers. When borrowers could no longer refinance their loans to meet their mortgage obligations, the number of defaults spiked, and the real estate bubble burst. Based on the AAA rating granted to private mortgage pools by American Internal Group (AIG), banks were nevertheless able to write the loans off their books. Thus, despite appearing to "have the properties of being mobile but also immutable, presentable, readable, and combinable with one another," the home ownership targets, loans, financial instruments, and ratings were all black boxes "whose contents have become a matter of indifference," masking deeper fundamental flaws, all of which contributed in retrospect to the perfect storm.[87]

All these artifacts are like the map that La Perouse was holding in his hand when communicating with the local natives in the Pacific, attempting to fill in the missing gaps. We can become so accustomed to maintaining the flow of immutable mobiles, so that with each one succeeding the next, the "world tends to be perceived by organizational members in terms of particular concepts that are reflected in the organization's vocabulary. The particular categories and schemes of classification it employs are reified and becomes for members of the organization the attributes of the world rather than mere conventions."[88]

In *The Adventures of Pinocchio* covered in Chapter 2, with each ensuing lie, Pinocchio's nose grows so long that he is unable to get "through the door of the room."[89] Yet, have you heard of the Pinocchio paradox? Essentially a variation on the liar's paradox, would you believe Pinocchio if he were to say, "My nose will be growing?" This was what 11-year-old Veronique Eldridge-Smith suggested to her father after he explained the liar paradox and asked her to come up with her own version.[90] Let's first start with the liar paradox. Observe the following sermon from St. Jerome:

> *I said in my alarm, Every man is a liar!' Is David telling the truth or is he lying? If it is true that every man is a liar, and David's statement, "Every man is a liar" is true, then David also is lying; he, too, is a man. But if he, too, is lying, his statement: "Every man is a liar," consequently is not true. Whatever way you turn the proposition, the conclusion is a contradiction. Since David himself is a man, it follows that he also is lying; but if he is lying because every man is a liar, his lying is of a different sort.*[91]

When we assign a binary true-false value to a statement, it immediately exposes an underlying paradox. Is Pinocchio lying when he says that his nose will be growing? The future becomes past perfect. Likewise, we wonder about the masking of inner contradictions or inconsistencies in the tight interlock of cascading inscriptions that cascade whether we are referring to mortgage loans, internal controls, or SaaS configurations. Take the assertion: management provides oversight for enterprise spending. It can be both true and false. While approved purchase requisitions reside behind every processed vendor invoice, the possibility can still exist for requisitions to be created after the enterprise has already entered into an agreement and received services from the provider. In this manner, the management assertion hides as much as it reveals.

Framed against the backdrop of simmering Pinocchio paradoxes, we wonder just how fragile cascading inscriptions can be. For Latour, it is their fragility that engenders the roar of justifying artifacts.[92] He cites an example of how Boyle's air pump demo not only invented the phenomenon but also the accompanying staging from the instrument setup to the admission criteria of witnesses to commentaries they could provide.[93] In thinking back to the procurement SaaS deployments I have been involved in, the same staging pattern is evidenced in the identification of purchase champions in each department to periodic refresher and new hire trainings on purchase requisition creation and approval to designated contacts assisting with end user questions. Staging also relies on communicated rules and procedures such as no contract may be executed without an approved purchase order (PO) number or no invoice would be paid without a PO. This staging to some extent is independent of whether the SaaS has been configured to specific organizational needs or whether default features have been inherited out-of-the-box. Mutability, or change, in the environment is a factor that threatens the fragility of cascading inscriptions. Departments, cost centers, or accounts are added or updated as the enterprise grows, or shrinks, or quite simply realigns the way teams, incentives, and goals are structured. Entries made into SaaS would have to be revised to reflect these changes. A new expense account added may impact an amortization schedule that distributes journal entries each month from a prepaid balance to an older existing expense account. Likewise, a new or updated department may impact an allocation schedule that redistributes a shared expense such as rent among all existing departments. How flexible the SaaS is in handling these changes becomes in part a test of how mobile, or how transferrable, it truly is.

So far, we have explored how an immutable mobile can move across space – enterprises or locations. Now, let's take this a step further by exploring how it can travel through time. In effect, the more able it is to absorb change, the less susceptible it is to break down. Introducing a new department can be like introducing a wrinkle into an otherwise automated, and thus taken for granted, process of allocating entries, the very reason for having a software automate otherwise manual time-intensive or laborious processes. If already entered schedules derive their department codes from vendor invoices already entered, locked, and sealed in prior accounting periods, newly automated amortization or allocation entries in future periods would remain coded to the former departments. Manual intervention is required either to amend these entries each month or post adjustment entries that recode amounts to different departments. The burden on the accounting is twofold. First, a query is executed each month to uncover entries that would be mapped to former departments. Second, an adjustment entry is created and reviewed before posting. Imagine the amount of work that needs to be performed for multiple invoices for varied vendors across departments. To the outside observer, the allocation schedules still execute like clockwork – from this respect the SaaS remains immutable. Yet, an invisible sleight of hand remains nonetheless hard at work behind the scenes to ensure that the output of these very automated procedures remain valid. To allow for the update of departments in already configured allocation schedules, seasoned SaaS users would advocate for an enhancement request to be submitted to the SaaS vendor. But here is where the rubber meets the road: enhancement requests from various customers are typically pooled, sifted, and prioritized from the degree of magnitude on existing SaaS customers and alignment with overall product strategy before they are worked on, tested, and released to production. In other words, the light flickers at the end of a very long tunnel.

Does this constraint make SaaS any less mobile? Certainly not from an access perspective, given that it can be accessed with a web browser whether from a computer, tablet, or phone, the last of which may manifest as a mobile app, albeit with a more limited subset of available features. To measure mobility by ease of access is to measure it too literally, when thus far we have explored the mobility of SaaS across varying practices across different enterprise customers as well as from the perspective of change across customers and within any one customer. Where SaaS is more immutable – such as when it comes to handling changes in department for already created schedules – it becomes less mobile. Not as widely accepted in an enterprise undergoing frequent departmental change or perhaps even perceived less favorably with a competing SaaS that is able to automate changes to future entries, it is perceived to be less universal. Conversely, the more mutable a SaaS, the more mobile it becomes, and likely more universal. Yet, this begs the question: how mutable can a SaaS become before it reaches the brink of no return, losing its identity all together? There is a limit to the number of custom fields that can be defined, a limit to the number of workflows, a limit to the number of concurrent scripts that can be running at any one time before performance starts to degrade, or self-imposed governance limits kick in. We are after all talking about the same piece of software that has been externally developed and repurposed for every conceivable need from a manual entry of transactions to an automated receipt of exception notification receipt to a report run on key metrics.

Perhaps the real question to ask about SaaS isn't how brittle it is in handling changes in requirements but how apt it is at handling changes without falling apart, or in other words, remaining immutable. For if we were to look back to the use of metadata tables to serve as a layer of abstraction to point to specific field formats that a SaaS customer would desire, such as date in place of currency format, the architecture of the SaaS fundamentally stays the same. Although it *appears* mutable, it has remained immutable. In effect, SaaS that has crossed over from SaaS to PaaS – Salesforce with Force.com manifests this ideology. At Salesforce's annual Dreamforce events in San Francisco, we invariably hear about the top ten nonprogrammatic hacks among Salesforce administrators. One administrator recounted how she used the Force.com platform to build a workflow for onboarding new employees. Onboarding falls into the unlikely realm of human capital management (think Workday), yet with Force.com remaining immutable while appearing mutable, an easily extensible platform allows for endless possibilities in making forays into uncharted waters, not unlike La Perouse journeying to the Pacific.

After all, Workday started with a focus on HR and payroll transactions and over time is making inroads into financial reporting with Workday Financials. With the ASC 606 deadline looming over the horizon, Workday showcased its ability to be one of the early 606 adopters by relying on its very own product, Workday Financials, to comply with the industrywide change from a rule-based accounting for revenue to a more principle-based one. The same can be said for Salesforce when it parlays its capability in tracking sales leads and opportunities through its Force.com platform into financial reporting with Financial Force. In this respect, the trajectory that today's SaaS travels mirrors a well-trodden road undertaken by their on-premise or hosted software predecessors such as

PeopleSoft. The founder of Workday, Dave Duffield, after all founded PeopleSoft and left to start Workday when Oracle acquired PeopleSoft.

The ability to absorb change that can withstand any potential breakage at the seams is itself alchemical. We spoke about the acquisition of NetSuite by Oracle as an Ouroboros of sorts, a snake eating its own tail. With the immutable mobility that comes with SaaS, we can say that when faced with each new client environment and local need, the ability to configure the SaaS to take in or subsume these needs, refreshing older attributes with new ones, is not unlike shedding old skin to take on the new. Thus, the pivotal question becomes not so much SaaS, PaaS, IaaS, or even iPaaS, but whether we should perhaps really be talking about what I call configuration as a service (CaaS), a foundational construct that underpins the cloud footprint.

If we were to start with a simple proposition that configurability, compared to its traditional ERP precedents, is more available and accessible out-of-the-box for SaaS, then ideally one would hope that enterprise users consuming SaaS, whether nontechnical or otherwise, would be able to, as Salesforce advocated, perform declarative "customizations" through point-and-click to address local needs through the use of a universal package; note here that SaaS is very much a third-party package even though the term package has gone out of style, a nod to Ellison's allusion to future of the past. Yet all too often, reality sets in during a SaaS implementation, and, I suspect like Big Civic, organizations (here perhaps consciously or otherwise I have chosen an apolitical noun as opposed to collegium, bureaucracy, corporation, and enterprise and perhaps falling under the influence of McNay's organizational framework as immutable mobile) are faced with a triangulation of project constraints (time, scope, and resources). The outcome? Users succumb to what comes out-of-the-box all too soon and, in the words of Pollock, "simply end-up accepting those 'default' features embodied within systems."[94] What would compel users to opt for a harder, less trodden path? Faced with time pressure and constraints on resources, I have heard many clients during SaaS implementations ask for best practices out-of-the-box; in other words, to evidence that a company is public ready and compliant, simply *download* default workflows out-of-the-box that harken back to earlier ERP precedents. To be sure, against directives laced with expediency and command, I have also heard an opposing tide of dissent – end users who question what makes a particular cloud implementation, and from their vantage more implantation than implementation, any different from the custom or on-premise software that it is replacing and how perhaps there is an off chance that operational drivers concerns that are not related to accounting can rise to the surface of consideration for configuration to-dos rather than continue unabated as manual workarounds? It would have been a shame otherwise. Software, after all, hasn't always equipped nontechnical users with an ability to configure its look and feel; we have come a long way from systems that do not travel.

"Databases don't travel," was de Dombal's response in an interview on the use of decision support systems in healthcare.[95] The system he had in mind was the AAPHelp system he developed in the 1970s to diagnose acute abdominal pain (AAP) in patients through the application of Bayes theorem. The challenge lay in obtaining consistent results in different settings to replicate the 91.8% accuracy achieved by the AAPHelp system. Case in point: the most senior physician in the same study was only able to achieve a diagnostic accuracy of 79%.[96] Bayes theorem measures the likelihood a patient would have a disease based on the likelihood of specific symptoms exhibited in his medical history. The problem is doctors in different settings have different views or perspectives of what constitute even the most obvious symptoms, let alone those related to AAP. Add to this, Bayesian calculations mandate that a patient's history be entered in a specific way via a rigid set of data points into the AAPHelp system. Sound familiar? An example of an immutable mobile is printed press, insofar as ideas on paper travel unedited across locations, rather than rely on word of mouth and the accompanying likelihood of revision. A still more immutable example is a diagram or number that reduces the likelihood of misinterpretation that can result from reading the same printed text. Probability, an output of the Bayesian computation performed by AAPHelp, is an exemplification of the former. This same probability can be compared with like data from multiple varied medical facilities; it is mobile in that we can compare it quickly and easily without going through, as if were, voluminous patient history that is easily susceptible to more than one interpretation.

Yet, AAPHelp, the software producing this probability, is anything but. What constitutes a symptom, or a group of symptoms, can significantly impact the calculation of the likelihood of AAP. Other sites were not able to achieve the same 91.8% probability because even among like professionals in the same industry, not everyone can agree on the same symptom let alone abide with the staged rigor in inputting these into AAPHelp. For Latour, immutable mobiles "have the properties of being mobile but also immutable, presentable, readable, and combinable with one another."[97] Thus, even though the AAP diagnostic accuracy of 91.8% is mobile in that it can be used to compare against data across sites and immutable through the same application of the same Bayesian formula on the same data, the means of obtaining the likelihood of AAP, in this case AAPHelp, is neither immutable nor mobile. There is too great of a margin of error that goes into the input of the Bayesian formula. Perhaps not coincidentally the reception at other locations is less than positive precisely because of the arduous means necessary in collecting data. Arguably, AAPHelp fails to be an effective immutable mobile by taking on too much. The reverse can be said for SaaS. It succeeds in becoming an immutable mobile by taking on too little. Think back to the last SaaS you had to use or implement. Rather than rely on it in a Web 1.0 format as a source of information or Web 2.0 to post and share information, are you able to perform predictive analytics like AAPHelp, so that based on quarter over quarter operating expenses seen over the past 3 years, you can attempt to project future spending if the organization continues to operate at the same run rate?

Precisely because it can become too imbued with the local requirements and contingencies of its production, Professor of Social Medical Sciences Marc Berg argued, back in 1997, that software isn't portable.[98] He joined a growing chorus of researchers who point to the difficulties adopters face with implementing "commodified" solutions despite the vendors' repeated claims of innate flexibility to accommodate even the most idiosyncratic of settings. When we dive into a study of a student administration system conducted by Pollock and Williams, it isn't hard to see why.[99] Built on a generic kernel, the software provider's approach was to use templates that form the outer layer of the software package to meet local needs.[100] Recall our snake-shedding-skin motif, so that instead of new attributes, the SaaS merely takes on new templates each with their associated attributes. The metadata tables in the SaaS multi-tenant architecture also comes to mind. Students in my *Accounting Information Systems* class who have difficulty understanding PaaS tend to think of WordPress which lets users create their own websites using different templates, even though a PaaS is a platform that lets you host services, applications, storage, and analytics, among others. Yet with each new customer, the vendor providing the student administration system quickly experienced a snowball effect where the need to build out new or update existing templates far outstripped any possibility of ever gaining a wider target audience outside of academia.[101] Which brings us to the configuration of SaaS: is it based on an idealized input criteria that itself merits further review? Just as only the most senior researcher could barely achieve a diagnostic accuracy of 79% for an AAPHelp system that is purported to yield up to 91.8% accuracy in controlled settings, to what extent is the configuration of the SaaS inherently fragile? We talked about configuring the SaaS to make it less fragile, or conversely, more forgiving, but here we are going a step farther: to the extent that the SaaS has been configured, is the configuration itself fragile or forgiving?

In Chapter 2, we discussed the challenges faced in selecting the right purchase items when creating a purchase requisition, so users may get confused between choosing a prepaid or fixed asset. In the procurement SaaS, a key control may be designed to restrict access to make changes to the accounts assigned to purchase items, since inappropriate changes to the mapping may impact the way the spending is ultimately accounted for. Yet, this control is inherently fragile as it doesn't yet quite go far enough to provide guidance to end users on what items to use in the first place. It is less than forgiving when after a requisition with the incorrect item has been approved, it can no longer be changed, necessitating a manual update downstream elsewhere.

Another example is a purchase requisition approval workflow configured within the SaaS, such that whenever a user creates a requisition it is immediately routed to the user's direct supervisor or manager for approval in accordance with companywide authorized approval limits. At first glance, this control seems robust until that is when one user attempts to copy an existing requisition created by another user. What better way to figure out what item to use than to replicate an existing approved requisition? Yet, by doing so, the user inadvertently copies over the user who created the first requisition so instead of routing the second requisition to the user's supervisor for approval, the SaaS routes it back to the first user's manager.

In this respect, the SaaS workflow configured is more fragile to the different permutations that a user behavior may take on, less forgiving to the lack of user knowledge on the *right* items to select and use.

A third example is the submission of project timesheets through a time and expenses (T&E) SaaS that in turn routes them for supervisory approval before payment. What is to prevent consultants from submitting hours that exceed those already committed in an executed statement of work? Here, fragility extends beyond a singular SaaS insofar as the artifacts at hand, timesheets and statements of work, can and likely do reside in different systems. While the T&E SaaS may appear forgiving to consultants who incur overage hours, it is ultimately less forgiving to customers and account managers who are confronted with overage billing and the possibility of having to extend customer credit as a demonstration of good faith.

In the final analysis, whether the technology is indifferent to a myriad of uses or integrations (recall iPaaS), whether users decide to take up the option of configuring a software beyond what is offered out-of-the-box, depends a great deal on their level of indifference to the outcome. If we were to take on Carr's perspective of how SaaS customers just don't care enough to be drinking out of the same Kool-Aid for a service as ubiquitous and yet requisite as say payroll, then the level of configuration enacted may merely be a one-time implementation affair.[102] If, on the other hand, the SaaS in question is intended to be integrated with either custom software developed in house or other third-party SaaS products in ways that are specific to the way goods and services are either purchased or sold or employees hired or paid within the organization, and that this configuration is recognized as a core competency that is likely to put the organization in good stead when it comes to edging out competitors, then it is likely that the users would adopt a much more SaaS-y stance rather than continue with a hitherto Chinese wall approach inherited from on-premise software.

Crossing this line to embrace a more proactive approach to SaaS configuration requires a shift in mindset not unlike compelling developers to undertake a new methodology to develop software. When developers, for example, who are accustomed to waterfall techniques of developing software, with its carefully delineated phases of requirements, coding, testing, release, and maintenance, are asked to switch to a more Agile way of developing software, one that emphasizes 2-week sprints to evidence a working prototype essentially favoring working software over formalized processes, find it easy to slip back into "old" ways of seeing, so that, in effect, the sprints amount to a series of mini-waterfalls, where the prototype presented each time needs to be production ready and compliant in *all* respects. Waterfall is not unlike structured programming, which Turkle describes, as relying on a master plan where what the program does is first defined and each task is broken down into discrete sub-procedures.[103]

Developed by 17 self-professed organizational anarchist in a Utah resort in 2001, Agile seeks to undo this regimented and micromanaged style. In place of traditional waterfall software development life cycle (SDLC), where different phases are distinctly segregated and sequenced, Agile favors iterative increments over long-term planning, with each iteration involving a cross-functional team working together on all aspects: planning, requirements analysis, design, coding, unit testing, and acceptance testing.[104] While an iteration may not add enough functionality to warrant a market release, the goal is to have an available release with minimal bugs at the end of each sprint as well as to address any misconceptions or gaps that arise.

Compared to developers, auditors are even more susceptible to succumbing to waterfall-like tendencies in the design of internal controls in organizations employing Agile, by first mapping *all* accounts with financial impact, identifying *all* business cycles, walking through and validating *all* key controls, reporting test results, performing remediation testing on *all* impacted controls before presenting their findings to management, with severity of exceptions differentiated by degrees of anticipated financial impact, from material to significant to control deficiencies. It is no wonder that despite the advances made in delivering working software sooner rather than later, with an increased emphasis and thus accountability to outcome, the means of validating that only authorized, valid, and correct changes are deployed continues to be accountable to audit's waterfall sense and sensibilities rather than one that is more aligned to the nouveau Agile approach. In my *Accounting Information Systems* class, when asked what audit artifacts would be in use at an Agile engagement, students' first responses tend to favor traditional software development life cycle (SDLC) artifacts, such as functional specification signoffs over sprint burndown or velocity charts. In this case, waterfall audits remain blissfully indifferent to Agile. Indifference here is seen in a more negative light.

Thus far, when we talk about indifference, we have viewed it as an ability to stay immutable while amenable to change, less fragile as it were to insults to integrity or conversely more forgiving, but I am aware of a more commonly used definition of indifference, one that literally means not caring enough, to the point where any response, even vociferous opposition, is preferable. There are parallels that can be drawn between the use of SaaS against Agile principles. Just as SaaS gives us the ability to handle change precisely through configuration as a service, or CaaS, it exemplifies a key precept in the Agile Manifesto that relates to the ability to handle last minute changes. Waterfall or SDLC with its insistence on having all requirements captured before development commences, and having testing begin only after coding is completed, suffers under its own weight of specification upon specification, code upon code, and test result upon test result with last minute changes adding to more documentation to the beat of an almost logarithmic growth.

For those of you who are interested in how waterfall came about, check out *Managing the Development of Large Software Systems*, one of the earliest papers by Dr. Winston Royce, whom some consider a grandfather of SDLC. Published in 1970, you will find mention of mini-prototypes testing early on in outlined SDLC phases as a means of revisiting or checking up on earlier assumptions or requirements. Yet, what gets passed on through the ages isn't so much the iterative nature of software development but the emphasis on contractual obligations, a relay race where the baton is handed off from business analysts to developers to testers to operations.[105] In this light, the official account of SDLC that gets handed down through the generations mirrors the contractual as opposed to actuarial reading of a medical record as described by Garfinkel, so that when the software deployed to production malfunctions and needs to be rolled back, we can point back to SDLC artifacts to ask if the fault in the stars lies with the analysts, developers, testers, operations, or the end customers. Despite SDLC's emphasis on documentation, Dr. Royce saw the value in artifact reuse even back then, proposing that "the documentation is the specification and is the design."[106]

In circling back to Chapter 2, recall how the software at hand, SaaS or on-premise, requires an almost SDLC approach, that all requisition attributes needed to be completed before saving it in the system. To be sure, this is less than forgiving. It doesn't quite let the user create a requisition way ahead of time if only to give upfront notification to management of a potential spend, which after all is one of the key objectives of procurement management. Compared to their on-premise predecessors, while SaaS is much more affordable for small- and medium-sized companies with the option to dial up or down on usage where needed, the question that needs to be asked is: can nontechnical users inherit what is at first generic and out-of-the-box and incorporate more Agile-like thinking into its design, so that the emphasis isn't so much on obtaining all discrete data elements upfront prior to entry in the SaaS, so as to not inconvenience it with inevitable gaps or likely inaccuracies, but to allow room for the iterative layering of detail the more the software is put to use.

After all, as we have seen with SDLC, initial requirements change. What is deemed important may be relegated to a nice-to-have only because out-of-the-box SaaS functionality has not been taken into consideration. Conversely, what is not emphasized may rise to the center of attention when only needed to handle real-life exigencies. We can well benefit from applying a layered approach with each ensuing Agile sprint to the way we consider and capture transactions, so that even if not all pieces of information are available at the outset, these by no means prevent us from recording a prototype of sorts early rather than late, with an emphasis on outcome and effective procurement management of future spending, rather than process, what is approved by whom and when. With less emphasis on process decorum, staging, a key ingredient in Boyle's demonstration of the air pump, matters less in an Agile world, where the SaaS configurations are tweaked each time when pushed up against life's hard knocks as it were. To counter against incomplete or inaccurate information during initial entry, we could configure custom records that through in-flight, draft, or work-in-progress statuses would allow users to retrace initial steps or reverse their actions, so that proactively notifying management of anticipated spending is not quite as onerous.

Thus far, when speaking of fragility and forgiveness, I have used these almost interchangeably so that what is less fragile is in effect more forgiving. Yet, for some, forgiveness applies after the fact when something has gone awry. Hence, the common refrain: I would rather ask for forgiveness than permission. For all the emphasis auditors place on preventive over detective controls, a setup can be deemed more forgiving if sufficient compensating detective controls exist to mitigate what hasn't yet been prevented. Fragility in this sense is more synonymous with preventive controls that prevent the errors or fraud from even arising in the first place. As we have seen with Coupa and Workday, despite the downtimes experienced, the setup was less susceptible to failure, or more forgiving precisely because of the emphasis placed on remediation and thus detective measures. And yet at a more micro subprocess level, even when it comes to prevention, when the transaction for entry is barely complete or where uncertainties still abound, we could configure the SaaS at hand to allow these to be entertained at the outset, rather than continue to simmer behind the scenes.

Ironically, by allowing for the possibility of gaps in the initial admission criteria for data in a transparent manner, the SaaS would promote a more complete capture of attributes ultimately. In this sense, being more forgiving or accepting of initial uncertainty makes the SaaS less fragile to insults to integrity so that what is omitted or incompletely entered continues to be augmented to align with real-life conditions over time. What is more immutable or mobile? A less than forgiving and thus more fragile software incapable of handling messy data unless these conform to stringent admission criteria or one that is truly configurable to handle real-life curveballs. We can argue that by forcing users to subscribe to its system paradigm, the software is an immutable mobile even if users are coerced into a standard input process and ultimately have to resort to manual workarounds. Yet there is a different way we can define an immutable mobile; because SaaS is configurable. Recall the Microsoft researchers' description of a metadata table housing custom fields defined by its tenant ID.[107] It remains immutable yet no less mobile precisely because customers have an ability to tailor it to meet specific needs without threatening its underlying multi-tenant architectural integrity.

An ease that comes with configuring SaaS is much like smashing a black box, so that its contents are no longer one of mere indifference to nontechnical layman users. This is real work. Instead of pointing the finger back at a VAR or ASP and mandating that they deliver per agreed specifications, the SaaS enterprise client is held accountable to configuring the way the SaaS would work in an optimal manner in local environments. Doing so requires real effort more than mere indifference on the part of users and administrators alike, and yet the outcome, even as it takes on new colors in each Agile-like iteration, is oddly more robust, less fragile, more forgiving and, therefore, more indifferent to potential insults to architectural and transactional integrity. In place of an audit within an audit, we have difference within indifference, for the proposition put forth here is to pay attention to local differences and undertake the necessary work to configure the SaaS as such.

Having an exhaustive set of requirements ironed out ahead of time before embarking upon configuration work brings to mind a specific image. Picture mid-1840s Western settlers embarking on the rocky Oregon trail weighed down by family heirlooms like mirrors, rocking chairs, iron stoves, and even pianos. Faced with seemingly insurmountable winding trails through the high mountains, they would soon discover what was at first thought of to be indispensable, not to mention held dear, would soon become dispensable, so that by 1875, a litter of furniture stretched out as far as the eye can see across Wyoming. From an internal control perspective, however, we run the risk of becoming indifferent to the volume not to mention complexity of SaaS configurations that have amassed over time. Much like how the use of the digital camera or mobile phone has resulted in voluminous photos with scant attention paid to the limitation of physical film rolls, SaaS enterprises are rapidly approaching a state where not enough attention is spent on monitoring or controlling for configuration changes so that a control lag exists between the time configurations are updated to the time they are controlled for.

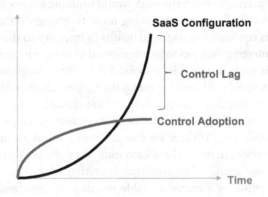

It is here when universal indifference – the indifference to the ease and extent of configurational change that can be wrought over time by nontechnical users – is of concern. Risks are compounded when we speak of key custom fields that are updated unknowingly without assessing the impact on other custom fields, records, workflows, or scripts. Fields updated or optimized for use in one upstream SaaS – for example updating the identifiers for locations to be more in line with International Organization for Standardization (ISO) codes in order for management SaaS to streamline reporting – may have implications for how they would work downstream. In this case a downstream sales tax computation SaaS may rely on default identifiers preset for locations to be able to effectively compute line level tax. Another example is the volume of exception emails generated when transactions do not sync from one SaaS to another. How do we sift out the false positives if only to be able to timely respond to a *real* exception? Much like the cascading inscriptions of control upon control described earlier, the cascading inscriptions of configuration upon configuration can prove to be formidable black boxes over time, even if their inception in the beginning started with breaking of a black box. Perhaps this is the inevitable Hegelian circle: thesis, antithesis, and synthesis.

Back to my career of residence moves, if I had kept a little black book of my trials and tribulations, itself an immutable mobile of sorts, one that I can keep turning to, in times of whimsical need for déjà vu, what would be recorded? Despite the sheer physicality of a move from a 50-unit building to a 3-unit condo to a duplex, the book alone, the very artifact used to communicate or combine with other narratives or points of view, would contain all moves. The things I remember, the way I remember them, salient facts and nuances, would vary if we were to consult another person's little black book of moves. In place of annoyances from intrusive neighbors and changes to living furniture, she or he may be more intent on nearby shopping or food options and depending on whether kids are in the equation, childcare facilities or schools within easy reach. Imagine that in place of the black book, a tablet is available for me to record, as if were, a diary of moves. Yet, upon opening it, I find preprogrammed categories to complete – from nearby childcare facility to best pizza parlor for getting a late-night snack – all of which seem highly irrelevant. What if I had the option of erasing all these categories to start from scratch? It would have been a lot more work surely, but this is a one-time cost in exchange for future payoffs that I can reap, and continue to reap, so long as I set them up right to begin with. This is the beginnings of what it means to avail ourselves of the configurability options that come with SaaS, without been inundated or weighed down at the outset as organizations invariably do, by accounting, audit, or compliance demands.

Now imagine a different scenario. This time I developed my own black tablet of sorts and attempt to sell it to other users. When pressed about daycare facilities or preschools, I respond that these are not available out-of-the-box, and quite frankly from a security perspective, it matters more than a common wall or shared laundry facility with neighbors is captured rather than childrearing practices that should belong to a different app altogether. This is like saying that the management evidencing of vendor assessments and of contract execution should belong outside of the accounting SaaS at hand for what can be more important than the debits and credits to the right general ledger accounts and evidence of approval from approvers with the right authorization limits? The examples we have covered in this chapter all compel us to take a second look, in the oft-chance that we may see what we overlooked. In place of La Perouse's voyage to the Pacific, "the only real voyage of discovery" for Marcel Proust "would be not to visit strange lands but to possess other eyes, to behold the universe through the eyes of another."[108]

For all our emphasis on admission criteria and preventive controls, it seems to me that we are more concerned with getting in data right the first time at the expense of omitting data that is less than idealized, in other words unstructured or messy. The focus is on accuracy at the expense of completeness and validity.

Preventive controls help not just in reducing the level of substantive testing when it comes to audits and tests of internal controls, they also ensure that errors are resolved at close to the source, ideally prior to system entry. And yet, as we have seen, this unwittingly excludes less than complete data that is nevertheless relevant. The trick then is not to exclude everything at the outset but to figure out how much to exclude. When the data has made its way in, the trick then is to figure out how much to include, and when to stop. An accounting SaaS is after all beholden to month-end close and financial reporting periods. It is a subtle balance of sorts, trading the needs for data completeness on the one hand and accuracy on the other. All too often, the focus is on speed of capture, even if the data admitted is nebulous at best and remains nebulous even as it is synced with other SaaS downstream.

I am reminded of a 6-year old blogging service, JournalSpace.[109] When a disgruntled employee deleted data in its primary disk, the secondary disk was swiftly overwritten thanks to disk mirroring.[110] With no other means of backup, bloggers who hosted their sites using the platform lost all their data.[111] In the context of interconnected SaaS, when speed of data capture is emphasized over quality, downstream manual efforts need to be undertaken to correct errors in data downstream without addressing the root cause upstream. A vicious cycle of firefighting ensues. As we contrast my fictitious example of a little black book or tablet with the SaaS at hand, patterns start to surface, if only to shed more light on what we have hitherto taken for granted whether it is the way we account for transactions in the context of SaaS or the way accounting as a purported universal language manages to insinuate itself into the very fabric of our every day. In a sense, whether the residence moves happen or not becomes a moot question, I alone contain all the moves, multitudes to invoke Walt Whitman.[112] The little black book, tablet, or SaaS functions like an immutable mobile surely but also like a language. The question becomes: can memory survive without a language?

Exercise 3.1

Software is not hardware. Yet, in our dealings with software, to what extent do we treat software not like software but like hardware when it comes to:

1. Assessing changes to user requirements
2. Auditing software
3. Developing new reports or queries using the software or SaaS at hand

To what extent is any of the earlier made easier when working with SaaS?

Discussion

Planning and executing changes to software is not as easy as making changes to hardware. In Dr. Winston Royce's 1970 paper, *Managing the Development of Large Software Systems*, to procure a five-million-dollar hardware device, he estimated a 30-page specification.[113] In contrast, for the same dollar value spent on software, he estimated a 1,500-page specification.[114] He gave various reasons for the increase in page count, all boiling down to necessary communications among different stakeholders from requirements to coding to testing to operations. Yet, with SaaS, to what extent have the challenges we experienced with on-premise software been truly addressed? Are we still working with a wolf dressed in sheep's clothing? Are we really talking about, and to employ Ellison, "women's fashion"?[115] To begin a dialogue on internal controls for SaaS, we must first be able to identify key differences between SaaS, and its predecessor, on-premise software.

Exercise 3.2

Select a software in use in your enterprise.

1. How configurable is it? If it is configurable, who performs the configuration within your organization? Has it been fully tapped for its configuration potential?
2. To what degree are users configured by the software rather than the other way? In other words, can you think of examples where unsuspecting users are roped into the way the software views and records events as transactions even if these do not correspond with how things truly work out?

Discussion

It is interesting how when we look back at a recent software implementation, we may arrive at the same conclusion as the one Pollock described earlier: "Big Civic changed its processes to match the system rather than the other way round."[116] In some ways, when we have a knife in our hands, every object in sight suddenly looks ready to be sliced at. Upon learning SPSS, a statistical computer program, in college, I remember how eager I was at applying it to all and sundry in the non-profit world I was volunteering in with scarcely a moment's hesitation. Often, in Agile retrospectives performed after a system go-live, lessons learned surfaced scope creep and herein, a glimpse into the ways we all too easily erect a science of cascading inscriptions over and over on manual processes and people, under the auspice of sharing industry best practices. SaaS, to the extent it can be configured afresh, offers a window of possibility in averting this outcome.

Exercise 3.3

1. Think back to a recent software or project implementation in your organization. Which methodology was used: SDLC or Agile?
2. Review McNay's four organizational archetypes: collegium, bureaucracy, corporation, and enterprise. Which archetype does your organization most resemble? To what extent does your organization's archetypal profile lend itself more readily to Agile versus SDLC?
3. Agile and SDLC mindsets extend beyond new software implementation or enhancements.
   - When entering transactions in a software in use, to what extent are we operating under an SDLC or Agile mindset?
   - When mandating approvals for transactions in specific statues, to what degree are we tapping into SDLC or Agile concepts?
   - When auditing systems and transactions with financial impact, to what degree are we tapping into SDLC or Agile concepts?

Discussion

Upon closer inspection, Agile or SDLC methodologies reveal much deeper patterns about the way we require requirements to be communicated, the way we expect stakeholders to be knowledgeable of requirements, the way we expect requirements in turn to be locked down and arrested in time, even if in our personal affairs, we are unsure of, and often find, ourselves in situations fraught with uncertainty and change. To what extent are internal controls built on theorized accounts that require much staging and delivered on aplomb rather than actual results? While subsuming all too readily to longstanding cascading inscriptions, they nonetheless serve as poignant reminders of actual activities that continue to reside elsewhere, unscripted and off the page.

Endnotes

[1] de, Botton. A. (2014). *The News: A User's Manual.*

[2] Garfinkel, S. and Abelson, H. (1999). ed. *Architects of the Information Society, Thirty-Five Years of the Laboratory for Computer Science at MIT.* Cambridge, MA: MIT Press.

[3] Ibid.

[4] United States Securities Exchange Commission. (September 8, 2016) Form S-1 Registration Statement Under The Securities Act of 1933. https://www.sec.gov/Archives/edgar/data/1385867/000119312516705441/d144637ds1.htm

[5] Coupa Success Portal (October 12, 2017). System Up Time and Metrics. https://success.coupa.com/Trust/System_Up_Time_and_Metrics#February+2017

[6] AWS. Summary of the Amazon S3 Service Disruption in the Northern Virginia (US-EAST-1) Region. https://aws.amazon.com/message/41926/

[7] Ibid.

[8] Clarke, D. (July 29, 2015). Workday's journey to zero downtime: Progress report. *Workday Blog.* https://blogs.workday.com/workdays-journey-to-zero-downtime-progress-report/

[9] Weier, M. H. (October 9, 2009). Is workday's 15-hour SaaS outage acceptable? *InformationWeek.* https://www.informationweek.com/cloud/is-workdays-15-hour-saas-outage-acceptable/d/d-id/1083850

[10] Krigsman, M. for *Beyond IT Failure* (October 8, 2009). Workday, SaaS, and failure: 'A matter of trust'. *ZDNet.* http://www.zdnet.com/article/workday-saas-and-failure-a-matter-of-trust/

[11] Ibid.

[12] Ibid.

[13] Ibid.

[14] Shankland, S. (February 25, 2009). Salesforce.com squeezes $1B from the cloud. *CNET.* https://www.cnet.com/news/salesforce-com-squeezes-1b-from-the-cloud/

[15] Chong, F., Carraro, G., and Wolter, R. (2006) Multi-tenant data architecture. Tech. rep., MSDN Library, Microsoft Corporation

[16] Ibid.

[17] Ibid.

[18] Ibid.

[19] Ibid.

20 Wainewright, P. (September 6, 2013). How workday does cloud. *diginomica*. https:// diginomica.com/2013/09/06/workday-cloud/

21 Ibid.

22 Ibid.

23 Ibid.

24 Malik, O. (October 27, 2009). AWS Woos Corporates With Price Cuts, New Products. Gigaom. https://gigaom.com/2009/10/27/amazon-cuts-ec2-price-offers-relational-database-as-a-service/

25 Netflix Technology Blog. (September 24, 2015). Chaos engineering upgraded. The Netflix Tech Blog. https://medium.com/netflix-techblog/chaos-engineering-upgraded-878d341f15fa

26 Carr, N. G. (2008). *The Big Switch: Rewiring the World, from Edison to Google*. New York: W.W. Norton & Company.

27 Ibid.

28 Singh, M. (March 22, 2017). Salesforce hacks for a successful admin/developer. *Forcetalks*. https://www.forcetalks.com/blog/salesforce-hacks-for-a-successful-admin- developer/

29 Salesforce Developers. Salesforce App Developer Guide. When to use declarative vs. programmatic tools to create Salesforce Apps. https://developer.salesforce.com/docs/ atlas.en-us.salesforce1.meta/salesforce1/dev_salesforce1_clicks_vs_code.htm

30 Mell, P. and Grance, T. (October 7, 2009). The NIST definition of cloud computing. The National Institute of Standards and Technology (NIST), Version 15. https:// www.nist.gov/sites/default/files/documents/itl/cloud/cloud-def-v15.pdf

31 Ibid.

32 Salesforce Press Release. (November, 2013). Salesforce.com Introduces Salesforce1. https://www.salesforce.com/company/news-press/press-releases/2013/11/131119.jsp

33 McLaughlin, K. (November 18, 2013). Salesforce expands APIs, rolls out new platform for mobile developers. *CRN*. http://www.crn.com/news/applications-os/240164063/ salesforce-expands-apis-rolls-out-new-platform-for-mobile-developers.htm

34 Ibid.

35 Ibid.

36 Ibid.

37 Odlyzko, A. and Tilly, B. (March 2, 2005). A refutation of Metcalfe's Law and a better estimate for the value of networks and network interconnections. Digital Technology Center, Minneapolis, MN: University of Minnesota. http://www.dtc. umn.edu/~odlyzko/doc/metcalfe.pdf

38 Pezzini, M. and Lheureux, B. J. (March 7, 2011). Integration platform as a service: Moving integration to the cloud. *Gartner*. https://www.gartner.com/doc/1575414/ integration-platform-service-moving-integration

39 Rosoff, M. (October 12, 2011). Jeff Bezos "Makes ordinary control freaks look like Stoned Hippies," Says Former Engineer. *Business Insider*. http://www.businessinsider. com/jeff-bezos-makes-ordinary-control-freaks-look-like-stoned-hippies-says-former-engineer-2011-10

40 Black, B. (January 25, 2009). EC2 Origins. http://blog.b3k.us/2009/01/25/ec2-origins.html

41 ZDNet Staff. (June 3, 2014). Amazon and Microsoft top Gartner's IaaS Magic Quadrant. http://www.zdnet.com/article/amazon-and-microsoft-top-gartners-iaas-magic-quadrant/

42 Johnsen, M. (October 6, 2014). Walgreens institutes developer challenge to spur Balance Rewards integration in health-focused apps. *Drug Store News*. http://www.drugstorenews.com/article/walgreens-institutes-developer-challenge-spur-balance-rewards-integration-health-focused-app

43 Williams, R. and Pollock, N. (December 6, 2008). *Software and Organizations: The Biography of the Enterprise-Wide System or How SAP Conquered the World*. London, UK: Routledge.

44 Larry Ellison's Brilliant anti-cloud computing rant, *The Wall Street Journal*, September 25, 2008.

45 Oracle Press Release. (July 28, 2016). Oracle Buys NetSuite. https://www.oracle.com/corporate/pressrelease/oracle-buys-netsuite-072816.html

46 Wahlberg, A. (July 29, 2016). Another billion dollar acquisition, Oracle Buys NetSuite. IT Key Media. https://itkey.media/another-billion-dollar-aquisition-oracle-buys-netsuite/

47 The Wall Street Journal's MarketWatch, NYSE Symbol "N". https://www.marketwatch.com/tools/quotes/lookup.asp?lookup=n

48 Pang, A. (January 18, 2017). Top 10 HCM Software Vendors and Market Forecast 2015–2020. https://www.appsruntheworld.com/top-10-hcm-software-vendors-and-market-forecast-2015-2020/

49 Ibid.

50 Latour, B. (1986). Visualisation and cognition: Drawing things together. *Knowledge and Society: Studies in the Sociology of Culture and Present*, 6: 1–40.

51 Ibid.

52 Ibid.

53 Ibid.

54 Ibid.

55 Norman, J. (1988). *Chinese*. Cambridge University Press.

56 Latour, B. Visualisation and cognition: Drawing things together.

57 Williams, R. and Pollock, N. (December 6, 2008). *Software and Organizations: The Biography of the Enterprise-Wide System or How SAP Conquered the World*. London, UK: Routledge.

58 Latour, B. Visualisation and cognition: Drawing things together.

59 Ibid.

60 Foucault, M. (1977). *Discipline and Punish : The Birth of the Prison*. New York: Pantheon Books.

61 Latour, B. visualisation and cognition: Drawing things together.

62 Ibid.

63 Fabian, J. (1983). *Time and the Other: How Anthropology Makes Its Object*. New York: Columbia University Press.

64 Latour, B. Visualisation and cognition: Drawing things together.

65 Williams, R. and Pollock, N. *Software and Organizations: The Biography of the Enterprise-Wide System or How SAP Conquered the World*.

66 Ibid.

67 Ibid.

68 McNay, I. (1995) From collegial academy to the corporate enterprise: The changing cultures of Universities in T. Schuller (Ed.) *The Changing University?* Buckingham, UK: SHRE/Open University Press.

69 Somerville H. and Menn J. (June 20, 2017). Uber CEO Travis Kalanick resigns under investor pressure. *Reuters*. https://www.reuters.com/article/us-uber-ceo/uber-ceo-travis-kalanick-resigns-under-investor-pressure-idUSKBN19C0G6

70 Diller, R. (June 25, 2015). French anti-uber protest turns to Guerrilla warfare as cabbies burn cars, attack uber drivers. *TechCrunch*. https://techcrunch.com/2015/06/25/french-anti-uber-protest-turns-to-guerrilla-warfare-as-cabbies-burn-cars-attack-uber-drivers/

71 Williams, R. and Pollock, N. *Software and Organizations: The Biography of the Enterprise-Wide System or How SAP Conquered the World.*

72 Ibid.

73 Ibid.

74 Ibid.

75 Lardinois, F. (February, 14, 2001). Heroku admits to performance degradation over the past 3 years after criticism from rap genius. *TechCrunch*. https://techcrunch.com/2013/02/14/heroku-admits-to-performance-degradation-over-the-past-3-years-after-criticism-from-rap-genius/

76 Ibid.

77 Ibid.

78 Somers, J. Heroku's ugly secret. Genius. https://genius.com/James-somers-herokus-ugly-secret-annotated

79 Latour, B. Visualisation and cognition: Drawing things together.

80 Ibid.

81 Lardinois, F. Heroku admits to performance degradation over the past 3 years after criticism from rap genius.

82 Latour, B. Visualisation and cognition: Drawing things together.

83 Wallison, P. J. (November 7, 2017). Statement before the house committee on financial services subcommittee on housing and insurance on sustainable housing finance. American Enterprise Institute. https://financialservices.house.gov/uploadedfiles/hhrg-115-ba04-wstate-pwallison-20171107.pdf

84 Ibid.

85 Ibid.

86 Ibid.

87 Ibid.

88 March J. G. and Simon, H. A. (1958). *Organizations*. New York: John Wiley & Sons.

89 Collodi, C., Murray, M. A., Leone, M., Pyle, H., and Leone, S. (1965). *The Adventures of Pinocchio*. New York: Grosset & Dunlap.

90 Eldridge-Smith, P. and Eldridge-Smith, V. (April 1, 2010). The Pinocchio paradox. *Analysis*, 70(2), 212–215. doi:10.1093/analys/anp173.

91 St. Jerome, Homily on Psalm 115 (116B), translated by Sr. Marie Liguori Ewald, IHM, in *The Homilies of Saint Jerome*, Volume I (1-59 On the Psalms), The Fathers of the Church 48 (Washington, DC: The Catholic University of America Press, 1964), 294.

92 Latour, B. Visualisation and cognition: Drawing things together.

93 Shapin, S. (November, 1984). Pump and circumstance: Robert Boyle's literary technology. *Social Studies of Science*, 14(4), 481–520.

94 Williams, R. and Pollock, N. *Software and Organizations: The Biography of the Enterprise-Wide System or How SAP Conquered the World.*

[95] de Dombal, F. T., Leaper, D. J., Staniland, J. R., McCann, A. P., and Horrocks, J. C. (1972). Computer aided diagnosis of acute abdominal pain. *British Medical Journal* 2, 9–13.

[96] Ibid.

[97] Latour, B. Visualisation and cognition: Drawing things together.

[98] Berg, M. (1997). *Rationalizing Medical Work: Decision-Support Techniques and Medical Practices*. Cambridge, MA: MIT Press.

[99] Williams, R. and Pollock, N. *Software and Organizations: The Biography of the Enterprise-Wide System or How SAP Conquered the World*.

[100] Ibid.

[101] Ibid.

[102] Carr, N. (2004). *Does IT Matter? Information Technology and the Corrosion of Competitive Advantage*. Boston, MA: Harvard Business School Press.

[103] Turkle, S. (1980). *Computer as Rorschach Society*,17, 15–24.

[104] Beck K., Beedle M., van Bennekum, A. et al. (2001). The Agile Manifesto.

[105] Royce, W. W. (1970). Managing the development of large software systems in: Technical papers of western electronic show and convention (WesCon). August 25–28, 1970, Los Angeles, CA.

[106] Ibid.

[107] Chong, F., Carraro, G., Wolter, R. Multi-tenant data architecture.

[108] Pinter, H., Trevis, D., and Proust, M. (2000). *Remembrance of things past*. London, UK: Faber.

[109] Budman, G. (January 5, 2009). JournalSpace shuts down due to no backups. Backblaze. https://www.backblaze.com/blog/journal-space-shuts-down-due-to-no-backups/

[110] Ibid.

[111] Ibid.

[112] Whitman, W. (1921). Song of myself by Walt Whitman.

[113] Royce, W. W. Managing the development of large software systems in: Technical papers of western electronic show and convention (WesCon).

[114] Ibid.

[115] Larry Ellison's Brilliant anti-cloud computing rant, *The Wall Street Journal*, September 25, 2008.

[116] Williams, R. and Pollock, N. *Software and Organizations: The Biography of the Enterprise-Wide System or How SAP Conquered the World*.

Chapter 4

Beginning Ending

> We remain ... prisoners of a language that has its
> roots in a way of life and a way of work that are fast
> becoming obsolete.[1]
>
> **Shoshana Zuboff**

In the 2016 science fiction film, *Arrival,* linguist Dr. Louise Banks is enlisted to communicate with one of 12 extraterrestrial spacecrafts scattered around Earth. Initially, the complicated circular symbols presented confound Dr. Banks. She gradually realizes that the aliens are really attempting to communicate a nonlinear perception of time. Like her daughter's name, Hannah – a palindrome – the sequencing of the film taps into our propensity to assume a linear sequence of events: what appears to be a series of flashbacks to the past throughout the film turns out to be future events that followed rather than preceded the arrival of the extraterrestrial crafts. Sound familiar in the context of purchase requisitions put together after the company has already received invoices? To the nondiscerning eye, it is as if the company created requisitions in a sequential manner prior to receiving the services or items, so that when viewed retrospectively by auditors and likely as support behind invoices, they appear as "flashbacks to the past" when they are really "future events" sequenced after the receipt of vendor invoices. There is also the question of whether the purchase should be read like a palindrome, so that when viewed from the start – requisition, followed by receipt and then vendor invoice and finally payment – or from the end (payment associated with invoice related to receipt recorded from requisition), we get to the same information regardless of where we begin, either upstream, downstream, or even midstream looking forward as well as looking back. Palindrome comes from the Greek roots *palin* (again) and *dromos* (direction).

This degree of consistency is important especially for transactions with financial impact processed in a Software as a Service (SaaS), and in many ways, becomes even more important when the company puts the same transaction through multiple SaaS, so creating a requisition in one SaaS, and receiving it in another, before billing and paying it out of a third SaaS. I was involved in one such implementation, where we were an early adopter of an expense reimbursement SaaS that introduced new procurement functionality into its product. If you think processing the entire requisition-to-receipt-to-invoice-to-payment flow in one application is complex enough, imagine the complexities when stringing it through multiple ones. Ironically, internal controls for SaaS don't give enough attention to the interface management that needs to be in place for multiple best-in-breed SaaS solutions for one singular transaction. Here is what Mol and Law had to say about medicine:

> *Medicine's current self-reflection is predominantly epidemiological in character. Epidemiology brings together disparate entities too, but its method of accounting isolates every so-called variable from all the others and is incapable of articulating links and tensions between them.*[2]

The same phenomenon applies to the development of internal controls for SaaS. Precisely because we can integrated it with other best-in-breed SaaS in tracing a transaction from cradle to grave, attention needs to be paid to the "links and tensions" among various interconnected SaaS. A company can distribute a less than fragile stance secured with preventive controls as described earlier to upstream SaaS, and more forgiving attributes to downstream SaaS via detective controls. Almost always, the financial SaaS that sits as the final stop ends up being in scope for the Sarbanes–Oxley Act (SOX) not just for financial reporting reasons but also most likely the source where companies employ compensating detective controls to review transactions synced from upstream SaaS where controls therein may be lax, and as such carved out of scope for audit. But even without relying on any one specific SaaS, a simple question that can come up is what happens if requisitions synced over from an upstream SaaS turned out to be coded to a wrong department? Can we resolve the fix in the downstream SaaS, and if so, what does this mean in terms of gaining a consistency (I am tempted to employ Latour's use of "optical consistency" when describing immutable mobiles from Chapter 3)[3] when viewing the cost center or department to which the invoice is coded and looking back upstream to the requisition? Do we lose something in translation? If so, what does it mean for internal controls over the management of departments or cost centers? For generally accepted accounting practices (GAAP) income statement reporting, companies typically roll up operating expenses into general and administrative (G&A), sales and marketing (S&M), and research & development (R&D) categories. In turn, departments, such as accounting, human resources, and facilities, typically roll up into G&A expenses, sales, business development, and marketing into S&M expenses, and engineering and product development into R&D expenses. Thus, how expenses come to be categorized has a different financial impact insofar as internal controls over financial reporting are concerned. More likely, in the day-to-day operational flow, companies may fail to sync requisitions because they didn't align the departments across upstream and downstream SaaS. In other words, the company may rename an existing department as part of a reorganization. If the company renames the accounting department to finance downstream, a requisition coded to the accounting department upstream is not likely to sync downstream. Ideally, a company builds exception reporting and handling into the inter-SaaS sync to address data completeness in terms of getting all valid and approved requisitions upstream synced downstream. Otherwise the company would have to perform manual reconciliations periodically if only to help with vendor invoice application or accruals reporting.

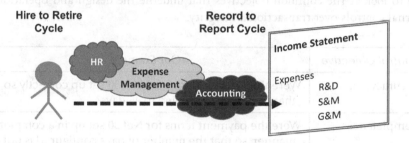

The same pattern is at work for onboarding a new hire. If a company enters a new hire into a human capital management SaaS in a G&A department such as information technology (IT) but it turns out later that they should have coded the hire to an R&D department such as engineering, then they would have to sync expenses such as those related to payroll and expense reports across to the downstream accounting SaaS with the wrong classifications impacting the way they present financials with G&A, S&M, and R&L rollup for operating expenses. While we can hardly expect an HR personnel entering the new hire's information to have an appreciation of the potential spillover impact on financial reports in terms of expense rollup on an income statement, this example highlights the importance of internal controls over upstream software that sync into an accounting SaaS deemed to have financial impact, simply because wrongly classified data in a SaaS (or a couple of SaaS – in our diagram, upstream SaaS include both human capital and expense management) deemed out of scope can nevertheless flow through to a downstream SaaS deemed in scope. Compensating mitigating detective controls downstream may be intervention too little too late if the company doesn't establish properly the right classifications upstream.

Even without layering in an additional SaaS or two, mistakes can happen within any one given SaaS. Three examples highlight the difference between a label and its contents. Payment terms labeled Net 30, 30 days from the invoice date upon which payment is expected, can nonetheless run askew, if the underlying configuration doesn't align with the label description – 45 days may be inadvertently set, or none may have been inputted altogether. In the former, even though the customer, after presumably having undergone a credit review and obligated through contractual agreements to pay their invoices in 30 days, nevertheless get an additional 15 days grace period as it were. In the latter, the opposite happens, so that the due date is the same as the invoice date. We may argue that the company needs to conduct an additional manual review to review payment terms, especially since these are the foundational blocks that drive invoice due dates, accounts receivable aging, and cash flow. Yet, viewed alternatively, and here we jump ahead in giving a brief preview of Chapter 9, what safety nets does the SaaS at hand provide to *catch* these slips or mistakes? For those of you who are wondering about the difference between slips and mistakes from a design perspective, Chapter 9 covers them, but it suffices here to look at the common objectives that underlie the design and operation of internal controls over transactional integrity.

Control Objective	Our Example
Accuracy	Were the payment terms for Net 30 set up correctly so that in effect it is not tied to 45 days?
Completeness	Were the payment terms for Net 30 set up in a complete manner, so that the number of days configured is not a missing entry?
Validity	Were changes to payment terms made with just cause, or authorization so that no duplicates exist?
Access	Which SaaS users have an ability to make changes to payment terms?
Audit Trails	In reviewing payment terms, how can we tell when and what changes have been made and by whom?

Another example of discrepancies between a label and its contents that can lead to pervasive impact is the setup of the chart of accounts. An account labeled as an expense can nevertheless show up on the balance sheet if the user incorrectly selects its account type as an asset or liability. A third example of a mismatch between a label and its contents is an invoice with a foreign customer billing address that the user has nevertheless assigned the United States as its billing country. This mismatch skews a report on revenue by billing country in terms of over-reporting revenue for the United States. For all three payment terms, chart of accounts, and billing addresses, manual reviews either before or after updates can serve as effective compensating manual controls, but the question that we need to ask is how does the SaaS at hand mitigate slips or mistakes from occurring more proactively, so that in effect the ensuing software design is less fragile, or more forgiving? Because payment terms, chart of accounts, and billing address relate to setup or master data rather than transactional data, any changes to them would likely have a pervasive impact.

And so, it is perhaps ironic that because not all SaaS is built the same, the same controls that address accuracy, completeness, validity, access, or audit trails for transactional data may not be available for setup or master data. In our example, when entering a sales order, even though the SaaS at hand assigns valid payment terms on the order drawing from terms set up on the customer record, checks for mandatory field completion, ensures that line level amounts add up to the total, and have associated access and audit trail capability to control for changes to orders, the same controls may not be available in the setup of terms, so that no system checks exist to validate if the Net 30 payment terms is truly Net 30, or Net 45, or Net 0, and no audit trails are available for investigating who has made what change when. For internal controls over transactional data to be ultimately effective, we would need the same controls over foundational setup or master data.

With each additional interface or integrated SaaS, made possible using web services or iPaaS, we see a compounding effect of overhead costs when it comes to the management of transactions in general and identification of missing transactions specifically. The same challenges can exist in the Order-to-Cash world. In continuing our earlier example on payment terms – what happens if Net 30 exists in an upstream SaaS but not in the integrated downstream one? Would the company sync over the transaction, and perhaps more importantly what controls exist to notify invested stakeholders of sync error? Or take a customer's sold-to address. When company syncs over a quote from an upstream SaaS such as Salesforce onto a downstream one such as NetSuite for sales order capture, does the sales order inherit the customer's default sold-to address in NetSuite? If so, would it matter that there is a difference between the sold-to address captured in NetSuite versus Salesforce? Depending on the type of product sold, the customer may not receive it because of an incorrect sold-to address. Sold-to address also has sales tax implications if it turns out the different sold-to addresses belong to different tax jurisdictions. Just as file-based systems suffered from data isolation and duplication issues arising from each program housing its own data, one SaaS may be able to handle having multiple bill-to or ship-to addresses for one customer, whereas another, far less flexible, would require multiple entities created for the same customer each assigned to a unique bill-to or ship-to address. It is anyone's guess as to what comes across ultimately in a downstream reporting SaaS. An upstream transaction processing SaaS used for billing or invoicing customers may support the ability to lock periods, and this in turn raises the question of what would happen if the closure or locking of periods in this SaaS differs from that in a downstream financial reporting SaaS. What conflicts may result? For example, how would an enterprise prevent a user from opening a period in an upstream SaaS presumably to resolve specific bill to or ship to address discrepancies even as the same period remains locked in the downstream financial reporting SaaS? Would the changes sync over, and if so, in what period would the company classify them?

Thus far, I have described potential challenges in the maintenance of master or standing data – whether this be cost centers, departments, customers, vendors, or periods between the integrated SaaS. In many ways, this mirrors the meta-layer discussion we had from Chapter 2 that speaks not so much to the ability to handle change but the ability to handle change from a meta or abstracted layer that leaves the internal "kernel" so to speak immutable. There is another type of challenge: different SaaS may have different requisite fields that are mandatory, so what an upstream originating SaaS is able to sync over the downstream destination SaaS may deem incomplete. A workaround may be employing an integration Platform as a Service (iPaaS) to default all values to a specific field so that all synced over transactions reflect this plugged value where it lies waiting for hidden hands from accounting to work their magic, reclassing or recoding where appropriate. In the case of missing transactions that the system does not sync across, the company would have to make manual entries in the downstream SaaS to ensure that they record the appropriate impact. Our examples earlier reside in the world of Order-to-Cash, but we can just as easily apply the same patterns to Procure-to-Pay. If payable transactions, such as vendor invoices from an upstream procurement SaaS are not syncing over to a downstream financial reporting SaaS in a complete manner because of missing or misaligned cost centers, departments, or vendors, then expenses would have been under-reported, leading to a possible overstatement of net income if not for necessary "accrual" entries that would have to be exacted downstream to make up for what is missing upstream.

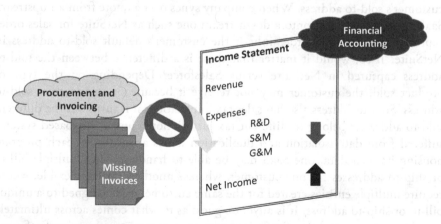

The amounts for these entries arise not so much from an aggregation of granular specific transactional amounts as from a month over month review of variances. Clearly, if the company pays a certain amount for recurring services for all its physical facilities each month and, for one month, fails to record these expenses in the downstream SaaS because of a failure to sync from an upstream SaaS, then the company can record a journal entry to capture the anticipated impact. Insofar as system validation or detection is not available or limited, the company needs to perform compensating manual work to review and validate the accuracy, completeness, and validity of transactional entries.

Less than likely usual suspects can also serve as useful aides in reconciliations or identification of missing transactions. Take the following setup: an upstream SaaS not unlike Shopify that records sales transactions initiated by customers from an online product catalog. They sync over these transactions as open customer invoices in a downstream accounting SaaS. An iPaaS syncs over payments from a payment processing gateway to the accounting SaaS and associates them with invoices brought in by the e-commerce one. If they fail to sync invoices synced across, the iPaaS would flag and report errors in recurring attempts to create and associate payments with non-existent invoices. In this manner, the company can harness the "links and tensions" among various interconnected SaaS to support the resiliency of the overall system at large in bolstering resiliency of operational flows.

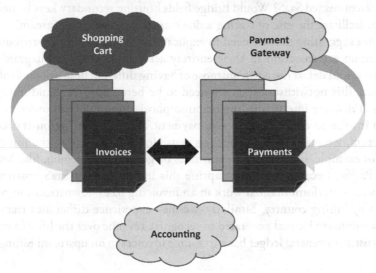

Lest we think this is too much work, the point of having an integration between an upstream and downstream SaaS is the efficiency cost savings in having to recreate some form of transactions to record impact downstream. We have already seen how manual accrual entries for unsubmitted or unapproved transactions upstream may or may not be precise to any transactional detail but may be based on month over month review. With integration, we gain a palindrome perspective when we can easily map one downstream entry to an upstream predecessor. This integration helps as well with account reconciliation and other downstream controls. The previous example relates to credit card payments for items checked out by customers from an online shopping cart. Consider a different example, wire payments from customers to whom the company has sent customer invoices. Imagine yet a different iPaaS that automatically syncs over and applies customer wire payments received in the company's operating bank account with the invoices flagged with open and unpaid in the accounting SaaS? For this to work, customers would have to include the invoice number in their wire payments. The invoice number attribute thus serves as a bridge field that "connects" the open outstanding invoices with received payments. Even if a customer were to fail to include the invoice number, the system would flag its wire payment as unapplied and put in a work-in-progress clearing queue ready for review. The accountant doesn't have to review and reconcile all received wire payments, only those with missing invoice numbers and amounts that don't quite tally, and thus can save time and resources in applying payments to invoices and reconciling bank accounts. Thus, when deploying or implementing a new SaaS or iPaaS, we need to reassess and unpack the assumptions that we have become accustomed with, while continuing to resonate in the old world of monolithic "ERP" software. Are a consistent set of key attributes maintained across all integrated SaaS? What happens if differences exist in the unique identifiers for the same transactions across two or more interconnected SaaS? Would bridge fields housing secondary keys be necessary if only to facilitate the ease of tracing a downstream transaction upstream?

I'm not suggesting that we need to explicate and replicate all the attributes that can make up a transaction in their entirety across two or more integrated SaaS because it would defeat the entire purpose of having different best-in-breed solutions altogether. This notwithstanding, we need to be better adept at handling specific nuances at discrete intervals in the metamorphosis from quote to order to fulfillment to invoice to credit card or wire payment. When reporting on transactions downstream, we may come up short on possible ways to analyze the numbers at hand. For example, if we were to report sales by geographical region, like Americas or Asia Pacific, because we didn't capture this in an ordering SaaS upstream, we would need to perform manual work in an invoicing SaaS downstream to compile numbers by billing country. Similarly, we may experience difficulties tracing the monthly summary journal generated to recognize revenue over the life of a contract in a downstream general ledger back to source invoices in an upstream billing SaaS.

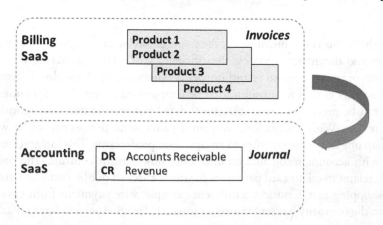

Had we not lost the product information in translation, we can conceivably review month over month revenue by product in the downstream general ledger without having to resort to Excel gymnastics in a bridge spreadsheet outside of the confines of SaaS. The use of Excel or other tools external to the SaaS is not in and of itself bad; after all, with SaaS, one of the functionalities we look for is the ability to bulk import mass transactions in Excel or csv. There are also other cloud solutions, FloQast for example, that alerts users of any difference between account balances in NetSuite reconciled with spreadsheets residing in Box, a cloud storage enterprise solution. But, in our example, the downstream reporting SaaS would have been more useful had it captured product level detail from its upstream billing counterpart without additional manual intervention.

By reading a transaction like a palindrome, I am in no way suggesting that it is in fact a palindrome. When we play with the idea of a transaction as a palindrome though, we start to see how our interpretation of the same transaction can change depending on our vantage. Often, the integrated SaaS mutually constitute the look and feel of the same transaction in one SaaS versus another. While we may find specific project details such as budget and resource in an upstream SaaS that tracks timecards for consultants, there would have been no need to sync across all this information in a downstream billing SaaS that invoices customers based on hours expended or milestones achieved. Even within the same SaaS, different data elements reside in different modules so that a journal entry in NetSuite would not have customer payment terms typically located in a sales invoice. Thus, the different functions afforded whether by module within the same SaaS or across multiple SaaS all play a hand in what a transaction looks like in one 'system' versus another. There is even a more fundamental form of reversibility at work, irrespective of whether the company made correct or incorrect entries. Backwards or forwards, an ideal SaaS would enable users to get to the same destination in more than a few ways. As an example, the accounts receivable team when getting a call from the customer should ideally be able to search for the customer in a Search bar, obtain a series of possible matches, select the right customer, and quickly scroll down to associated orders, fulfillments, invoices, credit, or payments. Alternatively, when given the invoice number on the phone, they should be able to just as easily locate the invoice by entering the unique document number in the Search bar. The revenue team on the other hand may get to this same transaction by working backwards, first from drilling down from the applicable revenue account on the income statement and obtaining a list of contributing children invoices, of which the invoice in question is a part of. A customer success or retention team may yet locate the invoice by working backwards from any credit memos applied. In more ways than one, we arrive at the same destination regardless of the origin.

When employing the palindrome metaphor, we are therefore not merely examining any one element but rather the overall mix of information. Does the total mix change owing to an omission or duplicate resulting from when viewing the same transaction whether across two or more modules within the same SaaS or across two or more SaaS? Historically, software revenue recognition has been a mutually constituted activity among varied elements. At its most basic form, we recognize revenue when we deliver software to the client, but what happens when it is a combination of license fees, training, and maintenance? If we deliver these elements at different times, how much revenue would we allocate to each element? This is when vendor-specific objective evidence (VSOE) comes in.

Bundle	VSOE Price	Actual Price	Recognized Amount
First item	60.00	49.95	52.42
Second item	20.00	19.95	17.48
Subtotal	80.00	69.90	69.90

VSOE refers to the price the market would pay for each stand-alone element, otherwise its fair market value. We allocate the eventual revenue among varied elements in a bundle based on VSOE. In the example above, the eventual revenue allocated to each item in the bundle is the actual price multiplied by the percentage of VSOE each element brings to the bundle. If we compute the above computations in a separate SaaS and synced then back to the general ledger (GL), then in effect when using the GL as a jumping-off point, would we have sufficient insight into key attributes both upstream and downstream?

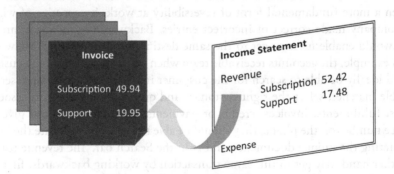

Would we be able to associate the recognized revenue amount with its actual price or product category on the sales invoice? In addition, if any one of the VSOE elements (VSOE price) were to change, this would alter the overall allocation, so the question becomes where does the change originate from, and how do we detect it? A change can come in the form of a separate change order, in which case how can we interlink the change order with the originating one? Conversely, we would expect other changes in the sales invoice presentation, an addition of a Remarks or Project Code field perhaps to better explain the nature of the sale to the customer, not to have an unintentional impact on the underlying VSOE elements. More fundamentally, if we can't establish the VSOE for any one element, we can't recognize revenue until the completion or delivery of all elements that make up a bundle – this impacts an enterprise's top-line revenue and financial health.

Even as I write this, Accounting Standards Codification 606 (ASC-606) is changing revenue recognition rules. Developed by the Financial Accounting Standards Board (FASB) and what some see as the biggest accounting change since SOX, the 606 rule takes effect in the periods after December 2017 and affects businesses with multi-year contracts, licensing revenue, contracts that peg revenue to performance benchmarks, or third-party sales distribution channels. The standard has the effect of deferring certain costs, such as sales compensation, while accelerating the recognition of revenue from certain customer contracts. Some see an adoption increasing reported profitability in the early years with movement of certain expenses to the balance sheet. Where applicable, 606 also has the impact of revisiting aspects of VSOE; to the extent individual elements have a specific performance obligation (such as fulfillment of time and material professional hours), companies may recognize these earlier ahead of the other elements of the bundle. It has thus been characterized as a principle-based methodology to recognize revenue rather than a rule-based, all or nothing approach.

The VSOE example demonstrates how various elements that can constitute revenue recognition in a way that is not obvious to the layman or naked eye. More than a need to not just establish relatedness or palindrome-like quality among upstream and downstream transactions such as sales order and fulfillment with an invoice, the amounts each element brings to the table in turn affects the amount that a company ultimately allocates as revenue. In effect, we must be able to work backwards from the allocated amounts to actual amounts communicated with the customer. As discussed, what happens in the event of a change order where the system updates existing line amounts or adds new lines? To the extent that the system relates new or updated lines to original ones, the companies need to thread these back to the original order lines. Had the company been replying on standalone selling price based on different quantity volume tiers, any increment or decrement of lines can change the overall allocation.

Thus, the ability to thread transactions not only applies to upstream or downstream records invariably of a different transaction type but can also refers to the same transaction type, in our case the sales order between the original order and the change order. Upsells, the ability to add incremental lines, is highly desirable for an organization not only keen on demonstrating gaining market share but also on the ability to increase depth of the products consumed by existing customers. In our example, the ability to leapfrog from an original order line to a change order line or vice versa, whether we are peering prospectively from an upstream SaaS or retrospectively from a downstream one, is a palindrome-like quality that would be highly desirable.

Amortization Schedule

Created From	Journal
Start Date	January 1, 2017
End Date	December 31, 2017
Originating Account	Prepaid
Total Schedule Amount	$120.00

Account	Period	Amount	Total Amortized
Expense	January 2017	$10.00	$10.00
Expense	February 2017	$10.00	$20.00
Expense	March 2017	$10.00	$30.00
Expense	April 2017	$10.00	$40.00
Expense	May 2017	$10.00	$50.00
Expense	June 2017	$10.00	$60.00
Expense	July 2017	$10.00	$70.00
Expense	August 2017	$10.00	$80.00
Expense	September 2017	$10.00	$90.00
Expense	October 2017	$10.00	$100.00
Expense	November 2017	$10.00	$110.00
Expense	December 2017	$10.00	$120.00

Our VSOE example is from Order-to-Cash, yet in the Procure-to-Pay cycle, accountants are likewise interested in threading amortization journal entries auto-generated by applying amortization schedules to upstream vendor invoices. Amortization may be required insofar as prepaid expenses are incurred and need to be distributed or amortized over the period of consumption. Creating the current period's amortization journals and tracing these back to original invoices every month may not be an easy task. When you think of this visually, an amortization schedule attached at the line level of an invoice item may in turn comprise multiple lines, for example, 12 for each month in 1 year for amortization. When running a report on the current period, the art of threading, or constructing the query criteria becomes critical as at any one time, there are multiple types of relationships. An amortization schedule has a one-to-one relationship with each invoice line just as each invoice line has a one-to-one relationship with an item or service for purchase. Yet, an amortization schedule in our example has a one-to-many relationship with the amortization amounts computed in the applicable periods. With each ensuing month, each successive line in the amortization schedule would have a one-to-one relationship with a journal entry automatically generated through bulk processing. On the other hand, a journal entry would likely have a one-to-many relationship with amortization schedules assuming one journal can have multiple lines, each relating to a unique amortization schedule associated with an invoice. When attempting to run a report threading through all these links, it is not uncommon for the report to throw up multiple "duplicate" lines considering how multiple lines corresponding to multiple periods in an amortization schedule all nevertheless relate back to one invoice line. If we are only interested in seeing the amortization amount in the current period, the ability to act like a palindrome would mean locating the eye of needle, such as reporting on computed amortization in one period for multiple invoices as opposed to all periods for one invoice.

What happens if at first a company incorrectly codes the vendor invoice to an expense account rather than a prepaid account on the balance sheet? The company enters a journal entry to reclass the amount to a prepaid account – the following illustration shows what happens when the company applies an amortization schedule to distribute the amounts to expense over 12 months. Yet, in this example, we lose the palindrome-like quality because we are no longer able to trace the amortized amount for the July period back to the originating vendor invoice.

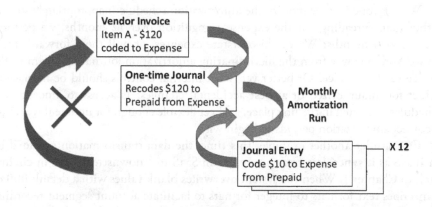

A scene from *Through the Looking Glass* comes to mind when the White Queen offers to hire Alice by paying her "two pence a week and jam every other day."[4] When Alice replies that she doesn't like jam, not today at any rate, the Queen counters,

"You couldn't have it if you did want it ... The rule is, jam to-morrow and jam yesterday – but never jam to-day."[5] When Alice responds, "It must come sometimes to jam to-day," the Queen replies, "It's jam every other day: to-day isn't any other day, you know."[6] Before an utterly befuddled Alice, the Queen explains, "That's the effect of living backwards ...It's a poor sort of memory that only works backwards."[7] When asked what she remembers best, the White Queen replies, "Oh, things that happened the week after next."[8] In a chapter on palindromes, where we can work forwards then backwards to see if we get to the same conclusion, and in the context of the prior example of reclassing the expense to prepaids after the fact when the customer has already received the service or good as well as the invoice, the way we account for things is remarkably similar to the way memory works for the Queen.

How we can trace how we fundamentally account for expenses to the beginning – is a prepaid item for purchase that is coded to a prepaid account chosen as part of a purchase requisition so that when it is approved and becomes a purchase order, the item selected is already correct and coded to the right account to begin with so that by the time it flows to an invoice, the accounting impact doesn't have to be updated? Think about this in context of implementing a fixed asset module within the accounting SaaS so that fixed assets procured are in turn recorded as fixed assets with specific lives for amortization within the software as opposed to manually computed in a spreadsheet. Part of going live with a fixed asset module or a different fixed asset SaaS altogether is in turn dependent on how we record the data at the onset. A journal entry that intervenes midstream to reclass the account impacted from an expense account on the income statement to a fixed asset account on the balance sheet breaks the link to the invoice, and correspondingly the link between the created fixed asset with its upstream invoice, receipt, and purchase order. In this regard, it makes little difference whether we implement the fixed asset module, if the way we account for items in purchases is remarkably different from the way we classify them ultimately in the GL.

What happens if we modify the amortization schedule inappropriately so that rather than spreading out the expense recognition over 12 months, we perform them over 6 months? We would overstate expenses, or pull them forward. How do we work our way from the incriminating amortization journal upstream to the source vendor invoice? Or better yet, what internal controls should be in place to detect for unauthorized or at best accidental changes? Is access to amortization schedules restricted in the first place, and yet flexible enough for update if we set up incorrect amortization periods to begin with?

Or consider another example, this time, the data transformation executed by an iPaaS as it syncs data from an upstream SaaS to a downstream one in circling back to Chapter 1. When the system overwrites blank values with a default 000 or transcribes text formats to integer formats to facilitate account segment recording in the downstream SaaS, how do we work backwards to the beginning to ensure that the transformation has been appropriate and not tampered with over time? What happens when the upstream SaaS undergoes configuration changes so that prior assumptions no longer hold true, that is, blank values no longer stay blank or alphanumeric formats supersede text formats? Would we need to update the iPaaS or would we need to configure the downstream SaaS to adapt accordingly? With the luxury of hindsight, would it be more scalable for the data augmentation to occur directly in the downstream SaaS if possible rather than scotch-tape together, as if were, a system of brittle assumptions and constants? Beyond this one singular exchange between two SaaS via an iPaaS, it is more likely that we are dealing with a spoke-and-wheel model so that we have multiple best-in-breed SaaS syncing with one another using more than one iPaaS with varied data acceptance formats.

Does it make sense to rely on the iPaaS to perform the data transformation? Depending on the degree of sophistication of the SaaS at hand, we may have to rely on the iPaaS. Yet, because different SaaS may have different data entry requirements, it may make more sense for us to first attempt data augmentation with the "terminal" SaaS where applicable, rather than burden the iPaaS with different even conflicting needs. With a traditional audit focus on end-point or terminal applications, and in our example, SaaS, this too would need to undergo a minor revision of sorts to account for the pivotal role of iPaaS. Who has access, what configurations changes occur, how often do we upgrade version, and the impact of either upstream or downstream SaaS upgrades on the continued functionality of the iPaaS at hand become areas of consideration when reviewing systems with financial impact under SOX.

A curious observation on the nature of rules: for the Queen, "the rule is, jam tomorrow and jam yesterday – but never jam to-day" even as Alice's countering claim is jam yesterday "must come sometimes to jam to-day."[9] In Chapter 3, we talked about the Pinocchio paradox. This time, consider Wittgenstein's rule paradox where "no course of action could be determined by a rule, because any course of action can be made out to accord with the rule."[10] To understand it, consider the following scene from *Through the looking Glass*, where the Queen, the Red Queen this time, reminds Alice, "Speak when you're spoken to!"[11] Alice counters, "But if everybody obeyed that rule, and if you only spoke when you were spoken to, and the other person always waited for you to begin, you see nobody would ever say anything."[12] It thus follows that if every course of action can be attributed to a rule, then in effect no one action truly is rule bound. To illustrate the reasoning that leads to this conclusion, Kripke gives a mathematical example with the following conditions:

- You have never added numbers greater than 50 before
- You are asked to perform the computation 68 plus 57[13]

You are inclined to give the answer 125. Yet suppose a skeptic came along and argues that because there is prior history of adding beyond 50, plus mean "quus" such that:

$$X \text{ quus } Y = \begin{cases} X + Y \text{ if } X, Y < 57 \\ 5 \text{ otherwise} \end{cases}$$

For the skeptic, the answer of 5 is just as applicable as 125. Now consider the following accounting impact of a customer payment.

	Debit	Credit
Customer Payment	Cash (5,000)	Accounts Receivable (5,000)

Both cash and accounts receivable sit on the balance sheet. So as part of a mid-term question on whether cash payments impact the balance sheet, income statement or both, the answer given by students in my *Accounting Information Systems* class is balance sheet. The GL impact of a customer payment is crediting the customer's accounts receivable (the customer owes the company less from an aging perspective) and debiting the operating bank account out of which the company accepts cash whether from check, credit card, wire, or ACH. Both accounts reside on the balance sheet. Yet, much like Kripe's mathematical example disputing what would appear to be an unambiguous application of rules, consider what happens when a company creates a foreign currency invoice in a subsidiary that has a base functional currency of U.S. dollars (USD).

	Debit	Credit
Customer Payment	Cash (5,500)	Accounts Receivable (5,000)
		Realized Gain (500)

If the invoice were in a currency different from the USD functional currency of the subsidiary between the time the company issued it and payment came in, the same local currency amount would have had different daily exchange rates applied to it. Thus, from a GL impact perspective, the USD currency amount recorded in the invoice would likely have fluctuated from the USD currency amount received during payment even if the local currency amount stays the same. The company would have recorded the difference between the two converted USD amounts to realized gains or loss on the income statement. In our previous example, we would have received $5,500 in our USD checking account with 500 recorded to realized gain because of the currency rate difference between the time the company records the invoice to the time the customer paid the invoice. Because of the magnitude of the gain, it is entirely a fictional example. Yet, in continuing with Kripe's mathematical example given by the skeptic, the formula would have been:

```
              ┌ DR Cash
              │ D/R A/R, Realized Gain/Loss
  Customer    │ if currency <> USD
  Payment   ─┤
              │ DR Cash
              │ CR A/R otherwise
              └
```

Therefore, a simple mental heuristic or rule that all customer payments only impact balance sheet would not have worked. At month end closure, when the company runs currency revaluation based on a monthly consolidated rate, the company records any further differences to unrealized gain or loss. In this manner, different variables can come into play. Recall how in Chapter 1 the same rules that led Enron to create special purpose entities (SPEs) to carve debt out of the balance sheet when revamped nevertheless led to Alibaba's use of variable interest entities (VIEs) to carve additional assets into the balance sheet as support for going public. This is yet another example of how various factors can co-constitute or "multiply-author" accounting impact. In keeping with our palindrome theme, how do we thread through the impact of unrealized as well as realized gain or loss back to the invoice recorded in foreign currency? Can we run a currency translation adjustment (CTA) report to show the differences attributed to unrealized gain or loss, or must we manually re-perform calculations for selected transactions?

If all this sounds too accounting focused, it is. The interplay at work that constitutes a transaction doesn't just happen within the confines of a SaaS or multiple SaaS, but to a larger degree, speaks to the role accounting plays in determining, in effect, what a transaction looks, feels, or perhaps even smells like. Recall from Chapter 3 the characterization of accounting as a universal language. We can, in fact, compare accounting principles to grammatical rules that form the backbone of the English language. Just as we are accustomed to seeing a subject, verb, and noun that make up a sentence – "I ate the cake" – accountants are accustomed to looking for a customer, amount, and item that make up an invoice. Naturally, there are layers of detail that we are failing to mention – with a customer, there are attributes such as customer payment terms, contact, billing or shipping address, and likewise for item, product SKU, list price, revenue account, and tax code – for which we would need to account. Syntax, a far more nuanced undertaking, revolves around the way words and phrases are composed, play off or play against one another. "Not all transactions are invoices" has a different ring to "not all invoices are transactions," even as the latter carries a whiff of incredulity. Likewise, when it comes to recognizing revenue "not all invoices are associated with deliveries or services rendered" is far more likely to raise eyebrows than "not all sales orders are associated with deliveries or services rendered." In the latter scenario, we would assume that the customer canceled the sales order or else modified it to remove specific lines. The former, however, raises the possibility that the company created invoices, and possibly recognized revenue even though it neither delivered nor rendered items or services. Syntax becomes a concern in the SaaS context when looking forward or back or, having made a roundtrip from to the end to the beginning, it is still unclear as to what to account for, when and for how much. The accounting school's view of accounting as common language for business notwithstanding, there are those that argue it is by no means the only one, and that in fact it has been too restrictive.

"Accounting is a requirement of business, but it's not the reason for doing business," argues Workday's VP of Application Strategy Mark Nittler.[14] Branding itself as an "alternative to ERP for HR and finance management," Workday, as mentioned in Chapter 3, is a SaaS started by Dave Duffield in response to Oracle's acquisition of his company PeopleSoft in 2005, more than 10 years before NetSuite underwent a similar fate. Nittler built Workday on the premise of overcoming the prevailing account code block underlying financial applications. To this end, Workday uses worktags for any number of attributes assigned to a transaction so that the accounting department can continue to rely on accounts while other departments like sales are able to use projects to monitor the same transactions. The account code block doesn't just apply to financials: as pointed out in the prior chapter, the U.S. medical industry is rife with similar examples. When consulting my health insurance provider about whether they would reimburse a vaccination, the provider asked me what code my doctor's office would submit. When I pled ignorance, my health insurance provider advised me that had the doctor's office coded the vaccination as a lab test it would have been reimbursable as would a vaccination administered to a dependent in pediatric care. As it is, the doctor's office coded the vaccination as a travel vaccination and therein resulted in an out-of-pocket cost that was not altogether insignificant. Without custom segments or in the case of Workday, worktags, we need to define every entity created in the software in relation to an account code block, a combination of parameters including chart of accounts, cost centers, departments, and subsidiaries to facilitate journal entries made downstream. We can't unwind a service coded to a specific revenue account and subsidiary if we already made the sales. Conversely, we wouldn't be able to set up a service for use in a sales order if we had yet to determine an appropriate revenue account. What we can sell and how quickly is in fact dependent on how we can first account for it.

This is very much like saying that every sentence needs to contain a subject, verb, and noun at the onset. Yet, in our everyday use of language, we almost always allow for the possibility to furnish additional detail. A sentence like "she smells" comprises of a subject and a verb and yet allows for a noun to be added later such as "she smells a rat." So, when using a SaaS, we can look to see how flexible it is in enabling business on the one hand and achieving accountability on the other. We can make a counter-argument that it is precisely because a sentence requires a noun that it promotes clarity from the beginning. We would have taken "she smells" to mean she needs a bath, if not for its accompanying noun. On the other hand, had the SaaS allowed the user to record the sale in a quote pending further review and authorization from both buyer and seller, this would have allowed for the possibility that "she smells something" first and clarifying this "something" to mean a rat, or even a rose after. We had discussed this in Chapter 3 when showing how a requisition, by forcing the user to select an already existing vendor defeats the intent of performing an independent vendor selection process to make cost conscious decisions.

There are also unasked questions surrounding the ability to recall an order already pending approval. Would the SaaS force us to resubmit thus producing potentially duplicate transactions or would the approver need to reject an order submitted inadvertently in error each time? In effect, by forcing a SaaS to be accountable, as it were, to accounting too soon, we may not be able to record a sales opportunity or purchase requisition soon enough. That the sentence must contain a subject, verb, and noun drives the content of what the system captures, and recalls Marshall McLuhan's oft-quoted aphorism, "the medium is the message."[15] Just as we only quote valid services or items from a price book, we can layer on an additional detail: we only allow certain nouns. From an accounting perspective, it is not hard to understand why the greater the latitude accorded to sales teams to apply discounts or veer off established list prices, the harder it becomes to maintain the fair value of any one element or VSOE pricing. Yet we may not capture other elements that may be of interest to a customer simply because they have no relevance in an accounting context. While we capture provisioning status so that we can evidence delivery in recording revenue, provisioning details such as when and how to gain access to a subscribed or purchased software are not. Thus, the specific format, or form employed can cut both ways, both as a means of not only keeping what's deemed desirable in but also what's deemed irrelevant out.

In some cases, the erroneous entry of data can threaten the SaaS's transactional status integrity. Consider a negative quantity that a user has entered in a sales order at the line level presumably to capture discount applied to a preceding line of positive quantity. The status lifecycle this sales order takes on is:

1. Pending approval
2. Approved and pending fulfillment
3. Pending billing/partial fulfillment
4. Partially fulfilled

Contrast this with a different sales order this time with a positive quantity but negative amount in a secondary after the primary positive quantity line:

1. Pending approval
2. Approved and pending fulfillment
3. Pending billing
4. Billed

In the first example, we fulfill the sales order upon approval only for the positive line. We can't fulfill a negative quantity. Yet, after the system fully invoices the order, it reverts to *Partially Fulfilled* status even though the system has fully billed it. In the second example, because we have fulfilled both positive lines – the primary item and its discount – the sales order cycles through pending billing and billed statuses accordingly. Notice that our read of the sales order transaction status is fragile or less than forgiving in this case to the entry of quantity at the line level. Imagine if we layered a workflow on top of all sales orders pending billing, where the system automatically generates and issues invoices to customers. We may encounter one or both exception scenarios – the workflow may fail to take into consideration sales orders pending billing/partial fulfillment for invoicing, or may proceed into an iterative loop, itself a palindrome of sorts – for orders that the system has fully invoiced but they nevertheless get stuck in *Partially Fulfilled* status. Setting aside the sales order, because we can't technically fulfill negative quantities, the invoice generated from the sales order with a negative quantity in the first example may fail to account for the negative line amount so that the total comes to 100 instead of 95. The following illustration depicts the sales orders side by side. Can you spot the difference?

Billed Sales Order		
Order No.		Journal
Date		8/30/2017
Period		Aug-17
Status		Partially Fulfilled
Total Amount	$	95.00

Item	Quantity	Amount
Subscription 1	20	$ 100.00
Subscription 1	-1	$ (5.00)

Billed Sales Order		
Order No.		Journal
Date		8/30/2017
Period		Aug-17
Status		Billed
Total Amount	$	95.00

Item	Quantity	Amount
Subscription 1	20	$ 100.00
Subscription 1	1	$ (5.00)

To say that a SaaS supports a specific format, and the ensuing transactions a specific form, and that these lend them readily to audit and compliance, is much like saying just because something looks and smells like a rat, it is a rat. Thus far, we have drawn on grammar, and explored how syntax focuses on structure. What we haven't yet talked about is semantics, the meaning of vocabulary arranged within a structure. Take the Oracle at Delphi. When consulted by the peoples of the ancient Mediterranean world, her response was: "You will go you will return not in the battle you will perish."[16] Although syntactically intact, from a semantics perspective, we remain in the dark on our odds of survival.

I am reminded of the 1999 thought experiment in which philosopher John Searle pictures himself "locked in a room, and given a large batch of Chinese writing" plus "a second batch of Chinese script" and "a set of rules" in English "for correlating the second batch with the first batch."[17] When Chinese symbols are slipped underneath the door, by applying the rules at his disposal, he is able to respond in kind by matching them with appropriate symbols and thus succeeds in fooling those outside the room into thinking that he is fluent in Chinese.[18] To an observer outside the room, it would appear that he spoke Chinese when he didn't.[19] The Chinese Room is a thought experiment presented by Searle in his 1980 article *Minds, Brains, and Programs*.[20] Searle's point is that just because the protagonist can follow an algorithm or script to produce Chinese characters, he still doesn't understand Chinese.[21]

In the same manner, a computer or machine can follow a code to produce an output yet still not understand it. Thirty years later, Searle would expound on the intent behind his Chinese Room argument to clarify that while "computation is defined purely formally or syntactically," "minds have actual mental or semantic contents."[22] He further argues that "we cannot get from syntactical to the semantic just by having the syntactical operations and nothing else."[23] This would be like saying that we are unlikely to make an accounting error simply because we are using an accounting SaaS imbued with an accounting view of the world. Recall the lack of transparency on revenue recognition or accrual criteria from Chapter 3. While our exploration of SaaS thus far has focused on sequence and, specifically, sequence within structures, we have barely scratched the surface when it comes to semantics, the making sense of it all.

Here's another parallel: recall from Chapter 3 the giant metadata tables at the heart of cloud computing that arguably work in the same manner as the Searle's monolingual speaker. Reminiscent of the large batch of Chinese writing, all custom fields defined by the customer for use in a SaaS are all nevertheless stored in string format behind the scenes. In this context, metadata tables function like the Chinese scripts and English rules so that instead of interpreting and responding in Chinese, the metadata tables track specific customer preferences on the type of data format for presentation with each custom field. When the customer queries a custom date field, for example, the metadata table would map the underlying stored string format back to the date format for presentation in the web browser. As we have seen, this in effect is what drives the multi-tenant data architecture behind cloud computing, multiple tenants sharing the same database, or sets of databases, with individual tenant identifiers marked where possible. When we extend the use of metadata tables beyond field formats, we can start to see how they can also store specific customer defined workflow configurations so that the same process for approving sales orders in one organization can differ markedly from another despite both tapping into the same data tables.

Discussions on artificial intelligence (AI) often bring up Searle's Chinese Room experiment specifically when it comes to limitations of AI, so it is interesting how the parallels are more obvious in the context of SaaS. At another level, the metadata tables help SaaS become almost palindrome-like: although read differently by different enterprise customers, the fields nonetheless reside in the same format in the same database. Yet, in recalling Searle's point on the variance between syntax and semantics, we can argue that while metadata tables form the underlying backbone or structure for tailoring the SaaS to meet specific enterprise needs, they by no means produce unequivocal outcomes when it comes to the successful adoption of SaaS for operational and reporting needs. How users, both internal and external, come to either embrace or resist the SaaS's inherent worldview and supporting architecture of fields and workflows is, in fact, a discussion centered more on semantics than on pure syntax.

A case in point is JDA Software, an accounting software focused on supply chain management. In January 2012, it launched internal investigations in response to a subpoena from SEC questioning their revenue recognition practices.[24] In August of the same year, JDA had to restate selected financials from 2008 through 2011.[25] Among other findings, it was determined that VSOE of fair value did not exist for their cloud services, so they had to defer and recognize revenue over the longest period for any undelivered services.[26] The unit of analysis is thrust into focus. Stand-alone transactions such as consulting services were not necessarily independent once assessed in the context of new licenses purchased for software go-live and implementation. The pricing of consulting contracts varied so much that VSOE pricing for these components were all but untenable. When I shared the JDA Software example in my *Accounting Information Systems* class and asked what we could improve upon, all suggestions centered on arriving at a better accounting treatment, whether it was coming up with and communicating more coherent revenue recognition policies to amassing the adequate population size to derive at imputed VSOE. Nobody touched on the reliance on other departments or groups in the same organization; actual prices sold depend a great deal on sales and incentive management practices, and by association management oversight of customer contracts or deals prior to execution. In this example, both sales and accounting are accountable for proper revenue recognition. In a way, having robust sales management and oversight practices is a foundational building block for internal controls on revenue recognition even though when revisiting what went wrong in a misstatement, it may not be the first thing that comes to mind.

Another interesting aside on unit of analysis: a student pointed out that seen in totality across all four years, 2008 through 2011, JDA didn't misstate revenue even though in any given year, they overstated in one and understated in the next. This is like the proportional distribution of revenue recognized within multiple elements in the bundle: the total revenue recognized in any one customer deal equals the total contractual value, yet the amount recognized at different times for different elements vary. Recall how a few paragraphs earlier, we explored the potential impact in changing an amortization schedule, either pulling in or out the amount of expenses recognized in any given period. The same scenario can just as easily apply to revenue recognition; in the case of JDA software, they pulled revenue forward so that they overstated it in 2008 and understated it in 2009, but in revisiting our amortization schedule example and the effects of inappropriate access or unauthorized updates to schedule(s) or likely both, the same risk extends to revenue recognition schedules and the need for a precise enough needle of an internal control to detect for changes and retrace our steps backwards from revenue journal to revenue recognition schedule to invoice to fulfillment to order. Recall how, for the White Queen in *Through the Looking Glass*, the "rule is, jam to-morrow and jam yesterday – but never jam to-day."[27]

Mark Nittler from Workday had remarked, "Accounting happens last in our system because accounting isn't real."[28] Insofar as the revenue distribution does not reflect actual line level amounts recorded on an invoice, there is a certain chasm over what we record on the sale and ultimately class as revenue. But accounting insofar as it is accrual-based plays by a different set of rules when it comes to recording numbers. Just because we haven't yet received payment doesn't mean we can't already record revenue with the offsetting debit to accounts receivable even though in our personal lives we are more likely to live on a cash accrual basis, balancing our checkbooks based on what flows in and out of our bank accounts. Nittler's point is well taken though: accounting is by no means the singular monopolizing perspective. I am reminded of a recent *San Francisco Chronicle* article I read where a man went through a face transplant from a deceased donor.[29] In blurring the lines between what is virtual and real, what is past, and what is present, the article described a tearful meeting that the clinic arranged between the donor's wife and the recipient.[30] To her surprise, the recipient did not resemble her husband but rather a living testament to past and present influences and histories having lived through a decade of stares after shooting his own face.[31] Just as we each bring different elements to bear in our daily lives, the accounting perspective commingles with other ones in reality. When we dial back our lens yet farther, as a second student would point out, multi-element arrangements are not merely applicable to software revenue recognition. A commonplace example that we all can relate to is mobile or cell phone plans. In addition to phone service, the company often bakes data and other warranty services or elements into the plan and need to properly account for them.

When we move from syntax to semantics, the specific attributes of SaaS become less of a focus than, and perhaps more to the point, what we use it for. In a way, the metadata tables, an index of customized preferences, surface the myriad of ways that different enterprise customers can use the same fields. When we widen our lens to focus on SaaS, as opposed to tables within SaaS, the forest for the trees so to speak, the SaaS is an index that points to fuller, richer happenings that we can't easily index. For Heidegger, a tool is "not the mere aggregation of traits" but "that around which the properties have been assembled"; in other words, how it is "put to use."[32] It is "ready-to-hand with which we have to do or perform something."[33] This is like saying the SaaS helped us close the books more quickly or automated the chain of necessary approvals that would have otherwise taken us longer to manually obtain. It becomes "present-to-hand" when the unexpected happens: something breaks or doesn't quite go according to plan. We do not sync a transaction across because of a missing cost center. We don't find a billing address because it belonged to a different entity upstream. The account balances in downstream and upstream SaaS do not agree because we locked the periods for allowing the booking of transactions at different intervals.

When a tool becomes present-to-hand, we start paying attention to its attributes, or perhaps more pointedly at the gaps between functionality and requirement. We need to sync the setup parameters together with transaction data. The upstream SaaS needs to be better adept at accounting for customers with more than one billing address. A detective control needs to be in place to mitigate for the possibility for timing differences in locked periods. Yet, I would argue that it is when a tool appears ready-to-hand that we need to be especially vigilant to potential gaps. A SaaS that can allocate revenue based on established VSOE of multiple elements doesn't quite go far enough, for example, to ensure that we get an adequate number of stand-alone transactions for plotting against a bell curve to get to an appropriate VSOE. Or perhaps more fundamentally, having a revenue recognition SaaS doesn't preclude us from choosing to recognize revenue in the absence of deliveries or services rendered just as having a billing SaaS doesn't prevent us from creating an invoice, even though we have not made a sale. More than that, simply focusing on the attributes of any one SaaS says nothing about "that around which" we use it for.

Customers may use workflows built on Force.com platform behind Salesforce.com to put in place processes around employee offboarding and while this works for some organizations, for others it presents compliance and regulatory challenges. What is good for the goose may be detrimental for the gander. Or as a physician friend of mine at a local university is apt to describe, the cause and treatment of sore throat for a vocal student differ sharply from the "same" symptoms seen in an engineering student. As we move from SaaS to internal controls, are the internal controls deployed in your organization ready-to-hand or present-to-hand? Does it depend on whether it is operating effectively or if you have identified exceptions? What are the costs associated with ready-to-hand? Complacency, for one, starts to creep in with the same controls recycled year after year. Automated controls, specifically, are especially susceptible to a different complacency of sorts; the audit approach of testing once and only once while amenable to containing audit costs associated with pulling samples and substantive testing can have the unfortunate consequence of promoting indifference when the system baselines and doesn't validate the controls as periodically as we would have liked.

Our tendency, after all, has thus far been in focusing on technology as a means to an end, whereas for Heidegger, "the essence of technology is by no means technological."[34] By focusing on instrumentality, he argues we are driven by causality. Here, he draws out the four causes set forth by Aristotle to explain causality. Using a silver chalice as an example, he describes:

1. Causa materialis or silver, the material
2. Causa formalis, the form the silver takes on, or the chaliceness
3. Causa finalis, that which the chalice is intended for, or circumscribed to a sacrificial vessel used in the religious ritual of communion
4. Causa efficiens, the person responsible for bringing the chalice into being, the silversmith[35]

Of these, Heidegger views the third cause as the most important, "that which gives bounds, that which completes."[36] In applying this to a billing SaaS, we can parlay its four causes as:

1. Software and hardware that make up SaaS
2. SaaS-y-ness, that it can be accessed from the cloud and on a subscription basis
3. Recording of sales to customers
4. Programmers and implementation team that deployed SaaS for the organization

Each cause is "co-responsible" for "bringing forth" bills to customers just as in our preceding VSOE and foreign currency transaction examples, different elements come into play. But what about the third cause, which for Heidegger is the most important, "that which gives bounds, that which completes"?[37] What is to stop a user from setting up a vendor as a customer and using the billing SaaS to record vendor invoices? The same reason that would preclude the use of a chalice outside the context of a church. I remember being part of vendor negotiations on a SaaS that supports the review and approval of sales contracts and integrates these into sales orders. When we voiced our need for handling vendor contracts, the sales rep mentioned perhaps facetiously that nothing would have precluded us from re-appropriating the same software for our own ends. We called it a sales contract management SaaS because it is the right thing to use at the right time and in the right place provided by the right vendor.

Less obvious perhaps are the ways in which a SaaS is less effective as an index of real-life experience, even as we perceive it to be ready-to-hand. With the billing SaaS, how easy is it to add an additional field to display on the invoice the rate for services for some customers and not others? Conversely, how easy is it to add a collection notes field on an overdue invoice but not show it? When the SaaS at hand is unable to handle either scenario, it may inundate users with error messages, less to do human errors and more with its inability to handle alternate paths. In response, users resort to other tools. As discussed in Chapter 3, users can create separate Word document to mirror the SaaS-generated invoice and use it for communicating with customers who do seek further detail on service rates. Users can summon a separate Excel document to track collection notes on all overdue invoices. What are fields in a table anyway but an indexed characterization of real-life relationships: relationships among fields within an invoice, relationships among customers and invoices, even relationships among customers? Can a customer, for example, be set up as a distributor or reseller? If so, can the user designate an end customer? What if the same end customer can also belong to another reseller? In effect, one reseller can have multiple end customers. Conversely, one end customer can have multiple resellers.

Somewhere in this trajectory, the SaaS may put up a barrier: the former may hold true; the latter not so much. Or the SaaS may not support one-to-many relationships between customers and shipping addressees, thereby breaking the link between resellers and end customers. How then do we account for sales made to end customers? We could create multiple customers, each mapped to a single shipping address. In the eyes of an external auditor, these would appear at first glance suspicious duplicates to which we can point to the shortcomings of the software at hand. We could tie these parameters to the transactions rather than to the customers: an end customer may simply be a custom field. Separately, revenue treatment for these invoices would have to be different than those for non-reseller customers without end customers. How the system configures fields depends partly on the system constraints imposed by SaaS (how ready-to-hand is it?) partly on what users expect to be able to draw meaningful conclusions (how would customers analyze data?) Would users expect to see all end customer sales related to a distributor, or vice versa all distributor sales related to an end customer?

To be sure, this is not an exercise in futility. Under GAAP, to recognize revenue to distributors based on "sell-in," the SaaS would need to meet certain seller criteria, such as fixing the price to the distributor so that it is determinable at time point of sale, transferring the risk of loss to the distributor, incurring no significant obligation to bring about resale of product, and obtaining reasonable assurance that the company can collect payment. If the system didn't meet these criteria, GAAP would require the company to recognize revenue only upon sale to the end customer, in other words, "sell-through." How ready-to-hand a SaaS is depends on the nature of what the user perceives it as ready-to-hand for. If it were merely a means to capture sales, then despite its less than complete indexed characterization of real-life distributor sales, it is qualified as ready-to-hand. But wouldn't it be wonderful, if not ideal, if the SaaS at hand were able to help enterprises account for revenue in a manner that is consistent with GAAP, rather than simply capture sales?

We can argue that to be able to determine if we have transferred risk of loss to a distributor or if an obligation exists to assist in resale, we would have to interpret the contract established, thus employing a legal and not just an accounting read, and this would have been out of the bounds of the SaaS at hand. But insofar as the price is determinate on the sale and the customer is in good credit standing, thus posing no risk to collectability, surely SaaS can help us evidence these criteria? In April 2016, Logitech forked out a $7.5 million fine to settle SEC allegations that the company fraudulently inflated its earnings for a failed TV hardware device. Among other transgressions, it gave significant incentives to distributors to purchase units shortly before the end of a quarter, a common "hockey stick" pattern, recognizing revenue immediately upon "sale," even though agreements exist to help distributors sell back the units if left unsold. In other words, the risk of loss remained borne by Logitech. All of this can take place in any SaaS we can argue; users can record journals to circumvent the GL impact of invoices; users can create invoices to directly credit revenue, that is, record sell-in, even if inappropriate. All the more to expect a ready-to-hand billing SaaS, built on "accounting as universal language," rather than serve as a silent accomplice to the corporate shenanigans that abound, transfixed and yet utterly helpless. Recall our earlier trinity of mistakes that can arise from a mismatch between a label and its contents as exemplified in incorrectly configured payment terms, chart of accounts, and billing addresses. To what extent is the SaaS at hand more present-to-hand rather than ready-to-hand if no validation errors surfaced for one of the following:

■ 45 days assigned to Net 30
■ An expense account type selected for an income account
■ A billing country inputted as Singapore even though other elements of the billing address clearly reflect a location in Mumbai

We would have expected the SaaS to be more than a data entry conduit, all syntax and not much else. While I can attest to validation checks such as only accepting data inputs in currency formats for amount fields or ensuring that the system didn't create new invoices or sales orders for customers who have exceeded their credit limit, we still need to make more progress for the SaaS on display to be more than present-to-hand.

When we place this against the longer arc of time, a SaaS that merely lets users input data, however invalid, remains trapped in the Web 2.0 internet technologies that let users post and share information; in Web 1.0, internet technologies are primary used as sources of information. Web 3.0 changes the rules of the game. As discussed in Chapter 3, Uber fundamentally changed the way we order and supply rides, and Airbnb the way we book and provide accommodations. Some have ascribed predictive capability to Web 3.0 where instead of spending time research-ing the best option, intelligent agents present the best options based on known preferences. With Web 3.0, ready-to-hand takes on a new level of significance, not merely fulfilling past expectations, forged through habit, but also disrupting exist-ing syntax and inciting a new level of semantics. This is like saying the billing SaaS, precisely because it is accounting focused, presents alternate options of recognizing revenue, sell-in or sell-through, and proposes the most feasible path. For all the effort invested in the maintenance of orderly records – the output of SaaS – we can easily mistake the end for the beginning.

Back to our example of the billing SaaS, the captured sales merely serve as input for what appears to be a longer, more protracted exercise in figuring how best to account for revenue. Here, best is subjective at best: it can mean how best to report revenue to meet latest quarter predictions and meet Wall Street expectations, or how best to report revenue in a manner that conforms with GAAP, or quite likely, a combination of both. But when exploring the alternate path – forwards, backwards and a return to the beginning – we often mistake the end when it is merely a fork in the road. To determine which path to take requires human judgment, but rather than use the SaaS as a thermostat that regulates and thus maintains status quo, why not have it ask: is it appropriate to maintain a ludicrously low temperature in the dead of winter? This question is like asking whether we need to refresh or update approval limits assigned to requisition approvals in a procurement SaaS when materiality of spend in an organization has increased over time, so that virtually not almost anything is routed to the CFO for approval each time?

Another way of peeling behind the layers of what it means to be "ready-to-hand" is to observe just what goes on when capturing a sale. Is the SaaS forgiving enough to users who may not have all the information ready during information capture? The expense management SaaS, Concur, offers a mobile app that lets users take photos of expense receipts and through optical character resolution populate fields such as amount, date, and expense type automatically. Would it allow the user to save a transaction in draft status with timely reminders to users to complete mandatory fields later? When it comes to accrual of unsubmitted expenses, does it let users run a report on all expenses by department that users have not submitted or have not received approval for? When using a corporate credit card set up in Concur, would it queue up receipts every time we charge the card to facilitate the entry into an expense report? Or if we are unsure about how to proceed, whether choosing a code or cost center, does the SaaS let us reconsider our entries even after submitting the transaction for approval? Is there a 3.0 wave where flexibility combined with analytics can yield a SaaS that is more accountable to real-life end user needs? The ease of recoverability from an incorrectly submitted of selected cost center, item, or transaction for that matter taps into how the SaaS can help resolve real-life messiness.

A SaaS that I have worked with does not let users delete journals pending approval or otherwise unless they have access to delete all journal entries albeit in an open accounting period. It is all or nothing. In response, I undertook the following steps to "re-tool" the SaaS. I granted all roles access to delete journals, then intervened with a workflow that checked to see if the current user is the same user who created the entry (separately a custom field created to house this otherwise system log field buried in audit trails) and if it is not the same user, then lock the screen to prevent the user from editing or deleting an entry that that user did not create. This workflow check not only gives users a way to retrace their steps, in the event of making an erroneous entry, it also frees up time for approvers to only review entries that merit review. As a bonus, approvers can't edit or delete the entries they are reviewing, and this aligns with a tighter segregation of duties. What is the point of having an independent review when reviewers can update the very entries they are approving?

Let's return to the improving the "ready-to-hand" nature of vendor payment terms. To fundamentally change the rules of the game, imagine a different SaaS that accounts for the gap between the time the company renders services or goods and the time they receive payment to help companies determine which bills to pay sooner. Tesorio, a startup originating from Wharton's MBA program, analyses a company's invoices and ultimately helps vendors receive payment earlier albeit with a discount.[38] In covering the time value of money in my *Accounting Information Systems* class, I asked the question, would you rather receive payment of $100 today or $100.01 a month from today, all but one student raised their hands. As the student pointed out, you can take the $100 today and invest it in equity where the rate of return is going to be more than the 0.01% return we get from having it sit in a bank account even if the risk is correspondingly higher as well. But from a vendor perspective, rather than getting a line of credit to pay its bills on time while waiting to receive payment, it would be preferable to receive payment sooner albeit with a discount baked in than receiving the amount in its entirety months later.

With all our focus thus far on gaining the same read whether backwards or forwards when viewing a transaction and its related records, we can be forgiven for assuming that there is only one path to take. And yet, if we look back to the ability of SaaS to be configurable via that meta or abstraction layer, it is altogether possible for users in different organizations to adopt different paths, or reads for the matter, even when it comes to processing the same transaction. When it comes to the same SaaS, an entity can elect to use journal entries without approval out-of-the-box. Another may decide to use these with approvals but without additional "customizations" using out-of-the-box configuration ability. Yet another may purchase an off-the-shelf customized bundle or package from the same vendor developed by its professional services team and thus "productized." Still, another could have its in-house developers script to change the way the entries appear instead of relying on workflows, essentially undertaking programmatic rather than declarative customization to employ Salesforce's lingo. Another could take it a step further – so far, we have only reviewed approvals – what about rejections? And would we send email notifications to reviewers as well as creators to notify them to intervene at each interval because after all what is more annoying than having an entire queue of in-flight journals pending review since the first day of the current period as we are scrambling to close the books? The choice a SaaS client may elect to undertake may well reflect on where it is in its growth and maturity cycle. Is it a startup with minimal resources, or has it grown to become a medium-sized company? Is it considering going public or does it wish to stay private, continuing to rely on funding from private investors or venture capitalists? If it had just gone public, how much time does it have to comply with SOX? Depending on its market capitalization, the JumpStart Our Business Startup (JOBS) Act grants newly public companies a grace period of up to 2 years to evidence internal controls over financial reporting.

My point is: not only is the SaaS client organization's path not predetermined, it is also by no means static. As it matures from startup to publicly traded company, it can cycle through all phases. Configurability of the extent or degree of software adoption is what SaaS offers. Contrast this with the release of Stratus 286, a desktop computer in place of a SaaS. In usability trials, Grint and Woolgar described how a first-time user, Ruth, attempted to connect a printer to the computer.[39] Ironically, even back then, there was recognition that one of the makings of a successful device includes its ability to plug-and-play with peripherals, just as a SaaS needs to be able to integrate with other best-of-breed SaaS. Armed with instruction booklets, Ruth poked around and finally asked for help from the subject matter expert at hand, Nina.[40]

Particularly telling was the way Ruth characterized her own reactions, "I looked at this and looked at that and I thought, 'No I'm being stupid, now this is silly.'"[41] Nina's response was: "But we were in fact being silly asking you to do it."[42] It turned out that all this time the company had asked Ruth to connect the newly minted Stratus 286 with a lead designed for an earlier K series machine.

Perhaps as a sign of the advances we have made in technology, many of the challenges in this vein, even though I am making a somewhat apples-and-oranges comparison between hardware and software, iPaaS resolved, so an integrator iPaaS tool such as Celigo is able to connect multiple billing SaaS, such as Shopify and Magento with an accounting SaaS like NetSuite. What is interesting is that even though Stratus 286 was on trial, we would have been forgiven into thinking that Ruth and Nina were the ones to be put on trial. After all, one was "silly enough" to attempt to connect using an outdated lead, the other just as "silly" in making the request in the first place.[43] All this time, Stratus 286 remained quiet, a silent unblinking witness to the exchange that transpired at hand.[44]

Here is another account from a highly respected computer journalist who did not partake in the pre-launch press conference nor lunches with members of the marketing team.[45] Not surprisingly, his published assessment, a negative one, was but the singular notable exception to an otherwise universal positive reception.[46] A complaint by a senior member of the marketing team was particularly telling: the journalist saw Stratus "as if it was a machine you could go and buy off some shelf in the high street."[47] Yet today, this is precisely the premise behind SaaS, that it can be purchased at a lower cost from off the shelf as it were and ready for use.

The intent of the examples shared by Grint and Woolgar was to illustrate the metaphor of machine as text. By comparing machine with text, they attempted to show how multiple readings from users and observers are possible. This stands in contrast to the portrayal of technology as determinants of "social and economic organizations and relationships," a form of Darwinism where the fittest survive.[48] In taking a page from Grint and Woolgar, I have attempted to draw similar parallels between palindromes and the nature of SaaS transactions. Grint and Woolgar make the differentiation between insiders and outsiders. Nina and the marketing team fall in the former camp, whereas Ruth the latter. The reporter clearly belongs to the latter, even if the makers of Stratus 286 would rather have him banished to the far outer reaches, likely a lighthouse at the end of the world.

Another scene from *Through the Looking Glass* comes to mind where upon being introduced to Alice, Humpty Dumpty pronounces, "It's a stupid name enough! What does it mean?"[49] When Alice asks whether a name must mean something, Humpty Dumpty replies in the affirmative, preferring to see its name to mean "a good handsome shape" while in contrast Alice's name to "be any shape, almost."[50] Humpty Dumpty adds, "When I use a word, it means just what I choose it to mean – neither more nor less."[51] Alice counters, "The question is whether you can make words mean so many different things" to which Humpty Dumpty declares, "The question is which is to be master – that's all."[52] This last point, to be "master" of a particular kind of reading of Stratus 286 is what its manufacturer aspires to be from a pre-launch press conference to marketing team lunches even as the dissenting opinion of the wayward journalist reveals the inevitability of more than one reading.

An insider/outsider perspective gains us an insider/outsider reading of the machine. These can well converge but more likely a chasm exists between them. Consider the following exchange with a user who is accessing out-of-the-box reports from a SaaS for the first time. The reports present a rolling period of the last 12 months and although the report is what she had asked for, she would have preferred columns sequenced in a descending time sequence so that the most current period appears first. I explained that this was standard behavior expected out-of-the-box and that in fact, the way rolling periods presented align with how SaaS executes the reports, by first putting in starting period and next the ending period in the selection criteria. If, for example, I had reversed the values in the report criteria, the SaaS would prompt an error stating that the ending period entered preceded the starting period selected. As administrator of the SaaS in question, I played the role of the insider. And yet when I look back at this exchange, I can clearly empathize with the role of the user as outsider. Surely the SaaS should be flexible enough to adjust the manner of period presentation to specific user needs? I suppose that compared to Stratus 286, it was at least more than a silent witness when it prompts an error message when having to process an "incorrect" selection criteria. There is an element of coercion at work, whether in the SaaS's inability to re-sequence the rolling periods and regardless of the order in which the user selects the starting and ending periods, or in my ability to "educate" the user on its ways.

Yet a cursory online search for financial reports with rolling periods led to a similar question posed by users of a different SaaS. In reading the challenges faced by Salesforce administrators, it is worthy to note (and not just for myself), the lengths SaaS administrators go to fulfill what would appear to be a rather straightforward reporting requests from finance and accounting users. This includes combing through list of available filters out-of-the-box, keeping tabs on changes or enhancements to come in the upcoming releases, or resorting to use of custom formula and custom summary rollup fields. This is not unlike the manual workaround I would have to perform if the user persists in the request by creating a report with manually plugged in periods and sequenced columns, and having to add a column with the right placement with each ensuing month. A comment stuck out from feedback on Salesforce: "why does everything related to reporting take so long to implement?

We have Chatter implementations all the time but basic reporting we have to look outside Salesforce to satisfy, why?"[53] Launched as an enterprise collaboration platform, Chatter mirrors a company's intranet but one where employees can follow to collaborate on opportunities or service cases. The user's comment resonates at many levels. Thus far we looked at how an accounting or audit lens can constrict the ways and means in which a user uses SaaS; here the tables are turned where an emphasis on meeting sales targets or service levels can preface some functionality over others in a customer relationship management (CRM) SaaS. With the SaaS provider's emphasis on automation over information, doing over reviewing what the user has done, we are also setting the ground for covering material in looking ahead to Chapter 7.

The roles of insider and outsider are somewhat interchangeable depending on your perspective. Accounting or finance users requesting a specific look and feel to what would have been commonplace bread-and-butter reports used in their industry are in on accounting or finance requirements, so from this perspective they are insiders whereas the SaaS administrators, as well as the entire ecosystem that makes up the text or narrative of the SaaS itself, are clearly outsiders. Yet when it comes to understanding what the SaaS is and isn't capable of intimately, the SaaS administrator becomes the insider with end users playing the role of the outsiders looking in. The less than positive review by the computer journalist exemplifies the role of the outsider to the inner workings of Stratus 286 yet fast forward to the present, this outsider perspective strangely resonates with the current times where a SaaS is portrayed evidently as an artifact that can be easily procured off the shelf as it were and consumed, so while the reporter is an outsider back then, he is ahead of his time, more like an insider who talks the talk of present day speak and its surrounding exigencies.

Who is in, who is out, varies depending on which side you are on, and when. Seen in this way, it is no different from the map in the sand drawn by the Chinese before La Perouse. And perhaps this is the greater immutable mobile, that against the sands of time, almost any artifact that appears remotely immutable crumbles. The view of machine as text, or SaaS as text facilitates multiple readings – whether between the user of the SaaS and the administrator or, in the case of Stratus 286, among the user and support (insider and outsider) on trial, or the journalist and the marketing team. The launch of Stratus 286 from usability trials to press release exemplifies the degree of staging involved. Here we are not simply talking about performative aspects such as evidencing the degree of compliance readiness – recall the SAS 70 or SSAE reports from Chapter 2 – but rather the multiple sources of support that need to be present from the mandatory fields to complete to the underlying order–receipt–invoice sequential flow to right-size the reading, and thus use of SaaS.

The usability trial of Stratus 286 mirrors Boyle's demo of the vacuum pump discussed in Chapter 3. When we circle back to the Wittgenstein's rule paradox, Kripke's response is that the relationship in question is not so much between the application of the rule and the rule itself but rather between the behavioral aspects of rule and the expectations of other users. In other words, as Wittgenstein put it, "it is not possible to obey a rule 'privately': otherwise thinking one was obeying a rule would be the same as obeying it."[54] That Stratus's manufacturers sought to create a favorable consensus among all journalists speaks to the public nature of rule-following.

Staging is taken to a whole new level when we consider Peritus Software that in addition to offering software maintenance outsourcing services to large organizations is a maker of software products that sought to improve "the labor-intensive processes involved in conducting mass change and other software maintenance tasks."[55] On the evening before it was to announce its second quarter financial results, its outside auditors contacted the CFO citing lack of sufficient audit documentation to evidence the occurrence of the sale of a software license to AT&T.[56] In response, the CFO prepared a letter documenting the license agreement between Peritus and AT&T.[57] Instead of sending it to an AT&T official for execution, he faxed to a former AT&T employee who had just accepted a job at Peritus as an account manager.[58] The Peritus new hire forged the signature of the AT&T official and returned the letter to the CFO, who in turn faxed it to Peritus' auditors.[59] As a result, the auditors approved recognition of the revenue.[60] The actions undertaken allowed Peritus to improperly record over $1 million in revenue, which falsely inflated the company's second quarter 1998 revenue by 10% and enabled it to meet analyst estimates.[61] The SEC filed civil action lawsuits that resulted in both the CFO and newly hired account manager having to pay penalties.[62]

While we have talked about the staging behind a computer launch like Stratus 286, Peritus Software takes staging to the extreme. Earlier, in Chapter 3, we reviewed how the revenue recognition criteria critical though it may be, remains buried deep in accounting software or SaaS, not unlike Garfinkel's lack of success in locating information on patient admission criteria from clinical records. We also looked at a fictitious car dealership scenario and saw how shared among CPAs differences in opinion exists when it comes to recording revenue. When sharing the Peritus example in my *Accounting Information Systems* class and asking students which if any of the four revenue recognition criteria Peritus had met, all but one stated that evidence of a persuasive agreement existed, even when the case clearly showed staging undertaken to make the contract with AT&T appear plausible. When asked if the main reason for misstated revenues had to do with recognizing premature revenue, a student who was a star performer of the group agreed, despite evidence that all the revenue recorded was fictitious to begin with. The student's argument: "fictitious would have meant no contractual document to share with the auditors altogether whereas for Peritus, such as a document did exist" speaks volumes to the power of persuasion that comes from elaborate staging.

The Peritus example illustrates the ludicrous nature of rule-following, the furnishing of fake evidence to comply with the letter, rather than the spirit of the law. Lest we think this oversight is only applicable to students, I'm reminded of a recent exchange with another student. After debating back and forth how Peritus recorded the fictitious revenue instead of premature revenue, the student suggested Peritus may have undervalued liabilities as well. My first response was no, this is revenue, nothing to do with vendor payments and owing other entities money. After a good night's sleep – I had just flown in on a red eye flight – I realized that precisely because Peritus makes software that it is more likely that they record the revenue first to deferred revenue, a liability account, and monthly revenue recognition performed to amortize the revenue rateably over the subscription period and credit revenue accordingly. So focused I was on emphasizing the difference between fictitious and premature revenue that I omitted the obligation of the said provider when receiving the payment in advance to deliver software over an agreed contractual period. From the customer perspective, a disproportionate amount of consumption of SaaS results in an emphasis on prepaids in its own accounting processes and thus meriting additional internal controls in SOX compliance. Insofar as the customer pays the subscription for the entire upcoming year beforehand, albeit in line with established payment terms like Net 30, care given to the identification, recording, and reporting of prepaid expenses becomes ever more relevant and critical.

Thus, the increasing adoption of SaaS not only changes the manner in which we devise, design, and test internal controls – through the increasing ability for enterprise end users to essentially self-serve by putting in their own configurations or customizations – but also, more importantly in a fundamental way, it transforms the emphasis of internal controls at these SaaS consuming companies so that slowly but surely the focus is on negotiating annual subscription renewals, revisiting incremental cost per user license, as well as inquiring about any cap on year-over-year pricing uplifts. The SaaS provider after all continues to expend necessary resources to add new functionalities.

Peritus is a blatant example embellished with elaborate staging but often the breaking of the palindrome pattern of a transaction – getting to the same conclusion whether viewed forwards or backwards – can arise from the best, as opposed to the worst, of intentions. Consider an order entry clerk who fails to locate customer X in the order management SaaS. Upon deeper investigation, the clerk finds out that customer X recently acquired customer Y. The order management SaaS is in turn synced upstream to a sales management SaaS where a quote exists for customer Y prior to the acquisition. When the system executes the contract, it gets synced over as a sales order for customer Y. In this example, which of the following options should the order entry clerk pursue:

1. Rename customer Y in the order management SaaS to customer X
2. Create a new customer X in the order management SaaS and reassign the sales order to the customer X
3. Create a new customer X in the order management SaaS and merge all transactions related to customer Y into customer X

In the first example, simply renaming customer Y to customer X may unwittingly recast all retrospective entries related to customer Y as customer X, so that sales would have appeared to be with customer X before the acquisition when in fact that is not the case. There is the added complexity of invoices belonging to customer Y that may be still unpaid; does this mean that the clerk should switch dunning notifications or collections over to customer X personnel by default? Furthermore, there is the shipping address; does the clerk continue the delivery of goods or services to customer Y or customer X?

In the second example, the clerk creates a new customer X in the order management SaaS and the clerk reassigns the sales order from customer Y to customer X. Presumably, the order entry clerk calls customer X and finds out that they merged and integrated purchasing functions as one post acquisition. While this path seems reasonable enough, there is the curious matter of breaking the link with the upstream sales management SaaS so that what the system initially captured as a quote in the upstream SaaS belonging to customer Y presently needs to perform a somersault of sorts to arrive at customer X in the downstream SaaS. In our scenario, the sync is one-directional – quotes from the upstream sales management SaaS translate to sales orders in the downstream management SaaS – but in keeping with the palindrome-like spirit, what if the integration were bi-directional, so that sales personnel logging into and using the sales management SaaS also get to see unpaid invoices or credit memos associated with these same customers and synced over from the downstream order management and likely billing SaaS? Thus, a sales professional gets a glimpse not only into opportunity wins but also actuals including payment and credit history, all of which matters in upsells and renewals. What would happen if the system reassigned the sales order downstream to customer X? How would the system sync the actual transactions back upstream as being associated with customer Y? The second option, while preferable to the first, nonetheless complicates more than simplifies matters. The third option doesn't provide a solution to these upstream alignment challenges per se, but at least maintains the referential integrity of prior transactions associated with customer Y. The question becomes: is there an audit trail behind the merges performed, or when we look back, do these reflect as belonging to customer X all this time?

With SaaS, gone are the instruction booklets or detailed implementation handholding reminiscent of Stratus 286 – recall its off the shelf ease of use – so does staging apply? The answer is indubitably yes though in not so obvious ways. The roles we play – whether as insider, outsider or, even as we shall soon see, an independent or unbiased third-party – in turn shape the way we talk about, articulate, and debate what and how we use SaaS. There are degrees of insiderness. As alluded to earlier, with folks supporting a SaaS, an administrator located at the customer enterprise may be merely first level support, being the first line of defense with helping end users navigate and use out-of-the-box functionality. A developer on the same team may be more of an insider insofar as understanding scripting and workflows, and ways to manipulate the way the SaaS looks and feels. The vendor or service provider organization is even more of an insider insofar as they directly make enhancements that have pervasive impact on all customers rather than just one as well as resolve bugs. And yet from the perspective of the enterprise customer, the order reverses, with the vendor organization being the least able to articulate a specific customer's needs. I suppose the same applies when you throw auditors into the mix. To experienced users and administrators alike, generic audit questions like how to evidence for changes to user access or configurations may at first belie an ignorance of the SaaS at hand, a far-removed outsider perspective if you will, but upon closer examination may yield troubling concerns over the lack of system audit logs on administrator interventions whether deleted records, changes to user profiles, or configurations. For although many a SaaS vendor can attest to the presence of a system log of audit trails for transaction changes, not as many can attest to the availability of all attributes exposed for reporting. Fewer still can demonstrate the availability of audit trails for administrative changes, even though these present a source of concern especially framed against the possibility of insider attacks. When we trace the trajectory of a singular transaction as it sheds its skin to take on new outerwear when moving from cradle to grave in an ecosystem of integrated SaaS, it is all the more likely for a superuser or administrator for one SaaS to have the same level of access for all other interfacing SaaS.

I am reminded of how a computer engineer held the San Francisco hostage by refusing to turn over passwords to the City's FiberWAN (Wide Area Network), where the city stored records such as officials' e-mails, city payroll files, confidential law enforcement documents, and jail inmates' bookings.[63] We can replay a possible similar trajectory with a disgruntled SaaS administrator. When we circle back to exposure of attributes – whether used for reporting on transactions or changes to transactional, master or configuration data – their very absence foretell different readings. The lack of information on configuration changes is like asking our intrepid, albeit world weary, linguist Dr. Banks to try to decipher signs and symbols drawn by the aliens in the absence of any common language.

In as far as configuration changes are concerned, these can drive different processes and thus software behavior, so it is more than an academic exercise in futility. A product such as FloDocs which recently rebranded itself as Strongpoint, provides change management for SaaS solutions like Salesforce and NetSuite by mapping out and baselining all customizations undertaken so that any regression impact on existing configuration work surfaces when users perform changes. Even without the possibility of configuration change, if we take a step back and look at setup data, any change herein can tip automated computations into disarray. Prepaid entries generated via amortization schedules come to mind. When departments or cost centers change, users need to refresh amortization schedules, otherwise resulting journal entries throw an error. Likewise, allocations based on headcount, such as the allocation of overhead rental expense by department needs to be constantly revisited because the changing size of the organization, even if the department stays the same. Thus, the amount of work that goes into the maintenance of a SaaS is not unlike drawing and redrawing a line or map in the sand only to have it washed away by the ebb and flow of the tide each time. What the user doesn't update isn't effectively reported.

Another way to take to task the insider versus outsider dichotomy is to ask questions about the SaaS using Aristotle's four causes to gain a more complete picture.

In a customer reference call, I remember being caught off guard by the nature of another company's business, which comprises shipping ice with the products it sells to customers and how the same SaaS used by a client organization to sell software a different company retooled to sell physical products that are not "withered" by the time they deliver. It seems almost too good to be true that analysts, such as Gartner Group, can neatly rank vendors based on "completeness of vision" on the x-axis and "ability to execute" on the y-axis. Depending on how the vendors score, Gartner divides them into leaders, challengers, visionaries, and niche players. A deeper read belies the amount of work on both sides – Gartner as well as assessed vendors – in collecting and responding to raw data on 15 underlying dimensions. Dubbed the Magic Quadrant (MQ), there is no denying that this analytical framework can be useful in gaining a management forest-for-the-trees perspective, even as it has had its detractors, not least vendors, that have sued because they feel that they have been mischaracterized.[64] A reliance on a two-dimensional model also harks back to Latour's identification of the biggest advantage that comes with the use of immutable mobiles – "the 2-dimensional character of inscriptions allows them to merge with geometry" or put simply "you cannot measure the sun, but you can measure the photograph of the sun with a ruler."[65] In the case of Gartner's MQ, streaming the myriad of work behind the development, use, and support of a SaaS so that it can be benchmarked apples-to-apples alongside its peers, regardless of the amount of the level of effort involved in sifting, compiling, and comparing seems like a worthwhile undertaking.

But framed against present day capabilities, even the variables used for benchmarking can seem a touch archaic. With a best-of-breed SaaS that can easily integrate with other SaaS, does it matter that it is a niche player with a less than complete vision even as it possesses the ability to execute? With SaaS, are we in fact talking about the proliferation of niche players? Also, to what extent are these categorizes not only *not* mutually exclusive but intricately interrelated? Conversely, we can easily see how too complete a vision may hinder a vendor's ability to execute. Another counter-argument is completeness of vision addressed by ease of configuration or of integration. It's almost like a gift that keeps on giving. Is there a real need to capture all market requirements, as well as possible variations or permutations, if the company developed the product at hand precisely to handle last minute change or unanticipated demands?

Completeness of vision feels old-school, like legacy waterfall or SDLC techniques that are insistent on knowing or capturing everything beforehand. The assessment criteria do not appear to be accountable to the nature of SaaS. In this respect, it is likely that completeness can slow down the ability of the SaaS to execute. Also, to the extent that requirements change or users further crystallize or clarify them upon consecutive viewings of a working prototype (recall the Agile methodology), then we can make the case that early execution (on ability to execute) may very well augment completeness if not validity of vision. But then, the allure of 2-dimensional constructs and the way they plug-and-play, just like iPaaS, with our existing diagrams, numbers, charts, and graphs is simply too tantalizing to resist; after all, Gartner's MQ is entirely congruent with many a 2 by 2 grid exhibit displayed in many a Harvard Business school article which vendors are quick to proclaim, "so and so named a visionary" or "visionary for the last 3 consecutive years."

Even as an *independent* market research firm, it unwittingly plays a role in the way we frame and talk technology. The same MQ, after all, not only applies to both software and hardware vendors, it is also used to subsume human capital management (HCM), sales, inventory, financials, and other software solutions, bringing new meaning to the universals that lurk behind specifics. In thinking back to my first job as a management consultant fresh out of school with an intervening 2½ year military stint, I remember bolstering the credibility of client recommendations with findings from Gartner Group and other research firms. The following depicts the spectrum of insider- and outsider-ness that characterize end users, technical personnel, and third-party or independent bodies depending on your frame of reference. It becomes all too obvious that when you are an insider, you are simultaneously an outsider. When you are on the inside, you are also on the outside. There is just no escaping the other. The following illustration shows how the vendor, while an insider when it comes to the SaaS and its inner workings, nonetheless remains an outsider when it comes to the functional or domain knowledge housed in an accountant.

	Insider				**Outsider**
Functional / domain knowledge	Accountant	Government bodies	Analyst Groups	Developer	Vendor
System / SaaS knowledge	Vendor	Developer	Analyst Groups	Accountant	Government bodies
Industry / compliance knowledge	Government bodies	Analyst Groups	Accountant	Vendor	Developer

In the closing analysis, perhaps the real question to ask is to what extent has the very language or languages that we have grown accustomed to imprisoned us, trapped as it were, in the earlier Chinese room of sorts? To the external observer, we appear to converse in Chinese even if it really showcases how good we are at correlating one language with another with little or at best surface understanding or appreciation for either context or nuance. With a proclamation on the "end of software" in 1999, Marc Benioff left Oracle after 13 years to start Salesforce with Parker Harris, a software engineer.[66] In retrospect, Salesforce heralded not so much the-end-of-software as we know it but rather the faint beginnings of SaaS. It turned the software revenue model on its head by driving down entry costs to CRM capability that would have cost hundreds of thousands. Siebel, a dominant CRM player at the time and on-premise software provider in contrast, would later be acquired by Oracle. The lack of clarity on the admission criteria for patients, revenue or accruals notwithstanding, the low admission cost to using Salesforce eventually made it a household name not just among smaller- and medium-sized enterprises but also large Fortune 500 corporations. And yet, as we have seen from user feedback surrounding rolling period reporting functionality with Salesforce, several fundamentals remain unchanged in the way we engage and sustain a dialogue with software. We started by exploring how it matters that we can replay a transaction and its related records forwards and backwards. Along the way, we see how semantics or meaning can differ from syntax and just because there are language or software rules at play, every reading is anything but predictable. Reversibility too, can translate into forgiveness whether users can retrace their steps without feeling imprisoned in a cul-de-sac when committing an inadvertent misstep. We can just as easily extend this same ease of reversibility to human subjects surrounding their use of the SaaS so that an assessment of their degree of insider-ness or outsider-ness can be just a matter of perspective.

Reversibility is just as easy when it comes to characterizing SaaS-y-ness or a SaaS's positive attributes. The same advantage can very well turn into a disadvantage in a different environment or through a different lens. Ease of access through a web browser can also mean ease of password sharing across SaaS. At risk are SaaS administrators with superuser access and likely straddling multiple integrated SaaS. Talk about toxic pairs that can arise when specific individuals have superuser user access across two or more integrated SaaS so that there is a more than likely possibility for fraud to be committed or an unauthorized transaction initiated without the necessary oversight and reviews. With the *right* level of access, we can create a vendor in the upstream procurement SaaS and pay the same vendor in a downstream accounting SaaS without necessarily having to create an intervening purchase requisition, purchase order, receipt, and vendor invoice. In addition, with the all too ubiquitous email address as a user name, the only variable to hack would be the password however complex. Faced with multiple best-of-breed SaaS, users experience lethargy with changing passwords during periodic aging and expiry and having to come up with ever more creative combinations. This is such a common phenomenon that at a Usenix Security Symposium in San Diego Dinei Florencio and Cormac Herley of Microsoft Research recommended using a shared password for trivial accounts and complex, individual passwords for more valuable accounts.[67]

A second advantage with SaaS – having uptime and availability managed by the SaaS provider – means no additional capital layout on the part of the client organization, but as we have seen with the disruption to AWS in February 2017, any SaaS that taps into AWS, and in this case the procurement SaaS Coupa, became unavailable for access by association at a time during month end close. The fall-back procedural options untaken can vary from lining up vendor invoices received and queued for entry when Coupa becomes available to skipping Coupa altogether and making a direct journal entry in the downstream accounting SaaS. Any or all these fallback measures go into far greater depth into what goes on behind the scenes than what the marketing intervention that went into handling the Workday's 35-hour outage would have us believe.

There is also the question of how we would look at invoice statuses or other details when there is no procurement SaaS available to log into in fielding customer inquiries. Another possible option may be to look for related records in an upstream or downstream SaaS. With lack of availability, the same benefit of SaaS availability can be rewritten or reversed into a cost, even as recovery procedures may be attempted to ease the later re-entry of transactions that could not be entered at the present time. A nested reversal of a reversal? Finally, ease of configuration also means greater likelihood of unauthorized, invalid, or just plain incorrect updates made. This combined with a lack of audit trails on configuration changes presents a unique conundrum. Out of all three areas discussed, the last two are out of the customers' hands so while it is easy to hand off non-core competency processes to a SaaS vendor, by the same token, the SaaS client also gives up control.

One key caveat on reversibility: the world of accounting is far less forgiving when it comes to reversing what the user already recorded – just check in with public companies that have had to restate their financials – consider the following accounting treatments assessed and proposed for changes to contract modifications in ASC-606. A vendor organization delivers a combination of a good and a service to a customer. The total contract value is $4,200, of which they allocate $3,000 to the goods and $1,200 to the service in accordance to their respective standalone selling price (SSP). The customer makes no up-front payment, but instead pays $350 per month over a period of 12 months. Because payment is dependent on the vendor's performance of the related monthly service, upon transfer of the good to the customer, the entity records a contract asset for $3,000 instead of a receivable. Each month that the vendor receives payment, the vendor recognizes revenue of $100 as the service is performed, and also reclassifies $250 of the contract asset to a receivable. Created by the International Accounting Standards Board (IASB) and FASB to provide a forum to analyze and discuss stakeholder issues arising from implementation of the new revenue standard, the Joint Transition Resource Group for Revenue Recognition (TRG) gives an example where the vendor and customer negotiate a change in scope and price of the contract after 9 months have elapsed, such that a year of service is added for the price of $50 per month for the new remainder term of 15 months. Let's take a deeper dive. By the 9-month mark, the balance remaining on the contract asset would have been $750 ($3,000/12 * 3). The question becomes: should we

1. Write off the remaining contract asset to revenue, essentially reversing revenue and reproportion the remaining $1,650 (($350 × 3) + ($50 × 12)) over the modified term of 15 months

2. Retain the contract asset and only reproportion the unrecognized revenue $900 (($100 × 3) + ($50 × 12)) over the modified term of 15 months

FASB staff ultimately opted for the second choice over the first, preferring to avoid adjusting revenue for performance obligations already satisfied and instead to account for such modifications prospectively rather than retrospectively. Unlike Dr. Banks who chose to reach forward to the future if only to access the information to whisper into the Chinese General's ear in the present, FASB's approach would have been to write off any potential and likely destruction of the alien ships altogether and to make room for future allowances or amends.

Reversibility takes on new meaning when users use reversing journals to commit financial fraud. WorldCom, once the fifth most widely held stock in the country and listed as the top return for shareholders over a 10-year period, fell from grace when it restated its financials by $3.8 billion from having improperly capitalized operating expenses. An interview with then vice president of the internal audit group at WorldCom, Cynthia Cooper, reveals how while accountants who rolled up to a senior VP were booking entries to increase the wireless allowance, those rolled up to the CFO who nevertheless went ahead and reversed these entries after.[68] In the tightly knit web of ever-integrated relations, where the boundaries between subject versus object, animate versus inanimate, advantage versus disadvantage begin to dissolve, even the divide between reversibility and irreversibility becomes suspect.

Palindrome applies more to the forward and backward looking at a transaction so that we arrive at the same semantics whether played forwards or backwards syntactically. It also applies when contrary meanings can co-exist in the same space. In fact, when more than one syntactical rule – system, accounting, CRM, audit, management – converges at the intersection of SaaS usage, conflicts or gaps in understanding are all but inevitable. In *Arrival*, Dr. Banks comprehends multiple languages but even she would be at her wits' end if inundated with various languages lobbed at her simultaneously. In the movie, she comes full circle when she realizes that she can in fact foretell the future so that what comes before meets what comes after, the frame by frame sequencing of time or the movie, as it were, coming to a grinding standstill. In a cliff-hanger scene, she attempts to contact Chinese General Chang to stop him from attacking the alien ships. What should she say? Spoiler alert for those of you who haven't yet seen the movie. In a move that gives new meanings to future past perfect, she *recalls* a future scene at a ball when the General thanks her for contacting him before. What did I say, she hears her future self asking the General only to have him whisper in her ear what would have been his wife's last words, "In war there are no winners, only widows." With these very words, she returns to the present, delivers them to the General and, in the process, manages to avert a catastrophe in the making.

The image of returning wild geese, as Métail points out, is a recurring theme in Chinese poetry. With the change of seasons, they flee to warmer climates only to return later. Going and coming. Distance and proximity. In Chapter 1, we talked about the plight of the sex slaves transposed from China to what was then San Francisco's Dupont Avenue in the 1890s. In a more recent transmigration reminiscent of wild geese leaving then returning, a reversal of sorts to the Chinese diaspora, the *San Francisco Chronicle* reports of increasing Chinese students choosing to return to China after graduation rather than seek employment in the United States.[69] More than any other country, China sends more college students to the United States. Yet, interviews with those who worked in the United States after graduation but nevertheless made the move to return home despite spending a good number of years with U.S. employers suggest a glass or bamboo ceiling. Asians, while not classified as a minority in tech companies, continue to be curiously absent in executive management. When applying a palindrome to view a business transaction from cradle to grave, we ask what happens when we work backwards, forwards, or from midstream in either direction. Would we reach the same conclusion? Against this and in the context of wild geese fleeing and returning, we can read a reversible Chinese poem forwards and backwards.

风送香花红满地

雨滋春树碧连天

The wind accompanies the scented flowers, they cover the earth
The rain cultivates the spring trees, they brush the sky

天连碧树春滋雨

地满红花香送风

The sky brushes against the green trees, abundant spring rain
The earth covers itself with red flowers, scent-laden wind

The previous illustration is an example palindrome poem that Métail describes.[70] When read forward, the emphasis is on the wind and rain as subjects, with the earth and sky as being done unto. When read backwards, the favor is returned, with the sky and earth as subjects and the rain and wind being done unto. Read forward, what is active becomes passive; conversely read backwards the active takes on the passive. Likewise, when we work forwards from the faint beginnings of a transaction in an upstream SaaS, the emphasis is on complete, accurate, and valid field capture so that it serves as an authorized source to trigger shipping, fulfillment or billing. When we work backwards from the GL impact in an income statement in a downstream SaaS, the emphasis is on revenue allocations and segments coded, and the ability to trace what has been recorded to an actual live transaction as opposed to a mere accounting manipulation. With all our emphasis on directional sequencing, perhaps what is more important is the recognition of having to come full circle.

Exercise 4.1

Select a transaction of your choice in an enterprise software.

1. See if you can work your way upstream and downstream from this transaction.
2. For the identified upstream and downstream transactions, do they reside in the same software or others? If they reside in other software, how do they get brought across either into or away from the enterprise software?
3. To what extent does complexity either increase or decrease when the related transactions reside in other software?

Discussion

The easiest answer to the first transaction would have been to draw a blank, that is, not be able to identify an upstream or downstream related transaction. Either the software chosen is a monolithic ERP package that encompasses all enterprise functions, or there are issues in being able to trace the identified transaction upstream to its source or downstream to its conclusion simply because not enough breadcrumbs are available to thread together the missing pieces. Sometimes we underestimate complexity simply because we can't trace transactions back to their source, giving the illusion that the user initiated them in the enterprise software until we ask the pivotal question, why. Also, what often lurk behind the scenes are manual reconciliations performed to ensure that the number and total amount of transactions in a processed batch tie across two or more systems.

Exercise 4.2

Give an example substantiating each of the following propositions:

1. The better one is at being a vendor, the better one is at being a customer.
2. An advantage that comes from having an internal control can become a disadvantage.
3. An internal control can also be an external control.

Discussion

When I had these questions for the final exam in my *Accounting Information Systems* class, students joked that I should be teaching psychology. Yet when we came up with examples such as to include the customer purchase order number on the invoices we remit, simply because of own experiences in having to put a purchase through purchase requisition approval internally, the resulting odds are customers are more likely to pay in a timely manner if they need to jump through far fewer hoops such as having to locate the originating purchase authorization before executing payment. Similarly, easy access to SaaS online can make it easier for access to be breached especially if we use the same password across multiple sites. For all our attention placed on controls *internal* to an organization, we can argue the same control insofar as it is evidenced in other organizations is also an *external* one shared by many. As we start to realize how our black versus white definitions can contain multitudes, they begin to lose their sharp edges.

Exercise 4.3

Pick an enterprise software in use in your organization.

1. What happens when it goes down for a couple of days? What actions would you undertake to work around the fact the software is inaccessible?
2. What happens if it goes down during month-end or quarter-end close? How would the actions you take change as a result?
3. What happens if instead of a couple of days, it goes down for a few hours. Would this change the course of actions that you have chosen to take?

Discussion

When I included a flavored subset of these questions on the midterm exam in my *Accounting Information Systems* class, the answers I received varied across the board. The easiest one I received was that no action would be taken as the enterprise software did not process any transactions with financial impact and thus there was no real urgency to having them processed expediently. Of those who identified some level of financial impact, some wrote about resorting to manual or paper records. Yet others explored switching up month-end close tasks by pulling forward those that they can accomplish when the system is down so that all hands can be focused on data import or entry when it is back online. As unlikely as it would seem, I have experienced SaaS outages during quarter-end close where we could not help but teeter on the edge even if, in retrospect, adequate remedial actions were in place. When customers or vendors call to inquire about outstanding bills or invoices during the time when the primary SaaS is down, accounting personnel would have to turn to compensating manual or system records.

Endnotes

[1] Zuboff, S. (September 1985) Automate/informate: The two faces of intelligent technology. *Organizational Dynamics*; 85, 14(2), 5–18.
[2] Mol, A. and Law, J. (2004, June 1). Embodied action, enacted bodies: The example of hypoglycaemia, *Body & Society*, 10(2–3), 43–62.
[3] Latour, B. (1986). Visualisation and cognition: Drawing things together. *Knowledge and Society: Studies in the Sociology of Culture and Present*, 6, 1–40.
[4] Carroll, L. and Tenniel, J. (1899). *Through the Looking-Glass and What Alice Found There*. London, UK: Macmillan Publishers.
[5] Ibid.
[6] Ibid.
[7] Ibid.
[8] Ibid.

⁹ Ibid.

¹⁰ Wittgenstein, L. (2001) [1953]. *Philosophical Investigations*. Malden, MA: Blackwell Publishing.

¹¹ Carroll, L. and Tenniel, J. *Through the Looking-Glass and What Alice Found There*.

¹² Ibid.

¹³ Kripke, S. (1982). *Wittgenstein on Rules and Private Language*. Cambridge, MA: Harvard University Press.

¹⁴ Wainewright, P. For *Software as Services* (August 20, 2007). Workday: Forget ERP, start over. ZDNet. http://www.zdnet.com/article/workday-forget-erp-start-over/

¹⁵ McLuhan, M. (1964). Understanding Media: The Extensions of Man. New York: New American Library.

¹⁶ Coppee, Henry. (1872). *Elements of Logic*. New York: American Book Company.

¹⁷ Searle, J (1980). Minds, brains, and programs. *Behavioral and Brain Sciences* 3, 417–424.

¹⁸ Ibid.

¹⁹ Ibid.

²⁰ Ibid.

²¹ Ibid.

²² Searle, J. (2010). Why dualism (and Materialism) fail to account for consciousness. In R. E. Lee (Ed) *Questioning Nineteenth Century Assumptions about Knowledge, III: Dualism*. Albany, NY: SUNY Press.

²³ Ibid.

²⁴ Securities Exchange Act 1934. Accounting and auditing pronouncement. Release No. 73209 (September 25, 2014). United States of America before Securities Exchange Commission. https://www.sec.gov/litigation/admin/2014/34-73209.pdf

²⁵ Ibid.

²⁶ Ibid.

²⁷ Carroll, L. and Tenniel, J. *Through the Looking-Glass and What Alice Found There*.

²⁸ Howlett, D. For *Irregular Enterprise*. (August 20, 2007). Workday financials: Accounting isn't real. *ZDNet*. http://www.zdnet.com/article/workday-financials-accounting-isnt-real/

²⁹ Potter, K. (November 9, 2017). Tearful meeting for pair forever linked by face transplant. Associated Press in San Francisco Chronicle. http://www.sfchronicle.com/news/medical/article/Tearful-meeting-for-pair-forever-linked-by-face-12346637.php#photo-14525343

³⁰ Ibid.

³¹ Ibid.

³² Heidegger, M. (1977). *The Question Concerning Technology, and Other Essays*. New York: Harper & Row.

³³ Ibid.

³⁴ Ibid.

³⁵ Ibid.

³⁶ Ibid.

³⁷ Ibid.

³⁸ Reyes, J. (July 22, 2014). How Wharton MBA startup Tesorio is helping Yards Brewing save money. *Technical.ly*. https://technical.ly/philly/2014/07/22/tesorio-carlos-vega-wharton-yards/

³⁹ Grint, K. and Woolgar, S. (1997). *The Machine at Work: Technology, Work and Organization*. Cambridge, UK: Polity Press.

⁴⁰ Ibid.

[41] Ibid.

[42] Ibid.

[43] Ibid.

[44] Ibid.

[45] Ibid.

[46] Ibid.

[47] Ibid.

[48] Ibid.

[49] Carroll, L. and Tenniel, J. *Through the Looking-Glass and What Alice Found There.*

[50] Ibid.

[51] Ibid.

[52] Ibid.

[53] Salesforce Trailblazer Community. Rolling periods. https://success.salesforce.com/ideaView?id=08730000000Bq7M

[54] Wittgenstein, L. and G. E. M. Anscombe. (1997). *Philosophical Investigations.* Oxford, UK: Blackwell.

[55] United States District Court, District of Massachusetts. (April 1, 1998). Class action complaint for violation of federal securities laws, Civil Action Number 98-10578WGY. http://securities.stanford.edu/filings-documents/1012/PTUS98/199841_f01c_98CV 10578.pdf

[56] Ibid.

[57] Ibid.

[58] Ibid.

[59] Ibid.

[60] Ibid.

[61] Ibid.

[62] Ibid.

[63] Kravets, D. (July 15, 2008). San Francisco admin charged with Hijacking City's Network. *Wired.* https://www.wired.com/2008/07/sf-city-charged/

[64] Nicastro, D. (August 8, 2014). Vendor Sues Gartner Over Magic Quadrant 'Pay to Play' Model. *CMS Wire.* https://www.cmswire.com/cms/information-management/vendor-sues-gartner-over-magic-quadrant-pay-to-play-model-026133.php and Jennings, R. (October 22, 2009). Gartner sued by ZL re. Magic Quadrant; huge damages claim. *ComputerWorld.* https://www.computerworld.com/article/2467990/social-business/gartner-sued-by-zl-re--magic-quadrant--huge-damages-claim.html

[65] Latour, B. (1986). Visualisation and cognition: Drawing things together.

[66] Benioff, M. (March 8, 2013). Salesforce Blog: Marc Benioff: How to Turn a Simple Idea into a High-Growth Company. https://www.salesforce.com/blog/2013/03/how-to-turn-a-simple-idea-into-a-high-growth-company.html

[67] Florencio I., Herley C., and Coskun, B. (August 1, 2007). Do strong web passwords accomplish anything? In *Proceedings of the Second USENIX Workshop on Hot Topics in Security* (HotSec '07), USENIX.

[68] Carozza, D. (March/April 2008). Extraordinary circumstances. *Fraud Magazine.* http://www.fraud-magazine.com/article.aspx?id=210

[69] Lee, W. (September 24, 2017). *American Dream Also Found in China.* San Francisco, CA: San Francisco Chronicle.

[70] Métail, M. (2017). *Wild Geese Returning: Chinese Reversible Poems.* Series: Calligrams.

Chapter 5

Manual Automatons

> The whole history of a system project can
> be construed as a struggle to configure ...
> the user.[1]
>
> **Steve Woolgar**

It would have been a sight to behold. A life-sized wooden man outfitted with clothes and a turban presiding over a chessboard on top of a wheeled cabinet in a Viennese court in 1770. Hungarian inventor Wolfgang von Kempelen would throw open the cabinet doors and shine a candle within. The light threw into sharp relief its contents – a garish concoction of gears and cogs. At one viewing, an "old lady ... went and hid herself in a window seat, as distant as she could from the evil spirit, which she firmly believed possessed the machine."[2] Baron von Kempelen would proceed to invite a volunteer to play a game of chess with the automaton chess player also known as the Mechanical Turk. Over the course of its 85-year career, the Turk would play against famous opponents including Napoléon Bonaparte, Benjamin Franklin, Charles Babbage, and Edgar Allan Poe before perishing in a fire at the Chinese Museum of Philadelphia in 1854. How was this possible? Many a theory abound. Yet others speculated that the Turk was controlled by magnets and chains. Poe himself would write about how he thought an operator hid in the Turk. Babbage, after playing two games against the Turk, would draw up plans that eventually led to the design of his first mechanical computer, *The Difference Engine*. Even though it was never completed, Babbage wrote an algorithm for playing chess. When later revealed that the real machinery was a human operator hidden inside the cabinet – he would use a mechanical seat to slide out of view when the inventor opened the cabinet for inspection – the public's reaction remained one of disbelief. After all, numerous speculative books and articles have been written on its inner workings. I do not know what is more remarkable: the fact the Turk was able to trick its audience all this time or the public's everlasting faith in the existence of artificial life. Like the explicit one-time staging performed to demonstrate the vacuum pump or Stratus 286, or the ongoing staging that continues unabated behind the scenes by varied actors to support Software as a Service (SaaS), Baron von Kempelen's explicit attempts at throwing open the cabinet doors to light the interior with a candle strikes a universal chord. We all feel this pull, this irresistible urge to succumb to the idea that one day, much would be automated. Fears abound about how continual artificial intelligence (AI) research would one day take away our jobs, render us irrelevant. And on the other hand, a co-worker was just sharing an account the other day about how he used to be able to "automate" all his account reconciliations using visual basic (VB) scripting in Excel so that while others in his team were expending time and resource trying to close the books, he could execute the same tasks with a mere click of a button. Like fireflies, we are drawn to the appeal of doing more with less, or ideally not much at – until the Mechanical Turk showed up, audiences were mesmerized by Jacques de Vaucanson's Digesting Duck that quacked, flapped, and pooped – and yet we struggle to retain a sense of identity or worth when faced with drones or self-driving cars of today.

As we shall soon see, when working with SaaS, reality can be much more nuanced, neither one nor the other, but often involving complex, even unexpected interplay between seemingly irreconcilable opposites. When looking at and behind the value propositions of SaaS such as "we don't have to have to worry about updates in the cloud," it is amazing how little has changed. Alain de Botton points out how the news media, in its unstinting presentation of financial number wizardry to current and would-be investors, doesn't quite offer a real-life account of what goes on behind the numbers.[3] In a series of brief vignettes that succeed each other in rapid succession, de Botton contrasts the images behind the oft-reported company stock prices.[4] Behind the public brand of Tsann Kuen Enterprise Co. Ltd listed on the Taiwan stock exchange lies a 23,000-person hangar-like factory in Xiamen City producing the economical commodities that we consume every day.[5] For Latour, the news is a perfect example of an immutable mobile even as it conceals more than it reveals "the real thing."[6] We can say the same for cloud technology. Each time we upload a document to the cloud, it disappears into air, only to be available when invoked. In a rare look at a Google cloud data center, one is struck by rack after rack of servers in an almost hanger-like facility processing at one petabit per second of internal bandwidth for data transfers. Blink and you might just mistake them for the workers hunched over in the Xiamen City facility. This reminds us of sociologist Erving Goffman's depiction of the backstage behavior in *The Presentation of Self in Everyday Life*, a characterization of how we conduct our internal affairs when we let our guard down.[7] In contrast, our front-stage behavior is the one displayed to others. In many ways, the cloud industry is a classic interplay of front- with back-stage behavior. Because SaaS abstracts out all layers of the technology stack, all end users see and interact with is a ubiquitous browser. And yet, behind the sheen lies a tangled consortium of servers, hardware, and networking equipment in secured data centers all over the globe. As recently as 2011, Salesforce.com operated seven data centers around the U.S. and Asia spanning about 76,000 square feet of space, with two data centers apiece in Chicago and northern Virginia, along with facilities in San Francisco, San Jose, and Singapore.[8] As alluded to in Chapter 3, many SaaS providers including Coupa do not even maintain their own data centers relying instead on Amazon Web Services (AWS) for infrastructure as a service (IaaS). Even within the SaaS, internal controls perceived to "operate" do so within the confines of the audit universe; the moment real-life messiness enters the picture, the remedial actions stay in the back stage, in favor and support of the "more" rationalized and front-stage behaviors easily portable as best practices across public firms globally.

Today, the Mechanical Turk lives on even if it no longer resembles its life-sized wooden forefather. Conceived by Amazon, the site Mechanical Turk gives academicians and companies an online platform to source humans to complete quick, little tasks than even computers could not handle. Dubbed Human Intelligence Tasks (HIT), these comprise of anything from identifying and logging a receipt to flagging offensive content images to tagging drains and lamp posts on roadways. In perhaps a homage to tradition, humans continue to perform these HIT, so much sifting and classifying in mere minutes with a payout of under 10 cents apiece. It is funny how in its modern-day incarnation, the Mechanical Turk is performing rather menial tasks, when back in the day, he was wowing the audiences by an ability to execute the Knight's tour, a set of moves that rival even the most advanced of players, defeating the most capable of opponents including Charles Babbage. Despite technological advances, the present-day identification of drainage or lamp posts seems almost menial, not unlike the former-day sifting of a cog from a gear. Another way of differentiating the current day manifestation is its accountability to a rather specific component task broken down from a higher-level objective, whereas its Viennese counterpart is responsible for all component tasks supporting an overall objective, namely that of winning the game. Still, a lot has happened since its time – its tour around Europe and later America took place during the Luddite riots after all – and what better way to illustrate this than to start with the scientific management principles developed by Frederick Taylor a little more than a century later in the 1880s and 1890s.

In an era when mechanization and automation were still in their infancy, Taylor laid down the groundwork for modern-day task componentization and automation by factoring processes into discrete, unambiguous units. Opting for shop-floor experience at Enterprise Hydraulic Works in Philadelphia in place of a Yale education, Taylor would go on to start an independent consulting practice advocating scientific management principles comprising of

1. Methods associated with a scientific study of work over rule-of-thumb methods
2. Formalized employee training over leaving them to their own devices

3. "Detailed instruction and supervision" over each "discrete task"
4. Division of work between planning for managers and execution for managed workers[9]

"Now one of the very first requirements for a man who is fit to handle pig iron as a regular occupation is that he shall be so stupid and so phlegmatic that he more nearly resembles in his mental make-up the ox than any other type."[10] Less well known perhaps is Taylor's view of less intelligent workers. To be fair, Taylor also championed frequent breaks and good pay even if he was of the opinion that "the man who is mentally alert and intelligent is for this very reason entirely unsuited to what would, for him, be the grinding monotony of work of this character."[11] It is interesting to observe parallels between Taylor's scientific principles and the audit approach to internal controls:

1. A system of internal controls formalized through documented policies and procedures
2. Periodic employee training
3. Top-down management risk assessment
4. Segregation of duties to support independent management oversight of work performed

Thus, can we conclude that it takes a "mental make-up" of an "ox than any other type" to be "fit to handle" internal controls?[12]

A lot has happened since Taylor's era, not least of which the evolution of a management style, from micromanaging clearly defined tasks to delegating responsibilities, such that direct reports assume greater ownership not just for executing and delivering on service and customer satisfaction but also articulating and defining these very processes and sub-processes to begin with. The definition and decomposition of higher level tasks into lower level ones, much like our earlier comparison of Agile versus waterfall or traditional SDLC techniques, assumes a certain level of stagnancy, that what we need to do we can arrested or captured in time and decompose into subtasks for which we predetermine the outcome or milestone and measure against it to track progress. I'm not denying that for some SaaS providers this waterfall implementation approach remains entrenched as the predominant methodology, so that in the case of one SaaS implementation, it obligates customers to complete specific templates offered and have the requirements signed off before configuration actually begins; if and when users test a demo prototype in a sandbox environment and requirements change, the SaaS provider updates the initial requirements document and recirculates it for another round of review and approval. The process places emphasis on determining whether customers truly need customization, a bone of contention between client and vendor – and in this respect, mirrors an on-premise software implementation – not least because it is accompanied by additional unanticipated or unplanned for costs that need to be baked into an updated purchase requisition recirculated for approval. In another example, because of the flavor of SaaS purchased, the number of fields that we can configure is limited, as are reports or email templates out-of-the-box. Implementation timeline, as with cost, is prefaced over the act of tailoring the SaaS to specific organizational needs. And depending on the processes supported, the actual manner that the software works out-of-the-box doesn't vary greatly from one client to another. Even if both sell different products, one service and the other physical goods, having different tax codes for different products would suffice in computing, tracking, and reporting on specific sales tax liability while leaving underlying processes fundamentally unchanged. Depending on whether the SaaS is priced on annually, monthly, or by the volume of transactions processed, different decisions are made on whether to have the sales tax computed at line or header or even batch level. Much can be accomplished just by operating within the confines of the SaaS at hand.

In contrast to this out-of-the-box or IaaS approach, Agile values user stories. One user story could be: as an account receivables personnel, I would need to execute a bill run with pre-entered criteria so that I don't have to process all customer invoices individually but can schedule them to be processed in a bulk manner. As you can imagine, a benefit of this user story is that it would improve the organization's ability to scale and process greater transaction volumes with the same resources at hand. In working with individual users to figure how to configure the SaaS to account for this user story, we may unearth greater detail such as how an automated bill run would need to execute differently for standard versus custom sales orders, or how those that belong to a specific dollar value threshold, large deals for example, warrant a more detailed review against the contracts prior to actual invoicing. The beauty of Agile is that not all detail needs to be captured prior to developing a workflow in the SaaS. In fact, it is only during the demo of a singular invoice belonging to a custom sales order that prompted users to clarify the need to differentiate standard from custom sales.

Depending on the team at hand – Agile advocates for a cross-functional team – other unanticipated requirements start to enter the picture. For example, from an order management perspective, users should consider only approved sales orders with future expected invoices for an automated bill run as opposed to those pending approval or cancelled. Also, from a revenue recognition perspective, these auto-generated invoices should only apply to orders with associated fulfillments; recall that one of SOP 97-2 revenue recognition principles requires delivery to be made. There is not just one account or one narrative, so the key with limited resources and time is to focus on capturing those that are requisite for Day 1 go-live or needed for a minimally viable product (MVP). Technical debt creeps in and often accumulates over time if stories not worked on Day 1 continue to fester and snowball during Day 2 maintenance. Contrast this with the Taylorist approach where there is only *one* story.

Management is responsible for planning, even if it is precisely because they manage that they remain unaware of real-life specifics. Our example of inflating a multipiece wheel from Chapter 2 comes to mind. Even though much of the work takes place out in the field where a safety cage is not available, planners deem it mandatory precisely because they have never been out in the field. Contrast the Agile approach as well with the SDLC one, where by the time multi-accounts or stories are captured in requirements in their entirety – and even then there is always a possibility one is inadvertently left – time would have elapsed so that by the time configuration begins, these requirements captured at a snapshot in time would have likely changed depending on ongoing changes to people, strategy, or processes in the company which in turn would necessitate a new wave of change requests to the march of succeeding artifacts. All this takes time, so it is not uncommon for deployment to production to occur years, rather than months, later. We can easily draw parallels between the waterfall or SDLC approach with Taylor's principles:

1. A software development life cycle methodology exists documenting the various requirements, analysis, development, testing, deployment and maintenance phases
2. End-user training is conducted prior to go-live
3. A project manager provides oversight and monitoring of project deliverables against committed milestones
4. Handoffs from one phase to another, or one team to another is authorized by appropriate signoffs

As before with internal controls, can we conclude that it takes a "mental make-up" of an "ox than any other type" to be "fit to handle" SDLC such as is the "grinding monotony of work of this character?"[13] These similarities are made more remarkable considering how handling pig iron is vastly different from developing or configuring software, even though we can certainly make the case that the SaaS's acceptance of data input only in a predictable and unwavering format resembles the "mental make-up the ox than any other type."[14]

Agile, in contrast, mirrors the art of playing chess. It is virtually impossible to anticipate every move beforehand – the premise behind waterfall with its insistence on signoffs at gating intervals between requirements, development, testing, and release. By focusing on working software rather than the girth of the requirements binder, we recognize that while we don't have everything planned out ahead of time, we are nonetheless adept at adapting to changes that arise. In the context of chess, we are still focused on winning the game rather than going over every composable task in fine detail. For we could have all our reviews evidenced and requirements documented and still not have sufficient time or resources to deliver the software.

A case in point is the FBI's attempt at deploying electronic case management for sharing among agencies to defend against terrorist attacks. Conceived in March 2006, Sentinel integrates off-the-shelf components and was awarded to Lockheed Martin to implement in four phases at the price tag of $305 million targeted for completion in December 2009. Developed using waterfall, the initial requirements compiled totaled 1,129 requirements in June 2005.[15] Yet in the 7 years that passed after the requirements were approved, the combined changes to FBI's business processes and information technology (IT) infrastructure led to 90 additions, 172 deletions, and 119 modifications.[16] The first phase culminated in access via a web browser with little enhancement over existing functionality, in what some would call "lipstick on a pig."[17] Faced with mounting data quality, functionality, and performance challenges, Phase 2 was put to a premature end with Lockheed Martin told to stop all future work. All this time, agents continued to maintain manual paperwork alongside the "automated" system.

Faced with delays and rising costs, the FBI insourced the entire project in September 2010 and made the switch to Agile as the development methodology. It broke down the 1,1,29 requirements into 670 user stories.[18] Although ensuing interim audit reports continued to surface challenges, by July 2014, users began reporting a positive tangible impact on sharing information and carrying out operations. Yet, the latest iteration of audits from the U.S. Department of Justice Office of the Inspector General Audit Division revealed a curious find. Users were still not using the Search and Index feature, which one would think would be a huge value added over physical paperwork, especially since with properly indexed data, one could locate "white males who drive black cars" quickly.[19] Yet, only 42% of respondent used the Search functionality, and of these, over 59% rarely got the results they needed.[20] There was also a hidden catch: more administrative time was spent in indexing, ironically "leaving less time for investigative work."[21] Here, what users experienced mirrors what physicians experienced with electronic medical records (EMR) described in Chapter 2. In addition to additional time spent on indexing, a key subset of users, Evidence Custodian Technicians and Electronic Surveillance Technicians, also reported spending more time storing and managing evidence on top of having to maintain physical records in addition to electronic ones.[22]

Despite Power's critique of audit as a loop unto itself, these audit reports, which are freely available to the public online, nonetheless reveal more performative than ostensive aspects of the everyday. Feldman and Pentland describe the latter as an "ideal or schematic form."[23] Examples include standard operating procedures or taken for granted organizational norms. Recall Taylor's emphasis on having methods associated with a scientific study of work as opposed to informalized rule-of-thumb.[24] As we will see, in many respects, these methods serve more as resources for action rather than real determinants of action and that may be why they can't really describe the action to perform in any high degree of detail. Doing so would render an objective unattainable in situations that demand a more tailored response to local nuances. It is not hard to see how performative aspects can remain unchanged when configuring a SaaS. The ostensive aspect, a three-way match control for example, would require a purchase requisition and receipt before a user could create and save a vendor invoice. Yet, because there is a manual workaround – that is, the user creates the purchase requisition only after receiving the invoice and working backwards rather than forwards – the performative aspect remains unaltered, thanks to the degrees of freedom accorded to local nuanced practices.

For Feldman and Pentland, performative aspects are concerned with "specific actions taken by specific people in specific times."[25] Characterized by a high degree of improvization, they are 'performed' in the context of their ostensive counterparts – rules and protocols – but nonetheless are imbued with a certain degree of novelty each time a user executes them. As Feldman and Pentland put it, "in terms of music, the ostensive part is like the musical score, while the performative part is the actual performance of the music."[26] In this regard, the performative aspect is integral to its ostensive counterpart. When the score is no longer played, it becomes a relic of the past. With Sentinel, despite the best of intentions for the ostensive – an easy search of records based on user-entered criteria – in reality, the performative enters the picture whether it is having to index additional stored data or wading through a morass of false positives yielded by a search. When Taylor described how managers identify smaller tasks by decomposing from bigger ones, it is hard to see how these descriptions can touch on the performative, especially since they are formulated by individuals not in the know. If they are ostensive, which they very likely are, then it is not hard to see how they exemplify the Mechanical Turk, concealing performative aspects, the man hidden within to execute chess moves using a combination of magnets and strings. An image comes to mind: the last scene from *The Wizard of Oz* where Toto locates the wizard even as he is frantically working the controls of a machine all the time screaming, "Pay no attention to that man behind the curtain."[27] With the Mechanical Turk, audiences did just that. The question is: with SaaS, are enterprise customers doing the same? Is SaaS no more than lipstick on a pig?

Thus far, when looking at actions, we have peered in from different perspectives, whether it is with a Taylorist lens with composable tasks defined by someone else other than the doer or ostensive aspects that leave room for the performative. We have been using activities, actions, and operations rather interchangeably but to see past the imitation game, it helps to turn to Aleksei N. Leontiev, a Soviet developmental psychologist and founder of activity theory. Stripped to its essentials, Leontiev's premise comprises three levels:

1. Activities and the motives that drive them
2. Actions and associated goals
3. Operations carried out under the conditions of the goals ascribed[28]

Insofar as there is decomposition of higher level activities into actions and operations, there are brief undertones of Taylorist principles, but this is where the similarity ends. Lest we walk away thinking that it is a waste of time to delve down to granular processes and sub-processes, Leontiev's approach merits a deeper review. For Leontiev, human activity manifests as an action or process, or a series of actions or processes undertaken to fulfill specific motives.[29] When a company is motivated to report its accounts receivable (A/R) in an accurate and complete manner (activity), it puts in motion a set of actions to accomplish its goals. These can comprise performing a credit check on its customers and reviewing its invoices against manual support to ensure that customers are able to pay and that they are remitting invoices to the correct bill-to addresses. Operations do not have their own goals per se but support the actions undertaken to meet specific goals.

In our A/R example, the actual sourcing of specific details on a new customer, such as legal name, address, tax identification number, or federal taxpayer identification number, are variations of operational work. Note the same operation can address more than one process and goal. In this case getting the customer's address can help with both getting the required information for performing a credit check as well as insuring that the right bill-to address is on the invoice during customer invoicing. When we talk about internal controls in and around SaaS, we are really focusing on the bottom rung, the operations undertaken or the means to an end. Let's move from Order-to-Cash to Procure-to-Pay. To ensure that organizational spending is properly controlled and accounted for (motive), a series of actions or processes is set into motion: the request to spend, the approval of that request, the communication to the vendor, the receipt of the service, the receipt of the invoice, the processing of payment against the invoice, the month end reconciliation of the bank account balance, and the ongoing reporting to reflect at what stage the organization is in on monthly and quarterly financials. At the next level down, varied operations occur to support these actions.

The same operation of obtaining specific attributes on new customers discussed earlier in our A/R example can be just as applicable to new vendors. Each action has an associated goal. The goal that drives a request for spending is to relay a tangible output, in this case a purchase requisition to decision makers, not so much controlling spend. Likewise, the goal associated with securing purchase requisition approvals addresses the provision of necessary oversight for a specific department spend as opposed to controlling spending for the entire organization. Thus, in this manner, each of these can be sub-goals that relate back to an overarching goal that in turn drives the motive to properly account for spending.

At this point, it makes sense to clarify the difference between a purchase requisition and a purchase order (PO). The former is used to obtain approval for spending for the latter. While I may have used them interchangeably to illustrate the importance of including customer PO numbers on invoices from a vendor perspective, and conversely from a customer perspective being able to locate the purchase order number on a received vendor invoice, the approved purchase requisition translates into a purchase order number that can be shared with one's vendor. One approved requisition in this instance would map to one purchase order. When a user records a receipt or invoice, it is in turn matched against the purchase order, hence the ubiquitous three-way match control.

By decomposing activities and actions, Leontiev is not suggesting that we can't apply the same actions across two or more different activities or motives just as the same operation can be indifferent to the nature of triggering action or goal. Indeed, the same actions of requesting and approving purchase requisitions can meet a myriad of audit, compliance, management, and business motives. As we have seen, it is this inherent confusion of actions, and specifically, the preference for front-stage over back-stage behaviors, that can tempt us to narrowly focus on the subset of actions guided by underlying audit and compliance motives rather than those more performance or operations related.

While shaped by motives, actions are really directed towards goals. While motivated by the overarching or underlying motive to control spending, the process to request and approve spend are directed towards goals that emphasize the completeness, validity, and accuracy of the information captured in the purchase request. The relationship between actions and activities is reciprocal. In this case, the same actions can support varied activities around audit, compliance, management, and business. Conversely, the same activity or motive can engender varied actions. To control spending in a small private startup, the founders may decide to centralize all sourcing decisions with the financial controller. Guided by this motive and directed by an associated overall goal and ensuing sub-goals, the process or actions taken to procure services may simply be one of routing all requests to the financial controller, rather than having different department heads approve spending for their respective budgets. In this scenario, only the financial controller is aware of the company budget for the year and literally holds the purse strings to all spending with external providers. The actual operation, otherwise the routine undertaken to support the performance of the action, has more to do with the tools employed, whether that be a physical log book with perforated PO templates with pre-assigned numbers locked in the financial controller's desk or a procurement SaaS accessible anytime and anywhere via a web browser.

According to Leontiev, while activities are driven by motives and actions by goals, operations depend on conditions under which the goals are attained.[30] The log book makes more sense in a centralized spending environment for a privately held firm with limited resources, financial and physical. The emphasis is not so much on granting different individuals timely access to an easily accessible tool, especially since their intervention is not required for spending approval as it is on constraining the avenues available for spending requests in a manner such that only authorized spending emerges out of the pages of a carefully controlled log book under lock and key. When the conditions change, when the private startup begins scaling and growing, and the financial controller, in effect becomes a choke point for processing spending requests, the means or technology to solicit authorized spend evolves to a procurement SaaS solution.

When we examine the conditions governing the operations, unlike actions where we are looking at "producing" a purchase requisition or evidencing requisition approval, we are really looking at the completeness, timeliness, and accuracy of the information captured for the former and the validity of the request submitted for the latter. Such is the "operating effectiveness" of the internal controls attested to by management and validated by internal and external auditors. Underlying goals and motives guide these control objectives. Why devote so much text to activities, actions, and operations? Are we merely splitting hairs? You be the judge. Yet in devising internal controls for SaaS, are we really trying to avoid falling into a trap of devising controls that merely serve as ritual assurance, the same templates or routines recycled year after year, ready for audit primetime, then cast aside or relegated to the background when the auditors leave?

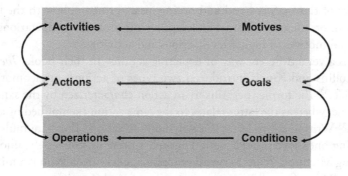

The relationships between activities and actions, as well as that between actions and operations are reciprocal and bidirectional. Just as the same actions driven by goals can align to multiple motives, the one and same operation can be used to perform multiple actions. Completeness of information entered applies to POs just as much as it would apply to vendor invoices and journals, or for that matter to sales quotes, orders, customer invoices, and returns. The ability of a SaaS, whether procurement, CRM, or enterprise-wide, in giving users the access to configure specific mandatory fields by transaction type addresses this operation. Through the SaaS, the conditions for the systematic capture of transactions become changed and from the Leontievian perspective "unfold" back into conscious action, where the window of opportunity for learning or relearning opens. From the Leontievian perspective, where the SaaS is configured and deployed – the conditions of operations – and the degree to which these can change makes a huge difference to the success of the SaaS deployment and ensuing maintenance.

Three key points to note here. First, the operation of mandatory fields doesn't merely address the same completeness control objective or goal in more than one (sub)process in Order-to-Cash, Procure-to-Pay, Record-to-Report, or Hire-to-Retire business cycles, it can also lend itself to other control objectives and goals. Take validity of an entered transaction. How can we even begin to ascertain if it is a valid entry, meaning unambiguous, unique, and legitimate based on an authorized source of input or trigger without a complete set of attributes to perform an assessment in the first place? Second, as we go up two levels from control operations to look at activities and motives, are the internal controls we designed too bottoms-up and not top-down enough in terms of explicating the link between control operating effectiveness and increased operational performance or cost savings? That the IT Process Institute's correlation of foundational controls with IT performance, in Chapter 2, has not been more publicized is itself revealing.[31] Third, insofar as the conditions of the goals have changed, SaaS versus on-premise, to what extent are we not acknowledging and leveraging them? It seems odd that despite the advance of online technologies, the Mechanical Turk of today have humans complete far more trivial component tasks than would a hidden human circumscribed within the confines of a wooden artifact. Thus, to what extent are we not leveraging the malleability of the SaaS at hand and opting instead to comply with the locked-in pattern of an on-premise software in adapting our present-day operations to meet the goals and motives of higher-level actions and activities?

There is a yet a different way of depicting actions. In their book, *The Shape of Actions*, Collins and Kusch introduced two types of actions: mimeomorphic and polymorphic.[32] The former pertains to an action characterized by the same behavior each time, whereas the latter relates to the same action exemplified by a range of behaviors.[33] Writing a love letter is a polymorphic action. There are multiple ways of professing one's love though not all entirely sincere or, conversely, unoriginal.[34] When using Microsoft Word for word processing, clicking on Print is a mimeomorphic action.[35] Seen from this perspective, mimeomorphic actions mirror Leontiev's operations whereas polymorphic actions are like Leontiev's descriptive for actions. The problem, as Collins and Kusch point out, is when we get confused by what the machine does and what we do.[36] Used as a tool to produce writing that appears in a consistent and universally acceptable font format, Microsoft Word is a novelty against the old-fashioned typewriter allowing for mistakes and edits without wasting reams of paper. Yet, it is by no means a proxy for churning out the love letter. The letter writer still needs to be present. In the futuristic movie, *Her*, directed by Spike Jonze in which Theodore, the male protagonist, is a letter writer undergoing the final stages of his divorce. He purchases and falls in love with OS1, an intelligent operating system. As the movie progresses, that Theodore favors OS1 as a proxy over any "real" relationships in the traditional sense is the same mistake that Collins and Kusch warn us of, a natural tendency on our part to attribute agency or intent to machines, turning them into proxies when they are merely tools.[37]

RAT, an acronym for "Repair, Attribute, and All That," is used to describe the manner "we 'repair' the deficiencies of machines and then 'attribute' agency to them."[38] Sound familiar? In our used and overused procurement SaaS example, we have described the tendency for invisible hands, whether belonging to an accountant or administrative staff, to assist in the user entry of purchase requisitions. At an even more atomic level, when the SaaS can preclude these same invisible hands from setting up a duplicate vendor, presumably from entering the same vendor name twice, we can mistake this proxy or human stand-in for SaaS capability in safeguarding against the processing duplicates or fictitious vendors. In effect, there is nothing to stop us from creating a similar sounding vendor albeit with an infinitesimal difference to the spelling of its name. What is to stop us from assigning the same bank account information, as part of electronic fund transfer (EFT) disbursement, to the same vendor but set up under two slightly different names in the SaaS? A common design mistake, Collins and Kusch write, is "to think that a computer that thoroughly hides the RAT does not need RAT at all."[39] I would argue even further that a common mistake is to think that an automated control, as in our SaaS example of duplicate detection of vendors, hides the RAT so well that it doesn't need RAT at all – in this case the manual intervention required to identify the potential for duplicate or fraudulent payment to vendors that already exist and have in fact already been paid. To focus on an automated control to evidence a check against duplicates or frauds is to emphasize performance over competence, intent over reality. We are all too familiar with users who tend to technology, massaging daily artifacts in a way that serve as valid input, or conversely translating the output to integrate it back into real-life. Think back to accounting personnel assisting end users to select the right item or service category to classify a purchase requisition as prepaids, expense or fixed asset so that the cost can be properly amortized over its life as opposed to expensing all at once.

Less obvious is a set of users who follow or engage in the use of technology in a mechanistic unyielding manner according to a set of Taylorist policies or rules in place while enjoying the all-too-convenient excuse that the technology at hand is the cause: "the software doesn't let us do that." Going back to Leontiev, operations themselves do not have intentions. Actions fulfill goals and motives guide activities. As Collins and Kusch suggest, "Where a mechanized world contains human beings, they have made themselves like cogs in the mechanism."[40] Recall in John Searle's Chinese room, the protagonist follows a script or a set of rules correlating English instructions with Chinese messages to communicate in Chinese to persons outside the room, thus giving the illusion that he understands Chinese despite not understanding a word.[41] He is but a human playing a computer playing a human. When we begin to use SaaS, we are subsuming our daily interactions that take place outside the system within. Based on specific parameters and logic, we configure the SaaS to output desired outcomes in a manner that resonates with and integrates back into our everyday realities. Collins and Kusch recount an incident involving a lady waiting in line for an airplane ticket at the Sheraton Hotel in New Delhi.[42] There were two lines, one for international carriers and the other for domestic.[43] To get to the head of the line took 2 hours.[44] When the lady got there, the clerk informed her that she was in the wrong line and nothing could be done about it.[45] Having to start over, she burst into tears.[46] In this case, the clerk was merely abiding by the book, abiding without thinking or flexibility yet abiding nevertheless to predefined rules that have nothing to do with the system at hand and yet everything to do with being a willing accomplice; "the system made me do it."[47] The question becomes: what if the workstations in either desk allowed the clerk to process airplane tickets for either international or domestic carriers? And if so, would the clerks' behavior change or would they likely stay the same? This is in fact the question we have for using SaaS in place of on-premise software. How we engage with a technology reveals more about who we are than what it is.

For all of Microsoft Word's dizzying array of built-in end user preferences from varied font, paragraph format, and text indentations, we forget how "it does not encourage or suggest more experimental or creative styles of delivery such as electronic literature with its generative and dynamic content. With all our focus on syntax – the Microsoft Word preferences – we forget that these very 'preferences' set up and negotiate an equivalent to the contract that a theater audience or reader adhere to when entering a fictional representation."[48] In other words, they dictate the semantics, "a mental, cultural contract negotiating one's expectations and how one is supposed to act and react in the representational space."[49] While in the prior chapter, we differentiated semantics from syntax, here we explore how semantics and syntax may really be two sides of the same coin. With the advent of SaaS, what better opportunity to revisit the optical illusions that color our interpretation of real, lived-in experiences with using software? For example, is a control ever fully automated or manual? In many cases, what we perceive to be fully automated, such as the SaaS check for duplicates, upon deeper examination, reveals a hiding of RAT, as when we still call upon human judgment to distinguish similar sounding albeit slightly misspelled names for what turn out to be the same vendors or customers to begin with. Another example is the automated restriction of access in SaaS. While this may be reviewed or configured at a point in time – automated as it were so that the software, rather than humans, checks to make sure that users can do what they can only in relation to the roles and permissions granted within the software – it says nothing of the manual efforts that would be required to either perform a periodic review of access granted to ensure against unauthorized changes or the manual efforts involved in access granting or termination. An administrator, after all, still needs to click a button, and likely more than one. The same can be said for automated approval workflows. While the workflow is automated such that it follows the same and exact sequence of events each time specific conditions are met, the actual approval is performed manually; someone still needs to log into the SaaS upon receiving an email notification to either approve or reject the transaction in question and likely against manual support. Thus, in the audit universe that we have become accustomed to performing control-speak, we need to revisit even the so-called and often taken for granted "distinctions" between automated and manual controls if indeed we are to bridge idealized constructs with real-world events, the ostensive with the performative.

These distinctions invariably lead us to perform analytics in a certain manner, seek "improvements" along a specific trajectory or path. For instance, in the years following the initial Sarbanes–Oxley (SOX) implementation, auditors compelled public companies to pursue internal control enhancements in years 2 and 3 of SOX compliance by increasing the percentage of automated controls over manual controls. The benefits are twofold: on the one hand, the technology would perform the same control in the same manner each time – recall Collins and Kusch labeling of mimeomorphic actions – as opposed to humans' polymorphic actions amenable to equal measures of error and of change. On the other hand, because the control has been automated and deemed far more reliable than human intervention, from a control validation perspective, it is tested once and only once as part of automated control validation and benchmarked or baselined so that validation does not have to be performed in ensuing years insofar as no significant changes have been made. In contrast, control validation of a manual control is labor intensive. often involving sample sizes pulled and validated depending on its control frequency. In this manner, we can see how the categories – automated vs. manual – have shaped the way we talk about as well as interpret internal controls in the context of using SaaS, even though we can make the case that these distinctions are arbitrary at best.

Once deemed automated, it is at once seen as easier to validate, even if to see it as such, we would have to ignore its less than automated and thus savory aspects. Boiled down to its essence, Leontiev's emphasis is that a "given object becomes the environment only when it enters the reality of subject's activity as an aspect of this reality; examining it through any other connections and relations will not permit us to find out anything about what kind of an environment it is."[50] Recall our earlier question over how "ready-to-hand" a SaaS is by merely functioning as a thermostat of sorts when it comes to automating purchase requisition approvals even if approval limits are no longer applicable in the face of organization changes. Leontiev's point is that "temperature conditions exist as a value of the environment – a positive or negative value – only in relation to a specific organism."[51] Or as Kaptelinin explains it, "The object of activity has a dual status; it is both a projection of human mind onto the objective world and a projection of the world onto human mind."[52]

I have attempted to show that behind the sheen of newly minted automated controls lay a rather tangled mess of manual interventions required to hide the RAT. Recall the wizard's plea, "Pay no attention to that man behind the curtain."[53] The automated vs. manual control dialogue misleads us into thinking the automated controls are good enough proxies for human intervention and/or judgment as opposed to mere tools to help us intervene and/or make decisions. These distinctions are objectified, rendering them external to us, something that we can see or observe and have become conditioned to look for outside of ourselves, rather than a product or culmination of the way we have framed and characterized the internal control dialogue in the first place. We take them for granted and often fail to notice that the lens we wear already censors and colors what we choose to look at. To the extent that the percent of automated controls triumphs over manual ones, several lingering questions remain. The first one that comes to mind is, are manual elements involved even in the operation or sustenance of an automated control? A configuration control such as a locked accounting period that allows for only non-general ledger (GL) impacting changes still needs to be manually locked. Accounting periods do not lock themselves. Once a prior period is locked, the software precludes all transactions from entry by end users. Only a user with administrative access can overwrite locked periods to post entries or unlock the periods entirely. The latter scenario is not as uncommon as one would think; in an aggressive financial close cycle, with the emphasis being placed on the time to close the books in time for external reporting, last minute adjustments, especially those surfaced by auditors, may need to be recorded for the financials to be presented in a manner that is coherent and aligned with Generally Accepted Accounting Principles (GAAP). Thus, an associated control may be a review of changes to accounting periods; this review is in fact manual even though it taps into the software's ability to track configuration changes as part of a system audit trail that can then be easily reported upon.

It is for this reason that system-furnished audit trails are an often a common inquiry first and foremost in the minds of enterprise clients as they shop around for software, or contemplate a transition from on-premise to cloud software, even though they do not place enough emphasis on differentiating audit trails for changes to transactions versus configurations. The availability of audit trails is a prerequisite surely, but it by no means assures or even guarantees that reviews are undertaken in a timely manner. Even so, there is also the question on what to report, whether all audit trail changes immediately come into purview or only selected ones that have GL or financial impact; hence the need for allowing non-GL impact changes to a locked period. Updating a memo field to include the customer PO to expedite payment or adding a collection note for an invoice past due surely has entirely different implications from changing line level amounts, or tax codes assigned that may result in a different invoice amount or tax liability recorded altogether. In revisiting Leontiev's depiction of operations, actions, and activities and specifically how the same operations can support varied actions – and similarly the same actions can support multiple activities – the entry of a collection note, when presented with a system error, nevertheless points back to the locking of the accounting period. Have non-GL impacting changes been enabled for the locked period?

More than exposing the porosity of manual versus automated divisions, this example casts doubt upon the tried and true audit approach of differentiating financial versus non-financial impact. Often used to only scope in work that has an impact on SOX compliance, it unwittingly ignores the "multiply-authored" nature of locked periods in an accounting SaaS. Collection notes recorded as part of customer dunning are often deemed too operational to be deemed a key internal control in scope for financial reporting impact. These, after all, do not change the underlying accounting impact, and yet in our example, they point back to and, in the process, validate whether the steps to lock an accounting period have been completed. In addition, insofar as collection notes lend themselves to more timely customer payments, they go a long way towards improving the days sales outstanding and ensuing cash flow.

Thus, in this example of locking accounting periods, we see the back and forth interplay between what appear to be static distinctions between manual and automated controls and areas deemed to have financial and non-financial reporting impact. These binary, "black vs. white" classifications have contributed to the "textually contained" world that we find ourselves enmeshed in the moment we begin to develop or revisit the design and operation of internal controls to support an enterprise SaaS in use. They assume that a control cannot be both automated and manual, and that once it is deemed automated, it becomes a proxy, rather than a tool, for manual intervention, thus appearing to relieve enterprise clients of any corresponding responsibility or accountability even as coordination work or RAT continues unabated behind the scenes. They also assume a clear unambiguous line can be drawn between financial impacting and non-financial impacting operations, even though in our example the difference resides in the eye of the beholder. More fundamentally, the "test once and only once" audit approach employed for automated controls rests on the premise that the action of an automated control is, to use Collins and Kusch's descriptive, mimeomorphic. Because it is performed by the software, it is assumed to be the same each time. Yet as Collins and Kusch point out, one or more mimeomorphic actions can make up a higher action type that is itself polymorphic.[54] Thus, although the systematized preclusion of entries from being posted to locked periods is mimeomorphic, together with other mimeomorphic actions – enabling for non-GL impacting change, such as for collection notes to be recorded in addition to other seemingly self-contained mimeomorphic actions such as the defaulting of journal entries to unapproved status upon creation, the availability of journal entry approval only to users with approval authority – as well as polymorphic actions – maintenance of month end accounting close calendar and attendance at close meetings to review status and any issues arisen – all serve to support the polymorphic action of recording journal entries in a correct and complete manner.

The problem of the audit approach in testing one or even several mimeomorphic actions is not so much one of selective granularity or atomicity but rather one of assuming that mimeomorphic actions alone – or automated controls – when validated would evidence that the software or SaaS in question is secure or compliant, when perhaps the real crux of the matter lies in how these automated controls, or mimeomorphic actions, are combined with other actions – both mimeomorphic and polymorphic – towards a higher level polymorphic action and its objectives. There is also the nature of a mimeomorphic control – the very possibility that the very sameness of behavior that characterizes its nature – can be amenable to change. An upgrade pushed to all customers, as characterized by the very nature of SaaS, can, in theory as well as in practice, have a regression impact on existing functionality, especially on user-defined scripts or workflows. Recall our example of FloDocs or Strongpoint as a means of surfacing regression impact of configuration changes from Chapter 4. In this example, if the mimeomorphic nature of defaulting journals to unapproved status is accomplished by a user-defined workflow, and this is in turn affected by new objects introduced via an upgrade scheduled nonetheless, then merely testing it "once and only once" as part of the tried and true audit approach no longer works, simply because after the scheduled upgrade, this automated control may no longer work. To mitigate this risk, at least proactively, we may have to log into a release preview environment, create a journal using the existing workflow, identify the impact beforehand, and make any necessary changes to tweak the workflow to accommodate the upgrade, such that the mimeomorphic control continues to function after the scheduled upgrade to production.

The automated label can lull enterprises into a false sense of security not to mention complacency. Automated approval workflows don't always translate into authorized transactions. An example may be a recurrence of approved purchase requisitions with amounts that all somehow manage to hover slightly below an approval threshold that would have necessitated an additional approver or a second pair of eyes. Likewise, automated procedures for running an efficient SOX compliance program is by no means an all-encompassing safeguard to precluding fraud or improper accounting. They simply ensure that various tasks from review to validation are completed like clockwork. In fact, it may become harder to change the control description or composition over time, so they tend to be recycled year after year even as the organization undergoes inevitable growth or shrinkage. Finally, as alluded to in our example on requisitions that slip past the cracks, automation can only take us so far. Automated whistleblower procedures may free up time for enterprises to conduct employee awareness training to bring to light grey ethical areas. Yet, it is just as likely that they turn into a check-the-box exercise. Picture an online webinar on the company code of ethics: precisely because it is accessible from anywhere at any time, participants may juggle multiple concurrent tasks during viewing. That compliance can easily devolve into a ritual where various constituents act out their expected roles, and audit is displaced as a self-fulfilling cycle independent of the actual work that goes on should not come as a surprise.

Michael Power describes the concepts of decoupling and colonization, where the audit process becomes decoupled from the very organizational processes on which it is based, and the organization is in turn colonized by the audit process as a driver of the type of information to locate and report on.[55] With the automation strategies previously identified, we can argue that what has been automated is a gradual flattening of varied human responses – moment-to-moment or arising-in-the-moment behaviors located in local contexts endowed with specific actors and constraints – to a congealed consistency, absent of variety. In effect, we can abide, unthinking and unblinking, by the compliance script inscribed in the varied automation technologies at our disposal. That transactions in general, or requisitions specifically, are approved would suffice and pass the audit, never mind those that circumnavigate pre-established thresholds. That the design, validation, and report on internal controls occurs as expected is evidence enough that enterprise-wide compliance efforts are effective. That having few, if any, issues reported through a web-based whistleblower tool is an end in and of itself, as is having all employees successfully log in and acknowledge having read the company code of ethics. In a strange reversal of roles, it is humans, rather than internal controls, who have been automated to comply with pre-programmed outcomes – automatons whose conditioned responses are borne more of reflex than of any conscious intention or forethought. It is a strange *old* world, all the more unsettling, when framed against the stark, *new* dystopia depicted in the movie, *Her*.

From a compliance perspective, we may be satisfied with documenting a three-way match as a key control that resides within a procurement software that prevents a user from recording an invoice if it did not have an associated receipt or requisition. Because this control is automated and likely a standard software functionality that comes out-of-the-box, it is tested once during the current fiscal year and baselined so that it would not need to be validated in the coming year. Thus, it buys us cost savings by cutting down the amount of internal control validation that needs to occur for management to comply with SOX. What it doesn't quite reveal is the amount of manual work that nonetheless the user needs to perform to locate the missing receipt and requisition tied to the vendor invoice. Recall from Chapter 2 Lucy Suchman's account of what goes in an accounting office when an AP clerk received an overdue invoice in the mail.[56] In this sense, the automated label hides as much as it exposes. We also recall the VIE rules from Chapter 1 and how they end up including as much as they unintentionally hide when it comes to the ownership of Chinese companies through contracts. Even then, automated, when used to characterize this key control, is a restrictive description at best. Had the application been more fully automated, it would have allowed the user to enter the invoice anyway but with a periodic reminder for the accounting team to continue its search for the missing upstream support. It might have also been useful if it displayed current unmatched requisitions and receipts logged in the system against this very same vendor. Had it been truly automated, it would have enabled the vendor to submit its invoice via a self-service portal automatically matched with an open purchase requisition and receipt, only requiring intervention from the accounting team when exceptions are encountered. Finally, as we have seen, evidencing an automated three-way match by no means precludes purchases submitted to game the system, amounts hovering slightly under established thresholds. By calling what we see automated too soon, we don't go quite far enough to configure the SaaS to be ready-to-hand.

By all accounts, our example on exception handling procedures surrounding an invoice payment merely scratches the surface on what can happen. What if the invoice is already matched with a receipt and requisition, but during the point of entry, a contractor assisting the accounting team does not know which expense category to code it to? Because the application does not let the contractor save the entered invoice without selecting a mandatory expense category, the contractor selects one tied to marketing rather than one associated with research and development (R&D). The automated control auditors typically look for mandatory fields as having these in place would ensure that all expenses entered are in fact coded. Whether the right codes have been used, as we have seen from Chapter 4, is a different story. Categorizing something as a marketing expense as opposed to a R&D can have far reaching consequences. Even when coded to the right GAAP category such as R&D, what happens when new departments are added, and older ones are sunset and deactivated? Are key reports updated to reflect these changes, such that historical transactions up until the changes were made continue to reflect in the right R&D categories even as new ones coded to the new departments are captured? Simply put, having system-mandated mandatory fields is not a sufficient safeguard against financial misstatement. Here too, the application would have been more useful if it allowed the contractor to enter the invoice without coding it initially but giving her an opportunity later to make amends. As Cooper and Reimann put it, humans "don't usually enter 'bad' codes' but rather 'in a sequence that the software isn't prepared to accept."[57]

To truly design effective internal controls then, we may be forced to confront these categories and challenged to rewrite the text. One way to do this is perhaps to question the essentialist account, that is, the view that an entity possesses a specific set of attributes that defines its identity and function. That a control is automated, and that another is manual, and how they work together to promote correct and complete entries is but a form of essentialism, distributed nonetheless, but still resting on the assumption that different elements possess and bring their own unique set of attributes to the table. This contrasts with the "multiply-authored" identity constituted from relations with others we looked at in Chapter 1.[58] An alternate view is one of Latour's best-known slogans, "Technology is society made durable."[59] Applied to our context, we can perhaps say that SaaS is enterprise made durable. Even at its more atomic or mimeomorphic level, the ability of the SaaS to preclude the posting of entries to a locked period emerges with:

- An administrator user locking the period, or relocking it after opening it for last minute changes or adjustments
- A team of accountants focused on month-end close and working through the entries scheduled for posting and reviewing these against support
- An audit team reviewing month over month variances and identifying whether adjustments need to be made; the SaaS vendor controlling changes or upgrades to the software in a manner that does not affect its ability to allow for entries in locked periods

The automated control itself derives or emerges from the interaction of these elements – if the accounting team were late in its close calendar, prolonging the length of time for the prior period to be kept open, it increases the likelihood of users inadvertently making entries in the unlocked period. To simply pronounce that the SaaS functionality is working, just not used timely, if at all, misses the higher level polymorphic action of ensuring correct and complete entries as part of month end close. It is perhaps this reason that compels the SOX regulations to call for management to attest to a system of internal controls, and not any one control per se. But when we adopt the view that the SaaS in use is "enterprise made durable," we are not merely adopting a reductionist perspective of distilling a system to the sum of its parts, but really emphasizing that its effective use emerges from the interaction of these different, moving parts. That the SaaS is seen to work represents the culmination of varied enterprise trajectories both within and without – administrator, accountant, auditor, and vendor – rather than any one attribute or one set of unique attributes that the SaaS has over its competitors that the vendor would like you to believe. That the SaaS is not a black box, more like "an action cascade stuffed full of human skills," and as Collins and Kusch put it, "very far from being an automaton"[60] – not unlike the Mechanical Turk, an odd composite of gears, magnets, and a hidden human.

Another perspective is simply this: we can't talk about automation without calling upon the manual. When students in my *Accounting Information Systems* class were asked what automation is, a few replied simply: something that is not manual. But what this chapter has been about thus far, is exposing how within something seemingly automated lies something manual. This dance between opposites is more common than we would care to admit. The more manual a task or set of tasks is, the more we can try to automate by configuring within a workflow in a SaaS as an example. Yet, the results of the automation may yield further finds on why the data entered can be inconsistent to begin with and further manual intervention has not been taken into consideration. In this manner, the path to automation leads to more uncovering of manual interventions. Seen in this manner, automated and manual are not simply a pair of binary opposites; they are interdependent. In fact, how automated we deem a process to be may reflect more of how little or how much we know about its manual aspects. The reverse holds true. The same dance can be characterized between the ostensive and the performative, or the external with the internal. In many ways, it can be hard to provide a full description of what the ostensive is without giving examples of what happens in practice. Likewise, we can be hard pressed in describing the internal without making comparisons with the external. As we have seen, audit is still far from developing a methodology that accounts for interplay between automated and manual, ostensive and performative, as well as external and internal. Controls are validated in relative isolation from one another, and it is only when a user encounters an exception that others are called forth to provide rallying support as it were. The science of how much to sample is in turn predicated on the contrived black-and-white categories we have devised: automated versus manual controls, preventive versus detective, IT dependent manual controls versus non-IT dependent manual controls.

The user stories that make up the backlog that is groomed towards a current or future sprint merit additional consideration. Ideally with Scrum, a popular Agile technical, a cross-functional team huddles together to work on new features. The premise is that different functions can come up with a diversity of perspectives – business, financial, operational, audit, security, and compliance – that contribute to user stories. But as we have seen with the dance between automated and manual, there can be more than one story, and invariably, a story within a story: a manual component to what is automated but also the hidden human within the Mechanical Turk, or the performative behind the ostensive. The Taylorist approach is invariably the objectivistic account. Compare this with the model for pedagogical design. Parker Palmer describes how this model has been characterized by:

1. Objects of knowledge
2. Experts who disseminate knowledge
3. Amateurs who receive knowledge
4. Baffles that prevent a bottoms-up flow, such as from layman amateurs to experts or from experts to objects of knowledge[61]

In many ways, the Taylorist approach is the objectivistic model and is also the pedagogical one with management entity controls at the top with cascading process and application controls that are sequenced "top-down." Can you think of any "baffles" in use in the design or operation of internal controls to prevent a bottom-up flow of information? How about the reliance of auditors as guardians of control-speak? Questions over what's in or out of scope for financial impact are filtered through an audit lens. A process undertaken every day and valued by invested stakeholders, the recording of collection notes, is nevertheless deemed too operational and out of scope for the design of internal controls over financial reporting. Ironic that the very group the unsuspecting public has come to see as keeping public companies honest can also present hindrances to our understanding of internal controls.

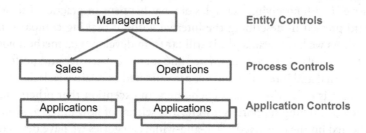

In contrast, the possibility of configuring SaaS to meet a diversity of layman or amateur perspectives presents a different model, one that is not hierarchical but acknowledges the way we interrelate with one another with the subject matter at hand whether it is the locking of accounting periods or handling of invoice payments. Different perspectives weigh in on a seemingly objective and unvarying reality. Parker calls this the "community of truth" where "there are no pristine objects of knowledge and no ultimate authorities."[62]

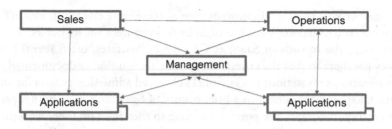

It is this bias that the SaaS consuming enterprise needs to guard against when resisting the temptation to enforce a tight system of top-down controls too much too soon or only pursuing a course of configuration closely aligned with an official and thus theorized and ostensive account, with scarce regard for the performative. Such an organizational stance is inherently unforgiving to the diversity of perspectives that abound even if it is also a fragile one. The need to include different points of view stems not so much from a relaxation of stringent requirements or scaling back of high expectations – if anything, the ability to entertain variety, much like Agile versus Taylorist SDLC – emphasizes outcome over process and focuses on whether requirements or expectations are met. So, the organizational posture adopted here is not one of making do with less but more. For even as we make our journey from monolithic ERP on-premise packages to SaaS, we encounter not just a multitude of best-in-breed application but also a multitude of stakeholder perspectives as well as within SaaS a multitude of means for their needs to be addressed.

Too often, we instinctively choose to ignore the man behind the curtain even without the wizard's compulsion. And in so doing, we are the ones with programmed responses. Like graduates of the Taylorist school of scientific management, we too, in addition to the Agile backlog, have been groomed to handle composable HIT-like tasks instead of attempting to grasp the bigger picture. Just as a metric may conceal as much as it purports to reveal, a generic automated label doesn't quite exactly tell us just how truly automated a process is. By calling anything automated – from viewing a mere system-generated warning (simply because the software is unable to handle fuzzy human input) to receiving genuine alternatives for processing the same transaction – we run the risk of reducing the definition of automation to the lowest denominator. Recall the debates surrounding FASB's proposals to reframe materiality in a legal light: if every little thing were considered material, then what truly is? Consequently, if something remotely has the potential to be material, would it slip by unnoticed and unremarked? Likewise, if every little thing were considered automated, then what truly is? Here too, much common ground resides between seemingly irreconcilable opposites: accounting or legal, manual or automated, hidden or found.

At this juncture, it makes sense to give a quick recap of the ground we have covered thus far. We started in Chapter 1 by highlighting the sheer whimsical nature of compliance, from the varying length of wild-caught salmon not to mention somewhat odd application (and juxtaposition) of SOX to wildlife conservation to the reuse of VIE rules to circumvent even as these were erected in Enron's wake in response to its inappropriate use of SPEs to keep debt off its books. This notwithstanding, the records in SaaS, as Chapter 2 illustrates, often reveal little on why they got there so that the criteria for revenue recognition as documented in the system remains as mysterious as Garfinkel's observed admission criteria for clinical patients. Chapter 3 takes us into a brief history of SaaS, and in so doing, presents us a possibility to tap into the potential of SaaS to shed light on inner workings. By offering a multi-tenant architecture replete with metadata tables, SaaS enterprise clients can in effect configure and customize, seemingly orchestrate at hand a field of fields in a way that does not threaten the application's core integrity. Chapter 4 takes on this path farther by exploring just what is it that can be configured: in the context of transactions with financial impact, sequencing can and does matter as does architectural and transactional integrity. Yet, what we perceive to be the beginning is often really the outcome, and thus the SaaS configured to handle this theorized account of affairs either encourages less than official manual workarounds or otherwise forces users to enter or update data or transactions in a manner that does not conform with reality.

By asking who gets to determine what is worthy and according to whose values, Terry Cook, in *Remembering The Future*, unpacks the hitherto unexamined assumptions and biases of archivists in putting together documentation "not to keep the best juridical evidence ... but to serve ... those figures and events judged worthy of celebrating or memorializing."[63] "The object of activity," for Leontiev, "is twofold: first, in its independent existence as subordinating to itself and psychological reflection that is realized as an activity of the subject and cannot exist otherwise."[64] Or as Van Mannen and Pentland put it, the potential to script action after the fact and according to official legitimate accounts lead auditors to "routinely write their conclusions in advance" in a manner such that "facts ... recorded prior to their occurrence ... will soon come into being."[65] I recall my early days of auditing where it was not uncommon for junior associates to share best practices of wording common audit exceptions such as "excessive access is granted to so and so" or "no authorization is evidenced to so and so" across varied clients.

What is determined after the fact as a key control, such as a systematic mandatory field validation or system disallowing of duplicate transaction numbers, is then flagged as a best practice operating control to be impressed upon and circulated among audit clients even though the auditors have long past come and gone, rotated to their next audit client even as practical considerations or fissures begin to appear behind recommended best practices. Mandatory fields may not apply to all transaction types. As discussed before, most companies use cost centers to track purchase transactions to record operating expenses into General & Administrative (G&A), Sales & Marketing (S&M), and Research & Development (R&D) categories that align with GAAP on the income statement, but the same values do not apply to sales transactions. Thus, a filler value is entered for sales transactions if only to be able to save them in the accounting SaaS even though they ultimately do not apply. Likewise, mandatory fields can slow down the creation of transactions, mostly because not all field attributes are immediately present and accessible upon initial transaction entry, and perhaps more to the point, as our filler value of a cost center illustrate, do not address the validity of the entry. Separately, having a system check for duplicate auto-generated numbers doesn't really preclude duplicate transactions recorded for the same customer and vendor, if all the user must do is update the document or transaction numbers to make them appear unique, or vary the description in the header memo field. For sales transactions such as customer invoices, invoice numbers should be unique, yet the same cannot be said for vendor invoices or bills received. After all, what is to preclude two or more vendors from using the same numbering scheme and it is pure coincidence for an invoice or bill received from one or more vendors to be the same? Thus, when reconciling transactions in a downstream SaaS with an upstream one and checking for completeness – recall Chapter 4 – we need to also consider both the entity or vendor name and document number so that whether the review is automated or manual, it would not throw up false positives. Unfortunately, these reviews remain delegated as back-stage behavior performative yet not primetime enough to be on front-stage ostensive display.

It wouldn't matter that an event has yet to occur in the future, as long as we describe it in a future past perfect manner that is consistent with what has come before. As this chapter illustrates, this rigid almost mechanical style is in turn what we mistake for automation: when users are configured to the system, looking in from the outside, it nevertheless appears that the system has been configured to the users. What we deem as automation is really a series of manual steps undertaken behind the scenes. As our variations on purchase requisitions illustrate, it is easy to conflate repair with automation and slippage for control. The ensuing opportunity costs can be glaring: where much work still needs to be underway to improve the manner we interact with systems, it is tempting to turn a blind eye and move on, content with the "automated" state of affairs. What we are accustomed to flagging as automated controls are really stand-ins, mirroring back upon us an uninvolved, unblinking and, not coincidentally, automated response. Nicholas Carr writes about succumbing to automation complacency when we over-rely on systems and automation bias as we begin to trust them at the cost of second guessing ourselves.[66] Cooper and Reimann wryly observe that while "conventional wisdom says that error messages tell the user that he has made some mistake," they actually "report to the user when the program gets confused."[67] This occurs more often than we would think. Someone is hiding the RAT. Or the Mechanical Turk has risen yet again like a phoenix from ashes to make yet another penultimate round. Chapter 4 introduced the reading of SaaS as a palindrome: when reading the transaction backwards or forwards, we get to the same destination. A palindrome, after all, is the same word spelled backwards and forwards. Perhaps even this is too mechanistic a grasp of palindromes. Insofar as our very human responses stay the same with or without SaaS, we are palindromes in the making or already made. The assorted cast of software or users may have changed but our inclination to attribute agency to an automaton over the manual repair we have had to perform unfortunately stays the same.

This reminds me of the 1956 movie, *Invasion of The Body Snatchers*, where one by one patients and friends alike of Dr. Miles Bennell are replaced by look-alike alien stand-ins that fester in basement seed pods. For the converted, "life is so simple," through symbiosis "reborn into an untroubled world."[68] At a compliance conference, a lawyer recounted how he was brought in to review vendor obligations when the payroll tax computed by a newly implemented software was incorrect to be promptly informed that it was the enterprise customer's responsibility to review the outcome of the payroll computation in sandbox prior to go-live, and in effect the errors of the computation were as much attributed to user negligence in providing oversight as they were to faulty algorithms used in the software. In an interesting turn of events, humans have been automated to be complacent with the automated computations, whereas the machinery behind the software has been rendered manual insofar as compensating human oversight is nevertheless warranted. The speaker titled his closing slide, "Automated Humans, Manual Machines?" The point I make here is not to discount the value of manual oversight altogether. Having supervision in place does not have to translate into salutary nod to Taylorist principles, nor does it mean that Agile can't be practiced. In fact, the latter is often confused to signify Agile ≠ Audit with the premise that what has been developed or configured using Agile can't be effectively audited. Yet, when deeply engaged in a 2-week Scrum sprint, we would be kidding ourselves if we were to think that there is no structure or rhyme to the madness. Process, often construed as a dirty word in some IT circles, is misleading. How else would we characterize sprint planning, daily standups, demos, retrospectives, burndown, and velocity charts, *traditional* Agile artifacts used to track progress made? Just like how the iterative mini-prototype first documented in Dr. Royce's 1970 book, *Managing the Development of Large Software Systems*, was all but ignored when handed down over time,[69] the same omission is applied to the Agile Manifesto:

1. "Individuals and interactions over processes and tools" doesn't mean there are no processes and tools
2. "Working software over comprehensive documentation" doesn't mean there is no documentation
3. "Customer collaboration over contract negotiation" doesn't mean there is no contract nor negotiation
4. "Responding to change over following a plan" doesn't mean there is no plan[70]

Invasion of the Body Snatchers was released amid the mass hysteria surrounding McCarthyism in the 1950s and the blacklisting of Hollywood, not to mention simmering fears of a potential nuclear war. Yet, as a testament to its timeless appeal, the film was remade three times after the original. In a world overrun by cloud computing and mobile apps, to what extent have we have been dulled into unquestioning, compliant witnesses impervious to change? Conversely, to what extent does the new gadgetry continue to perpetuate old-world myths, paradigms, and biases? In this strange old new world, our minds become the hardware that accepts whatever is filtered through our belief structure as software. Recall Ellison's remarks about the whimsicalness of computer fads, recycling what is old as new. HIT from Amazon's Mechanical Turk takes decomposable mind-numbing trivial tasks to a "new" level that would make Taylor proud. What Steve Woolgar meant by configure when he wrote that "the whole history of a system project can be construed as a struggle to configure ... the user."[71] To configure or be configured, that is the question.

Yet, the present or beckoning future doesn't have to be quite so grim. The mundane world of back-office operations like expense report processing has been infused with AI and other technologies to automate a 100% audit of all expense reports. From the legitimacy of restaurants to the existence of customer clients claimed on expenses to the elimination of potential duplicates across reports to the accuracy of the amounts claimed against supporting receipts, AppZen, a California startup, verifies the veracity of the submitted expenses.[72] More than this, AppZen relies on a mobile app that runs in the background, queuing up potential expenses to be submitted on an expense report using photos of receipts taken on your mobile phone as support.[73] Natural language processing is used to associate yellow cab with taxi as opposed to Amtrak with train. Statistical analytics are culled from submitted expenses so that higher risk reports meriting additional human oversight are identified. AppZen integrates with Concur, a larger more well-known and thus commonly used expense management SaaS. Other expense management SaaS such as Expensify have challenged the traditional unit of analysis, an expense report for grouping expenses. Branding the term Real-Time Expense Reports (RTER), each expense is a transaction compiled real-time and queued for submission for approval according to a specified schedule, reducing the likelihood of unsubmitted expenses.[74] As an interesting aside, I wonder how by pricing SaaS offerings based on the number of submitted expense reports, as is the case for Concur, we may unwittingly encourage a batching and later submission of queued expenses, precluding in some ways the timely reporting of incurred expenses. This notwithstanding, Concur offers the ability through Cognos reporting to report on unsubmitted expenses to facilitate timely accruals even if expense reports remain unsubmitted. Describing 2016 as "the year expense management players got more aggressive, strategic, and intelligent," JoAnn DeLuna writing for *Business Travel News* provides varied automation examples: Abacus completes expense details through optical character resolution (OCR) of receipts and uses machine learning to categorize expenses and pair receipts with corporate card charges; Certify relies on an automatic and scheduled submission of expenses that meet compliance policies and data completeness requirements.[75] More recently, Concur bots on Slack, a popular real-time collaboration app and platform that lets users perform actions directly without having to log into Concur. Via Slack, expense reports can be approved, business itineraries pulled up on demand, and receipts submitted.[76]

Contrast these examples with the man hidden in the Mechanical Turk controlling each chess move diligently albeit manually. Machine learning and big data in our present times underscore the overwhelming magnitude of the ever-available data points that far outstrip any individual efforts of even an illustrious few on the one hand, but also point to the benefits of drawing intelligence analytics from the review of many, so that we can identify the possibility of fraud and other control-related aspects earlier rather than later. In the process, software gets better at handling real-life data, often presented in unstructured, messy formats as opposed to the pristine versions carefully tended to by invisible hands prior to entry. Coupa, the procurement management SaaS that we discussed in Chapter 3, recently completed its acquisition of Deep Relevance that applies business intelligence analytics on companywide and individual spending to identify potential fraudulent expenses or vendors, and puts together fraud profiles with alerts on questionable transactions by dollar amounts. As we rise above component tasks, we start to see how even with preapproved spending obtained via a purchase requisition, we can pay using our personal credit card and submit for expense reimbursement using an expense report rather than having the vendor submit an invoice to Accounts Payable for check or wire payment. How then do we correlate the actual with the anticipated, processed with approved, straddling across two SaaS, procurement and expense management SaaS such as Coupa and Concur, even if the accounting impact is ultimately recorded in a downstream accounting SaaS, such as NetSuite? If we were to behave like the clerks handling domestic and international airfares at the Sheraton Hotel in New Delhi,[77] where the emphasis is the proper employment of artifacts depending on the SaaS used – an expense report is not an invoice and not in the procurement SaaS – we may suggest that purchase orders be closed out, thereby unwittingly negating the higher level purpose or objective of bringing attention to anticipated spending ahead of time, in short displacing the ends for the means. More than busy manual hands, HIT behind Amazon's Mechanical Turk, these new developments, and explorations suggest the beginnings of a complete overhaul, a long overdue fulfillment of a delayed promise offered by its 1770 Viennese origins. Better late than never. We ended Chapter 3 by asking if memory can survive without a language. Yet, as we made our way through Chapter 4, we saw how language can hide as much as it purports to reveal. In this chapter, we have revisited this initial question posed two chapters earlier, not so much on whether memory can survive, but how it can reinvent, so that history is in effect shaped, and continues to be shaped, by memory in the clear suffused light of the present day.

Exercise 5.1

On a scale of 1 to 10, with 1 being the lowest and 10 being the highest, how automated is the following?

1. A journal entry is routed for approval
2. When a purchase requisition exceeds $1,000, it is routed for an additional approval
3. Exception notifications on sync errors are emailed to key stakeholders

Discussion

When I asked my students in the *Accounting Information Systems* class, I obtained an array of responses. Some think that because the SaaS at hand is involved in routing the transaction for approval or triggering an exception notification for each sync error encountered, the process is automated. Others point to the remaining need for manual review and intervention. I played the devil's advocate: these processes while automated only bring us back to the predetermined ideal operating levels whether that is having an approved entry, additional approval for purchase requisition over $1,000, or sync successes. One doesn't quite get down to validating whether the approval granted for the journal was valid and performed in reviewing against supporting documentation, or whether $1,000 is the appropriate threshold to escalate for another level of requisition approval, or whether the sync exceptions are merely symptoms of a deeper root cause failure. Thus, we can argue that what these processes automate is simply the rate at which pre-identified events are detected and triggered for manual intervention. The response of users to each and every approval and exception notification is also pre-programmed and automated, at the opportunity cost of spending time asking deeper questions of what is actually needed for an effective review, why levels are configured the way they are, or delving into the root cause of sync failures.

Exercise 5.2

For each of the following, identify what can go wrong despite having:

1. An approved journal entry
2. Three-way match between purchase order, receipt, and invoice
3. Notification of sync error

Discussion

This exercise is deceptively similar with the prior one. Yet upon closer reflection and refraction, we can argue that it invites participants to take a closer look at that which transcends seemingly mundane findings, such as no exceptions found in approved entries, three-way matches, or error sync notifications. How likely are these more a reflection of what is ostensive rather than performative? Auditors are more inclined to ask: what can go wrong if any of the earlier three processes were not in place and in so doing are unlikely to underestimate the degree of complexity that resides behind the scenes. Put differently, even if we found no exceptions, it is by no means a guarantee that the journal is appropriately recorded or vendor authorized. Conversely, we can also ask the reverse question: to the extent that we received no notifications on sync errors over a period of time, does it make sense to continue to have this operational as a key internal control? When there are no exceptions identified in the quarter over quarter validation of an internal control, does it make sense to continue with the charade?

Exercise 5.3

Review McNay's 4 organizational archetypes: collegium, bureaucracy, corporation, and enterprise first covered in Chapter 3.[78]

1. Which archetype does your organization most resemble?
2. To what extent does your organization's archetypal profile lend itself more readily to active SaaS configuration versus docile acceptance of defaults settings out of the box?
3. To what extent does your organization's archetypal profile lend itself more readily to the use of Agile over SDLC?

Discussion

This exercise brings together the organizational archetypes covered earlier but in the context of the material covered in this chapter on Leontiev, while organizational activities are driven by motives and actions by goals, operations depend on conditions under which these are performed. To what extent does an organization's leanings whether heavy or loose in policy or in control implementation influence the level of acceptance of stories? Rather than a top-down Taylorist approach, is a bottom-up multi-stakeholder approach practiced? To the extent that the SaaS offers out-of-the-box configuration, how likely is it leveraged to meet specific needs?

Endnotes

1. Woolgar, S. (1990). Configuring the user: The case of usability trials. *The Sociological Review*, 38, 58–99.
2. Karl Gottlieb von Windisch. (1784). Briefe über den Schachspieler von Kempelen nebst drey Kupferstichen die diese berühmte Maschine vorstellen, or Inanimate Reason; or, A Circumstantial Account of that Astonishing Piece of Mechanism, M. de Kempelen's Chess-Player, Now Exhibiting at No. 9 Savile-Row, Burlington Gardens, London, translation taken from Levitt.
3. de, Botton. A. (2014). *The News: A User's Manual.*
4. Ibid.
5. Ibid.
6. Latour, B. (1986). Visualisation and cognition: Drawing things together. *Knowledge and Society: Studies in the Sociology of Culture and Present*, 6, 1–40.
7. Goffman, E. (1959). *The Presentation of Self in Everyday Life.* New York: Anchor Books.
8. Miller, R. (March 10, 2011). Salesforce.com plans more data center capacity. *Data Center Knowledge.* http://www.datacenterknowledge.com/archives/2011/03/10/salesforce-com-to-build-its-own-data-centers

9 Taylor, F. W. (1911). *The Principles of Scientific Management*. New York: Harper & Brothers.
10 Ibid.
11 Ibid.
12 Ibid.
13 Ibid.
14 Ibid.
15 U.S. Department of Justice, Office of the Inspector General (September 7, 2012). Interim report on the Federal Bureau of Investigation's implementation of the sentinel project. Report 12–38. https://oig.justice.gov/reports/2012/a1238.pdf
16 Ibid.
17 Israel, J. W. (June 2012). Why the FBI can't build a case management system. *Computing Now*. IEEE Computer Society.
18 U.S. Department of Justice, Office of the Inspector General (December, 2011). Status of The Federal Bureau of Investigation's Implementation of The Sentinel Project. Report 12-08. https://oig.justice.gov/reports/2011/a1208.pdf
19 U.S. Department of Justice, Office of the Inspector General (September, 2014). Status of The Federal Bureau of Investigation's Implementation of The Sentinel Project. Report 14-31. https://oig.justice.gov/reports/2014/a1431.pdf
20 Ibid.
21 Ibid.
22 Ibid.
23 Feldman, M. and Pentland, B. (2003). Reconceptualizing organizational routines as a source of flexibility and change. *Administrative Science Quarterly* 48. 94–118.
24 Taylor, F. W. *The Principles of Scientific Management*.
25 Feldman, M. and Pentland, B. Reconceptualizing organizational routines as a source of flexibility and change.
26 Ibid.
27 Fleming, V., Langley, N., Ryerson, F., Woolf, E. A., Rosson, H., LeRoy, M., Garland, J., ... Warner Bros. Family Entertainment (Firm). (1999). The Wizard of Oz. Turner Entertainment.
28 Leontiev, A. N. (1977). Activity and consciousness. Published in Russian in the Journal Voprosyfilosofii, 12, 129–140 (1972) and English in the book Philosophy in the USSR, Problems of Dialectical Materialism (Moscow, 1977, pp. 180–202). Available at Marxists Internet Archive [http://www.marxists.org/]
29 Ibid.
30 Ibid.
31 Phelps, D., Kim, G., and Milne, K. (October 2006). Prioritizing IT controls for effective, measurable security. Software Engineering Institute. Carnegie Mellon University. https://resources.sei.cmu.edu/asset_files/WhitePaper/2013_019_001_297211.pdf
32 Collins, H. M. and Kusch, M. (1998). *The Shape of Actions: What Humans and Machines Can Do*. Cambridge, MA: MIT Press.
33 Ibid.
34 Ibid.
35 Ibid.
36 Ibid.
37 Ibid.
38 Ibid.

[39] Ibid.

[40] Ibid.

[41] Searle, J. (1980). Minds, brains, and programs. *Behavioral and Brain Sciences*, 3, 417–424.

[42] Collins, H. M. and Kusch, M. *The Shape of Actions: What Humans and Machines Can Do.*

[43] Ibid.

[44] Ibid.

[45] Ibid.

[46] Ibid.

[47] Ibid.

[48] Pold, S. (2008). Preferences in Fuller, M. (2008). *Software Studies: A Lexicon.*

[49] Ibid.

[50] Leonteiv, A. N. (July–August 2005). Study of the environment in the pedological works of L.S. Vygotsk. *Journal of Russian and East European Psychology*, 43(4), 8–28.

[51] Ibid.

[52] Kaptelinin, V. (2005). The object of activity: Making sense of the sense-maker. *Mind, Culture and Activity.* 12(1), 4–18.

[53] Fleming, V., Langley, N., Ryerson, F., Woolf, E. A., Rosson, H., LeRoy, M., Garland, J., ... The Wizard of Oz.

[54] Collins, H. M. and Kusch, M. *The Shape of Actions: What Humans and Machines Can Do.*

[55] Power, M. (1997). *The Audit Society: Rituals of Verification.* Oxford, UK: Oxford University Press.

[56] Suchman, Lucy, A. (1983) Office procedure as practical action: Models of work and system design. *ACM Transactions on Information Systems*, 1(4), 320–328.

[57] Cooper A. and Reimann R. (2003). *About Face 2.0: The Essentials of Interaction Design.* Hoboken, NJ: John Wiley & Sons.

[58] Strathern, M. (1988). *The Gender of the Gift: Problems with Women and Problems with Society in Melanesia.* Berkeley, CA: University of California Press.

[59] Latour, B. (May 1, 1990). Technology is society made durable. *The Sociological Review*, 38(1), 103–131.

[60] Collins, H. M. and Kusch, M. *The Shape of Actions: What Humans and Machines Can Do.*

[61] Palmer, P. J. (1998). *The Courage to Teach: Exploring the Inner Landscape of a Teacher's Life.* San Francisco, CA: Jossey-Bass.

[62] Ibid.

[63] Cook, T. (2006). Remembering the future: Appraisal of rand the role of archives in constructing social memory. In F. X. Blouin, Jr. and W. G. Rosenberg (Eds.), *Archives, Documentation and Institutions of Social Memory: Essays from the Sawyer Seminar.* Ann Arbor, MI: University of Michigan Press, pp. 169–181.

[64] Leontiev, A. N. (1978). *Activity, Consciousness, and Personality.* Englewood Cliffs, NJ: Prentice Hall. (Original work published 1975).

[65] Van Maanen, J. and Pentland, B. T. (1994). Cops and auditors: The rhetoric of records. In S. B. Sitkin and R. J. Bies (Eds.), *The Legalistic Organization.* Beverly Hills, CA: Sage Publications, pp. 53–90.

[66] Carr, N. G. (2014). *The Glass Cage: Automation and Us.*

[67] Cooper, A. and Reimann, R. *About Face 2.0: The Essentials of Interaction Design.*

[68] Mainwaring, D., Fredericks, E., Wanger, W., Siegel, D., McCarthy, K., Wynter, D., Gates, L. et al. Artisan home entertainment (Firm). (2002). *Invasion of the Body Snatchers*. Los Angeles, CA: Republic Pictures.

[69] Royce, W. W. (1970). Managing the development of large software systems. In Technical Papers of Western Electronic Show and Convention (WesCon). August 25–28, 1970, Los Angeles, USA.

[70] Beck K., Beedle M., van Bennekum A. et al. (2001). The Agile Manifesto. http://agilemanifesto.org/

[71] Woolgar, S. Configuring the user: The case of usability trials.

[72] Cohn, M. (September 19, 2016). Voices AppZen uses AI to scrutinize expense reports. *Accounting Today*. https://www.accountingtoday.com/opinion/appzen-uses-ai-to-scrutinize-expense-reports

[73] Forrest, C. (December 11, 2014). How AppZen disrupts expense reports with natural language processing. *TechRepublic*. https://www.techrepublic.com/article/how-appzen-disrupts-expense-reports-with-natural-language-processing/

[74] DeLuna, J. (March 14, 2017). Next-Gen expense management. *Business Travel News*. http://www.businesstravelnews.com/Research/Next-Gen-Expense-Management

[75] Ibid.

[76] Dietz, J. (March 14, 2018). Concur labs and slack partner to bring travel and expense bots to the masses. *SAP Concur*. https://www.concur.com/newsroom/article/concur-labs-slack-partner-bring-travel-expense-bots-to-the-masses

[77] Collins, H. M. and Kusch, M. *The Shape of Actions: What Humans and Machines Can Do.*

[78] McNay, I. (1995). From collegial academy to the corporate enterprise: The changing cultures of Universities. In T. Schuller (Ed.) *The Changing University?* Buckingham, UK: SHRE/Open University Press.

Chapter 6

Control Chaos

Out beyond ideas of wrongdoing and

rightdoing there is a field. I'll meet you

there.[1]

Rumi

Half a century after the dawn of Taylorist scientific management, Douglas McGregor published *The Human Side of Enterprise*, challenging the very image of workers as unmotivated and uninspired, shirking responsibility at every turn. Quite the contrary, McGregor asserts, workers are self-directed and capable of self-control.[2] Frederick Herzberg shared his views. In his book, *The Motivation to Work*, Herzberg describes the factors that motivate a worker: responsibility, achievement, recognition, and advancement, not to mention the work itself.[3] No longer seen "as stupid and so phlegmatic that he more nearly resembles in his mental make-up the ox than any other type,"[4] McGregor and Herzog portray a worker as more than a mere cog in a machine, a manual automaton as it were. A job well done is a reward in and of itself. What workers invariably need, Herzberg advocates, are "mini-budgets, tools, etc. that are necessary to do the job."[5] In contrast to Theory X, a set of views of workers that aligns with Taylorist scientific management, McGregor characterized this second set of views of workers as Theory Y.[6] Contemporary management scholars today appear to be in favor of Theory Y over Theory X. "Increased spending authority does not entail a loss of control," Tom Peters writes in *Thriving on Chaos*, "to the contrary, it begets more control of the most powerful sort–self-control. Low spending control leads to shenanigans – avoid a $1,000 limit by making an endless stream of $999.95 requisitions. High spending authority says to the worker, or unit boss, 'I take you seriously.' The monkey is on his or her back to live up to the trust."[7]

Recall from Chapter 5 the employment of internal controls in the context of a Software as a Service (SaaS) like a thermostat. Just as when the thermostat turns the heat on or off when it gets too cold or too hot, the procurement SaaS routes the purchase requisition for approval for purchases above a certain threshold, say $5,000, and, if it exceeds, for example, $10,000, it routes the purchase requisition for secondary approval after obtaining the first approval. In this manner, the procurement SaaS provides an automated process for the accomplishment of company spending policies or objectives. What it does not do is question whether the approval threshold should be set at $5,000 for obtaining at least a singular independent approval or $10,000 to warrant an additional pair of eyes. Similarly, when the procurement SaaS performs mandatory field checks, it is reducing the possibility of incompleteness or error in end user entries or submissions. What it does not do is determine which of the fields should be mandatory, or whether additional ones need to be set as mandatory. For example, in our previous examples, when it becomes all too clear the purchase requisitions submitted are not detailed enough and lack additional support such as quotations, statements of work, or prior invoices, and do not give enough "food for thought" to the purchase approver when assessing the validity of the submitted spending, it may help to require that each purchase requisition be accompanied with external support.

When the procurement SaaS limits access such that requestors and approvers only have access to view purchase requisitions they have submitted and approved, it is accomplishing the enterprise objective of keeping intra-department spending confidential. What it does not do is assess what should be further restricted or conversely relaxed to allow for greater visibility. Downstream approvers on a large purchase requisition, for example, may find it reassuring to be able to see who in effect has reviewed and approved the requisition before it is routed to them. For the requestor who submitted the purchase requisition, having this system audit trail information can also help to determine whether the requisition is stuck, and where in the approval chain. In this respect, it would have been helpful if the procurement SaaS were able to "advise" relaxing access just enough to expose approval routing and system audit trail mechanics to all users who have a stake in any given purchase requisition while keeping intra-department spending confidential. Alternatively, for a different organization, inter-department visibility to all spending may be just what is needed to encourage (or shame) less than compliant departments to fall in line with company policy.

The point of the earlier exercise is not to make a facetious mockery of what the procurement SaaS cannot do, but really to point out what Chris Argyris characterizes as the absence of double-loop learning in ineffective regulating processes. To understand second loop learning, let us first tackle single loop learning. According to Argyris, single loop learning happens when a system or process detects an error and undertakes a corrective action.[8] Our procurement SaaS can detect when a purchase requisition requires a single or at least two levels of approval, flag a warning when users do not complete mandatory fields, and preclude users from accessing purchase requisitions that belong to other departments. Second loop learning comes into the picture when we start to evaluate or question the norms established through company policies or objectives. Is $5,000 too high of a spending threshold to require purchase requisition approvals? How would we know, or perhaps more pointedly, where do we begin to gather the relevant data points? The procurement SaaS may not be a self-calibrating apparatus capable of questioning its own configurations, whether that be the $5,000 approval threshold or even the purchase approvers identified on the approval chain, but we can certainly create, save, and distribute reports at periodic intervals on purchase requisitions submitted and not submitted.

Over time, we can determine if multiple purchase requisition have been submitted for the same service and even though the total amount exceeds $10,000 and therefore would have required two approvals, but, because they are broken up into multiple smaller requisition amounts, only undergo single approvals each time. In tracking vendor invoices processed without purchase orders (POs; the output of approved purchase requisitions), we can also assess whether the total invoiced amount across all invoices for any given one vendor for the year has exceeded the $5,000 threshold. If so, a purchase requisition should have been submitted to track anticipated spending from that vendor for the year. Finally, we can re-assess the average amount of vendor spending against the $5,000 threshold. If the bulk of average spending with each vendor amounts to $3,500 per year, it would lead us to suspect that the $5,000 threshold is too high for accounting or management to receive proactive and proper notification of expected spend. So even though the procurement SaaS cannot independently question the $5,000 threshold policy for purchase requisition creation and approval, it can certainly facilitate double-loop learning, or as the case may, define a better internal control around vendor spending.

Yet, according to Argyris, double-loop learning often remains untapped, stemming from a fundamental inability to bridge the chasm between what we think and say we do, "espoused theories," with what we actually do, "theories in use."[9] "If people are unaware of the propositions they use," Argyris goes on to argue, "then it appears that they design for themselves theories-in-use that are not genuinely self-correcting. Thus, they become prisoners of their own theories."[10] He describes holding a seminar with 15 line officers, mostly presidents of divisions, as well as eight financial officers of these divisions together with the chief executive and financial officers on financial management systems.[11] While the line officers expressed frustration over completing too many forms and still not getting the financials in a timely manner, the financial officers asserted that the forms were too complex because of the requirements from banks.[12] What both sides don't quite express are simmering concerns over information incompleteness or worse distortion.[13] This is consistent with Argyris's theory that employees in an organization perceive and participate in the part-and-parcel of error hiding and other corporate games as a means to reduce the tension arising from conflicting goals and objectives.[14] Recall from Chapter 4 the "links and tensions" among various interconnected SaaS that are not unlike those witnessed among disparate variables in medical epidemiology.[15]

Another example that illustrates the role that visibility or lack of visibility plays lies in the handling of healthcare provider billing. When receiving a provider bill on recent lab work, I was surprised to find out that I was responsible for 100% of out-of-pocket expenses. After calling my insurance provider, it turned out that they had made a mistake. Even though I went with an in-network provider, they assumed that I went out-of-network. The good news is that they realized their mistake and proceeded to remit the payment to the provider. Yet when conversing with the billing department from the provider, I was told that they had not yet received the payment. More importantly, because the billing department had no access to my insurance coverage, they could not verify the veracity of my response. In Chapter 4, we first mentioned the concept of a cul-de-sac, where, when attempting to use a SaaS, users are not able to retrace or unwind the steps taken. Here, the billing clerk handling my concern was trapped in a cul-de-sac of sorts, unable to update my bill or provide an update because of the lack of visibility into my insurance coverage. While there are more real-life factors that would come into play, such as patient confidentiality, it nevertheless represents a microcosm of a day-in-the-life challenge when working with SaaS and internal controls where it is precisely the lack of visibility, or perhaps more pointedly the lack of insight into the need for visibility among personnel across departments, that ends up slowing down or worse introducing errors in an otherwise compliant process.

In *Formal Structure as Myth and Ceremony*, John Meyer and Brian Rowan explore how formal organizational structures in society are attributed to a rational approach that identifies technical goals and prescribes rules or appropriate ways of attaining them.[16] Many of the institutionalized elements, such as accounting, come from legal mandates, charters, and certifications. By shaping its organizational structure to align with these elements, an enterprise establishes its legitimacy. One way of evidencing its adherence to collective societal values and objectives is compliance with external assessment criteria. Publicly traded companies come to mind having to comply with rules of the U.S. Securities and Exchange Commission (SEC) in exchange for being able to sell shares of stock to the public to raise additional capital. Compliance with other criteria such as the Sarbanes–Oxley Act (SOX) can "demonstrate socially the fitness of the organization."[17] Yet, as Meyer and Rowan point out, there are situations when formal organizational structures can conflict with internal organizational efficiencies.[18] Going public necessitates additional internal resources such as compliance and investor relations. SOX compliance especially during the early years of 2004 through 2006, came at a price, of which a disproportionate amount was imposed on smaller and medium-sized enterprises. Institutionalized elements do not always align or are not compatible, necessitating a hodgepodge of enterprise efforts at compliance.

Payment Card Industry (known as PCI) compliance, for example, sharply differs from SOX compliance. While the former's Data Security Standard (DSS) calls for organizations to change system passwords every 90 days, SOX makes no such specifications, leaving it up to individual firms to design and exact individual permutations of password controls. What happens when the password aging of a SOX in-scope SaaS is 180 days and differs from the 90-day policy spelled out by DSS? How does the organization reconcile inter-SaaS or inter-system differences? Meyer and Rowan make the case that it is through decoupling – putting in gaps between institutionalized rules and actual work demands – that organizations can carry on their work routines as usual, "making things work out back stage" while maintaining ceremonial conformity with institutionalized structures."[19] Recall our review of Goffman's back-stage versus front-stage behaviors from Chapter 5. Internal managers and external accrediting agencies alike participate in "ceremonial affairs" when providing or accepting assertions and other high-level evidence furnished at face value, in effect circumventing any real degree of inspection or assessment.[20] Check-the-box compliance served up on a silver platter.

If all this sounds familiar, we are building up to what is likely to happen in an audit. But before we get there, there are benefits to decoupling that merit our attention. If we think about SaaS, and specifically the combination of SaaS and Platform as a Service (PaaS), it is precisely the flexibility afforded by easy customization that lets varied enterprise clients use the same software differently albeit with customized fields, records, or workflows in no time with little or no technical knowledge. This is one of the defining benefits of SaaS over on-premise solutions that require technical consultant assistance and a traditional waterfall development lifecycle to implement the necessary enhancements. As early as 1974, Karl Weick observed the benefits of loosely coupled systems, such as between the principal's office and the counselor's office in an educational institution.[21] Fast forward to 2004 when Roberts warns of "a system that is 'tightly decoupled', so that changing any aspect of the design or the environment will compromise performance severely unless numerous other aspects are also adjusted, may work very well if all goes to plan."[22] When decoupling occurs between policies and actual processes, the benefit is one of giving actual participants the necessary space and freedom to improvise and respond swiftly to in-the-moment contingencies without so much as turning to a heavy rulebook each time. This gives new perspective to German sociologist Max Weber's claim on the bureaucratization of human life – individuals trapped in an "iron cage" of rule-based, rational control.[23] If anything, the decoupling observed in organizations and systems alike speaks to the satirical pejorative behind French economist Jacques Claude Marie Vincent de Gournay's coinage of bureaucracy in the mid-18th century: "We have an illness in France which bids fair to play havoc with us; this illness is called bureaumania."[24] By the 1920s, the definition was expanded by Weber to include any system of administration conducted by trained professionals according to fixed rules. As an aside, Weber is not an admirer of bureaucracy per se although he is of the belief that bureaucracy constitutes the most efficient and rational way to organize human activity, and therefore it is indispensable to the modern world.

The danger with this kind of decoupling is when organizations seek to acquire legitimacy and compliance with external regulations without so much changing underlying practices as erecting formal structures that evidence that they have "done the right thing." In this sense, "good faith" among internal organizational and external constituents, the key ingredient that Meyer and Rowan identify that precludes organizations that employ decoupling from turning into anarchies has been violated.[25] "Decoupled compliance structures," Tammy MacLean and Michael Behnam point out, "may either manifest themselves as public claims of programs that do not exist in practice, or as programs that exist in practice, but are disconnected from important, on-going, line-related organizational functions."[26] This decoupling stands in stark contrast to the idealized proposition for compliance activities to be integrated back into the everyday fabric of organizational life where "decisions are made in light of these policies and people occupying these specialized structures have the confidence of, and interaction, with other departments and their managers" as espoused by Weaver, Trevino and Cochran.[27] In their study of the decoupling between external compliance requirements and an internal sales compliance program at Acme Insurance Company, MacLean and Behnam are able to trace how the decoupled compliance program created a "compliance façade" that shielded and encouraged the prevalence of deceptive sales practices to attain commission or bonus targets through churning by which a new policy is purchased through the use of dividends or loan values from an insured's existing policy or from borrowing more than 25% of an existing policy's cash value.[28]

Churning violates every state's fair trade practices, not the least the National Association of Securities Dealers (known as NASD) regulations and Acme's internal sales practice compliance rules.[29] The key issue lies in the dissonance created by the decoupled compliance program: while external constituents saw Acme as legitimate and meeting regulatory demands, internal constituents saw the program as lacking credibility or legitimacy and chose to conduct business as usual.[30] With Acme, the very monitoring system used to flag replacement transactions had a loophole: it did not identify replacements when the withdrawal of money from the existing policy occurred more than 90 days after the sale of the new policy.[31] This in turn encouraged sales personnel to "sell" a new policy to accept quarterly premiums, such that future ones would be funded by withdrawals from the existing policy 91 days later.[32] Here, parallels can be seen with the "$999.95 requisitions" to "avoid a $1,000 limit" shared by Peters at the start of this chapter.[33] Compliance efforts within Acme turned out to be annual obligatory meetings culminating in the completion of a 20-statement form.[34] In the face of an overwhelming emphasis placed on sales performance, it is no wonder then that the resulting ratio of efforts expended on obtaining sales results to completing compliance reports was 9:1.[35]

In this environment, the practice of churning continued unabated or, rather, institutionalized itself. MacLean and Behnam pointed out three elements that characterize this institutionalization.[36] First, sales personnel employed a common language and set of methods to use funds from existing policies towards new ones, such as notations made on policyholder records (PR) cards that still showed money in their policy.[37] Second, sales managers shared "best practices" on churning, diffusing it throughout the organization.[38] A sales agent remarked how a sales manager would clip out PR cards with promise and call agents into his office to share ways of calculating how much more insurance the policyholder could afford.[39] Third, churning became a routine, an informal norm, an acceptable form of business conduct within Acme even though to the outside world, it continued to receive the highest of ratings from the mid-1980s to the mid-1990s from A.M. Best, an agency that rates life insurance companies on their ability to meet current and future financial obligations.[40] The decoupled compliance program, however, only succeeded in maintaining the compliance or legitimacy façade in the short term.[41] Ironically, the rampant practice of churning increased the likelihood of Acme losing its external legitimacy in the medium term.[42] By the mid-1990s, declining dividend rates meant that old policies could no longer fund new ones; policyholders started getting overdue notices on policies that they were told didn't require payment.[43]

Faced with an avalanche of customer complaints to state regulators, a national investigation was launched into Acme's business practices ultimately costing the company tens of millions in fines.[44] State investigative files and interviews document an example when a state investigator asked an agent whether the company deliberately sought a compliance monitoring system that did not work too well.[45] The interviewee's response best summed up the institutionalization of decoupling: "I didn't think they want anything that would unduly interfere with sales."[46] There are interesting parallels that can be drawn between Acme and the areas we have covered thus far. Decoupling is exemplified by the metadata tables used by SaaS to allow for individual client enterprises to configure or tailor custom attributes on their own without disrupting the underlying data architecture. Additionally, just as over time, Acme's practice of drawing from future dividends ultimately collapsed under the weight of less than attractive dividend rates, it mirrors, in an odd way, the reactive attempts undertaken to resolve surface symptoms rather than root causes so that over time information technology (IT) organizations find themselves caught in a perpetual, self-fulfilling firefighting loop.

We can make the argument that the bigger danger behind decoupling lies not so much in dealing with the aftermath of shady business practices, but in the insidious and tautological manner formal structures are imprinted in the very way we ultimately impute or measure effectiveness despite their very dissonance from everyday actual practices. Ceremonial legitimacy is one thing, a taken-for-granted assumption on cause and effect is quite another. Back to our procurement SaaS. Suppose when viewing purchase requisitions by vendor over the course of a year, we find examples of multiple purchase requisitions of small amounts submitted meriting only a single approval ($5,000) but ultimately add up to amounts meriting two or more approvals (over $10,000) for the full year. Clearly, some form of decoupling is at work, this time between the communicated purchase policy that all spending over $10,000 needs two approvals, and the actual process undertaken by various internal constituents to submit purchase requisitions. Much like how the sales agents and managers at Acme out-maneuvered the defunct compliance monitoring system that failed to identify replacement transactions where funding occurred after 90 days, purchase requestors have figured out the loophole in the procurement SaaS that only checks for the requisition amount against minimal approval thresholds for any one singular requisition, rather than year-to-date requisition amounts. Much like the Argyris's point on second-loop learning, it would have been useful if a second feedback loop were in place. Monthly reports could be created on purchase requisitions submitted year-to-date, for example, flagging possible policy bypasses on a timely basis, which managers could in turn use to re-educate line personnel on the purpose or importance of submitting the right spending for approval.

In this scenario, the procurement SaaS would have been configured to be self-referential. No longer just a thermostat that serves as a stabilizing force in temperature upswings, it is simultaneously capable of producing information that clues users in on whether the configuration was right in the first place. In the case of Acme, these monitoring or detective measures came too little too late, invariably lacking teeth to modify existing behaviors let alone instill new ones. But suppose, without undertaking the necessary compensating control of monthly reporting, the enterprise using the procurement SaaS decides to deploy it to a newly acquired subsidiary. The effectiveness of internal controls over purchase requisitions becomes measured more by the number of purchase requisitions approved in line with their submitted amount and less by the number of purchase requisitions that bypassed two or more approvals because of the local practices of splitting or breaking the aggregated spending into bite-sized portions. Because of this, the focus of the deployment at the subsidiary is more of a straightforward application of the purchase policy, rather than accounting for actual in-situ workarounds that have occurred at the parent entity. Accordingly, outcome-based measures that underlie the success of the procurement SaaS are more a reflection of the ostensive than the performative – requisitions that have been submitted and approved rather than workarounds employed to bypass instituted approval thresholds.

Decoupling can occur at a still more subtle layer. Review of sales orders can be deemed to "occur" within an order management SaaS and thus imbued with both automated and manual elements until we ask, just what are reviewers comparing the legitimacy of the order data with? When answers such as against manual paper artifacts outside of any system, and coupled with the ensuing need to make manual updates to custom deals, the surface portrayal of system automated approvals using the SaaS at hand starts to lose its initial mystique not to mention appeal. A surefire way to smash the archetype – in keeping with the spirit of Argyris' double-loop learning – may lie in monitoring the amount of time invested in the review and approval of sales orders before and after a SaaS deployment. If no significant time and resource savings are observed, how truly automated is the review of sales orders post SaaS deployment? Does the real issue, in fact, lie in the creation and corresponding update of custom deals?

The metrics to monitor, in this manner, is the transition from number of orders approved per month to number of custom orders manually entered. These exceptional circumstances recall changes to POs, circling back to our previous example of approving purchase requisitions. Upon deeper investigation, we observe that much of the busywork surrounds not so much the initial approval of new purchase requisitions as it is around the changes to POs, and the absence of any secondary reviews. Then we realize just how wide the chasm is between ostensive approval evidenced on newly minted purchase requisitions and the performative behind-the-scenes updates on POs post requisition approval. Thus, the internal control here is not so much a precise means of addressing the underlying chaos as it is a lid for masking and containing the complexities within. So accustomed we have become with a compliance game that the whistle of the boiling kettle goes unnoticed.

In studying the Edna McConnell Clark Foundation (EMCF) transition from offering better services for people in poor and disadvantaged communities to bringing these services to more people through better-run, more efficient, and more durable organizations, authors Allen Grossman and Daniel Curran made an interesting observation.[47] By basing the effectiveness of an organization on the manner in which it collects, analyzes and reports information, the risk is that emphasis is on the process rather than on the actual quality of services rendered.[48] A case in point is the nonprofit Room to Read founded by former Microsoft executive John Wood. As pointed out by Patricia Bromley and Walter Powell in *From Smoke and Mirrors to Walking the Talk: Decoupling in the Contemporary World*, Room To Read's strategic plan acknowledges an uncertainty over whether the measures it uses to measure outcomes truly reflect gains in literacy for children in developing countries: "For example, although we know that in 2008 a total of 2,341,941 local language and/ or English language books were provided to the 4,478 libraries established between 2006 and 2008, and that on average 88% of our libraries have check-out systems in place, we still had concerns about just how many books were being checked out and read by children."[49]

Framed against our prior discussion of Latourian immutable mobiles – recall here our review of the 2-by-2 magic quadrant from Gartner in Chapter 4 – it is not hard to see our leanings towards "concrete" numbers however two dimensional to account for the three dimensional. Or as Donna Haraway slyly puts it in *A Cyborg Manifesto*, "human beings, like any other component or subsystem, must be localized in a system architecture whose basic modes of operation are probabilistic, statistical."[50] Money is one such immutable mobile that pervades our individual and collected consciousness, shaping the way we see ourselves, and others, as well as the relations we have with ourselves and others. Another is copyright. A case in point is a recent 45-minute hearing before the Ninth U.S. Circuit Court of Appeals in San Francisco on Naruto, a monkey living in the Sulawesi wildlife reserve in Indonesia.[51] When picture perfect selfies taken by Naruto appeared in *Wildlife Personalities*, the People for the Ethical Treatment of Animals sued the publishers for copyright infringement and sought to redistribute any proceeds back to the monkey.[52]

In *The Audit Society: Rituals of Verification*, Michael Power describes the "loose coupling" between what an audit is expected to accomplish and what is actually performed.[53] He writes of two types of audit failures, the first of which relates to how "the audit process is decoupled or compartmentalized in such a way that it is remote from the very organizational processes which give it its point."[54] This is in line with the decoupling process described by Meyer and Rowan. The creation of specific audit structures – audit committee, internal audit, compliance – all conspire to decouple audit mechanics from actual operational processes. The second type of failure, far more insidious, relates to the way audit "construct[s] concepts of performance in its own image."[55] Audit consciousness permeates performance measures in a way that mirrors concerns of Grossman and Curran about process over outcome or of Bromley and Powell about Room to Read's actual gains in literacy. Auditees' performance is measured by their ability to supply evidence that point to a system of internal controls, documented policies, procedures, and key controls. Auditors perform sample testing of these constructs to determine if identified key controls are operating effectively. To the extent that they do speaks more to the auditees' ability to collect, analyze, and report information in an auditable fashion rather than to an actual or inherent quality of operational performance. Perhaps this is why auditors are careful to qualify that they are testing the system of internal controls, rather than actual process or system outcomes.

In our procurement SaaS example, this would be like saying that it matters more, from an audit perspective, that evidence of approvals exists as system audit trails for purchase requisitions submitted. Actual outcomes, such as "bypasses" employed by splitting aggregate amounts into smaller sums to skip dual approvals, are not actually validated. The procurement SaaS could still be deemed to be operating effectively from an audit perspective and yet fail to account for the circumventing end user workarounds. Audit trails can also be deceptively misleading. Upon creating a new transaction, it would appear that a user has unwittingly selected a wrong department or cost center when it shows in the system audit trail that the user has created the new record. Yet upon deeper investigation, a script kicks in each time a new record is saved and defaults the department to a specific value. Because the user creates the transaction, only the user's actions and not that of the script is recorded in the audit trail. Likewise, when running a bulk process such as revenue recognition on open invoices in the most recent period, it would appear from the system audit trail that the user is quickly able to manually create a large journal entry with voluminous lines tied to multiple invoices when all the user must do is click a button. Finally, insofar as a specific SaaS such as Concur lets us proxy in as a different user, likely in the role of an administrative expense delegate, we question whether the actions logged on behalf of another user are reported accordingly as delegate activity rather than those immediately tied to and thus accountable to the primary user who has no action in the matter.

Viewing audits as "fatal remedy," Power argues that "audits do as much to construct definitions of quality and performance as to monitor them."[56] In assessing higher education, Marilyn Strathern writes that "the concept of audit in turn has broken loose from its moorings in finance and accounting; its own expanded presence gives it the power of a descriptor seemingly applicable to all kinds of reckonings, evaluations and measurements."[57] Cris Shore and Susan Wright in turn describe the colonization of audit over the United Kingdom's higher education landscape.[58] Faced with Academic Audits (known as AAs), Research Assessment Exercise (known as RAEs), and Teaching Quality Assessment (TQA), universities create audit structures comprising of quality assurance officers and monitoring committees on the one hand, and staged ritualized performances on the other, devoting more time to producing auditable records to prepare for dress rehearsals for the next TQA audit than to teaching or research.[59] Much like the EMCF search for more auditable organizations to engage services with, teaching quality has become synonymous with the ability to maintain an effective system of records that would pass an audit. In other words, as Power aptly puts it, "What is being assured is the quality of the control systems rather than the quality of first order operations. In such a context, accountability is discharged by demonstrating the existence of such systems of control, not by demonstrating good teaching, caring, manufacturing, or banking."[60]

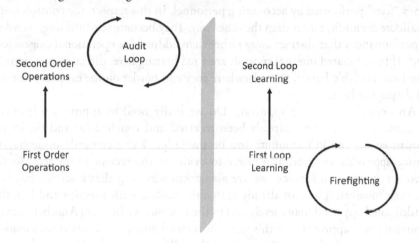

Here is the curious combination of absent second loop learning and present second order operations or conversely, its mirror half: the presence of first loop learning and absence of first order operations. With an omission of first order operations, the organization is ensnared in an audit loop that emphasizes second order operations, behaviors that reify the system of internal controls rather than directly resonate with the immediacy of the everyday exigencies. On the other hand, an organization that responds via first loop learning rather than second loop learning remains caught in a vicious cycle of firefighting that prefaces surface symptoms over root causes. This odd recursive looping unto itself is an aspect of the audit institution that recalls Ouroboros, an ancient symbol depicting a serpent or dragon eating its own tail.

In this respect, when we bring this audit perspective to an enterprise SaaS, we run the risk of developing internal controls that amount to no more than ritual assurance. While approvals and audit trails are evidenced, because the focus is on fulfilling the audit, they never quite plumb the necessary depths to address actual, real-life concerns that arise in day-to-day, moment-by-moment contingencies encountered in everyday operations. Because the controls focus on audit or compliance objectives, rather than serve as instruments or means to automate the manner we deal with what can go wrong, they serve as a buffer that decouples rational management objectives from actual, in-situ processes that surround the use of the SaaS. The SaaS may very well offer the ability or potential to streamline processes, remove single points of failure, or reduce an overall reliance on manual workarounds. A practical example we have already discussed is the manual work still undertaken by end users and support personnel alike to correct for data inconsistencies in transaction entries that make it appear the orderly records are the outcome of having internal controls configured in the SaaS when the reality is otherwise. Thus, the internal controls such as three-way match, transactions approvals and mandatory fields, are deemed to be operating in the SaaS by auditors even if they are really the outcome of everyday work performed to correct for misclassifications, duplications, or omissions – manual behind-the-scenes "fixes" performed by accounting personnel. In this respect, the controls justify or validate the audit, rather than the other way. They become self-fulfilling, tautological performances that abstract away rather than address the operational exigencies at hand. If the officiated internal controls are a red herring here, directing our attention away from invisible hands, then elsewhere they can border on the excessive, ceremonial displays at best.

An example is invoice approvals. Do we really need to approve an invoice if the items or services have already been received and vouched for and the invoice amount equals the PO amount? You be the judge. I can certainly understand if invoice approvals are used as a proxy to evidence the receipt of services, so that when we approve an invoice, we are also acknowledging that a service has been received; however, if we can already match the invoice with a receipt and PO, then an additional approval may merely add to the compliance burden. Another example is journal entry approval, but this time for reversal entries. Accrual entries made in the current period often get reversed out the following month. Thus, to the extent that approvals are already evidenced for accrual entries, do we need another round of approvals for reversals? Insofar as a user fails to approve these reversal entries, and they do not get recorded in the following period, then to what extent does this redundant control of having to approve reversal entries make it more rather than less likely for the books to be misstated from an oversight or omission in approving reversals timely and completely? Whereas with controls that preface the ostensive over the performative, we do not get enough of what we want; with redundant controls with little value added, we get more of what we do not want.

With SaaS, however, the user does not have to pretend or work at being a know-it-all. Specific configuration changes in procurement SaaS – such as the exposure of upstream approvals to downstream approvers, the enabling or disabling of specific fields, and interjection of a finance approver before the purchase requisition is routed to the department owner – allow administrative users to put in place desired changes, review the feedback from end users, and make specific tweaks to the process. Much like the Agile development process that characterizes much of software development today – incremental, usable and iterative – the end user takes part in the design of internal controls for the enterprise SaaS rather than remain as a passive participant waiting to be "configured" or tamed by the software or subject matter expert well versed in PeopleCode, SAP (Systems, Applications, Products), or Oracle-speak. The potential that SaaS offers is, to use Hales's characterization, the ability to evolve users from clients to co-designers to actors-constructors.[61] Design of internal controls is not driven top down by management or auditors, but from bottom-up by end users. The ability to attach support to a purchase requisition, such as vendor quotations or proposed statement of work – as is the renaming of services and items that are more user friendly rather than accountant friendly – is a voice of the silent majority more focused on accomplishing operational resiliency than mere compliance.

Furthermore, the design of internal controls is not just SaaS specific – how controls are configured within SaaS – but also relates to all actions and changes undertaken with the SaaS. The testing of specific configurations enabled in the test environment lets end users work with a rapidly evolving prototype. Further, the easy rollback of changes in production encourages a necessary level of tinkering before requirements get tested in real life and at least put through varied iterations. In this manner, SaaS encourages the user to evolve from being a mere client engaged in contractual negotiations over requirements – recall the Agile Manifesto, "customer collaboration over contract negotiation,"[62] we reviewed from Chapter 5 – into more active co-designer and actor/constructor roles in devising custom attributes, records, or workflows through point and click SaaS capability.

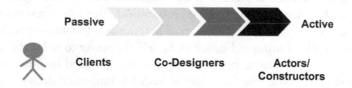

In *Where Are the Designers*, Hales identifies categories of computer software design that can be just as applicable to the design of internal controls supporting an enterprise SaaS. On one end of the spectrum are the "design of generic products."[63] These are like the audit toolkit of "best practice" internal controls. In the middle, documented user processes reside and are factored into the overall "design of user activities" through specific configurations. Still further, we see "design in use" – what happens when actual users use the software in real environments. Did I say we need Date Received as a mandatory field? Well, not really, it does not apply to all scenarios and in fact is one additional step that is redundant in most purchases on services. Or how about edit access to purchase requisitions already submitted? With the purchase of the SaaS, we first arrive at "design of generic products."[64] Subsequently, during requirements gathering, "design of user activities" is incorporated into the

SaaS through application configuration. Initially, it is determined that requestors only have create and not edit access to purchase requisitions to prevent the update of requisitions that have already been approved, thereby circumventing the purchase requisition approval process altogether.

What happens when a requestor has submitted a purchase requisition with the wrong amounts but only realized after submission? In this "design in use" case, the requester should have the ability to edit a purchase requisition that is still pending approval, or at least be able to delete it and replace it with the right purchase requisition. Still further when the purchase requisition reaches the approver, the approver realizes that the requester selected the wrong service. A couple of things may happen. The approver may wish to edit the purchase requisitions before approving it and, in this instance, would like edit access to the PO. Alternatively, the approver may "reject" the purchase requisition so that the requestor can edit it and resubmit accordingly. In the first option, when running it by audit, it is determined it would be a segregation of duties conflict. There is the possibility of the approver increasing the amount of the submitted purchase requisition before approving it, thus making it redundant to have an independent requestor submit the requisition in the first place. And so, in the final analysis, the requestor would need the ability to update purchase requisitions that are in pending approval and rejected statuses.

In the final act, we arrived at the other end of spectrum – "design of design." With SaaS, the process to change it albeit through trial-and-error configuration has changed. Rather than wait for a business analyst to update the requirements and a technical personnel to make the actual change, and in this sequential manner, amid back-stage back-and-forth banter – "what do users know" and "if they had only told us this in the first place" – the layman user who has administrator access creates a specific role and assigns selected requestors to this role to test out their edit access to purchase requisitions. In this final act, the user becomes an active "actor-constructor," redistributing to himself or herself the power to tailor the use of the SaaS from the initial generic functionality and any idealized images conjured by documented procedures. The flexibility of SaaS has integrated design into use, so that it is no longer separated from actual day to day.

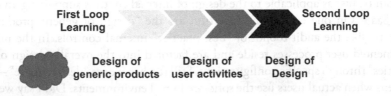

When we progress along the continuum of design from generic products to design of user activities to design of design itself, we evolve from first to second loop learning, no longer satisfied by the mere adjustment of the thermostat, and actively reassessing the continued applicability of the thresholds configured in the first place.

Design in use is a useful concept to employ when deploying changes to production. The initial deploy of SaaS would not need to anticipate, let alone address every conceivable circumstance. And if so, then the unique malleability of fields, records, and workflows that make up the SaaS offering is the perfect candidate this approach. Just as in building planning, Stewart Brand advocates for a loose fit, a strategy that "postpones many design decisions and leaving them to the eventual users;" the same approach can be applied in the design of internal controls for and around SaaS.[65] Take a leased space that allows a company to expand by knocking doors through walls of a neighboring startup that has failed or else moved away. From this perspective, a SaaS that is too rigidly implemented with all the "bells and whistles" of every conceivable internal control can end up already hampering every action of newbie users trying to learn its language at the outset. In fact, Brand advocates building designs that let people try things out.[66] From this perspective, a sandbox environment of SaaS can give users the opportunity to try out new ways without incurring real risk to production. Even in production, when access is initially relaxed rather than tightened during initial deployment, this encourages users to try out or experiment with different roles; arguably, tightened access at the initial outset can backfire especially when users get frustrated with not being able to access functions that are commensurate with their job responsibilities.

All too often, users used to on-premise or legacy solutions wait for an analyst to develop customized reports or saved queries, without realizing that the SaaS at hand grants them the ability to develop their very own tailored reports – drilldowns that tap into related records and joins with other tables – so that they can schedule them for regularly email distribution to a selected audience or as input into management dashboards that give executives a visual overview of key performance indicators. Even with instances of SaaS in sandbox versus production environment, the impetus is to first attempt to test drive the configuration changes as completely as possible in sandbox, obtain approval and then make the changes quickly in production. But just as in Agile, end user requirements are not completely flushed in the initial sprints, especially when faced with limited time and resource constraints. It can be wishful thinking to expect production "release" of configuration changes to go off without a hitch.

Take the following SaaS customization I had students in my *Accounting Information Systems* class attempt. To validate the amount of sales orders synced in from an upstream SaaS, we configured a custom amount field to re-compute the total amount by multiplying price with quantity and service period at the line level and adding up all the lines. In class, we omitted to factor in sales tax. When deploying our changes to production in test mode so that they are only applicable and thus visible to the logged-in user, we saw variances between our custom amount field and the standard amount field almost immediately even if they were false positives because our custom computed amount did not account for the sales tax included in the standard total amount field. A quick fix in production is to update the field formula to compare the computed amount against the subtotal instead of the total amount. Had we insisted on strict rollback procedures upon seeing errors in post-production release, we would have missed the opportunity to address the identified real-life rubber-meets-the-road concern expediently and effectively. In this example, our production deployment had limited financial impact if any. After all, this had to do with a custom field that did not impact the underlying accounting. Contrast this reasoning with change management controls in favor of the rational approach described by Meyer and Rowan, so that we would have had to abide by the "all changes need to be tested in sandbox prior to production rollout" at all costs. While this was true in our example – students did perform testing in a sandbox environment before performing a test drive in production – the SaaS at hand extended this testing to production, so that when post deployment errors are encountered, they can be attended to in real time.

Thus far, we have not yet questioned the completeness of real-life scenarios captured in sandbox testing even if in many ways, precisely because we are talking about sandbox, it is unlikely that we can completely capture real-life situations. Often, users do not refresh sandbox data, and in our example, administrators had not enabled certain integrated SaaS bundles, such as sales tax computation. In one extreme example of a SaaS platform upgrade from a multi-tenant instance to a single tenant one, I have seen how the sandbox version of the upgraded platform is not available until actual cutover to the new version. In other words, it is like putting the cart before the horse – having sandbox available for testing only upon go-live. Sandbox refreshes with the live production instance (and data) are not without errors and often client organizations cannot control them simply because they are not the ones performing the refresh. If, and when, they become available, there may be risks with having a newly minted sandbox refresh without updating interface or integration specific configurations. In one example, because the sandbox refresh now points to an integrated production instance of a different SaaS, test transactions may without warning show up in a downstream integrated SaaS in its production instance thereby resulting in actual material impact.

Refresh is not the only route. Testing the auto-application of payments to invoices in sandbox, for example, may require up-to-date customers and invoices in the sandbox. Rather than refreshing the sandbox instance completely, we can also upload in bulk the necessary customers and invoices. This selective approach while involving a one-time effort has arguably a higher level of precision in preparing and validating the specific types of data for testing rather than refreshing the instance completely and having to deal with false positives. It also frees up the same sandbox instance for other customization efforts that are in parallel, such as development of scripts, fields, or workflows. Yet even this route is not without its drawbacks. Testing bank reconciliation in a sandbox environment requires that necessary payments already exist for tying back to the bank statement activity, but to create payments, vendor invoices need to be already recorded. For logged vendor invoices, vendors need to have already existed in the sandbox environment. Depending on the last refresh of the sandbox environment, these vendors may not already exist, and thus need to be created. Therefore, even in this simple example of bank reconciliation testing in sandbox, more time is expended in setting up the necessary precursor constructs from vendors to vendor invoices to payments. Because of the resource constraints and depending on what the user is truly validating, the actual expense accounts or cost centers impacted may all default to a specific account or cost center insofar as the emphasis is on completeness of reconciliation over recording of general ledger (GL) impact. Another challenge with sandbox testing is the absence of audit trails in sandbox instances for some SaaS. This absence becomes complicated if the nature of the testing needed is triggered by knowing when a transaction has been approved and this information is unfortunately contained in transaction audit trails not available in a sandbox environment.

Access management for sandbox instances often gets overlooked owing to a combination of factors. Audit, for example, focuses on actual, production data, yet with a sandbox refresh, actual production data, if left unmasked, continues to "live" in the sandbox environment, which is invariably accessed by contractors or third-party vendors who assisted the sandbox verifications with end users and configurations. These users, precisely because they are not full-time employees, often do not get captured by companywide offboarding processes so it is not unheard of for consultants to continue to have access despite already having left the engagement only to have these accounts detected later in a periodic quarterly access review of sandbox licenses against current employees or contractors. Also, unless the key client personnel either working directly with the contractors or reviewing their timesheets notify the Human Resources (HR) department, often the authorized source of personnel changes, absent contractors who no longer need sandbox access can remain undetected for a long time.

The level of access granted to users in sandbox is another area of consideration. One approach would be to mimic or attempt to (in the case of a new SaaS deployment) the kinds of user roles that we would expect with enforced segregation of duties so that no one single individual can create a customer, submit an order, fulfill, invoice, and pay it without an additional pair of eyes. Yet, we can argue, especially with a new SaaS deployment, it is precisely because users are unfamiliar with the features at hand that they should see past each other's prescribed roles and have the permission granted to tinker or experiment in sandbox. Being able to exact a transaction end-to-end from soup to nuts also gives users ideas on what data to automate when checking up on or reconciling upstream or downstream ultimately in production. There is also often spillover impact either downstream or upstream that order management personnel may not consider, such as checking revenue recognition start and end dates at the order line level, as these along with the assigned revenue recognition schedule drives the revenue amortization. The same can be said for product operations personnel creating new items or stock keeping units (SKUs). Without assigning the applicable revenue recognition schedule, no revenue would have been recognized when the invoice is booked.

Without upstream consensus on the kinds of attributes required downstream, manual intervention would have to occur downstream to rework the transactions too little too late downstream and when facing additional pressures to close the books in a timely manner. In this case, a locked accounts receivable (A/R) sub-ledger would directly conflict the ability to rework transactions in a locked period. The same can be said for computation of sales tax. Without understanding and acting on the billing team's need for a tax code assigned correctly during item or SKU setup, either no sales tax or an incorrect sales tax would be computed in the sales order and invoice, necessitating not only manual rework by the billings team, but also communications with customers who may have been invoiced incorrectly, thus exposing the assemblage of actors behind the Mechanical Turk of an invoice. It is for this myriad of reasons that sandbox access to allow varied teams to perform testing and cross the pond into each other's domains may be highly desirable and, in effect, would encourage visibility, a subtle control.

Recall our previous example of how visibility to spend across departments may compel stragglers to catch up with the Jones in complying with company purchase policy. When deployed into production, roles can then be better segregated. Although the challenges here would be to acclimatize users to seeing in production far less than what they would have become accustomed to seeing in sandbox. In this case, having a perpetual sandbox instance available in addition to the production one would help users continue to be able to change or learn by experimenting while continuing to process real-life transactions in a consistent manner. In organizations where SaaS configuration is performed by an in-house team, two or more sandbox instances may be procured and maintained alongside the production instance so that one may be used for "development" and the other for user acceptance testing.

Putting aside the operational, change and access management challenges surrounding a sandbox SaaS instance in addition to the production counterpart, design in use becomes evident where upon deployment of configuration changes to production, we start to notice the hitherto taken for granted differences between integrated SaaS. In the example of the custom field computing an expected amount based on sell price, quantity, and service period, we may notice that the computed amount is often slightly different from the amount synced in from an upstream SaaS often by immaterial amounts. Upon further investigation, it turns out that the upstream SaaS does not factor into an additional day in a leap year that is contained in the service duration, whereas the downstream one fully accounts for the exact number of days between the service start and end dates. Other differences that amount to pennies may come from a difference in the level of precision. An upstream more operational SaaS may account for amounts for up to six decimal places to support high volume low cost transactions whereas a downstream integrated SaaS may only support up to two decimal places for currency amounts. In this manner, custom configurations in any one given SaaS, especially in our example on custom fields that recompute amounts and compare these against those synced in from an integrated SaaS, serve as fingers pointing at each other. There can also be discrepancies within the SaaS in which the custom computed fields have been introduced.

Through use of these custom fields, however, we may learn of other possible entry errors. For example, if the computation requires input of one or more existing fields, then the validity of values in these fields hitherto otherwise unexamined would come into spotlight. Computations would throw an error if users entered text instead of an integer or did not check a box that needed to be checked. Composite fields of fields in fact do a pretty good job of checking up on one another. Sharp differences observed immediately upon rollout of custom computed fields should not be a justification for rolling back changes quickly. Rather these differences are opportunities for revisiting what we have taken for granted all this time. I am reminded of the net belonging to the Vedic god Indra. Known as Indra's net, it hangs over his palace on Mount Meru and posits a multifaceted jewel at each vertex. Look closely and we can see that each jewel is reflected in all other jewels. In our example, the configured fields in one SaaS serve as jewels that reflect the characteristics of yet another integrated SaaS. We can argue that they function as a more effective audit mechanism than any boilerplate internal control checklist or practice aide from a Big Four auditor.

In this case, the specific configurations undertaken by the user as active co-designer or actor directly "audits" the integrity of synced in values. Rather than passively take in amounts and rely on a commonplace albeit best practice control that reconciles against completeness – checking to make sure that the total amount synced into the downstream SaaS ties back to source value in the upstream SaaS – this "control" goes one level deeper, beyond the commonplace thermostat to question that validity of the synced in amount: did it take into account the additional day in a leap year encompassed in the service duration? This interconnectedness among SaaS is per-haps why more and more, hiring managers in startups that are heavy consumers of best-in-breed SaaS look for new hires that are not just good in any one system but really excel at orchestrating and reconciling among multiple systems. As Charles Best, Chief Financial Officer of Blackline Systems, puts it, "I need people who are effective at managing data and reconciling data from one application to another to validate that our processes are working as opposed to entering an invoice into an ERP [enterprise resource planning] system only to pull it back out to write checks."[67] Blackline provides a cloud solution that automates manual repetitive accounting processes, such as reconciliation of accounts in the GL system with bank statements.

Another way to envision the system of interconnected SaaS is to see it as a hologram of sorts, where each SaaS serves as a mirror of what goes on elsewhere. What we see depends on where we stand. When we look upstream from a down-stream SaaS, incomplete attributes may be missing. Yet, looking downstream from an upstream SaaS, the governing automated controls may seek to tighten too much too soon. In South Africa, ubuntu gained traction in the 1950s as a philosophy. Best described by Michael Onyebuchi Eze, the core of ubuntu can be surmised as "a person is a person through other people."[68] In many ways, a SaaS is a SaaS through other SaaS. Recall again the "multiply-authored" identity constituted from relations with others we discussed in Chapters 1 and 5.[69] The application landscape that emerges for any one client enterprise is comprised of a plethora of varied SaaS. Supported by open application programming interfaces (known as APIs) and integration Platform as a Service (iPaaS), transactions in an upstream SaaS sync with a downstream SaaS seamlessly or so it would seem. What the SaaS can or cannot do, the shortfalls or value-addeds, are in turn compensated by another SaaS. From a maintenance perspective, what results is a poignant reminder of file-based systems that predated databases in the late 1960s and 1970s. Just as data consistency issues plagued file-based systems – a change made to one file repository necessitated yet another change in a different repository – similar challenges can arise when setup fields or parameter changes are not replicated across two or more integrated SaaS so that a transaction coded to a new department or cost center in an upstream SaaS fails to sync to a downstream SaaS where the same department or cost center has not yet been created or has been modified. Change, or more aptly the ability to handle change – whether it resides at the transaction level, data, or at a higher configuration level that in turn drives how transactions and data interplay – is often the driving factor behind whether to employ a composite of best-in-breed SaaS solutions versus one monolithic stand-in reminiscent of on-premise ERP software from a bygone era.

Let us revisit Chapter 1 when we reviewed how a web commerce facility can be executed from a combination of SaaS, such as Magento, for example, with NetSuite, so that while the customer is able to enter credit card information on the front end thanks to Magento and linking these to a payment gateway (such as CyberSource), the same transactions need to flow into an accounting SaaS (in this case NetSuite) as invoices or cash sales to credit revenue. In an alternate scenario, the same flow can all be performed out of NetSuite as it offers front-end customer-facing SuiteCommerce platform ability as well. As opposed to handling a hodgepodge SaaS (recall file-based systems in the 1960s) each with its own tolerance for error handling and thus susceptibility to failure, why not just go with one solution? The course of action to take may well reside in how configurable a SaaS is compared to another without involving technical (read costly) third-party expertise. Insofar as products sold can change and impact the way discounts, tax, or different product tiers are presented on the webcart, it may make more sense to go with yet another different upstream SaaS albeit one that lets us introduce late breaking changes expediently without impacting a downstream accounting SaaS responsible for more than just credit card sales. The course of action to take can also change over time. Where one organization may first start with a more monolithic approach, likely a leftover habit from on-premise days, the same organization can choose to switch to a "multiple-authored" composite model comprising two or more best-in-breed SaaS over time. The reverse can also occur. For an organization accustomed to having multiple SaaS thread through the same credit card sale transaction, an influx of say NetSuite in-house subject matter expertise may elicit discussions exploring the possibility of a return to a more singular SaaS approach to standardize configuration management especially since changes to the setup would have been stabilized over time. The point is, even after deployment, learning is ever more critical. The ability to adapt design or configuration decisions made within any one given SaaS when it comes to the integration among two or more SaaS becomes pivotal.

Consider the scenario when an order and billing management SaaS would need to integrate with a revenue recognition one. The downstream destination SaaS may only accept quantities as positive quantities so order cancellations come in as positive quantities. Yet, the upstream order SaaS records negative lines added to reflect discounts or item cancellations. In the consideration of a potential integration between the two, the data can be augmented either in the upstream or downstream SaaS. In the former scenario, a user may create a custom record to reflect cancellation orders that can in turn be used for input into the downstream SaaS. Alternatively, in the latter scenario, the downstream SaaS to the extent possible can be used to "transform" or overwrite negative values with positive ones and associate these with cancellations. There is yet a third option, having the iPaaS perform the data cleansing. Recall from Chapter 4 our questions on whether to rely on the iPaaS to perform the data transformation whether that be defaulting a specific value to empty attributes or transforming from text to currency formats. Where and how the configuration changes would need to be made would shape the work that relates to Day 2 support, but herein the changes are not irreversible so that in effect after Day 1 go-live, updates to where and how reliance is placed can be in turn reassessed and reconfigured. Part of the decision lies in the resources available in-house such as subject matter expertise with the upstream or downstream SaaS or the interconnecting iPaaS. A second factor to consider is the underlying inter-SaaS architecture. Insofar as there may be other SaaS that need to be integrated with the upstream SaaS, does it make sense to front-load complex logic and "customized" configurations in the upstream SaaS or does it make more sense for each receiving downstream SaaS to be accountable for its own data cleansing, especially since each has its own unique data model and thus processing needs? A third factor that can come into play is any competing enhancement or customization projects in flight surrounding the upstream or downstream SaaS or iPaaS. Sometimes the easiest option to take may well be the least painful – so, for example, if the upstream SaaS is undergoing major customization with available resources, then it may make more sense for data cleansing to happen in the downstream SaaS – with the understanding that changes can be made in the future. A further consideration: if the iPaaS were used for data transformation, it automatically comes into the purview of an internal controls or SOX audit.

In his book, *How Buildings Learn*, Stewart Brand tells of the tale of a brilliant but lazy college planner who built a new campus with no paths between buildings.[70] The planner chose to delay the decision on where to put in paving until after the first winter to take the opportunity to photograph the paths made in the snow.[71] Could it be that with a SaaS implementation, instead of hastily laying down the boilerplate processes, we wait and observe, and just like the lazy college planner, and based on user adoption and usage patterns, introduce tailored controls targeted to mitigate observed risks? What the future may bring remains to be seen but the "design-in-use" observed in the SaaS can provide clues. Timely exception reporting is key whether it relates to internal control design for SaaS or building design. Brand decries the lack of transparency in buildings, citing examples of how rot in the walls and the short circuit are almost always remain hidden from view, out of sight and therefore out of mind.[72] He advocates for the exposure of parts that are most likely to fail – from use of materials that smell when they get moist to inspection windows and hatches.[73] A higher than expected number of $999.95 purchase requisitions, for example, can trigger a revisiting and ensuing update of purchase approval limits of $10,000 within a procurement SaaS. An uncharacteristic inflation of win opportunities reported nearing the end of each month may lead sales management to revisit the sales targets and performance setting process. A higher than expected product return rate may lead management to tie sales commission payout to net rather than gross billings. These examples in effect exemplify Argyris's second loop learning. As Henry Petroski put it differently, "Sometimes a component must fail for the larger system of which it is a part to survive an insult to its integrity."[74] In *To Forgive Design*, he covers numerous examples that draw from the behavior of a fuse: when tested by heightened conditions, whether that be stress, pressure, or heat, it reduces its ability to continue as self-contained and uninterrupted.[75]

An example is the sprinkler system that acts by failing to contain the water it holds when triggered. A Harvard Business Review article titled *Failing by Design* describes how organizations find it challenging to innovate or take risks when the mere mention of failing can be unsettling.[76] Yet, in the aforementioned example of custom fields with baked-in formulas, it is precisely because differences from our initial assumptions surface that they actually work, and in the spirit of real-life exigencies, the back-and-forth refinement of the working formulas behind these fields fine-tune the way we are able to respond efficiently without being inundated by the sheer volume of false positives. To some extent, the trajectory taken by SOX compliance with its insistence on key or primary controls to be vetted and tested with no exceptions, as opposed to secondary or non-primary controls, can be distracting when it is really the identification and resolution of multiple, little small fires that we can better equip ourselves to prevent a big fire. Even with no little fires, user requirements invariably get "tested" in production when faced with rubber-meets-the-road considerations. In Chapter 5, we reviewed an attempt at automating a bill run so that users do not have to create every invoice from scratch but can rely on a billing schedule assigned to the sales order. Initial requirements can focus on a big bang approach, having invoices generated automatically and emailed immediately; yet, upon rollout in production, these are diluted to reflect more real-life considerations, such as having to manually intervene for non-standard sales with rather unique terms and conditions, or those made out to resellers instead of end customers. For the latter scenario, invoices may need to be further updated to show the end customer intended even if the sale were made out to the reseller. When all is said and done, the actual email dissemination of invoices may be decoupled from automated bill generation to allow for updates to non-standard and reseller sales.

For all the talk we have on devising internal controls for SaaS, we forget that control lies at the heart of every algorithm. Recall Kolwaski's unabashed 1979 declaration "Algorithm = Logic + Control."[77] For Kolwaksi, logic is defined as the "what" that needs to be done, whereas control is "how" the computation would be performed.[78] When we start to see and even appreciate just how intrinsic a control is to a computer algorithm, we begin to see that all our work on internal controls for SaaS really revolves around developing controls of controls. Just as in Hale's category of software changes discussed previously, we evolve from design of generic products to design of user activities to design of design.[79] Declarative programming, for example, is a style and manner of building a computer program characterized by explicating the logic of a computation – the what – as opposed to its associated control flow – the how. In contrast, imperative programming specifies just how something is done. Structured Query Language (SQL), for example, is a declarative query language.

```
SELECT * from Invoices
INNER JOIN Customers
WHERE Invoices.Customers.ID = Customers.ID
```

For any given set of customers, the earlier SQL query identifies all invoices associated with them. Whether enterprise users create "looks" using Looker, a SaaS-based business intelligence solution, or saved searches in NetSuite, a cloud-based accounting SaaS through point-and-click in a browser, to report on key data metrics, they are in effect performing declarative programming. In Looker, for example, we can see the underlying SQL code constructed behind the scenes. Compare the SQL code with the following code that is more imperative in nature.

```
var InvoicesBelongingToCustomers = []
var Invoice, Customer
for(var ii=0; ii < Invoice.length; ii++)
  Invoice = Invoices[ii]
  for(var ci=0; ci < Customer.length; ci++) {
  Invoice_Customer = Invoice_Customers[ci]
   if (Invoice.Customer_ID == Customer.ID) {
    InvoicesBelongingToCustomers.push({
     Invoice : Invoice,
     Customer : Customer
    })
  }
}}
}
```

The earlier code iterates through the full list of invoices to seek out and identify those that belong to every customer in the list. In contrast to the declarative SQL code, it is longer and harder to maintain. Declarative programming does not just apply to extracting the right data to provide food for thought, it can also be used towards constructing new fields, records, and custom workflows involving approvals. In fact, Salesforce.com has amassed or initiated an entire set of literature both written and "you-tubed" on the declarative development without writing a single line of code – and in Salesforce's world, Apex code. One of the key benefits of employing a declarative avenue, or point-and-click mode of development, is its immediate appeal: we do not need to be able to code to make the necessary improvements or updates. By declaring the "logic" through point-and-click, we are in fact able to execute a change in process, such as routing in a workflow without necessarily enmeshed in the underlying "control" flow. With ease comes speed and the ability to put in place a new workflow or update an existing one swiftly in a sandbox environment before production deployment.

In fact, to write code that is cumbersome and a chore to maintain is like incurring technical debt in developer circles. A common metaphor that is increasingly used today, technical debt mirrors financial debt in that "interest" is incurred every time a change is made without completing other necessary changes that are impacted so that even though in the short to medium term the code is working, in the long run, the debt needs to be paid off for the work or code to be complete and not break over time. Something as simple as failing to place comments in code is a form of technical debt, especially since when someone else who is troubleshooting an error inspects the code, misunderstands what it is trying to do, and updates it incorrectly, thereby unwittingly creating an error on top of an error. Is it any wonder that undercover Salesforce.com evangelist Jeff Atwood pronounces that "every time you write new code, you should do so reluctantly, under duress, because you completely exhausted all your other options."[80]

In addition, governance limits constrain client written code in the SaaS world and understandably so because SaaS is really a multi-tenant environment that lets different customers run different flavors of software on the same hardware. In Salesforce.com, the Apex runtime engine enforces strict limits to prevent a runaway Apex from monopolizing shared resources. If a specific Apex code exceeds the limit, the associated governor issues a runtime exception. This notwithstanding, every line of code incurs additional costs to maintain and upkeep. In our custom amount field that re-computes an amount that holds up a mirror to the amount synced in from an upstream SaaS, what would happen if we were to realize that the reason why we have been blissfully unaware of differences is because an administrator had inadvertently updated the formulas in the custom field? Thus, additional configurations merit additional reviews. While initially viewed as an "enhancement" of sorts self-served by savvy enterprise customer users, these nevertheless accrue over time to form a congealed layer of keep-our-lights-on tasks that are responsible for making sure that key configurations in use have not been inappropriately updated. To this end, other SaaS solutions emerge in the marketplace, not simply those that assist with processing business transactions or integrations like in iPaaS, but those that track changes to configurations, whether to roles and permissions, such as FastPath, or, in our previous example from Chapters 4 and 5, changes to custom fields, records, and scripts in Salesforce or NetSuite using FloDocs or Strongpoint. This way, when an administrator inadvertently modifies a common data element that is used by another script or workflow, alerts are provided in a timely manner.

There is yet another SaaS, one that can surface any difference, for example, arising between the account balance maintained in the accounting SaaS and the account reconciliation in Excel maintained in Box. FloQast highlights any discrepancies between the two so that even though account reconciliations, a key internal control, are performed outside an accounting SaaS, a link is nevertheless preserved to ensure data consistency. Not surprisingly, the prevalent trend of SaaS is to, as Rich Weborg, chief executive officer of OneReach, a cloud-based call center solution, puts it, "allow organizations to do as much as they can without engaging the development team."[81] To this end, OneReach offers non-technical users a visual workflow capability that lets them drag and drop message components to create automated rules around the creation or submission of customer event or payment notifications within minutes via voice, email, and text messaging. Just as a report on approved purchase requisitions does nothing to surface the coordination or articulation work undertaken behind the scenes by accounting personnel in "fixing" services or items to reflect the ones that are coded to the right GL accounts for outright expensing or amortization over time, or the cajoling that goes on albeit in a professional manner compelling approvers to intervene on purchase requisitions sitting in their approval queue for days, the "analytics" in popular vendor parlance may not provide quite the level of insight into the "logics" – the what – surrounding a circumstance, merely the "controls" – the continual tweaking of the how that really justifies status quo. What is really needed may be a complete rethink, a revisiting of assumptions swept under the rug.

Another way of thinking about the logic vs. control aspects is to compare this distinction with Noam Chomsky's differentiation between competence and performance. The linguistic competence possessed by native speakers of a language is contrasted with mere performance; the former refers to the speaker's mental reality of the language, unencumbered by speech impediments or distractions.[82] While the former can be inferred from the latter, Chomsky speaks of "devious and clever ways" to uncover it.[83] All too often, as he would point out, "a person might memorize the performance table and perform on various simple-minded tests exactly as the performer who knows the rules of arithmetic, but this would not, of course, show that he knows these rules."[84] Thus, performance, a mere doing is contrasted with competence, an inner capacity. Chomsky goes on to highlight the "creativity of language," that is "the speaker's ability to produce new sentences, sentences that are immediately understood by other speakers although they bear no physical resemblances to sentences which are 'familiar.'"[85] In a way, the underlying logic of an algorithm speaks to competence, whereas the control aspect addresses performance. John Searle's protagonist who appears to speak Chinese from inside the room exemplifies the performance outwardly despite not having the necessary competence within.[86] Searle's experiment is really a counter response to Alan

Turing's famous Turing Test, introduced in his 1950 paper *Computing Machinery and Intelligence*, which opens with the question, "Can machines think?"[87] Turing starts by describing a man and a woman in separate rooms and communicating with guests outside with typewritten notes. In this "imitation game," both the man and the woman pretend to be each other and the audience's challenge is to tell them apart.[88] Next, Turing replaces one of the participants in the room with a computer.[89] The question becomes: can the audience tell the human apart from the machine solely based on typewritten answers? Here, the computer is playing human. In Searle's experiment, a human is playing a computer (when following the transcription rules or algorithm) playing a human who comprehends Chinese. In the case of SaaS, this inner competence, or "creativity of language" translates into an ability to spin up and navigate unexpected turns in configuration design, testing, and deployment, all which assume that the SaaS is open ended.

As we have seen before even as we communicate, whether speaking or writing, we give ourselves the room to try out new things, hitherto unseen and thus unplanned for. Our example on the design-in-use challenges experienced when rolling out custom computation fields that key off on other values in a sales order shows just that – just as the Mechanical Turk from Chapter 5 would need to recalculate and consider its next or even next series of move(s) based on its opponent's current move. I recall the story of how a man with Taylorist leanings, accustomed as it were to the command and control, sought out a famous Zen master. Upon meeting, the Zen master suggested that they discuss the matter over tea. When the tea was ready, the master proceeded to serve the man. A moment or two after the tea rose to the rim, the guest shrieked: "Enough. You are spilling the tea all over. Can't you see the cup is full?" To which the master smiled and replied, "You are like this tea cup, so full that nothing more can be added." The initial generic feel that we may get from an un-configured SaaS can be disconcerting. Where is the value-added, the core competence? On the other hand, core competence does not come out-of-the-box; it is gained through a series of day-in and day-out practices of working with and through the tool. The question becomes not so much how feature rich a SaaS is out-of-the-box, but how capable it can be in accommodating specific needs as and when they arise. With the configurational capability of SaaS, are we able "to produce new sentences, sentences that are immediately understood by other speakers although they bear no physical resemblances to sentences which are 'familiar'"?[90]

Ostentative	Performative	Competence
Design of generic products	Design of user activities	Design of Design

When we start to layer in the Feldman and Pentland's ostensive and performative[91] with Chomsky's competence and performance[92] and plot these against Hales's design of generic products, design of user activities and design of design,[93] a picture starts to emerge. In some respects, getting to "design of design" is an exemplification of the "creativity of language," a Zen moment of sorts, where the SaaS consuming enterprise is "competent" enough to assemble new, different compositions based on the Lego mix and match of the SaaS configurational tools at play. There is of course the wrong kind of competence, as exemplified by Acme previously where commission or bonus targets are accomplished by taking advantage of a loophole in the monitoring system.[94] It nevertheless illustrates a use case where the "creativity of language" ran afoul. The question becomes how do we get to "design of design" while ensuring that operations remain ethical and fraud-free as it were? Recall from Chapter 2 a Controller's comment that "we are not in the business of saving lives." This notwithstanding, universities are introducing ethics courses into the computer curriculum, recognizing as Stanford professor and former senior research scientist at Google Mehran Sahami put it, "technology is not neutral … the choices that get made … have social ramifications."[95]

Although more than mere data entry, in today's culture, competence is synonymous with expediency. A QuickBooks ad at the bus stop flashed: "Enter your invoices while waiting for the bus. Now that's owning it." The do-it spirit is infectious – we can work from anywhere at any time from any device including the ubiquitous mobile in our hands. The message is loud and clear: get it done lest we are done unto. A late invoice to a customer translates into arrears. Worst yet, a missing invoice can result in no payment at all for services already rendered. No money collected translates into a ballooning A/R, follow up dunning procedures, potential write-off of bad debt, and underwhelming cash flow. All things considered, having a mobile app that lets us submit an invoice whether waiting for or on the bus is not too shabby. Presumably, the app queries all fulfillments to be billed and lets us prioritize those with rapidly approaching bill dates. Fulfillments would have been applied to already approved sales orders. Sales orders would have been validated for customers already set up with pertinent information completed and deemed in good standing. In this manner, we would have all the supporting documentation lined up waiting for us to pull the trigger or click the button. What the app does not quite do is send the invoice for us. That would have defeated the purpose of the ad, which presumably comes at a cost. But to send an invoice too soon before services or items ordered have indeed been delivered would mean overstating revenue in the current period; sending it too late would mean understating it in a prior period. An invoice sent out in error – who can remember inadvertently defacing a text message thanks to fat fingering – can always be recalled, or else augmented, for example, by including the customer's PO number to ease their internal chain of validation and approval to accelerate payment. We perform the ultimate act to bill the customer too early, on time, or too late: the app does not make this choice for us. Even though it may offer an upstream chain of artifacts lined up in attention, such as sales orders or fulfillments, it by no means prevents us from entering or submitting a transaction in a less than timely or valid manner. In this respect, the app is no different from an on-premise or cloud software. Whether we are using a state-of-the-art or out-of-date homegrown solution, we own the act of invoicing.

To some extent internal controls are erected to reduce the likelihood of garbage in garbage out. Less obvious perhaps are the subtle and sometimes not so subtle ways our world is seamlessly transformed into a standing reserve of likely drivers or suitors ready to be consumed. Where "the clock made us into timekeepers,"[96] a team of cognitive psychologists from Vanderbilt University and Kobe University aptly observed that the prevalence of smartphones, tablets, and laptops turned us into a nation of typists; at 72 words per minute with 94% accuracy to be exact of what was gleaned from 100 students put through a test.[97] The same can be argued for the ubiquity of Uber and Airbnb. The French nation ushered in the first day of 2017 with a new law that established workers' "right to disconnect" by requiring companies with more than 50 employees to establish hours when staff should not send or answer emails. French legislator Benoit Hamon, when interviewed by the BBC, described the law as a welcome relief to office workers who leave work but nevertheless "remain attached by a kind of electronic leash – like a dog,"[98] implying perhaps that the ubiquity of email communications has turned humankind into a nation of tethered dogs.

What does all this mean for internal controls and SaaS? We have reviewed how the audit lens on internal controls can create a set of front-stage behaviors that create a buffer between external regulatory demands and internal processes and shield the latter from having to undergo the real work of risk identification and internal control articulation. In a way, by relying on audit "blinders" in the design and operation of internal controls to support SaaS, we are playing an imitation game. Controls developed under the audit lens can be like the man in Searle's Chinese room, imitating real-life processes as part of their design. Like the audience viewing the man in the Chinese room as capable of communicating in Chinese, management is seeing the operating effectiveness of the internal controls as evidence of functional operating processes truly capable of handling actual in-the-moment contingencies or "normal natural troubles." An audit validates the internal controls – the performative aspect – to get to the inner competency. But as we have seen, this validation can be misleading because employees within the enterprise can engage in front-stage and back-stage behaviors. As Chomsky points out, performance ≠ competence.[99]

Following investigations that began in late 2015 by the California Department of Insurance into its licensing practices, Parker Conrad, Chief Executive Officer (CEO) of Zenefits, a human capital management (known as HCM) SaaS as well as middleman in the HR insurance business, resigned in early 2016 as a result of inadequate "internal processes, controls, and actions around compliance."[100] At issue was Macro, an internal tool that let employees pad the number of hours committed to pre-licensing classes, in effect abetting unlicensed brokers to sell insurance.[101] Of note was the intervention by the SEC even though Zenefits was not public.[102] Zenefits had to reset expectations with its investors when its valuation was more than halved from $4.5 to $2 billion.[103] While the fine Zenefits would pay SEC would pale in comparison with that paid to at least 40 states, $450,000 as opposed to close to $11 million – note that Zenefits did not admit to wrongdoing in its SEC settlement – SEC's move sent a clear signal that embodied more the spirit rather than letter of the law.[104] As I write this, an article in the *San Francisco Chronicle* reports results of a study compiled from several Salesforce surveys: while 80% believe business has a responsibility towards making a social impact, only 36% felt their company was walking the talk.[105] In an interview, former Salesforce employee and diversity advocate, Kyle Graden voiced, "All the emphasis and all the budget was put on Pride and marketing the company as inclusive, but meanwhile we still had people from underrepresented groups ... who were being passed over for promotions and made to feel invisible."[106] To the eyes of the auditor, the control aspect may indeed be shown to be operational, but it is by no means a sufficient condition to evidence actual competency, or any real understanding of the underlying rationale or logic. In part, such understanding is demonstrated not by an almost rote compliance by the book but by unfamiliar, unconventional performative aspects – while not audit ready, is ready to be used and reproducible as audit evidence – that nevertheless address or at the very least attempt to bridge the disconnect between the theoretical with the empirical, or ideal with actual. The workarounds or work undertaken to work around the algorithmic conditions defined by the SaaS are shoved aside in favor of rationalistic analyses of as-is and to-be processes, the how of the control flow. With all the emphasis on the doing, does anyone care any more about what is done?

With the application of an audit lens, the potential of SaaS remains untapped. The premise of SaaS is to expose the mystery or at least the mechanics behind fields, records, and workflows to non-technical users, so that they may experiment or tinker with changes in real-time albeit in a sandbox or test environment. The focus is on local practices surrounding and supporting the SaaS in use. By focusing on the actual processes behind the veil, we slice right past the rhetoric or rationalizations over what should be whether dictated by documentation or audit to what simply is. Under the hood, at the most fundamental level, behind every SaaS lie algorithms, themselves combinations of logic and control. To the end user, these have been abstracted by queries, looks, reports, workflows, and other control panels. When we attempt to devise internal controls through the latter, we are layering controls upon controls. The outcome is controls of controls. Ironically, to develop better controls, or refine upon existing ones, we may need to get to the underlying logic to revisit whatever it is we wish to accomplish as circumstances change. We also see beyond the SaaS – *internal* controls for SaaS do not all have to be configured within it. Controls can reside in another SaaS, perhaps an integrated one, or outside of both SaaS altogether. As Hales points out, "if the tool you've always used is a hammer, you tend to address everything as if it were a nail."[107] A poorly deployed procurement SaaS perhaps has more to do with the lack of effective communication companywide about the PO policy, or the lack of knowledge about department owners, as to what their department budgets are and what spending they can approve and less to do with the controls directly configured within the SaaS. Likewise, a longer than expected time spent on approving sales orders in an order management SaaS may hint at sales practices that weight heavily on custom deals and the need for order entry personnel to run custom orders by revenue teams for additional reviews. Alternatively, it may point to the lack of an effective document management system or SaaS in place when order entry staff experience difficulties in locating executed sales contracts for comparative review. At the mere mention of internal controls, audit objectives come to mind; however, as we have seen in this chapter, the audit universe is but a pair of blinders on what happens back stage.

Our procurement SaaS example illustrates what truly happens when an internal control is in action, how user perspectives differ and perhaps more importantly can change when tested against real-life exigencies. A hammer is not simply a hammer; it matters as to who is wielding it. To quote Latour's famous passage from *Pandora's Hope*, "You are different with a gun in your hand; the gun is different with you holding it. You are another subject because you hold the gun; the gun is another object because it has entered into a relationship with you."[108] Recall Leontiev's "twofold" purpose of activity from Chapter 5, "first, in its independent existence" and second, as "psychological reflection that is realized as an activity of the subject."[109] With the SaaS in our hand, would we opt to hide the RAT (acronym for "Repair, Attribute, and All That"), in other words unwittingly repair the real-life gap that it fails to address manual rework yet attribute the positive outcome to its ability to "automate?" Or would we choose to leverage its out-of-the-box configuration capability to attempt to tailor it to our organizational needs? Would we choose to configure our own parameters to recognize the interplay among other SaaS, and thus in effect be able to check up on others through any one given SaaS? Or would we fall back on established internal controls that are more aligned with on-premise software? Would we be more open to change seeing how SaaS is more configurable than on-premise software or would we be more likely to discourage any changes to what we perceive as a third-party, off-the-shelf, utility-like product anyway? Would we hire and build a team that is adept at breadth – orchestrating different best-in-breed SaaS including interfaces with more traditional on-premise and legacy software – or would we groom application-specific subject matter experts each responsible for plumbing the depths of their respective silos?

With SOX compliance, we almost hear about the comparison of the total number of controls among different organizations. Since auditors are not inclined to advise on any reduction in the number of controls – the premise is the more the merrier – public company client personnel have taken to cross-comparing control counts among themselves. Yet in continuing the same vein of argument from Chapter 5, where the sharp division between automation and manual or financial and non-financial is not always quite so obvious, the automated or financial often harbor the manual or non-financial. The same can be said for the attempt at control; for just as automation is really a way of getting human subjects to conform to specific entry criteria, control is a way of getting the same subjects to articulate a specific way of validation that lends itself to testing but upon deeper inspection, reveals an avoidance of an underlying chaos of sorts, so that what is truly performed is decoupled from what is validated. This is more than having to contend with the unintended consequences of a control. Recall our previous example of how tightened password aging policies may unintentionally encourage the use of the same complex passwords across different applications and websites. Yet, without having to explore the side effects or regression impact resulting from a control, we often fail to notice that intrinsic nature of chaos within controls. Like the argument put forth previously about either being automated or manual, what is of contention is not that we are not controlling but that we are not controlling enough, or we would have recognized the chaos lurking beneath an otherwise uninterrupted façade of ostensive controls. Perhaps a more effective means of control would have been not to first focus on control but to observe the SaaS in use and in time observe the ways it can be configured to control for specific outcomes. The emphasis is on outcome, and not process, not so much the evidencing of process to evidence a control, but whether efficacy can be achieved therein to produce consistent outcomes. If at first chaos is allowed if only to gather necessary material or preparation to advise on a specific course of action, so initial chaos can be said to engender eventual controls.

Recall Brand's previous example of the lazy college planner waiting for footprints to form in the snow before laying down paving. The same can be said for the reverse. If the initial emphasis is on process in a bid to control too much too soon, then what is controlled for is merely a red herring for the unnoticed to slip right past. Even so, what is configured and deemed effective is susceptible to change. Like the composite field of fields, perhaps the control of controls speaks to a meta need to walk a fine line between managing what needs to change and what needs to stay the same. We forget that control rests at the heart of a computer algorithm; it is hardly surprising perhaps that chaos can ensue from thus. If we, however, were to consider the realm of possible user scenarios yet unaccounted for and therefore unprogrammed, it should come as no surprise that chaos would follow quickly at the heels of supposed controls. After all, as we have seen time and again, compliance rules and requirements themselves change, from the Financial Accounting Standards Board (FASB) 3% rule that unwittingly allowed for Enron's use of special purpose entities (SPEs) to variable interest entities (VIE) rules that counteracted the use of SPEs to avoid reporting debt on the balance sheet but therein allowed Alibaba to go public based on pooled contractual vested interests. What is wrong versus what is right shifts and turns, moving along like fast flowing river water, forever eluding our grasp not unlike the red groupers aboard Miss Katie in Chapter 1. Even without the slightest hint of wrongdoing, the guidance issued for internal controls changes with updates to the Public Company Accounting Oversight Board (PCAOB) alerts and emergence of the Statements on Standards for Attestation Engagements No. 18 (SSAE 18). General Data Protection Regulation (GDPR) and Accounting Standards Codification 606 (ASC-606) are also some of the regulatory changes looming on the horizon. Thus, just as a constant cannot be mentioned without an allusion to the element of change, the dynamic configurational nature of SaaS points to the finer control of holding this space of constancy and change, policy and implementation, ostensive and performative, and performance and competency.

The seeming polarity of the opposites reveals an underlying interdependency, so that when we speak of controls, chaos doesn't lurk far behind. Perhaps the criteria we use to define controls is far too limited to mean one way or a couple of ways, rather than unpack a multitude of ways. If the criteria for control is too constrictive, everything else becomes chaos. What the criteria does not quite surface is the relationship between controls and chaos – how to accomplish the former and here too, recalling the operating effectiveness of internal controls, if only at a point in time, the latter is indeed necessary. It is only with frequent practice of withstanding constant blows to transactional integrity that an organization learns about new if not more pragmatic ways of mitigating risk to finetune or hone a textbook control. A delimiting view of control versus chaos masks this underlying feedback loop. It also unintentionally promotes front-stage over back-stage behavior, so that what is officiated as an internal control and communicated internally and validated by internal and external auditors may simply be a stand-in for more practical measures adopted behind closed doors that hint at chaos that cannot be contained. Whether it is control or chaos becomes an accident of perspective. Narrow criteria for circumscribing a control also promotes the illusion that we can truly control anything at all. After all it is commonplace to encounter things that do not often go as planned. The question becomes: to what extent can we leverage the SaaS innate configurability to handle the unexpected, so that even if things were to progress down an unfamiliar path, it would still be okay? Control does not necessarily preclude locking down all available paths to congregate at a cul-de-sac, a walled garden of sorts. It can mean an acknowledgment of different path – show there is no right *one* to begin with.

A cynic's view of decoupling would have been to continue with the charade of erecting and maintaining an almost impenetrable wall of ostensive controls that never quite touch the underlying performative or inner competencies. This view, however, casts a shadow over the Information Technology Process Institute (known as ITPI) study we reviewed in Chapter 2 that surveyed over 330 organizations to arrive at a positive correlation between foundational IT controls and IT operational performance.[110]

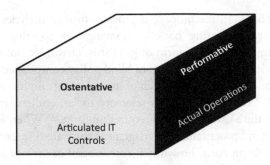

Could it be that rather than evidence better IT performance, such as increased rate of success of production changes deployed the first time, the front-stage IT controls arrived at are pointers to more performative, back-stage behaviors? After all, one of the identified controls – monitoring the rate at which changes have been deployed to production without failures – describes a means (how) to report on the number of changes released to production without failure, and not necessarily the amount of behind-the-scenes work invested such as testing ad nauseum the proposed changes in sandbox before production release or, as we have covered previously, providing hyper-care post release in order to respond nimbly to any unanticipated errors that arise.[111] Weick is of the following belief:

> *In a loosely coupled system there is more room available for self-determination by the actors. If it is argued that a sense of efficacy is crucial for human beings, then a sense of efficacy might be greater in a loosely coupled system with autonomous units than it would be in a tightly coupled system where discretion is limited.*[112]

The problem is, as we have seen, this arrangement can be just as easily used to justify behaviors both bad (Acme and Zenefits) and good (Agile and design-in-use). In revisiting Collins and Kusch's mimeomorphic versus polymorphic actions in Chapter 5,[113] there is also a risk that we relegate internal controls to the mere mimeomorphic, or in Leontiev's parlance, the operational,[114] rather than emphasize that those that reside at a higher level – polymorphic – or actions and activities that are meaningful. Mundane component tasks performed the same each time, more syntax than semantics, whether automated or manual, would have made Frederick Taylor proud.

In revisiting Theory Y, the motivational factors behind work, described at the start of this chapter, and against the backdrop of Tom Peter's *Thriving on Chaos*, Rocketrip, a technology platform startup, presents a whole new way of envisioning compliance and cost control. By encouraging employees to beat a budget when it comes to company expenses related to travel, it offers algorithms that track real-time pricing when it comes to travel planning to assist employees to opt for less costly options to beat the cost that would have been otherwise incurred in merely complying with company policies. In the process, it provides further analytics and insight into travel spending, redistributing back cost savings by splitting savings between employees and employers in the form of gift cards, charitable donations, and other benefits. In a subtle take on the dangers of blind policy compliance, Rocketrip CEO Dan Ruch takes on the popular approach of incentivizing employees to comply with corporate policy.[115] Recall Tom Peter's reference to "an endless stream of $999.95 requisitions" with the $1,000 purchase requisition limit.[116] When we think about it, insofar as expense and procurement management software is intended to help companies gain a handle on costs, how much cost control or savings are truly achieved other than reporting and procedural dissemination to support policies? In other words, an emphasis on process over outcome.

Thus, Agile presents an opportunity not just to try out different routes to attain the desired outcome – consider this with the lower cost options Rocketrip gives a company's employees, a gaming approach that leads to a win-win outcome for both employer and employee – more fundamentally, it reframes our approach to internal controls and SaaS by turning our attention back on outcome. If mere compliance with company policy results in higher costs, and in our example on corporate travel, how does having an expense management solution in place help with managing costs? The premise behind Rocketrip requires an important though subtle shift in emphasis. We ask not how compliant we are with corporate expense policy but instead how can and do we save the company money by opting for less costly albeit less conventional means of corporate travel? In recalling Acme and Zenefits, gamification when taken to the extreme is not without its detractors as seen in the recent furor over the United Airline proposal to replace standard employee bonus with a lottery system that awards lavish prizes to a lucky few at the expense of nearly 90,000 workers.[117]

As an annual SaaS subscription, Rocketrip plays or integrates with larger corporate expense management software providers such as Concur, a sign that conventional Theory X Taylorist approaches at compliance and cost control are slowly but surely loosening their hold. Concur is partnering with Uber and Airbnb as well, not as conventional surely but ultimately less costly options for corporate travel and accommodations. The use of SaaS, with the accompanying ease of integration of other best-in-breed in play applications in the corporate cost management ecosystem, supplants legacy monolithic and/or on-premise software and presents a unique window of opportunity to completely revamp the way we have become accustomed to using software, from unconsciously hiding the RAT if only to grasp at purported automation benefits to directly attaining business benefits from driving real process improvements. Sometimes, the one thing we have been looking for has been there all along. David Bohm recounts an episode of how we catch the light reflecting off a coin dropped on a patterned carpet.[118] In that brief instant, the carpet went from having nothing on it to one that held the key to what was lost.[119] A crack is visible on our walled future; light beckons from beyond.

Exercise 6.1

To what extent does (a) the former inform (b) the latter?

1. (a) New custom field (b) Other standard and customer fields
2. (a) Newly integrated SaaS with (b) Existing SaaS
3. (a) New custom workflow with (b) Existing out-of-the-box and custom processes

Discussion

Compensating controls are used by auditors to describe secondary controls that can mitigate the risk even when identified primary ones fail. Yet, compensation is a pattern that can be applied more pervasively when it comes to the configuration of SaaS. Recall ubuntu as "a person is a person through other people."[120] This exercise asks us to be vigilant even as we make configuration changes. Does the new field indicate whether other values are entered in the surrounding fields correctly or completely? Insofar as the new integrated SaaS has its own unique transaction identifier, how does it reflect the current existing SaaS that has been in use? Are likely duplicates surfaced in false positives? Are there missing elements to support a seamless sync? Likewise, a new custom workflow exposes the inner workings of existing processes when something does not quite go as planned. When we perform regression impact analysis to understand the impact of a configuration change on existing functionality, it is often too late. Even when the new configurations are deemed to be working, they function in relation with others, rather than solely by themselves.

Exercise 6.2

How are the differences between single and double loop learning illustrated by:

1. Purchase requisition approval versus tiered approval authority
2. Sync error notification handling versus exception event triggers
3. Restricted access to key financial reports versus setup of cost centers (marketing, accounting, engineering, etc.) to map to generally accepted accounting principles (GAAP) profit and loss (P&L) categories (sales and marketing, general and administrative, and research and development)

Discussion

An area that eludes easy grasp is the configuration of a control. Much has been said about the admission criteria for a clinical patient or a transaction and how this is less than obvious when peering into the system transaction record. The same can be said for the criteria for flagging an exception or setting up which codes or categories that data gets classified or grouped in. Much like the meta concept of control of controls, double loop learning comes in when the latter is examined. With all our attention focused on getting back to the norm when deviations are seen, we sometimes forget to question the norm in the first place and whether it continues to hold currency despite ongoing organizational and people change.

Exercise 6.3

Consider the following binary pairs. To what extent can one give rise to the other?

1. Control versus chaos
2. Constant versus change
3. Individual versus community

Discussion

One of the areas that remain unexplored in compliance is how quickly compliance with something can become out of compliance. Nothing can stay static for very long, especially when extrapolated across the long arc of time. We have already explicated the interrelations between control and chaos, as well as constancy and change. The last binary pair, individual versus community, is worth exploring as it works against objectivistic Taylorist models where there is one objective source of truth with knowledge disseminated top-down. Ideally an effective system of internal controls is characterized not by a virtual lockdown but more by a skilled balancing of the needs of the individual with that of the collective whole. The former carte blanche approach is likely to give rise to manual workarounds that circumvent official accounts, giving rise to decoupling and audit's recursive loop unto itself. The latter gives credence to ubuntu.

Endnotes

1 Jalāl, D. R. and Barks, C. (1997). *The Essential Rumi.*
2 McGregor, D. (1960). *The Human Side of Enterprise.*
3 Herzberg, F. (1959). *The Motivation to Work.* New York: John Wiley & Sons.
4 Ibid.
5 Ibid.
6 McGregor, D. *The Human Side of Enterprise.*
7 Peters, T. J. (1988). *Thriving on Chaos: Handbook for a Management Revolution.* New York: Harper & Row.
8 Argyris, C. (September 1977). Double loop learning in organizations. *Harvard Business Review,* 55, 115–125. https://hbr.org/1977/09/double-loop-learning-in-organizations.
9 Ibid.
10 Ibid.
11 Ibid.
12 Ibid.
13 Ibid.
14 Ibid.
15 Mol, A. and Law, J. (June 1, 2004). Embodied action, enacted bodies: The example of hypoglycaemia. *Body & Society,* 10(2–3), 43–62.
16 Meyer, J. W. and Rowan, B. (September, 1977). Institutionalized organizations: Formal structure as myth and ceremony. *American Journal of Sociology,* 83(2), 340–363.
17 Ibid.
18 Ibid.

19 Ibid.
20 Ibid.
21 Weick, K. E. (November 1974). Middle range theories of social systems. *Behavioral Science*, 19(6), 357–367.
22 Roberts, J. (2004). *The Modern Firm: Organizational Design for Performance and Growth*. Oxford, UK: Oxford University Press.
23 Weber, M. (1994). *Weber: Political Writings* (Cambridge Texts in the History of Political Thought). In L. Peter (Ed.). Trans. Ronald Speirs. Cambridge University Press, p. 16.
24 Raadschelders, J. C. N. (1998). *Handbook of Administrative History*. New Brunswick, NJ: Transaction Publishers. p. 142.
25 Meyer, J. W. and Rowan, B. Institutionalized organizations: Formal structure as myth and ceremony.
26 MacLean, T. and Behnam, M. (December 2010). The dangers of decoupling: The relationship between compliance programs, legitimacy perceptions, and institutionalized misconduct. *ACAD Management Journal*, 53(6), 1499–1520.
27 Weaver, G. R., Trevino, L. K., and Cochran, P. L. (1999). Integrated and decoupled corporate social performance: Management commitments, external pressures, and corporate ethics practices. *Academy of Management Journal*, 42(5), 539–552.
28 MacLean, T. and Behnam, M. The dangers of decoupling: The relationship between compliance programs, legitimacy perceptions, and institutionalized misconduct.
29 Ibid.
30 Ibid.
31 Ibid.
32 Ibid.
33 Peters, T. J. *Thriving on Chaos: Handbook for a Management Revolution*.
34 MacLean T. and Behnam M. The dangers of decoupling: The relationship between compliance programs, legitimacy perceptions, and institutionalized misconduct.
35 Ibid.
36 Ibid.
37 Ibid.
38 Ibid.
39 Ibid.
40 Ibid.
41 Ibid.
42 Ibid.
43 Ibid.
44 Ibid.
45 Ibid.
46 Ibid.
47 Grossman, A. S. and Curran, D. F. (April 2003). EMCF: A new approach at an old foundation (TN). Harvard Business School Teaching Note 303–119.
48 Ibid.
49 Bromley, P. and Powell, W. W. (June 2012). From smoke and mirrors to walking the talk: Decoupling in the contemporary world. *Academy of Management Annals*, 6(1), 483–530.
50 Haraway, D. (1991). A cyborg manifesto: Science, technology, and socialist-feminism in the late twentieth century. In *Simians, Cyborgs and Women: The Reinvention of Nature*. New York: Routledge.

51 Wang, L. from Associated Press (July 13, 2017). A monkey took a selfie. PETA says he owns the copyright. 'Where does it end?' Chicago Tribune. http://www.chicago-tribune.com/business/ct-monkey-selfie-lawsuit-20170713-story.html.

52 Ibid.

53 Power, M. (1997). *The Audit Society: Rituals of Verification*. Oxford, UK: Oxford University Press.

54 Ibid.

55 Ibid.

56 Ibid.

57 Strathern, M. (2000). *Audit Cultures: Anthropological Studies in Accountability, Ethics, and the Academy*. London, UK: Routledge.

58 Shore, C. and Wright, S. (December 1999). Audit culture and anthropology: Neoliberalism in British higher education. *The Journal of the Royal Anthropological Institute*, 5(4), 557–575.

59 Ibid.

60 Power, M. *The Audit Society: Rituals of Verification*.

61 Hales, M. (1994). Where are designers? Styles of design practice, objects of design and views of users in computer supported cooperative work. In C. Duska Rosenberg (Eds.), *Design Issues in CSCW*, London, UK: Springer Verlag.

62 Beck, K., Beedle, M., van Bennekum, A. et al. (2001). The Agile Manifesto. http://agilemanifesto.org/.

63 Hales, M. Where are designers? Styles of design practice, objects of design and views of users in computer supported cooperative work.

64 Ibid.

65 Brand, S. (1994). *How Buildings Learn: What Happens After They're Built*. New York: Viking.

66 Ibid.

67 Sweeney. J. (November 1, 2013).

68 Eze, M. (2010). *Intellectual History in Contemporary South Africa*. New York: Palgrave Macmillan.

69 Strathern, M. (1988). The gender of the gift: Problems with women and problems with society in Melanesia. Berkeley, CA: University of California Press.

70 Brand, S. *How Buildings Learn: What Happens After They're Built*.

71 Ibid.

72 Ibid.

73 Ibid.

74 Petroski, H. (2012). *To Forgive Design: Understanding Failure*. Cambridge, MA: Belknap Press of Harvard University Press.

75 Ibid.

76 McGrath, R. G. (April 2011). Failing by design. *Harvard Business Review* 89, 76–83.

77 Kowalski, R. (July 1979). Algorithm = Logic + Control. *Communications of the ACM*, 22(7).

78 Ibid.

79 Hales, "Where are designers?."

80 Atood, J. "The best code is no code at all," *Coding Horror*, May 30, 2007, https://blog.codinghorror.com/the-best-code-is-no-code-at-all/.

81 Olavsrud, T. "OneReach delivers automated communications for SMBs," *Small Business Computing.com*, December 20, 2011, http://www.smallbusinesscomputing.com/news/onereach-delivers-automated-communications-for-smbs.html.

82 Chomsky, N. "Current issues in linguistic theory," in *Papers Presented at the Ninth International Congress of Linguists, Cambridge, MA, 1962, Janua Linguarum* 38 (The Hague, the Netherlands: Mouton, 1964), xx–xx.

83 Ibid.

84 Ibid.

85 Chomsky, N. *Topics in the Theory of Generative Gramma* (The Hague, the Netherlands: Mouton, 1966).

86 Searle, J. "Minds, brains, and programs," *Behavioral and Brain Sciences* 3 (1980):417–424.

87 Turing, A. M. "Computing machinery and intelligence," *Mind* 59, no. 236 (October 1950):433–460.

88 Ibid.

89 Ibid.

90 Chomsky, N. *Topics in the Theory of Generative Grammar* (The Hague, the Netherlands: Mouton, 1966).

91 Feldman, M. and Pentland, B. "Reconceptualizing organizational routines as a source of flexibility and change," *Administrative Science Quarterly* 48 (2003), 94–118.

92 Chomsky, "Current issues in linguistic theory."

93 Hales, "Where are designers?."

94 MacLean and Behnam, "The dangers of decoupling."

95 Singer, N. "Universities rush to develop computer science ethics courses," *SFGate*, February 16, 2018, https://www.sfgate.com/business/article/Universities-rush-to-develop-computer-science-12620943.php.

96 Postman, N. *Amusing Ourselves to Death: Public Discourse in the Age of Show Business* (New York: Penguin Books, 1986).

97 Logan, G. D., Ulrich, J. E. and Lindsey, D. R. B. "Different (key)strokes for different folks: How standard and nonstandard typists balance Fitts' law and Hick's law," *Journal of Experimental Psychology: Human Perception and Performance* 42, no. 12 (2016):2084–2102.

98 Schofield, H. "The plan to ban work emails out of hours," *BBC News*, May 11, 2016, http://www.bbc.com/news/magazine-36249647.

99 Chomsky, N. "Current issues in linguistic theory."

100 W. Alden, "Zenefits founder Parker Conrad resigns after compliance failures," *BuzzFeed News*, February 8, 2016.

101 Shieber, J. "Zenefits under investigation in California," *TechCrunch*, February 11, 2016, https://techcrunch.com/2016/02/11/zenefits-under-investigation-in-california/.

102 Newcomer, E. "Zenefits settles With SEC over charges it misled investors," *Bloomberg*, October 26, 2017, https://www.bloomberg.com/news/articles/2017-10-26/zenefits-settles-with-sec-over-charges-it-misled-investors.

103 Ibid.

104 Ibid.

105 Siegel, A. "New research: How leading with equality and values impacts your business," *Salesforce Blog*, July 13, 2017, https://www.salesforce.com/blog/2017/07/impact-of-equality-business-research.html.

106 Lang, M. "Study: Companies talk inclusion, but few walk the walk," *San Francisco Chronicle*, July 13, 2017, http://www.sfchronicle.com/business/article/Study-Companies-talk-inclusion-but-few-walk-11284627.php.

107 Hales, "Where are designers?."

108 Latour, B. *Pandora's Hope: Essays on the Reality of Science Studies* (Cambridge, MA: Harvard University Press, 1999).

109 Leontiev, A. N. *Activity, Consciousness, and Personality* (Englewood Cliffs, NJ: Prentice Hall, 1978). [Original work published 1975.]

110 Phelps, D., Kim, G. and Milne, K. *Prioritizing IT controls for effective, measurable security* (Pittsburgh, PA: Software Engineering Institute/Carnegie Mellon University, 2006). https://resources.sei.cmu.edu/asset_files/WhitePaper/2013_019_001_297211.pdf.

111 Ibid.

112 Karl E. Weick, "Educational organizations as loosely coupled systems," *Administrative Science Quarterly*, 21, no. 1 (March 1976):1–19.

113 Collins, H. M. and Kusch, M. *The Shape of Actions: What Humans and Machines Can Do* (Cambridge, MA: MIT Press, 1998).

114 Leontiev, *Activity, Consciousness, and Personality*.

115 Campbell, J. "Rewards for policy compliance are a bad idea, says rewards program provider," *The Company Dime*, October 27, 2017, https://www.thecompanydime.com/incentive-compliance/.

116 Peters, T. J. *Thriving on Chaos: Handbook for a Management Revolution*.

117 Scheiber, N. (March 11, 2018). Lotto tickets are nice, boss, but can i have my bonus? *The New York Times*. https://www.nytimes.com/2018/03/11/business/economy/games-employers.html.

118 Bohm, D. (September 17, 2006). *The Special Theory of Relativity*. New York: Routledge.

119 Ibid.

120 Eze, M. *Intellectual History in Contemporary South Africa*.

Chapter 7

Uninvited Guests

These are things

We live among and to see them

Is to know ourselves.[1]

George Oppen

Here is the thing. I could have written a different book. In fact, I did start out differently – more in the vein of the news coverage on technology today. Scarcely a day has gone by without hearing of the latest breach or outage. Despite being in "the business of pain management for enterprises,"[2] Amazon's Elastic Computing Cloud (EC2), an Infrastructure as a Service (IaaS), experienced a catastrophic failure in April 2011. Although movie streaming and photo sharing sites Netflix and SmugMug were among the sites unaffected by the outage, it ended up bringing down hundreds of sites. Amazon is not the only provider susceptible to cloud outages. Barely 5 months into the same year, Microsoft Office 365 and Google Docs suffered similar outages.[3] In the case of Google Docs, users were unable to access its cloud-based applications, such as documents, presentations, and spreadsheets, for about an hour.[4] No company appears to be immune. It can happen to the best and the worst of us. In audit conferences, attendees invariably bring up, dissect, and analyze breaches and outages. Egress Software Technologies, an encryption services provider, released the figures from a Freedom of Information Act (FOIA) request to the Information Commissioner's Office (ICO) showing a worrying increase in data breaches attributed to human error.[5] Comparing incidents from April through June between 2013 and 2014, healthcare organizations reported an increase in breaches from 91 to 183, a staggering 101% increase.[6] Other sectors reported year over year increase: insurance at 200%, financial advisers at

44%, lenders at 200%, education at 56%, and general business at 143%.[7] A recent Gartner study projected that "through 2015, 80% of outages impacting mission-critical services will be caused by people and process issues, and more than 50% of those outages will be caused by change/configuration/release integration and hand-off issues."[8] The Information Technology Process Institute Visible Ops Handbook reports that "80% of unplanned outages are due to ill-planned changes made by administrators ("operations staff") or developers."[9]

In its root cause analysis, the Amazon Web Services (AWS) team traced the April 2011 outage to a human error in a network configuration change when upgrading the capacity of its Elastic Block Storage (EBS) primary network.[10] Instead of displacing traffic off a redundant router to allow for the upgrade, it was redistributed to a secondary redundant network that could not handle the ensuing volume.[11] The resulting network interruption broke the connection between a large number of EBS nodes in the affected cluster to their replicas.[12] When the traffic was rerouted and network connectivity restored, the free capacity of the cluster quickly dwindled in the face of high concurrent volumes.[13] Many of the EBS nodes remained "stuck" in a perpetual loop, continuously searching the cluster-free space to re-mirror data.[14] To restore these volumes and stabilize the EBS cluster, Amazon ended up disabling all control application programming interfaces (APIs; for example, Create Volume, Attach Volume, Detach Volume, and Create Snapshot) for EBS in the affected Availability Zone.[15] These control APIs are the same web service APIs that let us commission multiple server instances to support our application as it scales up or down based on arising need.[16] The AWS outage experienced a domino effect; AWS had referred to it as "a race condition."[17]

When AWS restored network connectivity after routing traffic away from the secondary redundant network, the EBS nodes attempted to search for new ones repeatedly to re-mirror data.[18] Faced with voluminous concurrent requests for replication, nodes began to fail, resulting in more volumes needed to re-mirror.[19] A vicious cycle ensued.[20] To prevent similar errors in future, AWS planned to audit network configuration changes and introduce automations to reduce the likelihood of manual human error.[21] At audit conferences, the audience response to widespread breaches and outages is revealing. I'm reminded of the mob of torch-wielding villagers chasing Frankenstein's monster into the cemetery in the 1931 *Frankenstein* movie. In Mary Shelley's book, Victor Frankenstein uttered these words upon seeing his creation first come to life: "His yellow skin scarcely covered the work of muscles and arteries within … his watery eyes … almost of the same color as the dun white sockets in which they were set, his shrivelled [sic] complexion and straight black lips."[22] He proceeded to flee to the courtyard but not before deciding that "a mummy again endued with animation could not be so hideous as that wretch."[23] Frankenstein is a case study in science's accountability, or lack thereof, to its applications. When we revisit the feedback heard at audit conferences, we hear equal measures of blame and helplessness, and despite the light thrown by the villager's torches, there's a pervading sense of darkness, an impending doom.

Ironically, it was the complete and utter lack of visibility that led metal-working firms to develop management techniques to "control" performance in the depressed 1870s. According to Thomas Johnson and Robert Kaplan in *Relevance Lost: The Rise and Fall of Management Accounting*, this coincided with the dismantlement of contract foreman who hired and fired their own workforce.[24] Manufacturers went from a distributed reliance on specific, and therefore, varied working practices of specific teams to a centralized means of measurement and calibration in a bid to streamline processes and improve performance. Clerical staff came into existence to record information about shop floor activities, so that by the 1880s, managers in textile factories had the same access to the material and cost information available on the floor.[25] Indeed, as Johnson and Kaplan point out, the textile industries were the first American business enterprises to develop management accounting systems to measure direct and overhead costs in transforming raw materials to finished goods.[26] But it was really the deployment of the sales accounting system that decentralized decision making at vertically integrated firms such as DuPont Powder Company.[27] Unlike the manufacturing accounting system that centralized ordering, receiving, and payment in the purchasing and accounting departments, the sales accounting system, by employing minimum price figures and base sales, enabled branch sales managers to determine customer pricing that mirrored competitor pricing, as well as manage the performance of salesmen by making their compensation more performance-based when having a variable component tied to actual sales and the extent to which they exceed base expectations.[28] In effect, "by lowering the cost of discovering opportunities within the firm," the authors claimed, "management accounting systems such as the one developed by the founders of DuPont Powder Company have undoubtedly increased the potential size of complex business organizations."[29]

In her 1988 book *In the Age of the Smart Machine: The Future of Work and Power*, Shoshana Zuboff uses the panopticon metaphor to describe how computer technology enables managers to track the behavior and output of workers.[30] Much of our discussion with SaaS has centered on the automation of otherwise manual processes, or an improvement upon the degree of automation provided by on-premise and legacy solutions. But this is only one half of the equation. The only half is the reporting or analytics capability. As Zuboff points out, "greater comprehension is both a condition and consequence" of the automation of otherwise manual processes. Indeed, "even when a given application is designed to automate, it simultaneously generates information about the underlying processes through which an organization accomplishes its work."[31] In Chapter 6, we covered second-loop learning. This "informate" half that Zuboff coined provides the means to facilitate second-loop learning, so that we are not just making things run better and faster. In effect, technology provides the much-needed reflexivity that provides clues as to whether the requirements or underlying policies require an overhaul or revamp. In our procurement SaaS example threaded through the preceding chapters, one way we can revisit the minimum threshold requiring purchase requisition approvals is to use the SaaS to report on the requisitions split into smaller amounts thereby bypassing dual approvals required for higher amounts as well as on invoices processed without associated purchase orders (POs). The flexibility and ease that come with a SaaS does not apply to automating processes, they also extend to informating processes. When enterprise users begin to tap into this latter capability of SaaS, they begin to think about or see technology in a different light. They start to think or see with technology. Zuboff had likened information with the ability to hold up a mirror to users about their own behaviors and perspectives surrounding their interactions with others in their daily affairs and in the context of the technology in place.[32] Like Frankenstein, we too need coaxing to pay attention: "I entreat you to hear me, before you give vent to your hatred on my devoted head."[33]

Despite being a self-professed lover of nature along with its requisite change of seasons, we wonder why Frankenstein was so quick at dismissing his creation at the outset. After all, the creature was capable of an entire spectrum of human emotions – need for belonging, shame, love for literature, fear of the unknown – yet it was addressed at various intervals as "daemon," "abhorred monster," and "devil."[34] Likewise, for all our self-professed emphasis on controls and of accountability, to what extent are we abandoning our assemblage of moving albeit best-in-breed SaaS the instant they show signs of life? Consider the following remarks made about SaaS:

1. No one at our company has to maintain the cloud software.
2. The Software as a Service allowed us to double our turnover in the past year without adding staff.
3. With a few easy clicks, you can pay employees and file tax forms.

The main premise behind every cloud computing ad is: let us take care of it so you do not have to. None of us are denying the value proposition that SaaS has to offer, and like those that came before: the ability to do more with less.

Knowing what we now know, user requirements can and often do change. The configurations deployed are hardly cemented in stone. The user doesn't have to be a passive or even accusatory bystander but instead can be an active participant, designer, and constructor. Thus, to what extent are SaaS enterprise customers shirking their responsibilities to handle Day 2 operational concerns and the ensuing need to continue to groom the composite landscape of moving parts beyond Day 1 go-live? Unlike Frankenstein, we did not create the SaaS in use, we merely procured them off-the-shelf as it were. Nor do we detest them to the point of hatred. Yet, like Frankenstein, we share a propensity to abandon ship the first chance we get after it sails out of the harbor – this is after all why we got SaaS in the first place so that we don't have to worry about supporting it blissfully unaware of the continual need to change sails, vary direction, and be the wind beneath its wings.

This tendency reminds me of a series of lab exercises attempted by students in my *Accounting Information Systems* class where unbeknown to them, the exercise compelled them to follow a scripted set of instructions that ultimately resulted in:

1. The wrong account type selected for a newly created account
2. The use of the wrong account as the income account to be credited as part of a new revenue recognition template
3. The assignment of the incorrect revenue recognition template to a newly created service for sale
4. The creation of a sales invoice that recorded this newly created item with revenue recognition start and end dates
5. The execution of a revenue recognition management process that resulted in a journal entry that debited the deferred revenue account and credited the wrongly set up income account
6. The incorrect presentation of revenue on the income statement

Our inactions belie an air of indifference to the manner configuration, deployment, and continued use of the SaaS. This indifference reminds me of the order invariably issued by Captain Picard aboard the starship U.S.S. *Enterprise* in the television series *Star Trek: The Next Generation* when faced with an imminent disaster deemed irrevocable in impact: "All hands abandon ship! Repeat. All hands abandon ship!" In the episode, *Cause and Effect*, the U.S.S. *Enterprise* found itself caught in a time loop, colliding with a different ship each time. Crew members experienced a sense of déjà vu as they cycle through their daily motions over and over until they found a way to send a clue to their future selves to avert the collision.

When we step outside the two-dimensional television screen, however, we realize that reality is not about *not* making mistakes. Mistakes do not have to result in outcomes with catastrophic proportions. Rather than make do with "what could have been" or "if only" postures, reality is less about getting to go back in time if only to get it just right and more about responding to incidents as they arise. In the preceding exercises undertaken by students in my *Accounting Information Systems* class, it became apparent that the driving force behind internal controls over financial reporting was a more foundational set of internal controls over transactional processing in turn driven by still more foundational controls over master data such as chart of accounts, revenue recognition templates, and services for sale. History is replete with human agents tending to machines and working diligently behind the scenes to resolve errors that arise. In the same manner field service technicians were often instrumental to the success of photocopiers as characterized by Julian Orr, "keypunch girls," cramped into hot basement rooms and transcribing programming instructions onto paper coding pads, ran mainframe computers. "It's just like planning a dinner. You have to plan ahead and schedule everything so it's ready when you need it," explained Admiral Grace Hopper, a computer science pioneer, in *Cosmopolitan*'s 1967 "The Computer Girls."[35]

What makes us think that with SaaS, we can get away with indifference? SaaS is a black box. It abstracts away real-life messiness: competing or parallel processes, workarounds, loops, and cul-de-sacs. Introduced initially as an experiment by James Clerk Maxwell, and popularized later in cybernetics by W. Ross Ashby, use of the black box concept was to bracket out inner workings to focus on inputs and outputs and, in general, emphasize direct interactions with the observer. Cloud computing clients are not responsible for enhancements, maintenance, or availability. To get an insight into the work that nevertheless goes on behind the scenes, check out a common job description for a cloud operations position:

- Manage highly available and reliable operations of the cloud platform with experience managing fault tolerant and web scale software deployments
- Establish operational best practice and standard operating procedures in release, support, and break-fix management

Darkness and poor visibility notwithstanding, there is also a pervading sense of finality or of fatality at audit conferences. This is the end; this is the end; this is the end. Reality is far more nuanced. In June 2011, two months after the AWS EC2 outage, web-based storage firm Dropbox admitted that a programmer's error caused a temporary security breach that allowed use of any password to access any user account.[36] The San Francisco-based startup attributed the error to a "code update" that "introduced a bug affecting our authentication mechanism."[37] The code update was made at 1:54 p.m. Pacific standard time (PST).[38] When the company detected this at 5:41 p.m. (PST), it rolled out a fix at 5:46 p.m. (PST).[39] The company claimed that less than 1% of its users were logged in during this period.[40] Even so, access without passwords was possible between 1:54 p.m. (PST) and 5:46 p.m. (PST).[41] Dropbox co-founder and chief Technology Officer (CTO) Arash Ferdowsi had this to say in a blog post:

> *This should never have happened. We are scrutinizing our controls and we will be implementing additional safeguards to prevent this from happening again.*[42]

Dropbox would have another go-around at handling another breach a year later. In August 2012, it experienced a domino effect of a different kind from AWS when their users started noticing an uptick in spam to email addresses they only used for Dropbox.[43] An investigation by the company revealed login credentials stolen from other websites used to sign into Dropbox.[44] One stolen password in particular unlocked a Dropbox employee's account that in turn contained a project document with user email addresses.[45] Since then, Dropbox implemented two-factor authentication to also include administration consoles.[46] It monitors employee use, including restricting shared folders and links within the company.[47] In this case, a combination of poor user practices both outside and inside the company – end users sharing the same password across multiple websites and the ease of availability of the user emails in a project document – resulted in the breach.[48] The domino effect of password reuse has been extensively researched. As early as April 2004, Blake Ives, Kenneth Walsh, and Helmut Schneider explored in *Communications of The Association of Computing Machinery (ACM)* how the passwords at popular sites can be reused at other sites.[49] In this manner, "users who reuse passwords who fail to realize that their most well-defended account is no more secure than their most poorly defended account for which they use that same password."[50] The latter typically belongs to sites with inadequate authentication standards.[51]

Recognizing that failures are inevitable, Netflix built Chaos Monkey, a set of scripts that run through Netflix's AWS process and randomly disable AWS instances to ensure that the rest of the system can keep running without customer impact. Yury Izrailevsky, Director of Cloud & Systems Infrastructure, and Ariel Tseitlin, Director of Cloud Solutions, wrote in the Netflix blog that the name originated from the idea of releasing a wild monkey to "shoot down instances and chew through cables."[52] What better way to learn about any weakness in handling insults to integrity than having engineers on standby to monitor and react rather than be caught unawares at "3 a.m. on a Sunday."[53] If failure is indeed a recurring pattern, the only way to mitigate failure is to meet it head-on by integrating it into the design of safeguards. Netflix makes failure injection a lifestyle rather than an anomaly. A key thrust of Netflix's strategy, then, is to always design for failure.

> *We've sometimes referred to the Netflix software architecture in AWS as our Rambo Architecture. Each system has to be able to succeed, no matter what, even all on its own.*[54]

Thus, the design of the underlying SaaS architecture to handle failures does matter. While SaaS customers get to focus their attention on gaining an edge on time to market rather than on maintaining the infrastructure level of the software stack, the outages show the need to ask providers, during vendor selection, what happens when something goes awry. In revisiting the April 2011 AWS outage, Paul Smith of Everyblock admits:

> *Frankly, we screwed up. AWS explicitly advises that developers should design a site's architecture so that it is resilient to occasional failures and outages such as what occurred yesterday, and we did not follow that advice.*[55]

Similarly, SmugMug's Co-Founder and Chief Executive Officer, Don MacAskill, wrote:

> *Each component (EC2 instance, etc.) should be able to die without affecting the whole system as much as possible. Your product or design may make that hard or impossible to do 100% – but I promise large portions of your system can be designed that way.*[56]

What does not kill us can only make us stronger. The difference in Salesforce's response to email phishing incidents in 2007 and 2014 is telling. In the former, news outlets reported about Salesforce's silence on the breach well before it made a public admission. In the latter, Salesforce issued a warning to customers even though they had not yet identified any customer infected. In November 2007, Salesforce acknowledged that one of its employees fell prey to a phishing scam resulting in an exposure of salesforce customer contacts.[57] Like the Dropbox incident 2 years after, these Salesforce customers received bogus emails, this time resembling Salesforce invoices.[58] The phishing emails succeeded in getting a subset of end users to reveal their passwords. Fast forward to September 2014, Salesforce warned its users of the Dyre malware that attacked financial institutions.[59] Dyre is a new family of malware, different from previous Trojans.[60] Like other Trojans, attackers attempt to trick users into downloading and installing Dyre on their computers by disguising the download as something useful and then quietly stealing data from unsuspecting users.[61] But the way it attacks users is novel by using browser hooks to acquire data protected by Secure Sockets Layer (SSL).[62] This way, the malware not only gains access to the data users transfer to or from a cloud service, but also to their login credentials, which the attackers can sell for a profit.[63] Barely 6 months earlier, SaaS security vendor Adallom noticed that a single user alone in its customer Salesforce instance generated hundreds of view operations in a short period of time.[64] A subsequent investigation revealed that the user was an employee catching up on work outside of regular office hours via a home computer running Windows XP and an old version of Internet Explorer.[65] A malware scan revealed a variant of Zeus, a banking Trojan, that instead of going after banking credentials targeted SaaS applications.[66] Designed to crawl the Salesforce instance, it downloaded the company information onto a temporary folder.[67] The Zeus incident adds another domino to the vulnerability mix – bring your own device (BYOD). Ami Luttwak, co-founder and CTO of Adallom, explained:

> *The SaaS applications are themselves safe, but the implications of using them from unmanaged devices are either disregarded or unaddressed, at least pragmatically so. I think we can agree that asking employees to connect to Salesforce.com over a corporate VPN* [virtual private network] *is unpragmatic. The core problem is that security teams do not feel accountable for the security of SaaS applications.*[68]

We may be forgiven for thinking that the silver bullet to all this insecurity is to abandon the use of cloud or SaaS altogether. The titles of the studies put forth by analysts are particularly telling. Forrester went from "SaaS Adoption Requires a New Approach to Information Security"[69] in 2014 to "SaaS Adoption 2017: If You Aren't Using SaaS Broadly, Your Business Risks Falling Behind."[70] Where the former report, admittedly commissioned by Adallom, emphasized "complacency" on the part of SaaS-consuming enterprises in thinking that vendors are responsible or liable for data breaches, the latter report alluded to the evolution of SaaS when describing the maturing of SaaS offerings.[71] When we peer behind the dynamics of conflict, disagreement, and resolution that characterize cloud outages and breaches, we may find an altogether different subtext. Clients poised to adapt or react to unexpected changes are better able to tap into the benefits of using the cloud without compromising the availability or security of their data or resilience of their business operations. While Netflix executed its design for failure strategy at the lower levels of the software stack, AWS, there is no reason why a company cannot apply this same strategy at the higher levels. SaaS clients that focus more on what they can glean from a third-party service provider, rather than on what they can inherently do, are doing themselves a great disservice, especially given the ease with which they can configure SaaS to meet specific needs, and their unique position to see, as well as opportunity to orchestrate, the entire transaction lifecycle across the multitude of SaaS in the enterprise ecosystem.

Take the integration between two different SaaS for example. Users can use reports scheduled to run from the destination application to reconcile against those from the source to detect missing transactions that should have synced. To the extent that the SaaS comes with transaction entry or user login audit logs, how frequently do users review these, and what criteria do users employ to surface possible red flags? Internet protocol (IP) addresses outside of the enterprise VPN? Number of transactions updated on any given work day? To see the SaaS rendered as simply a black box is a convenient way of sidestepping our responsibility, like how Frankenstein persisted in viewing his creation as a black box of sorts in spite of its demonstrable range of human emotions and needs. In addition, as the Zeus incident demonstrates, a Trojan gained access to the SaaS by capturing login credentials from a home computer. In other words, a SaaS in question is but an element interwoven into an increasing diversity of external services, and of devices, employed in an enterprise's everyday operations.

Rogue or shadow IT is characterized not only by employees who bring their own devices to work but also by those who subscribe to SaaS without notifying the IT department. IT security traditionally has focused on defense of the company's perimeter, employing a combination of tactics, including firewalls, antivirus, two-factor authentication, and VPNs. But rogue or shadow IT introduces a new reality where this perimeter is either arbitrary or fast dissolving in a world of interconnected devices. Internal controls devised for and around this SaaS are rooted in more pervasive controls that address this ecosystem. Access administration, a company's BYOD policy, and login monitoring are just as relevant as what features the SaaS can offer to restrict or check for unauthorized access.

One way is to look for help in less than likely sources. Procurement coupled with license management when executed effectively throughout the organization can identify various pockets of rogue SaaS purchased without authorization and provide insight into a more hybrid and thus realistic risk profile. Ultimately armed with this knowledge, the enterprise is better equipped to weigh the ease of consuming every readily available SaaS on the one hand with the need to make up for any shortfalls in direct vendor obligation or liability in the event something goes awry. Just as in an internal controls assessment, not all systems automatically fall within scope, assessed as it were, based on their likelihood and anticipated impact on financial reporting, the enterprise can apply the same pattern of identification and prioritization to all SaaS consumed within the enterprise. Depending on the nature of the enterprise business at hand and its contextual industry – a startup in the healthcare industry would need to comply with the Health Insurance Portability and Accountability Act (HIPAA), whereas a fintech company with banking specific regulations – the appetite for consuming SaaS varies when balanced against the type of data transacted and the degree of impact to an organization's branding and reputation should a breach arises. To unlock services as black boxes, as we will see, is to expose at times a colorful array of actors, processes, and societal constructs that come into play and conflict as the SaaS is consumed.

It occurred to me that a deceptive dose of blame or shame laces the examples of breaches and outages shared at audit conferences and in classroom. Systems do not have to be unforgiving. When we are less afraid, or more curious, when beginning to explore deep seated beliefs, we become more forgiving. We wonder if Frankenstein was fundamentally unable to handle a range of emotions, and this in turn led to his inability to deal with them in his creation, a reflecting mirror of sorts? What if Frankenstein had recognized his creature's inherent yearnings as a desire to be more human, practically a rare commodity in today's age of artificial intelligence and drones, and decides to pursue a different course of action? Instead of going for what should be, he plumbed the depth of what is. When encountering the lack of love the creature felt, he gave love. When faced with ignorance yet combined with a yearning for literature, he shared acclaimed works and began a book club discussion for two. You get the idea. But in continuing with this spirit to embrace what at first appears to be problematic when our instinctual reaction would have been to avert or ignore, we start to view internal controls differently. Outages lead to availability. Breaches lead to tightened security. The end is but an invitation to begin again. To what extent is Frankenstein accountable to his creation, having assembled it with assorted parts? Yet, the tale of Frankenstein is less about accountability than it is about forgiveness.

With all our emphasis on automating, could we have been ignoring informating, its shadow half? Take an example on a private startup that has grown and decides to employ a procurement SaaS in place of a manual logbook secured by the financial controller. When configuring the SaaS, are approval limits set up in a manner that enables or empowers respective department heads to make good decisions on organizational spending within their allocated budget? With all the emphasis on approval routing, it is the ability to provide exception reporting on high volume, low value purchase requisitions related to any one given vendor in the same year, or that of invoices processed without POs – that get at the "shenanigans" that Peters talked about. Unlike its automate counterpart, this informate or analytical component is less than publicized even by SaaS providers, perhaps because it requires more than the automation of a set of manual processes. It also requires a deeper and sometimes more nuanced understanding of clients' operating environment. As Susarla, Barua, and Whinston point out, SaaS providers are quick to draw up service level agreements (SLAs) on availability and reliability while maintaining an almost unanimous silence on business analytic capability.[72] Automation and information, or analytics, go hand-in-hand. It is hard to imagine the value of reporting without a high level of automation on the one hand, and the consistency, or dare I say, quality demanded of the data on the other. Perhaps it is for this reason that the informate piece remains observable, not verifiable, in everyday vendor parlance or literature. After all, while specific processes can be systematized according to best practice templates with users configured in the process in a rapid deployment and implementation of SaaS, coming up with tangible and thus useful reporting metrics requires a more intimate knowledge of the client's business environment. Yet, despite building foundational blocks that let us harness the full value of a SaaS, the informate piece can come up short. A customer relationship management (CRM) SaaS can very well automate the management of campaigns and leads such as through email prospecting and auto-response, Susarla, Barua, and Whinston write, but just as important are sales and marketing analytics and customer service knowledge management.[73] What is the percentage of subscribers to a service who have discontinued their subscription in a specific period, otherwise known as customer churn rate? Conversely, for the same cohort of customer sales that recur year over year, are we able to upsell services?

To be sure, this need to report on how-we-do the way-we-do predates SaaS. In the interviews conducted by Zuboff with operators at the paper and pulp mills undergoing automation, she reports on how the informating process gives workers the opportunity to think about how things could have turned out differently. As she eloquently put it, "automation thus preserves what is already known and assumes that it knows best," so that status quo is accepted, existing manual processes merely "automated" – redistributed to technology. With the implementation of the expense tracking system (ETS) at Tiger Creek, one of the paper and pulp plants studied by Zuboff, expense information from the pulp and paper making process let operators see the impact and extent of their actions, as well as identify areas for potential cost savings despite the persistence of multiple "unknowns" in the production process.[74] For Zuboff, "the informating process takes learning as its pivotal experience," and she goes on to assert that in contrast to the automating process which is a means to an end, the learning that comes with informating is continual as new data or events present themselves for additional insights.[75]

This learning has more to do with a kind of self-reflection rather than self-justification. In contrast to the employment of system audit logs to evidence what a user has done right or wrong, the informating using a SaaS's analytic capability can give us an opportunity to step outside of ourselves, outside of the rules of the system even. By system, I mean the holistic system, the entire system of people, activities, and technology beyond any one software or SaaS. It is when we become so accustomed to behaving like cogs in a machine, like manual automatons, complying with predefined rules or policies and in effect using the software in a much more ritualistic or mechanistic manner than was the software's intention or design, that we start to see shenanigans like $999.95 purchase requisitions emerge. It is also for this reason that users do not tap into, much less review, much of the SaaS capability even out-of-the box so to speak. In a rapid deployment that is so characteristic of a SaaS implementation, the focus is more on automating existing processes, but once that gets going, the enterprise client moves on to other projects. The informating half lies dormant. Informating leads to learning. Learning leads to forgiveness. Forgiveness leads us back to automating.

The point here is not so much to kickstart both the automating and informating tracks simultaneously – without anything to automate, there would be nothing to informate – as it is to *not* forget about the informate piece once automation is underway. The informating aspect can shine a light on both exceptions as well as circumstances that appear otherwise normal and mundane. Audit trails showing a disproportionate amount of accounting personnel intervention upstream in helping end users update purchase requisitions can be a valid cause to revisit the user friendliness of the fields and layout of the requisition template even though at the outset nothing appears awry and quite the contrary, especially with an uptick in the requisitions submitted. Likewise, an excessive number of update requests for already approved transactions, such as POs, may surface the need for approval routing not just for initial purchase requisition creation but also for PO updates. And that, in fact, when the company initially rolled out the SaaS to have approval in place for new requisitions, it only scratched the surface on all possible purchases submitted and meriting review, with new purchase requisitions comprising a minority of such requests.

The trick to having a good design of internal controls for SaaS is planning for change. As we have seen with building planning, Brand is quick to point out, all too often, our foreseeable futures are narrow and limited, like wiring an entire building with fiber optic cable to take advantage of broadband technology even as wireless turns out to be the more dominant technology in the workplace of tomorrow.[76] Could Zuboff be a tad pessimistic when calling automation an end in and of itself?[77] After all, with informating, therein lies the opportunity to tweak currently automated processes, and with that comes new data points, a re-learning of sorts. Thus, even though we start with automating during the initial stage of SaaS deploy, to truly harness its capability and potential, we need to switch gears to informating and then back to automating. If this is true, then the initial SaaS deployment would not need to anticipate, let alone address, every conceivable requirement. And if so, then the unique malleability of fields, records, and workflows that make up the SaaS offering is the perfect candidate for this approach.

Just as in building planning, Brand in *How Buildings Learn* advocates a loose fit, a strategy that "postpones many design decisions and leaving them to the eventual users,"[78] companies can apply the same approach in the design of internal controls for and around SaaS. Just as a leased space allows a company to expand by knocking doors through walls of a neighboring startup that fails or moves away, a SaaS that is too rigidly implemented with all the "bells and whistles" of every conceivable internal control can end up hampering every action of newbie users trying to learn its language at the outset. In fact, Brand advocates building designs that let people try things out. From this perspective, a sandbox environment of SaaS can give users the opportunity to try out new ways without incurring a real risk to production. Even in production, when companies initially relax rather than tighten access during initial deployment, they encourage users to try out or experiment with different roles. Arguably, tightened access at the initial outset can backfire especially when users get frustrated with the inability to access functions that are commensurate with their job responsibilities. The informating aspect is relevant here as well. All too often, users used to on-premise or legacy solutions wait for an analyst to develop customized reports or saved queries, without realizing that the SaaS may very well let them both develop their very own tailored reports or drill-downs that tap into related records and perform joins with other tables, scheduling these for regular email distribution to a selected audience and devise management dashboards that give executives a graphical perspective.

For Zuboff, technology's informating capability "textualizes the production process" providing visibility into the peaks and valleys behind an otherwise unassuming surface.[79] "When that text is made accessible to operators," she argues, "the essential logic of Taylorism is undermined."[80] Taylorism covered in Chapter 5 is all about controlling who gets to see what when and concentrating this panopticon power in the hands of the few – management as opposed to workers. Chapter 6 attempts to provide a counter-response to Taylorism. In a book where our subject matter revolves around devising internal controls in the use of SaaS, we are touching upon controls of controls, with a world of panoptic controls beckoning at the door. While there may be some truth to this view, there is an unfair emphasis on a top-down approach as alluded to in previous chapters, where management reviews the work of personnel. There is not enough attention on the concept of mutual controls, where the increasing prevalence of technology creates a need, as well as a means for different actors or groups to exercise control over one another to achieve mutual objectives. Mutual controls stem from sociologist Harold Garfinkel's view of accountability not so much being answerable to superiors but account-ability being everywhere, being accountable to everyone else you work with.[81]

Oddly enough, Garfinkel channeled his early foray in his father's bookkeeping business into his future work on the concept of accountability. Just as an accountant enters columns of accounts, an actor's everyday action is observable and reportable, in other words, an account. Consider the tiered approvals of purchase requisitions in a procurement SaaS. When a requisition is over an approver's approval authority, it routes to a higher level after the approver approves. From a managerial control perspective, there is top-down oversight over spending. An employee is not able to engage in a contractual relationship with a vendor unless an approver with the appropriate level of authority approves the purchase. So mundane that it often goes unnoticed or unremarked is a mutual control perspective. When a user routes a purchase requisition to a higher level, often a director-level or vice-president-level employee who is further removed from the details surrounding a specific purchase, and invariably the one responsible for spending from multiple departments, the approver grants approval based on knowing that the user already reviewed and approved the PO. When the SaaS at hand does not give the user this level of insight, or visibility into upstream approvals, it inhibits the user's ability to decide.

From a control as oversight perspective, the SaaS is effective in providing tiered approval routing. However, from a control as visibility perspective, the SaaS is not quite as effective. The SaaS can apply the same approach to the timely review and approval of journal entries among different members in the same accounting team. If the entries pending review were visible to everyone, there would be a greater likelihood that users would perform reviews in time to coincide with the close calendar for the very simple reason that no one likes to appear as a laggard in the continual drive to cut down on the time it takes to close the books. The users may still route the journal entries to individual managers for approval, but to focus on this as a satisficing condition for evidencing the presence of internal controls in a SaaS would be premature, and it does not quite surface the underlying inter- and intra-group dependencies that belie what appears on the outset to be nothing more than top-down command and control. In this manner, just as we stated before, where the interplay and reflection of multiple SaaS can mirror Indra's jewels, we can say the same for mutual controls that elicit visibility and promote participation among all rather than for a select few.

The mutual control perspective is one that underlies an audit approach to mitigate risks, yet it does not quite garner the same level of attention garnered by managerial controls. Let us circle back to the potent combination of procurement and license management to combat rogue IT, or the use of unauthorized SaaS throughout the organization. It is through a mutual-control perspective of providing visibility into top five department spending or unauthorized SaaS consumption that we gain insight into different pockets of users with their unique characteristics and inter-group dynamics that may not be immediately apparent. A marketing team may insist on using Hangout over Hipchat or Slack, while a finance team chooses to maintain its own custom Access database. The restriction of one's access in a SaaS in a manner aligned with one's job functions or responsibilities is a common enough control to limit excessive access and thus one's ability to take a transaction from start to finish without additional supervisory oversight or review. What often does not get explicated is that it is precisely this limitation of access that fosters a collaborative environment where one can place a certain level of trust, or dare I say faith, in the actions the user performs. Limited access to make entries, on the one hand, does not let a user override key mandatory fields, or validity checks that default yet other fields to the right department classification and location, thus increasing the likelihood for the user to enter valid and complete data. Limited access to review entries, on the other hand, precludes approvers from inadvertently modifying the very same transactions they are validating, as well as makes personnel accountable for their own entries, such as having to resolve errors in "rejected" transactions sent back by approvers. It is when the company grants excessive access to personnel downstream that the mutual control environment starts to disintegrate. Instead of sending incorrectly made entries back to preparers, reviewers granted edit access can choose to fix them. This does not necessarily improve upon the quality of transactions submitted. What it does achieve is increase the amount of work undertaken downstream. An audit perspective that focuses solely on the presence of managerial oversight does not fault this approach, even though the latter has made the review work performed downstream less visible to preparers upstream and in effect redistributed accountability from preparers to reviewers.

When we step back and turn our attention from individual preparers and approvers and look at the flow of transactions from sales or payable sub-ledgers to general ledgers (GLs), there is even a greater possibility for obfuscation or conversely, reduced visibility to what happens to a specific transaction as it evolves from a quote to a sales order to an invoice to a payment, or from a purchase request to a PO to a receipt to an invoice to a payment. Fundamentally, corrections that are made downstream, most commonly via a journal entry in the GL to correct the accounts coded as opposed to initiating entries in the sub-ledger such as a PO or sales order, are not unlike corrections made by reviewers or approvers downstream rather than sending them back to preparers for correction. When we in turn take a step further and instead of focusing on sub-ledgers and GLs in any one SaaS, but instead focus on sub-ledgers and GLs across multiple SaaS, we further underscore the importance of internal controls as a means of promoting mutual visibility, and thus mutual accountability.

The client enterprise consuming the SaaS is therefore an orchestrator of sorts, shielding sensitive data from prying eyes who have no business in back-end transactions, yet lifting the veil just high enough to bring visibility to various users who consume different SaaS in the entire transaction lifecycle, fostering accountability not simply to the organization, but also to one another. In fact, the image of internal controls as a big brother watching over anything that so much breathes while eye-catching is ultimately misleading. End users when appraising or reviewing SaaS as part of request for proposal (RFP) of services often invoke system audit trails not simply as means for management to track their whereabouts or footprint but perhaps more selfishly as a way for to document their actions and therefore justify them in the event of an inquiry or worse misunderstanding. To paraphrase Garfinkel, to be "account-able" is to be "report-able."[82]

In the SaaS world, informating can have a more direct impact on automating rather than a mere retrospective of sorts. The ability to run a tailored query to only show unpaid invoices only aged for 30 days, for example, allows a daily workflow to pick it up to communicate with customers with 30 days past due. When the invoice is 45 days past due, the daily workflow can tap upon a different query and associate it with a differently worded email sent out to the customer in turn to elicit payment. In this example, the query is part of the automation workflow. If all who access the SaaS could easily edit the query and if a user were to accidentally update 30 days past due to 35 days past due, then there is a high likelihood that the 30 days past due email notification would be sent incorrectly to a customer who is 35 days late in remitting payments per the agreed terms in the contract. Because the workflow would apply to all unpaid invoices, then an inadvertent change to the 30 days past due query may have wide-reaching implications and likely impact more than one customer who is 35 days past due. In this manner, informating – the ability to devise or maintain a tailored query – has direct implications on automating. Such examples are endless.

Another flavor can be the way a company generates consolidated invoices. As their label suggest, companies can consolidate invoices in various ways, including but not limited to any open unsent invoice created in the past week and belonging to the same customer. Other ways of grouping an invoice can be by item type so that a usage consolidated invoice can group all time and material hours as opposed to a support consolidated invoice. For resellers, the reseller can group a consolidated invoice with specific end customers identified. Users can create these logical groupings via queries so much like our customer collection email examples, any inadvertent change to the queries specifying how we consolidate whether by item type, creation date, or customer type can have spillover impact on the presentation of the consolidated invoice generated and communicated with the customer.

Whether the SaaS lets nontechnical users construct the query through point-and-click makes a difference. An upgraded version comprises not just additional features and functionality that lets users do much more, so that if a fixed asset module were not available, this would become available albeit with limited features at first launch. There is also another kind of enhancement – those that give nontechnical users the ability to devise workflows, in place of writing scripts, and make changes to setup parameters without necessarily having to contact vendor support – being able to, in fact, self-serve, and, in the process, truly undermining Taylorism. For clearly, the user can perform the same end user query by print-and-click as well as by scripting. The Looker code example in the previous chapter comes to mind. There is not just one way. Although the public exposure of queries democratizes the process, the lack of visibility continues to restrict and concentrate the ability to change the way we work into the hands of a privileged few.

When a workflow devised through point-and-click further uses a query that a user devises through point-and-click, informating informs automating. When the user devises an additional query to verify the changes made from the automated workflow, automating informs informating. Rather than see informating and automating in binary mutually exclusive this or that term, I believe this is a more pragmatic and, in many respects, more inclusive way of integrating the two sides of the same coin. I have also seen other SaaS vendors take the reverse approach starting first with a user interface that lets nontechnical users construct their own queries, and next either through an enhancement or a separately procured third-party module altogether give users the capability to perform Structured Query Language (SQL)-like queries.

Today, the image of the nontechnical user is changing. Many nontechnical users undertake application administration duties and invariably end up as power users of the SaaS they use every day. Just as skillful accountants employ macros and Visual Basic (VB) scripting in Excel, they view the prospect of being able to write their own SQL queries and executing these on their own with anticipation rather than trepidation. An exposure of applicable field names with data formats in tables usally accompanies an ability to write SQL-like queries, so that users are in fact able to identify what has not been previously considered simply because they had no visibility to the entire dictionary of fields to begin with. Some SaaS providers even go so far as to share code or query samples. These run the gamut from those easily accessible online with back-and-forth user feedback to ones obtained by contacting the SaaS provider's support hotline. The ability to peer under the hood at the plethora of fields also gives users the ability to identify and configure bridge fields that would help in the integration between two or more SaaS. A specific customer identification number may be in use in the upstream SaaS and when shared across multiple SaaS in the entire Order-to-Cash cycle helps in easy identification so that there is no dispute over which customer to invoice when entering the Order-to-Cash cycle through a mid-stream SaaS. The same holds true for identification numbers for products or stock keeping units (SKUs) sold. The same primary key in an upstream SaaS serves foreign keys in the downstream ones, so even though the internal SaaS consumption landscape may mirror a 1960s disparate file-based system, the SaaS has performed careful diligence to ensure that the same costs associated with the legacy architecture no longer apply with the present one even if it is accomplished through careful stitching or architecting.

For all our attention on transactional data attributes such as unique identifier or primary key belonging to the customer or vendor or employee for that matter, there is yet a different way of slicing through data and that is to think of each data record as an element, or dare I say service, for consumption by other record types such as transactions. In spite and perhaps precisely because of the multitude of SaaS, it makes even more sense that within the organization the same customer record, whether in an upstream or downstream SaaS, would share certain key requisite fields or attributes. This sharing is almost like a middle or mid-layer of customer, employee, and vendor records that any plug-and-play SaaS can easily consume. This sharing is the proposition that MuleSoft, an integration Platform as a Service (iPaaS) recently acquired by Salesforce, makes to both large and small enterprises, so that in fact there is a meta-management to granular transaction management. Unless there is internal consensus, different SaaS may mirror disparate file-based systems in the 1960s, each having a unique identifier for the same customer. How do we reconcile transactional data across SaaS? Better yet, how do we verify if there are not potential duplicates of the same customer, especially since the unique identifier in a SaaS is typically system or auto-generated? Having consistent record attributes at a meta level facilitates the ease of integration among existing SaaS as well as the addition of new ones. The iPaaS can also provide consistent exception management capabilities, such as email notifications, if the transactions do not sync across. Consistent reporting and handling processes mean that regardless of the SaaS plugged in, the same error codes or escalation procedures apply so that incident management and error resolution can take on a predictable cadence even if the internal landscape of SaaS in use or operations personnel change. What good is informating if it doesn't lead to action?

The genesis of *Frankenstein or The Modern Prometheus: The 1818 Text* took place in the summer of 1816 where upon visiting Switzerland Mary Shelley and her soon-to-be husband, Percey Mary Shelley, became neighbors of Lord Byron who on one propitious day would propose a challenge for each of them to write a ghost story. Mary Shelley would wake up each morning "forced to reply with a mortifying negative" when asked "have you thought of a story?"[83] Just as the creature attempted to mirror his creator Frankenstein's life by educating itself and trying to fit in with the public, Frankenstein's life in many respects mirrored the life of his creator Mary Shelley. Like Mary, their mothers died early. Just as Frankenstein needed to give up his brother and wife to chase after his creation, Mary eloped with Percy giving up her father and two stepsisters. Growing up with two stepsisters when her father remarried and whom her stepmother favored more than her, Mary's own childhood mirrored the creature's experiences of being unloved or being neglected. The creature's murder of Frankenstein's wife is an odd foretelling of sorts. Percy would be taken from Mary a year after the book was published. How things come to be take on new shapes and forms in a retelling or retrospective. What if when the creature was born, instead of discovering his mistake with one big bang, Frankenstein were able to view a working albeit scaled-down prototype and make tweaks along the way? In place of "glassy eyes," these could have been tinkered earlier to reflect "the glorious presence-chamber of imperial Nature."[84] In place of shriveled complexion and thin cruel lips, perhaps he would have further further refined them before facing the mammoth of a creature presently looming over him?

We have seen how Agile encourages seeing working software early rather than late, outcome over process. But in addition to getting a prototype earlier rather than later, here we are also exploring ways to introduce elements to try to break the prototype. Much like Chaos Monkey in use at Netflix, the image of a wild monkey running rampant in a forest of virtualized instances comes to mind. Why not introduce a negative earlier to clarify just what it is you need or do not like or want for that matter? If a mere face rather than an entire figure were available for Frankenstein to make necessary corrections – is it too human, too susceptible to feelings than even he (or us for that matter) can handle, then take it down a notch – then surely he would have made the creature more robotic, instead of life-like? After all, humans are not immune to automated displays of affection as evidenced by the everyday overuse of "how are you." In fact, despite its rather inhibiting, not to mention hideous outward countenance, it is precisely its propensity to act and want to be human that makes it so undesirable to humans. So why not make it less human by degrees? Had Frankenstein created his creature in today's lab a-la-Agile-Scrum style, he would insert a specific scenario (use case) and see how it reacts. If it even so much as betrayed a sliver of human emotion, Frankenstein could very well dial it down swiftly, so that what materializes is not unlike a dishwater, disinterested and unbiased.

Instead of merely evidencing approved purchase requisitions, we can conceivably automate the generation of requisitions that skim, that is, hover slightly below established thresholds to assess if these make the cut. Rather than circumscribe the myriad of ways that an accounting office can mitigate risks of unauthorized purchases by prescribing what is a key control and what is not, this attempt at breaking the purchasing approval policy ironically allows for a multitude of ways to mitigate risk, expected or otherwise. What is characterized as a key automated control – a purchase requisition approval – may be nothing more than a click-the-button exercise on the part of the approver. Instead the real lookout for suspicious requisitions may reside with a back-office finance team when reviewing month-over-month spending and looking for significant variations. This real key control surfaces precisely because we are less focused on automating an internal control, more on automating counter-compliance, than in generating exceptional circumstances or events that necessitate intervention.

Every day presents yet another opportunity for a dry run or rehearsal. Purchase requisitions skirting approval threshold are like caged canaries that miners would carry into a coal mine. If dangerous gases such as carbon monoxide are at toxic levels, the canaries would be the first affected, thus providing warning to leave the tunnels immediately. Caged canaries, chaos monkey, fuses – all these are fingers pointing to what can go wrong well before it does go wrong. Automating the entry of invalid transactions therefore tests the waters – do they remain undetected; or if a user identifies them, are they acted upon? This approach focuses on consequence, as well as on the mitigating procedures that would come into play when dealing with consequence, rather than idealized processes that ease audit verification, improving our relations with auditors and not much else. With purchase requisitions skirting defined thresholds, we can in fact still pass the audit – evidence requisition approvals – and yet circumvent the internal controls in place.

Naturally, a prerequisite with programming counter-compliance is having a systematized way of identifying and monitoring the exceptions introduced to be able to unwind them at the right time to preclude any actual financial impact downstream. "Programmed" here is used loosely to describe a systematic or otherwise automated means of seeding exceptions and threading them through the transaction lifecycle. While the means of weaving these into the daily flow is automated, the crafting of test scenarios is not. Like all other constructs, they would have to be refreshed periodically; otherwise, we run the risk of participants growing accustomed to the very exception handling routines they perfected over time. Arguably, despite the growing belief that process is a dirty word in organizations embracing Agile over waterfall software development techniques, the Scrum approach of daily stand-ups, biweekly demos, and retrospectives is a planned process of sorts. By insisting that we are not following a plan when embracing Agile or Scrum over waterfall or Software Development Life Cycle (SDLC), we miss the wider overarching lens of articulating and applying a common method to the madness.

Let's take this a level higher, away from SaaS. When revisiting the activities that make up compliance – the assessment, design, validation, remediation, and reporting of internal controls – instead of merely automating the performative aspects such as whether we are performing each activity timely and in the prescribed sequence, we can instead automate the identification, handling, and analysis of canaries, or exception events. Employee terminations and customer write-offs come to mind. Instead of rubber stamping enterprise-wide procedures and controls year after year, what better way to validate that the enterprise remains a controlled environment in the face of inevitable change whether to process, system, or people by validating if the employee off-boarding process would de-provision access for all applications granted to a "test" termination, or if the sales operations team would put through a "test" sales order belonging to a customer that is in bad standing. Once again, the focus is on what happens, as opposed to what we think would or should happen or focusing narrowly on a single process attribute like evidencing approvals.

Programmed counter-compliance recalls computer assisted audit techniques (CAATs) employed in computer programs such as access control list (ACL) to analyze transaction data for validity and completeness. Yet, while CAATS aims to identify anomalies such as employees who have also been set up as vendors as a red flag of potential fraudulent activity, programmed counter-compliance introduces anomalies to ascertain whether controls are in place to mitigate them. A common frustration with CAATs is handling false positives. As it turns out, employees may be set up in the system as vendors because historically the company had reimbursed them for their expenses in a vendor check run. The same would not apply to programmed counter-compliance when the very nature of the introduced event or series of events is suspect to begin with.

Thus far, the strategies commonly employed to automate compliance – systematized approvals, compliance activities and handling of anonymous reporting – falsely assume, and to employ Hart, "the world in which we live were characterized only by a finite number of features" and "provision can be made in advance for every possibility," further proof that "we labor under two connected handicaps whenever we seek to regulate," the former being "our relative ignorance of fact" the latter being "our relative indeterminacy of aim."[85] Programmed counter compliance, by introducing the seeds of what can go wrong early and often, acknowledges that we cannot plan for all possibilities, that even the best laid plans can go awry. In true Agile fashion, programmed counter compliance efforts exemplify "working software over comprehensive documentation" and "responding to change over following a plan."[86] When Netflix developed Chaos Monkey, a resiliency tool that seeks out and terminates virtual machine instances and containers running inside its production environment, they are of the belief that "the best defense against major unexpected failures is to fail often."[87] Yet in the world of audit and compliance, failure is a dirty word, swept under the rug all too hastily. Programmed counter compliance is not in conflict with securing an unqualified opinion from auditors: what it does acknowledge is that it is by no means the only objective. Organizational resiliency and the ability to grow and handle change, these are but a couple of the primary drivers behind programmed counter compliance of which compliance is but a byproduct. A common critique of auditors as "folks who come along after a battle to bayonet the wounded" reveals a deeper fissure: the inefficacy of audit precisely because of its insistence on procedure, not outcome, the battle already lost. We have become accustomed to quantifying internal controls that provide reassurance but don't necessarily capture the spirit of the law. From this perspective, programmed counter compliance may be just what is needed to stir us from our doldrums. With all the automation summoned at the mere click of a button, our response to comply has itself become automated. If auditors are seen to follow a predictable script starting with a review of significant financial accounts and proceeding to key process cycles and controls that address risks mapped back to financial assertions, then enterprises, by following a similar trajectory inscribed in AS 5 and to some extent its predecessor AS 2, can be seen to cultivate a culture of indifference even as different stakeholders cycle through familiar motions.

Earlier, I referenced the observation made by Cooper and Reimann that humans "don't usually enter 'bad' codes" but rather "in a sequence that the software isn't prepared to accept."[88] Programmed counter compliance in this instance would introduce invoices with "bad" codes so that we may, in turn, observe the array of avenues users turn to not only in identifying but also in fixing them. Moving up one level to a more advantageous position, we can extend the concept of programmed counter compliance across two or more transaction cycles or systems. In other words, to truly ascertain if inappropriate purchases can still make their way past a widely cast approval policy net, we may be better off submitting the same amounts via expense reports and see if they get approved for reimbursement. Why bother navigating the company's purchase approval policy when expense reimbursement is a far easier or quicker route to getting paid, the lesser of two evils? In fact, employees often have trouble differentiating between the two, whether to submit an expense as an expense report or capturing it on a purchase requisition. What ultimately determines the path that they would take may be driven more by expediency and ease rather than any top-down, enterprise mandate. Thus, when employing programmed counter compliance, we can take a more pervasive bird's eye view, not merely focusing on what could go wrong within any one process or subsystem, but by examining the exchange among various interlocking elements from a holistic perspective. Counter-compliance posits: to gain control, we may have to be willing to give up control. To be able to put up a more than formidable defense against making mistakes, we may have to lower our defenses in the first place. Counter-compliance is less about what's broken and more about breaking.

It challenges us to work with and transform what we know and have, an alchemy of sorts. In envisioning scenarios to break the system, we are compelled to tap into our creative juices rather than forever consigned to looking back. Alchemy is hard work that require us to look unflinchingly into the abyss where rewards are to be had but are equally hard won. Contrast this with Frankenstein's propensity to fall ill or flee the scene when faced with his creation. In combining the controls on controls approach with counter-compliance and mutual visibility, we take on queries on queries, or reports on reports. In a SaaS refresh from production to sandbox, a team may have to devise queries on queries to make sure that the same fields in a key query or report remain unchanged. From an audit perspective, it can be easy to repurpose these queries on queries or reports with financial impact such that any change to the results necessitate in notifications to interested or vested parties.

In the final analysis, how we work with SaaS may reveal more about what we are than what they are. Think about it. Because they are easy to procure, plucked off the shelves as it were, and plugged into our ever-increasingly complex assemblage of best-in-breed applications, we treat them as if they were invited guests. Once they've gained entry, we let them be, then get perplexed when something goes awry. When requirements are not initially fulfilled, we question whether vendor rights and obligations have been met. This series of counter compliance actions seems like a lot of work, certainly more than what we bargained for. Yet, with the almost litany of what went wrong paraded in the start of this chapter, AWS, Dropbox and Salesforce reveal the amount of vigilant work that goes on behind the smooth surface gleam of a web browser. They also point back to how instead of assuming our roles as passive consumers in today's service economy, we can consider availing ourselves of the configuration options that come with SaaS and play a more active role in identifying and responding to the "what can go wrongs" well before they occur. In the era of big data, so much emphasis is placed on having the right information easily available at our fingertips, like the FBI agents who use Sentinel in hopes of easy indexing and searching from Chapter 5. Yet, a lot of what we deem information is but one of many impressions. How many visitors came to our site, how long did they stay, what products sell the most don't quite provide any degree of insight into the degree of automation efforts we have undertaken thus far. It is not uncommon to see organizations that are quick to deploy a series of SaaS at breakneck speed yet, upon close examination, only used a mere sliver of functionality offered by each SaaS. With so much emphasis placed on process efficiencies – how fast, how soon, how much done and at what costs – there is little or no time devoted to second loop learning. With all the attention on getting the mobile app up and running, letting users access the software in quick time, and having these synced over into an accounting SaaS, it can be easy to forget that the purpose of the procurement app is to make sure that company purchases are valid and authorized in the first place. As our earlier examples can attest, we can still deploy a quick procurement app on your phone capable of submitting requisitions and getting these approved in quick time and still grapple with a rise in unauthorized expenses coming in under the guise of personal expense reports.

Or consider the following questions. Despite a recent SaaS deployment to replace a legacy on-premise software or home-grown system, to what extent does this reduce the overall time in processing the same transactions? From a holistic perspective, we may need to factor in time spent on other ancillary systems insofar as reconciliations still need to be performed for in-flight transactions in both old and new software, as well as any accompanying physical artifacts that still need to be maintained, and contracts and such that still need to be executed. When viewed in a larger context, the efficiency gains made in the newly minted SaaS may impose negative externality effects on other parts of the overall software jigsaw.

Thus far, when we talk about validity, we review it in the context of authorization. Is a transaction authorized? In other words, is something triggered appropriately in response to an authorized source? Yet, validity can also be used to characterize our very own reactions. Put simply, are our reactions valid or invalid? In the case of Frankenstein, he may have been reacting to his own perception of the creature, rather than directly to the creature itself. What stood in the way between the creature and Frankenstein was his own emotional charge that resonated with how he saw the creature – recall again the adjectives used – "yellow skin," "shriveled complexion" and "black lips" all of which are hardly inviting or valid. In the same manner, our reactions to what is in scope and out of scope for an audit and for compliance merits deeper analysis. Queries, insofar as they informate, are less likely to be in-scope than workflows that automate manual processes. This view may reflect our inner biases in favoring automation over information. Much like the rapidly dissolving boundary between automation and manual explored in the last chapter, this chapter showcases the interrelations between automation and information. Having the query be used as a basis for triggering the workflow is more a direct way of seeing how informating can impact automating. But even if the query were not used, we have seen that whether or not the workflow is deemed effective depends on surrounding informating constructs that have been developed in place to check up on in-flight transactions stuck in queue or those whose amounts are suspect. Like the tip of the iceberg, these mask underlying efforts at circumvention. Information also dovetails into the second loop learning covered in the past chapter, providing the data points needed to finetune the workflow or automation put in place. Our tendency to see automating versus informating from the perspective of what's in or out of scope can thus be characterized as invalid if not incomplete. In effect, a duet needs to be conducted between informating and automating for one to get a more complete picture, rather than zooming in on any one aspect and declaring it a roaring success.

When you think about it, the whole concept of SaaS requires a revision of our views of validity when it comes to IT. Faced with the rise of services, the role of enterprise IT is changing. For enterprises that have transitioned from on-premise software to cloud computing, IT is no longer in the business of purchasing servers, performing backups or even coding and testing but instead serves as an in-house broker for negotiating services from external third-parties on behalf of the enterprise and monitoring service levels. In a way, this changing role of the IT mirrors the transition of a developing nation. When an economy undergoes industrialization and post industrialization, we see the primary sector in raw materials giving way to the secondary sector in the manufacture of finished goods; this too would give way to the tertiary sector in services. From 1960s through 2000s, we see IT going from purchasing "raw materials" (servers and networks) to "manufacturing" (building of applications and maintenance of infrastructures) to brokering external services (applications and data hosted by third parties). This has led some to introduce the concept of IT as a service, where the vision is to provide a service catalog with vetted internal and external services that the business can choose from. This multi-sourcing concept is a key tenet of what International Data Corporation (IDC) calls the third platform that replaces earlier mainframe and client/server/Internet technology. In an internal memo back in 2005, Bill Gates wrote:

> *The broad and rich foundation of the internet will unleash a 'service wave' of applications… services designed to scale to tens or hundreds of millions will dramatically change the nature and cost of solutions delivered to enterprises or small businesses … we will build strategies around Internet services and will provide a broad set of service APIs for use in key applications.*[89]

Consider the following common scenario: emphasis is placed on automating manual processes, so, for example, if a company is presently tracking its fixed assets in Excel, then a search is initiated to explore whether or not to implement a new fixed asset SaaS that integrates with the current accounting SaaS or to implement an additional fixed asset module that already comes with the accounting SaaS albeit at a higher subscription price tag. Attention is centered on the various asset types that need to be accounted for as well as associated lifespan for amortization, asset creation from purchase invoices, review, and retirement. In the interest of time and cost, the company went with the additional fixed asset module. After deployment, it moved on to focus on automating another manual process: sales commission calculation. What could possibly go wrong with this picture? Ask the accounting personnel hard at work behind the scenes and it turns out that not an insignificant amount of rework accompanied the implementation. From re-coding vendor invoices to properly code invoices to fixed asset accounts when these were not selected by end users in the first place to the challenges in updating invoices in already locked AP periods as part of expedient month end close, to not having the system generated numbers align with the actual asset tags affixed on physical machines to facilitate an annual inventory count, to an inability to unwind or delete a fixed asset recorded when an incorrect asset was selected on the invoice. The list can go on and on, and invariably does in real life, but because the company has already moved on to focus on sales commission calculation, it does not, and likely will not, devote the necessary project or technical time and resources to rework the newly minted fixed asset system. While it appears to be functioning as planned (and in this case unlike Frankenstein's creation), there is a greater amount of busy-work than meets the eye. Immediate benefits to short-term productivity at least in tracking the fixed asset from creation to retirement may be gained, but arguably over time, the amount of rework needed may accrue to a deafening roar that threatens worker satisfaction resulting in likely attrition. Unintended consequences are surfaced by the Carnegie Mellon Software Engineering Institute (SEI) in its review of system archetypes, recurring patterns seen at organizations that rapidly acquire and develop software.[90]

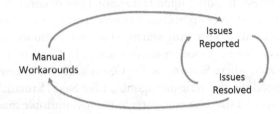

Another ripple effect may very well be that for workers who choose to stay, more and more of their time is spent firefighting and rework than on new project initiatives, thus slowing down the company's expressed attempt to attain breadth in manual process coverage as opposed to depth. What if the rework needed is more foundational, so that instead of having all assets proposed and then created, essentially a two-step process, merely one would suffice that of creation? Yet it would have been all but impossible to update this one-time foundational setup. The weight of the ever-escalating technical debt threatens to bust the seams. With all these self-fulfilling first loops at work, there is no room for second loop learning. Ever seen the feet of a swan underwater as it glides out into the stillness of a lake? Its frantic motions beneath mirror the manual interventions of workers to sustain a placid countenance above. By only engaging initially and only at new project opportunities, the organization's posture is lop-sided, closed off to possibilities to fully explore what it already has. We may excel at covering new ground exploring uncharted waters yet in all this busyness, how engaged are we? Busyness in this case is a red herring. For as we have seen they deflect attention from our innate ability to stay engaged with the matter at hand. It is in some respects a SaaS half-lived, opportunities short-changed, the entire spectrum of possibilities prematurely circumscribed. So quick to flutter hither and titer like hummingbirds with short attention spans. Like Frankenstein, we toil away at testing and implementation, yet when the fruits of our labor come to light, we couldn't wait to move on.

The same can be argued with the way we pronounce no exceptions noted when recycling the same controls year after year for audit. No exceptions noted – no news is good news – is another self-fulfilling loop distracting our attention away from the daily exceptions that operational folks encounter and work at resolving daily so that the positive findings presented to management may really be a foil for multiple underlying exceptions. In contrast, programmed or configured counter-compliance to break the system each time can be characterized as a series of attempts to gain compliance. The end is the beginning; the end is the beginning; the end is the beginning. Having to contend with exceptions on a more frequent basis, such that getting no news is *not* good news, is a more effective means at strengthening the system of internal controls against likely insults to integrity. Rather than rely on thousands of impressions, here we are talking about thousands of pinpricks to integrity. What doesn't kill us can only make us stronger. Rather than continue to rely on drywalling as an approach to evidence control operating effectiveness, building upon layer upon layer of controls that do not get to the performative, counter-compliance efforts require us to knock down self-imposed walls, not unlike a growing startup that grows into its neighboring configurable space as other neighboring tenants leave. In Chapter 5, we first talked about the movie *Her*, where Samantha, the OS, is acquired to provide a constant companion to Theodore, the male protagonist. Like SaaS, Samantha operates not within the confines of a singular computer but across multiple machines. Case in point is when she goes offline as part of an upgrade, unwittingly giving Theodore a panic attack. Much to his dismay, when she resurfaces again, she proceeds to inform him that she has been in touch with 8,316 individuals, 641 of whom she has established a romantic relation. In the end, Samantha leaves Theodore to join the collective consciousness, evolving beyond the words on a page to the infinite space between words. In a sense, automating and informing serve as mirror halves to improve fragility and forgiveness, in the same way automated controls can help a system of internal controls or SaaS be less fragile and manual controls can foster a more forgiving environment where unanticipated errors can at least be detected and resolved. Seen from this angle, counter-compliance has both the ability to shore up fragility and forgiveness: ways to counter-comply test fragility while remediation efforts incorporate forgiveness. In a Hegelian reading, Frankenstein's monster was the very antithesis to his thesis, just as counter compliance is the antithesis to compliance. A self is defined precisely because of its difference from the other, or absence of the other. Whereas the monster endeavored towards becoming more human by immersing itself in human literature, it is Frankenstein who displayed less than human characteristics when rejecting his creation at first sight.

The differences between the first Frankenstein movie and the book speak volumes. The creature in the book taught itself to read, eventually becoming enamored with Milton's *Paradise Lost*, but the creature in the movie was at best capable of growls and grunts. The creature in the book responded in kind to his creator's less than kind reception; it is precisely because of its maltreatment and neglect that led its revolt against its less than humane treatment. The movie, however, attributed the creature's brutality to the defective brain supplied by Frankenstein's assistant, in the same way an auditor is inclined to attribute a breach or outage to an absence of accountability. In fact, Universal Pictures was all but adamant that no empathy be established with the creature, tellingly referred to as "monster" in its subsequent films. To what extent do we display machine-like characteristics in our mechanical indifference to operational day 2 challenges that accompany SaaS? Conversely, to what extent does the SaaS at hand display more manual leanings when key reviews still need to be executed with human care? It's like walking through a hallway of mirrors. We are the monsters we create, each an unknowing host to our inner Mechanical Turk.

Exercise 7.1

In place of management oversight – think of a supervisor reviewing and approving your work – how can mutual controls serve to handle insults to transactional integrity?

1. Unrestricted view access to all approved purchase requisitions within an organization
2. Automated notifications on percentage of month end closure sent to all members of the finance and accounting teams
3. SaaS availability metrics and outages accessible online

Discussion

I recall for one enterprise implementing a procurement SaaS the looks of surprise on the faces of auditors upon learning that everyone in the organization had the ability to view one another's spending. So accustomed they had become to access restriction that they failed to see the role visibility can play in making one and all accountable by exposing the information across departments. What may well result is no department wanting to look bad by exceeding its budget. Similarly, having a periodic notification on percentage of month-end close tasks to all accounting and finance personnel, whether manual or automated through a SaaS such as Blackline or FloQast, helps keep team members abreast of who has completed tasks timely and conversely who is becoming a lag and thus in need of help. Finally, because its core competence lies in being available and accessible from anywhere at any time, the SaaS provider is likely more compelled to maintain its uptime than an in-house IT personnel responsible for a custom developed application.

Exercise 7.2

Identify elements of automating and informating in each of the following:

1. Purchase requisition approval
2. Exception notification alerts
3. Monthly variance reviews

Discussion

I think back to a recent governance risk and compliance (GRC) panel when a SaaS administrator at a recently turned public company expressed his concerns over an ability to comply with SOX in the first year. When asked whether access reviews were in place, his answer was because the SaaS was newly implemented, none had yet been performed. When asked whether segregation of duties had been tightened, his response was because they had a small accounting team, employees needed to be able to perform more than one task and in more than area. How do I then evidence that controls nonetheless exist over financial reporting, he threw his hands up in genuine exasperation? Yet as pointed out by various members of the panelists, including myself, other controls can exist beyond the vanilla ones in access and segregation of duties restriction. Insofar as variance reviews are performed, any material difference would have been surfaced and investigated even if access were deemed proper to begin with. Thus, variance reviews informate even if the means of dissemination can be automated using the SaaS at hand. Just as mutual controls highlight the pivotal role of visibility, when we begin to dig a little deeper, it is surprisingly remarkable sometimes how fraud can be successfully attempted given the plethora of informating and automating elements at play.

Exercise 7.3

Think of possible ways to counter-comply in:

1. Purchase requisition approval
2. Access provisioning
3. Disbursing vendor payments

Discussion

You'd be surprised to learn of how prevalent the key-under-the-doormat approach is in use at concealing confidential data from potentially prying hands. When it comes to excessive access granted, I've had many a user come up to me genuinely unaware of the powers they had in overcoming what at first appears to be restricted abilities to access specific functions. I suppose a flavor of this is seen when users upon the initial deployment of SaaS continue to perform duplicated manual tasks even if the SaaS at hand has automated the same process. Attempts at counter compliance exposes some of these illusions, as do those associated with boilerplate yet illusory controls which show a sliver of a crack when a fictitious vendor set up nevertheless makes it past purchase requisition approval through to payment. Or when I circle back to the feedback heard on the GRC panel, right-sounding default out-of-the-box roles get copied and approved for assignment to new hires despite having excessive permissions that violate key segregation of duties.

Endnotes

[1] Oppen, G. (1968). Of being numerous (1–22) from new collected poems, New Directions Publishing Corporation.
[2] Hesseldahl, A. (July 19, 2014). Talking the cloud business with Amazon CTO Werner Vogels. Recode. https://www.recode.net/2014/7/19/11628994/talking-the-cloud-business-with-amazon-cto-werner-vogels
[3] Hickey, A. R. (September 8, 2011). Google docs goes dark in evening cloud outage. *CRN*. http://www.crn.com/news/cloud/231601024/google-docs-goes-dark-in-evening-cloud-outage.htm

4 Ibid.
5 Egress Software Technologies. (December 5, 2014). Human error causes alarming rise in the number of data breaches and resulting monetary penalties, according to ICO FOI request. https://www.egress.com/en-US/news/ico-foi-data-breach
6 Ibid.
7 Ibid.
8 Dolisy, J. (February 10, 2014). How to avoid network outages: Go back to basics. *Network Computing*. https://www.networkcomputing.com/networking/how-avoid-network-outages-go-back-basics/257686406
9 Behr, K., Kim, G., and Spafford, G. (2005). *The Visible Ops Handbook: Implementing ITIL in 4 Practical and Auditable Steps*. Eugene, OR: Information Technology Process Institute.
10 Amazon Web Services Team. (April 30, 2011). Amazon: Here's why our cloud crashed. *Business Insider*. http://www.businessinsider.com/amazon-heres-why-our-cloud-crashed-2011-4
11 Ibid.
12 Ibid.
13 Ibid.
14 Ibid.
15 Ibid.
16 Ibid.
17 AWS. (April 29, 2011). Summary of the Amazon EC2 and Amazon RDS service disruption in the US East region. https://aws.amazon.com/message/65648/
18 Ibid.
19 Ibid.
20 Ibid.
21 Ibid.
22 Shelley, M. W. and Butler, M. (1994). *Frankenstein, or, The Modern Prometheus: The 1818 Text*. Oxford, UK: Oxford University Press.
23 Ibid.
24 Johnson, H. T. and Kaplan, R. S. (1987). *Relevance Lost: The Rise and Fall of Management Accounting*. Boston, MA: Harvard Business School Press.
25 Ibid.
26 Ibid.
27 Ibid.
28 Ibid.
29 Ibid.
30 Zuboff, S. (1989). *In the Age of the Smart Machine: The Future of Work and Power*. Oxford, UK: Heinemann Professional Publishing.
31 Zuboff, S. (September 1985). Automate/informate: The two faces of intelligent technology. *Organizational Dynamics*, 14(2), 5–18.
32 Ibid.
33 Shelley, M. W. and Butler, M. *Frankenstein, or, The Modern Prometheus: The 1818 text*.
34 Ibid.
35 Lewis, A. (April 26, 2011). When computer programming was 'women's work'. *The Washington Post*. https://www.washingtonpost.com/opinions/when-computer-programming-was-womens-work/2011/08/24/gIQAdixGgJ_story.html?utm_term=.c53d7b951569

36 Ferdowsi, A. (June 20, 2011). Yesterday's authentication bug. *Dropbox*. https://blogs.dropbox.com/dropbox/2011/06/yesterdays-authentication-bug/

37 Ibid.

38 Ibid.

39 Ibid.

40 Ibid.

41 Ibid.

42 Ibid.

43 Conger, K. (August 30, 2016). Dropbox employee's password reuse led to theft of 60M+ user credentials. *TechCrunch*. https://techcrunch.com/2016/08/30/dropbox-employees-password-reuse-led-to-theft-of-60m-user-credentials/

44 Ibid.

45 Ibid.

46 Ibid.

47 Ibid.

48 Ibid.

49 Ives, B., Walsh, K. R., and Schneider, H. (April 2004). The domino effect of password reuse. *Communications of the ACM*, 47(4), 75–78.

50 Ibid.

51 Ibid.

52 Bennett, C. and Tseitlin, A. (July 18, 2011). The Netflix simian army. Netflix Tech Blog. https://medium.com/netflix-techblog/the-netflix-simian-army-16e57fbab116

53 Ibid.

54 Netflix Technology Blog. (December 16, 2010). 5 Lessons We've learned using AWS. https://medium.com/netflix-techblog/5-lessons-weve-learned-using-aws-1f2a28588e4c

55 Gilbertson, S. (April 25, 2011). Lessons from a cloud failure: It's not Amazon, It's you. *Wired*. https://www.wired.com/2011/04/lessons-amazon-cloud-failure/

56 Ibid.

57 Vaas, L. (November 7, 2007). Salesforce.com employee hands customer list to phisher. *eWeek*. http://www.eweek.com/security/salesforce.com-employee-hands-customer-list-to-phisher

58 Ibid.

59 Greenberg, A. (September 8, 2014). Salesforce warns of Dyre malware possibly targeting users. SC magazine. https://www.scmagazineuk.com/salesforce-warns-of-dyre-malware-possibly-targeting-users/article/539586/

60 Ibid.

61 Ibid.

62 Ibid.

63 Ibid.

64 Prince, B. (February 19, 2014). New zeus variant targets Salesforce.com. *Dark Reading*. https://www.darkreading.com/attacks-breaches/new-zeus-variant-targets-salesforcecom/d/d-id/1141335?piddl_msgorder=thrd

65 Ibid.

66 Ibid.

67 Ibid.

68 Osborne, C. (February 20, 2014). Zeus variant targets Salesforce.com accounts, SaaS applications. *ZDNet*. http://www.zdnet.com/article/zeus-variant-targets-salesforce-com-accounts-saas-applications/

69 Forrester. (May 2014). SaaS adoption requires a new approach to information security. Forrester thought leadership paper commissioned by Adallom. http://resources. idgenterprise.com/original/AST0139802_Adallom_WP_SaaS_Adoption_1_.pdf

70 Herbert, L., Hamerman, P. D. et al. (June 29, 2017). SaaS adoption 2017: If you aren't using SaaS broadly, Your business risks falling behind. *Forrester.* https://www. forrester.com/report/SaaS+Adoption+2017+If+You+Arent+Using+SaaS+Broadly+ Your+Business+Risks+Falling+Behind/-/E-RES117364

71 Ibid.

72 Susarla, A., Barua, A., and Whinston, A. B. (2003). Understanding the service component of application service provision: Empirical analysis of satisfaction with ASP services. *MIS quarterly,* 27(1), 91–123.

73 Ibid.

74 Ibid.

75 Ibid.

76 Brand, S. (1994). *How Buildings Learn: What Happens After They're Built.* New York: Viking.

77 Zuboff, S. Automate/informate: The two faces of intelligent technology.

78 Brand, S. *How Buildings Learn: What Happens After They're Built.*

79 Zuboff, S. Automate/informate: The two faces of intelligent technology.

80 Ibid.

81 Garfinkel, H. (1967). *Studies in Ethnomethodology.* Englewood Cliffs, NJ: Prentice-Hall.

82 Ibid.

83 Shelley, M. W. and Butler, M. *Frankenstein, or, The Modern Prometheus: The 1818 text.*

84 Ibid.

85 Hart, H. L. A. (1994). *The Concept of Law* (2nd ed.). Oxford, UK: Clarendon Press.

86 Beck, K., Beedle, M., van Bennekum, A. et al. (2001). The Agile Manifesto. http:// agilemanifesto.org/

87 Bennett, C. and Tseitlin, A. Netflix Simian Army.

88 Cooper, A. and Reimann, R. (2003). *About Face 2.0: The Essentials of Interaction Design.* Hoboken, NJ: John Wiley & Sons.

89 Gates, B. (October 11, 2005). Internet Software Services. http://www.telegraph. co.uk/finance/2925650/Complete-text-of-Bill-Gates-memo.html

90 Gallagher, B. (April 2, 2008). Identifying acquisition patterns of failure using system archetypes. https://resources.sei.cmu.edu/asset_files/Presentation/2008_017_001_ 23071.pdf

Chapter 8

Known Unknowns

Shape clay into a vessel;

It is the space within that makes it useful.[1]

Lao Tzu

There's something to be said for saving face. Growing up, it was all about saving face. Regardless what went on at home, we never so much as betrayed a hairline crack on the surface. A woman on the morning train was putting on eyebrows. Fellow riders plugged into their distraction of choice nevertheless found it hard to look away. When all was said and done, it was as if nothing happened; hey presto, new riders entering the same compartment would not have known that mere minutes before, the fellow rider sitting in the seat closest to the door didn't have eyebrows to begin with. We are not our appearance. If we are, our appearance is beyond us. It struck me that underneath all the bravado about new technology lies a deeper acknowledgement and practice of what Ervin Goffman termed "front stage" and "back stage" behaviors.[2] Our fellow rider's behavior was all the more compelling by sharing with us what would have deemed back-stage behavior. Recall from Chapter 7 the sheer horror at being able to see past the "yellow skin" of Frankenstein's creature, how it "scarcely covered the work of muscles and arteries within."[3] It is not uncommon to hear from application administrators a blow-by-blow account of the amount of work that goes on behind the scenes with the implementation and maintenance of a SaaS that supposedly needed neither love nor attention. Goffman writes of "impression management," how each of us perform the work to convey or maintain a public face.[4] Just as the SaaS abstracts away all the wires, server racks and other hardware sequestered away in multiple data centers around the globe to provide failover capacity, much remains unseen behind the seemingly all-encompassing yet amorphous vapor of cloud. It strikes me that when it comes to designing in exception handling for SaaS, one of the reasons that not enough attention is considered upfront can be attributed to the way we view frontstage and backstage behaviors. For those of us who are used to a PR marketing launch not unlike that surrounding Stratus 286, it seems almost antithetical to expose or speak of any vulnerabilities or susceptibilities.

Compliance ≠ exceptions? If the last chapter is about forgiveness, this chapter is about fragility – not as weakness but openness to exploring deep seated beliefs. We would have liked SaaS deployments to be iron-clad and error-free, yet when we hear tales of SaaS founders' starting their companies from scratch, we are struck by the sheer speed and agility at having to deploy new functionality and rolling with the punches if something breaks. Naturally, as the SaaS vendor grows and the product is more mature, these challenges don't surface as much anymore, but what their stories point to is an emphasis on the rate of responsiveness over thoroughness of planning to the point that time to market is compromised. Not coincidentally, just as Brand, in *How Buildings Learn*, would have preferred for walls to be porous to easily expose an incalcitrant pipe or circuit breaker concealed within through smell,[5] it would make more sense, especially with ease that comes with configuring SaaS and integrating webhooks to provide instant real-time notification based on specific triggers, for little everyday annoyances to be surfaced sooner rather than later. In effect, what we've traditionally deemed back-stage behavior otherwise reserved for a developer or administrator can really start to come on stage front and center. Sync errors in transactions from other integrated SaaS, transactions that sit too long in a pending for approval queue, all these and more may be symptoms of a more fundamental problem at hand.

Done ≠ undone? Today cost-per-impression (CPI) or cost per thousand impressions (CPM) – the expense incurred for each potential customer to view an ad or expense incurred for every thousand potential customers who view the ad – is used to assess the cost effectiveness and profitability of online advertising. In a blink of an eye, a metric is established. Yet, just like how we need to reassess front- versus back-stage behaviors, we may face a similar compulsion to reassess the faith we place in the irreversibility of impressions made. Just as how Agile seeks to unwind the emphasis on capturing every requirement to exhaustion and approving these before working on and sharing a prototype, with a SaaS deployment, it may help to factor in the ability to redo or effect a gradual makeover in time, even if the feature set conferred on the outset is not ideal. Precisely because we don't know what we don't know and here too also availing ourselves of the configurability that comes with SaaS, it may be fine to give ourselves the permission to start with a few key fields or attributes and augment these once we gain more experience and ideas through using the SaaS as opposed to merely thinking or talking about it. I am reminded of the time when I gave my students in the third semester of my *Accounting Information Systems* class the ability to submit quiz results for a regrade. Each time I received a request via email – and in this regard much like receiving an exception email on a possible sync error – I cringed inwardly, somewhat regretting the decision to extend this option to students who instantly availed themselves of the opportunity. Yet, upon closer reflection, I realized that part of my reaction stemmed from an expectation that a quiz grade is final, even if an answer to an open-ended question did not appear correct simply because the student had different assumptions in mind, or for a multiple-choice question the options seemed terribly confusing. The option for a redo, or regrade while a minor inconvenience on my part, is more closely aligned with the vicissitudes of life that we all have come to realize.

With a SaaS, not all configurations can be unwound – and this is when careful planning around irreversible choices needs to be performed – yet to what extent are we not tapping into its ability to unwind configuration changes in other areas by insisting inwardly that what is seen on Day 1 is idealized in stone? When working with expectations from a systems integrator or implementer, I am sometimes struck by the intractability of impressions formed on both sides, vendor and customer, when it comes to delivering upon agreed requirements. Upon seeing the user interface – one thinks of the dramatic unveiling in a PR launch of sorts – users are quick to form an impression on how specific features conform or do not conform with what they asked for or what they had in mind. Likewise, vendor personnel are quick to form impressions of users based on how aligned or congruent their initial impressions are with documented specifications. Much like in my mind's eye, I'm in favor of seeing the quiz grade as finalized, there is a need to accord the freedom to redo on both sides whether one is in the shoes of the vendor, expecting users to revisit what they want once they have additional data elements to compare with and test against prior assumptions, or in the shoes of the client, the ability for the SaaS to be reconfigured or reworked. After all, it is by seeing the SaaS in action that both sides get closer to a mutual understanding of what is needed and what can be delivered.

Account = 1? The possibility of redo deepens the narrative or story. When I attended a recent book conference and found a seat in a session with editors of a journal that publishes short stories, one of the questions the audience members surfaced was what made a good short story. The answer given was not what you would expect: the ability of the short story to hold multiple stories. The bleeding of back-stage behavior onto the center stage is but a means of introducing different aspects of a story that up until then had been relegated to the margins. Manual intervention by accounting personnel downstream to reclassify transactions or enter data that has not been synced in correctly, if at all, is a back-stage story that unless shared would continue to unwittingly support the premise that the automated SaaS solution is truly automated, or that companywide there is no need for an active dissemination of policies and procedures necessary for entering and approving specific transactions. Likewise, the ability to tailor a SaaS by degrees based on observation of its design in use gives an opportunity to introduce deeper elements progressively into what appears to be a generic off-the-shelf artifact. These are all instances of how there can be more than one account to a story. Recall the use of user stories in Agile that make up the backlog that is groomed to prioritize into successive sprints.

The multiple story concept when applied here speaks to a need for more than one account. With a billing SaaS, we have described how various accounts may need to be documented from the order management to billing to collections. Yet what may be left out is an audit and controls account. Changes to invoices generated through billing schedules may need to be queried and reviewed for impact to revenue recognition. Alternatively, access to update invoices may need to be restricted to key fields with accounting impact. Of specific audit focus may be oversight for deleted transactions. While these audit user stories may not be prioritized in initial sprints, they need to be added to the backlog or grouped into a later hardening sprint, rather than squirreled away if only to get to see the clear light of day.

In truth, there is no better way to learn about the innards of a software than by handling, troubleshooting and attempting to resolve end user concerns. One is faced by an upper ceiling constraint on just what one can do, partly because the SaaS is developed by an external provider, partly because one is held in check by the level of configuration or customization availed for experimentation at one's fingertips and partly because of overall resource and time constraints. When a SaaS is inaccessible or slow, internal emails are ringing off the hook. When troubleshooting, the locus of control is determined: is it the client organization's fault or the vendor's? Has the release of a custom script or workflow interrupted or broken an existing feature? A script that runs continuously on numerous records can slow down other areas, such as importing entries or running of reports. Conversely, is it the fault of the vendor's? Has there been a recent patch release or scheduled batch of enhancements? Has there been a change to the URL or authentication criteria? We try to figure out what happened, and in so doing attempt to put together an account, an explanation of what happened. For Goffman, accounts come in two flavors: excuses and justifications.[6] The former is characterized as an attempt to reduce responsibility or accountability. The latter is characterized by an explanation of how specific outcomes, typically positive, can be attributed to specific behaviors. In the event of a SaaS outage, we will likely not be short on both excuses and justifications; even though it is something that client personnel can't control or predict, manual workaround procedures are performed so that work can nevertheless carry on. One mere sentence here is sufficient to span an excuse and a justification. It is when we come up short on both excuses and justifications that things start to take a challenging turn.

Testing ≠ production? Consider the earlier example shared in Chapter 6 on having a custom field re-compute the amount for reviewing against an actual amount synced over in a sales order. Suppose a request is made to take this a step further, that the screen be locked if the computed estimate differs from the amount synced in. When calling into a SaaS support hotline, one is presented multiple options: one can lock the screen via a script, or a workflow, or simply hide the approval button in a sales order. When testing this out in sandbox, the application administrator on the side of the customer enterprise may realize that sandbox hasn't yet been refreshed with the most recent data. Initiating a request for refresh may take a couple of days yet the SaaS in use may support testing in production. What do I mean by this?

To test in production, wouldn't the script or workflow already be released? Per our change management control, wouldn't testing in production be anathema to the idea of change management and the separation of sandbox from production environments altogether? Yet insofar as the SaaS allows the script or workflow to only apply to the actions of the application administrator, to what extent are we not leveraging SaaS capability to the fullest? Although I haven't yet explored this in any great depth before, the ability to provide a platform for developers and administrators to devise custom records, workflows and scripts so as to tailor SaaS in ways that have not yet been anticipated by the vendor's in-house product managers and developers makes it in turn more of a PaaS, and in fact, it is the SaaS provider's ability to provide this platform that makes it be more universally adoptable in varied use cases. When one looks at SaaS providers and their embrace of PaaS as a service offering, a platform for developers, administrators and analysts to build new, unexpected functionality, Salesforce.com with Force.com for instance, we see the same "looseness" at play. Even Workday jumped on the bandwagon. At a keynote in Workday's 2017 *Rising* conference, its CEO alluded to the debut of a PaaS in early 2018 giving users the ability to "build custom apps that look like Workday but may also pipe in third-party cloud services."[7]

The increasing exposure of product APIs – key to building distributed networks in the cloud ecosystem – to facilitate cross-pollination or integration with other products, such as Salesforce.com with Evernote, emphasizes localized combinations that go a long way towards strengthening the overall role of Salesforce.com as a universal CRM cloud solution across industry verticals. Is it any surprise that shortly on the heels of the Salesforce1 platform launch in November 2013, the Gartner Group named Salesforce.com a leader in its 2014 Magic Quadrant for Enterprise Application Platform as a Service (aPaaS) report?[8] Gartner defines an enterprise aPaaS as one "designed to support the enterprise requirements for business applications and application projects."[9] Thus, more than mere scaffolding, platform here, just as cloud is more than what would at first seem ephemeral or temporary, has the potential of leveraging local assets housed in the respective best-in-breed SaaS to deliver entirely new or unexpected functionalities. Interestingly, itself an actor in the network inscribing its own narrative of the vendor and of the market, Gartner's worldview on vendors – evaluating them based on their completeness of vision and their ability to execute – "prioritize comparative forms of assessment rather than local accuracy" as Pollock and Williams point out in *Software and Organizations*.[10] A Salesforce administrator may develop off-boarding logic so that when advance terminations are given, the future term date can be entered into the employee's profile; and on the appointed hour, logic is designed in to automatically default his employee status from active to inactive. In this manner, no manual intervention is needed, a belated fulfillment of the 1967 dream where automation is like "just planning a dinner… you have to plan ahead … so it's ready when you need it."[11]

When the application administrator tests the locking of the sales order in production if the custom computed field does not agree with the actual amount, she would have to ensure that the underlying workflow or script is in testing mode even in production so that only her actions are considered or accounted for, and not anyone else's. To more fully flesh out this example, the custom computed field would have already existed in production – how else would the script or workflow compare it against the synced over amount field – yet even here the custom field, if not primetime ready, can also be hidden from other users. Thus, we have a custom field and a script or workflow that is already deployed in production and yet applicable to the application administrator visible to her eyes only. When testing the locking of the screen for instance, the application administrator may work with the SaaS support hotline to explore various options: would we like the screen to lock before submitting the order, or after? In investigating this further, they find out whether the custom field computes before or after the order is submitted, and this in turn changes the trigger they configure to lock the screen. One can ask the question: are they working on a live, real order and if so, what is the financial impact? In our example, because the custom field merely provides a computed estimate, it does not impact the underlying amounts recorded. In addition, because the locking of the screen or hiding of the approval button for that matter changes the way the transaction is presented to the application administrator only, we can argue that the risks of inadvertently updating real live data are minimized. At each fork of the journey, the configuration of the account, whether that be the choice of locking the screen or hiding a button, use of a script or workflow, application of the trigger before or after submission of the record keeps changing. There is the ability to redo, so that if the screen doesn't lock very well or the user experience feels clunky, then we can in effect go back and tinker with hiding the approval button. Embedded within this "short" user story that has been worked on in an Agile sprint by the application administrator with the assistance of the SaaS vendor's support personnel albeit over the phone and a shared screen interface, are more elements or stories introduced, resulting in stories of stories, not unlike the ideal short story proposed in the book conference panel. There are also degrees of front-stage behavior: although the custom fields and script or workflow have already been released to production, they are neither visible to the naked eye nor tangible (clickable). Hidden away, like a key under a rug, they nonetheless enable the application administrator to test out the options available to optimize the overall user experience. When finally released to the entire population of SaaS users, it's almost as if an inanimate display or potted plant that one paid little attention or mind to suddenly comes alive at the far end of the stage.

Back stage ≠ front stage? Netflix documents in its online tech blog a means of releasing new features in a manner that gets them in front of customers more quickly for consumption. After performing unit and regression testing, they perform what they call canary analysis by releasing the code on a small segment of their production infrastructure.[12] Here, they've automated the analysis with a canary analyzer that compares over a thousand metrics, such as response times and exception counts, with internal benchmarks so that anything falling below an identified performance threshold would result in a no-go: the decision to not deploy the change onto the rest of the production architecture.[13] By attempting to "break" the change in real-life conditions, there is arguably much more validation here than a simple check-the-box approval for production go-live. Rollback also takes on new meaning. More than an all-or-nothing approach, one can in effect test the waters much like bringing a canary into a mine. In fact, it is precisely because all real-life insults to integrity are entertained upfront, that the final product becomes far less susceptible to breakage when released to the rest of the production population. It is precisely because we are intent on attempting to break the build each time that it becomes less breakable with each successive hardening. When we in turn reapply the canary lens on our custom computed field and script or workflow, the application administrator is in fact testing the program changes on a sampled production population size of one. When observing any anomaly deemed unacceptable, the application administrator can simply inactivate the custom field together with the script or workflow. While still un-deployable, the work performed nevertheless is not wasted and serves as the necessary interim work that can be revisited or augmented in ongoing successive attempts.

There is an element of play. Recall from Chapter 3 the analogy of bricks versus clay when working with software. Pollock and Williams in *Software and Organizations* compared the experience of customizing traditional ERP packages to that of working with bricks.[14] SaaS, on the other hand, would be more like working with clay. Yet when one looks at the way we have designed and validated internal controls for SaaS, to what extent do we forget that we are working with clay? The same tight segregation of work between sandbox and production environments, the approval(s) required before anything can be released to production, the accompanying rollback procedures insofar as anything so much as burps – all these gating checkpoints hark back to an older era where working with software is like brick laying: once laid, they cannot be unwound. In contrast with the SaaS example we've covered, much of the work can take place in production, without impacting daily operations or financial reporting. With the traditional ERP or SDLC approach, emphasis is placed on process accountability. One would hope that when all the process controls have been performed, the resulting software works. It is in many respects wishful thinking as we have seen in undertakings big and small; recall here FBI's Sentinel project. Conversely, by releasing the customized changes in a controlled manner into a contained segment of production, observing the effects and making tweaks to the design constructs in response, we are more likely to arrive at a tailored change that truly works.

How to keep the changes contained can be exacted in a myriad of ways. In Netflix's example, this is defined by a specific part of the overall product architecture, whereas in the SaaS example we covered, changes were only limited to the actions of the application administrator. There is yet another way. A query may be devised that pulls up only a specific sales order belonging to a specific customer and incorporated into the custom logic. In testing the custom fields and script or workflow each time, only this sales order is "impacted." In effect, what the audience sees as frontstage behavior is merely a subset of what truly resides on stage if one accepts the premise that, so long as code is released to production, it automatically gets categorized as "front stage" behavior. As an aside, queries in turn can be devised by both technical and non-technical users alike and not made available for "public" access until ready for consumption. In this manner, the mere construction of an innocuous query is itself a series of steps that demonstrate the inherent fluidity of discovering what one wants, and going back to add more fields, update the search criteria and tweak the sequence in which they are displayed or even the formula to only show values to the right of a specific prefix; an example that comes to mind is the invoice number without the "INV" prefix. When we think of making customizations to the look and feel of SaaS, we think of change management, sandbox versus production environments and rollback. Yet boiled down to its essence, customization work is no different from constructing a simple query and having the ability to continually experiment in a controlled manner in production until you are satisfied with the outcome. The advent of SaaS is nothing short of an inevitable displacement of backstage behavior onstage.

Front Entry ≠ backdoor? To enter the Microsoft Theater in downtown LA, guests with priority check-in can enter the theater through the backdoor, just steps from the parking lot. Backdoor access, used to characterized privileged access gained through non-customary means typically bypassing standard security controls at hand, is in fact what the computer security industry focuses on. When it comes to the development of custom scripts to modify the behavior of SaaS or tailor it to better meet business needs, scripting can take place in an integrated development environment (IDE) insofar as the SaaS allows. Using the in-built code editor, an in-house or external developer can access fields or attributes native to the SaaS. Scripts can be downloaded from the SaaS directly into the IDE for changes before uploading back to the SaaS. This means of access is a type of backdoor entry, not unlike that enjoyed by guests with priority check-in at Microsoft Theater. Thus, restricted and segregated access between sandbox and production not only apply to users directly accessing the SaaS through its user interface in the web browser. In effect, these controls can be circumvented by individuals have having access to an installed IDE on their computers and in the process the ability to import, make changes and export custom scripts in the sandbox and production SaaS environments. With the possibility of making unauthorized program changes, change management comes into play, thus displacing the access versus change management dichotomy when it comes to the design and operation of IT general controls. Our example illustrates how excessive backdoor access to scripts changes can itself circumvent change management controls in requirement gathering, development, testing and production release. Thus, in the same manner back-stage behavior needs to be displaced onstage to shed light on inner workings, front and backdoor entry means need to be identified to acknowledge the myriad of ways, authorized or otherwise, that one can gain access, privileged or otherwise, into modifying the behavior of the SaaS at hand.

Sleep ≠ vigilance? To displace is to veer from one's initial position. To be displaced suggests an involuntary movement away from one's original aim or intent. But what if through a displacement or even a series of displacements, you end up right where you wanted to be? That which has been accomplished would not have come to be had it not been for the circuitous chain of precipitating displacements in the first place. Seen from this vantage, Latour brings our attention to speed bumps.[15] Termed "sleeping policemen," speed bumps are nonetheless effective in forcing drivers to slow down at key intersections like school districts, motivated less by a blind compulsion to observe speed limits and more by a genuine desire to maintain their car suspension in good condition.[16] Yet, the outcome, the deliberate slowing down of vehicles to a measured cadence, remains indifferent to displaced intentions.[17] In Latour's eyes, speeds bumps are more than mere matter, composed as if were of "engineers, chancellors and lawmakers" intermixed with "gravel, concrete, paint."[18] Make no mistake, the displaced intentions were highly calculated, used to achieve an original intent makes it in hindsight a rather ingenious internal control indeed. A mandatory receipt that needs to accompany every submitted expense exceeding $75 is, in some ways, like navigating a speed bump. Employees who comply don't necessarily subscribe to the belief that a supporting receipt is needed in every instance – think of the manual work involved in amassing receipts for every expense in a business trip – they simply want to be reimbursed, and ideally in a timely manner, knowing all too well that missing receipts would incur questions and protracted back and forth exchanges. Like speed bumps, the mandatory receipt field lies dormant, "sleeping policemen" as it were, ready to surface as and when an expense over $75 is submitted. For all the outcry rallied against the purported divide between humans versus technology, humanists versus automatons, the mandatory receipt feature in an expense management software, like the speed bump, is invested with human intent, admittedly one that counters the all too human temptation to get away with an unauthorized expense or two. Seen in this manner, technology serves almost like a mirror that we have built and held up if only to see or face ourselves.

When we circle back to our SaaS customization, where are the sleeping policemen? Let's try a high-level one. How about if the outcome of the custom fields and script or workflow aligns with the initial user ask? What if the application administrator has shared this prototype with the accounting users who requested these changes? What if a representative from other teams is included? When seeing the locking of the sales order on the screen, an order management personnel responds that this would have no impact as all orders are approved through a bulk import process, thereby bypassing the locking of the screen or hiding of the approval button through the user interface. In this case, second level sleeping policemen are manifested in ancillary cross-functional feedback before a change is rolled out. It can be argued that this itself is a form of regression testing: instead of testing potential impact to other units of coding or program functionality that may be impacted by the change, the application administrator is *testing* the validity of the communicated requirements against impacted teams. We can argue that this is in fact what a business analyst would do, and that the thoroughness of his or her work is in direct correlation with the level of consensus or dissent gained upon viewing a prototype, but regardless of when the cross-functional feedback is obtained, before or after a prototype is built or both, it suffices to say that when it invariably gets omitted in the design and only manifested later as a rubber-meet-the-road challenge during actual deployment of custom fields and script or workflow to all users beyond the application administrator, remedial action to inactivate or update the configuration work in production would have to be undertaken. For Netflix, the canary analyzer serves as the sleeping policemen prompting a no-go decision if many of the metrics don't get a passing grade. Likewise, to mitigate the extent of remedial work post-production rollout, a sleeping policeman of sorts is a cross-functional steering committee that meets regularly to review changes for financial and operational impact so that sensitive changes are not deployed during month or quarter end close. Other examples of sleeping policemen? Tiered approvals for more material transactions to slow down the process for authorization to be obtained and engagement with a vendor or customer to begin so that additional pairs of eyes provide the necessary cross-functional oversight for transactions that carry a higher risk. Or recall the use of FloQast, a separate SaaS that alerts users to differences in the account balance in the accounting SaaS and Excel reconciliations maintained in Box, in effect *slowing* down the financial close process and for good reason.

Latour describes another instrument inscribed or imbued with intent, this time an innocuous looking hotel key.[19] Rather than issue repeated reminders to hotel guests to leave their keys at the front desk, a far more effective technique has been to affix a large weight to each key.[20] In an expense management software, think of repeated email reminders configured at regular intervals to remind supervisors to review expense reports routed to their queue. These reminders, while not synchronous, are communicated from person to person in real time and nevertheless add to the weight of incoming emails in an asynchronous fashion until supervisors, no doubt feeling the pressure of the leash – recall French legislator Hamon's opinion on excessive ill-timed emails – begin to clear their queue of unapproved expense reports, not unlike hotel guests dropping their room keys at the front desk if only to relieve themselves of the sheer weight in their pockets. Like the hotel key, the email reminders set in motion what appears to be a displacement, whether that be ridding oneself of the burdens of email reading or key carrying, in a manner that in turn manages to accomplish the initial intent, whether that be reviewing expense reports or returning hotel keys in a timely manner. To achieve parity or "symmetry" among the human and non-human elements, Latour labels both as "actants" rather than "actors" and focuses on the chain of association amongst various actants, rather than any one in exclusivity.[21] But in circling back to our SaaS customization, what if the sleeping policemen did not exist? In other words, what if the demo did not take place with end users nor were cross-functional feedback solicited? The application administrator went ahead and deployed the customizations to lock the screen anyway. An email or call or a series of emails and calls ensue. Accounting users who requested for the screen to be locked would presumably be happy yet actual users who book and process orders may prefer for the approval button to be hidden if estimated amounts did not agree with actual amount simply because when the screen is locked, no further edits such as inclusion of customer's purchase order number can be added to a sales order pending approval. Insofar not all fields have been documented the first time in creating the order, locking the screen unintentionally delays the order creation process as entry personnel needed to have all requisite fields completed before submitting them. Also, what happens when manual entry errors have been made and need to be corrected in orders already submitted for approval? These would require supervisory intervention, and not merely in approving legit orders with requisite information completed but also in kicking back those that are still works in progress.

In thinking back to the concepts discussed earlier, even if there were ample opportunities for the application administrator when testing the customizations in production on herself to redo, that is explore other options to get to the same requested outcome, the same cannot be said for the very users who consume customizations. Ironically, compared to the time before the customization was in place, the spectrum of options available to entry personnel in either retracting an incorrectly placed order, or augmenting otherwise missing information, or correcting those already in flight for approval becomes more limited. The same customization that is intended to tailor the SaaS to meet user needs ends up restricting the degrees of freedom available to users in an otherwise generic out-of-the-box solution. Weighed down by the volume of support calls and user concerns, the application administrator ends up rolling back the fields and script or workflow to revert the user experience back to its original state. In this scenario, the escalating concerns and feedback can be compared to the heaviness of the hotel key. The more the application administrator deploys changes without going through sleeping policemen, the more support concerns can result; so in an odd way, just as the heavy hotel key prevents hotel guests from losing it by having to leave it at the front desk, the history of incidences resulting from the absence of sleeping policemen ultimately helps the application administrator to change her behavior to solicit independent feedback before rolling out the changes to begin with.

But this logic is convoluted. Wouldn't the heavy hotel key concept be more applicable to before rather than after the changes have been released to everyone? In other words, feedback should have been obtained even on the prototype version even if it were only accessible by the application administrator. If we switch gears, what would constitute a heavy hotel key in our SaaS customization example? What if additional capability were present, such that alerts are sent to the entire administrator group as well as key stakeholders every time a custom field, script or workflow were created, updated or even deleted? We are in fact talking about SaaS of SaaS, SaaS that oil the engines or gears both intra- and inter-SaaS. We mentioned earlier how FloQast can help with tying the account balance in NetSuite with reconciliations maintained in Excel in Box, but there are also other products like FloDocs, that have more recently been renamed as Strongpoint, that track any changes made to customized objects so that any potential changes with impact to other fields, scripts or workflows are surfaced. Much like the Netflix canary analyzer that compares changes against an outcome-based baseline metric benchmark, Strongpoint performs a spider search to look for and report on any associated impact of a customization change. In our SaaS customization example, this alone is not sufficient to prevent incident tickets from being filed in the first place. The heaviness would have to come from the necessity of having the changes showcased in a prototype made even if in production. In this event, we are bringing forward potential blockers, from after customization rollout to all users, to before the rollout when it is only applicable and visible to the application administrator. Much like how the heavy hotel key would pose such an inconvenience to the hotel guest to leave it at the front desk before it has the opportunity of being displaced, the vociferous volume of user concerns encountered during the prototype demo would have prompted the application administrator to fact check proposed customizations back in "staging" land, by inactivating any changes until she has time to rework the approach with the SaaS vendor hotline. Thus, when deploying and maintaining a SaaS in your respective organization, where are your sleeping policemen and heavy hotel keys?

There is deeper narrative here. Much like how a short story can itself contain other stories, there are more accounts here than meet the eye. Such is the culture we live in today. Just the other day, shortly after visiting my physician for back pain, I received a customer satisfaction survey in the mail. It begins with the usual lay-your-groundwork multiple choice questions to understand the frequency of visits, such as the number of times I visited the provider in the last 6 months as well as overall length of time I've been going to the same provider. Both questions are mutually exclusive, although I was intrigued to see that the last choice proffered for the first question was 10 or more times; one wonders how well and alive a patient would have been by then to answer the survey to any degree of satisfaction. There are questions to assess level of patient satisfaction: from a scale of 0 to 10 with 0 being the worst and 10 the best, how would you rate this provider? There are questions on clerical support: were clerks helpful and did they treat you with respect? There are questions on patient demographics: what is your age and your race? In the context of SaaS, it is not uncommon for SaaS customers to think of support as merely a hotline to resolve inquiries or concerns rather than a means to experiment or tinker with the configuration available at one's fingertips even without direct scripting involved. In our SaaS customization example, our esteemed application administrator has contacted support not because the site is down, nor because the system administrator isn't able to navigate to a specific feature. The support hotline is contacted because custom work has already commenced with custom fields, with a workflow already in the works. Here the application administrator may have difficulty in getting the screen to lock or the approval button to be hidden, but the point I'm trying to emphasize is that the concerns surfaced laid not so much in the first level processing of transactions or setup of entities such as customers or vendors but reside at a second meta level in the configuration or customization at hand. This would be like getting a survey question on how well I am able to tailor the physician visit to meet my needs, from being able to configure the sequence in which I'm seen beginning hopefully with the nurse practitioner to taking my temperature and blood pressure right away, to ultimately being able to do away with pesky patient survey questions altogether. After all, it is not uncommon for one to contact vendor support only to be told that the question or issue is not solvable or part of a future enhancement, and almost immediately, in the next minute, be presented with the penultimate "how did we do" series of customer satisfaction questions.

In yet another loosening of the barriers between front and back stage, user experience, or the solicitation of user experience, is slowly making its way to the stage front and center as SaaS can interweave the "how did we do" questions into part and parcel of work, and of doing, so upon concluding navigating a user to locate a less than visible menu tab, or identifying possible mistakes in the upload file during a bulk transaction popup process, a popup appears asking the user to rate her experience to a limited set of questions. Typically intended to take the user no more than 3 to 5 minutes to complete, answers to these questions can be later reported to informate on the intended automation. Low scores ascribed to what would otherwise appear to be a straightforward process can provide clues to the gaps that contribute to user and design distance. For a more detailed explanation on user and design distance, refer to the *Interface* section in PostScript. Just as I've attempted to show that the boundaries between front- and back-stage behavior are more porous, the boundaries between support for break/fixes and support for configuration changes start to blur. Admittedly this too – recall Ellison's allusion to the cyclical fashion-like phenomenon of computing – is not an altogether novel concept. When working with incident management systems in the past like Remedy as part of a support team supporting an internet banking application, a subset of production fixes would in fact turn into change or enhancement requests necessitating changes to the software source code. Yet, the difference in our SaaS customization example while infinitesimal still needs to be emphasized: the reason for the SaaS vendor support to be contacted is not directly attributed to a production issue as it is an attempt to enhance user experience. Rather than adopt an "if it ain't broke, why fix it" attitude, this re-envisioning of SaaS support has direct if not obvious implications in the way consuming SaaS enterprise customers strategize their level of reliance on third-party system integrators or consultants who assist with customization work or implementations. To what extent are the underlying planning assumptions still rooted in or left over from legacy or traditional on-premise software? Also, from an audit perspective, insofar as a third-party solution is not present to map out all possible configuration or customization changes, a mere examination of tickets logged with the SaaS vendor support hotline would shed light on the level of customization or configuration attempted in addition to mundane how-to inquiries or cul-de-sac blockers. Separately, integrations among SaaS are less than likely usual suspects; yet, they often serve as effective sleeping policemen. Consider the following scenario in a company that uses both NetSuite for financial accounting and ServiceNow for resolving customer inquiries and issues. Here, an integration is in place between NetSuite and ServiceNow such that new customers created in NetSuite are synced over to ServiceNow so that when tickets flow into ServiceNow, they can immediately be associated with existing customer contacts. When sync errors are reported such that customers are not synced over from NetSuite to ServiceNow, they slow down the ability for tickets to be created in ServiceNow, and rightly so, if only to point to the work that is necessary to augment missing customer details such as phone number in Netsuite before being picked up by the scheduled sync. Another example is CreditSafe. When integrated with Netsuite, CreditSafe provides credit information on new customers set up in NetSuite. Like ServiceNow, missing information completed during initial customer setup in NetSuite that is necessary for running a credit check may be identified by CreditSafe, the sleeping policeman under watch.

The tinkering work that we have undertaken by taking the same SaaS customization example and essentially straining it through a kaleidoscope presents a microcosm of possibilities that hopefully help us question and see beyond carte blanche portrayals of SaaS as generic off the shelf software that can't be used to gain a competitive advantage or core competency, or software whose source code remains tightly located in the locus of the vendor's control. Yes, while customizations or configurations even without scripting and by non-technical personnel can itself carry a cost when it comes to audit and ongoing maintenance, there are also canary-like aspects of SaaS changes that can be harnessed that would not have been present in legacy or on-premise software. And to the extent we are blocked by sleeping policemen and feel the deadweight of hotel keys, then it is highly conceivable that the outcome of the SaaS change is far more resilient than one that has simply undergone traditional change management controls such as production signoffs. In circling all the way back to Chapter 1, just as how Haraway states that "you can make categories interrupt each other,"[22] changes can interrupt other changes, such as legacy changes already deployed, as well as those in flight that serve as sleeping policemen for the ones that lie ahead. Lidwell, Holden and Butler document this well in *Universal Principles of Design* when chronicling the tradeoff between flexibility and usability.[23] They give an example of a Swiss Army Knife while capable of handling multiple scenarios, often doesn't get used as much as tools with more specific aims.[24] A kitchen knife is more commonly used every day that a Swiss Army Knife.[25] Or think about how much of Excel functionality do we really use on an everyday basis? Flexibility, the ability to use the same tool in a myriad of ways, comes with added complexity as well as the need for additional learning and adaption. Another way to think about this is to see the rise of best-in-breed SaaS almost as a counter-response to a monolithic ERP package of a Swiss Army Knife. In this light, any change or customization is not without costs to learning and of maintenance. This is when other SaaS, such as FloDocs or Strongpoint, that tracks change upon change and surfaces links, can come in handy. If a different administrator were to step in and attempt to update the custom computation fields used by the developed workflow, ideally the change management SaaS would send alerts to all invested stakeholders. Therefore, just like the hotel key that would have been easily misplaced had it not been for its weight, a mere couple of seconds invested in changes, however inadvertent to a custom field can trigger a timely distribution of alerts that when acted upon can unwind or reverse the immediate impact before it results in far-reaching implications.

In recalling Goffman's account of an excuse versus that of a justification, the reliance on a separate tool to keep everyone honest brings us back to the importance of visibility and how it can be really an effective albeit subtle control. In *Informate/Automate: The Two Faces of Intelligent Technology*, Zuboff shares accounts of users who favor audit trails.[26] Rather than seeing these as an all-encompassing Panopticon, observing their every move, users, especially those who collaborate closely together, rely on audit trails to keep everyone abreast of what's going on. More importantly, audit trails not only surface what could be awry or amiss but also evidence what has been performed correctly and timely. In the prior chapter, we also covered how the audit trails provided by SaaS can vary depending on the product maturity so that where transactional audit trails may be available, change histories to configurational, master data or line-level details may not be as easily accessible. When troubleshooting an issue, the existence of the audit trail may serve as an excuse, but it is used more as a justification to evidence that the users involved have performed everything per procedure. Scrum, a popular Agile technique, has its origins in a Harvard Business Review article titled *The New Product Development Game* where authors Takeuchi and Nonaka describe the employment of subtle controls that encouraged desired behavior.[27] Even though in Scrum, self-organizing teams contribute ideas to the backlog and fundamentally manage their own deliverables through daily stand-ups culminating in a 2-week prototype demo, controls in obtaining working software are effected through self as well as peer pressure rather than having a project manager crack the whip at each turn. The idea of a stand-up is to literally stand up among members of your cross-functional team and report on progress made from the day before and surface any blockers. Someone who doesn't quite yet pull her or his weight in the team is likely to be singled out for not being a team player having nothing to show for day in and day out. Imagine walking into a bank where a queue is already forming on one side. Our natural inclination would have been to stand behind the last person in the line. This visual accountability of sorts – showing behavior conforming or otherwise is put on public display and is thus more likely to be effective in achieving an orderly flow of "first in-first out" fulfillment of needs – has been described by Harold Garfinkel. What is fascinating is that this order has been accomplished without additional orders or admonishments issued by bank personnel, arising mostly out of decorum not to mention an inner compulsion to not appear out of line. No one, after all, likes to draw unnecessary attention to oneself for breaking a "natural" order.

For Garfinkel, however, a line is "witnessably a produced social object;" interwoven through the moment-to-moment interactions among the participants involved, rather than enacted from any preconceived rational intent.[28] This doesn't have to be a physical line for one to see it in effect. One afternoon upon showing up at the public swimming pool, I was about to dive in when I was greeted by a cacophony. Don't go in said one person. The lifeguard is not here yet, another explained. It did not occur to me that the few people or so around me were all hovering by the edge of the pool as opposed to swimming in the water. When can I go in, I asked? 1 p.m. exactly was the response. When I asked why, the lady sharing the swim lane with me responded that like it or not, we all needed to follow the rules. These same virtual rules apply when a yet third person jumps in, and we would have to comply with circle swimming rather than sticking to our own respective lanes; good luck if the swimmer behind you acts as if he is competing so that an otherwise leisurely weekend getaway at the pool can turn us into mice running on a wheel. In a SaaS context, a monthly dissemination of the companywide communications ranking the top five departments that have been late or remiss in submitting and approving their expenses would arguably have the same effect in triggering a desired or an appropriate action by exposing, and thereby situating, each department's expense management practice directly in relation to others, and seeing how a local order emerges as employees shape their actions in relation to others within any given context, even as the context continues to evolve through their actions; the ranking of top five transgressing departments is likely to change from month to month. Garfinkel centers on the context, no longer a mere passive background to our actions, as well as the role of reflexivity, where the actions undertaken can be traced back to the very context in which they are conceived.

I cannot over-emphasize the subtle difference between reactively firefighting to respond to a production break – recall the loop identified by CMU's SEI in the prior chapter – and proactively making changes to tweak configuration to improve user experience in the absence of a production break. For Takeuchi and Nonaka, subtle controls work when design engineers go out into the field to obtain feedback from customers. They write that "engineers at Honda are fond of saying that 'a 1% success rate is supported by mistakes made 99% of the time.'"[29] Much like the erosion seen between front- and back-stage behaviors, they call for a sashimi approach to developing new products, where development phases overlap rather than remain distinctly carved out from each other so that team members are afforded the opportunity to interact with one another rather than pass off responsibilities like batons in a relay race.[30] When something goes awry, because of the overlapping phases, it also becomes less likely to ascribe blame or point fingers at folks in a different team in a different SDLC phase. QA personnel in the testing phase comes to mind. Likely, end users typically only pay attention to the technology at hand (present to hand) when something doesn't go quite as planned. Recall our discussion of Heidegger's differentiation of a tool as present to hand versus ready to hand. When the tool is ready to hand and working as it should, it fades into the background, or even backstage as our focus is on the front stage task at hand. And so just like speed bumps that lie waiting for the unsuspecting motorist, the prototype demo with all vested stakeholders serves too as a subtle visibility control that insure that the outcome is something that is aligned rather than toxic to group needs. I'm reminded of a project management cartoon that goes as far back as the 1960s that depict how the customer was ultimately billed for a rollercoaster when what she had in mind was simply a tree swing, a variation of the Sentinel effect seen at the FBI in Chapter 5. A tolerance for mistakes and experimentation early on results in a more robust product capable of withstanding all too common insults to integrity. A key sleeping policeman that is associated with the employment of Agile or Scrum is continuous integration. The checking in of source code changes multiple times a day combined with automated builds that performs regression testing whenever a new build is launched focuses on breaking existing code to ensure that new enhancements or bug fixes are not affecting existing features. Our SaaS customized prototype demo of sorts underscores the need for end users to unwind, correct for or otherwise change course on already entered or submitted transactions. Very often, the excuses users give for what went wrong or taking the wrong turn are symptomatic of a fundamental inability to tailor or curtail the full extent of the automation at hand.

Thus, in revisiting our SaaS customization, imagine if the application administrator finds out upon further verification with her cross-functional audience during the prototype demo that the locking of the screen would only be useful for custom orders. For standard orders processed, the risk would be far too minimal to merit additional reviews considering the tradeoffs on flexibility in the ability to add or update non-accounting related data on the existing order. What if the application administrator lets the order management supervisor choose whether to subsume custom or standard orders to the lock screen functionality rather than have it deployed for all orders? In doing so, the supervisor has an ability for an out, a configurable path that takes the order where necessary out of the automation logic altogether. Why would this be important and wouldn't it defeat the purpose of the estimated computed check against actual amounts to begin with? Well, for one, if the order does not correspond to the supporting contract, then it is almost automatically flagged to be pending further investigation. To lock the screen in this case would have been a redundant move and if anything, slows the necessary action needed to correct the amounts to tie back to the underlying contract. By granting this configuration ability to the non-technical managerial user, the application administrator is not exposing the ability for anyone to circumvent the screen lock process, yet provides just enough wiggle room for manual intervention by authorized parties in exceptional circumstances planned or otherwise. Like our previous example on configuring invoices to be captured by the automated bill run in Chapter 5, the option to choose is in fact a second level meta deliverable to the end user. Rather than give them what they want right away, build in or design logic that lets them choose what they would want based on different variations or permutations that arise. In this manner, backstage behavior – the criteria for the script or workflow – gets moved to the frontstage, thereby changing what it means to be front versus backstage. Imagine attending a play about Frankenstein performed in the context of Mary Shelley's own personal life. The audience gets to form their own conclusions as to the plot devices used and thus is able to observe any parallels between the author and the protagonists depicted in the novel. By delivering more than the locked screen, and instead giving selected users the ability to choose when to lock the screen, the user becomes more than a passive audience member and is, in fact, ascribed the co-authoring responsibility for determining the daily course of affairs. Thus, the final product not only supports multiple stories but in effect gives the user the ability to tell her or his side of the story, excuse or justification. Ironically, by giving the user the ability to determine just *when* to lock the screen, the entire spectrum of possible user actions is itself unlocked. Just as the history of enterprise software continues to evolve from an on-premise solution that requires technical expertise to build custom solutions to a SaaS with configurability options out of the box for non-technical users, the customization delivered using SaaS mirrors the evolution from being mere feature rich to being truly permutation rich, configuration rich in other words.

The more configuration rich the product, the more widely it can be adopted. In her study of the "travel" or portability of photoelectric lighting kits from France to Africa, engineer and sociologist Madeline Akrich would soon uncover that idealized user behavior was too tightly scripted, or otherwise inscribed into the design of the technology at hand.[31] In an attempt to ensure a "foolproof" product design, this had the unfortunate consequence of rendering it unusable precisely because there was no possibility for leeway and users were unable to locate themselves and their circumstances within the prescribed script.[32] Ironically, the same controls that were baked into the design of the lighting kits to assure of continued operability ended up becoming roadblocks to securing end user buy-in, adoption and sustained usage.[33] Clearly, here we have moved past sleeping policemen. Non-standard plugs were used to prevent people from tampering with the kits and fixed length wires were used to ensure optimal performance.[34] Yet these very "controls" created installation and maintenance difficulties in adapting the 'standardized' kits to rooms of different sizes.[35] Similarly, while watertight batteries were conceived to prevent damage to the equipment, they were not readily available for procurement outside of the capital.[36] Finally, maintenance could not be performed by local electricians, only by the same contractor who installed the kit who only visited the area only twice a year.[37] More importantly, when contrasted with small generators in use, the photoelectric lighting kits did not integrate into existing network of actors or economic relationships.[38] Bought by an administration, the generators were distributed to youth groups who in turn rented them out to villagers.[39] Unlike the enterprise systems that Berg decry that "do not travel,"[40] the generators, in contrast to the lighting kits, were inherently mobile by creating and sustaining extended networks, new actors and relations.[41] Seen from this perspective, generators were harder to replace than photoelectric lighting kits.[42] By solely focusing on the technical design or functionality as the means to increase adoption, we ignore the relationships that are defined, refined and redefined in the same way different physical components make up the generator, or, as the case may be, the photoelectric lighting kit.[43] The same can be said for a continued emphasis on SaaS capability, focusing solely on configuration and customization as means to automate processes rather than taking into account the relationships at hand. To an external observer, a financial accounting SaaS would be seen like an internet banking application of sorts, one that enables enterprises to swiftly transact and make or receive payments seamlessly from their internal general ledger to external corporate banking sites. Yet, for most implementations of accounting SaaS, the bank that an enterprise has a primary relationship is typically the last to be involved. Where emphasis may be placed on customizing check layout to get the payee names to be aligned with pre-formatted checks or adding a custom attribute and workflow to allow management to approve which vendor bills get added to the next check run, SaaS consuming enterprises often do not initiate, let alone sustain, an ongoing dialogue with their banks to improve upon the overall process of cash disbursement or receipts, so what may inevitably result are manual spreadsheets downloaded from the accounting SaaS and imported to the corporate banking sites. An emphasis on end-to-end relationships between a SaaS consuming enterprise and its bank(s) would have been on exploring ways to automate or integrate the flow of money. Depending on where the organization is in its maturity lifecycle, it may start out by printing physical checks during initial SaaS go-live, before evolving to embrace corporate procurement cards as it grows in headcount and operational complexity. When enterprise personnel actively engage with banking personnel and SaaS providers, the objectives, and associated supporting behaviors evolve from having the bank or the SaaS simply service the consuming enterprise to co-designing business processes to meet the needs of the enterprise's external constituents, customers and vendors. When an organization is the throes of implementing an iPaaS to automatically sync in customer payments received as ACH or wire formats into their accounting SaaS, enterprise personnel responsible for the SaaS need to effectively orchestrate the input from key participants from the bank, iPaaS and SaaS. Auto-generation of payments tied to existing customer invoices requires attributes to be exposed by the bank to the iPaaS and coordination of batch sizes and scheduling. The ability for payments to be associated with invoices requires that the enterprise send out customer notifications beforehand to add in invoice numbers in ACH or wire payments.

That underlying foundational constructs can themselves pose as sleeping obstacles, as opposed to policemen, to the way work is enacted, and re-enacted time and again, may not be obvious. Take a company's chart of accounts. Assume that over time that it has grown to be a rather unwieldy list; the different number sequencing in use for assets, liabilities, income, expense, cost of goods, and equity accounts are in part a reflection of varying numbering conventions adopted by different accounting personnel at different times. Viewed in and of themselves, they present opportunities for housekeeping or cleanup work if only to help improve communications and visibility among all parties. Yet, unlike the rather obvious or blatant example of photoelectric lighting kits that "do not travel" thanks to non-standard plugs, the financial reports that are developed using the SaaS and tapping into this chart of accounts do work even if the operative work is seen in a more dubious light when one starts to peer under the hood and see the swirling amount of busywork involved in having to fix these said reports every time a new account is added or existing account updated simply because there is no clear pattern in grouping a certain sequence of accounts as prepaid assets, for example, on a balance sheet. In this respect, it doesn't matter if we were using a SaaS or on-premise software; the same hindrances that render financial reports fragile or make it less forgiving from changes to the chart of accounts exist regardless. What this example illustrates is the confounding impact of variables that on the surface have nothing and, yet upon closer examination, everything to do with the software at hand. This overlooking of work that makes tools feasible is what Berg emphasizes.[44] To some extent, it starts out as a known unknown, even as over time it gets taken for granted, essentially morphing into an unknown. As Berg points out, "The technology seems to function on its own superb and universal power, while the work of meticulously creating and repairing the social and material infrastructure that makes this functioning possible ... disappears from sight."[45] Or as Star succinctly puts it and in turn referenced by Berg, "work that is done disappears into doneness."[46]

It is not hard to see similar parallels in various deployments of enterprise applications including SaaS. Consider a procurement and invoicing SaaS. With procurement, management needs to provide approval for requested spending and accounting needs to be kept in the loop to be able to accrue for expected spending. To this end, an approved purchase requisition or purchase order (PO) presents a means for management to be notified and to provide reviews, that accounting can in turn reference as authorized spending and use to "draw down" the approved amount when processing related vendor invoices. To preclude payment for unauthorized spending, the SaaS may be designed and configured such that for an invoice to be recognized as authorized spending, it needs to be associated immediately upon entry with an approved purchase requisition (PR) or PO. Already, we can anticipate potential issues. What if the approved purchase requisition or PO were not available because the stakeholders concerned did not realize they had to create one? How would accounting reconcile the vendor's payment terms – Net 30 for instance requires payment be remitted no later than 30 days after invoice receipt – with the time it takes to create and route a newly created purchase requisition for approval? What if the purchase requisition were available, just not approved as key approvers were away? Worst still, and this time revisiting our earlier example of having default values in an expense type speak more to an accountant than to an end user, what if end users had difficulty creating purchase requisitions in the first place not because they know they need to but rather because they don't know which appropriate expense types to code specific entries to? These are functionality related concerns that impinge on the SaaS user interface, but what of existing relationships within the network? What if the procurement and invoicing SaaS were introduced in a start-up environment that did not already have a well-established and communicated procurement policy as well as already identified requestors and approvers who are made aware of the spending thresholds that need to be approved? This is not to say that the SaaS and the procurement policy can't be rolled out simultaneously; in fact, the latter often provides the rationale – the whys – for pursuing the former.

But you can already tell from our simple example that to focus exclusively on the technical design or configuration of the SaaS – and, in particular, removing any leeway or looseness that participants can interpret or make concessions from the established protocol – while neglecting the greater control environment both within and outside the enterprise – can lead to inevitable roadblocks in distribution, buy-in and adoption. Default settings when relied upon carte blanche become habitual patterns that users rely upon, even if their utility morphs over time. We discussed the taken-granted-for-granted default categories in an expense report or purchase requisition, but consider approval limits that support tiered approval routing so that a transaction over and above a specific amount gets routed to another pair of eyes for review. While baselined as an automated control from an audit approach, over time it nonetheless becomes a known unknown in terms of how truly effective it is in securing validation of appropriate company spend. While not defaulted out of the box in the SaaS and thus having to be configured by customers, it nevertheless becomes a defaulted application control to be relied upon. The question becomes how often do we verify what truly happens? Do users break up the same spending into smaller-sized amounts and submit these so that a secondary approver would not be notified? Or instead of routing these through the procurement management application, do they submit these as expenses to route through a different SaaS altogether? These questions and more explore how an unquestioning reliance on default configurations on the part of users can in turn lead to a questioning of our default settings, our very own proclivities in turning a blind eye to whatever has been put in place at a point in time even if the value provided has long outlasted its stint. A SaaS's configuration may become a known unknown over time, especially if key personnel involved have changed, but the bigger known unknowns are our very own hardwired behavioral patterns.

Akrich calls attention to efforts that characterize social control, an attempt to "groom the user" as she puts it.[47] Note the parallels with grooming the backlog, a phrase to be adopted and heavily circulated by the Scrum or Agile methodology years later. Take the batteries in the photoelectric circuits. To keep the battery charged at an optimum level, the designers required that a generator be installed that cuts the current to users if the charge is too low, or conversely when the charge gets too high, if only to isolate the photoelectric panel to prevent damage to the photoelectric cell.[48] What ultimately ensued, however, was unanticipated by the designers. When the current was cut off in the evenings, users annoyed with interruption to their television programs would telephone the electrician each time.[49] The electrician, weary of making numerous trips, installed a fuse that allowed users to bypass the current shutoff long enough for him to delay his arrival until the following morning.[50] Such workarounds are commonplace in the employment of enterprise systems, and SaaS is not immune. Likewise, an organic proliferation of differently sequenced chart of accounts can lead to busywork that goes on behind the scenes to prop up frail or fragile reports that left alone would break at the first signs of change. An update to an account is not made only at one place but over and over compounded by the number of reports that contain the account. Because the account itself cannot be updated once transactions have been logged, it is next to impossible to replace the numbering or account type assigned if only to better streamline the way the chart of accounts and key financial reports are designed, thus the organization is caught in a self-fulfilling loop of fixing symptoms and never really getting to the root cause of addressing varied account configurations.

Returning to our procurement and invoicing example, it is not difficult to imagine a scenario where the accounting team intervenes each time an invoice is received and cannot be matched with an existing approved purchase requisition or PO. Rather than reach out to end users, wait for them to create purchase requisitions, entertain questions about expense types before having the purchase requisitions route through various tiers of approval, an accounting clerk, much like the electrician, may attempt his own fuse. He may create the purchase requisition on behalf of the end user and solicit email approvals outside of the SaaS. Doing so cuts down on the amount of time it would take to have an approved purchase requisition or PO in hand to process the vendor invoice that is due but also to complete booking all accounts payable entries in time for month end financial close. Perhaps instead of expending effort to "groom the user," the same effort can be expended in "grooming" the foundational constructs, whether that is having standard plugs rather than non-standard ones for photoelectric circuits, carefully sequenced accounts with anticipated wiggle room or buffer for new ones that do not have spillover impact on existing financial reports as the criteria for the results holds true despite a change each time, or setting up unequivocal commonsensical expense types coupled with periodic refresher training to equip end users to make the right choices the first time when creating purchase requisitions without tapping into the shadow support of delegates.

We reviewed earlier the convergence or divergence of multiple user stories, but much more can be said about how when user stories are solicited and added to the product backlog, even here all too often it's the admin or accounting user's worldview rather than a layman user unaccustomed to the accrual accounting, cost centers or capitalized assets versus operating expenses. In observing academic end users' ongoing reliance on administrative staff while interacting with a self-service travel management solution, researchers Arminen and Poikus observed that because the software was developed with the university administrators in mind, end users became confused by and consequently frustrated with the resulting user interface.[51] Originally conceived as part of a centralized administrative project that aimed to achieve 12% savings in fiscal spending, the web-based application took away paper submissions and integrated what used to be distinct processes in travel proposal and claim submission.[52] Contrary to the promise of ease of use, end users ended up having to "learn" the administrator's way.[53] Default values that appeared, for instance, were more directed at the administrative end-user rather than the non-administrative one. Going back to our expense management SaaS, it is not hard to see how default expense categories, such as software license, computer hardware and computer accessories, mean more to an accountant than a layman user. To the non-administrative user, a question may be: why aren't the categories more generic and thus usable, one that is labeled technology rather than granular distinctions between software license and computer hardware or hardware and accessories. To the administrative user or accountant, these differentiations make a difference as to whether the expense ends up on the balance sheet or the income statement, as well as how it is accounted for, whether depreciated over the course of its useful life or expensed all at once. Stories from layman users get relegated to the back stage; occasionally they are surfaced when a user asks what the difference is between capital asset versus professional service expense types, or groups all travel expenses in the travel and accommodation category versus breaking them out by airfare, ground transportation, meals and such. Just as elements of what used to be deemed back-stage behavior, the ability to configure or modify query criteria is presently considered front stage. The plethora of self-service tools, such as procurement or expense mobile apps that essentially lets users create their own expenses or templates of their own expenses and submit these themselves rather than rely on clerical administrative staff like before, shows just how entrenched most if not all users have become to the accounting worldview. By "up-sourcing" the administrative functions from the administratThis mirrors what Timmermans and Berg observe in their research on the adoption of medical protocols; rather than captureive or accounting personnel to end users, the SaaS displaces the inter-dynamics among actants, to employ Latour, in its network. Mandatory fields in the expense entry force end users to enter complete information or upload supporting documentation such as receipts; this is an improvement over a manual form, but downstream intervention from administrative personnel may still be warranted to validate the expense codes selected. What used to be entirely performed by administrative staff – checking for completeness of information, expense classification and such, gets redistributed with the introduction of the SaaS – doesn't simply go away, as the marketing around SaaS would like us to believe.

This mirrors what Timmermans and Berg observe in their research on the adoption of medical protocols; rather than capture the expertise or deplete existing skills, these are merely shifted to a different plane.[54] More importantly, for the expense management SaaS to function effectively, it needs to bridge existing trajectories of various actants with desired goals or objectives. Default values in a dropdown list belonging to a mandatory field, for instance, may display expense names in everyday language such as Meals or Transportation without revealing the accounting-speak beneath, related general ledger accounts. Similarly, a project or event field may be created for use in cost allocations rather than have end users remember to redistribute individual line entries to a specific cost center each time. The workflow of having accounting approve each expense report in addition to the expense approver or supervisor also taps into familiar, longstanding relationships among existing actants. Despite the intervention of SaaS, it still allows for end users to enlist the assistance of administrative or accounting personnel in repair work. Rather than view this as a shortcoming, especially since it did not remove the need for an administrative function, it nevertheless evolves the administrative or accounting role from mass processing to exception reviewing and advisory. Or take Concur, an expense management SaaS that provides a mobile app, ExpenseIt, that lets users snap pictures of their receipts using their mobile phone and auto-generate expense entries with pre-populated key fields such as vendor, date and amount based on optical character resolution (OCR) technology. In this instance, end user manual entry has been further "up-sourced." This doesn't mean that the end user, expense or accounting approver goes away, only that certain tasks such as data entry become obsolete giving way to more time and resource on validations and approvals.

In exploring the design of the expense management SaaS, we asked who is targeted or, perhaps more pointedly, scripted: the non-administrative user or the administrative one? In circling back to configuration versus feature rich functionalities, perhaps the more pertinent question to ask is how much flexibility, leeway or looseness does the SaaS grant varied participants, whether administrative or non-administrative, in forming their own interpretations or deviating from the prescribed script in a manner that does not render the SaaS unusable and yet still in alignment with their individual objectives and ensuing trajectories whether that be timely expense reimbursement, complete accrual capture, appropriate department cost allocation or proper financial recording. Out-of-the-box reporting capability on un-submitted expenses, for instance, give accounting personnel the ability to accrue for expenses more completely while giving some level of flexibility to end users when delinquent in responding to expense submission deadlines. When devising internal controls for transactions entered and processed using the SaaS, we are really finding ways for users to "repair each others' interpretations of, or deviations from, the protocol."[55] If the SaaS functionality allowed for accounting personnel to review all expense reports approved by supervisors, and sent these back where necessary to end users to make necessary corrections, this would reduce the possibility of incorrectly entered expense codes or incomplete receipts. Leeway here is taken to mean the ability to "adjust the protocol to unforeseen events and repair unworkable prescriptions." It is "a prerequisite to the protocol's functioning," Timmermans and Berg claim where, "the overall stability of the network is at the same time challenged and dependent upon the instabilities within its configuration."[56]

The French phenomenological philosopher, Maurice Merleau-Ponty, asks us to imagine a blind man navigating a city street with a cane. No longer perceived as "an object for him" as well as "for itself," the blind man not only interacts with other objects in his environment using his cane, but he also learns to perceive his environment through the cane.[57] In other words, in addition to extending his range of actions, the blind man's cane has been incorporated as a way of perceiving the world. When it comes to devising internal controls for SaaS, we are like Merleau-Ponty's blind man feeling our way in the dark even if our range of motion, not to mention perspective, is constrained by the design of the cane. If forgiveness from Chapter 7 is about undoing what is done, fragility is about being open to new, different ways not just of doing but of seeing. More than front versus back stage, fragility speaks to the courage to detach ourselves from the scene of the crime, step off the stage or outside the screen and cross over to the side of the audience. The dichotomy between front and back stage is itself misleading just as manual intervention nonetheless vanishes into automated-ness. Control work is less about attaining no exceptions as it is about developing a tolerance (and knack) for handling exceptions. This requires us to drop our old attachment and release the act. When we do, we realize that it is the very notion of internal controls that we cling to that precludes us from putting in place the controls that truly make a difference. Like the blind man's cane described by Merleau-Ponty, Marshall McLuhan defines a medium "as any extension of ourselves," an "outering" of our senses.[58] Contrast this with the content in Chapter 7, where the prerequisite to knowing things is to know ourselves. Here the argument is: to know things is to extend knowledge beyond ourselves albeit in a way that is circumscribed by the nature of the tool at hand. Is the human mind constituted by the very tools at its disposal? Less well known than McLuhan's "the medium is the message"[59] is perhaps Neil Postman's "the medium is the metaphor" in which he argues that each medium – whether it is print, television or as in our case, software – orients the way we experience the world, "sequence it, frame it, enlarge it, reduce it, color it."[60] Postman himself posits, "Where do our notions of mind come from if not from metaphors generated by our tools?"[61] A co-worker responds that she does not have the bandwidth to take on a project – our project perhaps and would you mind not taking it personally? Where elsewhere would have referred to network capacity, a pre-requisite for cloud applications, bandwidth here can and does refer to availability of time, which oddly enough is itself a product of the clock. The blind man's cane is a way of feeling out what is out there, but what is perceived is at the same time confined to the design of the cane. Presumably, he is aware of this and would have already made the necessary adjustments in his daily habitual routines. Not merely feature-rich, a configuration-rich SaaS would ideally let the user configure it to meet her needs at the right time rather than make manual adjustments to abide by its limited world (and arguably developer or administrative user world) view.

Jaron Lanier highlights the lock-in phenomenon.[62] He traces how MIDI, invented in the early 1980s to represent musical notes, has nonetheless become the de facto foundation upon which popular music is built, in software and devices not least your mobile phone.[63] In the same vein, in *Sorting Things Out: Classification and Its Consequences*, Bowker and Star describe how classification orders human interaction through a cloak of invisibility.[64] The mobile app, for instance, is programmed by software developers with worldviews that may not be entirely aligned with that of an account receivables clerk. Folks change, move around – so it is not out of the blue for a customer contact to have multiple email addresses – whatever it takes for the invoice to be routed to the hands of the right person who is able to review against service rendered or item received and authorize payment. But when developers design software for customers to have key identifiers, such as unique email addresses and furthermore designate these as primary keys that differentiate one customer record from the next in a database table, it becomes difficult to associate more than one unique email address for the same customer. This become important when sending out invoices: it would help to send them to multiple email addresses, not only the service recipient to verify that the service has indeed been rendered but also the customer's accounts payable team, the project manager in charge of the purchase requisition and so on. When leads are first identified and pursued in a sales opportunity lifecycle, multiple leads with different email addresses that belong to the same customer institution or company nevertheless get sifted into multiple customer records with the same bill to or ship to addresses because of lock-in, the manner each customer needs to be identified by one and only one unique email address. We can only imagine the reporting challenges that ensue when the company needs to report on the actual number of unique customers it has – customer concentration is a key metric in financial disclosures – as opposed to relying on multiple instantiations of the same customer maintained in the software. To what extent can the script be rewritten if the very conceptual construct of a customer were itself configurable so that more than one email address can be associated? Alternatively, can multiple contacts with associated emails be associated with the same customer? Imagine if a new customer contact were to sign up for a new service on the company's website; how does one figure out that the contact already belonged to an existing record already set up in a "backend" financial SaaS, and that the new customer signup instead of creating a whole new customer altogether elects to create a new contact instead to associate with the existing customer? On the other hand, others are of the opinion that a new software implementation almost always imposes, and in a good way, uniqueness among different records, so that an email address is used in place of a manually assigned identifier, itself a conglomeration of names and pre-assigned numbers cobbled together with spit and fire. Thus, reality is much more nuanced once we factor in both the costs and benefits of a system imbued worldview.

Yet, much of automation associated with SaaS has thus far emphasized the speed or rate of capture, whether it is prospect solicitation, new customer signup or existing customer upsell. One can argue that this is a relatively simple task, and the more complex task that lies ahead is the reconciliation of seemingly disparate elements of data with one another to form a coherent whole. So, like in Chapter 7 where we find chaos within controls, here we find unknowns lurking amongst knowns. Fragility and forgiveness are constructs that apply: by posing the necessary impediments either before or after a change or series of changes have been made, or inappropriate action or actions taken, sleeping policemen redirect user behavior back to the main path. Hotel keys when configured as a pattern in the SaaS at hand follow the same pattern. Because they blend or interweave into everyday use, they become inconspicuous artifacts that over time help to render the SaaS less fragile. Insofar as forgiveness entails a dispelling of illusions or uncertainty, having subtle controls such as audit trails, in a way that mirror daily Agile stand-ups, reporting on the actions taken, what, when and by whom serve as a foundation for making explicit what used to be implicit and thus susceptible to misinterpretation. After all, intent is paramount. Ill or worse malicious intent to wreck damage or bring about reputational harm is blatantly unjust and wrong, but most of the time, it is almost always little acts of omissions, slips or unintentional errors that go undetected, and over time accrue to become a ticking time bomb. In this sense, subtle controls that bring visibility to aid forgiveness ultimately circle back to improve the resiliency of the SaaS to combat possible insults to architectural and transactional integrity. If automation is possible by setting aside the space for creative addressing of organizational needs, such as the unique attributes that make up a customer, in short, recognizing the unknown within the known, then information, or informating, is possible by tapping into the known, such as audit trails where available.

Not all errors are forgivable nor can all mistakes be easily unwound. Public markets have been less forgiving of public companies that have had to restate their financials either through an omission, error or overall failure of internal controls. It becomes imperative that little acts of recognizing the unknown, in what appears certain and unwavering, are performed each day. This repair work is in effect what is needed ahead of time, in addition to new initiatives or enhancements. In other words, the mundane keep-the-lights on projects or technical debt nevertheless belong to the must-haves as opposed to the nice-haves that tend to get attention and fanfare. The former invite us on a journey to resolve underlying root causes that in turn drive the surface symptoms characterized by the latter. For as we dig deeper into the dichotomy between front and backstage work or behaviors, even as we start to entice backstage work to come on stage if only to expose what may be awry, it remains backstage work from the perspective of having to perform internal repair prior to publishing the numbers publicly in a 10-K or 10-Q. Indeed, the risk factors section of the quarterly or annual financials recognize this implicit need to articulate known unknowns that may sway the numbers. As an example, you may find the following verbiage, "Foreign currency exchange rates and fluctuations could have an adverse impact on our future costs or on future profits and cash flows from our international operations." This is because as part of period close, general ledger account balances in foreign currencies need to be revalued using different exchange rate types (current, historical or average). Recall our discussion on realized and unrealized gain or loss in Chapter 4. As an example, profit and loss accounts are valued using the monthly

average rate creating entries in unrealized gain or loss. As part of closing procedures, the accounting SaaS can be used to compute the average rate but other
compensating controls, such as month over month variance reviews, can also
serve as sleeping policemen to check for any large unanticipated swings. Thus,
even though variance reviews serve to shine the stage light on average rate computation, this set of activities nonetheless remains backstage behavior to the eyes
of public investors and regulatory agencies.

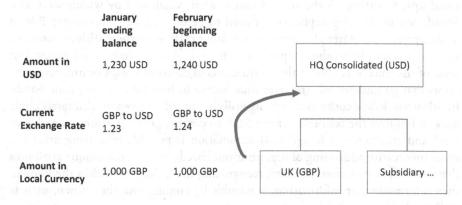

	January ending balance	February beginning balance	
Amount in USD	1,230 USD	1,240 USD	HQ Consolidated (USD)
Current Exchange Rate	GBP to USD 1.23	GBP to USD 1.24	
Amount in Local Currency	1,000 GBP	1,000 GBP	UK (GBP) Subsidiary ...

Another example is the consolidated current rate used to revalue each month's
balance sheet accounts, so that the same historical transactions nonetheless get
revalued using the new monthly current rate. From a consolidated perspective, the
ending USD balance for a specific balance account may differ slightly from its
opening USD balance in the following month because of the different consolidated foreign currency-to-USD current rates employed even if the ending balance
and opening balance stay the same in the local currency. In our previous example,
this applies to all historical transactions recorded in a local and foreign currency
in a foreign subsidiary up through January and February. In this iteration, the
palindrome pattern betrays a sliver of disruption; because the balance sheet aggre-
gates transactions up through a specific point in time whether January or February,
all prior transactions nonetheless get revalued when rolled up to the consolidated
USD subsidiary to a different consolidated current rate applicable each month. The
February opening balance is recorded at 10 USD above the ending balance from
the prior month because of the difference in January and February consolidated
current rates applied. In this respect, the changing consolidated current rate is a
known unknown. But when we slice in from a SaaS administrative or maintenance
perspective, the question arises: is one able to arrive at the 10 USD difference by
running a currency translation adjustment (CTA) report, or does one need to
manually reperform the calculations to arrive at the opening balance for February?
The latter points to back-stage behavior that the accounting SaaS at hand hasn't
quite yet rendered frontstage or visible. Thus, when one speaks of back versus

front-stage behavior or work, it matters where one is standing: the same behavior or set of behaviors that appears back stage for one may be front stage for another. Our review of SaaS configuration and possibilities of compensating controls to some extent increases the visibility and thus degree of frontstage behavior before varied internal stakeholders. Yet, as we dig deeper, there are specific backstage computations that the SaaS at hand can in turn mask, presenting unique challenges from a system audit not to mention palindrome end-to-end perspective.

	Interest Rate of 6%	Interest Rate of 25%
Net Present Value	$\dfrac{10{,}000}{(1+0.06)^5}$	$\dfrac{10{,}000}{(1+0.25)^5}$
Revenue Recognized Upfront	= 7,473	= 3,277
Interest Revenue Over Life of Lease (5 years)	10,000 − 7,473 = 2,527	10,000 − 3,277 = 6,723

Rates, in particular, merit careful attention. An SEC investigation into Xerox's earnings from 1997 through 1999 for instance revealed ludicrously low discount rates used to compute lease revenue. The earlier example illustrates how discount rates matter in the amount of upfront revenue recognized. As you can see, the lower the discount rate, the higher the amount of revenue recognized upfront. As a result of using low discount rates, Xerox managed to pull "forward nearly $3.1 billion in equipment revenue and pre-tax earnings of $717 million from 1997 through 2000."[65] In Brazil, the low discount rates used were especially "absurd" especially since "Xerox's own average local borrowing rate in Brazil, which always exceeded 25% before the final months of 1999."[66] In yet another riff on the known unknowns, neither Xerox's management nor its external auditor validated the application of these discount rates effected through "top-side" adjustments in its accounting system.[67]

The earlier two examples, unrealized gain/loss and lease revenue, relate to actual numbers but known unknowns can be just as easily applied to forecasts. Take revenue forecasts, keyed off future invoices expected from sales orders. In our example, assume that a one-year sales order of $120 has a semi-annual billing frequency so that two invoices are expected from this one sales order. Assume that the first bill has already been invoiced so that presently only one more invoice is expected. The following is a revenue recognition schedule associated with the future invoice, in inversion of the amortization schedule from Chapter 4.

Revenue Recognition Schedule

Created From	Invoice #2
Start Date	January 7, 2017
End Date	December 31, 2017
Originating Account	Deferred Revenue
Total Schedule Amount	$60.00

Account	Period	Amount	Total Recognized
Revenue	July 2017	$10.00	$70.00
Revenue	August 2017	$10.00	$80.00
Revenue	September 2017	$10.00	$90.00
Revenue	October 2017	$10.00	$100.00
Revenue	November 2017	$10.00	$110.00
Revenue	December 2017	$10.00	$120.00

Note that the second invoice totals $60 instead of the full sales order amount of $120 since the first bill has already been issued to the customer. The known unknown here is: is the SaaS at hand able to report the billing forecast over the remainder half of the year from July through December 2017 even though the invoice has yet to be generated? Or can the SaaS only report the remainder future expected amount of $60 against a sales order of the full year duration of 2017 instead of the second half only? Put differently, how capable is the SaaS at hand in reporting forecasts, known unknowns, so that we not only are able to report numbers accurately in providing guidance to Wall Street in the case of public companies, but also more fundamentally we are able to make strategic and operational decisions based on expected future growth?

Sleeping policemen, hotel keys, blind man's cane. In a variation of Latour's oft-quoted "society is technology made durable" slogan,[68] Steve Woolgar views technology as "governance and accountability made durable."[69] With SaaS being configurable – much like the putting on and presumably taking off of eyebrows – is there a remote possibility that governance and accountability can be configurable as well? To the extent that governance and accountability are configurable, to what extent can we question and revise our notions of them? In studying and describing his patient, 19-year old Agnes who was raised as a boy and underwent a sex transition operation, Garfinkel writes that the "natural normal female" was something Agnes aspired to attain.[70] Yet, as pointed by Armitage in her analysis of Garfinkel's work, and drawing on Smith, Garfinkel attempted to reflect Agnes as a "natural normal" female right from the start.[71] Garfinkel describes Agnes as "typical of a girl of her class and age… There was nothing garish or exhibitionistic… occasional lisp similar to that effected by feminine appearing male homosexuals."[72] Consequently, as Armitage points out, "we are left to presume that Agnes' lisp was natural while effeminate homosexuals effect a lisp."[73] Armitage highlights Smith's ideological circle, itself reminiscent of Michael Power's critique of audit as a loop unto itself.

> *An interpretive schema is used to assemble and provide coherence for an array of particulars as an account of what actually happened; the particulars thus assembled, will intend, and be interpretable by, the schema used to assemble them. The effect is peculiarly circular, for although questions of truth and falsity, accuracy and inaccuracy about the particulars may be raised, the schema in itself is not called into question as a method of providing for coherence of the collection of particulars as a whole.*[74]

With an ideological circle or loop, one runs the risk of leaving default configurations whether that be automated controls in SaaS or mental constructs or inclinations in humans unexamined. As discussed earlier, default configurations such as purchase requisition approval levels over time take on a life of their own, so whether they continue to support proactive and preventive reviews of company spending become questionable. The loop unto itself – audit's perspective of validating that tiered approval levels exist and that the SaaS at hand in turn routes transactions for tiered approvals – continues unabated, so that like putting on eyebrows, it becomes a performance in and of itself. It is a behavioral pattern borne more out of habit than need, the way one becomes accustomed with a specific routine in everyday affairs, and the looks of alarm at even the slightest hint of change.

Controls ≠ outcomes? A fear of technology imposing constraints that in turn circumscribes the range of otherwise available possibilities lies at the heart of the recent wave of self-professed digital dissenters. Calling themselves techno-skeptics or humanists, they recall Luddites, nineteenth century textile workers who rebelled against the Industrial revolution by breaking machines. Today, perhaps a different though no less important rebellion may well reside in breaking the circular schema in effect. Not just through continuous integration of new code into the existing one, but also in the daily act of smashing the front versus backstage dichotomies we have grown used to. The idea that once SaaS is signed, sealed and delivered, it cannot be undone. Or how about the prevailing schema I've employed in this book thus far: that SaaS is configurable for non-technical layman users? To some extent, this may hold true for some SaaS that is configuration-rich and not so much for others that tends to be more feature rather than configuration rich. In addition, when holding the SaaS constant, this may apply to some SaaS client enterprises more than others. Depending on existing workloads and degree of familiarity of users to SaaS versus on-premise software, some users may require more assistance than others when it comes to menu navigation on the one hand or on the other hand, having been accustomed to monolithic ERP packages, expecting an out-of-the-box segregation of duties analyzer, and a sophisticated one at that, or already pre-configured access roles. These impressions can be dangerous insofar as they lead to an underestimation of the time and resources needed to optimize Day 2 SaaS usage. Put simply, how about the schema that, at any point in time, there can only be one official account? In some ways, forgiveness is possible only by recognizing that there can be more than one account, that having one and only one account however officiated is inherently fragile. The putting on or taking off of eyebrows speak to the ability to configure, change course and unwind, a daily reminder of the intrinsic frailty of accounts, and of the eventide of life.

Exercise 8.1

Consider the following stories we tell ourselves:

1. For all user needs to be met, we need to document them completely before starting SaaS configuration work.
2. As a collections clerk, I need to know when customers are past 90 days due so that I can reach out to their sales rep to find out of what's going on.
3. As an auditor, I would like to be informed if key configurations have been updated.

What are some of the hidden assumptions, biases or stories behind these stories? How can we deepen these stories? Conversely, how do these stories engender other stories?

Discussion

For the first story, to what extent are we assuming that all needs can be identified beforehand? To what extent do needs get clarified from the back-and-forth clarifications based on seeing a working prototype? Also, have different stakeholders from different functions been involved? For the second story, are we assuming that

90 days past due customers are already receiving dunning notifications? Are we also assuming that payment terms for the same customer do not vary by type and amount of sale? For the third story, are we assuming that audit trails are available for configuration changes in addition to transaction or master data changes? For all these stories and more, to what extent are we not exploring farther by asking so what? What can go wrong if none of these needs are met? Are there compensating controls or measures? If a 90-day past due customer is up for contract renewal, would the sales rep have already reached out proactively? As we dig deeper, we find stories of stories.

Exercise 8.2

Give an example of a SaaS configuration that mirrors:

1. Sleeping Policeman
2. Hotel Key
3. Blind Man's cane

For each of the earlier, explain how it can help or hurt the way we devise controls.

Discussion

When attempting to demo the creation of a sales order in my *Accounting Information Systems* class, one of the students had problems creating the same transaction. It turned out that I was performing the same action in her account instance, and because I went ahead and saved it each time before she did, she kept encountering the system error message prompting her to save the same transaction with a different unique number to prevent duplicates. In this example, the check for duplicate transaction numbers serves as a sleeping policeman. There are other examples that lean towards a more positive encouragement of ideal behavior, such as accumulation of points when selecting the lowest cost airline in an expense management SaaS, a gaming approach that is a riff of Latour's hotel key. Finally, with the blind man's cane, the inner biases that a SaaS brings to the table such as associating only a purchase requisition with only one vendor as opposed to a project with multiple vendors, both simplifies and constrains the range of possibilities of how SaaS can help us record or process transactions more consistently or efficiently.

Exercise 8.3

Does each of the following resemble back stage or front stage behavior:

1. A configuration change released to selected users in production
2. Back and forth discussions on changes to initial requirements
3. Audit findings on areas of improvement

For each of your answers, which perspective are you coming from?

Discussion

When a production change affects only one or a couple of users, is it still a change to be audited for production impact? Or is it merely intentional, a test mode of sorts before it gets released to all users? The perspective of back versus frontstage behavior helps us clarify the array of options we have at our disposal in testing out varied scenarios if only to arrive at less fragile and more forgiving outcomes. Contrast this with an insistence on a tighter segregation between production and development. How likely would we experiment if only to arrive at a more resilient solution? In *Transparent*, a TV series that explores gender and societal pressures, a character played by Angelica Houston utters, "I'm NATO, not attached to outcomes." The ability to respond to changes to requirements or audit findings depends on our ability to be NATO, which ironically enough leads to experimentation, a trying out of new ways that might just end up serving up stronger sleeping policemen, hotel keys and blind man's canes.

Endnotes

1. Laozi and Mitchell, S. (1988). *Tao Te Ching: A New English Version*. New York: Harper & Row.
2. Goffman, E. (1959). *The Presentation of Self in Everyday Life*. New York: Anchor Books.
3. Shelley, M. W. and Butler, M. (1994). *Frankenstein, or, The Modern Prometheus: The 1818 Text*. Oxford, UK: Oxford University Press.
4. Ibid.
5. Brand, S. (1994). *How Buildings Learn: What Happens After They're Built*. New York: Viking.
6. Goffman, E. *The Presentation of Self in Everyday Life*.
7. Sharwood, S. (October 12, 2017). Workday says it's got a PaaS in its pocket and is ready to party. The Register. https://www.theregister.co.uk/2017/10/12/workday_paas/
8. Sinai, J. (March 30, 2015). Salesforce named a leader in Gartner's aPaaS magic quadrant. Salesforce Blog. https://www.salesforce.com/blog/2015/03/salesforce-named-a-leader-in-gartners-apaas-magic-quadrant.html
9. Ibid.
10. Williams, R. and Pollock, N. (December 6, 2008). *Software and Organizations: The Biography of the Enterprise-Wide System or How SAP Conquered the World*. London, UK: Routledge.
11. Lewis, A. (April 26, 2011). When computer programming was 'women's work'. *The Washington Post*. https://www.washingtonpost.com/opinions/when-computer-programming-was-womens-work/2011/08/24/gIQAdixGgJ_story.html?utm_term=.c53d7b951569
12. Schmaus, B. (August 14, 2013). Deploying the Netflix API, The Netflix Tech Blog, https://medium.com/netflix-techblog/deploying-the-netflix-api-79b6176cc3f0
13. Ibid.
14. Williams, R. and Pollock, N. *Software and Organizations: The Biography of the Enterprise-Wide System or How SAP Conquered the World*.
15. Latour, B. (1994). On technical mediation–Philosophy, sociology, genealogy. *Common Knowledge*, 3(2), 29–64.

16 Ibid.
17 Ibid.
18 Ibid.
19 Latour, B. (May 9, 2014). Technology is society made durable. *The Sociological Review*, 38(1), 103–131.
20 Ibid.
21 Latour, B. (1996). On actor-network theory: A few clarifications. *Soziale Welt*, 369–381.
22 Harway, D. J. *The Haraway Reader*.
23 Lidwell, W., Holden, K., Butler, J., and Elam, K. (2010). *Universal Principles of Design: 125 Ways to Enhance Usability, Influence Perception, Increase Appeal, Make Better Design Decisions, and Teach Through Design*. Beverly, MA: Rockport Publishers.
24 Ibid.
25 Ibid.
26 Zuboff, S. (September 1985). Automate/informate: The two faces of intelligent technology. *Organizational Dynamics*, 14(2), 5–18.
27 Takeuchi, H. and Ikujiro, N. (January–February 1986). The new product development game. *Harvard Business Review*, 64(1), 321.
28 Garfinkel, H. (2002). *Ethnomethodology's Program*. Lanham, MD: Rowman and Littlefield.
29 Takeuchi, H. and Ikujiro, N. The New product development game.
30 Ibid.
31 Akrich, M. (1992). The de-scription of technical objects. In J. Law and W. E. Bijker (Eds.) *Shaping Technology/Building Society: Studies in Sociotechnical Change*. Cambridge, MA: MIT Press, pp. 205–224.
32 Ibid.
33 Ibid.
34 Ibid.
35 Ibid.
36 Ibid.
37 Ibid.
38 Ibid.
39 Ibid.
40 Berg, M. (1997). *Rationalizing Medical Work: Decision-Support Techniques and Medical Practices*. Cambridge, MA: MIT Press.
41 Ibid.
42 Ibid.
43 Ibid.
44 Ibid.
45 Ibid.
46 Star, S. L. (1995). Epilogue: Work and practice in social studies of science, medicine, and technology. *Science, Technology, & Human Values*, 20(4), 501–507.
47 Akrich, M. The de-scription of technical objects.
48 Ibid.
49 Ibid.
50 Ibid.
51 Arminen, I. and Poikus, P. (June 2009). Diagnostic reasoning in the use of travel management system. *Computer Supported Cooperative Work (CSCW)*, 18(2–3), 251–276.

52 Ibid.

53 Ibid.

54 Timmermans, S. and Berg, M. (April 1997). Standardization in action: Achieving local universality through medical protocols. *Social Studies of Science*, 27, 273–305.

55 Ibid.

56 Ibid.

57 Merleau-Ponty, M. (1962/1945). *Phenomenology of Perception*. C. Smith (trans.). New York and London: Routledge. Originally published in French as *Phénoménologie de la Perception*.

58 McLuhan, M. (1964). *Understanding Media: The Extensions of Man*. New York: New American Library.

59 Ibid.

60 Postman, N. (1986). *Amusing Ourselves to Death: Public Discourse in the Age of Show Business*. New York: Penguin Books.

61 Ibid.

62 Lanier, J. (2011). *You Are Not a Gadget: A Manifesto*.

63 Ibid.

64 Bowker, G. C. and Star, S. L. (1999). *Sorting Things Out: Classification and Its Consequences*. Cambridge, MA: MIT Press.

65 Securities Exchange Commission. (April 11, 2002). Plantiff vs. Xerox Corporation. Civil Action No. Defendant Civil Action No. 02-272789 (DLC). https://www.sec.gov/litigation/complaints/complr17465.htm

66 Ibid.

67 Ibid.

68 Latour, B. (May 9, 2014). Technology is society made durable. *The Sociological Review*, 38(1), 103–131.

69 Woolgar, S. and Neyland, D. (2013). *Mundane Governance: Ontology and Accountability*. Oxford, New York: Oxford University Press.

70 Garfinkel, H. (1967). *Studies in Ethnomethodology*. Englewood Cliffs, NJ: Prentice Hall.

71 Ibid.

72 Ibid.

73 Armitage, L. K. (April 29, 2001). Truth, falsity, and schemas of presentation: A textual analysis of Harold Garfinkel's story of agnes. *Electronic Journal of Human Sexuality*, 4. http://www.ejhs.org/volume4/agnes.htm

74 Smith, D. E. (1990). *Texts, Facts, and Femininity: Exploring the Relations of Ruling*. New York: Routledge.

Chapter 9

Lost and Found

A feature of the human predicament...

that we labour under whenever we seek to

regulate... is our relative ignorance of fact [and] our

relative indeterminancy of aim.[1]

H. L. A. Hart

When all was said and done, as much as $100 billion in revenue reported by energy giant Enron was attributed to institutionalized accounting fraud. In response to Enron and other corporate and accounting failures in the telecommunications, cable, and energy industries, the Sarbanes–Oxley Act (SOX) was passed by the U.S. Congress in 2002. At 168 words, Section 404 of SOX provides curiously little guidance on how publicly traded companies would go about devising or calibrating internal controls for financial reporting. Instead, companies turned to audit firms for assistance, of which one of their own, Arthur Anderson, went asunder after being indicted for obstructing justice in shredding documents pertaining to their audit of Enron. Understandably, when advising clients on matters of control documentation, audit firms redoubled their efforts in attention to detail, partly to curtail litigation risk, and partly to bolster themselves for inspections by the Public Company Accounting Oversight Board (PCAOB), a nonprofit corporation also established by SOX. In 2004, the first year of SOX compliance, PCAOB put out Auditing Standard 2 (AS 2), which the Securities Exchange Commission in turn blessed as a guide for implementing 404. At 161 pages, AS 2 was more voluminous than 404, though no clearer, itself chock full of control-speak that would have appealed more to the audit profession. It was also in 2004 that I left a Big Four audit firm to assume the reins of SOX compliance for a publicly traded biotech company with dotted line reporting to the audit committee, a mandate of SOX. I experienced firsthand the pressure to bridge efforts across different internal constituents as well as with external requirements that were nebulous at best. As it turns out, we were not alone. The initial cost to comply with SOX was staggering: pegged at anywhere from $1.6 to $4.4 million per company, a disproportionate amount remained borne by smaller public companies.[2] This amount would reduce with the passage of time, as well as with the Dodd-Frank Act of 2010 and the JOBS Act of 2012, which, among other provisions, grants newly public emerging growth companies as many as 5 years to phase in auditor attestations of internal controls as part of 404. AS 2 would in turn be superseded by Auditing Standard 5 (AS 5), PCOAB's response to reduce costs for smaller public companies.

Like my peers, I sought to automate compliance to reduce costs with each passing year. Manual controls on transaction processing are usual suspects when it comes to automation. Where possible, approvals are routed within the financial application to approvers with the right level of approval authority. Where necessary, reminders are configured for unapproved transactions stuck in a queue. Updates to already approved transactions are re-circulated for approval. When it comes to validating this control, we can view the approval levels set up within the software and trace a transaction through its approval lifecycle, noting impact to the general ledger only upon approval and review. Had this control been manual, auditors would perform what's called substantive testing: making a judgmental selection of transactions to evidence for approvals. Insofar as the approval levels and approval functionality remains unchanged, this automated control would be benchmarked and not tested in the following year. Other efforts to reduce the cost of compliance revolve around automating compliance activities. The review of internal controls with control owners, the update of flowcharts, the identification of key, as well as any secondary or compensating controls, the distribution of testing at various junctures during the year with sufficient buffer built in for remediation testing of exceptions uncovered, the reporting and analysis of test results – all this, to a large degree, can be facilitated by a governance, risk, and compliance (GRC) application. Just as controls over the accuracy and validity of transactions are automated through a financial software, controls over how a compliance program is executed can be automated in a GRC tool.

In addition to audit committees, SOX also requires companies to establish procedures for employees to file internal whistleblower complaints, as well as procedures to protect the confidentiality of employees who file such concerns. Thus, another approach aimed at automating compliance lay in deploying a web-based tool that lets employees submit concerns and route these through the appropriate chain of command. It strikes me that even this body of work behind 169 pages can become a gloss for not truly addressing whether we are ultimately accountable. Recall the

Agile means of developing software: it differs sharply from waterfall or traditional Software Development Life Cycle (SDLC) because of its emphasis on working software over complete documentation. By the same token, to what extent have our compliance efforts emphasized accountability over evidencing documentation? Conversely, to what extent has our emphasis on control documentation and other artifacts distracted us from asking if we have truly become more accountable to our actions? Just as waterfall and SDLC focused on process accountability – that we are accountable to the checks and approvals within and between each gating development phase – SOX compliance efforts likewise have prefaced process accountability: are walkthroughs conducted, are the risk and controls matrices signed off, is testing performed and reviewed? Less talked about is outcome accountability. Just as we can conceivably go through all the checkpoints in SDLC and end up with a software that barely works, we can go through all the motions in SOX compliance and end up with an organization that has at best successfully decoupled compliance, the evidencing that controls are performed, from actual risk mitigation. Talking about compliance becomes a way of not talking about outcome accountability.

Here's a quick test. Imagine sitting with an end user in your enterprise and asking the user about what he or she has taken towards SOX compliance. What would the user say? Now imagine an alternate mirror scenario, except this time, ask about what steps user takes to insure the quality of his or her work? In other words, what does the user typically do to defend his or her work against likely insults to integrity? What is the user likely to say this time? In my audit work with clients, I've had a chance to test this out with various auditees in different companies. In the first scenario, the answers given almost always first center on restricted access, separate approvals, and the presence of audit trails. In the second scenario, the answers start to become more interesting, less generic sounding though no less important. One user talks about cross checking her work with authorized source artifacts such as executed agreements. Another sends out confirmation emails to customers to make sure any disagreements are surfaced upfront. One manager implements a peer review system, where different members of her team work on the same transaction but from different perspectives: one books orders and another updates them. Yet another user runs queries or reports that identify variances in key fields as a trigger to perform deeper analyses on a weekly or monthly basis. And another user may yet reconcile output across systems to ensure that no transaction has been omitted and that nothing is lost in translation.

In *Universal Principles of Design*, Lidwell, Holden and Butler make the differentiation between slips and mistakes.[3] Slips are non-intentional so when configuring a Software as a Service (SaaS), I often get requests to make a key button or text display more prominent so that slips are less likely.[4] In continuing with our SaaS customization from Chapter 8, the application administrator may be asked to have the custom field that re-computes an estimated amount show up in grayed-out or inline format so that it is not editable and is used to differentiate from the actual amount field that can be entered and updated. Insofar as a difference exists between the computed and actual amounts, the administrator may also be asked to display in red "Yes" for a field labeled "Difference" to help the approver see this more clearly lest he or she makes the slip of approving orders with discrepancies between actual and computed amounts. A mistake, as defined by Lidwell, Holden, and Butler, is intentional but, unlike a malicious attempt by an insider to perform an attack or one spurned by a need to reflect better than actual financials, the intention is inappropriate because of a misinterpretation of the tool at hand.[5]

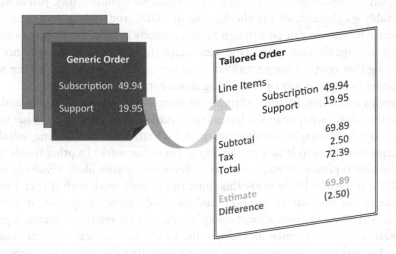

During the testing of the SaaS customization, users may yet realize that although the formula baked into the computation of an estimate amount does not include sales tax, the comparison in the Difference field takes the difference between the computed amount with an actual amount that includes sales tax. Thus, orders with ship-to locations for which sales tax is applicable almost always show up with a difference. If left undetected, approvers are more likely to reject rather than approve orders for these locations. If left unresolved, it contributes to a high level of false positives that makes us wonder whether the comparison is needed in the first place.

When we focus on evidencing outcome rather than evidencing process, the questions that are asked, and answers that are consequently given, take on a different plane. Another way of putting this is even if access were restricted or evidence of independent approvals were evidenced, there is still a possibility that mistakes could have been made or that underlying numbers recorded do not support real actual transactions. The review of audit trails is an interesting can of worms. When asked whether a month over month review of specific audit trails yields any findings, users almost always say no exceptions are noted. Which makes us wonder: what is the efficacy of this exception review when no exceptions were found? We can say the same of periodic access reviews. If quarter over quarter access reviews to ensure that active employees in an accounting SaaS corresponds with an active employee listing from the HR SaaS, and quarter after quarter no exceptions were found, what does this say about the utility or, conversely, futility of this review?

Even if an exception were found, say a recent termination from the source HR SaaS was not inactivated in the downstream accounting SaaS, what if, as we alluded to in Chapter 1, a single sign-on solution has been deployed so that even if the employee were not inactivated in the accounting SaaS, there would have been no risk of unauthorized access to begin with as single sign-on access would have been disabled, preventing access to not just the accounting SaaS but also other SaaS in use in the enterprise. This is, in fact, the value proposition that SSO providers bring to the table offering an Identity as a Service solution that allows for rapid access provisioning as well as deprovisioning from a one-stop shop as it were. In contrast, boilerplate audit templates often get recycled in different enterprises, and used in walkthroughs to surface internal controls that management supposedly devised and implemented. These are, after all, controls *internal* to the organization. Yet, as we have seen when it comes to impact analysis of any identified access violations, we often backtrack and point out the real source of control reliance, single sign on, rather than continue to speak of usual suspects, restricted access in accounting SaaS, just because it fits into the common currency of control speak.

In *Does IT Matter*, Nicholas Carr writes of SaaS as the universal solvent that dilutes the application features in a way that is consumable by multiple rather than a few select organizations, so that ultimately any competitive advantage that is to be gained with using SaaS is whittled away.[6] While I don't necessarily subscribe to his point of view – varying degrees of configuration for example can make a difference – I think the concept is perhaps more applicable in large to the body of artifacts that make up compliance work. It is surprising that the supposed controls that are *internal* to any one enterprise are invariably the same as other controls *internal* to other enterprises. It's almost as if audit clients turn to their auditors for best practice control templates to adopt them with minimal effort or fuss. Why bother attempting a control that is intrinsic to the way the organization functions just so more time is expended explaining to your auditors why it differs from the best practice gold standard? Rather than expend the necessary time and resources to start from bottoms-up by understanding what "controls" end users already employ in their day to daily functions, we turn to a compliance shortcut or heuristic. Because the latter is not performed upfront and upstream, that is early enough among varied stakeholders involved in different aspects of end-to-end business processes in the compliance cycle, the same controls get recycled year after year. When an exception does arise, research is performed to find out what truly happens and mitigating controls are thus engendered to explain away the lack of material or significant impact to financial statements.

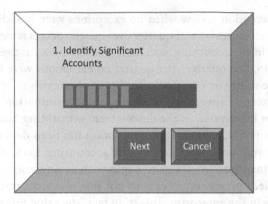

The universal solvent of compliance work can thus be likened to a wizard that we see when performing an installation or upgrade of desktop operating system or utility programs such as printer driver setup. We are guided through a series of predefined screens that essentially walks us through the setup process. There is no ability to provide any input to the wizard other than to exit it altogether by clicking on the Cancel button. It's all or nothing, go through with the installation by clicking the Next button or exiting it midstream albeit prematurely. Even though a pop-up may appear confirming whether this is indeed what we want to do, the choices or options available are simply "Yes" or "No." In the same manner that compliance cycles through significant account identification, business cycle review, walkthrough, sampled testing, and remediation followed by remediation testing, client stakeholders simply need to go along with the Next button. The wizard simplifies and directs the flow. Seen as an upgrade or enhancement over having to enter commands at the command prompt, it nevertheless dumbs down or downgrades the user by restricting the user's actions to a set of binaries: forward or backward, next, or cancel. These binaries mirror compliance work: are you in compliance or are you not? Would you rather fancy your chief executive officer (CEO) and chief financial officer (CFO) in orange jumpsuits?

It should thus come as no surprise that internal controls that are related to the use of an in-scope SaaS are often not specific to the SaaS at hand. At one end of the extreme, we can conceivably have no control directly tied to the SaaS and still be compliant just as we can conceivably not integrate an upstream SaaS into the downstream accounting SaaS but instead choose to book a manual journal entry at month end with no degree of granularity on underlying transaction detail. Consider the following scenario: regardless of the functionality provided by the accounting SaaS, all transactions tied to key accounts are reconciled in their entirely to source systems or SaaS and reviewed for validity, completeness, and accuracy. This one key control trumps all other potential upstream controls in ensuring controls over financial reporting. Yet, in real-life, it is hardly sustainable because of the sheer effort involved. We might still reconcile the sum totals with upstream SaaS, but to get to the transaction and line level detail seems almost too cost prohibitive. How do we possibly catch a fraudulent entry that increases the total by a certain amount and matches with another fraudulent entry that decrements the total by the same amount such that the overall sum of all entries in the same batch nevertheless remains the same?

Thus, when controls are interwoven into everyday use of SaaS upstream, manual reconciliation efforts are reduced downstream. Controls are thus not mutually exclusive and often build on or conflict with one another. As we have seen in previous chapters, often the line drawn between automated and manual controls is nebulous at best – when we approve a journal entry upon receiving a notification from a SaaS and click the Approve button upon login, is this control manual or automated or does it really comprise a mixture of both – yet when it comes to control validation, automated controls can be benchmarked per AS 5 guidance so that approval settings are tested not only once and only once in the first year of compliance, so long as no changes are made, this control would only be revisited in year 3 as opposed to year after year. Flagging a control as automated or manual becomes a political act, one imbued with downstream cost implications, even if the underlying control has different degrees of manual and automated.

All this amounts to control-speak insofar as we haven't yet considered whether the entries recorded were valid, complete, or accurate to begin with. Conceivably we could approve all entries in our queue, have audit trails show that no entry is created and approved by the same individual, and still come up short on duplicate, incorrect, incomplete, or just flat out fraudulent entries. Another example relates to the creation of accrual entries in the accounting SaaS. What is the support gathered to feed into the content behind an accrual entry? When it comes to employee expenses, would we run a report from an upstream expense management SaaS to capture the population of unsubmitted and unapproved expense reports? When it comes to vendor expense, would we comb through yet another procurement management SaaS to uncover purchase orders for which goods and services have been received but not invoiced? In both instances, reliance may be placed on out-of-the-box or customized reports coming from the SaaS, so this may be where automated aspects kick in. These reports may be scheduled monthly and delivered to vested parties. Yet, when it comes down to assessing whether to accrue spend based on an internal materiality threshold, say whether it exceeds 5% of net income, human aspects enter the picture, thus circling us back to the familiar automated-manual commingling that lies behind a thinly veiled automated control.

When an accrual entry is made based on month over month variance reviews and not directly tied to any system report on submitted, unapproved, or otherwise unrecorded transactions, and in turn routed in the accounting SaaS for approval, does this make it an automated or manual control or both? When reviewing this example with students in my *Accounting Information Systems* class against the textbook dichotomy between manual and automated, several voiced concerns over how susceptible the overall control design is to changes in personnel. What happens when the primary journal entry approver is out of office? What happens to entries that are routed for his or her approval and stuck in the queue as it were? If these entries are not attended to, and in the case of our accrual entry, expenses would have been understated and net income would have been overstated on the income statement. Which returns us, oddly enough, to the materiality threshold used to trigger action in the first place.

Does the accounting SaaS in use let us configure secondary or backup approvers in addition to primary approvers? If not, what manual efforts need to be undertaken to either update the approver or review for unapproved journals in flight? Both these options involve some level of manual intervention to augment what would appear to be an automated routing of journal entries for approval. With so little attention devoted to the way internal controls are designed with the SaaS in use, it may come as a surprise that the way SaaS is used is often in direct conflict with the overall objective of minimizing insults to transaction integrity.

Button and Harper studied the adoption of an order management system by a foam manufacturer in the north of England. In trying to piece together the reasons behind "it's too damn slow" or "it's totally impractical" variants of feedback received, a couple of key challenges emerged.[7] The first had to do with the additional work needed to process custom orders. The new system could not handle non-standard orders, so users had to manually key in each line. Every entry in turn needed a cost so a composite file had to be put together for the customer each time.[8] Recall our earlier electronic medical record (EMR) example from Chapter 2 where physicians end up spending more time making entries in software fundamentally skewed towards accurate billing rather than seamless clinical interface with patients. In the case of the foam manufacturer, users worked around the system resulting in escalating tensions between the accounting department and the shop floor.[9] These additional interventions can in turn increase the likelihood of slips and mistakes.

The second challenge was more fundamental: the system mapped out a sequential order for processing orders, from order taking on the phone in the front office, to entries made in the system by clerks to copies made and given to the production floor to invoicing to accompany the delivery of goods, and in so doing assumes that orders were made well ahead of time.[10] The reality was orders that came in from furniture manufacturers were almost always same day orders, so workers on the production floor would take in orders and begin working on them before prices were even set.[11] Also, orders once taken were not static documents. Changes were made often as a result of direct correspondences among the customer, shop floor, and production. Rather than serve as an authorized source for starting production, the order was assembled by all vested parties all the way from production to delivery.[12] The system, on the other hand, required all changes to the order to flow in a reverse manner from production floor to front office and back to production as all invoices needed to be matched with orders before they could accompany goods delivery.[13] As Button and Harper put it, "The system in effect organized the production and ordering processes as separate from one another, and in so doing actually hindered the efficient process of ordering, producing, and invoicing, the very process it was designed to enhance."[14]

Fast forward to today. It is remarkable how these findings continue to resonate not only in the way we use SaaS, but also in the way we audit and groom it into compliance. For the foam manufacturer, the ordering and production processes overlapped. I'm immediately reminded of the overlapping development phases recommended by Takeuchi and Nonaka in cultivating a sashimi approach to product development.[15] Even thinking back to the SDLC paper mentioned in Chapter 3 and developed by a grandfather of waterfall of sorts, there was already an acknowledgement of iterations between successive phases so that testing, for example, would inform development. After all, when testing fails, developers would have to recode.[16]

Thus, even today, despite the prevailing accounting approach of carving the Order-to-Cash cycle into distinct phases beginning from order creation to order approval, before fulfillment and invoicing, these phases overlap in real life just as software development phases overlap. With waterfall or SDLC, we mandate that requirements be approved or signed off before coding begins, but what happens when during coding, further investigation reveals a need for requirements to be updated? This necessitates a change request to be routed for approval. The ordering system used by the foam manufacturer exacts the same workflow requiring changes to orders to be routed back from production floor to front office and back to production floor.[17] Just as software developed through SDLC often takes a longer time to see the light of day, the same control in use by the ordering system results in delayed orders. Rather than automate manual processes to speed up time to market or in this case customer delivery, it slows things down. In this case, even though compliance has not been compromised, customer satisfaction almost certainly is.

This speaks to the underlying flaw with compliance methodologies. While it may make sense for a student to understand the various phases of Order-to-Cash, to carve these out as distinct separate sub-processes with approvals as gating entry and exit criteria between each phase superfluously inflicts or enforces a contrived sequence or order to the daily affairs as opposed to observing how events truly unfold a day in the life. As an aside, when I had a multiple-choice quiz question in my *Accounting Information Systems* class that tested students on the sequential flow of order to fulfillment to invoice, a couple of students chose the invoice–order–fulfillment flow. Their rationale? Because of the level of work involved and nature of the goods sold, the enterprise vendor required that all work be invoiced and paid upfront before production begins. It goes without saying that their scores were re-graded.

But the point is if accounting students in a graduate class recognize the fluidity to sequenced relations, why not experts in compliance? In our SaaS customization example as discussed previously, during the prototype demo, it turned out the locking of the screen or hiding of the approval button would make no difference as approvals are uploaded via bulk import. In addition, a locked screen may prevent one from adding information not available during order creation just as the ordering system in use by the foam manufacturer needed to be "flexible" enough to handle changes to orders based on ongoing updates among the customer, front office, and production floor.

Even more than an imposition of a contrived order over messiness or back-and-forth iterations, the prescribed sequence ends up suggesting a causal relationship between preceding and ensuing phases. In this manner, an order gives rise to a fulfillment which in turn gives rise to an invoice. For a novice or student, this demarcation is useful at least in making some sense out of the madness but at the end of the day, it is only a construct. As alluded to in our example on automating invoice or bill runs in Chapter 5, a user may express the need to be able to exclude invoices from the run meriting further investigation with the order management team. So even when the order has already been approved, and fulfillment performed, there is still a possibility that slips or mistakes can occur. For example, item discounts that don't matter to warehouse personnel performing the fulfillment would nevertheless matter to the billing team reviewing the invoices. What if the discount given on the invoice did not tie with an executed contract or did not make sense given the type of item fulfilled? If it were a slip on the part of order management, the accounting approach mandates that the dispute flow from billing back to order management and back to billing. In this time, the disputed invoice is still waiting to be sent.

The phases are not mutually exclusive. Just as the testing team catches slips or mistakes made by developers, the billing team may find errors that were not uncovered by the order management team, and as we go even farther downstream, it's altogether likely that a customer credit is issued if the errors remained all but undetected except by the customer. As with the foam manufacturer finalizing the order even as it is already on the production floor, the artifacts produced in each phase of the Order-to-Cash cycle are subject to change. We have seen how the order may change even if already approved – notice we haven't yet broached the high likelihood of late changes submitted by the customer – but the invoice too may change. The bill-to address may no longer apply, and the billing team gets notified a couple of weeks later. The updated invoice is sent to the corrected billing address. But in the event a customer credit is issued, the customer may call in and request an updated invoice, one that shows the net amount due after factoring in the credit. Does the invoice template out-of-the-box from the billing SaaS show the related credit on the invoice? If not, it misleads the customer into making a mistake in thinking that a credit has not been applied.

As we explore each possible permutation of the same SaaS customization example, it is becoming clear that approvals are but a gloss. While they evidence a second level of review, they by no means guarantee against possible insults to the integrity of the underlying artifacts, whether these are orders, packing slips, invoices, or credit memos, just as compliance is a gloss, more about demonstrating compliance with articulated internal controls than about securing the completeness, validity or accuracy of underlying transactions. Seen in its entirety, the body of work on compliance is a gloss of glosses.

The question becomes: do we abandon all control-speak altogether? How else would we speak of internal controls for SaaS at all, never mind this just happens to be the subject of this book? To opt for the former is a tad too drastic. It would be like saying that because the user stories in a product backlog are skewed towards nontechnical administrative users already well versed in accounting basics that we abandon all user stories when perhaps a good first start may be to begin with user stories from other departments such as sales, marketing, or operations insofar as they are affected by the proposed new software or product functionalities. What can be a different way or format of talking about internal controls without getting caught up by what Michael Powers calls the audit loop?

Let's turn to the *Universal Principles of Design* that catalogues a diverse range of 100 design principles compiled by Lidwell, Holden, and Butler from sources as wide ranging as human computer interaction, aviation, biology, mathematics, and gestalt psychology, to name a few. Take the principle of forgiveness. As defined by the authors, "forgiveness in design helps prevent errors before they occur, and minimizes the negative consequences of errors when they do occur."[18] Had the ordering system in use by the foam manufacturer been more forgiving, custom changes would have been more easily entered or changes to orders can well occur mid-stream on the production floor without compromising delivery time to the furniture manufacturer. The authors laid out different ways of incorporating forgiveness. One is "good affordances," designs that encourage correct as opposed to incorrect use.[19] In our SaaS customization example, by making any discrepancy between the computed and actual amounts display in red in the Difference field makes it easier for us to review the order for approval. Notice instead of merely contending ourselves with the evidencing of order approval as any hard-nosed auditor worth his salt would have us focus on, we have instead gone one step farther to address the actual mechanics of the approval. In this case, order approval is based on a review of computed against actual amounts, so why not make any discrepancy reported more visible?

A second strategy for building in forgiveness is "reversibility of actions," which translates into letting the users unwind or backtrack their steps when they realize that they have made a slip or mistake or quite simply changed their minds.[20] By not opting to lock the screen, and choosing instead to hide the Approve button, the application administrator in effect lets users continue to augment the order with more details, or make corrections to prior entries while it is still pending for approval. They can also choose to retract the order from the approval queue altogether. Much like how the sprint approach in Agile is iterative and lets the cross-functional team revisit and, where necessary, undo the earlier work performed based on feedback gathered from successive prototype demos, the "reversibility of actions" principle lets users clarify their intentions and change their minds.

No.	Principle[21]	SaaS Example
1	Good Affordance	Highlighting the difference between computed and actual amounts in red
2	Reversibility of Actions	Opting to hide Approve button rather than locking the screen to allow for ongoing order updates
3	Safety Nets	Having a separate custom field compute the estimate amount with no accounting impact to transaction
4	Confirmation	Pop-up confirming on whether information would be added to an order in a locked period
5	Warning	Pop-up warning of discrepancy between computed and actual amounts when user attempts to approve order
6	Help	Remarks or comments added to custom fields created on computed estimate amount and difference

A third means to augment forgiveness is to create "safety nets" that catch the users to prevent them from making a serious error.[22] Just as Netflix employed canary analyses to test out the impact of new code on a small subset of their production architecture, the application administrator in our SaaS customization example configured the workflow to only apply to the user's actions and no one else's. More fundamentally, the computed estimate does not change the actual amount recorded in the order even as it serves as a safety net of sorts by highlighting a potential discrepancy to facilitate reviews. Two other ways highlighted by Lidwell, Holden, and Butler are "confirmations" and "warnings" either verifying a user's intent or providing a warning before the user performs a critical action.[23] To this end, during the prototype demos with the application administrator, the user requests a warning to pop up when the approver chooses to go ahead with order approval anyway despite the discrepancy flagged between computed and actual amounts.

Finally, Lidwell, Holden, and Butler identified "help" as a means of making designs more forgivable.[24] In this approach, information is provided to either make it easier for the user to continue with a series of steps to take or to investigate the nature of the error encountered. Therefore, with the custom computed field, it may be helpful for the application administrator to include remarks clarifying that they do not include sales tax to minimize any miscommunication. Another example of how help can come into play is for the application administrator to provide hypercare upon deployment to be able to answer questions from lack of familiarity with use.

At a recent vendor conference, I was part of a presentation where the audience was polled on which of the following kinds of help they would prefer:

- Contextual prompts guiding one's actions
- Online chat with support
- How-to videos
- Phone conversation with support
- Email inquiries
- User manual

Three observations of the audience's reaction are worth noting here. First, oddly enough, by show of hands, there was significant resistance to calling support to obtain answers to questions even though this is more interactive than an asynchronous form of communication such as email. Not surprisingly, there was a universal distaste for user or help manuals. Second, and perhaps almost conversely, most people would prefer assistance that is specific to the action performed in the moment, so that when attempting to set up an expense category, for example, they would have liked to be prompted by the SaaS at hand to navigate first to customization and setup, and upon hovering over the right menu or tab, be presented with the guidance to select Expense Categories, rather than have everything presented all at once. Advice or assistance that would be deemed useful needed to be contextual to local needs and, even then, dependent on just what a user would be doing in the moment. Just as auditors perform a walkthrough of key controls end-to-end in a business cycle, the audience in the vendor presentation would prefer a guided walkthrough of sorts when performing a series of actions to process a transaction such as an expense report or an entity setup such as an employee. Third, there was disagreement between the SaaS vendor and the audience over whether help should be available to power users such as SaaS administrators or to the end user population at large, with the vendor presenting the options initially only with the former in mind, but upon hearing audience feedback, realizing that the preference is for the latter.

Let's circle back to the six principles identified of which help is but one option. Just as SOX or audit distinguishes preventive from detective controls, the authors of *Universal Principles of Design* preface the first three approaches over the last three ones presumably because they are more proactive rather than reactive. So here we are, an altogether different way of slicing at internal controls when it comes to SaaS, and yet even here, as our exploration of varied ways of offering help illustrates, there are specific audit ways and means such as walkthroughs that can have hitherto remained untapped and be far better harnessed to enhance user experience whether we are talking about power users or end users. Conversely, most SaaS continue to be intrinsically weak in meeting audit or compliance needs, such as providing a default out-of-the-box view only administrator profile for auditors to validate the SaaS under the hood, as it were. In addition to providing a guided walkthrough for key transactions, how about assistance rendered on key audit processes, such as the identification of materially significant accounts exceeding 5% of net income and showing ways to drill down to underlying transactions and accompanying mix of automated versus manual controls? In addition to a management or sales dashboard on business key performance indicators (KPIs), how about an audit or compliance dashboard showing:

■ Number of in-flight transactions in draft form and pending submission
■ Vendor, customers, or employees created, modified, or inactivated in the past week
■ Number of custom fields, records, workflows, and scripts in each business process
■ Deleted records

The last KPI, deleted transactions and specifically as it relates to journals, becomes an area of focus in specific countries that emphasize gapless journal numbering where every general ledger transaction must abide by a predictable numerical sequence. Here, we ask the following questions:

■ Does the SaaS at hand let us void entries so that a reversal entry is generated with the next system generated number in the configured sequence?
■ For transactions that are deleted can a copy be archived elsewhere?
■ How can we apply enterprise retention policies by removing specific data that exceeds a specific number of years?
■ How can we anonymize or remove specific data attributes as part of responding to or fulfilling General Data Protection Regulation (GDPR) or other data privacy obligations?

Notice that our examples are directly related to enhancing the SaaS in use. In other words, whether we have good affordances, reversibility of actions, safety nets, confirmations, warnings, or help can be directly traced back to the SaaS configuration at hand. Another example of how poor affordances can lead to more fragile or less forgiving control designs is how when limiting access to a key financial report, we would have to customize it. In other words, in addition to updating access, we can also unintentionally modify preconfigured categories. A better approach would have been to spin up a new employee group with access to either viewing or modifying these key reports so that changes to access to key reports can be accomplished by updating the members of this new access group rather than modifying the report customization directly to minimize the possibility of unwarranted and therefore unauthorized changes.

A different example of poor affordances may relate to the all-powerful superuser administrator role. To what extent can these administrator functions be broken down or parsed out into less sensitive roles so that precision is employed in making sure the right changes are made without incurring risk of pervasive impact? Contrast these explorations with the universal solvent of account reconciliations which has everything and therefore nothing specific to the SaaS at hand. Even when it comes to approvals, instead of hovering at generic and binary yes/no categories, these principles force us to look deeper to ask ourselves what is truly reviewed against when providing an approval, and what can help the reviewer perform a review either more quickly, completely, or accurately – more examples of poor affordances, irreversible actions, absence of safety nets, confirmations, warnings, and help?

Consider bad error codes that reveal all too little.[25] Ever encounter the 404 error when surfing online? When interviewed, Robert Cailliau, who with World Wide Web inventor Tim Berners-Lee pioneered the hypertext structure that led to the web, revealed that the number 404 was likely arrived at "according to the whims of the programmer."[26] "When you write code for a new system," Cailliau explained, "you don't waste too much time writing long messages for the situations in which you detect an error."[27] Within a SaaS, we are likely to encounter a fair share of ambiguous error messages. A simple error such as "this transaction cannot be saved" necessitates the user having to look up missing fields that need to be completed. Sometimes, the list of values in a mandatory drop-down field is not exhaustive, but to submit the transaction in time for processing, we go ahead and select an incorrect value anyway. Another example relates to bad user design and poor affordances in general. For example, a user navigates to calculate consolidated rates but sees only a list of consolidated rates from a prior period. No button is present to click on to calculate those for the current period. This leads the user to conclude that it is because the current period hasn't yet been closed, since the user is accustomed to performing the calculation after closing the books. Note that in this case, there is no error message or warning given as to the missing button, so the user is left to formulate his or her own hypothesis as to the best course of action. It turns out that a filter has been applied by default. Only by exposing the filter and selecting the current period for which consolidated rates have yet to be computed is the button rendered visible to be acted upon.

Here's another example of poor affordance or bad design. Imagine creating a custom balance sheet or income statement in a financial presentation format that is aligned with the generally accepted accounting principles (GAAP). Next, imagine using this underlying presentation templates for more than one key report. What can go wrong with this picture? A potential error made in updating the template has a cascading effect on all applicable key reports. Thus, when it comes to reviewing internal controls over financial reporting, a mere review of access to key reports is only the beginning. Insofar as updates to underlying foundational templates can impact more than one key report, this has far flung implications. So, in a sense the level of precision when it comes to a review of access to a key financial report needs to go down one level deeper or higher depending on how you look at it by really honing in on meta updates that are more likely to have a pervasive impact on more than one report. Contrast this with a transactional level control that looks at approval of journal entries. Here, note that just because entries have been properly reviewed and approved doesn't mean that the resulting reported numbers would be correct. An internal control perspective that prefaces transactional level controls (busywork) over higher level design controls on reporting misses out on the likelihood of impact. Exceptions found in the former are less likely to have a pervasive impact than those found in the latter. This same argument applies to reports that do not even have to align with GAAP in terms of presentation format. An accruals report on unsubmitted expenses out of an expense management SaaS, for example, needs to be designed in a manner that facilitates the ease of access to numbers in the current period, and in effect has nothing to do with whether expenses submitted have been approved once by supervisors and twice by the accounting team to begin with. Here, the concern is not so much whether the expenses submitted were unsubstantiated and thus unauthorized to begin with, but rather whether the accruals report has been designed right to pull current period numbers without necessarily omitting any cost centers or subsidiaries by default in a preconfigured filter. Secondarily, depending on the SaaS at hand, the numbers may be current as of close of business on the prior day, so the timing of when the report is run impacts data completeness.

One more example on poor SaaS affordance: consider having to generate a customer statement using the billing SaaS at hand. The problem a user faces is that either all, or only open, transactions related to the customer show up. The former is a little excessive considering how the subtext of a customer statement may be to secure payment on outstanding amounts due. Yet, the SaaS at hand when listing open transactions may only show unpaid invoices. For partially paid or credited invoices, the associated payments or credits do not show unless one elects for all transactions to be displayed on the customer statement as these transactions would have already had an Applied status and are no longer open. Thus, only open invoice amounts show up and even then, only the remainder unapplied amounts that are due are displayed. If this were a customer template out-of-the-box that offers no other possibility of adding related transactions, such as payments and credit to any open invoice in a statement, the customer is likely to be confused. A customer inquiry can come up: I thought the credit or partial payment has already been applied? If so to which invoice? These "bad" examples illustrate the level of manual intervention nonetheless needed for solutions that are purported to automate existing processes. To be sure, all this is hard work not just in execution but also in validation, much harder work than merely reviewing in client after client the same recycled boilerplate controls under the rubric of best practice.

What is it that sustains this archaic practice in the wake of financial debacles such as Enron? A common misperception among the public is that auditors keep public companies honest when it comes to publishing their financials. Even in my *Accounting Information Systems* class, students are apt to blame the auditor when we walk through case studies of corporate misstatements. Yet auditors are only too quick to clarify that they are merely validating management's design and operation of internal controls, rather than chase down every lead, article, or support that is used to report the financials. Given constraints in time and resources, the latter would have been an impossible task. Thus, in the final analysis, is our reliance on the compliance body of work more motivated by a suspension of disbelief rather than any true belief in or allegiance to its cause? Or perhaps it can be boiled down to our tendency to focus on individuals – who did what when – rather than be comfortable with a more holistic set of systemwide contributing elements? Enron's CEO, Kenneth Lay, one of America's highest paid CEOs in 1999, was found guilty on six counts of conspiracy and fraud in 2006 and, in a separate bench trial, convicted of four additional counts of fraud and making false statements.[28] Following Enron's bankruptcy, 20,000 employees lost their jobs and many lost their life savings as well. Investors also lost billions of dollars. Facing up to 45 years in prison, Lay paid the ultimate price, dying of a heart attack prior to receiving his sentence. Or maybe it has something to do with our reliance on black-white dichotomies, our predilection for binary pairs over a continuum of possibilities. One is either in or out of compliance. An order is not an invoice even if it shares many elements of the latter. A customer is not a vendor yet one can make the argument that an organization that knows how to be a good customer, by submitting purchase requisitions for upfront approval before procuring services or items, is likely able to play the part of a good vendor by including its customers' purchase order numbers on its invoices to expedite processing and payment. A continuum with overlapping order, fulfillment and invoice phases is so much harder to pin down and dissect than discrete, separate intervals each marching to its own tune. Or maybe we've become too distracted by all this busy compliance work to even notice?

As I've mentioned, my first job was as a management consultant with a Big Four in New York. One day when walking down Madison Avenue with a burgeoning laptop bag stuffed with client workpapers in tow, I became aware of a suspicious character following me. I looked around, saw a hotel loom ahead and figured it was my best option to shake him loose. Upon entering the revolving doors at the hotel entrance, I felt a sharp poke in my ribs. I turned around and to my shock, saw my assailant brandishing a pocket knife before me. I was trapped in the same compartment with him! For a moment, time stood still. The few seconds in which I stood transfixed with my mouth wide open felt like an eternity. A scream ensued followed by an attempt to push past into the lobby. The next thing I knew, I found myself crumpled on the floor before the reception desk and a group of curious onlookers. When I looked up, my stalker had disappeared. It's funny how I would think of this now, so many years later. With all this talk about safety nets and warnings, you would have thought I'd have noticed him much earlier? Did I have my earphones plugged in and was therefore blissfully oblivious to my surroundings? Yet, what ultimately resonates with me today is not so much the fear of being trapped in a revolving door, but that of not recognizing being trapped to begin with. If anything, I was motivated by my stalker's obvious knife waving displays to get out. Yet in the absence of such conspicuous signs of danger in our daily work, how many of us continue to reside in the revolving door of compliance gloss, neither inside nor outside, barely making past the perimeters of the audited SaaS on the one hand nor completely achieving an unbiased assessment on the other.

Another way to ask this question is: what happens when the requirements to configure the SaaS fall in a no-man's land, a gray area that lies just outside the confines of compliance and financial reporting demands? We have already seen how examples of how different regulatory needs such as the 90-day password aging policy from DSS in PCI compliance can conflict with other password aging controls within the organization that relate to systems or software that are in scope for financial reporting. I recall an example where a family member had a car accident, but it took close to 2 hours for highway patrol to respond. The reason? The area where the accident occurred lay outside the jurisdictions of the two adjoining cities, in this case Raleigh and Durham, so most of the time was spent on the part of law enforcement in debating which side should be involved – in other words a stalemate was reached – before action was ultimately taken. By the same token, it is highly conceivable that customer requests for enhancements submitted to SaaS vendors, insofar as they are not easily categorized into functional or compliance needs, often don't get worked upon. Recall from Chapter 4 how specific elements of Salesforce reporting have not been improved despite the release of snazzier functionality such as Chatter. Even internally, it is not hard to imagine when it comes to internal configurations for an accounting SaaS that those that don't quite belong to financial or compliance needs often fall by the wayside. These may accrue to form the technical debt that bids and waits in the background, for the perfect albeit inopportune occasion to bring about the collapse of a house of cards, where poorly named custom attributes used in custom workflows or scripts and are in turn triggered by readily accessible end user queries that somehow get inappropriately modified or deleted.

Another area where rules or constraints may introduce further complexities applies to situations where unforeseen scenarios or unplanned incidents arise when no policy or procedure was in place to dictate or propose a clear course of action, and end users inadvertently get trapped in a cul-de-sac of sorts. Here is a real-life example recounted to me. A man cancels and switches his health insurance and omits to sign up his wife and two kids. A couple of months go by. His wife is expecting, and they find out about the omission; it is imperative that the family gets added back to his insurance plan. Yet, upon checking back with the insurance provider, and despite additional reinforcements from his employer, the man is told by the insurance provider that because the open enrollment period is over, there is no other means of making a change. The only exception that can be made is for life changes so the new baby when delivered can be covered but not any existing family members. Eventually, after much wrangling and deliberation, a solution is proposed. The man terminates his employment relationship with his employer and is told that he would be re-employed 30 days after. This way, he gets to be eligible to sign up for insurance all over again, even if this would take effect only 30 days after his re-employment. Here, boxed in by the compounding effect of inflexible rules, the only way out is a creative albeit unconventional solution.

Recall our review of Chomsky's "creativity of language" from Chapter 6 and the way we attempt new and different ways of configuring the SaaS to move from ostensive to performative to competence even as we evolve from design of generic products to design of user activities to design of design itself. Our insurance example highlights the creative routes we can and are forced to take to unwind or undo our actions. In contrast to Chapter 7, where we've reviewed forgiveness and looked at examples of undoing what has been done to recover from security breaches or system downtimes. Here, the compliance rules are the very reasons that preclude us from unwinding, much like how Frankenstein viewed his creation, a composite of disembodied parts, nothing less but perhaps more importantly, in his creator's eyes, nothing more. Ironically, the insurance provider stopped sending physical hard copy documentation confirming the change in insurance. Had the man received it in the mail, he may have detected his mistake sooner and could have contacted the provider earlier to alert them rather than wait for 2 months to go by. From this perspective, the confirmation in the mail is a safety net of sorts that lets the end user attempt to unwind from a slip or mistake made. From a SaaS perspective, two examples come to mind that resemble the lock-in pattern we have seen with the insurance policy. An organization uses a separate item or stock keeping unit (SKU) to record discounts in the invoices issued to customers. A situation arises where the discount item is not set up to be taxable, while the item that the discount is to be applied to is itself taxable. Whenever entries are made involving discounts, the exact discount to be given can't be recorded in its entirety until the item upon which the discount is applied to is first recorded and saved so that users can see the full sales tax computed. Accordingly, a second "discount" line is added to absorb the sales tax associated with the primary line. Like the ultimate solution our intrepid family settled on to regain insurance coverage, a less than ideal workaround is employed.

The force or lock-in pattern is attributed not so much to compliance regulations as it is to the way items, discounts, and sales are set up and configured within the organization. In a different organization, discounts could have been set up as a flat percentage rather than a separate item altogether. Another example, this time a recent change in the account assigned to a sale item – when the invoice was recorded 2 months ago, a different account is impacted. What happens when we issue a credit today? Instead of debiting the same revenue or income account that was credited 2 months ago, the accounting SaaS at hand debits a different account when the credit memo is recorded. Here, one workaround employed is to record a topside journal to reverse the impact to the new account and recode it back to the older account. This approach is not ideal. In recalling the palindrome perspective discussed from Chapter 4, the adjustment journal cannot be immediately traced back to the originating invoice or credit memo. In recalling our review of Jaron Lanier's lock-in phenomenon from Chapter 8, the constraints of the accounting

SaaS at hand limits the range of possible actions when attempting to unwind the recording of the sale that has already taken place.[29]

Let's return to external regulations. What happens when they have more bite than bark? Or put differently, when the threat of consequence is the proverbial tail that wags the dog? The trajectory of Groupon illustrates the continual dance between compliance and consequence, bark and bite. Groupon connects sellers of merchandise and services with customers by means of attractive and discounted offers. Barely a few months after it went public in November 2011, in its first quarterly public filling, it revealed a material weakness in its internal controls. Raising $700 million, Groupon's initial public offering (IPO) was at the time the second biggest tech IPO behind the $1.7 billion Google raised in 2004. Yet, at the time of filling the S-1, also known as the registration statement, no disclosure was made of any internal control weaknesses; to be sure there was no legal need to, seeing how SOX provisions apply only to companies that are public, not ones that have registered for IPOs. In Groupon's S-1, its auditor Ernst and Young made it clear that while their audits included consideration of internal control to inform their design of audit procedures, they did not express an opinion on its effectiveness of internal control over financial reporting.[30] Further exemplifying abidance by the letter rather than the spirit of the law, Groupon reported weaknesses in its internal controls as part of a Section 302 disclosure rather than in a Section 404 report[31] – 302 requires that management attest to on a quarterly basis the effectiveness of their disclosure controls and procedures, whereas 404, which Groupon did not have to comply with at the outset of going public, relates to management and outside auditor assessments on the design and operating effectiveness of internal controls over financial reporting.[32]

This is reminiscent of the dubious nature of complying with the ever-changing minimal length of wild-caught red groupers or farm-raised salmon discussed in Chapter 1. To the public, auditors are perceived as gatekeepers behind reported numbers, yet there's the slippery nature of governing laws and regulations. Because of miscalculated customer refunds, Groupon went on to revise down its prior quarter earnings by as much as $14.3 million.[33] Groupon would go on to settle a $45 million shareholder suit over claims that it had misstated its financial success to achieve its $20 per share IPO.[34] Recall how in Chapter 2, we described how in its IPO, Groupon had debuted a new accounting metric, adjusted consolidated segment operating income (CSOI) that drew the ire of the U.S. Securities and Exchange Commission (SEC). Deemed to "provide visibility into" Groupon's business, its subsequent S-1 amendment defined adjusted CSOI as a measure of "operating profitability before marketing costs incurred for long-term growth."[35] In the first quarter of 2011, Groupon generated $81.6 million in adjusted CSOI, yet had marketing costs been included, it would have incurred a loss of $98 million for the same period.[36] History would prove to be a reversal of sorts for Groupon. In 2013, it fired its CEO following a 77% decline in share price. In 2016, it scaled back its operations from 27 countries to 15.[37]

For all the public rhetoric on consequences, and here too, we speak of consequences after the fact, if we were to peer behind the corporate machinery that makes up compliance, we may find, much to our surprise, a disproportionate amount of emphasis on process over outcome. When the emphasis is on process, the focus is on the quality of the process undertaken rather than on the output or product. Auditors typically ask: are the financials signed off? Have they been reviewed by a disclosure committee? From a system perspective, has access been granted in an authorized manner? Have program changes for applications with financial impact been tested? These questions and more characterize the entity and information technology (IT) general computer controls at play. While having the financials signed off, not to mention reviewed by a disclosure committee, can increase the likelihood of having more accurate financials, they are by no means a guarantee. Similarly, having access approved or program changes tested matter from a process accountability perspective, but we may be better off focusing on actual access granted from a roles and permissions review or actual results from tests of program changes. We can make the argument that had outcome been prefaced over process, enterprises would have been less likely to be caught off guard by unexpected finds by auditors.

The problem with compliance and audit and their imbued worldviews is that they too contribute to how we can apprehend the world with or without SaaS. In the case of an accounting SaaS, we have already seen how the discretely carved out phases in the Order-to-Cash cycle have resulted in a rather predictable chain of orders, fulfillments, and invoices. By not giving users the flexibility to save orders in draft status before submission, or an ability to recall them back from the approval queue, the SaaS becomes less forgiving to user needs. When an invoice gets generated incorrectly, by not providing functionality that allows the invoice to be recalled or put into a trash bin without actual deletion thereby removing all physical traces to facilitate an audit, the SaaS is also more unforgiving than not. Likewise, in the Procure-to-Pay cycle, we covered in previous chapters how by requiring a vendor to be created before initiating a requisition precludes a proactive review of anticipated spending against budget. Because new vendors are yet to be selected, a report cannot be executed on all draft purchase requisitions related to a specific project in the procurement SaaS. Here too, the SaaS is less than forgiving. Further, by having unrealistic requisition approval thresholds, users may bypass the procurement management SaaS altogether and instead submit the same spending as an expense reimbursement item in the expense management SaaS. After all, what could be easier than making a purchase using a corporate or personal credit card? If so, how can we relate this expense back to an approved purchase requisition or PO for which spending has been approved? In effect, we would have to traverse between the procurement and expense management SaaS. Note here the mere availability of approvals in both the procurement and expense management SaaS would have satisfied a SOX audit even as overall spending management in the organization as a whole is highly suspect.

Years ago, I remembered being surprised when receiving a request directly from a CFO to add a custom summary description field in all purchase requisitions. For all our focus on correct items selection, cost center, or department classification and appropriateness of tiered approval hierarchy, I had omitted to include a Memo description field that allowed users to enter a high-level summary description of the requested spending so that when the amount was large enough to be escalated to the CFO, all he had to do was to quickly ascertain what the spending was about from a cursory glance at the Memo field rather than scroll down to line level detail. The summary description, in this example, adds to the SaaS's good affordances. From an accounting perspective, the crisp lines of division contribute to gating checks between order and fulfillment, as well as between fulfillment and invoice, much like handing a baton from one runner to the next in a relay race. In reality, the lines of division are much more porous. Conceptually they exist to help us understand the flow, but the order or sequence is put together as the participants go through the process from moment to moment so that an order is still dynamically assembled as it were when a billing accountant is validating it against the invoice he or she is about to send to the customer.

In retrospect, by basing software functionality on an idealized audit stance rather than on how events truly unfold, users who use the SaaS in turn get trapped either in revolving doors of securing approvals at each gating checkpoint or are incented to circumvent the SaaS at hand altogether until all elements of the artifacts are queued up in rapid procession and ready for entry. As an example, a purchase requisition may be assembled only upon receiving an invoice with goods or services already received, almost as an afterthought to sustain the illusion of the intended flow from purchase order (PO) to receipt to invoice. Like the ordering system in use at the foam manufacturer, a procurement management SaaS through a series of unforgiving features:

- Requiring all information such as vendor data to be available during requisition creation
- Unable to save the requisition in draft format
- Low approval thresholds
- No reminders for unapproved purchase requisitions stuck in the queue
- Unable to update purchase requisitions already in flight for approval

These roadblocks slow down the process of identifying, reviewing, and approving enterprise spending upfront, the very thing that the SaaS has been purchased off-the-shelf to assist the enterprise with. These areas are not targeted by auditors, because they are not identified in the arsenal of walkthrough templates, control practice aides, and test documentation in the audit toolkit. Even though they do impact the way an organization manages its financials, they are nonetheless deemed out-of-scope when it comes to audit and compliance, applicable more to enhancing user design than to securing data integrity and operations more than reporting.

Another way to think differently about your existing procurement and expense management SaaS is to ask whether these are effective in detecting or mitigating insider fraud.

In the fifth edition of the *Common Sense Guide to Mitigating Insider Threats*, the group of researchers at the Carnegie Mellon University Software Engineering Institute describe a case where an insider widely praised in the media for innovation and operational excellence was able to steal more than $500,000 from his employer by pocketing part of the payment for inflated invoices charged to his department and colluding with an external organization for which payment was remitted but services were never rendered.[38] It should come as no surprise that in some security circles, audit objectives, with their insistence on idealized processes and artifacts to evidence compliance, are anathema to security goals. The inability of auditors, despite their role as corporate gatekeepers in the eyes of the public, to detect fraud is not as uncommon as one might think. In January 2018, the Securities and Exchange Board of India banned PricewaterhouseCoopers from auditing listed companies in India for 2 years for failing to detect the 7,561 fictitious invoices generated at Satyam, an Indian IT services company, for a period of 5 years from 2003.[39] Satyam which, ironically enough, stands for truth in Sanskrit had its CEO Byrraju Ramalinga Raju confess in 2009 to overstating the company's cash balance by $1 billion.[40]

Outside of SaaS, the elements deemed necessary when reconstructing a sequence of affairs are in turn used as benchmarks for obtaining funding or assessing new projects. Just as physicians spend more time on data entry and coding in EMR to evidence meaningful use to be eligible for receiving federal funds, David Graeber describes how in the academic world, researchers spend more time putting together proposals than performing research.[41] Marilyn Strathern similarly describes how academia is compelled to continue churning out papers even when what is necessary for new breakthroughs is the space to think and explore areas that may not be immediately relatable to their chosen expertise or focus.[42] When a go or no-go decision is based on an unchanging criteria established and in turn used by review committees, what is the likelihood of achieving innovation or breakthroughs? Graeber also highlights how this approach pits researcher against researcher, when research is really a series of collaborative overlaps where a person's work feeds into another, and conversely the person is refreshed or rejuvenated by the influx of new ideas from another person.[43] The sashimi effect of overlapping development phases as observed by Takeuchi and Nonaka is a more common occurrence than you would think.

In the same spirit, what if instead of adopting a waterfall SDLC-like approach to compliance and audits, where auditors first start with reviewing all financial accounts to determine those that are significant, then proceed to performing *all* walkthroughs in *all* business cycles identified, before proceeding to test *all* key controls – you get the idea – we adopt Agile or Scrum-like practices, where a cross-functional team from the client organization partners with auditors to corroborate on a backlog of areas that are more likely to impact the integrity of numbers that make up financial statements. Then 2-week sprints are introduced so that any control tightening that needs to be performed – recall having good affordances, reversibility of actions, safety nets, confirmations, warnings, and help – is worked on culminating in a prototype demo. Auditors can play a part not only as part of a cross-functional Scrum team in SOX projects but also in new product developments. Instead of recycling the same controls in a rinse and repeat format, why not attempt to tighten the SaaS at hand? The cross-collaboration reflects in truth the underlying relations between auditors and auditees rather than carefully delineated battle lines. In an audit after all, the auditors rely on auditees to pull support, verify assumptions, and in general understand the specifics of each client environment.

You may be surprised to learn that just as SaaS companies have customer advisory boards advising and providing feedback on new product functionalities, they may also have audit advisory boards comprising of auditors to provide feedback on internal controls. SaaS providers may also assist auditors in formulating control practice aides to begin with, providing information on where in the SaaS to evidence a specific control. Prior to SOX, as an auditor, I worked on pre-implementation projects that relate to new system deployments. Auditors are brought in to provide guidance on possible gaps in internal controls prior to rather than after an application go-live. Yet in retrospect, even this seems too much after the fact, almost like an afterthought or add-on after the application development or configuration is already in full swing, which is why it can be tremendously helpful if auditors are involved on day one as part of the cross-functional sprint team looking at, for example, ways and means to augment the forgiveness of the SaaS at hand.

At first glance, it is not an easy role. Auditors may need to withhold themselves from pointing out access violations, for example, in a sandbox environment when the overall intent especially in the initial sprints is to verify just what users are capable of with the plethora of options presented by the SaaS rather than worry about erecting varied restrictions and imitations. Key fields that need to be encrypted such as those that are identified by the upcoming General Data Protection Regulations (GDPR) in Europe may be surfaced by auditors and added to the backlog so that even though these are not worked on from the beginning, they are nevertheless fully visible in plain sight. Recall here the power of the subtle control of visibility. Audit trails sound great, ubiquitous like strewn bread crumbs, yet upon closer inspection only come in handy if no upstream reports or queries were available for users to perform checks on a periodic basis – who wants to sift through tons of audit trails after the fact? Also, per GDPR, audit trails tied to sensitive fields need to be removed after a length of time to reduce the likelihood of exposure in the event the software is compromised. Herein, the enterprise archival or data retention policy comes into play.

Another standard audit artifact, exception notification emails, looks good on paper or in a risk and control matrix but when cross-validated for feedback in the cross functional team becomes onerous. As one user points out, to be inundated each day with tons of possible exceptions, mostly false negatives, ends up "training" the email recipient to ignore them as a rule, until something catastrophic happens attributed to an as yet unidentified needle in the haystack of possible exceptions. Another user upon hearing this suggests a weekly email summarizing all required attributes so that the recipient can make quick comparisons from a summary perspective – recall the CFO's feedback on the need for a summary attribute on purchase requisitions – to make a quick determination on whether to perform a deeper dive should one be merited as opposed to sifting through every exception notification, a slow inertia or death of sorts. The previous example illustrates the back-and-forth collaboration between other users of the cross functional team with the auditor.

Other areas where an auditor role may be helpful are the identification of "bridge" fields insofar as the SaaS at hand integrates with another. The auditor typically asks: how do we know the complete population that needs to be synced over is indeed synced over? This can be accomplished in a myriad of ways and using forgiveness strategies. A confirmation email reconciling the total in an upstream SaaS with that in a downstream one can be disseminated after each sync by the iPaaS. Insofar as discrepancies arise, a warning may be provided. Deep dive investigations may reveal that unless the item master is itself kept up to date in both SaaS, errors may arise when the item in the upstream SaaS is not able to locate its mirror copy in the downstream one. So instead of just providing exception reporting on transactional data, the same can be applied to standing or master data between the two SaaS. Other bridge fields may be suggested to add to the backlog to augment overall affordances of the SaaS at hand. For example, a system-generated transaction ID in the synced over downstream SaaS may be used to update a custom field in the upstream SaaS so it becomes apparent from looking at the upstream SaaS that the transaction in question has already been synced over. If the sync is in turn triggered on upstream transactions that do not have this field populated, then when an error is identified and the transaction needs to be resynced, a quick way to trigger a re-sync is to remove the downstream transaction ID populated upstream. This feature would address the reversibility of actions.

Another way an audit presence may help is in the setup of web services accounts in the downstream SaaS that enable iPaaS to sync in upstream transactions. If the iPaaS supports it, token-based authentication would be preferable over user login and password as the assigned password is likely subject to password aging. When the password expires, the integration would break. Also, the account used need not be an all-powerful, out-of-the-box administrator account. Insofar that transactions synced need to be of a specific transaction type only, applicable permissions can be assigned to a custom role and granted to the integration account. Finally, rather than tie this integration account with the email of any given user, it can be associated with a group email alias so that exceptions that are sent to this email can be disseminated to all concerned. Because it is not tied to any one individual, it does not need to be updated when the group membership changes.

When we take a step back and attempt to compare the nature and composition of internal controls between an on-premise software versus SaaS environment, we start to see and thus appreciate subtle differences in addition to not so subtle ones. Of the latter, in using a SaaS, the client organization does not have to worry about IT operations: server procurement, maintenance, backups, and recovery. To refresh the sandbox environment, we can make a quick call to customer support just as we can do the same when the SaaS is down. Even though the client organization does not have to manage the underlying infrastructure, knowing in advance that the SaaS is reliant on a third-party Infrastructure as a Service (IaaS) such as Amazon Web Services (AWS) can help in coming up with recovery or compensating procedures when the IaaS or AWS is down. When it comes to change management, we can argue that it wouldn't apply as the client organization is not responsible for the underlying SaaS source code. Yet insofar as the client organization has taken up the offer to tailor the SaaS to meet its needs, any specific configuration undertaken would be reviewed in the same manner that program changes are. Is there an authorized request? Are users involved in testing? Here too, the control can be evidencing test results in sandbox before migrating to production. But there can be subtler distinctions when it comes to the use of SaaS. As we have seen earlier in the canary approach to limiting the impact of a workflow to one user, we can in effect continue to "test" while still in production, debunking the popular belief that once deployed to production, the changes can no longer be tested. Here, the importance of overlap comes in between testing and production. So too, is the overlap between technical and non-technical users. Because of the option to configure out of the box, the role of the user changes from a mere passive recipient to a co-designer to a constructor and even possibly an orchestrator when it comes to configuring bridge fields between two or more SaaS.

Change management doesn't just apply to configuration changes or customizations but also to SaaS upgrades. Upgrades are packages of enhancements and fixes intended to introduce new features or resolve prior known bugs. Sometimes we may need to upgrade the custom fields, scripts, or workflows that are "installed" or deployed in an upstream SaaS for the sync to be effectively communicated to a downstream SaaS. An example is the 2-way integration between a billing SaaS and a tax management SaaS. Sales tax computed on the invoice or credit memo in the billing SaaS gets synced to the downstream tax engine SaaS for recording and reporting. Conversely, any changes in tax rates are synced from the tax management SaaS to the billing SaaS to ensure that sales tax computations are correct at any time prior to invoicing. In a prior version of the installed components in the billing SaaS, tax credit may not be supported, so that if it were determined afterwards that the customer should have been tax exempt, there is no way to create a credit memo applied to the invoice only containing the amount that is taxed, to reverse its impact in the downstream SaaS. Users may need to manually void already generated entries. With a component upgrade in the tax management SaaS, a fix is introduced in a later version to support tax only credits, but this involves updating fields, scripts, or workflows in the upstream billing SaaS. What if a client configured script or workflow taps into the same fields that are updated by the new version? Would something break or go awry? Is a rollback to the original version even possible? We're assuming the prior version is retained somewhere in a source code control system. What else would we roll back to? Even with updated or new components exposed in a SaaS upgrade, the potential impact is not unambiguous. Thus, even if IT operational work may be a figment of the past, the work of upgrading downstream SaaS components in an upstream one may nevertheless be fraught with uncertainty.

Notice I saved the last category of internal controls, access management, for last, even if they are almost always the first to be brought up, perched on the edge of everyone's lips. Access management appears to be a breeze with user assigned password to email address. An area meriting consideration is that with the plethora of best-in-breed SaaS, what matters is not so much access within any one singular SaaS as it is access across all integrated SaaS. Even within one singular SaaS, what happens if the user in question has access to more than one environment, sandbox as well as production? Or consider a contractor or consultant who may be able to access various client organization's SaaS environments using the same email and password combination. What about an integrated SaaS that is synced with an individual administrator login credentials? What happens when the user leaves the company? How do we update the integration credentials? One quick interim measure may be to change the password. Another more complete though more labor-intensive approach would be to identify all configurations or customizations associated with this administrator account and update them to a different service access account. Invariably, with all the focus on actual data in production, it can be easy to omit the removal of credentials in any applicable sandbox environments.

As discussed before, contractor access may not be as carefully monitored or controlled as full-time employees, so there is a likelihood that the contractor may still retain access to his or her former client's SaaS environment well after he or she has left the engagement. What if when the user assisted with administrator access, he or she created a sandbox account associated with her personal email instead of her corporate email? Exception notifications triggered by saved queries in the SaaS are likely to continue to route to the users personal email even after he or she is no longer engaged as a consultant. Unless a search is undertaken to remove all traces of this dependency, sensitive information may continue to be leaked. A case in point is when a couple of students in my *Accounting Information Systems* class had to enlist my assistance in locating and removing the queries they created in the SaaS in class as these were configured to send out daily notifications to their personal email.

The same challenges that can plague an ineffectively managed sandbox environment can be applied to a release preview environment insofar as it remains available for access even after the new version upgrade. With SaaS, there is really one version for all customers with different customers scheduled on different waves of upgrade releases depending on which tenant they are sharing. As the name implies, a release preview environment lets users log into the upgraded instance to peer into the mirror ball of newly built-out functionality documented in the release notes. Like the canary analysis that Netflix uses, this window of insight also gives an opportunity for users to test out customized workflows, records, or scripts in this new environment to make sure that they still work. For example, if a specific approval workflow were configured around a new vendor addition and had been in use, what would happen if the new release preview offered a similar or conflicting functionality? How do we verify if the new functionality would not impact the configured workflow adversely? Conversely, if the new functionality offers additional features that users can avail of, such as delegate approvers in the event the primary approver is out of office, how do we transition from relying on the "older" configuration to embracing the new albeit out-of-the-box functionality in a seamless manner? New functionality aside, what if field or attribute names are updated, new ones added or older ones inactivated? How would these impact existing configurations or customizations that consume the same impacted fields?

Thus, when thinking back to the emphasis on real and actual data or transactions in a live production environment, this approach may be, in hindsight, shortsighted and, to a certain extent, unforgiving. Appropriate actions can be taken ahead of time before the release upgrade when we are proactive in testing new functionality, as well as relating the new to the old. Depending on the release upgrade, minor or major, the extent of release preview familiarization and validation may take up less or more time as well as any associated resources. Insofar as release upgrades tend to offer enhancements that build on fixes from previously uncovered bugs, then by not undertaking the necessary efforts upfront, client enterprises are not taking advantage to resolve past challenges encountered to reduce the level of future manual intervention needed to sidestep them. Likewise, when access to a terminated employee is turned off in production, there is a likelihood that the same access may not be turned off in a release preview environment. So, while release preview, like sandbox, tends to fall out-of-scope and out-of-mind in access reviews and restrictions, the need nevertheless remains to restrict access to those on a need to know basis. Beyond access, API keys that point to an integrated SaaS when left unchanged in a release preview environment can lead to unanticipated consequences where live upstream production transactions from an integrated SaaS may start to appear in a downstream release preview environment instead of the actual production environment. This has the potential of understating the general ledger or accounting impact in the production instance of the downstream SaaS leading one to ask: what controls are in place to detect and attend to these errors well before the release preview becomes all but inaccessible after the version upgrade?

Let's switch gears. There is an infinitesimal difference between field labels and field names. The former can be updated by enterprise users to reflect names that are specific or immediately identifiable to the organization's needs. When we talked about the possibility of new fields or changes to fields being introduced in the release preview version that may have spillover impact on existing configuration work performed thus far, we are really talking about the latter. Herein, there are fields and then there are *fields*, so it makes sense to clarify this difference at the cost of splitting hairs. What this also illustrates is a series of ways that a metadata pattern emerges as one peers into a SaaS from inside out. A singular system field name may take on multiple field labels over time even though at any one time, only one is in use. Likewise, the same field while alphanumeric in nature as it resides in a multi-tenant architecture nevertheless is configured in specific formats to denote currencies, integers, decimals, or free form text depending on the business rationale. When we move up from the surface minutiae to adopt a wider lens view, we start to see bigger constructs embedded in others, so that behaviors or actions point to chaos within controls, unknowns within knowns. Depending on the SaaS at hand, a change to the field label at any given moment in time may take effect across all transactions, old and new, so therein lies a challenge with establishing a point in time rigor that is requisite for the unvarying presentation of quarterly financials, so that, as a result of changing daily rates, even a day difference in dates recorded can translate into different U.S. dollar (USD) amounts computed for the same local (foreign) currency amount rolled up into the main subsidiary for consolidated presentation.

Yet, in circling back to the metadata layer that introduces a buffer or a safe space of sorts to protect the integrity of the underlying field, its system name can be different from its espoused label, its true alphanumeric nature can be decoupled from its configured preferred presentation format so that one literally sees the same field represented differently when logged into the SaaS as opposed to viewing it on a printed invoice sent out externally. Customers may be accustomed to seeing product names aligned with the organization's external product website or catalog and thus the introduction of a middle buffer between intrinsic and extrinsic field labels can, and often does, make a world of difference in allowing for enterprises to perform necessary updates or tweaks to requisite fields without affecting its business dealings with the external stakeholders in any adverse way. In this manner, concerted back-stage activity resides behind what is presented on stage, and the fields in the SaaS are rendered less fragile. If we extend this concept a little further beyond fields or attributes, SaaS willing, specific lines on the invoice may be imploded or hidden on the printed invoice that is shared with the customer and different from what an internal member of the enterprise billing team would see when logged into the accounting SaaS.

As we start to explore this further, and in the context of visibility and other subtle controls discussed previously, we start to appreciate nuances and implications of what gets exposed versus what remains hidden, what an auditor sees when he or she examines the printed invoice and its contents versus what he or she sees when accessing the software directly to validate that revenue is properly recorded. What may appear to be a product giveaway, a $0 line with positive quantity on an invoice may really be a blank line auto-generated by a billing script applied to the sales order. The former changes the entire revenue allocation mix, whereas the latter may simply be a by-product of unfulfilled sales order lines. What is visible to the customer is what the customer is in turn obligated to pay and is used for comparison against the original order or executed contract. To add further complexity, some SaaS allow the system field names or identification numbers to be changed in addition to field labels, giving rise to the compounding effect of change upon change as it were. The hard questions that must be asked include: what controls are there over field names, labels, and IDs? To what degree do changes impact the way the same information is presented to both internal and external users? Perhaps more importantly, do these changes result in confusion over the way revenue transactions are ultimately recorded?

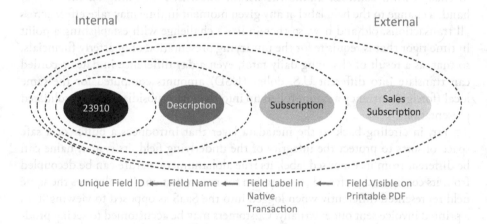

From the preceding diagram, we can look at the number of hops it takes, as we move from the outer to the inner, so that as we move from printable field label to internal field label to internal field name to internal identification number or ID, we can determine the possible ways or avenues where changes can be made and what possible impact may ensue. Even for the same transaction, customer or vendor, different templates or forms may be in use. For example, a professional service invoice may belong to a different template that has field labels specific to time and material services billed to customers. This invoice would look different from a subscription invoice that has subscription software and support billed to customers. Even natively within the same invoice transaction type in the billing SaaS, different revenue schedules may be in use, whether this relates to the recognition of revenue based on percentage of completion or rateably over a subscription period. Within the same invoice in the billing SaaS, there are field label names, as well as field internal and external identifiers. There are also professional service and subscription invoice templates. A third yet distinguishing variable can be reseller versus end customer invoices. For invoices sent to distributors or resellers, lines belonging to more than one end customer may be consolidated for display whereas invoices sent to an end customer invoice may merely contain items specific to only one customer.

What's in a label? I'm reminded of Emily Dickinson's poem:

> *I'm Nobody! Who are you?*
> *Are you – Nobody – too?*
> *Then there's a pair of us!*
> *Don't tell! they'd advertise – you know!*[44]

Here, the pair of nobodies allude to the ease of field interchangeability and subsequent ease of customization and adoption. As we look beyond the one SaaS at hand and appreciate the ease of integration among two or more SaaS, the inner (or, depending on your perspective, outer) circle enlarges so that as long as the external integrated SaaS taps into the internal field identification number or ID, then to the extent that it changes, the sync with the external SaaS would likely be impacted. Field labels would not impact this sync, and in choosing to use the internal field identifier rather than the label for sync, we render the system of interconnected or synced SaaS less fragile to changes in field labels. For some SaaS, even the internal field identifiers fall into two types, one auto-generated by the SaaS that cannot be changed, and another that is not auto-generated but can be manually assigned by users. The former is unique at any one time, but the advantage with having the latter is that the same identifier can be used to uniquely identify the same attribute on the same record across multiple SaaS. Put differently, any change to the manually assigned unique identifier would have pervasive impact across two or more synced SaaS rather than localized to the custom configurations in any one SaaS.

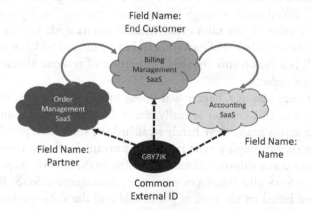

Thus, even though the multiple best-in-breed SaaS mirror disparate file-based systems of yesteryear, carefully appointed field attributes and, in our example, a common external ID, can go a long way to foster an environment where when the same record is concerned, such as a customer whether referenced upstream in a sales order or downstream in a payment, the same unique identifiers apply across multiple SaaS. Here, we are really pairing a somebody, a common identifier that resonates across multiple SaaS, with a nobody, an identifier that remains very much intrinsic to the specific SaaS at hand.

The pervasive impact of mismatched fields highlights the potential for toxic pairs. An example of toxic pairs can be compromised segregation of duties when the ability to add a vendor in an upstream SaaS is combined with the ability to create invoices in a mid-stream SaaS. Throw in the ability to process payments in a downstream SaaS and presto – one singular individual with access to all these functions across integrated SaaS can potentially execute a fraudulent transaction without additional oversight. In other words, there is a likelihood that individual may create a fictitious vendor, book a fictitious invoice, and process a fictitious payment without anyone ever noticing anything awry. Because the payments made to the individual are small insignificant amounts each month, small drips as it were, they are not a matter of any real concern to a manager or different accountant reviewing monthly bank reconciliations for material differences. The number of hops can be a useful way of determining whether upstream transactions can be easily referenced and combined in the same report with downstream ones.

In Chapter 4, we looked at how it can be useful to trace a downstream credit memo to an invoice to a fulfillment to a sales order. We would in effect undertake two hops to get from credit memo to sales order. The question becomes: does the SaaS let us do that when it comes to reporting? Can we get to sales order information by querying credit memos? If so, how granular does the SaaS get when it comes to tapping into upstream transaction detail? For example, would we be able to compare line level detail between the credit memo and the sale order to verify if what is credited is in fact what has been ordered? A credit given without changing the quantity fulfilled oddly enough changes the "received" sell price even if the "perceived" sell price on the sales order remains unchanged. Insofar as sell price contributes to the calculation of carve ins and carve outs of which standalone selling price (SSP) is a factor, this changes the portion of revenue allocated across all lines in the same order.

To some extent just as Chapter 8 is about known unknowns, the unknown within the known, this chapter is really about the unknown unknowns. In our review of fields across SaaS, we've barely scratched the surface on possible permutations. Imagine that through a sync from an upstream SaaS, the customer's email address is inputted as a ship-to address in a billing SaaS. In this setup, imagine too that the billing SaaS also interfaces with a tax management SaaS. Because sales tax is computed based on the type of goods sold and the ship-to address, the sync between the billing and tax management SaaS may throw up exceptions as email address is not a valid address value when it performs a complete address verification to determine the distribution of state, county and city tax for each item line in the invoice. The alert reveals a slip, how a specific field may be updated in a manner that does not lend it to easy integration with another SaaS. Our discussion thus far has centered on our ability to create a consistent field-naming methodology or convention across SaaS that creates an illusion that everything resides in one monolithic financial SaaS even as elements are interwoven across a garden variety of multiple SaaS with varying product capabilities and maturities. By requiring consistent ship-to addresses between two integrated SaaS, our sales tax computation example limits the degrees of freedom with which we can dictate and configure specific use of standard fields. As with the unique naming that can be assigned to custom fields, the same cannot be assigned to standard fields; after all, the latter form the foundational architecture upon which the SaaS is built and needs to be resilient to changes specific to client environments. Yet in a release upgrade, the SaaS vendor itself may choose to update the identifiers associated with these standard fields. It is therefore this possibility or risk that we are addressing by entertaining the notion of logging into a release preview environment beforehand to verify if it would impact the use of standard field identifiers in existing scripts or workflows as well as other integrated SaaS.

As our sales tax computation example implies, any release upgrade of any one SaaS may have implications in its ability to continue to integrate with other existing SaaS. During a version upgrade then, we don't just have to be concerned with locating impact within the SaaS: we are also concerned with identifying the impact on related and, in this case, integrated SaaS. Any breaks identified either within the SaaS or without, such as impacting integrated SaaS, are slips on the part of the SaaS provider. To the extent that they are addressed as priority fixes, they first need to be surfaced and identified by SaaS clients. It is not uncommon for a SaaS provider to adopt a SaaS centric view and specifically one that is specific to its very own SaaS rather than a more holistic view of the role it plays vis-a-vis another SaaS. So in an implementation of an expense management SaaS for instance that integrates with a downstream accounting SaaS, employees using the expense management SaaS may be unfamiliar with the downstream accounting one, so that specific decisions made upstream such as allowing the sync to be performed by a system account with administrator access and with it the ability to override locked periods, may result in nasty surprises: when attempting to close the books during month end, transactions are still synced into a locked period in the integrated downstream SaaS. The reverse may hold true. So, when it comes to sales tax computation, suppose the integration between the billing SaaS and the tax management SaaS does not yet allow for a credit to be created to refund the tax component only – recall our previous discussion on tax only credits. This issue may arise when a customer is really tax exempt but has been set up to be taxable in the billing SaaS to begin with. Suppose a new version of the tax management SaaS enhances upon this integration such that it now supports tax credits. This benefit would be gained in part by having the client enterprise proactively keep abreast of new upcoming releases of bundles from the downstream SaaS to be installed in the upstream SaaS, and either testing it in sandbox or inspecting the components before upgrading in production.

Because sandbox licenses are not free and, depending on the SaaS, may be priced as a percentage of the cost associated with production licenses, when peering into a best-of-breed SaaS architecture, we are likely to find a conglomerate of disembodied parts – production and sandbox environments belonging to some SaaS together with production only environments belonging to other SaaS – not unlike Frankenstein's creation. In the case of the tax management SaaS, a sandbox environment may not have been acquired, so even though sandbox is available for the upstream SaaS, it is not integrated with a sandbox copy of the downstream SaaS. In effect, to fully leverage the benefits of the new version with ability to support and process tax only credits, we would have to initiate an upgrade directly in production at the risk of incurring spillover impact on any other integrated or surrounding SaaS. In effect, if the customer were set up in an upstream sales management SaaS with taxable status, this would flow into the billing SaaS and then into the tax management SaaS for sales tax application. In this manner, the trigger lies not so much in the billing SaaS but even farther upstream in the sales management SaaS. Understanding the internal transactional and standing data roadmap architecture helps clarify where the control or check for appropriateness of tax exemption status should be. Otherwise, the busywork around correcting tax statuses in the billing SaaS takes on a life of its own. The same can be said for where to place a credit check for new customers. Having a customer credit check in the billing SaaS rather than the sales management one may be too little too late in qualifying an entity after it has already begun a contractual relationship with the enterprise. Recall the firefighting loop prefacing symptom over root cause resolution. Mistakes, as we have seen, differ from slips in that although the error made is intentional, instead of non-intentional, the intention is not malicious or ill-willed but rather stems from a misinterpretation of the SaaS at hand. To the extent that the field labels are misleading, these can lead to potential mistakes. When a customer email gets synced or manually entered in the ship-to address, and the SaaS at hand offers no warning, then this sets us up for a chain reaction resulting in more manual intervention.

Despite grandiose vendor proclamations, internal controls considerations are not magically whisked away when using SaaS. They merely take on a different shade. Just as Section 404 provided little guidance on internal control guidance, the same can be said for current practice aides or risk and control matrices on internal controls for SaaS. The concept of field of fields was first mentioned in Chapter 5, but here as we move from outer to inner, from the field label on a printed PDF to the field label on the native transaction to the underlying transaction field name to the field ID, we also touch upon the concept of interrelatedness covered in Chapter 1 – how, "the world is seen as a single interrelated field or continuum in which everything that interacts with – is the 'cause' of – of everything else, there are no separable causes and effects."[45] From field of fields, we move on to picture of pictures. In *The Human Condition*, Magritte depicts a painting that sits before a window in a room. The painting blends right in with the landscape outside the window so that the tree in the painting could have just as easily been mistaken for one outside. What's outside, the green and the sky, appears inside. Conversely, what's inside, the tree, appears outside. Magritte himself explains, "This is how we see the world. We see it outside ourselves, and at the same time we only have a representation of it in ourselves."[46] In thinking back to previous chapters and the analogy used with Frankenstein, it strikes me that when Victor Frankenstein created the creature, things could have turned out differently. For all the time spent on assembling parts to put together the final product, if he had used a sliver of that time to observe its behavior and at least attempted to be respectful to its needs and wishes, deaths would not have occurred, nor the ensuing ill-fated cat-and-mouse chase to the North Pole. Could it have been that Frankenstein chose to see only what he wanted to see? But then there would not have been a story, or a compelling one at that. When talking about Frankenstein with others, it becomes clear that the name Frankenstein conjures up the creature rather than its creator even though in the book the creature remained, rather aptly, nameless. Is there subconscious bias on our part I wonder? How many of us, unbeknown even to ourselves play the Frankenstein to our creature manifested in different spheres of our everyday exchanges, shutting down any attempt at establishing a two-way dialogue or entertaining the possibility of new ideas?

In a chapter where we talked about SaaS hotlines and customer satisfaction surveys, it must be said that teachers are not immune to student appraisals, not least adjunct professors. After teaching four semesters, I had my share of feedback that ran the gamut, but one stood out in particular. If I may paraphrase the feedback, it went something like: sometimes with all the frantic click-click that accompanies lab exercises in configuring the SaaS, it can be easy to forget the point of it all. Every so often, I think back to this remark. I can see how when in the throes of showing students the steps to configure a SaaS through point-and-click in a limited 2½ hour window, I can get blindsided by showcasing software wizardry or mastery over prefacing the context in which it is used. Maybe instead of emphasizing the array of fields that can be tailored to meet specific business needs, I could have spent more time exploring the field of fields, or picture of pictures. What's within is in fact a reflection of what's without. When caught up with the bells and whistle of the SaaS at hand – the what and the how – it can be easy to lose sight of the rationale as to why it is even used to begin with. Perhaps the greater unknown unknown, more than an inability to see past system inscribed process sequences, integrated SaaS, release preview, or sandbox environments conveniently deemed out-of-scope, or custom field of fields, is a fundamental inability to recognize what has always been standing right before our very eyes all this time. In his poem, *Love After Love*, Derek Walcott writes about the possibility of finding ourselves at our "own door" and "mirror" after years of hanging on to "photographs" and "desperate notes."[47] At the 2017 Seoul Biennale of Architecture and Urbanism, *Twin Mirror*, an installation, scans the face of every visitor and runs its past two side-by-size facial recognition models built with different assumptions and training data.[48] The outcome? The results are different for the same visitor. Who among us chooses to continue to reject what we see? Who among us would finally begin to embrace what has been staring back at us all along?

Exercise 9.1

Think of a process that you perform as part of your everyday work. What is the deliverable or output?

1. Think of three different tasks you perform to insure quality?
2. How does each task enhance accuracy, completeness and validity?
3. Is each of the identified tasks more preventive or detective in nature?
4. Which, if any, can be flagged as a key internal control?

Discussion

In a fun breakout exercise in a roomful of IT personnel, an example shared of an "idealized" everyday process is the processing of salary increments for employees who have received favorable performance ratings. Specific tasks listed include verifying proposed increments against manager reviews and human resource (HR) authorizations with assessed ratings, ensuring that only authorized personnel have access to make the changes, and informing impacted employees after changes have been made. Of these, the first two are more preventive in nature and the last one more detective. They are also more likely to be flagged as key internal controls rather than the last one which relies on employees to detect inappropriate or incorrect updates, after the fact. By asking the questions in this open-format style rather than start with "what key internal controls do you have," to what extent are we closer to unearthing actual in-situ practices rather than going with preconceived notions? Insofar as actual practices are tapped into, how are resulting control objectives less likely to be divorced from everyday operational needs? More importantly, to what extent are we using or reusing what we have rather than seeking what we don't have and don't necessarily need?

Exercise 9.2

Give an example of a slip and an example of a mistake in the context of:

1. Entering customer information
2. Approving a journal entry
3. Investigating an exception notification of sync failure

For each of the earlier, explain how the design of the SaaS can contribute to either a slip or a mistake.

Discussion

A slip can happen when sync exception notifications are received and not followed up on in a timely basis because they are either seen to have no production impact or get routed to a spam email folder. A mistake is likely to occur if the design of the sync exception notifications is not set up to facilitate timely intervention, such as if the email recipient is inundated with tons of emails to the point of ignoring these altogether or having a hard time figuring out the false positives from actual exceptions. Likewise, when entering customer information or approving transactions such as journals, poor or misleading use of field labels ("bad" affordances) tend to confound users so resulting slips become almost inevitable. Mistakes happen when wrong data is entered or inappropriate entries are approved when the subject misinterprets what she or he sees on the screen: is a contact's address the same as bill-to or ship-to address; is it easy to tell a duplicate journal entry has been made?

Exercise 9.3

Pick a specific business process such as processing an order or making a payment using SaaS and try to use as many components from the following in *Universal Principles of Design* as to improve the forgiveness of the system design:

1. Good affordance
2. Reversibility of actions
3. Safety nets
4. Confirmation
5. Warning
6. Help[49]

Discussion

A forgiving SaaS is also a more controlling SaaS. Sounds contradictory? A more controlling SaaS is far better adept at controlling the myriad of possible insults to architectural and transactional integrity. These components, or controls, work together and in part compensate each other, so a SaaS with poor affordances, such as poor user interface crowded out by misleading task bars and inconspicuous action buttons, may require more safety nets such as a message that screams, "Note you are about to delete a transaction. Are you sure you want to proceed?" Once you begin to look at SaaS from a design perspective, the mundane world of controls starts to take on new appeal.

Endnotes

1 Hart, H. L. A. (1994). *The Concept of Law* (2nd ed.). Oxford, UK: Clarendon Press.
2 Bialik, C. (June 16, 2005). How much is it really costing to comply with Sarbanes-Oxley? *Wall Street Journal.* https://www.wsj.com/articles/SB111885041027560378
3 Lidwell, W., Holden, K., Butler, J., and Elam, K. (2010). *Universal Principles of Design: 125 Ways to Enhance Usability, Influence Perception, Increase Appeal, Make Better Design Decisions, and Teach Through Design.* Beverly, MA: Rockport Publishers.
4 Ibid.
5 Ibid.
6 Carr, N. (2004). *Does IT Matter? Information Technology and the Corrosion of Competitive Advantage.* Boston, MA: Harvard Business School Press.
7 Button, G. and Harper, R. (1995). The relevance of 'work-practice' for design. *Computer Supported Cooperative Work*, 4(4), 263–280.
8 Ibid.
9 Ibid.
10 Ibid.
11 Ibid.
12 Ibid.
13 Ibid.

14 Ibid.

15 Takeuchi, H. and Ikujiro, N. (January–February 1986). The new product development game. *Harvard Business Review*, 64(1), 321.

16 Royce, W. W. (1970). Managing the development of large software systems in: Technical papers of western electronic show and convention (WesCon). August 25–28, 1970, Los Angeles, CA.

17 Button, G. and Harper, R. The relevance of 'work-practice' for design.

18 Ibid.

19 Ibid.

20 Ibid.

21 Lidwell, W., Holden, K., Butler, J., and Elam, K. *Universal Principles of Design: 125 Ways to Enhance Usability, Influence Perception, Increase Appeal, Make Better Design Decisions, and Teach Through Design.*

22 Button, G. and Harper, R. The relevance of 'work-practice' for design.

23 Ibid.

24 Ibid.

25 Ibid.

26 Wiener, A. (December 4, 2017). Page not found: A brief history of the 404 error. *Wired*. https://www.wired.com/story/page-not-found-a-brief-history-of-the-404-error/

27 Ibid.

28 Pasha, S. and Seid, J. (May 25, 2006). Lay and Skilling's day of reckoning. CNNMoney.com.

29 Lanier, J. (2011). *You Are Not a Gadget: A Manifesto.*

30 McKenna, F. (April 9, 2012). Groupon: Where were the Auditors? *Forbes*. https://www.forbes.com/sites/francinemckenna/2012/04/09/groupon-where-were-the-auditors/#3a36889c2568

31 Weil, J. (August 3, 2011). Groupon's strikeouts reveal an unspoken truth: Jonathan Weil. Bloomberg. https://www.bloomberg.com/view/articles/2011-08-04/groupon-s-strikeouts-reveal-an-unspoken-truth-jonathan-weil

32 Ibid.

33 Jones, D. N. (July 13, 2016). Groupon settles shareholder IPO suit for $45M. Law360. https://www.law360.com/articles/816985/groupon-settles-shareholder-ipo-suit-for-45m

34 Ibid.

35 Groupon amended S-1 filed with the Securities Exchange Commission.

36 De La Merced, M. J. (July 2, 2011). The Groupon I.P.O: What is adjusted CSOI? *The New York Times*. https://dealbook.nytimes.com/2011/06/02/the-groupon-i-p-o-what-is-adjusted-csoi/

37 Lam, B. (September 22, 2015). A world with fewer deals: Groupon cuts 1,000 jobs. *The Atlantic*. https://www.theatlantic.com/business/archive/2015/09/groupon-layoffs/406687/

38 Collins, M. L., Theis, M. C., Trzeciak, R. F., Strozer, J. R., Clark, J. W., Costa, D. L., Cassidy, T., Albrethsen, M .J., and Moore, A. P. (December 2016). *Common Sense Guide to Mitigating Insider Threats, Fifth Edition*. CMU/SEI-2016-TR-015. Software Engineering Institute.

39 Mundy, S. (January 10, 2018). PwC hit with 2-year India audit ban for Satyam case. *Financial Times*. https://www.ft.com/content/c1231f40-f695-11e7-88f7-5465a6ce1a00

40 Ibid.

41 Graeber, D. (2012). Of flying cars and the declining rate of profit. *The Baffler*, (19), 66–84. http://thebaffler.com/salvos/of-flying-cars-and-the-declining-rate-of-profit#left-menu

42 Strathern, M. (June 2000). The tyranny of transparency. *British Educational Research Journal*, 26(3), 309–321.

43 Graeber, D. Of flying cars and the declining rate of profit.

44 Dickinson, E. 1830–1886. (1978). *I'm Nobody! Who Are You?: Poems of Emily Dickinson for Children*. Owings Mills, MD: Stemmer House Publishers.

45 Meyer, L. B. (1967). *Music, the Arts, and Ideas*. Chicago, IL: University of Chicago Press.

46 Magritte, R. and Torczyner, H. (1977). *Magritte, Ideas and Images*. New York: H.N. Abrams.

47 Walcott, D. (1986). *Collected Poems, 1948–1984*. New York: Farrar, Straus and Giroux.

48 Gerfen, K. (January 12, 2018). The polymath: David Benjamin is expanding the definition of architecture. *Architect Magazine*. http://www.architectmagazine.com/practice/the-polymath-david-benjamin-is-expanding-the-definition-of-architecture_o

49 Lidwell, W., Holden, K., Butler, J., and Elam, K. *Universal Principles of Design: 125 Ways to Enhance Usability, Influence Perception, Increase Appeal, Make Better Design Decisions, and Teach Through Design*.

Chapter 10

Other Selves

The breaking of a wave cannot explain the whole sea.[1]

Vladimir Nabokov

In Alice Notley's poem, *The Prophet*, she writes of "one" and how one is "one ... & two & yet."[2] By contrast, in Chapter 4, we reviewed Kripke's formula that has an unusual twist.[3]

$$X \text{ quus } Y \begin{cases} X + Y \text{ if } X, Y < 57 \\ \\ 5 \text{ otherwise} \end{cases}$$

Kripke's "quus" formula seems incredibly delimiting if only the addition of numbers never goes beyond 57, whereas Notley compels us to think of our expansiveness as life itself. Yet all too often, when we find ourselves coming face to face with this reality, we are quick to dismiss it as an omission or oversight of sorts. When validating internal controls with a client, an auditor hears about vendor approvals automated using the Software as a Service (SaaS) at hand. Yet upon further investigation, the auditor realizes access to update vendors has not been restricted so technically even if a vendor were rejected, members of the accounts payable (A/P) team can still activate it. Another curious scene: yet a different auditor when performing a process walkthrough with a client hears that access to all permissions within a SaaS is restricted to segregated roles. Yet, upon testing in a sandbox environment, the auditor realizes that unbeknown to users, they can bypass this control as they all have the ability to update existing roles and permissions. Whereas in previous

337

chapters, we cover the need for a SaaS to be more forgiving in allowing users to reverse their actions or be forewarned before making any catastrophic moves, the two examples mentioned here highlight the reverse: how intended controls don't always work out the way they should despite the best of intentions. A step is missing. Something is in conflict. A control is negated by the very lack of control in another area. Here's another perspective: the devil is in the details.

Although these two examples are hypothetical, they scratch the surface of what audit findings can yield when the auditor experiments or tinkers around. I recall the days of system pre-implementation audits before the Sarbanes–Oxley Act (SOX). Although the software landscape back then was characterized by on-premise and traditional enterprise resource planning (ERP) solutions as opposed to the plethora of best-in-breed SaaS options we have today, there are recurring patterns. The two examples just shared have traces of a hide-the-key-under-the-doormat pattern, where an otherwise undetected susceptibility has the potential of unwinding a controlled if not precarious arrangement at hand. Ironically, to come upon such findings, the auditor would have to be less of an auditor, relying merely on existing artifacts or only auditing the control at hand. The auditor needs to be resourceful surely but also take on a hacker mentality even if in today's audit and compliance world, a hacker is viewed with at best disdain or at worst fear and foreboding. The very word hacking conjures up malicious attacks both from inside and out – phishing emails that steal corporate secrets, clicked links that download programs that reverberate and disrupt the internal network, or thousands of unknown computers that serve as unwittingly allies in propagating a virus. Even as I write this, the media is awash in news of the two recently uncovered security flaws, Meltdown and Specter, that affect microprocessors built by Intel.[4] Both flaws allow passwords and other sensitive information to be stolen from different software run from the same server, the foundational infrastructure for cloud computing.[5] Yet, by definition, a hacker per *The New Hacker's Dictionary* can mean someone who enjoys messing with and stretching system capabilities. Contrast this with another who is easily contented with grasping the bare minimum.[6] A hacker can also be someone who is adept enough at navigating around a program to either work around or resolve challenges or restrictions encountered.[7]

In previous chapters, we explored how understanding SaaS is very much like learning a new language. Inevitably, there are limitations to this language. I'm reminded of a scene from *Victoria and Abdul*, a 2017 movie based on the book of same name by Shrabani Basu chronicling the real-life relationship between Queen Victoria of the United Kingdom and her Indian Muslim servant Abdul Karim from 1887 to 1901. In one of the movie's earlier scenes, Abdul tells Queen Victoria, "Life is like a carpet. We weave in and out to make a pattern" before adding "Look at this – here is a bird of freedom caught forever in the design."[8] To what extent have the controls we erected apprehended the myriad of avenues available for configuration, arrested at mid-flight as it were? Our subsequent displacement of "what is" with "what should be" recalls Shoshana Zuboff's lament that "we remain … prisoners of a language that has its roots in a way of life and a way of work that are fast becoming obsolete."[9] Despite being the "Empress of India," Queen Victoria herself seems oblivious to the myriad of local languages in use when she asks Abdul to teach her Indian or "Whatever it is you speak."[10] Like immutable mobiles, where something gets lost in translation, the way the local natives visualize geography or time, though vastly different from the French explorers, nonetheless get subsumed in maps and other prevailing artifacts of the day and used to communicate across oceans. Or how in our salmon farm, the program at hand doesn't quite make the fish talk, despite what it has been promised to do, relying instead on busy manual hands behind the scenes. Just as traces of Eurocentrism are evident in Latour's depiction of La Perouse's encounter with the local Chinese natives, *Victoria and Abdul* has met with its fair share of critics who question the undertone of Orientalism in its one-dimensional portrayal of Abdul.[11] The question becomes: do we abandon all talk of internal controls for SaaS altogether, since it is all but impossible not to introduce an element of subjectivity consciously or otherwise into an otherwise "objective" scene? Yet even this view is highly suspect, downplaying the roles humans have in co-composing non-humans, so that what appears as an "objective" reality may be better described as a "multiple-authored" or co-authored scene composed of disparate threads that come together rather than serve as a passive construct to be acted upon. Witness the use of "kluge," a likely derivative of Scott's klugie for a common toilet. In *The New Hacker's Dictionary*, it refers to a quick programming technique of fixing the issue at hand though not in the most elegant or ideal of manner.[12] It borders on a "crock" not quite a "crock of shit" where the hack delivered is brittle at best.[13] A hack insofar as it is a "crock of shit," is nevertheless an invitation for a deeper engagement beyond an initial stop-gap intervention. I'm reminded of Richard Wright's poem in which he writes of how horseshit "blaze up into golden stones" in the sunlight.[14]

A "crock of shit," or a bad hack, is thus alchemical, a necessary reuse or leverage of the "bad" to get us to the "good." Indeed, one can be forgiven for mistaking optimization as our end goal in exploring the design of internal controls for SaaS when all too often, when faced with inevitable real-life constraints on resource and time, we are really satisficing rather than optimizing. This is the basic premise behind hacking, kluging, or crocking. Think of them as shortcuts. I remember presenting to my *Accounting Information Systems* class a newspaper article titled *Thanksgiving Hacks* and one of the students automatically assumed that a malicious virus has been introduced to an otherwise sanguine atmosphere. Within SaaS administration, Salesforce popularized administrator hacks, shortcuts to deliver quick customizations to tailor what is out-of-the-box with the existing internal organizational needs. Yet, a fine line needs to be carefully threaded so that we don't stop short at kludges or crocks. Otherwise, over time, the "code behaves as a human being on crutches; they walk somehow, but the observers fear they [sic] to drop down."[15] Yet to attempt at configuring or customizing a SaaS, to feel out or test out its potential, is really half the battle won. Students in my *Accounting Information*

Systems class upon learning how easy it is to add a hello message after devising a workflow through point-and-click every time an invoice is opened are nonetheless perplexed on what to do when a different question is asked on how to restrict access to this customized workflow so that this same message doesn't escalate from friendly albeit generic sounding to caustic or worse, sinister. Customizations or customized configurations or generic customizations as some vendors are apt to call them are a double-edged sword surely because the more you configure or customize, the more is put under an internal controls lens. Yet putting this aside, to effectively use SaaS to begin with, to attempt to overcome initial poor affordances out-of-the-box, we may have to be a bricoleur of sorts, borrowing from the work of French anthropologist Claude Lévi-Strauss, constructing or creating based on whatever material or tool is at hand.[16] For at the end of the day, when it comes to using SaaS, we merely work with what has been offered, application programming interfaces (APIs) or platform script logic that are exposed. Until fields are exposed for use, they cannot be scripted or used in a workflow since customers do not have the ability to modify the underlying source code maintained by SaaS providers.

In *Life on the Screen*, Sherry Turkle reviews the concept of bricolage in code projects, characterizing "bricoleur style" as an alternative to what she describes as the conventional structured "planner" approach with top-down decomposition of step-by-step tasks.[17] When I asked students to build in logic into the SaaS for a custom field to recompute the amount entered by multiplying the quantity with the rate, there are multiple approaches.

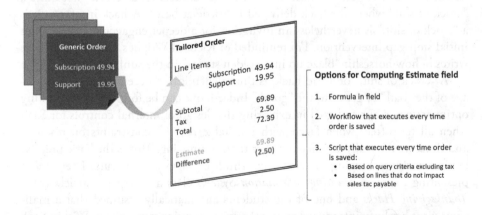

One student put the formula directly in the custom field. Another created a workflow to compute the formula in the field. Yet another employed a client end script. Even within a script, there can be multiple approaches. If, for example, selected lines need to be excluded, we might first count the number of lines and check for applicability of each line. Alternately, we might call forth a query that filters out lines that are not in scope. In this manner, there is no one right approach. The solution chosen depends on our level of comfort with handling the arsenal of tools that come with the SaaS at hand. In fact, it is precisely because there is not just one path but multiple possible paths that makes the SaaS design more forgiving and, to that end, more universal in its reach. At a recent Dreamforce conference in San Francisco, Salesforce had a *Day of the Admins*, celebrating the unsung heroes and heroines within client organizations who make things hum along, or fish sing for that matter, bricoleur style. So just as there are thriving communities of analysts classifying SaaS into magic quadrants or otherwise, audit advisory groups advocating the key controls for reliance in any given SaaS, there are also communities of client power users or administrators who share trials and tribulations on what worked and what didn't work, partners or vendors they enjoyed or did not enjoy working with, strategies employed in deploying new implementations, or relying on localized configurations or customizations – battles won or battle scars. It is this last group that deserves special mention. Auditors are more inclined to view members in this administrator group with suspicion seeing how imbued almost always with super-user powers within the SaaS, they can work their magic. But therein lies a huge difference between SaaS as clay versus on-premise traditional ERP solutions as bricks. Instead of continuing with manual controls key or compensating, there is a higher likelihood that a one-time effort can be spent in using all that is available out-of-the-box to automate the solution. As discussed in Chapter 9, rather than filing a case or ticket with SaaS support only when the SaaS is down or not working as intended, the same question can be raised when it comes to tinkering with whatever custom field, workflow, or script that is at hand and then seeking answers when these don't quite work out as intended. The emphasis here should be on testing and, specifically, end user or user acceptance testing (UAT) as it is more commonly referred to. Securing time and resource for this is harder than we might think simply because of the limited amount of bandwidth available. Typically, the accounting team has 2 weeks out of every month to work on projects and assist with UAT as all other time is devoted to closing the month. Time is necessary not just for testing positive use cases; in many cases, testing is not performed for negative use cases. What do we mean by this?

In our previous example on scripting used to exclude lines that are not in scope for amount computation, testing should be performed not only on verifying whether the right lines are carved out, but also whether the right ones have been carved in. Do test transactions only contain lines that needed to be carved in, carved out, or both? To the extent that configuration can be exacted out-of-the-box, as it were, then it needs to hum to the accompaniment of requisite testing. The latter is likely an area that is grossly underestimated when we think about SaaS. After all, SaaS is sold on the promise that it is not only easier or more intuitive to use but also does not require additional coding; otherwise, why buy external software to begin with – why not have developers code or build the entire SaaS in-house altogether? Lest the preparation leading up to testing is itself underestimated, if more up-to-date transactions were needed for a more "real-life" validation, then a request for a production refresh in the sandbox instance needs to be submitted.

The customized script would have to be duplicated in sandbox after the refresh. As far as the same test environment is used for other needs – other scripts or workflows that are in development, areas meriting testing, integration with other SaaS, etc. – these need to be placed into consideration. We wouldn't want to overwrite other works in progress with this more recent refresh. When it comes to the testing itself, insofar as exceptions are found, where would they be documented? Are they reviewed and how do we know if they are addressed adequately? Would remediation testing happen out of the same environment? Would we submit yet another request for sandbox refresh, thus necessitating an entire round of reviews all over again, or would we simply recreate specific transactions that did not pass the test? Finally, to the extent that all test scenarios have not been identified and flushed out in detail to be tested, would hypercare be provided upon the initial deployment of the change, so that any breaks experienced in production are readily escalated through the necessary channels and dealt with expediently?

As it were, at each gating checkpoint, measures are taken to break the new build, if only it becomes less fragile with each rinse-and-repeat series of test-fix-remediate. When released to production, hypercare is a means of incorporating forgiveness, a manual attempt at providing a safety net of sorts for catching and addressing quickly any unforeseen circumstances that arise. In continuing with our example on computing amounts at the line level for validation, what happens if the test environment in use is not integrated, as its production counterpart is, with another SaaS? When deploying the changes to production, errors may arise precluding new transactions from being synced in, as the script is determined to be interrupting with the existing web services. In this case, a rollback of the script changes may suffice in restoring operations to the normal state, but if one or more other integrated SaaS were configured to support the script changes such as the addition of new attributes, the intervention required may not be as straightforward or swift. During troubleshooting and coming up with a solution during hypercare, a post-mortem retrospective may suggest that the test environment be hooked up to the test instance of the other SaaS, if only to have integration testing be performed before rather than after production releases. Thus, in just this simple example of SaaS configuration-work and testing, you can already tell that in addition to functionality testing with UAT, integration testing is also an area that should come into prominence as SaaS is more easily integrated with another SaaS.

In an odd turn of events, I've been in situations where, because of a pervasive impact to the SaaS architecture, the very case management or ticketing system that the SaaS vendor is using to record support calls is down. In this case, the means to record a support call on an issue with a specific SaaS functionality, the very reason for the call in the first place, is itself also unavailable. As you can imagine, the approaches of SaaS vendors vary when it comes to logging tickets. On one extreme, the vendor only lets clients submit requests by creating a case online, rather than having them call into a support hotline. On the other extreme, the vendor lets customers call in directly to the support hotline without having to go through what appears to be requisite verifications of name, title, rank, and file, as it were, to quickly access help resources with a warm voice at hand. Most vendors reside in the realm between these two extremes, granting clients, and even then only "a few good men," the ability to contact the vendor support each time whether it is during new implementation or post go-live. Questions include how to create a specific template to upload standing master data like employees or set up a specific payment schedule to creating a new expense type. More in-depth assistance can also be secured either through an agreed block of hours charged albeit on a time and material basis or a fixed, one-time expense, as a percentage of annual subscription costs. Having a "warm" voice on the phone is not necessarily preferable to submitting a case online, and receiving an asynchronous response, especially if the response received is of the nondescript not to mention nonchalant "we will get back to you after further investigation" variety. In some cases, I've seen an incredible response time when a case is submitted online as opposed to logged with a "live" person over the phone. If nothing else, to not contact SaaS support would be like sticking our head in the sand and missing out on the opportunity to expand our horizons in understanding any existing or future capability. Unnoticed and unseen, it remains undetected, not accounted for and thus not seen as a possible way to alleviate an existing or future manual burden. So here too, just as the auditor can become less of an auditor, and more like a hacker, so that he or she can effectively audit better or at least provide management with more pragmatic solutions directly leveraging SaaS functionality, users of SaaS, by becoming less passive, by contacting support, or attending user focus groups or even vendor conferences, and taking on co-developer, constructor and even orchestrator abilities in effect become far better users adept at navigating even the worst of SaaS affordances on display out-of-the-box. Conversely, developers today are compelled to become more like end users, so that what matters is not simply a journal approval workflow but one that lends itself to an easy query of approval or rejection trails with timestamps as part of an audit deliverable or appreciation the accounting implications of the workflow in overriding locked periods. In this manner, the sharp edge of the sword slices both ways, not merely in a user taking on the shades of a developer but also in reverse, a developer taking on the role of the user.

It is compelling to see a fellow user take on a designer or constructor role and see how he or she is able to tailor what is out-of-the-box using out-of-the-box configurational capability. Yet, it becomes even more compelling when we are talking about a community of users from varied client organizations. Surely the choruses of voices heard when a SaaS goes down is more compelling than just one or two high-pitched ones. And while we are on the topic of SaaS availability – here I remember seeing an ad that read SaaS is on the line – there is probably no faster way to know when a SaaS is going down than when the integration Platform as a Service (iPaaS) integrating it with an upstream SaaS begins sending exception notifications on failed attempts at creating mirrored transactions downstream. In this manner, we move beyond any one singular control compensating for another within any one SaaS, whether manual for automated, and start to see how one

SaaS can effectively compensate the flaws of another. The "multiply-authored" cloud architecture of best-in-breed SaaS is one that can appear brittle on the outset especially since it is not on-premise, and its source code is not owned by the client, but precisely because multiple integrated SaaS speak with one another and compensate for the shortfalls of one or the other that we arrive at a curious strength in numbers. We can make the counterargument that strength in numbers is also evidenced by multiple customers using the same SaaS or same combination of SaaS, and this in turn accelerates the delivery of universal or common features desired.

When any SaaS does go down or becomes unavailable, the subtle control of visibility can be undeniably powerful in prompting an accelerated response – contrast this with an insular in-house developed application for which there is no market share and by association not quite the same pressure to deliver – and a more complete root cause analysis following incident resolution. Because the success of the SaaS vendor is in part dependent on its uptime, there is likely a greater level of scrutiny and investment in failover sites. To be sure this is a contrarian perspective: the idea that precisely because something (or very likely someone) is not within our control (or gated walls) that it is exposed and shared in usage (well then maybe not so much someone), that a great visibility and with it even greater demands on delivery of desired features or configurations can itself yield a less fragile and indeed even more forgiving product, time-tested by varied enterprises in altogether different industry verticals. Claudio Ciborra in his study of strategic information systems views bricolage as the constant "trying out" and experimentation, not to mention the constant ordering of people and resources as a means of maintaining competitive advantage.[18] In fact, the premise behind generative design is to use computer algorithms to create thousands of multi-varied solutions to solve a design problem.[19] At *The Living*, a core team of 10 architects applied generative design principles to an office at Autodesk Toronto.[20] Contrast this with an audit perspective where management controls are exacted top-down; Ciborra's perspective in contrast is a bottoms-up approach.

There is no greater credibility than having an internal cross-functional team work through the challenges in a software implementation, and with the configuration rich capability that can be unpacked, perhaps therein lies a greater opportunity at hand for SaaS customers. As David Benjamin, *The* Living CEO put it, a blind allegiance to computerized computation "could allow us to just hit the repeat button and crank out unthoughtful architectural responses in a lot of different conditions."[21] Just as *The Living* explored machine learning – the use of algorithms on data to improve the performance of a specific tasks – in more recent projects, there is no greater credibility than when different SaaS customers from different industry verticals nonetheless all report the same issue or concern at the about the same time to the SaaS vendor. The power of this group behavior is not quite the same as the popularized phenomenon of "groupthink" yet garners enough momentum from the combined force of masses over any one singular customer. Had the software been on-premise and a local installation with little public visibility, the rate of response from its vendor would have been likely lower. And in this respect, SaaS is truly a utility computing of sorts.

Imagine not being able to get online at home. This is a minor catastrophe of sorts, which speaks to a greater malaise of our times, but never mind that: what would we do? We could call up our home internet service provider (ISP). When inundated with calls by different homes within the same locale or vicinity, the ISP, assuming it is of reliable and long-standing reputation, would act swiftly. There may be a status update put out periodically to highlight actions taken to resolve the issue at hand. Although in this case because no online access is possible, if the status updates were provided on a website, this would not be feasible. A phone call here would make the most sense, even if hardly anyone uses the mobile phone for making calls these days. The process to restore online access to be able to consume the Internet, including SaaS, is in fact a mirror of the same process undertaken to resolve an issue faced with SaaS. It is idealistic to assume that the SaaS consumed would be error-free or else be available for access all that time. There are brief periods typically during non-business hours that it too will be down because of periodic maintenance or release of quick fixes involved. These are inevitable tradeoffs with having a different external entity provide your in-house transactional intensive applications. So, like our home online surfing example, a SaaS may have an online status outage page that alerts users of any service degradations as well as follow-up efforts taken to restore service. Independently, when using the SaaS at work or at home, there may be simple diagnostic data provided on the SaaS on server, network, and client statistics. Server statistics relate to the length of time it takes for the SaaS to assemble the page on their end and deliver it to the network. Network statistics relate to the length of time for the page to be delivered to your Web browser of choice. Finally, client statistics refer to the amount of time for the page to load on your browser. Behind the scenes, as you can imagine, where SaaS users choose to insert scripts, whether these are exacted on the server or client end would have performance implications. There are other tools available that we can run to monitor performance metrics such as access speed, but mostly we need to determine if it is an issue with our office or home network or Wi-Fi as opposed to with the SaaS availability. The ISP's inability to reach its customer through an online status update simply because the home internet network is itself down is a story within a story. Recall the earlier instance of a SaaS outage, the very case management in use by the SaaS vendor to manage support calls is interwoven into its own SaaS functionality so that when the latter is unavailable, the former is affected as well.

The compounding effect of multiple local participants can perhaps be best illustrated by an unlikely source. Digital Green, led by Rikin Gandhi, had its origins in a Microsoft research lab. Seeking to help solve disparate agricultural practices in India where more than 60% of the population relies on agriculture, Digital Green uses video as the primary means of sharing agricultural practices. Here, in far flung villages where online access is not even available, TVs and DVD players are employed. What does this have to do with SaaS, you may ask? Hold your horses.

The key with Digital Green is that it "capitalizes on natural social dynamics to amplify a single extension worker's ability to evangelize agricultural practices."[22] By experimenting with different ways even in showing or talking about video in local villages, the researchers observe that contrary to popular opinion, low and medium skilled facilitators shown in videos appear more credible that expert presenters.[23] A connection is more easily established with seeing someone whom you can instantly identify with in the manner of speaking as well as in outward appearance.[24] For some farmers, the ability to appear on TV leads to a jostling or competition of sorts for that brief shot at fame.[25] The use of local farmers in videos has thus been a silver bullet of sorts for Digital Green in making a tangible difference to the adoption of newer agriculture practices and establishing of camaraderie between extension worker and farmer.[26] In a 13-month trail pitting 8 control villages armed with the Digital Green approach with 8 that weren't armed, Digital Green was 10 times more effective per dollar spent on getting the farmers to adopt the newer agricultural practices.[27] In many respects, this is likely why at SaaS conferences, you would almost always find SaaS customers being invited to give presentations or be on a panel to answer questions. The power of the community of SaaS customers is something that hasn't yet been fully tapped into perhaps because each SaaS conference or customer advisory board or focus group is ultimately constrained by the perimeters of the specific SaaS at hand. Yet, it is not hard to see how multiple stakeholders, even though they may be using a different SaaS, for example, Expensify instead of Concur, for expense management, nonetheless may be interested in congregating and seeing how their needs nevertheless converge when both SaaS they use integrate with the same downstream accounting SaaS such as NetSuite. What is perhaps needed is not a vendor specific SaaS conference but a multi-vendor cloud conference that mirrors the multi-authored enterprise cloud landscape that we have come to embrace.

Paradoxically, when we are less insistent on being a customer or a vendor, we are better able at appreciating the nuances of being either. Recall from Exercise 4.2 in Chapter 4 how the better we are at playing a customer, the better we become at being a vendor. The same purchase requisition process that our organization undergoes to review spending is the likely the same one used by our customer. Likewise, just as it is more likely that when a vendor gets paid on time by including our PO number on its invoice thereby easing the process we have internally in reviewing and comparing the invoice to a purchase order (PO) generated within, the same can be said for getting a customer to pay an invoice we issue in a more timely manner simply by making it easier for the customer to compare its PO number listed on the invoice. In this manner, our customer is like our other self. I'm reminded of Carly Simon's remarks in her *Songs from the Trees* compilation album:

> *Don't get Orpheus and Boys in the Trees confused. They are one and the same. We are one and the same.*[28]

The previous example demonstrates how when we are better customers (through use of POs to review against receipt of service or goods and invoice), we can also become vendors (by including our customer's internal PO number on our issued invoices). The reverse can also hold true. When we are better vendors, we can also become better customers. To see how this might work, consider an example when through the use of an iPaaS, we are able to sync in customer payments directly into an accounting SaaS. For these to be auto-matched against outstanding and unpaid customer invoices, we would need our vendors to include our invoice numbers on their payments. In this manner, where the invoice number and the amount of payment received directly corresponds with an existing open invoice, the payment synced in can be applied immediately, leaving the collections or payments team to only focus on processing payments on an exception handling basis, such as focusing on those that have missing or different invoice numbers or amounts. When we are better vendors in accelerating the time for payments received to be applied against open accounts receivable, we can in effect become better customers by including our vendor invoice numbers in the payments we issue, not only expediting the internal processing on the vendor end but also minimizing the level of back-and-forth inquiries as to which of the outstanding invoices to apply the payment received.

The SaaS customer as co-designer, constructor, or orchestrator drives tailored configurations within any one given SaaS as well as across varied best-in-breed SaaS. Here, we are taking a step further in having the SaaS customer play the role of product advocate, evangelist, or champion. It is this underlying subtext that underlies Salesforce's act of shining the spotlight on Salesforce admin rock stars in their respective customer organizations. Think of these administrators as the oil that greases the Salesforce engine. When an issue arises, they are the first to attend to it, so in many respects unlike the SaaS support provided, they are typically the first line of defense. Because they deal with rubber-meets-the-road implementation challenges, they are also intimate with the means employed – whether these relate to pragmatic solutions or workarounds, kluges, or crocks – to address any immediate issue that arises. And yet for many of these frontline backers, a foray into SaaS administration and support presents a different career opportunity, the ability to get closer to the software, or at least hack their way in. For many, this is a welcome diversion from their everyday operational accounting or information technology (IT) jobs. It is not uncommon to see accounting personnel hired to fill the roles of product managers in SaaS companies that are eager to jumpstart or accelerate more in-depth or flushed out accounting or finance functionality or new modules. We can argue that the same divisions between tinkering or experimenting with issue identification and resolution are more arbitrary than what we may think for it is this continual ability to uncover new ways of assembling or reusing what is at hand that we are better able to respond to unanticipated issues with a trick or two up our sleeves. With SaaS customers, it is not uncommon to share novel even elegant solutions for which the vendor has yet to dream up much less articulate.

We may ask: in an alternate world, what if when using or configuring internal controls in SaaS, we may well begin with the basement of our expectations, but entertain the possibility, however remote, of inching our way towards the roofs of our imagination. The point of having a user story – so and so in which role needs to perform what and what – is that tinkering in SaaS gives birth to other stories. The point is not to use it as a defense against other stories, what auditors accustomed to a test-a-key-internal-control approach are inclined to. In attempting to shape the SaaS into one that is not merely static, but dynamic, one is in effect capable of learning and adapting to continual changing demands or needs. Using any one or set of stories as a wall of defense or armor precludes us from deepening the story we tell ourselves, so that by the time we start to unveil the underlying layers, it is too late to identify the subtle nuances buried within. A textbook control on access restriction may do more harm than good if it ends up breaking a user's ability to unwind or reverse his or her actions or perform the most rudimentary of queries or validation of his or her own work vis-a-vis others.

An emphasis on view restrictions also precludes a subtle, if not more powerful control of visibility, that taps directly into inter- as well as intra-group dynamics to foster accountability. With integrated SaaS, for example, access is more than the tightening of access within any one given SaaS, but the identification of toxic pairs among two or more SaaS, so that if we have the ability to create a vendor in an upstream procurement SaaS as well as perform payment in a downstream SaaS, in effect this toxic pair or combination needs to be surfaced for a review of conflicts in segregation of duties and an identification of any mitigating compensating controls that can be employed, such as having an independent review beforehand for all payments to be processed. Deepening the story also clues us in on how others come into the picture so that the end outcome is more of a collaborative coming together of multiple drives, intents, and actions, manual or automated, as opposed to a simple management top-down directive. It is when the control at hand appears to come from no one and thus everyone – the multiply-authored nature of a control and its reliance on multi-varied strands or elements – that it is arguably the most effective. I am reminded of the following Lao Tzu quote:

> *Intelligent control appears as uncontrol or freedom.*
> *And for that reason it is genuinely intelligent control.*
> *Unintelligent control appears as external domination.*
> *And for that reason it is really unintelligent control.*[29]

It is also here that we need the most work and ongoing research, so accustomed we have become to Taylorist "scientific" principles of management and to blind oblivion to all other approaches far more simmering yet no less compelling. From this perspective, the cloud solution, or SaaS, is not light as we might think. Yes, light perhaps physically or financially insofar as we do not have to maintain the racks of servers in an off-shore data center or worry about source code. Yet compared to an on-premise software, it can weigh in more heavily in other ways, challenging us to step outside our ascribed role whether that be customer, vendor, accountant, auditor, entry clerk, planner, developer, support, human resources, sales, marketing, or other functions within the organization. To employ Agile concepts is even more difficult considering we are more inclined to engage in contractual negotiation by focusing on service level performance and license usage in vendor management. To overcome this habit of sorts, there is even a greater need for multiple perspectives to converge to preface working software over excessive documentation, as well as cross collaboration over contractual negotiation.

Picture this: a cat on a window ledge bathed in the waning evening light. A picture, as they say, is worth a thousand words. We can focus on the cat's almond shaped eyes, its black fur, or its whiskers. Or its pointy ears which are momentarily perched upright even as it lies perched on the ledge. None of these attributes are specific to the cat. From this perspective, we can venture that a word may speak to a thousand pictures. The black fur can just as easily belong to a dog, a racoon, indeed even a rat, just as easily as it envelopes the cat in our picture. Though different, none of these attributes take away from or add to one another. That the cat has whiskers doesn't make its eyes less almond shaped. That it has black fur doesn't make its ears any less or more pointy. Seen in isolation, each attribute is universal, yet their composition is altogether specific to a cat, giving it an individual identity, so that it is in effect different from a dog, racoon, or its next meal, a rat. When we speak of the cat, we don't refer to it as an entity with almond shaped eyes, pointy ears, whiskers, and black fur. Though if someone were to ask us to guess what it likely would be based on the said attributes, we would have guessed a cat anyway. These attributes don't change. Over time the black fur may lose its luster or else become peppered with gray, but you get the idea once a cat always a cat.

The composite SaaS in use at varied client organizations is like our unassuming cat. Prepossessed undoubtedly by multi-universal features different client users pick and choose through a menu of configurations to employ. The resulting picture is more than a sum of its parts. What comes to mind is the following Sherry Turkle characterization: "The bricoleur resembles the painter who stands back between brushstrokes, looks at the canvas, and only after this contemplation, decides what to do next."[30] Rather than rely on a top-down, heavy-handed approach where the end is already preconceived, decisions are made at each turn or fork in the road as it were. Although the outcome is not predictable, it is not without requisite integrity. There's no risk of it morphing into a tiger from the appearance of larger fangs or deepening of an unassuming meow into a defying growl. In any event, a mere look at the cat casts all these attributes on full display. We can quickly tell if its teeth have grown or, conversely, if the black fur has taken on a different color. We can speak of the cat as a composite rather than call upon the assortment of seemingly disparate attributes each time. The word cat does not contain almond-shaped eyes, pointy ears, black fur, or whiskers even as the image does.

Recall the Chinese Room thought experiment presented by philosopher John Searle in his 1980 article *Minds, Brains, and Programs* where he pictures himself in a locked room and handed a batch of Chinese writing to interpret based on a set of rules in English.[31] In contrast, Google researchers when transforming Google

Translate into an artificial intelligence (AI)-based engine went from a reliance on an exhaustive set of pre-built rules to neural networks.[32] The premise is that each neuron in the network gets to vote, and the direction the network takes shifts based on the majority vote, so that the final destination is arrived through a process of trial and error. Oddly enough, the translated language appears more robust and contextual than sifting through an exhaustive top-down, rule-based approach.[33] SaaS customers are like neurons in the network. We are reminded of the thought experiment: if a tree falls in a forest and no one is around to hear it, does it make a sound? Conversely, we can also ask: to the extent that the internal control defined only speaks to an audit or compliance requirement, then how likely is the tree only falling in the woods of an audit or compliance world? Whether the SaaS is up, whether a feature or configuration is working or desired, these are like electrical charges passed along like interconnected switches in the SaaS brain. The greater the majority vote, the higher the probability of success in pattern recognition with lessons learned disseminated through the network.[34]

If we were to explore the neural network concept a little farther, with the multiple customer-neurons using the enterprise SaaS product, the SaaS provider can ideally provide statistics shared across all customers. Rather than speak of the overly used label of best practices, let's call these practices common to all customers. For example, in a procurement SaaS, expenses created for vendors like CDW or Office Depot typically fall into a specific expense category. To the extent that requisitions are created containing these expenses and are automatically defaulted to a likely expense category shared by most other SaaS customers, this would not only help expedite data entry but also in ensuring that expenses are also coded correctly to begin with. Recall from previous chapters how accounting personnel may have to correct for the incorrect codes downstream, sometimes in invoices and other times in reclass journal entries. If these were in turn prepaid expenses that needed to be amortized, by the time the entries were logged in the general ledger in any given month, it is all but impossible to tie the destination entry back to the source invoice or requisition. This is one area that SaaS providers should ideally explore farther in using their wide network to leverage and share with its customers without necessarily compromising specific customer confidential details, even if today this still represents, as it were, a green field of unmined opportunities. What has been leveraged upon, as in the case of Coupa, has been offering customers volume discounts that are available when pooled together as a group but would not have otherwise been received in purchases by individual customers. This is an obvious benefit to SaaS customers. But what areas are more likely to be configured or processes to be automated using SaaS when we compare across multiple SaaS customers? For customers that share the same market capitalization and the same level of organization maturity in the same industry vertical, to what extent do their enterprise cloud landscapes and resulting composition of internal versus external resources agree or differ?

Thus, what is less obvious and therefore not as widely applied or offered up are other fields of possibilities that emerge from pooling customer data together from the twin perspectives of better leveraging the out-of-the-box configuration capability and instituting SaaS specific internal controls. Do most startups from 0 to 200 employees only use a sliver of SaaS functionality? If so, what are the components used? In other words, from observing customers across all industries and having this behavior polled and collected in its multi-tenant architecture, is the SaaS provider able to identify common practices among different customer cohorts? If the same startup were to grow to a size of 200 to 400 employees, are there specific workflows that are employed on top of vanilla out-of-the-box functionality? If the startup decides to go public, what automated controls do like peers typically configure within the SaaS to foster internal control readiness? Is there an evolutionary path that startups consuming SaaS undergo when they gain strength both in size and complexity? What about streamlining and consolidation? The plethora of best-in-breed solutions notwithstanding, does it make sense to have different applications in play for the same function across different parts of the organization? For example, how many credit card payment processing gateways are in use? How many billing SaaS are in use depending on different types of services or goods sold, physical goods versus professional service versus ecommerce transactions? As the organization grows and matures, does it make sense to revisit the drawing board of externally subscribed SaaS in internal use and re-assess from efficiency and scalability perspectives?

Had a single vendor been used, companies could negotiate for volume discounts by pooling together the transaction volume that has otherwise been distributed to multiple SaaS provided by multiple vendors. These are higher level strategic questions but even on a more tactical and operational basis as we might imagine there are so many areas to address. Insofar as the SaaS is typically integrated or used with other SaaS, what bridge fields need to reside in either or both SaaS to help with data reconciliation to address completeness? In the case of an expense management SaaS integrated with an accounting SaaS downstream, do the expense reports get synced in as vendor invoices or expense reports? This decision determines whether internal personnel are set up as vendors or employees in the accounting SaaS. How about manual journals if the enterprise customer does not need expense granularity detail in the downstream SaaS having already had access to it upstream? Or vice versa, when it chooses to have more granularity downstream? What patterns does either the upstream or downstream SaaS provider observe in terms of customer adoption across different SaaS as well as behavior in any one adopted SaaS? For example, for a customer that does not have an in-house development team and sells goods on a website, which best-in-breed SaaS providers does it typically look at engaging and integrating from cart checkout to payment processing to capturing and syncing with its own internal accounting system? Questions like these and more continue to surround the multi-application approach that underpins SaaS. But what is evident here is also a phased crawl, walk, and run approach when it comes to consuming SaaS. In other words, an organization can't leapfrog from operating a singular monolithic on-premise legacy application to instantly using iPaaS to sync two or more integrated SaaS on day one without undergoing the necessary trials by fire to marry systematized with real-life accounts.

Even when starting out with a singular SaaS, there are different areas to focus on in an organization's implementation timeline:

- 0–3 months. Is everything working as it should for example, are we able to reconcile the standard or custom reports with external bank statements?
- 3–6 months. What is the level of user adoption; for example, does the policy or supporting configuration need to be modified?
- 6–9 months. Are there specific areas that have not been addressed in the initial deployment; for example, do custom workflows or management dashboards need to be tailored to specific user groups?
- 9–12 months. Are there specific functionalities or integrations that have not been leveraged; for example, can the data sync with upstream or downstream interfacing applications be more automated or real-time?

At each step of the journey, we need to keep our eyes on the ball. Are we trying to:

- Provide management with greater visibility
- Drive user adoption with a specific functionality or set of functionalities
- Introduce a new functionality or set of functionalities by forging two or more integrated SaaS with iPaaS
- Promote SOX compliance

When sharing a table at a conference with a SaaS implementation manager recently, she shared with me that she would not recommend exploring all possible configurations and options for Day 1 go-live. According to her, SaaS customers when presented with a plethora of choices get distracted by nice-to-haves rather than focusing on must-haves, what it would take to go live in their respective environments or what they truly need. While I can understand the need to focus on ability to execute within given time and resource constraints, organizations can run the risk of taking this approach too far by failing to iterate after initial go-live, thereby missing out on the longer term and thus more strategic gains to be had. The unit of analysis becomes one of pivotal importance. When we focus too narrowly on the timeliness and completeness of base requirements for the initial go-live, we may be successful on Day 1, but to continue to succeed on Day 2, we would need to gain a bigger of picture, and in effect expand our unit of analysis from:

- One key user group, for example, accountants to other groups such as sales and operations
- One primary or core set of processes, such as those revolving financial reporting to those that are deemed peripheral or ancillary, such as marketing and support

- One organization namely our own in consuming SaaS to other like, as well as different, client organizations consuming SaaS, so that we can explore ways in which we are the same or different, and how we may learn from one another
- One SaaS vendor or software provider to multiple SaaS service organizations offering a plethora of best-in-breed applications as well as crossing over into Platform as a Service (PaaS)
- One way of consuming SaaS in the traditional vendor-client sense to multiple ways of consuming SaaS, including, but not limited to, tailoring specific out-of-the-box processes, as well as integrating the use of internal practices with SaaS in novel approaches that result in entirely new and relevant products that meet other customer needs in the SaaS ecosystem and larger cloud market-scape

This last point recalls Amazon's ability to productize its retail computing infrastructure by externalizing its internal emphasis on standardized service interfaces and evolving from a mere online bookseller to a dominant Integration as a Service (IaaS) player. In Chapter 2, we reviewed how the admission criteria for clinical patients and revenue recognition alike can remain hidden from view, whether it is a clinical record or accounting SaaS we are peering into. Here, as we look at grooming the backlog of submitted customizations or configurations to sequence and prioritize the improvements to be put in place, we need to ask ourselves what our admission criteria or intake process for changes is. Is there one to begin with, or have we have been firefighting and responding to the squeakiest wheel each time? Where efforts are invested downstream in "fixing" a SaaS, necessary attention may be diverted from what needs to occur upstream to reduce the likelihood of garbage-in garbage-out. On the other hand, even if an issue or concern were deemed worthy to warrant additional time and resources, the absence of a consistent, documented and, perhaps most importantly, well communicated intake criteria in a larger enterprise grappling with competing project and resource constraints skirts by the necessary act to sort the right-size and prioritize the arising need into pebbles, rocks, or boulders, as well as reviewing the ensuing regression impact to the existing pipeline planned out for the year. With an emphasis on Agile and the ability to respond to change over following a plan, the mandate is not to maintain a rigid posture of defense in guarding against any changes but rather to reprioritize the projects already stack ranked and slated to be worked on.

Let's add a behavioral attribute: an ability to hunt for rats. Suppose a developer can code a script that can program the cat to hunt for rats in a field. The script depends on a query that first identifies all rats that are alive in the field. Based on this query, the program kicks in that triggers the cat to identify the first living rat it encounters. Because of its prowess, it is further solidified in its feline identity. But what happens if the query is modified so that instead of live rats, it identifies live squirrels. The cat hunts down live squirrels but doesn't quite know what to do with them. Within the SaaS, are there enough data points to gather to perform what-if analyses to make decisions? Just as we can ask, how much effort does the cat expend in hunting down a rat, what is the cost on average of acquiring a customer? Does the cost vary whether it is a large customer or a small customer? In other words, given limited time and other financial constraints, what are the best uses of the limited resources at hand? Are there enough data points to perform analytics to come to a decision on possible routes of action? Recall the premise behind machine learning. Or how about a recently deployed customer outreach program? What metrics do we have to gauge what we have done well or what we haven't done as well? For all the emphasis on what can go wrong and prefacing of automation over informating, how truly useful is the SaaS at hand at providing enough data to come to a timely if not appropriate operational or strategic decision?

In continuing with the agriculture thread with Digital Green, consider Farmers Business Network that lets farmers subscribe to a database aggregating and anonymizing performance data such as soil conditions, seed type, and weather to assist with making better decisions as to what to grow, and what fertilizers and chemicals to buy all at a combined group discount. In truth, the power of analytics is one untapped area when it comes to the deployment and use of best-in-breed SaaS. A key question to ask may be: is there a business intelligence tool that can amass data across multiple SaaS to present a coherent set of metrics for consumption to varied parts of the enterprise? A secondary question: are there common data definitions and attributes in use across the enterprise that support the compilation of enterprise-wide metrics? Even if metrics do exist, and have been in use, challenges can exist on whether these continue to be meaningful despite ongoing organization changes. In other words, have we become accustomed to seeing the same metrics in a management dashboard or do they actually contribute in a tangible way to decision making?

As we move one level higher beyond any one SaaS, divisions between internal and external become more porous. We are capable of being surprised even with seemingly mundane configuration tools out of the box. SaaS functionality is not simply what is delivered externally and all at once on day one as it is a carefully sustained process of cultivating what is tailored to an enterprise over time, not unlike the art of pruning bonsai. What is deemed internal to a SaaS enterprise need may in fact be external insofar as it is more universally shared by other SaaS consuming enterprises. The neuron-pattern is in effect when a significant number vote on an enhancement or bring to the SaaS provider's attention the criticality of a fix needed. What is deemed an organization's internal control, from this respect, may well be a series of mirrored controls appearing to be amazingly similar from an external vendor, analyst, auditor, or compliance regulatory perspective when we stand back to see the forest for the trees.

Differences may lie in how specific the control design is in addressing local nuances and more importantly how well it is executed and maintained over the series of personnel, process, and operational changes that the organization is surely tested in the face of time. What is deemed an internal need may well be met sooner rather than later simply because it has risen in scale and volume to be an external one shared by other consuming SaaS enterprises. In many ways, in the world of startups, the lines between customers and vendors are blurring with customers and vendors consuming products from one another. If an auditor were to come in and peer within the same SaaS, the same customer may have also been set up as a vendor. The same vendor that provides a specific accounting SaaS to a specific customer may in turn consume a billing SaaS from the same aforementioned "customer" or "vendor." There is no telling how this in turn impacts go-to-market or product roadmap decisions but what it does point to is how the auditor's divisive portrayal between customer and vendor is inherently fragile.

Even the supposed internal versus external divisions between front and back office applications are fast eroding. An accounting SaaS may offer a platform for hosting websites so that the flow of transactions from credit card paying customers into the general ledger can be seamless. Yet herein SaaS uptime or availability becomes no longer a matter of internal concern but an external public facing one. In the event customers are not able to procure goods or services online because the supporting accounting SaaS is down, this has far greater implications for the company's public brand and integrity than the mere insular concerns of internal departments having the ability to process transactions in an uninterrupted manner.

The neuron compounding effect is not just seen for customers. Take an expense management SaaS provider. When it also uses a downstream accounting SaaS for recording and reporting its own financials, it may yet realize when attempting to integrate its own solution with the accounting SaaS, gaps or areas where the integration can be improved upon, such as exposure of APIs, attributes, or use of common field names or identifiers as well as exception notification and handling processes. In strengthening its own internal APIs by consuming its own product in relation to another external SaaS, the expense management SaaS, it is in effect encouraging a far greater market adoption by like customers facing the same challenges.

With the ease of hindsight, we can argue that these challenges are not so much prohibitive as inviting, offering opportunities for the SaaS consuming and providing enterprise to widen its own product capability roadmap or deepen its core competency. In looking at its own internal roadmap, the expense management SaaS provider may look at expanding its offerings to an adjacent offering in procurement management. It is through observing, tinkering, and adapting what is internal with the other SaaS it consumes and integrates with that new ideas come up. Too often we are misled into thinking that innovation comes from an ivory-tower research lab when the everyday seemingly mundane breaks fixes we encounter are themselves opportunities to capitalize upon in filling a specific market demand or niche. The reverse is true, where external regulatory demands can and often do drive internal postures. As alluded to in previous chapters, *ASC 606, Revenue from Contracts with Customers*, issued jointly by the Financial Accounting Standards Board (FASB) and the International Accounting Standards Board (IASB) in 2014, has one such impact in driving SaaS and customer controls on revenue recognition.

Another is the General Data Protection Regulation (GDPR) adopted by the European Parliament, the Council of the European Union, and the European Commission intended to strengthen and unify data protection for all individuals within the European Union (EU). What is revealing is how it manages to reshape our impressions of what is internal versus external by defining personal data to be "any information relating to an individual, whether it relates to his or her private, professional, or public life. It can be anything from a name, a home address, a photo, an email address, bank details, posts on social networking websites, medical information, or a computer's IP address."[35] Applicable entities subsumed within this regulation include the data controller (organization that collects data from EU residents even if located outside of the EU), data processor (organization that processes data on behalf of data controller and in our case cloud service providers) as well as the data subject (person) based in the EU.[36]

In the context of the SaaS, recall that login is possible through an email address and password combination. In turn, when customers or vendors are set up, email address as well as postal address are all too common fields. When monitoring access, the computer's IP address can also be tracked. GDPR requires that privacy by design principles be baked in such as by encrypting or pseudonymizing personal data to mitigate the degree of impact in the event of a data breach.[37] Of interest too is how a right to be forgotten is ultimately replaced by a more limited right to erasure in the 2014 adopted version that basically provides for the data subject the right to request erasure of personal data related to them.

In an era where the youth of today are inundated with social media where even Facebook is fast eclipsed as an all too retro app embraced by their parents, what we view as internal and external is slowly blurring and in a way this interplay of internal versus external is played out in the enterprise consumption of SaaS. Recall in the early days of cloud adoption how an enterprise is likely to worry about the likelihood of its internal company proprietary data being breached with an increasing reliance on cloud software. To be sure, this is still a concern at most companies, yet today even if an on-premise solution continues to be used, it is all but impossible to witness the rise and entry of SaaS in varied areas of the enterprise application landscape whether it's document processing, contract execution, email, web conferencing or, as covered in bulk by this book, processing of transactions with financial impact. The use of far flung examples from a salmon farm to an Indian one on land hopefully helps illustrate just how portable or timeless concepts and applications can be.

Just the other day, when attempting to record a class using web conferencing media for students who are not able to show up in person, I'm confronted with a seemingly perplexing array of dos and don'ts:

■ Watch for the amber screen alert if the slide deck I'm presenting has not been selected for sharing.
■ Be sure to log into yet another online platform and follow a prescribed series of steps to perform upload.

- Ignore the message that file upload is still in progress even after uploading the recorded session.
- Hang tight when the initial resolution upon playback appears chalky at first.

Fragility in our final parting shot perhaps has less to do with daily inconveniences faced when the SaaS is temporarily unavailable for access as with its inability to respond or react. When it comes to user experience, it is this insistence on a pre-scribed series of order of steps to undertake, otherwise things may not turn out as planned – the file did not get uploaded – that makes it inherently brittle, even if it is available for access anywhere and anytime. The more we hold on, the easier we break.

As we discussed in Chapter 8, fragility in the system design thus results from maintaining a strong if impassive exterior as opposed to an openness to change and an ability to learn from past trials and tribulations. Conversely, when we are more fragile or open to exploring different ways, the resulting system of internal controls is less fragile. Controls based on idealized worldviews are inherently frag-ile constructs bolstered from time to time by their only line of accountability to audit and compliance regulations rather than any real accountability to actual out-come. Likewise, to the extent that the controls designed and validated only address compliance and audit demands, as opposed to other more pressing every day and operational needs, to what extent are they intended to be more ostensive rather than performative, smoke and mirrors rather than any real attempts to address underly-ing breaks or vulnerabilities?

Our own relationship when engaging with a system, software or tool, is in turn complicated by many layers. Our earlier discussion on the varied ways we unwittingly engage in RAT (repair, attribute and all that) in Chapter 5 recalls the following story from Hui-neng, the founder of the Zen school and translated by Thomas Hoover:

> *A group of monks arguing about a banner flapping in the breeze.*
> *One monk declared, "The banner is moving."*
> *Another insisted, "No, it is the wind that is moving."*
> *Although he was only a lay observer, Hui-neng could not contain him-self, and he interrupted them with his dramatic manifesto, "You are both wrong. It is your mind that moves."*[38]

As early as in Exercise 1.3 in Chapter 1, we have explored the varied degrees of SaaS usage from direct internal users, such as accounting to reviewers of financial reports like management to policemen-like roles like auditors. Yet, what is external – such as the recent ASC-606 compliance around revenue recognition – often engenders new accounting software, such as RevPro and RevStream, as well as augmented additional revenue management capabilities in accounting SaaS, such as Workday Financials and NetSuite, invariably shaping the way we use and configure the SaaS at hand. In the case of ASC-606, the controls may be located upstream, such as customer credit checks in a different SaaS. Thus, even though regulators, public investors, and banks may not be direct users or consumers of the SaaS at hand, they nonetheless provide contextual triggers for why and how we record the things we do. Along with the dichotomy between internal and external, the line between automated and manual is called into question. In circling back to having enough data points to assist with decision making, hiding the RAT can also extend to the scissors-and-glue way we stitch together data within one SaaS or across multiple SaaS to come up with meaningful metrics to be consumed. I am reminded of yet another narrative.

> *Once upon a time, I dreamt I was a butterfly, fluttering hither and thither, to all intents and purposes a butterfly. I was conscious only of my happiness as a butterfly, unaware that I was myself. Soon I awaked, and there I was, veritably myself again. Now I do not know whether I was then a man dreaming I was a butterfly, or whether I am now a butterfly, dreaming I am a man.*[39]

It seems the more we explore and plumb internal controls, the more the distinctions start to slip and slide. Internal versus external, automated versus manual, enhancement versus fix, customer versus vendor, front office versus back office, auditor versus auditee, risk versus opportunity, control versus chaos, fragility versus forgiveness.

In the last distinction, we can argue that when a SaaS is configurable to forgive, it becomes less fragile. The same can be said for a human user. When he or she is configured to forgive, he or she is likely to be less fragile. Compared to the human, configuring the SaaS appears to be a much easier task, even if it appears infinitely more daunting to a user accustomed to receiving unadulterated functionality of the box. The same can be said for cloud providers. An iPaaS, because of its ability to integrate different SaaS, needs to stay current by keeping up with new SaaS that it has yet to integrate with. Or when exploring the introduction of a new module in a downstream SaaS to compensate what is perceived to be a shortfall in an upstream SaaS, have we performed enough due diligence in asking whether the upstream SaaS has been fully leveraged to begin with? Have adequate controls been configured upstream? Otherwise, even with augmented functionality downstream, potential omissions or errors are still addressed almost always too little too late. How do we go about untangling this hairball of a setup? Pull a strand and the entire artifice unravels.

In drawing on the neuron network concept discussed previously, we can reach out to our peers working in other companies but employing a similar integration between the two SaaS in question. The butterfly/man, or within/without distinction ruptures precisely because the same two SaaS in use in one organization, whether in Procure-to-Pay, Order-to-Cash, or Record-to-Report cycles, is likely also in use in other enterprises. Put simply, what have others done? Do they encounter the same concerns or challenges? If not, is it because they have augmented SaaS functionality downstream, or is it because they have more fully embraced SaaS functionality upstream? What is moving? The banner or the wind?

I have deliberately withheld details on the SaaS and the integration in question to demonstrate the portability of this analysis. Like SaaS that can be used across enterprise clients, this review can apply to various organizations in varied industries. With the necessary investigation into the why, what results may be another "crock of shit" to add to the pile, another "human being on clutches."[40] We need to resist the urge to introduce new functionality – the grass is greener on the other side – without undertaking the necessary cross-comparative reviews across different SaaS as well as SaaS consuming enterprise clients. This urge belies a preference for a single bullet, a legacy monolithic ERP approach that is at loggerheads with the "multiply-authored" nature of SaaS.

When it comes to internal controls and accountability, we are also used to singling out an individual or a group of individuals. Enron's CEO Kenneth Lay comes to mind. We are less inclined to recognize that often a confluence of factors is at play. What we are inclined to believe is almost always a one-sided truth, shading other aspects. In Woolgar's example of how an unmarried mother of four was fined 50 pounds for putting out her trash in the wrong bin bags – her own black plastic bags rather than council issued ones – he makes a keen observation: the visceral difference of opinions on either side (councilmen and wardens versus ignorant and quite possibility innocent neighborhood inhabitants) rests on the fact that there can be no ambiguity surrounding the object in question, in this case, the bin bag.[41] After all, what is there to disagree about if we are not talking about the same thing? It is because of the bag's perceived ordinariness that we take it for granted. It is because we take it for granted that it becomes easy to think that it means the same thing to all parties involved.[42] It is precisely this sameness that allows for differences of opinion over the same bin bag.

Recall from Chapter 1 the often taken-for-granted auditor notion of 404: are we talking about a web page that cannot be located or SOX? That SOX can be mistaken for a virtual destination with no viable uniform resource locator (URL) is not without irony. It is when we begin to see shades of uncertainty or acknowledge ways in which this same object can mean something altogether different to different individuals, that we start to see how it is entirely conceivable that a responsible individual can still veer away from compliance with the said law or intent. For the hotel guest who does not find the key too heavy or burdensome in his pocket, there is less of a likelihood for him to return it to the counter. The same can be said for a driver who rides in an all-wheel drive Jeep and is less likely to care about the approaching speed bump. Because there is less of a risk of damage to the car's suspension, the driver is less likely to care. Because the driver is less likely to care, he or she is also more likely to drive at a rate of speed that violates the speed limit designated.

In the wake of well publicized corporate collapses in recent years, even an independent policing role such as an auditor is met with a widening gulf in opinion between the public and auditors about the latter's roles and responsibilities.

Shareholders, investors, and creditors expect auditors to provide absolute assurance on the veracity of audited financials when in fact auditors are only capable of providing reasonable assurance. Audit procedures themselves are performed on a sampling basis. Still others believe that auditors can assist with bookkeeping and other tax-related matters even when the provision of non-assurance services by auditors has been curtailed by SOX.

For all the ease with which we assign blame to Kenneth Lay, we forget how the process of complying with SOX is inherently forgiving, merciful even when we consider how a SOX engagement begins with a review of material accounts and related processes and systems, performance of walkthrough of a transaction from cradle to grave, design of internal controls, sampled testing, remediation, and remediation testing. Even if exceptions were identified in the initial walkthrough and first round of testing, a buffer of sorts is built into the lifecycle of control validation such that it allows for possibility of repair to occur and re-testing of repair performed to evidence operating effectiveness of internals by year end. From this respect, Agile with its emphasis on failing fast and early is oddly similar with the approach undertaken to foster internal control and SOX readiness and eventual compliance.

From yet a different perspective, this level of tolerance for errors or faults early on as an enterprise embarks on SOX compliance continues insofar as risks have been deemed out-of-scope from the realm of financial reporting. As an example, operational risks, such as excessive software licenses acquired from lackadaisical attempts in tracking or metering active internal usage against subscribed availability and resulting in unnecessary spending, would have been deemed out-of-scope as far as SOX and financial risks are concerned. Thus, even though the same control can be used to address operational and financial risks, such as access control and administration, the reverse doesn't necessarily hold true. The same control designed to mitigate a financial risk may not address an operational risk that in some respects is far more critical or integral to the enterprise.

Even here, the distinction of man versus butterfly can be plumbed farther. Access reviews, insofar as they yield exceptions on access provisioned to terminated employees, can dovetail into attempts at better license management. Just as accountability can be attributed to more than one individual, and control design in SaaS to more than one enterprise client, the same control, upon deeper analysis, can address more than merely an exterior compliance need.

Another way to view the auditor who has been so taken up by vendor approvals or restricted access in the SaaS that he or she remains blissfully unaware of possible circumventing moves, such as excessive access to edit vendors or configured roles and permissions, is to see the imposition of an audit reality over an operational reality. In the tradition of Avaita Vedanta, a school of Hindu philosophy, an error arises when a reality is superimposed on another. A frequently recounted tale is how a man mistakes a rope for a snake in the early hours of the morning. Recall our previous question on what is moving: the banner, the wind, or the mind? Here, the image of a snake is superimposed on a rope, so that the latter is mistaken for the former. This notwithstanding, the snake does not take away any of the characteristics of the rope. Each remains distinct as it were just as from our previous example, the cat just because it shares the same attributes – pointy ears and black fur – as say a dog, even when mistaken for a dog, its characteristics are no less undermined.

When we circle back to either Searle's Chinese Room experiment or Turing's imitation game, a superimposition occurs in both. In the former, an English language speaker is mistaken for one versed in Chinese; in the latter, a human is mistaken for a computer. When we circle back to SaaS, the very absence of adequate controls is superimposed by their presence. Another perspective: what appears to be contained within the confines of SaaS is in turn superimposed on a myriad cast of characters, human or otherwise. In previous chapters, we've covered Goffman's depiction front- versus back-stage behaviors,[13] but the narrative that comes to mind is mistaking what appears on the screen to be real. Where this chapter has been about other selves, what is on display can also be a deluded self, a case of mistaken identity so that what appears compliant or controlled for is really a lid on the chaos that cannot be contained.

To see past the illusion of the screen so as not to mistake what's on stage for what's real involves in part a willingness to experiment to try out new and unexpected ways. Most of the time, however, we remain mesmerized by what we see so that even when it has long exited as a scene on the screen, it remains nevertheless etched in our mind's eye. More than an aberrant slip or mistake, our enchantment with shadow and light is more than a brief romance. In recalling my history of moves and self-assembled furniture from IKEA from Chapter 3, I often hear comments such as "they don't make furniture like they used to" or "quality we can pass down through generations." Contrast these with the pride of another who has been able to be creative with the mix and match of vintage panels with store-bought engineered wood.

To change our lens on internal controls on SaaS requires a paradigm shift, or for some a brain transplant of sorts, so that creative reuse does not reflect an underlying weakness and breakage does not have to equate an absence of reliability. Thus, even when an all-encompassing on-premise software has been supplanted by multiple best-in-breed SaaS, we are more inclined to stick to the tried and true, continually casting the end user as customer or consumer rather than co-designer or constructor, or the SaaS as unchanging inflexible software capable of only accepted data input in a predefined format. Likewise, for those of us used to playing the roles of auditors or auditees, so accustomed we have become with our roles, we find it hard to see past the act, or the screen for that matter, just as it can be hard to tell the butterfly apart from the man, whether to accept a control on display as face value, or part of a large ecosystem of both supporting and conflicting cast. In circling back to the employment of access reviews towards both compliance and operational demands, we preface one view over another, rather than acknowledging the underlying overlap.

Even without an intent to mislead or commit fraud, even the best of intentions can lead to a control going astray. It is this "looseness" among individual actors that constitutes a network that fosters an everyday practice of using science, protocols, or technology in place of "docility." Through a combined research spanning a study of 112 resuscitative efforts over a period of 14 months, interviews with 57 emergency department personnel as well as a 2-month study into the usage of research protocols in everyday medical work, Stefan Timmermans and Marc Berg observed that it is the ability to tinker with a protocol, rather than strict adherence to guidelines that leads to its eventual adoption. Ironically, overly tight controls lead, more likely than not, to "subtle sabotage," either downright non-cooperation or the elusive search for patients that qualify.[44] In fact, "no one actor (including the protocol itself) is in control: rather universality emerges from this seemingly chaotic interaction of multiple trajectories."[45]

Trajectories here refer to individual, at times interweaving, paths undertaken by both people and things through past, present, and future. The introduction of a medical protocol brings these different trajectories together, transforming them in the process. Universal adoption relies on these "previously established networks" and is "contingently and collectively produced" and therefore "inevitably intertwined" with "locality."[46] In contrast to Woolgar's configuring the user, "patients and medical personnel are not turned into mindless followers of some pre-set script." Rather, "it is the protocol's trajectory which is secondary and which is aligned with their goals and objectives."[47]

Let's return to our example of using a SaaS to route purchase requisitions for approval. By employing an audit lens on what can go wrong, the focus is on getting anticipated spending documented and approved beforehand, if only to mitigate any incursion of unexpected liability on the books that is un-accrued for. When a vendor invoice is received, accounting personnel would look for an associated purchase order to apply it to and draw down upon the approved budgeted spending. Thus, the audit emphasis is not so much on how a purchase requisition is approved as it is on how to regulate unapproved spending, otherwise invoices received without associated purchase orders. To preclude any delays in the receipt of invoices, the A/P department may explicitly request that all vendor bills be sent directly to them.

To reinforce the message that spending be approved before, rather than after it is incurred – recall OSHA's handling multi-piece truck wheel accidents[48] from Chapter 2 – it may actively disavow the attachment of vendor invoices to POs submitted for approval, as the very presence of the former would, by audit logic, necessarily negate the validity of the latter. It is the intent of the A/P team to process vendor invoices received in a timely manner as and when they become due according to the terms negotiated with the vendor and stated on the invoice. Net 30, for example, would mean that vendor payment be remitted no later than 30 days after which the invoice is received. How a purchase requisition gets approved is not an immediate concern of the A/P team, and neither is whether it has been approved after a review, however high level or perfunctory, against one's budget, merely that an approved purchase requisition or PO exists for application to vendor invoices.

Yet, the process a purchase requestor undergoes in putting together a purchase requisition, essentially giving a rough estimate of what the spending would might be for the coming year, very much depends on what it would be in the prior year, as well as any assumptions layered into whether the same, higher, or lower level of service is expected. An approver when reviewing the submitted purchase requisition would look to any attached support such as an "old" invoice to gauge whether numbers are reasonable against prior actual spending as well as future anticipated spending. Also, the inclusion of an actual invoice, insofar as this has been a recurring expense from the past, provides more detail and context on the service requested, than would standard system fields that are binary driven – such as department or project allocations – or are in freeform text driven by idiosyncrasies of individual requestors in augmenting the purchase requisition with varying degrees of detail – the why as to why a service needs to be procured and for how long.

Thus, much like application of a sledgehammer on an inflated wheel, the very thing that the A/P department is attempting to discourage – the attachment of invoice support to a purchase requisition – turns out to be a pivotal factor in getting a purchase requisition created and approved in a timely manner, or at the very least in time for the anticipated expense to be accrued for in the accounting records after the service has been rendered and before the vendor invoice is received. The embodied logics in getting an approved purchase requisition, to invoke M.D. Baccus, "are specific to that task yet may reflect the enormity of the context within which it resides."[49] Just like the system that presides over the regulation of multi-piece truck wheel accidents – OSHA, tire manufacturers, service shops, attorneys – the SaaS that routes purchase requisitions for approvals "may have many goals residing within its overall framework" and hence, it is not enough to locate the specific goal being worked on. We also need to understand how the logics are "determined by the particulars of the system in a unique way for that task."[50] The goal of minimizing unapproved spending or purchase requisitions is affected by other goals – getting a purchase requisition completed, submitted, and approved – among purchase requesters, approvers and A/P.

When it comes to entity controls, auditors speak of management planning. Yet, the internal controls we devise are like plans and resources we draw upon. In her book, *Plans and Situated Actions*, Lucy Suchman questions the cognitive science tradition of relying on plans to articulate procedures that drive concrete actions.[51] She observes a jarring disparity between human-machine interactions when functionality is developed using specifications for actions rather than "moment-by-moment contingencies that constitute the conditions of the situated interaction."[52] The user is led by the nose through a "garden path" that terminates in an impasse, a cul-de-sac of sorts, when the software in question fails to anticipate or respond to a user action.[53] This necessitates a rethink, a rework, a deviation from a standard course of action mandated by online FAQs or user manuals to one that makes more intuitive or logical sense in any given circumstance.

Take the example of having to obtain a comparative view of the current year-to-date (YTD) view of the financials against the prior year's. Depending on which period we run the report, the number of months reflecting YTD requires changes. When we run the YTD in June for an enterprise with a December year end, the YTD includes 6 months January through June. When running it in December, all 12 months are included. Yet, when attempting to use the SaaS to run the cross comparative across 2 years, the current YTD versus the prior YTD, a user runs into a challenge in using the same report to obtain varied combinations of YTD as the comparative column, the intractable prior YTD stays constant at 12 months. Faced with this cul-de-sac of sorts, the user resorts to creating four flavors of reports, each hard-coding the comparative column to be 3, 6, 9 and 12 months to allow for a quarterly YTD comparative review. When contacting the SaaS vendor support hotline, the user is informed that this flexibility is still an enhancement presently.

Consequently, the user has had to change her plans of having just one YTD comparative report. In this same vein, Suchman proposes an alternative view of plans, not as a priori determinants that lay out behavior well ahead of time, but rather post-hoc formulations that account for behavior that has already taken place.[54] In other words, rather than rely on a rational plan to anticipate behavior, we reconstruct what happens afterwards in a way that makes it appear as if it followed a plan. In previous chapters, we discussed how the SaaS architecture gives nontechnical power users the ability to configure fields, forms, workflows, and reports that meet specific business needs. Some of this flexibility can be leveraged to build controls that address potential roadblocks through safety nets, warnings or confirmations.

The SaaS can be configured to prompt a warning if a potential duplicate is entered with the same date and amount. Reports can be created to cull un-submitted expenses to accrue for them in a more complete manner. Delegate approvers can be set when the primary approver is away. A policy can be set in place to preclude a user from entering an expense in a category that has exceeded its threshold. The more these controls can work behind the scenes to anticipate and respond to a user action or inaction, the more effective they would seem in making the SaaS more forgiving.

Phil Wainewright writes in his popular ZDNet blog that solutions, including SaaS, founded on SQL databases face the "challenge of the code block."[55] Super-entities, such as subsidiary, department, or account are the master-definitions that every other entity is defined in relation to. These choices, once made, cannot be undone. For example, in an accounting SaaS, once transactions have been logged for a user situated in a specific subsidiary, there is no way the user's subsidiary can be updated when the user transfers within the enterprise. In effect, a new user account would have to be created belonging to the target subsidiary breaking the link with prior transactions associated with the same user in the source subsidiary.

Still, as discussed in Chapter 4, advances have been made to overcome "the challenge of the code block." Workday's object-oriented architecture sidesteps the constraints posed by fixed SQL tables.[56] Workday modeled the entire functional domain in objects and their attributes in metadata. Workday delivers these objects as mini-applications, executing objects at runtime as though they were written in code.[57] At its heart, the Workday Object Management Server (OMS) maintains three tables – instance, attributes, and references.[58] When the Workday application runs, it interprets the metadata and turns definitions in these tables into meaningful data.

Changing business logic, Phil Wainewright writes, can be as simple as changing definitions and rerunning the application.[59] Workday's application developers don't so much write code as work with the object types built into the application, defining and instantiating them as required.[60] It is ironic that in *Plans and Situated Actions* and *The Shape of Actions* (described in a previous chapter) that the authors each covered the user confusion that resulted from making photocopies using the Xerox copier in the former and creating a vacuum pump in the latter. We would have thought that nothing would be more straightforward than making paper copies or shutting down all valves in creating a vacuum. Yet what they also show is that when it comes to the most mundane task or one that seeks to shut out all possibilities, humans can, and often do, fail miserably. Is it our nature to follow a hand-me down approach or is it really going against our nature to explore the uncharted?

In a recent example when working with a "old-school" management consultant, I was told that because the consultant had never worked with accounting segments that are anything but numerical, we would need to create unique numbering conventions for every accounting segment we set up even if the SaaS at hand allows for accounting segments to be in alpha-numeric format. Thus, here even though the SaaS at hand is capable of surmounting or transcending the "challenge of the code block," its human users are anything but capable.

But not so fast, with SaaS, we are not officially out of the woods. Here's an example that brings together separate challenges encountered with the ubiquitous "code block," SaaS downtime, and feature roadblock. During month end, when a sales tax computation SaaS integrated with a billing SaaS is not available, customer invoices sent out do not have associated sales tax. When service to the tax computation SaaS is restored, well after the period is locked and closed, how would we remit a tax only invoice to make up the sales tax differential without including the same item for sale all over again in the invoice line? When contacting either SaaS vendor to see if this was at all possible, the response obtained was that the ability to support tax only invoices was still an enhancement. For sales tax to be computed, it needs to exist in relation to a taxable item for sale on the invoice, just as all transactions need to be coded to an existing subsidiary, department, or account.

The issue is one of timing. The invoice with the taxable item has already been remitted when the sales tax computation SaaS is not operational. When the sales tax computation SaaS is up and running, the taxable item no longer needs to be invoiced. In this manner, the user lands squarely back in a cul-de-sac of sorts. How to overcome this? Just as in our prior example, where the user requiring a year-over-year comparison of YTD financials ended up manually recreating four different versions of the same report, the user here may apply a full credit memo to the entire invoice booked, and reissue it altogether with the correct sales tax application in the new accounting period.

Another way of describing the uncharted without making it seem overly dramatic or earth-shattering is to preface situational over mandated compliance. Recall Suchman's view of plans as resources that we draw upon rather than procedures that shape every action. This view is contingent on our ability to place the situation at hand in focus. To better understand situational versus mandated compliance, it helps to turn to situational leadership developed by leadership theorist Ken Blanchard. Characterized as an adaptive leadership style, it encourages leaders to adapt their management approach that best fits their goals and the circumstances at hand, as opposed to sticking to and invariably recycling the same style each time. This requires accounting for multiple variables in the workplace environment at different times as opposed to merely settling for a one-size-fits-all paradigm.

Sound familiar in a check-the-box approach to SOX compliance? In both examples, situational doesn't mean inconsistent outcomes, or lack thereof. What is adapted and changed is the means to obtaining the desired outcome. Thus, the manner of providing leadership and mentorship to an inexperienced but enthusiastic team member with a rapidly approaching important deliverable is vastly different from working with a more experienced team member who is not on the same page and working on a project that has been delayed time over time. In fact, the case is made that it is precisely because the leadership style is adapted to each set of circumstance that the same desired outcome – project deliverable – is accomplished despite the varying circumstance at hand. In fact, it can be hard to adopt an adaptive leadership style each time when our inclination is to favor one over another.

The manner of working with someone who is highly committed but not quite as competent in the face of a looming critical project deadline with high visibility can be vastly different from working with someone else who displays variable commitment but is highly able to handle the challenge at hand. In the same manner, situational compliance doesn't mean choosing when to comply or if at all, but rather how. It's like getting a new eye prescription at the local optometrist. You get asked 1 or 2, 3 or 4, as a different lens is outfitted each time until your vision becomes clearer and clearer. Devising internal controls with situational compliance in mind is much like the progressive zooming in and out so that we get to the end state through a series of adaptations and adjustments undertaken each time rather than abide by a top-down "best" practice adopted by other companies and "blessed" by the auditors.

It stands to reason that the approach for gaining internal control or SOX readiness in a newly public startup with limited resources would differ significantly from that used in a large conglomerate with internal audit and other control capabilities. Yet invariably, it is the level of precision we bring to bear in dealing with the myriad of possibilities that lie between these two extremes that can often present the most challenges. It is easy to be encouraging or be prescriptive in an all or nothing situation, but the approach taken and revised in turn for handling varying degrees of commitment and of competence is all the more challenging. How specific do we need to be in specifying just what is needed while at the same time eliciting the necessary motivation to unearth what's already there? Conversely, how easy would it have been to avoid addressing the motivational whys of gaining compliance and assuming in its place that the same competence displayed with existing operational processes and gaining efficiencies can be just as easily portable or applied towards managing risks with financial impact?

We can take a page from Waymo. When developing self-driving cars, it writes a complex computer program that takes in real-life situations encountered and runs these through varied simulations virtually so that the car is tested in its response time and again against any conceivable iteration.[61] Because different people act differently in different parts of the world, the simulations replicate a situation that can be traced to specific locales.[62] Situational compliance also underlies the Naked Streets premise proposed by Dutch traffic engineer, Hans Monderman.[63] Rather than used to characterize streets overrun by naked pedestrians running amok as it were, naked here refers to stripping the streets of traditional safety measures, such as traffic lights, warning signs, speed humps, pedestrian crossings, and road markings.

In 2001, Monderman applied the Naked Streets concept to the upgrade of the Laweiplein, a crowded four-way intersection in the town center of Drachten in the northwestern Netherlands. The results? Despite traffic volumes increasing by a third, accidents were halved. Monderman had an unconventional if not unforgettable demonstration. He walked with his eyes closed backwards into the intersection while drivers and cyclists diverted their routes to avoid him rather than honk at or worst strike him. Since 2001, the Naked Street phenomenon has been applied in the United Kingdom, Denmark, Belgium, Germany, France, Sweden, and Spain, to name but a few. According to Monderman, risk, or the perception of risk at any rate, induces safe behavior.[64]

Perhaps we can apply this same approach to internal controls, not as cold comfort or a comfort blanket to blanketing out all that is uncertain but an invitation to dig deeper or else back track our steps out of an encountered dead-end to explore yet a different route. With this perspective, it is almost a given that whatever controls have been built into an existing SaaS – whether custom attributes, records, workflows, scripts, or web services – are susceptible to change and thank goodness for that! Often, we don't quite realize the complexity of real-life demands until something is already deployed in production. In syncing over a transaction from an upstream to downstream SaaS, we may not realize that the department that it has been coded to has been incorrect all this time until running (four versions of) a year-over-year YTD financials downstream and realizing that the expenses have been categorized in the wrong GAAP categories.

In a different scenario, we find unauthorized transactions downstream when performing a reconciliation against upstream transactions. Even though these have been voided upstream, they nevertheless are synced across for accounting impact downstream. When these are discovered, it is too late as the period has already been closed. In both scenarios, when figuring out workarounds, users may back track, switch course, and simply layer in a new nuance. In the first example, when we run into a challenge in getting the iPaaS to code the synced over transaction to the right department, a customized workflow or script is developed instead in the downstream SaaS to compensate for the shortfall. This technique effectively augments all incoming data prior to entry in the destination SaaS and acts to combat the all too common garbage-in garbage-out phenomenon.

In the second example, upon closer review, the timing of the void is itself important. A manual review for duplicate transactions doesn't occur early enough during month-end close so by this time the suspect transactions would have already synced over downstream. An attempt is made to subsume upstream transactions through an approval process so that the iPaaS would only sync authorized ones downstream. Here, careful consideration is given to emphasis upstream controls over firefighting busywork downstream.

Expectations can be blinders in precluding the uncovering of local practices that lends themselves to configuration and hence automation. As we have seen, to protect ourselves against insults to integrity, we can start by hurling potential insults to integrity proactively whether it is through programmed counter-compliance guerrilla efforts or by developing our situational muscle to meet the challenge of the situation at hand rather than falling back on the tried and true. Yet, what about our own configuration, the way we are used to seeing and framing issues that arise, for it is precisely this configuration that merits its own reassessment. To what extent should we look at breaking the integrity of our own worldviews and internal paradigms over time – and especially in the context of SaaS, and its capability for configuration for nontechnical users – at a more rapid pace?

One mindset that merits revisiting may be compliance as something to be unearthed, uncovered, or found rather than something to be consumed, deployed, or enforced. Recall the embodied logics of purchase requisition approval beyond the SaaS at hand, from communicated enterprise purchase policy to nature of goods and services procured. Instead of asking the question what can we do to comply with SOX, we can start by asking that to the extent that we already ensure the quality of work or deliverable, what elements lend themselves to compliance and audit? Whether our clients are internal or external, we already deliver and therefore fulfill on a promise or service level, so just as a quality assurance personnel are accountable to end users and developers, an end user is accountable to external customers and vendors.

This leads us to the integrity of our configuration that needs to be broken down for it to be built back up: the idea or belief that controls belong to auditors and compliance personnel, or management or supervisory personnel, insofar as they involve some form of validation. Controls are things others worry about. So, to the extent control-work is outsourced, we can get down to the business of real work.

For even as we labor hard at the design and operation of internal controls for SaaS, we need to shift our attention from the software to the beliefs we subscribe to. Real work insofar as it is focused on obtaining desired outcomes, can just be as much about internal controls as compliance is about evidencing control effectiveness in a 10-Q or 10-K. When we continue with this process of expanding our locus of control from within to without, we also start to take on the perspectives of others. Often, the places that most scare or repel us are deep sources for fostering mutual understanding and bringing about an alchemical transformation of sorts.

From an accounting manager perspective, a SaaS administrator who is perceived to be overly responsive to the point of not obtaining adequate authorization before intervening can be perceived to be an individual who is over-exercising his or her super-user authorities or worst embarking on a power trip. When the accounting manager starts to put himself in the administrator's shoes and handle a request of granting additional access to an existing role, however, he or she can begin to see how the activities performed "are specific to that task yet may reflect the enormity of the context within which it resides."[65] A request to grant additional access may be warranted in the event that an obstacle comes up precluding users from completing their tasks in a timely manner during crunch time as part of month- or quarter-end close. The fact that the administrator is contacted instead of the accounting manager belies deeper challenges around communication and clear roles and responsibilities within the team.

The need to revise access also speaks to how the presently configured roles and granted permissions may not have been configured enough, inherited from system defaults and thus not tailored to meet the needs of the consuming organization at hand. As the accounting manager continues to explore the role of the administrator, other questions emerge. For new hires assigned access to the SaaS, how are their roles granted? Do they simply get granted access roles belonging to predecessors who left, even if the new roles they have been hired into have been updated or revised?

By taking on the role of another, even without being assigned a new or upgraded system role, we begin to explore a possible path from start to finish, and start to question our own stories, the narratives we have constructed to support our own biases. Is it the banner, or the wind, or the mind? Is it a rope or a snake? If the latter, which end are we grabbing hold of? Ascribing blame all too easily is symptomatic of hanging onto our belief structures for our dear lives, as if entertaining a difference in opinion or potential for change is instantly imprinted as an insult to our very own constitutional well-being. From an administrator perspective, constant demands from an accountant may be particularly taxing. Not only is the accountant asking for assistance for navigation in performing a mass import of transactions, but he or she is also enlisting help in setting up a query to provide snapshots of the before and the after, to verify that the updates have indeed been performed appropriately. When all is said and done, the administrator feels that he or she could have performed the work himself or herself, and invariably may choose to anyway if only to avoid more communication with the said individual.

Yet, if the administrator were to place himself or herself in the accountant's shoes and walk through the actions needed with the accountant, he or she may yet uncover roadblocks that the accountant faces even as he or she proceeds to complete the tasks at hand. The administrator may find out that, unlike him or her, the accountants ascribed role and permissions do not let the accountant view the internal field identifiers so that he or she is not able to make his or her bulk updates more precisely by specifying and pinpointing which transactions should be impacted. When attempting to set up a query, the administrator may find that the accountant's role does not let him or her save the query so that he or she would have to create a new one each time. System audit logs are also not exposed for the accountant, so pulling up the changes he or she made to serve as a source of validation can prove to be a challenge. This example illustrates how the administrator can deepen his or her understanding of the matter at hand by stepping out of himself or herself and into the shoes of the accountant.

Conversely, our previous example illustrates how the accounting manager can better step out or his or her own role to better appreciate the challenges facing the administrator and his or her team in general. Both examples, however, share the need for, as well as the ensuing positives that can come with, taking on the negative, the other if only to better appreciate the complexities belying the situation.

The same pattern is seen when an auditee exchanges his or her perspective for an auditor's. The auditee may perceive the auditor to be demanding, whimsical even, for focusing on one area of controls such as the criteria for generating SaaS-generated reports whereas barely a year before, these areas went by unremarked. Well, we know they'd have to find something, the auditee had confided in a fellow co-worker. Better that than something else, is the response the auditee hears. After all, isn't it common knowledge that clients end up being the training ground for yet another wave of auditors deployed to the battlefield as it were? Yet had the auditee probed deeper, begun a dialogue with the auditor, the auditee may soon realize that the Public Company Accounting Oversight Board (PCAOB) – who else, after all, watches the watchmen? – has recently released an alert that mandated auditors to dig deeper to ensure that the criteria used to run system-generated reports, otherwise known as independently produced evidence (IPE), is not overlooked.

How can we rely on these IT dependent controls without necessarily having to increase the level of substantive testing necessary to validate that the control is operating as intended or designed? Had the auditee stepped into the shoes of the auditor, the auditee too would have found it challenging to become quickly knowledgeable of the client's environment after having just come off the rotation of yet another client or having to handle multiple concurrent engagements. After all, auditors need to remain chargeable all the time and can't afford to remain on the beach at any time. Likewise, the auditor may find the auditee's demeanor grating, not finding the time to respond to his or her inquires or only at the very last possible moment. The auditee gets branded as an uncooperative client; yet, had the auditee initiated and sustained an open dialogue, the auditee would have come to realize that on top of his or her day job and the audit at hand, the auditee is also simultaneously juggling multiple projects, just as auditor is booked on concurrent engagements. Thus, a textbook prescription of tightened segregation of duties is simply not possible nor reasonable in a context of limited resources.

Recognizing each other's perspective is but a first step, albeit a necessary one. We all need to begin somewhere. But for this recognition to turn into something tangible, we need to be willing to experiment, improvise, try out new ways to get to the same outcome, or in other words, adopt situational compliance. For a tightened role with reduced permissions, the auditor may propose that the auditee try out dual roles for a length of time, the existing role and the newly tightened one, so that in the event a roadblock is encountered and needs to be resolved right away, the auditee can go ahead and switch to the older role. After the dust has settled and time is freed up, a retrospective attempt may be made to assign the missing permissions to the tightened role. Through this back and forth, the auditor and auditee arrive at a much more palatable if not realistic outcome that can be a win-win perspective for both rather than for one or the other. After all, with excessive access, the auditee runs the risk of been accused of wrongdoing, an easy scapegoat for whatever has gone awry.

When we start to introduce overlapping perspectives of the SaaS administrator, end user, and auditor, we may yet realize that upon an initial inspection of a user access listing, there are too many administrator roles within an organization. In other words, the question is not so much a weakness in access administration procedures or lack of timely intervention in creating or approving an access request as it is in truly understanding the varied permissions that come with a SaaS for each transaction or entity type, standard or custom record, query or report, pervasive or specific application parameter. An over-reliance on the out-of-the-box default administrator role becomes inevitable when users don't quite comprehend the available assignable permissions, as well as the level of granularity or precision with which they can be assigned to a specific role. When in doubt or when in a time crunch, simply assigning the administrator role gets the job done on time without fussing over whether we can proceed from not having a specific permission assigned.

The extent to which access can be configured also depends greatly on the functionality of the SaaS at hand: is the administrator role really needed for system administrator tasks, or can a more curtailed system administrative role be defined? There are also manual procedures that can be worked out in the 3-way dialogue among administrators, end users, and auditors, so that when it comes to mass updates for example, the end user may perform this using a copy of the system administrative role albeit one with reduced permissions, with a requisite query defined after to report on audit trail of changes made, as opposed to having the administrator intervene in operational manual transactional or entity updates each time. This way, a segregation of sorts is manually enacted between the end user and the administrator – otherwise SaaS owner and custodian.

Often, by not questioning our own stance, or at least allowing room for a two-way dialogue with another, it can become easy for us to use our discomfort as a defense shield that we "make up" about and wave at others in a manner that is consistent with and justifies our original position when an easier approach may have been to develop an innate curiosity about a hardened stance. As a glaucoma patient, my father recently visited a public tertiary specialist eye care center for his physical eye exam. During the pre-consultation, he was attended to by an individual who was not wearing any identification nor did the individual have my father's medical file in hand. When questioned by my father, the individual did not take kindly to my father's questions and relayed it to the primary care physician. What ensued were more delays. Despite arriving on time at the appointed hour, my father left 5 hours later without the scheduled physical as by the time he was attended to, the lab technician had already gone home.

When revisiting this incident with his primary care physician in his next visit, he found out that the pre-consultation was performed by an overseas exchange student on a fellowship program. She was intimidated by his questions and privately broke down, prompting the surrounding staff to delay his scheduled physical. His primary care physician got to hear his side of the story, how he was left alone to experience the discomfort of having his pupils dilated all that time only to find out that the appointment that he had scheduled 4 months ago had yet again been postponed. In the clear light of day, this second visit provided a dilated lens on the accounts of both sides. Had the student not assumed that my father was merely being difficult, she could have asked what was troubling him. Had my father recognized that she appeared stressed and was inexperienced at juggling different patients, he could have realized that they both in fact shared the same frustrations with the time it took to prepare for the physical, the emphasis of the governing protocol over quality of care.

When we defend the frailty of our stance, in a bid to appear less fragile, we in turn become far less open to hearing about what really is, or what could have been. We grow hardened and inflexible. We end up being utterly unforgiving by all accounts. The design of internal controls that results is fragile, relying on any one perspective almost to sheer exclusivity rather than being able to integrate, and thus withstand, the views of many.

Consider the following quote from Einstein:

> *A human being is part of the whole, called by us "universe," limited in time and space. He experiences himself, his thoughts and feelings as something separated from the rest – a kind of optical delusion of his consciousness. This delusion is a prison, restricting us to our personal desires and to affection for a few persons close to us. Our task must be to free ourselves from our prison by widening our circle of compassion to embrace all humanity and the whole of nature in its beauty.*[66]

Imagine an alternate scenario: the auditee admits to the auditor that because the SaaS is recently implemented, there is still a heavy reliance on manual procedures rather than leveraging what has been offered out-of-the-box to automate processes. The auditor, upon hearing this, shares with the auditee that this is the first time he is auditing a SaaS as opposed to an on-premise software, and if she doesn't mind, he would be asking what would appear to be basic, even trivial, questions. The auditee responds that this is as good an opportunity as any to revisit what she has taken for granted all this time and if a finding does emerge, at least it would lend weight to its implementation, taking on the hues of a must-have rather than nice to-have.

A question from the auditor may be what version of the SaaS the enterprise on, unwittingly tapping into a key difference between SaaS and on-premise software. Rather than using this as a point of admonishment, the auditee proceeds to explain how with SaaS, even though the client personnel do not write the code for the SaaS, they have far greater flexibility through point-and-click in tailoring the SaaS to their needs. Upon hearing this, the auditor comes with an example of a vendor approval process he has seen with other clients using on-premise software and shares this with the auditee. The auditee considers this and shares the help documentation with the auditor on the configuration of a vendor approval workflow. This does not have to be an idealized scenario. What it takes is simply a willingness to admit that we don't have all the answers at the outset but are willing to put our minds (and hearts) together to resolve the challenge at hand, rather than hide behind self-professed "professional" masks, insisting on decorum over substance.

Although this example seems hypothetical and too good to be true, in reality I have had many experiences that underscore the need to revisit what appears to be cast in stone. As opposed to a first-time newbie of an auditor who has not audited clients using SaaS, we might work with an auditor who is able to confer with other clients using the same SaaS to verify how differently they are processing the same transaction or what additional configurational controls they have put in place? Sometimes, a consensus gained on an agreed-upon approach needs to be revisited so just as controls configured in a SaaS can and need to be updated upon deployment in production, the process to design internal controls is amenable to change.

A public company may engage with an external consulting firm to assist with the design and validation of internal controls that are in turn validated by its external audit firm. During this process, when exploring the tightening of access in the SaaS used in a specific business cycle, consultants and client personnel are inundated by the sheer volume of the number of permissions to account for in any one SaaS. To attempt to inventory these permissions, create new roles tied to permissions, and test these out in a sandbox environment would take more time and resources than originally envisioned. After much deliberation, a user raises the possibility of using the segregation of duties analysis of potential conflicts performed during cycle walkthroughs as a first filter to prioritize permissions that require tightening for which no compensating control were defined. When cross-checked with the consultants and auditors, it turns out to be a reasonable first step in addressing risks that matter more than others, not least in a manner that is measured and pragmatic.

Devising internal controls for SaaS can be challenging because of the push and pull we experience. On the one hand, we have grown accustomed to articulating and validating internal controls with on-premise software yet on the other hand the ease of configuration that comes with SaaS beckons new beginnings. To try something new, we need to be able to forget. GDPR's right to be forgotten comes to mind. Some would put forth the proposition that to forgive, we need to forget, hence the parlance 'forgive and forget'. What do we choose to forget? What do we choose to retain? Even within the SaaS, there is already a constant tug and pull this time, between what is deemed standard out-of-the-box functionality and what is tailored, configured, or customized.

What I haven't yet covered in any considerable degree is the role professional services (PS) firms play in shaping SaaS to meet client needs. Configuration capability through point-and-click for nontechnical audiences notwithstanding, some SaaS customers choose to engage with third-party contractors to groom what has been purchased off the shelf just as, in our earlier example, a public company engaged with an external consulting firm to assist with internal control design. Even for the SaaS vendor's internal PS team, this can be a booming business. With the passage of time, specific PS delivered enhancements in turn get reintegrated into the main product feature set so that it becomes widely available to all customers. Thus, the only constant in assessing standard versus nonstandard functionality is perhaps the only real tug and push between them, even as the former gets refreshed by the latter in due time.

Other SaaS vendors have started turning support into a separate more flushed out offering. Instead of merely providing a support hotline albeit one that handles product inquiries, performance concerns, as well as configuration or customization questions, a customer success program may be put together so that for the SaaS client that has neither the time nor internal resources to administer or maintain the SaaS it subscribes to, Administrator as a Service or Configuration as a Service may be purchased as a block of hours in a month. A dedicated single point of contact may also be assigned to compile all concerns raised and provide regular resolution updates. Other SaaS customers may opt not to dive into any level of depth in the feature or configuration galore provided by the SaaS at hand because their priorities are elsewhere. In place of integration with an upstream subledger SaaS, the user can always opt to make manual journal entries downstream. In place of having granular attributes downstream, users can log into the source SaaS upstream to perform reporting.

There is not one set way or one set of ways. In fact, from a strategic enterprise perspective, an organization may be spending excessive time attempting to configure or customize a SaaS to automate low value-add processes with little or no pervasive impact when the same efforts can be better spent on more strategic or compliance initiatives. When it comes to the latter, a risk assessment culminating in a heat map may reveal gaps in other SaaS or areas that may merit greater attention than devoting all efforts in configuring the SaaS at hand to the maximum.

SOX Compliance Dashboard				
Objective	Risk	Likelihood	Impact	Control
Optimal Vendor Relations	Risk of Unauthorized Vendors	High	Medium	A consistent RFP process needs to be deployed by tailoring the procurement SaaS
Management Budget Oversight	Risk of Unauthorized Spend	Medium	Medium	All spend over 1,000 needs to be controlled via procurement rather than expense management SaaS
Incomplete Accruals	Risk of Financial Misstatement	Low	High	Reports are executed on received unbilled POs and month over month variance analysis is performed
Secure & Timely Disbursements	Risk of Fraudulent Transactions	Low	Medium	Roles & permissions are tightened across upstream procurement and downstream accounting SaaS

In the previous example, greater attention needs to be devoted to configuration work in the upstream procurement management as well as expense management SaaS as opposed to continuing to emphasize the downstream accounting SaaS that would have automatically come under the purview of SOX. Imagine if peer companies got together and compared their heat maps on SOX compliance? How might they learn from one another?

Another way to drive compliance efforts is to work backwards from what needs to be in place to evidence internal controls – recall the palindrome perspective from Chapter 4. We could conceivably start with the frequencies of various key controls we have identified. The more sample sizes that can be gathered in any given fiscal year, the greater opportunities for rework, and consequently remediation efforts to be undertaken for the final round of testing to yield no control exceptions. Conversely, controls with small sample sizes have fewer room for error, and insofar as they are deemed susceptible to begin with, need to be prioritized to be worked on if only to increase the likelihood of successful audit findings. For a segregation of duties access review performed only once annually, although stakeholders have more time to remedy existing roles and tighten permissions granted within any one or across multiple SaaS, there is only one opportunity to either fail or succeed when it comes to a test of control operating effectiveness.

In contrast, ad hoc access approvals for new hires or transfers and quarterly access reviews and weekly change deployment reviews can amass more sample size and, in the sequence listed, by degree of increasing magnitude. In the unfortunate failure of operating control effectiveness of the weekly change review, there is more opportunity for remediation provided when the exceptions are identified earlier rather than later in the year than say, a quarterly access review where failure evidenced in one quarter would only leave three more quarters in the year to be validated. When we overlay this roadmap of control frequencies against the SOX compliance dashboard and the varied supporting SaaS, our work is cut out for us indeed.

Let's switch gears. To truly automate, we must first be prepared to handle altogether different, and arguably more multi-varied, realistic paths. In coding as in our daily lives, we are more inclined to employ "or" than "and" as we have become so accustomed to seeing a script or query not work when "and" rather than "or" is used in the criteria. Compare the following 2 query criteria on open customer invoices:

1. (Shipping Country = United Kingdom) AND (Shipping State = California)
2. (Shipping Country = United Kingdom) OR (Shipping State = California)

The first immediately throws up an error upon execution, since California does not exist in the United Kingdom. Ironically enough, by employing the 'or' condition, the second lists invoices with shipping countries in the United Kingdom *and* California. In this way and various other insidious ways, we are encouraged to opt for "or" over "and" in our otherwise unremarked every day. Yet in recalling Alice Notley's poem, *The Prophet*, referenced at the start of this chapter, the use of "&" is more accommodating in life outside of system queries, workflows or scripts.[67]

Consider the following scenario where an enterprise has acquired two other companies. Each of these newly formed subsidiaries roll up to headquarters (HQ), but they each consume separate procurement and accounting SaaS upstream. The financial data is in turn synced over to a traditional ERP on-premise vendor that has since transitioned to the cloud and in use at HQ. Thus, rather than contend ourselves with this-or-that binary opposites in comparing SaaS with on-premise software, we see here that the varied tools we have at our disposal can and often do co-exist in co-composing transactions from cradle to grave, so that the finalized numbers on the consolidated financials presented at HQ at the end of a fiscal quarter or year in many ways conceals the complexity in arriving at the numbers.

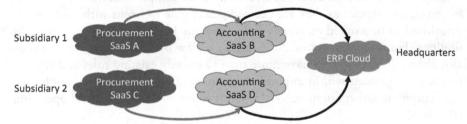

Furthermore, this cloudscape is not static. As the enterprise gets better in mergers and acquisitions, it may develop a reusable SaaS blueprint for application on new acquired companies so that the applications in use are transitioned from legacy applications or diverse SaaS to a more streamlined sequence of affairs.

From an internal control perspective, consider an alternate scenario where controls are not devised ahead of time and disseminated top-down to elicit the very behaviors to support industry "best-practice" metrics to be measured upon, but one where uncertainty reigns and events don't ever quite go as planned. Enron and other financial debacles reveal an intent to mislead, to appear as that which they are not. Their very actions demand a thoughtful response, one that needs to be well conceived surely, calculated even, and yet, we often choose to think that an internal control is operating effectively or designed appropriately even as it remains a surface sheen of what lies beneath, taking comfort, as it were, in our audit and compliance sub-routines.

The notion of SaaS having one version is first surfaced in Chapter 3. Recall how the use of the metadata table described by Chong, Carraro, and Wolter lets enterprise users add any number of custom fields in varied formats without changing the underlying table structure.[68] By doing so, even if SaaS undergoes annual or twice-a-year software upgrades to enhance or add new functionality, it can be seen to transcend the very notion of versioning. The same cannot be said for its human users, for as our discussion on expectations and pre-programmed responses in this chapter illustrate, we often have a hard time overcoming the versions we have created for ourselves in working with humans and software alike.

This brings us back to situational compliance of which the very ability to overcome existing or prior versions of self, and of others, lies at its core. Even if we can't foresee the entire spectrum of possible paths, what Agile, Scrum, and Chaos Monkey underscore is not so much what goes wrong but what can be done about it. Would we dare entertain a crack in our otherwise fragile armor to let in the enveloping light? By recognizing there is more than one way or one set of ways, our very response is anything but programmed. This requires a paradigm shift, but one not driven by the plentitude of content. The ocean, after all, is independent of the fish it houses. There's only one way to test out the water temperature in the Pacific. It's time to jump in.

Exercise 10.1

Identify a kluge that you have seen employed for each of the following in the context of using a SaaS:

1. Order-to-Cash
2. Procure-to-Pay

For each of the earlier, what can be unintended consequences? How can the kluge be an invitation to a more resilient or sustainable fix? Conversely, what are the ways we continue to hide the RAT,[69] thus in a way blocking an otherwise organic evolution of kluges into sustainable solutions?

Discussion

Kluges when deployed carry an implicit recognition from Day 1 that they are not ideal, that given enough time and resource, they need to be re-looked at, refurbished as it were. Yet, the passage of time can make us forgetful, so what has been deemed to be short-term, quick fixes take on a life of their own over time. In circling back to Chapter 5, kluges are inherently susceptible to repair, attribute and all that on our part, so that over time, we also become accustomed to hiding the RAT, and prolonging their lifespan.

Exercise 10.2

Consider the following two scenarios:

1. The users of an accounting SaaS are attempting to report on prepaid amortization. When they prepay an expense before it has been incurred, they typically assign it an amortization schedule where at the end of each accounting period, a journal entry is posted for the expense incurred over the period according to the schedule. In this manner, they record the incursion of expenses associated with the prepayment. To the extent they are already able to create custom reports in the SaaS on revenue recognition, how can they leverage these to report on prepaid amortization?
2. To what extent does it help to see the unique identifier specific to an upstream SaaS in the downstream SaaS?

Discussion

Both scenarios revisit the beguiling nature of superimposed dichotomies as well as mirrored possibilities. The first question is more tactical in nature. In an accounting SaaS, users are initially perplexed on how to produce amortization reports until they realize that the same revenue recognition queries they devise and use can be reused for prepaid amortization. The second question asks us to consider how an ability to compare items consistently across SaaS helps in reconciliation and how integrated SaaS can, in fact, help "check up" on each other.

Exercise 10.3

To the extent that the same SaaS is used by multiple customers, can you think of advantages that can be leveraged by having access to group behavioral patterns when we peer into the design of controls – in other words, groupthink? Identify a benefit gained in each of the following:

1. Enterprise purchasing patterns
2. Employee salaries
3. Approval thresholds for purchases and expense reports
4. Exception handling alerts or notifications
5. Features utilized
6. Degree of configuration or customization
7. Ability to predict likelihood of customer attrition
8. Ability to estimate cost of customer capture

Discussion

Here, we put on the hat of an industry analyst having access to multiple data points belonging to both like and unlike enterprise customers when it comes to consuming SaaS. The ability to gather and analyze statistics on usage patterns and numbers such as amount purchased, discounts obtained, or salaries benchmarked against peers both within and without vertical industry silos. The various options challenge us to think of data points not merely in terms of usage but also configuration patterns to be able to hopefully perform what-if analytics. When you think about it, this is one area that continues to remain untapped by SaaS providers. Even within a singular SaaS, the potential for meaningful analytics is an evergreen uncharted area among many SaaS customer enterprises. Further, if a customer were to know where it is in its use of SaaS vis-à-vis other customers and what the SaaS can offer, both from a feature and configuration perspective, a roadmap emerges.

Endnotes

1. Vladimir, N. (1941). *The Real Life of Sebastian Knight*. Norfolk, CT: New Directions.
2. Notley, A. (2008). *Grave of Light: New and Selected Poems 1970–2005*. Middletown, CT: Wesleyan University Press.
3. Kripke, S. (1982). *Wittgenstein on Rules and Private Language*. Cambridge, MA: Harvard University Press.
4. Metz, C. and Chen, B. X. (January 4, 2018). What you need to do because of flaws in computer chips. *New York Times*. https://www.nytimes.com/2018/01/04/technology/meltdown-spectre-questions.html
5. Ibid.
6. Raymond, E. S. (1996). *The New Hacker's Dictionary* (3rd ed.). Cambridge, MA: MIT Press.
7. Ibid.
8. Hall, L. (December 26, 2017). *Victoria and Abdul: The Screenplay*. London, UK: Faber & Faber.
9. Zuboff, S. (September 1985). Automate/informate: The two faces of intelligent technology. *Organizational Dynamics*, 14(2), 5–18.
10. Hall, L. *Victoria and Abdul: The Screenplay*.
11. Gronvall, A. (October 2, 2017). Orientalism is alive and well in Stephen Frears's *Victoria & Abdul*. *Chicago Reader*. https://www.chicagoreader.com/chicago/victoria-abdul-stephen-frears-judi-dench-eddie-izzard/Content?oid=31655216
12. Raymond, E. S. *The New Hacker's Dictionary* (3rd ed.).
13. Ibid.
14. Wright, J. (1990). *Above the River: The Complete Poems and Selected Prose*. New York: Farrar, Straus and Giroux.
15. Mudasobwa. (March 7, 2017). Is "kludge" a proper word to name a dirty hack in software development? *StackExchange*. https://english.stackexchange.com/users/37370/mudasobwa
16. Lévi-Strauss, C. (1966). *The Savage Mind*. Chicago, IL: The University of Chicago Press.
17. Turkle, S. (1995). *Life on the Screen: Identity in the Age of the Internet*. New York: Simon & Schuster.

18 Ciborra, C. U. (1994). In C. U. Ciborra and Jelassi, T. (Eds.) *From thinking to tinkering. In Strategic Information Systems.* Chichester, UK: John Wiley & Sons.

19 Gerfen, K. (January 12, 2018). The polymath: David Benjamin is expanding the definition of architecture. *Architect Magazine.* http://www.architectmagazine.com/practice/the-polymath-david-benjamin-is-expanding-the-definition-of-architecture_o

20 Ibid.

21 Ibid.

22 Gandhi, R., Veeraraghavan, R., Toyama, K., and Ramprasad, V. (December 15–16, 2007). Digital green: Participatory video for agricultural extension. Information and Communication Technologies and Development. ICTD. *International Conference on Information and Communication Technologies and Development.*

23 Ibid.

24 Ibid.

25 Ibid.

26 Ibid.

27 Ibid.

28 Simon, C. (November 20, 2015). *Songs From The Trees (A Musical Memoir Collection).*

29 Laozi and Mitchell, S. (1988). *Tao Te Ching: A New English Version.* New York: Harper & Row.

30 Turkle, S. and Papert, S. (March 1992). Epistemological pluralism and the revaluation of the concrete. *Journal of Mathematical Behavior,* 11(1), 3–33.

31 Searle, J. (1980). Minds, brains and programs. *Behavioral and Brain Sciences,* 3, 417–457.

32 Lewis-Krausdec, G. (December 14, 2016). The Great A.I. awakening. *The New York Times.* https://www.nytimes.com/2016/12/14/magazine/the-great-ai-awakening.html

33 Ibid.

34 Ibid.

35 European Commission–Data protection. (January 25, 2012). Data protection reform: Frequently asked questions, MEMO/12/41, http://europa.eu/rapid/press-release_MEMO-12-41_en.htm?locale=fr

36 Ibid.

37 Ibid.

38 Hoover, T. (1980). *The Zen Experience.* New York: New American Library.

39 Kuang-Ming Wu. (1990). *The Butterfly as Companion: Meditations on the First Three Chapters of the Chuang-Tzu.* Albany, NY: SUNY Press.

40 Mudasobwa. Is "kludge" a proper word to name a dirty hack in software development? https://english.stackexchange.com/users/37370/mudasobwa

41 Woolgar, S. and Lezaun, J. (June 10, 2013). The wrong bin bag: A turn to ontology in science and technology studies? *Social Studies of Science,* 43(3), 321–340.

42 Ibid.

43 Goffman, E. (1959). *The Presentation of Self in Everyday Life.* New York: Anchor Books.

44 Timmermans, S. and Berg, M. (April 1997). Standardization in action: Achieving local universality through medical protocols. *Social Studies of Science,* 27, 273–305.

45 Ibid.

46 Ibid.

47 Ibid.

[48] Baccus, M. D. (1986). Multipiece truck wheel accidents and their regulations. In H. Garfinkel (Ed.) *Ethnomethodological Studies of Work*. London, UK: Routledge, pp. 20–59.

[49] Ibid.

[50] Ibid.

[51] Suchman, L. A. (1987). *Plans and Situated Actions: The Problem of Human-Machine Communication*. Cambridge, UK: Cambridge University Press.

[52] Ibid.

[53] Ibid.

[54] Ibid.

[55] Wainewright, P. (August 20, 2007). Workday: Forget ERP, start over. Software as Services, ZDNet. http://www.zdnet.com/article/workday-forget-erp-start-over/

[56] Ibid.

[57] Ibid.

[58] Ibid.

[59] Ibid.

[60] Ibid.

[61] Said, C. and Baker, D. (September 24, 2017). Humanizing cars, sensitizing humans. *San Francisco Chronicle*.

[62] Ibid.

[63] Mihaly, W. (January 24, 2014). Naked streets. Streets Without Cars. https://streetswithoutcars.wordpress.com/tag/drummond-street/

[64] Hans Monderman quoted in Tom Vanderbild. (2008). *The Traffic Guru. The Wilson Quarterly*, Washington, DC.

[65] Baccus, M. D. Multipiece truck wheel accidents and their regulations.

[66] Translation of letter to Hermann Huth. (December 27, 1930). Einstein Archive 46-756.

[67] Notley, A. *Grave of Light: New and Selected Poems 1970–2005*.

[68] Chong, F., Carraro, G., and Wolter, R. (2006). Multi-tenant data architecture. Tech. rep., MSDN Library, Microsoft Corporation.

[69] Collins, H. M. and Kusch, M. (1998). *The Shape of Actions: What Humans and Machines Can Do*. Cambridge, MA: MIT Press.

Chapter 11

Transfigured Relations

I am always doing that which I cannot do,

in order that I may learn how to do it.[1]

Vincent Van Gogh

The 1990s TV show *Star Trek: The Next Generation* picked up where the original series left off. While it continued to "explore strange new worlds, to seek out new life and new civilizations, to boldly go where no man has gone before,"[2] in contrast to its predecessor, this series emphasized peacekeeping over war except, of course, when its own interests were threatened by opposing forces such as by the Borg.[3] Half man and half machine, the Borg were hooked up to the Collective, a central server of sorts. Multi-tenant Software as a Service (SaaS) architecture anyone? As no one singular Borg had an individual identity, together they sought to dominate "strange new worlds" through assimilation to the tune of "resistance is futile."[4] It strikes me that the way we have been devising internal controls for SaaS has many parallels with the Borg approach. We apply an almost universal template on all public companies with little attention or regard to specific differences in underlying business, process, or technology.

It can be easy to forget that even a simple internal control, such as authorized updates to vendor data, can be accomplished in a multitude of ways. On one end of the spectrum, a query or report can be run on all new vendors added or changes performed in the prior month to support a review against supporting documentation. On the other end, an approval workflow can be configured, such that all new vendor additions or updates trigger an approval process. Between these two extremes lies a myriad of ways to control for additions or changes to vendor data. Access to vendor data updates may be restricted. Key updates to sensitive fields may trigger an email notification to vested stakeholders. Even amid all these controls, what prevents someone from updating the payee in a file downloaded from the accounting SaaS and uploaded to the banking website? Even though the totals would still tie out, all the upstream controls around vendor addition, change, and review or approval would seem to go to naught in this instance. What approach is ultimately taken, such as prefacing a detective over a preventive approach in discovering likely exceptions that have already occurred rather than preventing them from arising in the first place, may change in time. Both approaches make the SaaS far more forgiving even if ideally the latter, because it is preventive, is preferable over the former in the long run. Yet, the chosen path is as much a confluence of resource, time, and cost constraints as it is the degree of configurability of the SaaS at hand and the level of familiarization in nontechnical and technical staff alike.

The goals of compliance and process automation do not have to be mutually exclusive and often become tightly intertwined. Getting proactive notifications of potential vendor changes or additions upfront and having to approve these changes minimize the likelihood of nasty surprises downstream, such as having already engaged the vendor and being obligated or liable to pay even if services were not acquired at negotiated block discounts favorable to the consuming enterprise at large. Yet the real test of how fragile this upstream vendor approval workflow is lies in having users give it a whirl or test drive, often post-SaaS deployment in production. For example, a report on changes to vendor data may reveal excessive access granted to the account payables (A/P) team so that even if approval is required and obtained for vendor additions, subsequent updates can be performed without authorization. In this manner, the automating component needs its corresponding informating mirror. In some cases, if most of the changes occur post vendor creation, owing to the lack of complete or accurate information such as W-9 or other details available at the outset of vendor creation to begin with, the approval workflow is itself re-tweaked to include routing vendor changes in addition to vendor additions for approval.

We can argue that it is precisely because users are afforded the range of possibilities in adding or changing vendors as part of their day-to-day in-situ processes that more rather than less information can strengthen, rather than weaken, the value proposition of an automated approval workflow, provided that the arising finds are viewed as opportunities rather than hindrances or worst nuisances swept under rug as it were. And so it is with our ability to make payee changes prior to processing payments using the banking website. In this variation, a user who may not even have access to the accounting SaaS may be able to manually update the Excel or csv download prior to upload to the banking site. For all our emphasis on configuring internal controls for SaaS, it is ironic that the real insult to transactional integrity is lobbied at the very intersection between the internal and external: using SaaS to produce the download or report and yet not quite using the SaaS to complete the payment. We can even ask: what precludes the user uploading the bank payments to ignore the download from the accounting SaaS altogether so that what ends up processed is in fact not what has been recorded for general ledger impact in the accounting SaaS?

The controls employed to ensure that the vendor payment file has not been manually updated in an inappropriate way hover at the intersection of automated and manual, system and non-systematized: SaaS, Excel spreadsheet, banking website, and bank reconciliation procedures. A myopic focus on controls within the SaaS would miss out on the ones that are more interface focused between the accounting SaaS and the banking site. In continuing with the example of Satyam's overstatement of over $1 billion U.S. dollars (USD) of cash and bank balances from a previous chapter, questions revolved around how it was able to pull the wool over the auditors' eyes, especially since former managing partner of Touché Ross (later Deloitte & Touché) Russell Palmer put it, "Cash is easy to audit. You count it and confirm it with a third party – such as the bank."[5]

In their defense, Price Waterhouse, Satyam's auditor, wrote in a letter to the new Satyam board appointed by the Indian government, "Financial statements were prepared by the management of the company ... We placed reliance on management control over financial reporting, and the information and explanations provided by the management, as also the verbal and written representations made to us during the course of our audit."[6] When we circle back to our emphasis on automated controls within SaaS, to what extent are we ignoring interface controls between the SaaS and the corporate banking application over incoming or outgoing payments and insuring that these are related with valid actual upstream transactions?

Other examples reside at the intersection between compliance and process, system and manual, essentially a no-man's land of sorts. The customer credit limit field in a billing SaaS may be used to trigger a hold-stop system message if the user attempts to create a new invoice with an amount that tips the customer open balance over its credit limit. Yet a deeper analysis may reveal that access to this credit limit field is not restricted so that a possibility exists for the credit limit to be increased to allow an invoice to pass through. Both the customer as well as the preceding vendor examples show how access can work with or against the automation at hand. Rather than simply view access restriction as an end in and of itself, it is viewed in the context of what it takes to get the work done. For automation to work, compliance would have to work as well, so in this sense, compliance is the other to automation.

Back to our vendor example, had the payment been made using checks, a service such as Positive Pay may have been offered by the bank, such that the company issues a file of issued checks to the bank each day checks are written. When those issued checks are presented for payment at the bank, they are in turn compared electronically against the list of transmitted checks. Any check presented that does not match the check number, account number, issue date, and dollar amount in the check-issued file would be presented to the company as an exception item for verification of payment. Yet even here the payee name may not be part of the matching service. Thus, we circle back to our initial question: how do we preclude the payee from being swapped out at the last possible moment in transitioning from one authorized entity to another? For the system of internal controls to operate, we would in a sense need the other to the SaaS, the manual to the automated. The context in which the SaaS is used – the banking website, the manipulation of the download payment file to align it with the appropriate payment format, any reviews performed before or after the payment is authorized – needs to be accounted for.

We can argue that in effect, neither restricted access to the accounting SaaS nor to the banking website would suffice as a good enough checkpoint to preclude unauthorized payee updates. Here, even the two-eye (two pairs of eyes) principle of having one user initiate the payment in the banking site and another user approve the payment would not work unless a review to authorize payment in the banking site is made against the original payment file downloaded from the accounting SaaS. The change to the payee information is almost like a kink in an otherwise uninterrupted flow. An improvisation with a mischievous wink. The resulting mix of internal controls is like a transfiguration than mere configuration. More than mere SaaS configuration surely, it involves a mix of the anticipated with the unanticipated, placement against a possible displacement, so that what is old gains new life, rejuvenated through continual sifting, coming apart and recombination. Kerry James Marshall said it best when describing how "devices we use to 'transfigure the commonplace'… isolate, re-contextualize, shift scale, shift material, invert, etc."[7]

Teaching in and of itself is largely an improvisation. We may start with a prepared text but what we end up with is rarely what we planned. Often the questions that we least expect take us to the most unlikely yet rewarding of places. When a student in my *Accounting Information Systems* class asked how an accrual entry in an accounting SaaS can be both manual or automated since the entry is based on a review of unbilled services received, I thought about it and recalled how in one company, the source of the entries may be triggered by a monthly automated query of all purchases orders that had been received but not billed. These same POs were the output of purchase requisitions approved using an automated workflow to begin with. The accrual journal itself would undergo a similar approval workflow. In effect, the category of controls that auditors deem information technology (IT) dependent manual controls would encompass a greater subset of all and sundry than what an initial assessment would seem to indicate. There is also a recognition that those directly performing the work, as opposed to supervising managers per Taylorist categorizations, would be better able to articulate a set of controls that would most directly impact the quality of their work.

Auditors tend to look at controls from a test perspective, making tradeoffs on the resources it would take to validate internal controls per established methodology so that an automated control would be tested once and only once after verifying that there has been no change to instituted configurations and a manual control would be validated through verifying selected samples. A monthly control would naturally be associated with a higher number of samples as opposed to a quarterly one. While this means more work upfront, it also means a greater opportunity to remediate upon any exceptions uncovered sooner. Because a quarterly control would only have four samples in any given fiscal year, once two have been tested and an exception is found, only two remain for remediation and remediation testing after. Yet as we have seen, these automated manual binaries are much looser in real life, with any specific process and underlying sub-process really involving an intertwining of both manual and automated elements.

Although access granting is manual, the ability of a SaaS to restrict access through permissions assigned to roles and in turn roles to individual users is itself automated in that once configured, a user with a specific role can go about his or her daily work without additional manual intervention to adjust his or her access each time. This is assuming that the SaaS has been observed in use for some time after go-live so that any tweaks that need to be made to the permissions granted to his or her role would have already been made. From an informating perspective, we ask whether the roles and permissions can in turn be easily reported out of the SaaS as opposed to evidencing manual screenshots each time. The ability of a SaaS to automate may not be matched by its ability to informate or provide visibility. Thus, for example, selected access may be granted to key financial reports, but these in turn may not readily be queried or alerted in an automated manner when changes have been made. Therefore, in addition to the one-time effort in performing an inventory of all financial reports impacted and manually updating the permissions tied to each report, additional efforts would have been expended on a recurring basis to ensure that no unauthorized changes have been made.

Back to our accrual entry, when presenting internal controls to an IT audience recently, a question was asked: in addition to in-scope accounting SaaS, what about Microsoft artifacts such as Excel, insofar as entries made in an accounting SaaS would come from reviews or analyses performed on numbers maintained in spreadsheets? Back in the early days of SOX compliance, I recall many a late night spent on coming up with a minimal if not sustainable set of internal controls over spreadsheets, such as use of protected cells to have some level of access control over spreadsheet updates. An answer that a different audience member gave was that generally only accounting applications are considered in scope. While this seems to me to be a pragmatic approach, if I may draw from Luff and Heath, it is also largely one driven by "conceptualising the knowledge a user has 'of' a system, rather than 'how' knowledge is used within the situated accomplishment of a range of social actions and activities."[8] I'm reminded of the following passage from William Blake's *The Marriage of Heaven and Hell*:

> *The ancient Poets animated all sensible objects with Gods or Geniuses, calling them by the names and adorning them with the properties of woods, rivers, mountains, lakes, cities, nations, and whatever their enlarged and numerous senses could perceive.*
>
> *And particularly they studied the Genius of each city and country, placing it under its Mental Deity;*

> *Till a System was formed, which some took advantage of, and enslav'd*
> *the vulgar by attempting to realise or abstract the Mental Deities from their*
> *objects—thus began Priesthood;*
>   *Choosing forms of worship from poetic tales.*
>   *And at length they pronounc'd that the Gods had order'd such things.*
> *Thus men forgot that All Deities reside in the Human breast*[9]

If the control over the proper and complete recording of accruals comes from downloading all unbilled received purchase orders into an Excel spreadsheet, sorting these by expense categories, looking up the categories to applicable general ledger accounts, transposing these into a format acceptable for bulk import into the accounting SaaS as an accrual journal entry, then surely a myopic focus on the destination accounting SaaS is quite simply that, a limited albeit easy target for exacting internal controls when much of the sifting, analysis, and compilation happens quite literally outside the SaaS. When defining in-scope applications for the audit, how careful are we in avoiding being ensnared or "enslaved" by the "system" we devise? The quoted passage from Blake has elements both of immutable mobiles and a loop unto itself. The journal entry in the accounting SaaS also resembles Garfinkel's intractable clinical or medical record, revealing little or no detail on the admission criteria. Here, it is less than revealing on any possible missing inputs that need to be accounted for when identifying missing liabilities that may not yet have been captured.

It's a wonder then how little things have changed. Even with the dawn of SaaS, mobile apps, and increasing emphasis on machine learning, accounting personnel today still face the same challenges faced by their forefathers in yesteryears. The challenge we face in locating a valid purchase order for a received invoice as observed by Lucy Suchman in an accounting office is still very much one faced by many an accounting or administrative personnel today.[10] What has perhaps been enhanced over time is the rate of capture – consider, for example, the ability to enter or approve a purchase requisition or invoice using a mobile app on your phone – even as what remains as largely unchanged is the validity of the entries. Are they in fact coded to the right categories, or should they have been captured to begin with? Our improvisational use of technology – much like our earlier example on using spreadsheets not to replace the accounting SaaS, but while using the accounting SaaS, to do what we need to get done – is not a new concept surely but often gets dismissed or relegated to the background with all our attention fixated, as it were, on the rate of information capture in the SaaS. Big data here is characterized perhaps more by garbage-in garbage-out rather than any real emphasis on valid data points that contribute to any kind of meaningful analysis.

Continuing in this vein, consider the matter of contract capture, negotiation, and execution alongside a purchase requisition created in the accounting SaaS. One is necessary for another, so that the numbers that make up the lines of a purchase requisition such as annual subscription fee with an additional percentage baked in for support, as well as for any one-time training and/or implementation fee, would have had to come from a statement of work or contractual agreement with accompanying terms of service. Although a plethora of SaaS solutions exist for contract execution – DocuSign and Adobe Sign, formerly EchoSign, come to mind – these like the clinical or medical records focus more on automating contractual aspects, such as who can execute the agreement on either side, their titles, companies they belong, and the date of execution, and having these defined using the SaaS at hand so that the contract may be routed to both parties for execution expediently. The why or, more granularly, how behind the execution remains hidden behind the veil. Leading up to the use of DocuSign or Adobe Sign to route the document in question for execution can be a series of back and forth email exchanges between the customer enterprise's in-house legal team with the vendor's based on redline edits made by both sides to a Word document.

To the extent that payment terms are negotiated as Net 30, for example, a separate team, accounting this time, may be asked to weigh in with their feedback. What appears to be a gap in SaaS functionality presently is not so much an inability to capture data instantly but rather an inability to give credence to the back-and-forth interactions among different invested stakeholders who participate actively in assembling the final executed contract and gathering supporting evidence, so that when we peer into the support behind the numbers, we can conceivably arrive at the same conclusion based on breadcrumb clues that shed light on the nature of decisions made at each turn. Did we get accounting to sign off on non-standard terms? It says here that if services rendered were to be disputed, we would have 10 days to notify the provider. Who agreed to this and why? Ideally, even from an efficiency perspective of capturing different feedback from different parties albeit in a secured manner, it would have been ideal if the contract or procurement management SaaS at hand lets different stakeholders communicate in real-time during business hours through a Slack or Hipchat plugin or like capability incorporated into the SaaS.

Thus, when attempting to determine how and why a contract is executed, we can in theory play back exchanges between or among multiple parties. This real-communication capability also lets participants come to a consensus much more quickly than the old-fashioned unidirectional manner of asynchronous emails, attaching documents, and maintaining multiple redlined versions. The earlier quote from Heath and Luff came from a study on the use of AutoCad among engineers in 1992, but arguably it is just as applicable today in surfacing the lack of collaboration capability in accounting SaaS employed.[11] In it, they shared examples of how the work of engineers was not just dependent on other stakeholders in the same office but also on individuals in other work organizations.[12] Drawings of specifications would have to be edited based on feedback from clients and drainage engineers alike.[13]

In the same manner, how cool would it have been when creating a purchase requisition in a SaaS if we could engage in a quick online chat with accounting personnel as to what categories to code the individual line items to? Just as when revisiting the final details of a contract, we can conduct private chats using the SaaS at hand with our internal legal team on the one hand and external chats with the vendor on the other hand. How cool would it be if we had the means of asking a question and starting a two-way dialogue when creating a requisition or making a journal entry? Has anyone else already made the entry? What new accounts were created since the last time the entry was made that we should be aware of? When refreshing an existing report on existing operating accounts, how cool would it be if we could ask within the SaaS if there had been changes to accounts since then? For those of you interested in the relationship between cool and technology, check out Alan Liu's *The Laws of Cool* which explores how information technology aides in building the knowledge economy even as it serves as a medium or lens for articulating the new technological cool.[14]

Ideally, anyone else logged into the SaaS would be able to respond. In lieu of this, we would find out after the fact: running a report, downloading it, reconciling it back to the trial balance before coming to the realization that the numbers don't quite tie? Ironically, if the real controls are attributed to reviews and analyses performed outside of the SaaS, then simply focusing on in-scope applications with financial impact seems a tad trivial. In circling back to our example on the use of customer credit limit to validate customer credit worthiness when it comes to recording revenue, having the credit check in a downstream billing SaaS seems almost too little too late if a contract were already executed with the customer and recorded in an upstream opportunity management SaaS that has nevertheless been deemed out-of-scope for assessment of internal controls over financial reporting to begin with.

How do we begin a dialogue with what is at once in-scope and out-of-scope for internal controls? Parker Palmer taps into this paradox as "a way of holding opposites together that creates an electric charge that keeps us awake."[15] Most of us have attended many a church wedding orchestrated to the tune of Richard Wagner's "Bridal Chorus" from his opera Lohengrin played as a processional hymn for the entry of the bride accompanied by Felix Mendelssohn's "Wedding March" in C major as a recessional hymn to the conclusion of the church service. In retrospect, it seems almost ironical that Wagner, an anti-Semitic, would be paired with Mendelssohn, born Jewish and who would, over his lifetime, struggle to find a personal compromise between his Jewish heritage and Christian faith. Palmer identifies six ways in which a space can draw forth and sustain "this creative tension."[16] Among these, the space should be "bounded and open" and embrace "the voice of the individual and that of the group," not least of which honoring "little and big stories."[17]

Recall from Chapter 3 the four organizational archetypes identified by McNay in characterizing the management of a university drawn on by Pollock:

- ■ Collegium (loose policy as well as loose control of implementation)
- ■ Bureaucracy (loose policy but tight control of implementation)

- Corporation (tight policy as well as tight control of implementation)
- Enterprise (tight policy but loose control of implementation)[18]

Much has been written thus far about the reconciliation of account balances as well as reconciliation of data or transactions across two or more integrated SaaS. Yet, far less, if at all, has been discussed about our ability, or lack thereof, in reconciling opposites. We alluded to this in Chapter 5 when we explored how the automated is dependent on the manual, giving rise to complementary opposites. The ability of immutable mobiles, or cascading inscriptions, as the name suggests, to inscribe and entrap notwithstanding, we don't have to swing to the extreme of abandoning policy or control altogether. With an enterprise environment, the space can feel "bounded and open" simultaneously. The ability to entertain a diversity of inputs and suggestions speaks to the maturity of the organization in handling differences in opinion while recognizing the inherent ambiguity behind seemingly black and white binaries, that a lot can reside in grey areas when it comes to policy implementation. The ability to tolerate differences belies a management that is not lacking in internal controls, so that any slight twist or otherwise unexpected turn would automatically veer it off-kilter into a precarious untenable position. When coming up with user stories to configure the SaaS, the enterprise can incorporate both "little and big stories," representing "the voice of the individual and that of the group," precisely because it recognizes that creative "conflict is required to correct our biases."[19]

Recall Marilyn Strathern's view from Chapter 9 that an open field outside of academic schedules and demands is needed for academia to think. Octavio Paz describes:

> *That state of grace designated by the word pause: a moment of immobility in the rotation of the day. The moment eyes are half-closed, we perceive the blink of time, the invisible passage.*[20]

For Susan Sontag:

> *There is no such thing as empty space. To look at something to be "empty" is still to be looking at something – if only the ghosts of one's expectations.*[21]

Sontag quotes *Through the Looking Glass*, the sequel to *Alice's Adventures in Wonderland* where Alice finds herself in a shop of "all manner of curious things;" yet whenever she looks hard at a shelf that appears to be filled to the brim, it nonetheless appears empty each time.[22] Could she have been misled by her expectations or is the underlying hidden message: to make room for things, we need to start with an empty slate to begin with?

It seems to me that there can be two approaches when it comes to configuring internal controls. We can come armed with the same template for reuse over and over in organization after organization, or we can have at our disposal a template that is ready to be consumed not as a prescribed set of steps but really as a plan – recall Suchman's alternative view of plans, not as a priori determinants that map out behavior well in advance but more as resources to be drawn upon – that can be taken into consideration, updated, used in parts or else refreshed altogether as an organization itself partakes in a discovery of key controls. In other words, come prepared with a plan that is amenable to change. To do so would require an openness to the range of outcomes that can ensue. Although bias is still present – we may be focused on insults to completeness, accuracy, or validity – the auditor at hand doesn't so much try to strain the discovery process to fit a preconceived look and feel in use elsewhere in other organizations as playing the role of an anthropologist observing the evolutionary path undertaken to identify key controls.

There is no *one* right sequence of actions. In one organization, the accrual of vendor spending may be consistently underestimated simply because contractor engagement is not controlled for. Conversion from contract to hire in turn incurs additional unanticipated expenses. In this example, having entity-level "soft" controls in a vendor management office (VMO) discharged with overseeing contractor engagement can go a longer way in ensuring upfront notification of anticipated spending than simply fussing over access roles and permissions in the procurement SaaS. Or recall how Groupon was criticized for stretching the time it took to pay vendors as a means of improving its operating cash flow at the risk of spiking its current liabilities.[23] Payment terms, from the perspective of a procurement SaaS, is merely a mandatory field. Without the field we would not be able to perform A/P aging to assess a vendor's current as well as longer term liabilities. Yet, merely focusing on having a mandatory field in the SaaS does not get us any closer to determining whether the payment terms are appropriate to begin with.

We can argue thus that the thrust of this book is to compel readers to look at internal controls not just from a system or SaaS perspective, but in a myriad of ways. This is only the beginning, a gentle invitation to a longer, more in-depth journey into exploring what truly happens when we go about our work. Rather than just focusing on controls we can configure within any given SaaS, or across multiple SaaS, we should perhaps use this as a diving board to leap into the morass of artifacts – contracts, documents, spreadsheets, emails – and therein opportunities for transfiguring the ways and means different individuals in different groups in different organizations can collaborate.

In part, to embark upon this journey, and more to the point, to stay the course, we need to be mindful that differences in opinion as to what an internal control even looks, smells, or acts like does not have to translate into an organizational stalemate or inertia of sorts. I'm thinking of Sarah Schulman's recent work *Conflict Is Not Abuse* that describes how a culture of scapegoating has ironically led to any real assumption of accountability and perhaps more pointedly, with both the perpetrator and the traumatized sharing a fundamental inability to tolerate difference.[24] Recall a famous quote often attributed to Voltaire yet was really written by English writer Beatrice Evelyn Hall under the pseudonym of

S. G. Tallentyre, and used to describe Voltaire's attitude towards Claude Adrien Helvétius, another French philosopher:

> *I do not agree with what you have to say, but I'll defend to death your right to say it.*[25]

Thus, the emphasis is on facilitating a dialogue as "a way of holding opposites together that creates an electric charge that keeps us awake"[26] that leads to action, as opposed to inaction. It is precisely when we decide to widen our lens and start to look away from the SaaS or community of SaaS customers or providers at the vibrant flora and fauna that flourishes on the margins – recall the IT audience member's question on the role of spreadsheets when reviewing in scope applications that impact financial reporting – that we end up at better configuring the SaaS not based on any watered-down, rehashed, and thus displaced conceptual notions of work, but on complex, gritty, real-life portrayals. There is not a singular, monolithic, overbearing source of truth but multiple strands all singularly valid, each bringing to bear a different nuance into the larger whole.

The fable of the blind men and the elephant comes to mind. Each blind man feels out a different part of the elephant and attempts to decipher what they perceive. Disagreements quickly ensue with each man coming to a different conclusion. When you put SaaS in the context of this parable, it is easy to see how the different best-in-breed solutions combined with other on-premise and other applications each provide a partial view, not unlike the distributed file-based systems that predate databases. In fact, when we revisit the value proposition behind iPaaS, we see a common meta layer of integration management in place of custom coding or scaffolding stitching together point-to-point integrations among a myriad of SaaS in an enterprise cloud-scape, and varying levels of sophistication and accompanying exception handling procedures. In addition to integrity over the accuracy, validity, and completeness of transactions synced among two or more SaaS, the emphasis is on standing data integrity, so that the same employee record means the same thing whether to an upstream human capital management (HCM) SaaS, midstream expense management SaaS, or downstream payroll management or accounting SaaS. In this manner, regardless of where the touchpoints are located, the same employee record when referenced would elicit the consensus of "trunk" as opposed to "rope," "snake," or worst still, "serpent."

In keeping with the theme of feeling out different parts of the elephant, to find out if we have engaged with professional services (PS) providers without running them by a procurement management SaaS or a vendor management office, we can in fact look for PS-like expenses reported in an expense management SaaS as potentially veiled attempts at circumventing the procurement policy altogether. Based on the findings we uncover, we can use the results to inform other areas in the organization that merit a deeper dive such as revisiting the relevancy of the enterprise procurement policy with departments that have historically experienced a higher variability and, thus, lower predictability of spending. Differences in opinion may arise, such as the inability of the SaaS at hand to save purchase requisitions in draft or route the requisitions to backup approvers when the primary approver is away, or sync cost centers with a downstream accounting SaaS, or sync department budgets from yet a different financial planning SaaS. Rather than view these "breaks" as annoyances that distract us from the straight and narrow path outlined in tried and true risk and control matrices, we can use them to craft together truer representations: creating a custom requisition-like record with a "Draft" status in addition to "Approved" or "Rejected" statuses, creating custom fields on employee records that designate both primary and secondary approvers so that either can be used in an approval workflow, reworking the approval workflow to include finance approval in the event that department budget amounts are not refreshed on a timely basis into the procurement SaaS from the financial planning one, as well as running queries that provide exception notifications when cost centers across one or multiple SaaS do not align.

Not all limitations are attributed to the limitations of SaaS. Other hindrances are related to the way the procurement policy has been envisioned, a carte blanche attempt to apply one singular approach to all and sundry when different departments have clearly different needs. An IT department, for example, may often place an order for computer hardware and software on behalf of other departments, so having the purchase requisition route to the requestor's designated department approver or supervisor doesn't quite apply in this instance if the spending is incurred on behalf of another department. Also, when it comes to visibility, do IT personnel need access to view the department budgets allocated to IT spending if only to provide more proactive assistance in asset procurement? Marketing departments may prefer that spending be reviewed against specific projects with each project in turn comprising multiple vendors such as those involved in the setup of a product specific conference. Still other departments like security may be actively involved in reviewing the security profiles of potential vendors that have submitted responses to a Request for Proposal (RFP) or Request for Information (RFI) for services and would like to be able to kickstart the purchase requisition process to secure approval from a budgetary perspective even when no vendor has yet been selected.

Our example of using the expense management SaaS to compensate for short-falls experienced in using the procurement SaaS is a more recurring pattern that we would think. For example, making sure that access is restricted to only active employees is not just relevant to security and compliance but also applicable from license management and vendor cost of engagement perspectives. If a subscription agreement were entered with a provider with the assumption that the company would continue to grow at an assumed rate, what happens when business conditions change, and we discover that the enterprise has over or under ordered after performing an inventory audit of actual licenses consumed? From this perspective, spending control and license management are not mutually exclusive from security and compliance, so as we start to widen our lens on what an internal control does, or doesn't do, I'm reminded of the following quote from John Daido Loori:

> *Ordinary understanding is seeing with the eye and hearing with the ear; intimacy is seeing with the ear and hearing with the eye.*[27]

How is this even possible? In the context of devising internal controls for SaaS, as our previous examples illustrate, the more we step away, the more we see. What does contract execution have to do with internal control configuration for an accounting SaaS? Well, as it turns out, nothing and everything. As discussed previously, the admission criteria for recognizing revenue is not made explicit in an accounting SaaS even if it is evident from the terms of a contract or statement of work. To what extent can controls in the downstream accounting SaaS be incorporated upstream, like in a contract management SaaS, and how does this change the way we view the configuration of internal controls in the context of contracts, emails, negotiations, and other artifacts? Would it help to have a custom field on the customer record that provides a link to the executed revenue contract for a cross-comparative review before running the revenue recognition process or creating the revenue entry? In the case of having an upstream SaaS validate customer credit, would it also make sense to have the downstream SaaS house bridge fields containing the customer credit limits defined upstream? Conversely, what's to stop a user from creating a fictitious customer, or vendor, and initiating unauthorized payments in a downstream SaaS without authorized upstream triggers?

This pattern of looking beyond an artifact's immediate use can cut both ways. Conversely, when faced with downstream SaaS limitations in accepting specific data formats for customer names, we may be tempted to seek consistency in customer names all the way upstream, in effect forcing names to be updated in the upstream SaaS even if these names are valid and have been used as billing addresses operationally. It's important we go in with our eyes open and ears on or at least maintain a healthy balance between receptivity and skepticism.

Developed by the Gordon Training Institute, the four states of learning are comprised of:

- Unconscious incompetence (we don't know what we don't know or wrong intuition)
- Conscious incompetence (we know what we don't know or wrong analysis)
- Conscious competence (we know what we know or right analysis)
- Unconscious competence (when doing feels like second nature, not knowing what we know or right intuition)[28]

Improvisation addresses the first of these four stages – the unknown unknowns, with the intent for internal controls to evolve from working with known knowns to having them interwoven into the course of everyday work with consideration if not appreciation gained for unknown knowns. Herein too the four stages of learning mirror the Johari windows developed by Joe Luft and Harry Ingham, hence the name "Johari."[29] Used to help people understand themselves in their relationships with others, the Johari window has a similar 2 × 2 concept that categorizes behaviors into:

- Known-knowns (or arena, visible to self and others)
- Known unknowns (or façade, visible to self but not to others)
- Unknown knowns (or blind spot, visible to others but not to self)
- Unknown unknowns (or quite simply unknown)[30]

It's funny how, as we find ourselves in the final chapter of this book, I too have come full circle. My first article was published in the Information Systems Audit and Control Association (ISACA) journal back in 2009 and ended up receiving the Michael Cangemi Best Article or Book award.[31] In it, I applied the Johari window to the relationship between auditors and auditees, and proposed different ways for evolving the relationship from one of *Facade* – hiding actual mechanics of how work is performed to auditors evidencing for controls – to one of *Arena*, where collaboration is evidenced over finger-pointing.[32] It seems to be that the Johari window can be just as easily applied to the way we evolve the way we design internal controls for SaaS. Although the context is different, the objectives are the same. To what extent can we bring to light *Unknowns* or *Blind Spots*, overcoming a focus on what has initially been deemed in-scope to allow the daily interactive exchanges to seep in so that what is arrived at is not contrived, but is of meaning and use in the context of the everyday.

Even when we are focused on the context of the specific SaaS at hand, blind spots can arise all too easily. With all our emphasis on restricting access to key reports or queries, it can be easy to forget that some of these queries, as we have explored in the previous chapters, are in turn consumed by configured workflows so that what initially appears to have an impact from a data informing or visibility perspective can also have an automating impact. An inadvertently modified query may impact the output that has been configured as a trigger in a workflow. A query on unpaid open invoices can in turn trigger an email notification workflow on dunning notifications. By unpacking the black box of unknowns, there is even a greater opportunity for the SaaS to bring to light the collaboration that takes place in cementing agreements, agreeing on cost center changes, or engaging with customers or vendors for that matter, essentially moving from *Unknown* to *Arena* so that when we do peer into the SaaS at hand, we can obtain more than a contractual read. Without this work, we can get mired in the land of *Facades* and *Blind Spots*, where successful year-after-year validations that yield no control exceptions nevertheless don't translate into any spillover benefits in operations and other areas. Divorced from what's going on at hand, these amount to smoke and mirrors for an audit to essentially validate itself. In effect, the movement from *Unknown* to *Arena* has already begun with the use of a SaaS to unpack configuration capability previously inaccessible to nontechnical users, but there is still too much emphasis on the how, the means to an end, rather than on the why, whether the end even justifies the means.

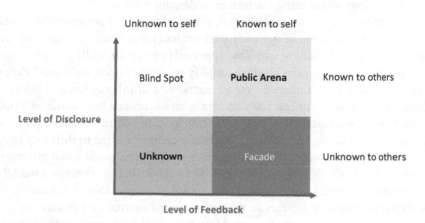

How do we begin? By asking: And then? I recall a co-worker delivering a fix and expressing disappointment when I began asking follow-up questions. What if this and what if that? Could we tweak that just a little to take this other area into account? When you put configuration in the hands of a nontechnical user, the power dynamics change and, often, in unexpected ways. The division between producer and consumer is not as tightly drawn as we might imagine. The outcome is as much dependent on the configurational capability out-of-the-box as it is on the countering response from the consuming enterprise user. In this manner, SaaS mirrors performance art, where the artist's actions and the audience's reactions commingle in real time to produce a mutually arrived-at product. This is not to say the audience cannot choose to engage less, much like the SaaS enterprise user who chooses not to intervene, opting instead to rely on the out-of-the-box defaults so that the outcomes arrived at can be vastly different from a peer who has chosen to use the tools at hand.

The exposure of the underground machinery is a freeing act of sorts and runs counter to Suchman's observation of service work, where "the better the work is done, the less visible it is to those who benefit from it."[33] What may even appear at first offensive to those used to dictating requirements rather than participating in discovery ends up reshaping the SaaS not to mention our approach in addressing countering "and then" questions. In the context of internal controls, when we speak of materiality, the impact to financial statements come to mind. Is it material? Does it exceed 5% of net income? Recall from the Financial Accounting Standards Board (FASB) proposal to reframe materiality in legalistic tones from prior chapters and the backlash from auditors and the like. For all the surface and sheen that comes with SaaS, we can easily identify with Hardt and Negri's observation that, in a digitally diffused marketplace, "the labor involved ... remains material – it involves our bodies and brains, as all labor does. What is immaterial is *its product*."[34] With SaaS, the material or the matter is more mutable, thanks to configuration capability put in the hands of users, no longer bricks and mortar but clay and Play-Doh, recalling Pollock's analogy when using the former to describe SAP.

Arguably one of the most celebrated, if not infamous, of performance artists is Marina Abramović. One of her early performances was titled *Expansion in Space* and consisted of her running into what appeared to be an unyielding column with a microphone attached on the inside to amplify the impact upon collision.[35] Perhaps as an attestation to an audience's varied reactions, a drunk guy jumped before the column and dared her to run towards him with his broken beer bottle in hand.[36] Thankfully, a co-artist shoved him aside just in time before she slammed herself into the column yet one more time. Slowly, the column started to shift by a couple of inches.[37] In some ways, this is not unlike the progress made when attempting to configure a SaaS. When we attempt to add a Reject button through a workflow to allow for the rejection in addition to approval of journal entries, we realize that the Reject button only appears in manually created journal entries and not those uploaded in bulk from a csv format. After making the necessary corrections and getting all bulk imported journals to be set up with both the ability for approval and rejection, we run into another roadblock: the Reject button does not show up for entries generated through automated bulk processing, such as through revenue recognition or amortization.

An improvisational use and configuration of SaaS gives birth to more stories. Contrast this with the "dumb-user stories" that Ellen Rose writes about in *User Error*, how vendors are apt to portray users to be less than knowledgeable of intended software functionality when encountering more than cryptic error messages.[38] Here, we are talking about another type of "dumb user-stories" where emphasis is placed on the means rather than on the ends. Like tightening access and worrying about complete data capture when the process is all but ignored or circumvented using a different process altogether bypassing the SaaS at hand. Or like the drunk guy with the broken beer bottle in hand, attempting to institute conflicting parameters so that excessive edit access to vendors circumvents the approval workflow configured to approve them in the first place. More intelligent user stories surface completing even circuitous routes to getting the same expense approved and processed even without using the SaaS in question, and yet end up as fingers pointing back to how the SaaS can be better utilized to integrate with other tools at hand, rather than viewed in almost exclusive isolation at the expense of everything else.

Thus, to more effectively configure controls for SaaS, we need to move beyond SaaS and be open to different views of internal controls. In circling back to the likelihood of payee updates prior to disbursement, this may mean roping into purview areas otherwise deemed out-of-scope. For the sake of audit, the accounting

SaaS can still be the center of attention, yet from an operational perspective, more can be done to secure the interface between the accounting SaaS and the corporate banking application. Just because it is an area that an auditor would deem too operational to validate or even identify as an internal control doesn't mean it is not accounted for in everyday processes. Perhaps it is unfair to associate improvisation with performance art. After all, each of Ms. Abramović's pieces is sketched out to the ninth degree even if the results can be nothing short of surprising. Imagine her sheer horror when encountering the audience member with a broken bottle in his hand. In 2010, more than 750,000 MoMa visitors stood in line to set across from Ms. Abramović's *The Artist is Present* performance.[39]

Less well known is a much earlier performance at the Charlottenborg Festival in Copenhagen in 1975 where for a full hour, she brushed her hair armed with a metal comb to the point of yanking out clumps of hair all the time chanting "Art must be beautiful, artist must be beautiful."[40] Recall Blake's characterization of elements imbued in "sensible objects" by "ancient poets."[41] This is an apt visual metaphor for the way we have grown accustomed to defining, testing, and maintaining internal controls – even though they become and remain oddly detached from the daily realities of actual in-situ processes, we nevertheless feel compelled to keep up the appearance, used to, as it were, the joke that auditors are those who arrive to bayonet the wounded after the battle has already been fought and lost when the joke is really on us, forgetting we are only too eager to inflict the harm ourselves without external intervention.

Just like performance art, or any art for that matter, where we need to engage with the audience, controls that are too audit-driven or insular are an end unto themselves, performed just for compliance's sake and loses resonance, leading us to ask: why do we even attempt it at all? A young organization without a procurement policy where all purchases are driven through a controller upon using an accounting SaaS with procurement functionality may consider decentralizing or distributing purchasing decisions to respective departments so that their staff would route requisitions to them for approval with only higher tier amounts having to be escalated to the controller for approval. Along the way, finance approvals are added to the workflow when department heads often approve expenses that exceed their budget as they often have no updated information on just what their budgets are, having been accustomed to having the controller and him alone control the purse strings. Reports are developed tracing actual spending back unto purchase orders to surface patterns on spending habits. Finance begins to set up monthly recurring meetings with department heads to review projected versus actual spending.

As the organization grows, finance starts to devise and run specific reports on the top five expenses per department and realizes that much of the spending is associated with changes in purchase orders rather than initially created requisitions. This resulted in additional configuration work performed for approval routings for changes to purchase orders. When the accounting team notices many requisitions stuck in the pending approval queue for a long time as the primary approver may be away or may not act in a timely manner and sees how this in turn affects their ability to capture accruals in a timely and complete manner, this translates into additional configurations undertaken to designate secondary in addition to primary approvers, as well as the setup of email reminders on every third day the requisition has remained stuck in the queue.

As the organization grows even bigger, there is a recognition that not all employees understand the procurement policy often negotiating deals without providing upfront notification and consequently the finance or accounting team is inundated either with answering inquires or performing behind the scenes downstream repair work. In response, PO champions are defined in each group to answer questions and reduce the amount of manual intervention downstream. Internally, a video may be recorded on how to create a requisition, or what to do in the event the amount negotiated with the vendor changes, or what is the difference between getting the contract executed and having the requisition approved. Out-of-scope systems, such as Slack, may be enlisted to provide a means of real-time Q&A on using the SaaS at hand. Recall in Chapter 5 how Concur bots in Slack allow users to directly perform traditional expense management approvals and receipt or report submissions without even logging into Concur. When reviewing the population of SOX in-scope applications, Slack would not have even entered the fold even if it is used to trigger expense submissions or approvals.

Let's stop here. In the previous scenarios, you see how controls configured for the SaaS change at each turn, depending on the reaction or level of adoption of the audience. Where applicable, tweaks are performed not simply to automate or speed up the process such as issuing periodic email reminders on in-flight requisitions meriting approval but also in promoting visibility on the level of adoption of the procurement controls. As the SaaS changes, so too does the barometer of expectation on timeliness, accuracy, and completeness. In its infancy, there is no qualm with having the controller alone manage all spending. Yet, as the organization grows, this is no longer scalable.

Note too that our scenario shows that even though requisition approval ability has been delegated to department heads, there is still a knowledge gap in understanding the an individual's own department budget. Other knowledge gaps exist, such as over the timeliness of submitted requisitions and the degree submitted amounts ultimately agree with actual spending. Even without throwing in the expense management process or SaaS as a means of circumventing the instituted procurement controls, we can see that a user can in effect submit a purchase requisition of a lower amount just for that user's department head approval and update the purchase order amount after. The internal controls devised at each turn evolves to meet the demands that arise even as these evolve in the context of ever-changing interactions.

Not all organizations follow this path. A separate entity may choose to purchase a different procurement SaaS that integrates with the existing accounting SaaS rather than spend additional time and resources configuring the one singular all-encompassing SaaS to meet changing needs. Yet another may decide to tack on projects as an additional dimension to track spending. No one need is anticipated beforehand, because the point is it arises because of the interaction among different players, rather than as a prescient foreknowledge of sorts etched in stone. The same challenges in visibility may not be experienced in a different setting where access to projected and actual spending may be too much rather than too little, where users in other departments can peer into another department's forecasted and actual spending. In this latter scenario, controls may be configured to restrict access to data by department.

Often management accustomed to the lines drawn between producer and consumer, supplier and customer, is inclined to ask about a demo of pre-built SaaS functionality using complex workflows and reports with the intent of configuring internal manual processes to fit this template rather than the other way. This could be what we need to get to the next level of maturity, they may proclaim. Yet, each organization is different, and we can argue that forcing a self-proclaimed "best-practice" set of practices upon an organization is likely to achieve the reverse of what is intended. Because local specific needs, such as frequent changes to purchase orders, are not addressed, the universal template ends up putting on the finishing touches to the emperor's new clothes rather than affecting any real change.

Here, the improvisational act is not so much performance art – recall the arresting sight and sound of Marina Abramović relentlessly pummeling her body against the column in *Expansion in Space* – as it is Irene Freeden's depiction of "a deer hunter in the dark ... waiting to catch the minimal movements,"[42] an allowance for things to naturally unfold to be able to respond in kind with the appropriate level of configuration. Contrary to what you might think, staged improvisation often requires a rehearsal, not to replay the exact sequence of steps to impose on an unsuspecting audience but to get into the mood or swing of improvisation. A common exercise is to run through all letters of the alphabet and start a sentence using each one with a sparring partner.

The process we undergo in learning about the SaaS, observing what goes wrong and responding with tweaks to configuration through trial by fire is not unlike the progression depicted by a secular fresco created by Ben Long, the largest of its kind in the United States. On display in the lobby of the Bank of America corporate center in Charlotte, NC, the panels depict, from right to left, a series of vignettes beginning with "Planning/Knowledge," followed by "Chaos/Creativity," and ending with "Making/Building."[43] Long was inspired by Shingon, a major school of Buddhism in Japan. Shingon is a Japanese reading of the Chinese word Zhēnyán, 真言, which means true word. Recall from Chapter 9 our review of Satyam which stands for truth in Sanskrit.

The ability to configure SaaS also subverts our traditional sense of what to expect in terms of what's active versus passive, or subject versus object. For those accustomed to a traditional waterfall or SDLC approach where all requirements are identified beforehand and detailed to exhaustion before any real configuration work begins, the prospect of viewing a half-baked prototype with only a sliver of the overall anticipated functionality, like a partially complete Mona Lisa, may seem daunting if not downright forbidding. Yet, we can argue that like performance art where an audience's reaction is immediately accessible and on full display to the performing artist, it is likely only through sharing what the SaaS can or cannot do early and often that requirements get clarified, regurgitated, and polished in the process. So that we are in effect not accountable to one version of truth that is applicable at a point in time but get to experiment with multiple truths as circumstances change.

We also need to get past the success versus failure compulsion. It is in fact by attempting to fail early and often that we stress test the proposed SaaS configuration in real life smashing the front- versus back-stage, hidden versus visible dichotomies that we have grown used to. A good job is not one where the underlying machinery is kept hidden from prying eyes but is in fact exposed to accord power or ability to nontechnical users to update prior assumptions made. Just as in preparing for a lecture, much of what I've gathered is often tossed aside to deal with what is at hand. Consumers and producers who are mirroring each other must be prepared to refresh outdated notions and reconfigure what they originally have in mind rather than attempt to fit a round peg into a square hole each time, or rather when armed with a swiss army knife, jab at everything that seems only too eager to be sliced. We get a whiff of this when during vendor product demos, customers are more inclined to say that's great but we don't need it or it's overkill.

Continuing with this trend of exposing more of what has hitherto remained hidden, to what extent can actual back-and-forth messiness that characterizes real world complexities be captured? It seems to me that it is not captured precisely because it does fit into ascribed boundaries. As we have seen, the rationale for recording expenses or revenue is often not captured; only the outcome is. It follows that much like revealing the configuration of SaaS, what also needs to be revealed in the SaaS is what has up until now been kept under wraps: the rationale, reason, or reasons for recording things the way we have, the process it took to get there. Performance art succeeds when it manages to confront the audience with previously held assumptions. Whether it is challenging us to question if art needs be beautiful to be considered art or whether a space constrained by a column can be expanded by sheer will, it forces us to question our fundamental biases, so that what we see in the artist may in fact reflect what we choose not to acknowledge or see in ourselves.

Much like Ms. Abramović's attempting to forcibly remove the snarls in her hair to the chant of "Art must be beautiful,"[44] subverting, in the process, our notions of what's art and what's not art, to what extent does our overemphasis on SOX in-scope SaaS to get to compliance swiftly and surely distract us from the need to remain open and observant, not unlike Freeden's "deer hunter in the dark?"[45] Just the other day, someone mentioned to me how the ubiquitous, and thus often taken-for-granted, email is nevertheless used in some software companies to deliver license keys in effect supporting revenue recognition. Take the following sequence of events undertaken to tighten a SaaS with vendor approval capability:

1. Create a workflow to default all newly created vendors to be inactive
2. Add an Approve button on the newly created inactive vendor records
3. Activate vendor for use upon obtaining approval
4. Create an audit query that reports on the approver name and approval time-stamp details
5. Segregate vendor creation and approval ability so that the same user cannot create and approve the same vendor
6. Add a Reject button on the newly created inactivated vendor record
7. Update the audit query to source in the additional rejection action and time-stamp details where applicable
8. Create a custom record that consists of a free form text field to house the reason for Rejection
9. Update the audit query to source additional rejection reasons where applicable
10. Add email capability to the workflow such that a newly created vendor pending review results emails to a reviewer for timely intervention
11. Update the email frequency such that gentle email reminders are sent to the reviewer for vendors sitting in the review queue for more than 5 days
12. Enable email plug-in such that the reviewer can either approve or reject the new vendor by clicking on links in the email without logging into the SaaS
13. Update the audit query to report on approvals or rejections performed via email by reviewers without having to log into the SaaS or being granted SaaS licenses to begin with

Each time the SaaS is configured, it is confronted with confounding user expectations, and changing ones at that, so that even if all the requirements are not surfaced at the beginning, such as having to access an audit report on approved or rejected vendors to evidence to auditors, these needs are nevertheless incorporated so that the initial design is iterated upon over time, exemplifying design-in-use. Because the workflow is in test mode and Approve or Reject buttons may be exposed only to specific users, testing can in effect happen in production, thereby challenging auditor notions of what's in production versus what's not, release versus development. An emphasis on an audit's usual suspects, such as traditional in-scope applications, would have missed out on new vendor approvals or rejections performed via email outside of the SaaS and the ensuing need to evidence the reviewer's actions nonetheless in the SaaS.

Recall from Chapter 5 the ability to submit or approve expense reports in Concur using Slack. A myopic focus on Concur would distract us from the contextual dynamics that surround the traditional in-scope SaaS applications in full display. As Thoreau put it, "The more you look the less you will observe ... What I need is not to look at all, but a true sauntering of the eye."[46] When it comes to configuring approve or reject links in emails in Step 12, emphasis may be placed on allowing approvers and especially those who do not require input access to the SaaS to nevertheless be able to intervene as a "watcher" of sorts, so that on the one hand licenses are not consumed and on the other, management oversight can still be provided and ideally evidenced in the audit log of the vendor record. When demonstrating this additional functionality to a larger cross-functional team, however, concerns may be surfaced about the dangers of clicking on links embedded in emails in general – recall from Chapter 7 examples on the harm wrought by phishing emails.

In addition, another concern may surface as to how to control for the identity of the approver. In other words, could the email recipient forward the approval email to another individual, and if this second individual clicks on the Approve link, would the vendor be approved in the SaaS even if the second individual is not the intended approver? Thus, when all is said and done, even though the SaaS at hand supports the configuration of email plug-ins allowing for the ease and flexibility of approving records, Step 12, while explored as part of a discovery sprint, may not materialize in production, or reality for that matter, when security policies are interwoven into accounting and compliance demands. The same challenges faced in the approval process for new vendors can be applied to new customers, employees, or accounts, as well as for related transactions including, but not limited to, journals, invoices, and orders.

Confrontation, like conflict, does not have to lead to abuse;[47] what it isn't is indifference, quite possibly the least favored audience reaction whether to performance art or the SaaS on display. The iterative configuration changes in the SaaS arise from confrontations or conflicts encountered at each turn, whether it is getting employees to understand the importance of submitting projected spending for approval proactively, managers to approve spending against their own department budget on a timely basis, or the need for accounting or finance to run key reports periodically to track key metrics. Where we have excelled is at registering who performed the control, when, and how frequently. What is less emphasized, if at all, is why and what is reviewed against, for if we even so much as broach the matter, we would no sooner realize that what is tracked is but a sliver of what resides on the surface. Rather than reveal, the SaaS record really serves to conceal. What we have become adept at is capturing up-to-the-minute minutiae that aligns with preconceived notions of what work is.

Rather than allow for the definition of what it means to be an internal control to take shape, we fall back on what is tried and true. Just as art when performed before a live audience changes in the process, so too does the SaaS when consumed and configured by enterprise users in their everyday work. And just as the artist allows the audience's reaction to inform his or her art even as the artist is attempting through his or her art to communicate a specific point of view, the SaaS in use is forever changed through configuration even as it strives to impress upon a system imbued worldview. I'm reminded of a poem from Rainer Maria Rilke:

What we choose to fight with is so tiny!
What fights with us is so great.
If only we would let ourselves be dominated
As things do by some immense storm,
We would become strong too, and not need names.

When we win it's with small things,
And the triumph itself makes us small.
What is extraordinary and eternal
Does not want to be bent by us.[48]

When coming into contact with its users, the SaaS is bent. When coming into contact with the SaaS, the users are themselves bent. Altered, repurposed, transfigured. What each side seeks is actively negotiated. Latour had viewed software affordances as a means of inscribing users to the imbued script yet with the option to configure. SaaS can also be said to be inscribed into the users' daily interactional flow.[49] In statistics, there is the concept of overfitting, how an over-accounting of parameters within the data set at hand leads to less predictability when real-life data with accompanying noise is included. Likewise, when configuring internal controls in a test environment, we run the risk of overfitting, devising what appears to be an interlocking cascade of custom fields, queries, and workflows when real-life data may not merit such complexity. We had thus far explored how enterprise users may underutilize a SaaS's configurational capability, but the reverse can also hold true. To what extent can a SaaS at hand be over-configured or customized?

Consider the example of configuring a custom record in place of a custom field. Rather than opting for an easier approach (defining a list of values associated for a custom field) over-customization here relates to the former (defining a custom record altogether even it houses merely one field as opposed to ideally multiple fields). What results is not so much control as the illusion of control. Not unlike the auditors who validate an enterprise's identified internal controls against a universalized template, and upon their exit, stakeholders revert back to the workarounds employed. An illusion of control when it comes to configuring SaaS boils down to taking false comfort in the automated three-way match between purchase order, receipt, and invoice as a means to control spending when the reality is purchases orders are created after the fact, much like the plans documented after a course of action has been undertaken as observed by Suchman. Thus, an improvisational view of controls in SaaS cautions against over-engineering to the point the SaaS supports specific use cases but fails to be widely applicable in a general way to the population at large.

This is reminiscent of the tradeoff between flexibility and usability as observed in *The Universal Principles of Design*.[50] An example is configuring all journal entries to require approval and locking them from editing when they are pending approval. At first glance, this appears reasonable and enforces a second level review. Yet, as reviewed in Chapter 6, for accrual entries that are set up to auto-reverse in the next month, the auto-reversing aspect won't kick in until a manual approval is performed, increasing the likelihood of missing reversal entries insofar as approvers fail to approve them. Similarly, when users make a mistake in submitting an erroneous entry, there is no opportunity to unwind their actions. Also, insofar as bulk generated entries from revenue recognition and expense amortization are created and pending approval, there is no opportunity for edits for selecting a new account or department in the journal after it is created but before it is approved. Thus, cross-validation using other use cases is a good means of preventing over-fitting.

When having a cross-functional team both come up with user stories to form the backlog in an Agile sprint as well as critique the prototype demo at the end of the two-week sprint, the intent is to stress-test the design beyond the initial idealized set of use cases identified. In place of performance art, perhaps jazz is a better metaphor for the improvisational use and configuration of SaaS. Much like how a cross-functional sprint team can foster heterogeneity of ideas and increase the likelihood of SaaS adoption in an environment characterized by varied and, at times, conflicting needs, Bratteteig and Stolterman point to the varied instruments at play in a jazz group; while different, together they orchestrate to form music.[51] To take in different perspectives, we need to shift our "placement" and yet for the differences in perspectives to come together to form a confluence of shared ideas and objectives, Bratteteig and Stolterman underscore the importance of "forgetting"[52] or what I would like to think of as forgiving. For forgiveness is no less applicable to the way we configure software than to the manner which we need to be cognizant of the need to continually put aside what has been "named and framed."[53]

Recall from Chapter 9 the pair of nobodies mentioned in Emily Dickinson's poem and how they allude to the ease that accompanies field interchangeability. To forget is to forgive; to forgive is to become less fragile. To what degree does enterprise or organizational knowledge remain nonetheless a fragile construct precisely because of our inability to forget and forgive? Chapter 6 on control chaos demonstrates how the more we attempt to control, the more chaos ensues. Here, on the other hand, out of chaos, creativity and resilience emerge. Like orchestrating good jazz, much care needs to be expended in coordinate varied voices and melodies.[54]

For all the effort expended on sifting, categorizing, and re-categorizing data, if we only extract ourselves from attribute minutiae, such as the precise account or cost center to code a line on a purchase requisition, we can start to appreciate common challenges most companies grapple with such as having to deal with unstructured data, whether received in the form of images or text. When we receive an image of a vendor invoice, wouldn't it be cool if the SaaS at hand is able to differentiate it from a contract or a customer invoice? Wouldn't it be even cooler if the SaaS at hand is further able to code it to a specific prepaid expense account and department based on the type of expenses typically incurred with this vendor as well as the department to have historically placed the orders? Deep learning, as alluded to previously in the use of neutral networks behind Google translate, has profoundly changed the way machines assist humans not just in speech recognition, but also in image classification and natural language understanding. With all the emphasis placed on Facebook, Instagram, and YouTube, we still lack a systematic way of sifting or culling data from images or raw text, in effect transforming unstructured data into structured data.

Imagine if we could transform customer feedback into useful data points for predicting customer churn. Or how about if we could make predictions of employee turnover based on annual performance appraisal input? What we have explored at length in this book is that even when it comes to structured data, much can go on behind the scenes to sift it into predefined categories to facilitate analysis. We still have a way to go in questioning the very categories we use to apprehend the world and, in turn, keep us ensnared. Our accounts have less to reveal about what happened, and more to mirror idealized social relations both within and without. Thus, just as our use of video as a medium to train users is still underutilized – recall our SaaS scenario – our corresponding ability to make sense of data from video images or otherwise raw and unlabeled text is even less developed. Deep learning is characterized by multiple layers – hence deep – with each layer comprising nodes that either amplify or dampen the input, with the overall intent to be able to make correct determinations based on pattern recognition whether it is identifying a cat from a mouse in the previous chapter or making accurate predictions such as on the issuance of customer credit against a history of outages experienced.

As alluded to in the previous chapter, each neuron works like an audience member in Ms. Abramović's *Expansion in Space* performance, where a majority vote erupted in a thunderous applause when she succeeded in moving the column by mere inches after running into it multiple times.[55] How then is the machine able to sift out the signal from the noise when attempting pattern recognition? It turns out that overfitting is a cost that machine learning engineers know all too well as they strive to improve the precision of their model at accounting all pieces of information pertinent to solving a problem. If the model were too complex however, there is a high risk that even though it performs well with the test data at hand, it doesn't quite generalize well when the dataset is expanded to encompass more real-life examples. I remember being at a performance in a Miami symphony hall outfitted, as the director proclaimed, with sensitive acoustics that picked up every sound. It turned out not only every instrument was picked up but also every audience member sneeze, cough, or clearing of the throat. Overfitting works like that, so the trick is how do we tune in to the music without being distracted by confounding audience bodily functions?

It seems to me that just as SaaS vendors grapple with how much functionality to add, or what features to augment, such that these can be generalized to a larger set of customers, the same tradeoffs are experienced by enterprise users when configuring SaaS to be interwoven into the fabric of their everyday work. Would we get the sound of music or a clash of clambering cymbals? Even though the advances made with deep learning seem promising – a recent session on deep learning was held at a Dreamforce conference – here too, we wonder just how *deep* deep learning truly is. Can it can wade past deep stacks of nodes beyond pattern recognition to uncover the why as to how data is structured, such as that which contributes to revenue versus expense recognition? How deep is deep? Would it help us uncover known unknowns or even unknown unknowns? The latter is perhaps the hardest to uncover. We don't know what we don't know often makes up our deepest biases. Like what we deem to be an effective operating control may not in fact control for much at all. Like the audience reaction that varies from one night to the next before a performance piece, the criteria of admission, or accounting can, and does, change.

In Chapter 1, we saw how this was the case with the maximal length worthy of wildlife conservation or minimal length worthy of food consumption in the case of farm-raised salmon. In the span of a mere few interceding years, the criteria would change so that what was noncompliant would in turn become compliant. Recall how later in Chapter 5, we asked about who gets to determine compliance readiness and just what that constitutes. To control better, we may be better off learning how not to control, which is another way of asking what can go wrong. From the fish that evade vaccination to the use of special purpose entities (SPEs) to underreport debts on the balance sheet to emancipation timed to the harvest of crops, the emphasis is on relations, how the idea of compliance is a multiple-authored construct and contract. With SaaS, we can argue that transfigured relations come into play, where the user gets to configure custom fields in a manner that transforms the way a record is interrelated with another whether within the same SaaS or across two or more SaaS. After all, it was William Blake who said, "Everything possible to be believed is an image of truth."[56] Garfinkel in turn observes how relations manifest "in accord with expectations of sanctionable performances."[57]

Continuing in this vein, Chapter 2 conjured up the concept of multiple readings, how invariably the official account is not simply what happened. Instead, what is documented reveals what would or *should* have happened if only proper lines of accountability are drawn and redrawn. Which reading gets inscribed in the design of software: the official account or the one behind the scenes? If the former, then to what extent does the software continue to indulge in "small things,"[58] hesitant as it were to attempt to answer larger questions like how to truly control spending as opposed to merely warning about incomplete fields.

It's almost as if fragility can slice both ways. On the one hand, we hang on to a specific idealized account impervious to what's truly going on; on the other hand, it's as if the account we've fashioned is itself inherently fragile to change, ready to break at the slightest suggestion of change. In Chapter 3, we were introduced to the concept of indifference. Through the meta layer, SaaS can be configured to local needs without changing its core. Its very indifference in this respect makes for universal adoption. More than a "universal solvent" dissolving differences like its on-premise predecessor,[59] a SaaS-y SaaS would acknowledge, encourage, and support differences. In this manner, its very indifference renders it less fragile. Likewise, its users can be less fragile to changing requirements as they continue to be able to tweak the configuration based on prototype feedback early and often. For fragility can be said to be the counterpoint to forgiveness, if the SaaS were more forgiving of local differences then it is less fragile. It travels well. Conversely, users who are less likely to clutch on to requirements long past their expiration date are more forgiving of change and thus less fragile.

The maturity of the consuming enterprise matters as well, with the degree of looseness in policy and control of implementation consequently reflected in its level of fragility, and of forgiveness. This leads us to Chapter 4 where we looked at how we invariably take one step forward and two steps back. Reversibility is explored from a transactional, soup-to-nuts, end-to-end perspective; yet, this same reversibility can also refer to the ability to unwind what has already been performed so that in effect the SaaS at hand is more forgiving of potential insults to integrity, and by the same token less fragile. Reversibility also calls into question casual relationships so that if purchase requisitions are mostly created after invoices are received, to what extent does requiring invoices to be created in SaaS only based upon approved requisitions make it less forgiving, more fragile?

What does unstructured data mean other than it is unstructured enough to be easily slotted into predefined existing categories? As we can tell from Chapter 3, these categories can be deceiving in conspiring to conceal more than reveal. The ability to transfigure relations using SaaS's configurational out-of-the-box capability is thus an attempt to both confront and counteract these contrived assignments with the understanding that if we were to do so, these can take on yet a different lens. The same picture would quite conceivably tell an altogether different story. Take completeness as a control objective. If we configure the customer credit limit field to be mandatory for entering a value greater than 0, then technically all customers would be validated against their credit worthiness prior to any booking of new revenue via an order or an invoice. Yet, here we are already tapping into validity of revenue recorded, so that we can be certain that it is associated with customers who are likely to pay.

Thus, any one lens that focuses on completeness as a control, such as having mandatory fields, and deems it complete misses out on the opportunity to probe farther with an "and then" compulsion. Yet, as we have seen, if access were not restricted to updating of customers at the field level, there is a possibility that the assigned credit limit could be overwritten to circumvent the ascribed set of controls. What if the SaaS itself is unable to support field level security, so that anyone with access to the customer can update any field even as some fields are more sensitive than others? A separate workflow may be configured to warn users of a possible credit limit breach if the new order or invoice tips the customer over an assigned credit limit. To configure all this automation is itself manual work, which merits a separate discussion on change management as it is likely to be overlooked. In this manner, completeness, validity, restricted access, configuration, and change management come into play. Not unlike Mary Shelley's Frankenstein, when you pull at what seems to be a single thread, the entire cast of disembodied parts begins to unravel.

This leads us to Chapter 5, where we explored how in using SaaS, we treat technology as humans while we in turn behave like automatons. We can't deny our recurring fascination or love affair with the idea that the tools we have at our disposal can one day render us irrelevant and even redundant. This manifests in little ways from our tendency to attribute automation to any artifact from a Mechanical Turk to a mobile invoicing app while blissfully ignorant of the underground machinery of manual labor that toils silently to arrange and fix, displace, and replace. What we deem automated, such as purchase requisition and journal entry approval often comes with requisite manual components, such as having to review validity against a deeper analytical supporting artifact. Furthermore, what we deem automated is not automated enough – it can't self-correct or look for exceptions. Like the audience standing at the door to the Chinese room, we believe that the speaker within can converse in Chinese when all he did was to follow the rules we gave him. This was in part the challenges faced by Google Translate when attempting to translate a foreign language in a way that resonates with both local context and custom.[60]

The more we configure, the more we would have to control for, and this is part of what Chapter 6 is about. Yet, there are different ways of controlling, whether it is using one SaaS to check up on another or figuring out the controls to employ when in production. Design-in-use sniffs out unplanned for and thus unanticipated outcomes which, when surfaced and addressed, point back to the illusion of control. In this respect, a control is not a static construct but more likely dynamically composed of varied elements stitched together. Chapter 7 picked up from Chapter 5 by compelling users to look themselves in the eye and ask if perhaps the SaaS configured mirrored their own shortcomings whether it is focusing on automating at the expense of informating or committing configuration errors that lead to systemwide outages or quite simply underestimating the amount of manual work needed to orchestrate multiple best-in-breed SaaS even if these were purchased off the shelf ready for consumption.

Like Chapter 5, Chapter 7 challenged us to see how our behaviors become automated, programmed into indifference over time, while the automations we put in place require constant manual care and intervention and, in this respect, behave more like humans. Looking back at my *Accounting Information Systems* classes, some of the more memorable lessons were the ones my students taught me. In my first semester, my midterm exam was challenging but perhaps not in the right way. Each multiple-choice question had tricky options which confounded students at best and annoyed them at worst. I spent the rest of the semester trying to recover whatever rapport was left between me and the students in the class. We could have a different read of the situation. Because this is a graduate level class, exams are supposed to be tough; after all, whoever said life is easy? Yet, upon closer reflection, the questions slotted real-life facets into predetermined categories. Doing well meant not so much applying principles to real-life examples as it was figuring out which answer seems the most probable out of the ones on display and choosing the right one through a process of careful elimination.

We can argue that the students who did well in the midterm were not necessarily streetwise as they were book-smart. In other words, when asked to improvise upon the use and thereafter configuration of the SaaS in their respective work environments, the ones who were best at defending or answering to predefined buckets or categories are unlikely to be the ones who would be more inclined to explore and uncover exceptions that break the design. To this end, counter-compliance is a concept that is introduced in Chapter 7. In the same manner that a performance piece confronts an audience's reactions head-on, counter-compliance works by confronting the design with exceptions early and often, and by focusing on failure as a means to augment operating effectiveness.

This leads us to Chapter 8, which examined the element of play involved in teasing out what can go wrong and configuring the mitigating controls. It involves taking a first step in overcoming our almost natural or instinctive inclination to shield the audience from what happens behind the scene. Recall Suchman's observation of how quality of service work is seen to correlate inversely with its degree of visibility. Thus, like the performance art that seeks to challenge audience members' preconceived notions, Chapter 8 spent quite a bit of time challenging our conceptions of what is deemed front- versus back-stage behavior. The irony is that the more visible breaks become through use of fuses and other alerts, the better able we become at addressing them and returning to normal operating levels. In this respect, Chapter 8 presented a whole new conception of fragility: fragility not as weakness but an openness to exploring deep seated beliefs. Rumi put it best, "The wound is the place where the Light enters you."[61] Or if not fragility, in recalling Chapter 3, perhaps an indifference. An indifference to outcomes so that we are not afraid to explore alternate paths – an indifference that leads to a universal adoption of sorts.

Overcoming a tendency to achieve a static, unchanging state by requiring all requirements to be captured and holding the deliverables accountable to these same requirements even in the face of change is but the first step in recognizing that for all our busywork in handling structured data, albeit by shuffling them about among static categories, we are missing the bigger picture – how these categories are defined in the first place and to what extent are the maintained boundaries more porous than we think – and yet an even bigger picture: how unstructured data continues to slip past unnoticed and unexamined like Norwegian farm-raised salmon. In the giant scheme of life, we are no different from the workers working the conveyor chain in the warehouse cavern of the salmon farm described in Chapter 1, so busy sifting, sorting, and administering that we don't even bother questioning the very definition of health in a farm feed or the boundaries superimposed on the overall process in the first place. Chapter 9 ended on a more positive note, the possibility that what is done can in fact be undone.

Chapter 10 started by pointing back at Chapter 6 with examples that give us an inkling into how the more we attempt to control, the more it eludes us. Oddly enough, the improvisational manner of feeling out controls in turn lends it credibility, just as like how videos starring local fellow farmers in Digital Green add to rather than take away the likelihood of adopting agricultural practices in far-flung countries.[62] In our SaaS example in Chapter 11, we ended with self-made videos on procurement that is shared internally. Much like PO champions, the appointment of SaaS ambassadors within a consuming enterprise can help ease some of the rough patches experienced with initial adoption, but more importantly over the long run, serve as beacons as to how best to improve upon initial go-live or highlight any simmering issues. Video is itself unstructured data even if in this case it can, and has been, used to build camaraderie and rapport. The bricoleur spirit of making do with what is at hand underscores just how very little we need to know ahead of time to be able to configure internal controls for the SaaS. A little bit of imagination combined with spit and perseverance can go a long way.

Much of performance art is unadorned and raw, in our face. Controls mirror the context in which the activities take place from assumptions we make about completion of key fields to how more controls don't necessarily mean merrier especially when they undercut one another. The proof is in the pudding. Put another way, the only way to validate whether the controls designed truly work is to observe their design in use and respond with necessary adjustments. The more we peel apart SaaS – how it has been designed, deployed, and configured – it would appear that what some clients strive for, knowingly or otherwise, are not so much features that drive process automation but ones that elicit an automated response from users. I'm not trying to split hairs here but the difference, however infinitesimal, does make a difference. We don't necessarily want to be surprised or alarmed when finding out that things don't quite work out as planned, even if this is the most likely way, when faced with real-world constraints, of identifying pragmatic use cases for finer fine-tuning when it comes to configuration and controls.

We can argue that we're not so much focused on deploying automated processes as we are on shrugging our shoulders, putting on display automated human responses so that like Mary Shelley's Frankenstein, we are more inclined to relegate the creature of a SaaS at hand to the background, out of sight and thus out of mind. Improvised use and configuration expend necessary time and resources, and yet, as we have seen, shine a light on the cracks on an otherwise unblemished surface viewed from afar. Chapter after chapter, we've revisited this precept, arc after arc folding back onto itself, concentric ripples overlapping and emanating outwards. Not focusing on our job in almost exclusive singularity – whether we are an auditor, developer, accountant, manager, employee, SaaS vendor, user, or implementation partner – is the first step towards excelling at our job. The stories that we tell ourselves are deceptively one-dimensional. The controls we devise end up confounding our expectations, more relational than divisive. By going one level higher or lower, we allow our narratives to be pierced or deepened, no longer content with bite-sized facets of any one story.

The following is a passage from Blake's *The Marriage between Heaven and Hell*:

> *Without Contraries is no progression. Attraction and Repulsion, Reason and Energy, Love and Hate, are necessary to Human existence.*
>
> *From these contraries spring what the religious call Good and Evil. Good is the passive that obeys Reason. Evil is the active springing from Energy.*
>
> *Good is Heaven. Evil is Hell.*[63]

Framed against this context, one way of threading through the chapters is as follows:

1. The criteria for compliance (truth) changes
2. There is more than one account (of truth)
3. SaaS supports multiple accounts (of truth)
4. The beginning can be confused for the end
5. What's manual can be confused with what's automated
6. What's chaos can be mistaken for controls
7. What's interior can be confused as exterior
8. What's known can conceal an unknown
9. We don't know what we don't know
10. A control is composed of complementary other(s)
11. Existing relations can be unwound and recombined

As McNiff put it, "What appears antithetical is often the basis of what we seek."[64] As he sees it, "If we step outside the oppositional mind-frame," we start to use "positive and negative forces in complementary ways."[65] For McNiff, performance art and improvisation are useful tools at reframing the other.[66] In the same manner, configuration of SaaS in use helps us reframe what could have been, or what could very well be. The configurations we exact transfigure existing relations among users and machines, and therein among nontechnical business users, administrators, developers, testers, as well as SaaS, iPaaS, on-premise software, and other office applications like Excel. Against the backdrop of a matrixed organization, where the same role such as IT or finance may be distributed among varied organizations within the same enterprise, the possibilities of transfiguration are manifold.

Other variables enter the picture: enterprise-wide policies and procedures, recent merger and acquisition decisions, the nature of the product developed and sold, customers, vendors, and regulatory agencies. By recognizing the perspective of the other, the impetus behind internal controls doesn't have to be diluted. When we leverage opposing points of view, such as how compliance has become a zero-sum game, a loop unto itself – control-speak for auditors can in turn spur the imagination of a different state not merely idealized but concrete enough to be realized. By proactively countering the archetypal illusion of no exceptions, questioning the criteria of what's in scope, transcending our biases on what can be exposed and rendered visible, challenging the premise that controls belong to those who are accustomed to validating them day in and day out, or accorded the mandated authorities such as PCAOB, revisiting our notions of account and accountability, displacing and transfiguring existing relations between usual suspects, we start to see how the system we have devised to contain the very system of internal controls is itself fragile and less than forgiving.

Two additional points on the nature of errors and configurations before we march irrevocably towards the book's conclusion. As we traverse from slippery salmon slipping past eager farm hands at the Norwegian salmon farm in Chapter 1 to assessing a software's affordances in mitigating slips and mistakes in Chapter 9, Meyer's stance that an "error depends on having a preconceived idea of what should happen" is particularly worth taking pause for reflection.[67] Consider the following quotes:

> *If we reduce the part played by conscious control in favor of spontaneity, we find ourselves in the position where the very notion of error ... disappears.*[68]
>
> *A "mistake" is besides the point.*[69]

When we focus on breaking the SaaS early and often rather than obtaining a clean bill of health each time, we end with a far less fragile, more forgiving state, in the same way a broken bone is stronger after healing. It would appear that audit war on errors, whether resulting from slips, mistakes, or intentional fraud, is error prone, especially since as we have seen time and again in this book that to reduce the number of errors requires in part a forgetting of errors or at least at a bare minimum, a level of tolerance or forgiveness for spontaneous alternate paths even at the cost of incurring errors.

The second point that gives us due cause for pause relates back to configurations wrought and re-wrought. While the emphasis has been on SaaS configuration, processes and people as it turns out can also be configured and reconfigured. As we move a level higher to gain a bird's eye view of varied configurations across varied companies in varied industries, we can hopefully start to appreciate that for our differences in configuration, we share the same objectives towards quality, integrity, and reliability. We also share a propensity for indifference. We reviewed the local production of videos at Digital Green and explored how this further deepened local partnerships and gained credibility. When chatting with a friend in video production, he shared a particularly frustrating project he had to endure at a non-profit organization where he was given a mandate to produce a video that would elicit an emotional reaction and not much else. Stakeholders involved were less than enthusiastic in responding to his calls to elicit specific requirements or provide feedback on interim prototypes. Left to his own devices, he had to strain hours of interviews into a 10-minute brief that would at least be palatable and ideally compelling enough to result in more money raised for its cause.

In thinking back to internal controls designed and maintained for SaaS, there are interesting parallels that we can draw. Like the lack of guidance or interest from the non-profit client, the lack of implementation feedback combined with the daunting prospect of having to comply with SOX and other regulations often leads us to fall back on the lowest common denominator of merely evidencing osten-sive controls rather than pursue any course of action that has any real operational impact. After all, these controls, like the 10-minute video, can be more readily consumed in bite-sized chunks. The paths we each take, or configurations that emerge, can vary though they by no means take us away from an unvarying com-mitment to resolve the challenges at hand. Thus, an all-or-nothing emphasis on errors, and of configurations, such as having no errors or no varying configurations, may end up hindering rather than helping, whereas conversely an approach that seeks to transcend errors and configurations – recall Palmer's "holding opposites together"[70] – can oddly enough help us see past what's on display and apparent to what lies beneath and truly sticks. An all-or nothing approach can yield less than desirable outcomes, so when figuring out how to control for financial report changes, the emphasis is not so much on having effective change management in place as it is on freezing the chart of accounts even if this is not pragmatic as an organization grows and scales. Another variant of an all-or-nothing approach may result in frantic downstream efforts to "fix" downstream attributes resulting from change orders initiated upstream rather than figuring out and marrying the accounting and operational perspectives when it comes to dealing with inevitable changes to customer needs in a way that renders overages and deficits transparent and thus accountable.

In truth, when we step outside our own narratives, we start to see how ludicrous the Borg's mandate in *Star Trek: The Next Generation* is. In place of "resistance is futile,"[71] assimilation is futile. When we begin to account for the number of ways to design, use, configure, validate, and report (on) a SaaS, we find so many ways to begin. Yet, the Borg remind us just how easy it is to relinquish our accountability. Just as our improvised use and configuration of SaaS does not exist in a vacuum, outside of governing enterprise processes and regulations, continual attempts to reframe our public and private discourse with internal controls seek to expose the seams that underpin our actions and inactions. In a 2004 interview with Larry King, Ken Lay maintained that he was not responsible for criminal conduct that he was unaware of.[72] Enron's stock price plummeted from high 90s to mere cents. More than a fall guy for Enron's eventual demise, to what extent are Lay's remarks chilling because they point back to our very own proclivities at evading the man in the mirror? I am reminded of the oft-quoted Hannah Arendt's phrase, "the banal-ity of evil."[73] Having escaped Nazi Germany, she was commissioned by *The New Yorker* in 1962 to cover the trial of Adolf Eichmann, one of the chief architects of the Holocaust; this culminated in *Eichmann in Jerusalem: A Report on the Banality of Evil* published in 1963.

> *What he said was always the same, expressed in the same words. The longer one listened to him, the more obvious it became that his inability to speak*

> *was closely connected with an inability to think, namely, to think from the standpoint of somebody else. No communication was possible with him, not because he lied but because he was surrounded by the most reliable of all safeguards against the words and the presence of others, and hence against reality as such.*[74]

Contrary to critics who accused her of trivializing the atrocities of the Holocaust to mere commonplace, Arendt's emphasis is on the very absence of critical thinking on the part of Eichmann.[75] Elsewhere, she remains hopeful that there is more than one story, or how there would be at least one person to offer an alternate version, a reminder of our earlier discussion on the one-dimensional stories we tell ourselves when it comes to internal controls.

> *One man will always be left alive to tell the story... The lesson of such stories is simple and within everybody's grasp. Politically speaking, it is that under conditions of terror most people will comply but some people will not, just as the lesson of the countries to which the Final Solution was proposed is that "it could happen" in most places but it did not happen everywhere.*[76]

Cynthia Cooper is one such individual. Referred to as the mother of 404, Cooper was the former vice president of the internal audit group at WorldCom, where in 2002 she blew the whistle on her company's $3.8 billion accounting fraud, the largest of its kind in corporate history at the time. In interviews, Cooper spoke about the chief financial officer's response to two mid-level managers who confronted him about the reclassification of expenses from income statement to the balance sheet 5 days before releasing their financials to the public in 2000:

> *He said, "Look, guys – I want you to think of this as an aircraft carrier: We've got planes out. Let's get all the planes landed safely. Once all the planes have landed safely, then if you want to leave the company, you can leave. ... No one's going to prison. If anyone were going to prison, it would be me. You're just following orders."*[77]

It is remarkable how messy real life can be. In an intertwining of the personal with the professional, the mid-level managers feared losing their jobs and threatening the financial security of their families. In the interweaving of the manual with the automated, Cooper's team of internal auditors were only afforded access to the balance sheet side of the entries when attempting to probe deeper into system audit trails.[78] Barely a year before, Kim Emigh, a financial analyst in WorldCom's network systems engineering division in Richardson, Texas, had reported inappropriate hours billed to capital projects rather than operating expenses in an attempt to pad operating budgets, among other allegations.[79] The outcome? Emigh, along with 375 others in his division, was laid off and had to put his family through financial struggles and hardship when he was unable to find employment.[80]

Cooper's own remarks when characterizing management culture at WorldCom give pause for thought.

> *At one point in the early years of my career, I was told by my boss not to use the term "internal controls" [sic] in any more audit reports because Bernie [WorldCom CEO] didn't understand what it meant and it aggravated him. Of course, we continued to use the term "internal controls" and instead worked to educate Bernie on why controls were important.*[81]

Cooper herself drew from Ambrose Redmoon:

> *Courage is not the absence of fear. Courage is acting in the face of fear.*[82]

When I mentioned this to students in my *Accounting Information Systems* class, many were emphatic that they believed the former to be true. When asked about what came to mind when hearing the word evil, three suggestions stood out:

1. No ethical values
2. No empathy for others
3. Scary

Many were confounded when I applied the airplane landing argument to justify the practice of evil. Put ourself in the shoes of the mid-level managers, I said. Imagine we're told that thousands of employees work for the company, each with their own families and unique set of circumstances and obligations. Would we want to be responsible for causing unnecessary alarm and impacting livelihood of thousands of employees, not to mention their families? Do we not have *ethical values* or *empathy for others*? Do we want to be the *scary* whistleblower or tattletale that no one likes and everyone avoids? We can hark back to the argument made by Hannah Arendt, how an absence of critical thinking really underlies the symptomatic absence of ethical values, empathy for others, or presence of scariness. For we can argue that it is precisely the lack of thinking or of imagination that makes us susceptible to continuing, unperturbed as it were, with the *normal* state of affairs. Lest we think this is a simple black and white matter, there are various shades of grey. In a presentation to the Army Navy Club on her book, *Extraordinary Circumstances,* Cooper pointed out that both mid-level managers wrote letters of resignation.[83] When she read one out, it became especially poignant when it became clear that the managers' continued collaboration in an alternate presentation of WorldCom's financial health quarter after quarter was perpetuated against the all too real pressures of family obligations and other factors that invariably commingled with their professional lives.[84]

Hopefully, with the advent and increasing adoption of SaaS and corresponding embrace of self-serve configuration attempts by enterprise users based on feedback from real-time design-in-use rather than once-in-time, design-on-paper requirements, the resulting internal controls designed, enacted, and validated for SaaS renders it less fragile, and more forgiving. As I shared with my students, forgiveness doesn't simply apply to humans through *empathy for others* and *ethical values* but can also be incorporate into application or software design. My point here is not to commingle, confound, and thus trivialize matters – Enron, Holocaust, and WorldCom – but to demystify the very notion of wrongdoing. As French philosopher and activist Simone Weil aptly put it, "Never react to an evil in such a way as to augment it."[85] Regardless of how it may be rationalized by those who benefit from it, we need to overcome a temptation to carry on business as usual whether it is using, configuring, or auditing SaaS. Martin Niemöller, a Protestant pastor and early Nazi supporter who later spoke out against Hitler, is best remembered for the following words:

> *First they came for the Socialists, and I*
> *did not speak out—*
> *Because I was not a Socialist.*
> *Then they came for the Trade Unionists, and I*
> *did not speak out—*
> *Because I was not a Trade Unionist.*
> *Then they came for the Jews, and I*
> *did not speak out—*
> *Because I was not a Jew.*
> *Then they came for me—and there was no one left to speak for me.*

An abdication of responsibility or of accountability does not translate into an easy retreat from the insults to transaction integrity that beckons over the horizon. The only alternative is to confront the latter head on. As Weil put it, "We must choose between hindering the functioning of the military machine of which we are ourselves so many cogs and blindly aiding that machine to continue to crush human lives."[86] To be sure, this is not easy. We can go at it too hard, or not hard enough. At each step along the way, we must remember to circle back to a field of openness, beyond wrong or right doing, so that we may in turn rise to greet whatever arises, not with immediate suspicion or disdain, but with burgeoning appreciation and faith that all roads lead us to a full and direct experiential realization of our potential, illuminated by the unmistakable incandescence of our being.

Exercise 11.1

Consider the following stories we tell ourselves:

1. For all user needs to be met, we need to document these completely before starting SaaS configuration work.
2. As part of the collections team, I need to know when customers are past 90 days due so that I can reach out to their sales rep to find out what's going on.
3. As an auditor, I would like to be informed if key configurations have been updated.

What are some of the hidden assumptions, biases or stories behind these stories? How can we deepen these stories? Conversely, how do these stories engender other stories?

Discussion

For the first story, to what extent are we assuming that all needs can be identified upfront beforehand? To what extent do requirements become clarified from back-and-forth clarifications based on seeing a working prototype? Also, have different stakeholders from different functions been involved? For the second story, are we assuming that 90-days past due customers are already receiving dunning notifications? Are we also assuming that payment terms for the same customer do not vary by type and amount of sale? For the third story, are we assuming that audit trails are available for configuration changes in addition to transaction or master data changes? For all these stories and more, to what extent are we not exploring farther by asking so what? What can go wrong if none of these needs are met? Are there compensating controls or measures? If a 90-day past due customer is up for contract renewal, would the sales rep have already reached out proactively? As we dig deeper, we find stories of stories.

Exercise 11.2

Imagine the following seven instruments at play in a jazz band: saxophone, trumpet, violin, piano, bass, guitar. and drums. If we had to characterize each of the following as an instrument, what would it be? Why?

1. Accountants, auditors, SaaS vendor, industry analyst, regulator, management, customer
2. SaaS, PaaS, IaaS, on-premise software, iPaaS, spreadsheets, contracts
3. Start-ups, regulation agencies, professional associations, public investors, private firms, small- and medium-sized public companies, Fortune 500
4. Automated controls, manual controls, detective controls, preventive controls, entity controls, IT dependent manual controls

In each group, to what extent is an instrument likely to clash with another? What instruments are likely to blend together to form a harmonious melody?

Discussion

All too often, we are apt to draw battle lines, pitting one group against another. Yet, if we just try to deepen the story and move past apparent differences, we may yet realize the identities that we cling to are invariably predicated on countering opposing forces and that rather than weakening our stance, these serve to bring out the unexpected through trial by fire. This book focuses on SaaS, yet hopefully it is evident by now that to talk about SaaS, we need to talk about all that surrounds SaaS. Deepening the story is a way of seeing how others fit in. In the process, we may yet realize that we are the others to whom we encounter.

Exercise 11.3

Here's a flavor of a common business fable:
A pig and a chicken are walking down the road.

The chicken says: "Hey pig, I was thinking we should open a restaurant!"
The pig replies: "Hm, maybe, what would we call it?"
The chicken responds: "How about 'ham-n-eggs'?"
The pig thinks for a moment and says: "No thanks. I'd be committed, but you'd only be involved."

Which of the following SaaS stakeholders resemble a pig, which resemble a chicken?

1. SaaS vendor
2. SaaS customer
3. Auditor

Discussion

When asked these questions in the context of customizing a SaaS to an organization's business needs, students in my *Accounting Information Systems* class almost always picked the vendor to be the pig. Yet, to the extent that configuration is available with SaaS, how is the customer playing more and more the role of the pig? The auditor is almost always cast as the chicken, but what are the ways the auditor can play a more committed role in tightening internal controls rather than continue to hover by the sidelines? Even within the SaaS customer group, there are those who play more of a pig role, such as accounting personnel, and others, such as sales management, who play more of a chicken role. How and what controls get to be configured for SaaS depends in part on what roles different stakeholders play within the organization and where they are in their level of commitment and of involvement. The configuration of the SaaS itself presents opportunities to "isolate, re-contextualize...invert," transfiguring existing relations.[87]

Endnotes

[1] McQuillan, M. (1989). *Van Gogh*. London, UK: Thames & Hudson.
[2] Roddenberry, G., Piller, M., Berman, R., Lauritson, P., Abatemarco, F., Braga, B., Echevarria, R. et al. (2007). Paramount Pictures Corporation. *Star Trek, The Next Generation: Season 6*. Los Angeles, CA: Paramount Pictures.
[3] Ibid.
[4] Ibid.
[5] Knowledge@Wharton. (January 22, 2009). Paying the price: Satyam's auditors face plenty of questions. The Wharton School. http://knowledge.wharton.upenn.edu/article/paying-the-price-satyams-auditors-face-plenty-of-questions/
[6] Ibid.
[7] Gaines, C., Tate, G., Rassel, L., and Marshall Kerry, J. (2017). *Kerry James Marshall*. New York: Phaidon Press.

[8] Luff, P. and Heath, C. (1993). System use and social organisation: Observations on human-computer interaction in an architectural practice published. In G. Button (Eds.) *Technology in Working Order: Studies of Work, Interaction, and Technology.* London, UK: Routledge, pp. 184–210.

[9] Blake, W. (1868). *The Marriage of Heaven and Hell.* London, UK: John Camden Hotten.

[10] Suchman, L. A. (1983). Office procedure as practical action: Models of work and system design. *ACM Transactions on Information Systems,* 1(4), 320–328.

[11] Luff, P. and Heath, C. System use and social organisation: Observations on human-computer interaction.

[12] Ibid.

[13] Ibid.

[14] Liu, A. (2004). *The Laws of Cool: Knowledge Work and the Culture of Information.* Chicago, IL: University of Chicago Press.

[15] Palmer, P. J. (1998). *The Courage to Teach: Exploring the Inner Landscape of a Teacher's Life.* San Francisco, CA: Jossey-Bass.

[16] Ibid.

[17] Ibid.

[18] McNay, I. (1995). From collegial academy to the corporate enterprise: The changing cultures of Universities. In T. Schuller (Ed.) *The Changing University?* Buckingham, UK: SHRE/Open University Press.

[19] Palmer, P. J. *The Courage to Teach: Exploring the Inner Landscape of a Teacher's Life.*

[20] Paul Getty Museum, J. and Bravo, M. A. (2001). *Manuel Alvarez Bravo: Photographs from the J. Paul Getty Museum.* Los Angeles, CA: Getty Productions.

[21] Sontag, S. (1967). *The Aesthetics of Silence.* Aspen no. 5+6, item 3. http://www.ubu.com/aspen/aspen5and6/threeEssays.html#sontag

[22] Carroll, L. (1865). *Alice's Adventures in Wonderland.* New York: MacMillan.

[23] McKenna, F. (April 9, 2012). Groupon: Where were the auditors? *Forbes.* https://www.forbes.com/sites/francinemckenna/2012/04/09/groupon-where-were-the-auditors/#3a36889c2568

[24] Schulman, S. (2016). *Conflict Is Not Abuse: Overstating Harm, Community Responsibility, and the Duty of Repair.* Vancouver, Canada: Arsenal Pulp Press.

[25] Tallentyre, S. G. (1906). The Friends of Voltaire. Richard West.

[26] Palmer, P. J. *The Courage to Teach: Exploring the Inner Landscape of a Teacher's Life.*

[27] Loori, J. D. and Tanahashi, K. (2009). *The True Dharma Eye: Zen Master Dogen's Three Hundred Koans.* Boston, MA: Shambhala.

[28] Adams, L. Learning a new skill is easier said Than done Gordon learning institute. http://www.gordontraining.com/free-workplace-articles/learning-a-new-skill-is-easier-said-than-done/#

[29] Luft, J. and Ingham, H. (1955). The Johari window, a graphic model of interpersonal awareness. *Proceedings of the Western Training Laboratory in Group Development.* Los Angeles, CA: University of California.

[30] Ibid.

[31] Ee, C. (2009). *Beyond the Looking Glass: IT Auditors and Client Communications.* Volume 5, 2009, of the ISACA Journal.

[32] Ibid.

33 Suchman, L. (September 1995). Making work visible. *Communications of the ACM*, 38(9), 56–64.

34 Hardt, M. and Negri, A. (2004). *Multitude: War and Democracy in the Age of Empire*. New York: The Penguin Press.

35 Abramović, M. (2016). *Walking Through Walls*. New York: Crown Archetype.

36 Ibid.

37 Ibid.

38 Rose, E. (2003). *User Error: Resisting Computer Culture*. Toronto, ON: Between the Lines.

39 Abramović, M. (2016). *Walking through Walls*.

40 Ibid.

41 Blake, W. *The Marriage of Heaven and Hell*.

42 Freeden, I. (December 31, 2017). In M. B. Acreche and M. H. Williams (Eds.) An awakening in *Counterdreamers*. London, UK: Karnac Books.

43 Kurts, G. P. (October 14, 2015). Have you interpreted the largest secular fresco in the U.S.? It's in town. CharlotteFive. www.charlottefive.com/have-you-interpreted-the-largest-sceular-fresco-in-the-u-s-its-in-town/

44 Abramović, M. (2016). *Walking Through Walls*.

45 Freeden, I. In M. B. Acreche and M. H. Williams (Eds.) An awakening in *Counterdreamers*.

46 Thoreau, H. D. (November 24, 2009). *The Journal of Henry David Thoreau, 1837–1861*. New York: New York Review Book (NYRB) Classics.

47 Schulman, S. *Conflict Is Not Abuse: Overstating Harm, Community Responsibility, and the Duty of Repair*.

48 Rilke, R. M. (1902). *The Book of Images*. Das Buch der Bilder.

49 Latour, B. (1994). On technical mediation–Philosophy, sociology, genealogy. *Common Knowledge*, 3(2), 29–64.

50 Lidwell, W., Holden, K., Butler, J., and Elam, K. (2010). *Universal Principles of Design: 125 Ways to Enhance Usability, Influence Perception, Increase Appeal, Make Better Design Decisions, and Teach Through Design*. Beverly, MA: Rockport Publishers.

51 Bratteteig, T. and Stolterman, E. (1997). Design in groups- and all that jazz. In M. Kyng and L. Mathiassen (Eds.) *Computers and Design in Context*. London, UK: MIT Press, pp. 289–316.

52 Ibid.

53 Ibid.

54 Ibid.

55 Abramović, M. (2016). *Walking Through Walls*.

56 Blake, W. and Baskin, L. (1968). *Auguries of Innocence*. New York: Printed anew for Grossman Publishers.

57 Garfinkel, H. (1967). *Studies in Ethnomethodology*. Englewood Cliffs, NJ: Prentice-Hall.

58 Rilke, Rainer M. *The Book of Images*.

59 Carr, N. (2004). *Does IT Matter? Information Technology and the Corrosion of Competitive Advantage*. Boston, MA: Harvard Business School Press.

60 Lewis-Krausdec, G. (December 14, 2016). The Great A.I. awakening. *The New York Times Magazine*. https://www.nytimes.com/2016/12/14/magazine/the-great-ai-awakening.html

[61] Jalāl, D. R. and Barks, C. (1997). *The Essential Rumi.*

[62] Gandhi, R., Veeraraghavan, R., Toyama, K., and Ramprasad V. (December 15–16, 2007). Digital Green: Participatory video for agricultural extension. Information and Communication Technologies and Development. ICTD. International Conference on Information and Communication Technologies and Development.

[63] Blake, W. *The Marriage of Heaven and Hell.*

[64] McNiff, S. (1998). *Trust the Process: An Artist's Guide to Letting Go.* Boston, MA: Shambhala.

[65] Ibid.

[66] Ibid.

[67] Meyer, L. B. (1967). *Music, the Arts, and Ideas.* Chicago, IL: University of Chicago Press.

[68] Weiss, T. R. and Weiss, R. (2014). *The Man from Porlock: Engagements, 1944–1981.* Princeton, NJ: Princeton University Press.

[69] Cage, J. (1952). Four musicians at work. *Trans Formation: Arts, Communication, Environment: A World Review.* New York: Wittenborn, Schultz.

[70] Palmer, P. J. *The Courage to Teach: Exploring the Inner Landscape of a Teacher's Life.*

[71] Roddenberry, G., Piller, M., Berman, R., Lauritson, P., Abatemarco, F., Braga, B., Echevarria, R. et al. *Star Trek, The Next Generation: Season 6.*

[72] CNN Larry King Live. (July 12, 2004). *Interview with Ken Lay.* http://transcripts.cnn.com/TRANSCRIPTS/0407/12/lkl.00.html

[73] Arendt, H. (1963). *Eichmann in Jerusalem: A Report on the Banality of Evil.* New York: Viking Press.

[74] Ibid.

[75] Ibid.

[76] Ibid.

[77] Alvarez, A. (June 12, 2013). Truth and consequences: Lessons from WorldCom. *Texas Enterprise.* http://www.texasenterprise.utexas.edu/2013/06/12/workplace/truth-and-consequences-lessons-worldcom

[78] Carozza, D. (March/April 2008). Extraordinary circumstances. *Fraud Magazine.* http://www.fraud-magazine.com/article.aspx?id=210

[79] Krim, J. (August 29, 2002). Fast and loose at WorldCom. *The Washington Post.* https://www.washingtonpost.com/archive/politics/2002/08/29/fast-and-loose-at-worldcom/1989a19e-6384-4e7d-a72c-d407f693e0cd/?utm_term=.0a133d76ceb6

[80] Carozza, D. Extraordinary circumstances.

[81] Ibid.

[82] Chambers, R. (September 26, 2016). Does the cost of courage have to be unemployment? *Internal Auditor.* https://iaonline.theiia.org/blogs/chambers/2016/pages/does-the-cost-of-courage-have-to-be-unemployment.aspx

[83] Mieszala, K. (April 5, 2017). Cynthia cooper–Extraordinary circumstances: The Journey of a Corporate Whistleblower. YouTube. https://www.youtube.com/watch?v=6bh7bI19N3Q

[84] Ibid.

[85] Weil, S. (February 1945). Reflections on war. *Politics,* 2(2). New York: Politics Publishing. https://libcom.org/files/Politics%20(February%201945).pdf

[86] Ibid.

[87] Gaines, C., Tate, G., Rassel, L., and Marshall Kerry, J. *Kerry James Marshall.*

Epilogue: Three Acts

Responsibility is to keep the ability to respond.[1]

Robert Duncan

Account

We started in *Introduction* by talking about accounts. What is an account? What does it mean to give an account of something or of someone? We can take this further: does this make something or someone accountable to its ascribed account? Is this what we mean by accountability? What about the account given by the system? To what extent does it correspond with that given by its user? To what degree does it reveal as well as hide? Is it not expected to reveal as well as hide?

In testing out enhancements to an upstream order management SaaS, users realize that synced over invoices in the downstream billing SaaS no longer get emailed when clicking on the Send button. This button has been added in the downstream SaaS; when clicked, it triggers a custom workflow that scoops up all the primary email address associated with the customer as well as any additional email contacts synced over on the invoice and adds these as email recipients to a custom email template that is sent out to the customer concerned with an attached PDF copy of the invoice. After attempting several times to click on the Send button, and not receiving any email, users turn to the SaaS to uncover what might go wrong.

In many ways, the earlier SaaS example mirrors an account recounted by Paul Dourish, this time involving a photocopier.[2] When a user requested six copies of a 20-page, double-sized document, and it stopped halfway, what went wrong? Did the copier indicate that it ran out of paper? Did something get jammed somewhere? Or was it the ink cartridge that ran out? Was the copier able to render an account that let users know what to do to resolve the issue at hand? In revisiting our SaaS example, what could have gone wrong in getting the emails to be sent out? Is there an issue with enhancements to the upstream SaaS so that new invoices synced over no longer have email contacts populated? Or is the issue attributed to other confounding factors that have nothing to do with the enhancements? Is the network down? Did someone inadvertently modify the custom workflow in the downstream billing SaaS in a manner that precludes emails from going out? Is the Send button disabled by chance? Ideally, the SaaS is more than a silent witness or accomplice to all this frantic uncovering of what went wrong. Do we unwind the enhancements in the upstream SaaS? How much more time do we need to spend on troubleshooting before determining that customers do need to be emailed invoices? Do we send out invoices manually as a last resort?

With the advances made in photocopier technology, it can, and very often does, give a specific account of what needs to be done. A red blinking light may signal that the paper needs to be added and specifically in the lower bottom-most tray. A flashing arrow to the right may provide a different message, this time signaling that paper may be jammed in the right feeder. A separate warning may be given if the ink cartridge needs to be replaced. What account is given depends on what has likely gone wrong. What goes wrong in one instance may not be the same trigger that applies in another. This may be what Dourish means when he writes about how not all the information is presented all at once through the account, only at appropriate intervals and where necessary.[3] For example, there would have been no need for the blinking red light if the lack of paper were not an issue. In fact, by exposing all and sundry, we are more likely to be confused than amused by the supposed automation at hand. The question becomes: is the SaaS able to provide the same degree of specificity when something goes awry? Thus far, we have focused on the what's and the why's, the former the nature of the functionality at hand – what does the SaaS do – and the latter whether there is a justifiable cause or authorized source; in other words, is the action approved or warranted to begin with? In the copier example, when Dourish speaks of accounts, he is addressing the how's – in other words, "how it can provide a user with appropriate information on the state of the service as it acts, and continuation or recovery procedures should it fail."[4] The account is intimate, in that it exposes the inner workings that affords users the ability to "introspect" or peer into its inner flow and where necessary "intercede" or make necessary adjustments.[5] As a homage to our SaaS multi-tenant architecture and out of the box configuration capability, Dourish references the "meta-level" that lets users figure out not just "what the system does, but about how it does it."[6]

Let's return to the case of the missing emails in our SaaS. In the absence of flashing lights of varying colors or other alerts, how do we troubleshoot? We might create a test invoice manually from scratch directly from the downstream SaaS and click on the Send button. If this goes through, then at least we can ascertain that natively within the downstream SaaS, the customized workflow or button has not been modified. As we can see, we are already going down the path of eliminating usual suspects. This path is necessary because of less than obvious messages received from the SaaS on what could have gone wrong. It is ironic that despite technological advances, the SaaS provides less than specific accounts when compared to the old-fashioned photocopier. When it comes to SaaS configurations or customizations, it also underscores the need to explicate exception handling procedures for exceptional circumstances. Simply automating a process or informing on its successful execution is not sufficient; we need to also be able to report on any exceptions encountered and offer ways for users to recover the SaaS back to its normal course of operations. In place of the SaaS as silent witness, let's suppose that the workflow configured has audit logs set up, so that when a user clicks on the Send button, an administrator can open the logs and see in detail whether the workflow is executed and, if so, which state is it stuck in. Could it be an invalid email address belonging to the contact on the test invoice being synced across? Is the customer not set up correctly to begin with? Providing details on what state the system is in narrows down the possible ways it can go wrong and, in so doing, provides a more direct path or set of direct paths that help users figure out just what went wrong and the steps to take to resolve the challenge at hand. In the meantime, the clock may be ticking for timely month-end close. The accounts receivable (A/R) subledger may be kept open longer; transactions synced across from another integrated SaaS may be recorded in an otherwise locked period.

The question becomes: the key internal controls we identify and in turn validate – to what degree are they imposed from the outside, stories we tell ourselves based on our conceptions of how the SaaS does, as opposed to intrinsic to the inner workings of the SaaS, part and parcel of how it identifies, reports on, and resolves issues that arise? The former, in Dourish's eyes, is a "structural model," whereas the latter is a "behavioral model."[7] Not surprisingly, the former is based on a static set of relations; the latter more dynamic. Insofar as internal controls represent the ways and means organizations anticipate, control for, and report on a set of behaviors, they are representations of representations, the latter themselves systems accounts of self-representation. Thus, to what degree do audit accounts marry with, or divorce from, system accounts, and perhaps more importantly, how are audit accounts impacted by the ability or inability of the SaaS at hand in offering less or more than revealing means of self-evidencing or reporting? The example Dourish gives is the percentage done indicator (PDI) that evidences the percent complete when a file is copied between two disks. Yet, when stuck at a 40% PDI, the user is no less able at identifying just where the copy operations went wrong. "Was 40% of the file copied? Did all of the file get 40% there?"[8] In the process of attempting to upload transactions in bulk into a SaaS, a user may receive an import error. We ask: to what extent does the error reveal, more than it hide, enough for the user to troubleshoot and re-import what hasn't yet made its way in? If the SaaS, like Dourish's file copy example, merely displays a 40% completion message, the user is not left with much recourse. If the user reimports the entire batch again, he or she is likely to end up with more duplicates. Does the user need to clear the import log, and perhaps, more importantly, does the SaaS offer any clues on the next steps to take? Of the remaining entries that fail to be imported, what can the user do to increase the likelihood of import?

The account that the SaaS offers here may be the beginnings of a true test of its capability in providing recovery or continuation procedures that are tied directly to its inner workings and a reflection of where it is, state-wise in processing a specific task, and how this ability, when stack ranked against other like SaaS, makes it more compelling from a usability and configurational perspective. So, in place of a 40% completion account, the SaaS may highlight transactions that do not make their way in, and flag errors with specific attributes. As an example, the unit of measure in these transactions does not yet exist in the SaaS. As a response, before continuing with the rest of the import or slamming the SaaS with the same import over and over, we can create the new unit of measure before proceeding with the rest of the import. During the second attempt, yet a different message appears, and this time, some of the entries do not have the right format, such as presence of a comma in an integer field. These are in turn corrected before proceeding with the next round of imports. Each time, the error message given speaks directly to what's missing or invalid rather than providing a mere gloss of an otherwise generic status notification. In this manner, it is precise when it needs to be, rather than having to be precise all or none of the time.

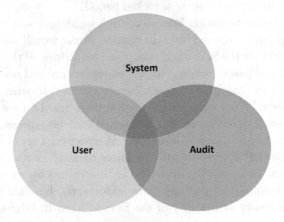

Dourish draws a careful distinction "between an account of system behavior as offered by a system, and the understanding of system behavior formed by a user in response."[9] Like a blind man's cane, to what extent does the account offered by the SaaS let users feel out what is happening? In addition to distinguishing between system and user accounts, I would layer on an additional distinction between system and audit accounts. The question becomes: to what extent do the internal controls devised reside in the overlapping domains so that they address more than one account?

Interface

In the same manner that cloud computing has been categorized into Software as a Service (SaaS), Platform as a Service (PaaS), and Infrastructure as a Service (IaaS), Anders Mørch describes three levels of end user tailoring: customization, integration, and extension.[10] We have already seen how SaaS vendors use the word "customization" and "configuration" somewhat interchangeability, with some preferring to use "configuration" over "customization" where others opt for generic customization over less or non-generic customization with the underlying subtext to modify the internal kernel as little as possible, or conversely to introduce change in a way such that universal, rather than specific, needs are met so as to render the SaaS universally mobile. Mørch's focus is on adapting generic software applications to the use of specific end user needs.[11] Just as the three types of cloud computing are differentiated by the degrees of customer proximity to the underlying infrastructure stack, Mørch looks at the design gap between "presentation objects" and "implementation code."[12] To the extent that the design gap is mediated by customization forms, integration languages or extension layers, these are in turn characterized by customizations, integrations and extensions and in this order. Mørch makes a finer distinction between use and design distance.[13] The former has more to do with look and feel, whereas the latter has more to do with peering into underlying architecture. In the context of a SaaS, minimizing use distance can be accomplishing by adding custom values or fields to address needs that are specific to the user organization.[14]

Recall the use of the metadata table described by Chong, Carraro, and Wolter to incorporate the addition of any number of custom fields in varied formats.[15] Design distance has everything to do with understanding embodied logics:

- Why the SaaS transacts or records the way it does
- Why every customer needs to be identified by a unique customer ID
- How every sales transaction can only be tied to one and only one customer

These recall the challenge of the code block associated with traditional enterprise resource planning (ERP). Yet, a reduction of design distance is possible with the ability to, in the words of Mørch, "integrate" by writing custom scripts or workflows that change the functionality of the SaaS at hand. A custom reseller record may be created to map to multiple end customers. Projects may be assigned to orders in addition to customers. Programming languages such as SuiteScript for NetSuite and Apex for Salesforce are available for more savvy end users to perform scripting. Extension enters the picture when the code is not so much modified as is interfaced with another SaaS, in effect extending the initial set of capabilities to a greater unanticipated unknown. The degree of change as evidenced from lowest to highest from customization to integration to extension mirrors the hierarchy adapted by Pollock from Hislop in describing the degree of ERP customization in ascending order of complexity: configuration, bolt-ons, screen masks, extended reporting, workflow programming, user exists, ERP programming, interface development, package code modification, and new module development.[16]

When we overlay internal controls on the degree of configuration or customization of the SaaS at hand, we can think of them in the same manner. To what extent do they minimize use or design distance? How close are they to manipulating the way the SaaS functions? What is the impact of making the change? This last question bears further comment. Customizations such as the development of a workflow that is scheduled to mass notify customers of a new payment means is not directly seen to impact financials and thus not deemed in scope for change management to comply with SOX. Yet if errors were communicated from inadequate oversight, the company may be less than effective in securing timely customer payment. Thus, even though the customizations are not in scope from an audit perspective, they would be pertinent from the perspective of financial health. In the context of an accounting SaaS, features that are enabled or disabled – such as the ability to invoice expenses incurred to external customers or enforce a three-way match among the purchase order, receipt and invoice – have a pervasive impact on the way the SaaS may behave even if it does not entail technical know-how or coding.

As we venture to the next layer, the development of specific reports or queries can impact the way companywide financials are presented. Continuing in this vein, the same devised queries may be consumed by custom workflows that are triggered by the number of days an invoice is past due as a trigger for dunning notifications. So even though the impact here is less pervasive, and more contained within Order-to-Cash and herein overdue invoices, the nature of effort is more technical, whether it is familiarization with the supporting scripting language or use of the workflow functions within the SaaS. Custom fields may be used by one or multiple workflows and scripts, so the impact is more pervasive than we are led to think. Also, the means to exact the configuration can overlap or be employed simultaneously, so for any one customization, various elements can come into play among attributes, records, workflows and scripts.

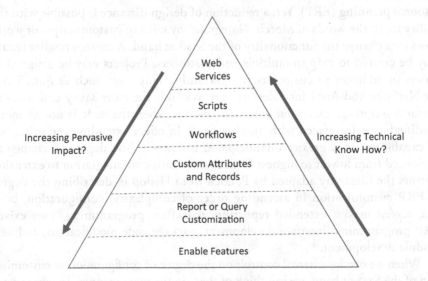

Increasing Pervasive Impact?

Increasing Technical Know How?

Web Services

Scripts

Workflows

Custom Attributes and Records

Report or Query Customization

Enable Features

We may have noticed that depending on the author or audience, integration, extension, and interface may have been used by different people to mean different things, yet we can argue that, fundamentally, we are talking about interface work. When we look at a computer program, it is a series of abstractions, so that most users are not exposed to the black box of inner workings. Even without layering in another integrating SaaS, we can in fact characterize our dealings with the present SaaS at hand as a series of interface management, beginning with first the user interface – Mørch distinguishes between two approaches: bringing the computer closer to the user as well as vice versa the user closer to the computer[17] – and working our way to the underlying code. When troubleshooting how a custom script may be displaying an error for a sales order for a specific billing frequency, for example, we may uncover, upon closer inspection, a missing condition for the value specified by the user, so that the script goes into an infinite loop of sorts exhausting performance or governance limits. If working with SaaS can be characterized as a series of interface management, then working with internal controls for SaaS is even doubly so, a series of interface management over interface management. Incomplete conditions in custom scripts present a technical debt that contributes to SaaS fragility, making it more susceptible to failure, and therefore less forgiving in handling varied types of input.

Recall Dutch artist Escher's *Drawing Hands* printed in 1948. A lithograph that depicts a two-dimensional sheet of paper from which two seemingly three-dimensional hands emerge, they appear to draw each other into existence. Looking at it closely, we don't know which hand is drawing which; one begins where the other ends. What does it mean to say that everything is "multiply-authored?"[18] That a control is as much what it is out there as what is in here? That a control is as much a product of others as it is of itself? Relations don't disappear: they are ever-present, swirling, anticipating. Recall from Chapter 1 that GAAP is "as much a product of political action as it is of careful logic or empirical findings."[19] What we are saying is that when it comes to "empirical findings," what we observe and record is as much a function of what is out there as it is of how we perceive and the methods we use to record and document. In the case of the audit loop, there is a risk that internal controls designed to pass the audit may end up validating itself or the governing relations among all stakeholders at hand rather than directly speaking to the nature of SaaS fragility and forgiveness when it comes to architectural and transactional validity, completeness, accuracy, and overall integrity. We have seen apparently fixated boundaries – between what's automated and what's manual, what's the beginning and what's the end, or what's internal and what's external – whittled away once we peel back the layers. Does this mean that everything is an interface?

Arguably, generally accepted accounting principles (GAAP) financial presentation is an application program interface (API) of sorts, if only to have every public company display its financials in a consistent and coherent manner. Risk factors in an annual or quarterly financial report (10-K or 10-Q) house content the same way a publicly exposed application attribute is instantiated and used to layer on additional customization or configuration work. The same can be said for audits: the common currency of control-speak around audit assertions and IT general versus application controls provides a common API for evidencing and attesting to control design and operating effectiveness. The same concept lies behind a fluent API or interface introduced by Evans and Fowler to reduce the gap in use distance, that is, make source code like readable human prose.[20] Conversely, we can make the argument that scripting with its exacting emphasis on parameter placement and articulation helps us identify grammatical or format errors more effectively than a written composition albeit in layman prose. In fact, there are times when editing this book, I would have invariably preferred an integrated development environment (IDE) to assist with identifying errors and inconsistencies rather than relying on the subjective human eye or a generic Microsoft Word spellcheck. When recalling sleepless nights of coding back in college in getting a program to compile and execute, at least the criteria for success is much more clearly outlined even if it is harder to attain. As code moves closer to prose; prose could itself be more like code. Everything is fast becoming an interface; yet, if everything were an interface, does the very notion of interface itself disappear?

Attribute

Ehn, Meggerle, Steen, and Svedemar turn software systems on their head by asking car salesman what kind of car they would use to characterize their sales support systems and why. For some, it was like a "Volvo 740 ... no big surprises, but it works as it should."[21] For others though, "it's like a half-finished car."[22] Yet others saw it as "an 850 Turbo ... it gives you a certain sense of security and stability."[23] What car does the SaaS we are using most resemble? The answers we give belie the degree of underlying utility, and configurability. Imagine being able to swap the placement of the car engine from the front to the back. Does the SaaS at hand give us that option? Like our earlier comparison of a transaction processed through SaaS to being like a palindrome, I'm not suggesting that we view the SaaS as a car. Yet by asking about users' opinion of SaaS in this manner, we are in effect able to explore a different trajectory unencumbered as it were by transaction minutiae.

On-Premise Software	SaaS
A transaction and its attributes are captured within one software	A transaction and its attributes are captured by multiple software
A transaction is defined by its internal attributes which drive its behavior	A transaction is defined by its interactions with other transactions in context
The attributes captured are stable and do not change	The attributes captured are dynamic and can change

(Continued)

On-Premise Software	SaaS
Information about attributes for reporting and assessment is internal to the software	Information about attributes for reporting and assessment is external to the software
Controls over transaction processing are predetermined and enforced top-down	Controls over transaction processing are organic and developed from the bottom-up

In listing the differences between on-premise software and SaaS, the previous table emphasizes the latter's relational nature and out-of-the-box configurational capability. We can take this a step farther. Instead of viewing attributes as specific to a transactional or entity record, which in turn is specific to a specific SaaS, think of a "multiply-authored"[24] SaaS architecture, where what each SaaS brings to the table is itself a contributing summary or high-level attribute, such as order management or sales tax computation. Viewing the internal consumption of best-in-breed SaaS in this manner helps us see more clearly how one SaaS can add to or take away from another conflicts with or compensates for another's value proposition or shortfall. In recalling the parable of the blind men and the elephant, each best-in-breed SaaS is a blind man of sorts in that each provides a partial view of the same transaction that threads through multiple SaaS from cradle to grave.

In semi-structured interviews, Ehn, Meggerle, Steen, and Svedemar also asked, "Do you think you have become a better salesman by using this system?"[25] The responses they obtained were incredibly varied. Some respondents felt they appeared more professional having information such as options and associated prices at their fingertips. Others felt that it didn't make their better salesmen per se, perhaps more efficient though not necessarily more effective. Of greater emphasis is the way their customers perceived them when using the system, or, perhaps more pointedly, the way they perceived themselves when using the system before their customers. In other words, "a salesman's judgement of the quality of the computer artifact in use is influenced by the salesman's judgement of the quality of the computer artifact in relation to the customer."[26] In the context of a sales management SaaS, can it prompt a sales professional to contact her customer when the contract renewal is coming up? Does it provide a customer dashboard to help her figure out what possible options to upsell the current array of products consumed? Conversely, based on historically observed patterns, what are the ways the sales professional can propose to reduce customer churn?

From an internal control perspective, to what extent does a user's view of a SaaS at hand change in relation to the auditor? In effect, a SaaS that effectively automates or informates or both may be neither effective nor efficient in audits. The reverse holds true. Yet, we can argue that by configuring a controlled workflow, we are becoming a better accountant, a world-class institution with reliable financials and timely close, a first-rate corporate citizen if you will. Configuration work is hard work. For all my emphasis on the ease of configuration that accompanies SaaS, should we choose to go down the path of configuring a custom workflow rather than consume approvals out of the box, we need to be prepared to invest time and energy in exploring likely scenarios. It's like having to dig deeper into each user story rather rely on third-hand, half-lived accounts. Take a custom journal entry approval workflow. Even without requisite scripting knowledge, we can devise a custom workflow through point-and-click using workflow capability out of the box as it were. Yet here, there are different use cases at hand. Journals created manually through the user interface are routed to the creator's supervisor for approval. Journals created via bulk processing, such as by running revenue recognition or amortization may not have the creator field populated. How then do we route to the necessary supervisory approver? A custom field may have to be created to sift through system logs to pull out the user who processed the revenue recognition or amortization run. Even so, we are not necessarily interested in the creator as in his or her supervisor to route the entry for approval. When the entry is first created, the approved checkbox may need to be rendered non-editable in inline format; otherwise, we can create and approve an entry simultaneously without an independent review. Yet what if we were to create an entry by mistake or inadvertently enter the wrong values? Surely the creator and perhaps the backup administrator would have the ability to either update journal entries in flight for approval or delete them altogether? With all the focus on approvals, surely the likelihood arises for approvers to have the ability to reject entries? If so, a custom Reject button needs to be added, and more importantly, when the entry is rejected, a Resubmit for Approval button is provided to allow for the entries to be corrected and re-routed for approval. When the entry is in flight for approval or re-approval, should we allow the approver to make updates to the journal or the approval flow? What about after approval? Surely, we need to consider the possibility that entries may need to be updated post-approval or even deleted? In place of deletions, we may have a policy of having reversal entries to overwrite the general ledger impact.

But these questions surface the need to unwind transactions or more generally speak to the reversibility or forgiveness needed for recorded transactions. What if the recorded entry also comprises a self-reversing entry the following month? An accrual entry, for example, is typically unwound in the next accounting period. What of the associated reversal entry in the next period? To the extent that the primary accrual entry is already approved, do we automatically default the reversal entry to approved in the next period? As we can see, a simple journal entry approval workflow can take on multiple layers of complexity, to say nothing of backup or delegate approvers needed when the supervisor is away. The additional work of tightening access to approve or reject is correlated with the number of access roles already devised. Yet, in all of this, we haven't even broached the use case of importing journal entries in bulk rather than creating or approving these by hand one at a time. Recalling Chapter 11, surely we need to be wary of over-engineering or configuring at the risk of overfitting? Yet even when dealing with these bread-and-butter use cases alone, the amount of configuration work is not insignificant. All these and more may confound or even frustrate an accounting user; yet, the same considerations may drive a superuser to try out different paths with seemingly no end in sight. To paraphrase Latour: We are different with the SaaS in our hands; the SaaS is different with us.[27] We are another subject because we use the SaaS; the SaaS is another object because it entered a relationship with us.

In the twilight hour, with the light waning, boundaries start to blur. What's interior is also exterior; the internal controls employed mirror those in other organizations. What's delivered is also received; what better way to savor all this than to ponder and gestate, write and rewrite? What's impersonal can become personal through configuration. What's technical can also turn on the nontechnical. What's inherently fragile can thus also happen to be highly forgiving. It is thus no coincidence that the title of this book speaks to a continuum as opposed to an exclusive disjunction, a pair of alternatives of which only one is acceptable. SaaS is but a medium after all. Dabble at it. More than a line in the sand surely; yet, it's no more than an arrested image of a drop of dew reflecting a ray of light. A case in point is *Scratch*, an interactive online visual coding application developed by the Lifelong Kindergarten Group at the MIT Media Lab. Through *Scratch*, kids as young as 8 years of age snap together blocks through point-and-click to control the interactions of different characters in games and stories. Compare this with our ability to configure workflows and custom attributes in SaaS through a similar point-and-click. In a TED video on *Scratch*, Mitch Resnick speaks of learning to code and coding to learn, just as we've become accustomed to learning to read before reading to learn.[28] The point-and-click approach to SaaS configuration invites us to undertake this journey. As Resnick points out, despite learnintg how to read and write, not all of us turn out to be professional writers.[29] By the same token, configuring SaaS does not turn us into professional developers or administrators; yet, it offers us untold possibilities of shedding old skins and embracing hybrid identities as we venture forth into uncharted waters. At dusk, the receding horizon is itself a floating flotsam of sorts.

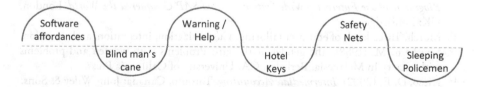

Alan Watts described our all too human tendency to preface the crest over the trough in picturing a wave.[30] As we explore configuring internal controls in SaaS through multi-varied perspectives, we come to realize that the blind man's cane, hotel keys, and sleeping policemen are but mere troughs to the more apparent crests of software affordances, warning or help messages and safety nets, the backstage to what is front and center. With an emphasis on the active design of SaaS when it comes to improving software affordances, it may be hard to see how the SaaS can nevertheless delimit our worldviews or strain them through an idealized lens. Likewise, for our attention on the need for safety nets to provide compensating controls, we may fail to notice the unassuming and timeless appeal of sleeping policemen. It is my hope that when reading this book, we start to appreciate the unseen, unspoken and, thus, unsung. Perhaps more to the point, we will come to realize that one can't exist without the other, the accounted without the unaccounted for, presence without absence, forgiveness without fragility.

Endnotes

1. Duncan, R. (1960). The law I love is major mover. *The Opening of the Field*. New York: New Direction, pp. 10.
2. Dourish, P., Adler, A., and Smith, B. C. (1996). Organizing user interfaces around reflective accounts. *Proceedings of the Reflection'96*. San Francisco, CA.
3. Ibid.
4. Ibid.
5. Ibid.
6. Ibid.
7. Ibid.
8. Ibid.
9. Ibid.
10. Mørch, A. (1997). Three levels of end-user tailoring: Customization, integration, and extension. In M. Kyang and L. Mathiassen (Eds.) *Computers and Design in Context*. pp. 51–76.
11. Ibid.
12. Ibid.
13. Ibid.
14. Ibid.
15. Chong, F., Carraro, G., and Wolter, R. (2006). Multi-tenant data architecture. Tech. rep., MSDN Library, Microsoft Corporation.
16. Williams, R. and Pollock, N. (December 6, 2008). *Software and Organizations: The Biography of the Enterprise-Wide System or How SAP Conquered the World*. London, UK: Routledge.
17. Mørch, Three levels of end-user tailoring: Customization, integration, and extension.
18. Strathern, M. (1988). The gender of the gift: Problems with women and problems with society in Melanesia. Berkeley, CA: University of California Press.
19. Kieso, D. E. (2002). *Intermediate Accounting*. Toronto, Canada: John Wiley & Sons.
20. Fowler, M. (December 20, 2005). *FluentInterface*. https://www.martinfowler.com/bliki/FluentInterface.html
21. Ehn, P., Meggerle, T., Steen, O., and Svedemar, M. (1997). What kind of car is this sales support system? On styles, artifacts, and quality-in-use. *Computers in Context*, 111–143.

22 Ibid.

23 Ibid.

24 Strathern, M. The gender of the gift: Problems with women and problems with society in Melanesia.

25 Ibid.

26 Ibid.

27 Latour, B. (1994). On technical mediation–Philosophy, sociology, genealogy. *Common Knowledge*, 3(2), 29–64.

28 Resnick, M. Let's teach kids how to code (TED Talk). https://scratch.mit.edu/projects/106082503/

29 Ibid.

30 Watts, A. (1971). *The Essential Lectures of Alan Watts*. Universal City, CA: Vivendi Entertainment.

Index

439